MANAGEMENT STRATEGY AND TACTICS

MANAGEMENT STRATEGY AND TACTICS

JOHN G. HUTCHINSON
Columbia University

HOLT, RINEHART AND WINSTON, INC.

New York   Chicago   San Francisco   Atlanta
Dallas   Montreal   Toronto   London   Sydney

The author gratefully acknowledges the following permissions:
granted by John Murray (Publishers) Ltd for world English language
rights to the excerpt from C.N. Parkinson's *Parkinson's Law and Other
Studies in Administration,* pp. 196–198; granted by Management Science
for "Coordinating Budgets with Forecasting," *Charting the Company's
Future,* 1954, on pp. 74–78, and for Figures 12.1–12.3 on p. 285; granted
by McGraw-Hill Book Company for Figure 14.1 from *The Human
Organization* by Rensis Likert. Copyright 1967 by Rensis Likert. Used
with permission of McGraw-Hill Book Company.

Preface

In a world where the need to make wise decisions is paramount, there is precious little tolerance to expend on wasteful academic debate over the relative merits of behavioral versus quantitative approaches to management education. Rather, the focus should be on using both approaches to help managers solve their never-ending problems. This book seeks to bring about such a result.

This text has three major sections: the first deals with perspectives on management; the second with key management problems and their most promising means of solution; and the third with special areas of interest for tomorrow's managers. The opening section leans toward the theoretical, but it closes with a set of conceptual models having practical overtones. The second unit identifies five major areas of managerial concern and indicates how to deal with them in behavioral and/or quantitative terms. The final unit offers managerially oriented approaches to labor relations, international management, research and development, and government relations. Since these three sections cover extensive ground, a companion book of readings, *Readings on Management Strategy and Tactics,* helps to provide added depth of coverage.

Throughout the text cases are used to emphasize key points and issues and assist the student in grasping abstract ideas in concrete terms. The cases are framed in varying degrees of complexity, which allows instructors to tailor the assignments to particular audiences. One text can thus be used in, say, the first course in a junior college or a beginning graduate course, even though its best fit is for junior-senior level students.

Every author has a group of people to whom he owes profound thanks, and I am no exception. My associates at Columbia—especially Deans George James and G. Chester Owens, former Dean Courtney Brown, and Professors E. Kirby Warren, William H. Newman, Victor Z. Brink, William D. Guth, and Boris Yavitz—were generous with advice and assistance. I also received guidance from faculty members at Arizona State University, the universities of Rhode Island and Massachusetts, the European Institute of Business Administration in France, and from my former colleague Charles E. Summer of The University of Washington. I also owe thanks to my secretary, Mrs. Harriet Laguna; to Louise Waller, Rosalind Sackoff, and Jere Calmes of Holt, Rinehart and Winston; and to Seibert Adams of The Dryden Press.

A final acknowledgement belongs to my wife, Jean, who helped to structure, edit, and type innumerable drafts of this manuscript.

—J.G.H.

New York, New York
December 1970

Contents

PART ONE
Perspectives on Management Strategy and Tactics

In Part One, historical perspectives on management are presented in terms of Shakespeare's famous comment, "the past is a prologue." Management is changing too fast to dwell long on historical musings, but careful study of evolutionary trends in management theory and practice provides a number of useful insights for modern managers. Even when the old wine comes in new bottles, it may still have sufficient flavor to please the contemporary palate.

The first chapter on "perspectives" reviews some of the more traditional doctrines underlying contemporary management theory. Many "modern" theories of management are based on certain premises or principles which are little more than reformulations of classical doctrines. A grasp of these historical philosophies provides a basis for developing perspectives on theoretical formulations purporting to explain the hows and whys of managerial activities. The second chapter in this part describes some of the more prominent modern theories of organization and indicates how current theories of managerial behavior are placing greater stress on findings taken from behavioral, natural, and physical sciences, and the arts. This second chapter also links the classicists and modern theorists and briefly illustrates how certain theoretical formulations have evolved into systems designed to identify key problems and provide for their solutions.

The final chapter on "perspectives" blends key portions of both traditional and modern theories and indicates how these general approaches can be wedded to solve specific problems. Strategic variables are related to long-term organizational goals, policies, and directions; and tactical means of implementing goals are integrated into the overall analysis. The various strategic and tactical approaches outlined in this chapter reflect a melding of both the old and new, and provide models for structuring and analyzing the critical problems facing contemporary managements.

Since many modern theories have not yet been validated by hindsight, they tend to generate a considerable amount of controversy. Each theory is represented as the "right one" by its advocates, and practicing managers tend to become disillusioned at the seeming lack of agreement among "expert" theoreticians. This lack of agreement breeds disenchantment, for even managers able to tolerate theoretical ambiguity must deal with real conditions. Like President Grover Cleveland, who justified a decision on a tariff problem by stating he was faced with "a condition, not a theory," modern managers must frequently act without the guidance of scientifically validated theories.

Admittedly, theory has its limits, but it nevertheless provides insights into the process and methods by which problems may be structured, analyzed, and solved. A sound theoretical framework can provide the formal means of handling a wide variety of critical problem areas, and it can thus become a useful tool for management. It is to this end that the theoretical models in Chapter 3 are directed.

CHAPTER 1
Management: Traditional Perspectives

Until the twentieth century theories and principles designed to guide managerial actions were virtually unknown, and for good reason. There was scant need for management theory in the one- or two-man shops flourishing in the Middle Ages. The guilds and small handicraft shops in the Renaissance had little or no need for theoretical formulations as long as the owner or manager could see his entire work force. Thus, conditions in the Middle Ages were not unlike those in effect in many small businesses today, underscoring the reason why managers of minisized businesses such as television repair shops, grocery stores, and cleaning plants have only moderate knowledge of, and no apparent need for, modern theories of management.

Given the nature of industrial production in the Middle Ages, it is not surprising that few organizations used formal techniques of management. The Catholic Church, the most complex organization structure extant, used principles such as the scalar chain, the exception principle, compulsory staff service, and other traditional management concepts described later in this chapter. Military organizations utilized formal principles of organization, with the concept of unity of direction and unity of command in authority relationships being the most obvious. Civil governments also adopted organization principles based on Roman approaches to public administration, but by and large there was little evidence in this period of what might be classified today as "management theory."

Though the development of modern management ideology can be traced to the period immediately following the Industrial Revolution, few really major contributions were made until much later. After the Industrial Revolution, which was, in sweeping terms, a change from manual to machine production, factories were still run in close to dictatorial fashion by entrepreneurs who were, in classic lord-of-the-manor terms, masters of all they surveyed. Machinery was king and the humanistic aspects of management were lost in a rush to take advantage of the fantastic gains in productivity provided by new technologies. In effect, the technologist had the last word in managerial practice and managers sought to increase output through technology rather than through a blending of all inputs entering into the production process. European technology, which had taken off from developments in the English textile industry, was exported to America and the same dominant emphasis on technology was exported along with it. Unfortunately, the same lack of concern for human factors that had shocked both Charles Dickens and Benjamin Disraeli in England emigrated to America along with British machinery and technical know-how.

It was not until another primarily European development began to influence the world that human factors were considered as particularly important in the production process; this movement was the rise of scientifically based inquiry, primarily in the physical and natural sciences. The basic underpinning of this approach, which eventually evolved into the "Age of Scientism," was the *scientific method,* a logical, rigorous, orderly means of testing ideas and hypotheses within the framework of a carefully devised analytical methodology. This methodology brought about sweeping discoveries in areas such as cell theory, medicine, physics, chemistry, biology, and evolution. It was only natural that this store of scientific inquiry should eventually spill over into other fields. In particular, business and industry soon utilized scientific techniques and approaches. As the trend toward scientism began in these areas, management thought entered its first formative stages. At first, the scientific method in industry was applied only to technical matters, but as sophistication grew, human factors were given more and more emphasis.

SCIENTIFIC MANAGEMENT

The person usually credited with publicizing the use of the scientific method to solve business problems is Frederick W. Taylor, the "Father of Scientific Management." Though others are frequently mentioned as being the real Bacon to Taylor's Shakespeare, debates surrounding the originality of Taylor's writings are subordinate to what Taylor advocated and publicized. Taylor, who was a trained industrial engineer and later the president of the Midvale Steel Company, laid out how the scientific method could be used to solve business problems. His works, which gained popularity at the beginning of the twentieth century, detailed a comprehensive recognition of the contribution that human beings can and do make to the production process. In recognizing the importance of both human and technical variables, Taylor espoused the modern concept of the manager as a coordinator of all factors of production, not just the technical ones. He was also one of the first writers to recognize formally the need to manage rather than just oversee the production process. In Taylor's mind the production manager made a positive contribution to productivity by entering directly into the organization, staffing, and layout of the various production operations.

In essence, Taylor's approach to managing production processes encompasses five steps:

1. Identify the job and develop the method (the "one best way")
2. Select the best man for the job
3. Train the man selected in the proper method.
4. Determine an expected level or standard of output.
5. Provide extra compensation for output above standard or expected levels (incentive payment).

Taylor outlined a scientific step-by-step approach which used techniques still in effect today. The concepts of time-and-motion study, wage-and-salary administration, personnel selection, and on-the-job training are inherent in Taylor's approach and they are widely used—and misused—in industry today. The utility of the techniques is proven by their ability to stand the tests of time. Indeed, most contemporary criticisms of these methods stem from inconsistent application rather than basic questions about their utility.

ENVIRONMENTAL AND HUMAN RELATIONS CONCEPTS

Taylor related the man to the job in a very precise manner, and his rigid formulation of work methods was criticized by psychologists who characterized Taylor as an engineer who saw men as appendages to a machine. They attacked him for taking skill and pride out of work by forcing a man to do a job in the "one best way" determined by an industrial engineer. Further criticism was heaped upon Taylor because his means for stimulating workers to greater production was based on monetary rewards, a concept disputed by many psychologists. "Give a man more money and he'll produce" was Taylor's approach to motivation. "Not so," said the psychologists, who believed in the motivating power of environmental stimuli. Taylors' ideas on time-and-motion study were thus much more widely accepted than his concept of monetary motivation.

Almost to a man, industrial psychologists trained in Watsonian traditions were particularly upset by Taylor's economic approach to motivation. In their lexicon, organisms are affected by sets of stimuli in the environment and they react in response to the stimuli presented at particular points in time. Their viewpoint is shown in oversimplified form in Figure 1.1. The set of stimuli (S) acting upon the organism (O) cause one or more responses (R). The responses chosen by the organism may change the stimuli or set off a series of actions that either change the conditions or the organism or create some new and more stable state of equilibrium. Information is fed back and forth through the system until actions taken bring a desired state of equilibrium into the system. To illustrate the *S-O-R* cycle, when sunlight (*S*) gets in the driver's eyes (*O*) he may pull down his sun visor (*R*) to cut down the sun's rays and thus bring about more satisfactory driving conditions (a new state of equilibrium).

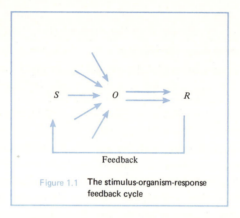

Figure 1.1   The stimulus-organism-response feedback cycle

One group of environmental behaviorists were quite disturbed with Taylor's concept of monetary motivation. They believed that environmental conditions such as light, heat, noise, and so forth were more critical determinants of behavior on the job than monetary factors. Further, they felt that physical working conditions could be controlled in such a way that man's on-the-job productivity would increase. In short, they said that changes in working conditions could affect productivity. These environmentalists were later called "moo cow" psychologists by one unionist because their ideas were based on the famous advertising slogan "You [can] get more milk from contented cows."

Though many of the ideas of the environmentalists have carried forward to the present day (witness, for example, air conditioning and color-coordinated offices), their belief that physical conditions in the environment were the key to greater productivity was discredited by a series of experiments performed in the late 1920s at the Hawthorne works of the Western Electric Company by a group of researchers from Harvard University under the direction of Elton Mayo, Fritz Rothleisberger, and William J. Dickson. These Hawthorne experiments were the basis for what is now known as the "human relations school" of management.

The Hawthorne project concentrated on one of the basic ideas of environmentalists. In their initial experiments, one of which was a scientific analysis of the relative impact of lighting on productivity, the Harvard researchers sought to test the hypothesis that increases in lighting intensity brought about increases in productivity. This hypothesis also served as a vehicle to determine whether a lowering of lighting intensities would bring about a reverse result.

In the first Hawthorne experiment the original conditions surrounding the job were recorded and changes were noted as the experiment moved through progressive changes in lighting intensities, methods of payment, hours of work, and so forth. In the face of varying lighting conditions, output rose. When rest periods were introduced, output also climbed. At the close of the experiment original conditions were restored, but output levels remained higher than those recorded at the starting point. The first and most obvious conclusion drawn was that no necessary correlation existed between lighting conditions, conditions of work, and productivity but that other factors seemed to exert important influence on these relationships. The second was an inference framed in the question, "If changes in environmental lighting did not alone determine productivity then what factors did cause the observed changes? "

The answer to this question became the focus of a series of new experiments which attempted to determine why productivity shifted during the original series of observations. In the words of Paul Homans, the increase in output "could be related to what only can be spoken of as the development of an organized social group in a peculiar and effective relation with its supervisors."[1] The hypothesis stated by Homans was tested more exhaustively and rigorously in experiments conducted in the bank wiring room at the Hawthorne works. These studies delved deeply into supervisor-worker relationships and eventually brought forth the general proposition that social relationships both within and between groups of people are the most important determinants of productivity.[2] In essence, they said that efficient operation depends on people functioning well within and between work groups in both social and work related activities. These findings, expanded upon in later researches, became the essence of the human relations approach to management.

PRINCIPLES OF MANAGEMENT

Both before and during the time Taylor and Mayo were conducting their researches and writings another group of management theorists were trying to develop and construct a set of universal "principles of management"—lists of prescriptive statements which spelled out how management organizations could operate most effectively. Taylor himself laid out certain principles, but his listings were concerned mostly with the concept of efficiency. Henri Fayol, Lyndall Urwick, Mary Parker Follett, William H. Newman, Harold Koontz, Cyril O'Donnell, and others developed much more complete sets of principles in their writings. This group was tabbed the "management process school" by Koontz in his widely read article, "The Management Theory Jungle." [3]

Lists of principles in circulation today build on the findings of both the human relations school and scientific management. They attempt to distill

---

[1] *Fatigue of Workers,* Western Electric Researchers, (New York: Reinhold Publishing Corporation, 1941).

[2] J.A.C. Brown, *A Social Psychology of Industry* (Baltimore, Md.: Penguin Books, 1954).

[3] *Journal of the Academy of Management,* vol. 4, no. 3 (December 1961), pp. 174–188.

the results of various studies of the managerial job into conceptual frameworks and then develop sets of principles or guidelines to help managers perform their various functions more effectively. Critics claim that these lists are overly prescriptive and fail to give individual motivation sufficient weight. To put it another way, they emphasize formal relationships at the expense of informal group relationships and individual differences. Critics also say that they merely detail *what* has been done in the past without generating any understanding of *why* things are done. Interestingly enough, most critics of the principles approach have explained *what* is wrong with principles without themselves identifying *why* they appear to be invalid.

Since principles and prescriptive lists comprise the basic core of traditional management doctrine, they deserve further elaboration. Criticisms, whether valid or invalid, can be assessed more clearly after an exploration of such lists in some detail. Indeed, the clarity of expression with which these lists are presented provides an excellent base from which to compare traditional management doctrines with more modern theories of organization and behavior.

Perhaps the earliest list of principles appears in the works of Henri Fayol.[4] Fayol's teachings were expanded by Harold Koontz and Cyril O'Donnell into fifteen principles that are perhaps the best known and most widely distributed set of principles in existence today.[5] A summation of these two lists appears in Table 1.1. Before Table 1.1 can be analyzed, some of its specialized terminology must be understood. A brief explanatory discussion appears below:

> The various "unity" principles are all related. *Unity of command* refers to having one and only one boss for each subordinate. *Unity of direction,* or *subordination* of individual interest means one plan and one head man for a group of activities having the same objective. *Unity of objective* indicates the extent to which organizational goals are known and the degree to which the organization is moving toward their attainment.
>
> *Division of work* deals with the extent of specialization in effect, while *parity of authority and responsibility* states that the authority granted to a subordinate should be great enough to accomplish the desired task.
>
> The principle of *responsibility* is similar to that calling for the use of a *scalar chain,* since both dictate that each subordinate should report to a single superior at each level of command and that each superior should be held accountable for the actions of his subordinates.
>
> *Balance* and *degree of decentralization* are also similar in that each attempts to determine a degree of decentralization to adopt in practice.
>
> *Stability* and *continuity* can be paired, since both represent the ability of the organization to continue on a given course of action in the face of change or diversity. The *flexibility* principle, on the other hand, refers to the organization's ability to adapt to changing conditions.

---

[4] *General and Industrial Management* (New York: Pitman Publishing Corporation, 1949).
[5] *Principles of Management,* 3rd ed. (New York: McGraw-Hill, Inc., 1964).

TABLE 1.1   MANAGERIAL PRINCIPLES

HENRI FAYOL	KOONTZ AND O'DONNELL
1. Division of work	1. Division of work
2. Parity of authority and responsibility	2. Parity of authority and responsibility
3. Discipline	3. Unity of command
4. Unity of command	4. Unity of direction
5. Unity of direction	5. Unity of objective
6. Subordination of individual to group interest	6. Balance
7. Remuneration of personnel	7. Scalar chain
8. Degree of centralization	8. Functional definition
9. Scalar chain	9. Efficiency
10. Order	10. Span of management
11. Equity	11. Exception principle
12. Stability of tenure	12. Responsibility
13. Initiative	13. Feasibility
14. Esprit de corps	14. Continuity
	15. Leadership facilities

Fayol's concept of fair, clear *discipline, equity* in treatment, personal *initiative,* and *esprit de corps* are similar to what Koontz and O'Donnell describe as the ingredients necessary for a favorable *leadership climate.* In essence, what is being sought is a work situation with high morale and a chance for individuals to exercise initiative.

Order involves having a material order for the efficient placement of things and a social order for the placement of people—a place for everything and everything in its place. If the order is correct and minimum cost situations are obtained, the principle of efficiency is being followed. Efficiency attempts to get a maximum or desirable level of output from a given level or quantity of input. It is usually considered to be a short-run concept since longer-term input-output relationships are most often measured in terms of the effectiveness of the organization in reaching its standing goals.

The *exception principle* specifies that only exceptional or unusual situations are sent to higher levels of command for decision. Once a bench mark is set, subordinates follow precedents and continue to make decisions until other unusual circumstances arise. The net result is the establishment of a series of precedents to guide subordinates making routine decisions. Only exceptional circumstances are forwarded to higher levels of management for resolution.

Remuneration of personnel should be in line with the difficulty and importance of the job.

Functional definition spells out the specialized authority of each department and its relationship to the total organization. The *span of management* is defined as the number of people reporting directly to another person.

It is not a person-to-organization relation. If six men report to a supervisor, his span of control is six. This is true even though all six men may work in the same department or unit.

In the opinion of the so-called operational school of management, the widespread application of these or similar principles would bring about a high level of organizational efficiency. Inevitably, the best principles are not followed carefully and negative situations appear. When this happens, principles may be reinforced or restated; but again, a new set of informal reactions may appear and the cycle repeats ad infinitum. In spite of certain changes, however, many of these formal principles have held over time, and, advocates of this theory hold, they apply to any activities involving managerial skills, that is, they are universal.

These lists of principles, along with the traditional teachings of economics found in the works of Adam Smith, Alfred Marshall, and writers in the field of managerial economics such as Joel Dean, were and are the underpinning of what today might be called the classical school of management theory. The major focus of these principles is on the job and on the person doing the job. This job orientation eventually brings about the classic planning-organizing-controlling cycle which is the essence of traditional management writings. Most modern organizations have been set up and have operated using those classical doctrines which tend to place efficiency and economic performance above the development of human resources. In recent years, however, greater emphasis has been placed on human resource factors, and the classical doctrines and principles have been revised and expanded to reflect this changing emphasis.

Though many classical management doctrines seem to have great validity today, not all proposals have gained universal acceptance. The most outstanding objections to traditional classical theory appear in the following set of criticisms:

Classical theory fails to explain motivation fully or looks at it too simplistically.

The individual is emphasized at the expense of the group, but group relationships and pressures are so important that they deserve careful, close attention.

The informal organization is not given adequate recognition. Formal structures fail to show what really occurs at the various levels in the organizational hierarchy.

The whys of operations are often taken for granted. Past practice is held up as "correct" without any attempt to uncover the cause-and-effect relationships which brought about certain results.

Factors and forces outside of the organization are given inadequate attention. Traditional theory handles internal matters, but is unable to cope with forces in the total operating environment.

The influence of outside factors on individual behavior in the organization is either ignored or understated. Man plays roles other than that of economic man, and classical theory fails to allow for this multifaceted aspect of individual behavior.

Specialization and efficiency are overemphasized. The net result is a downgrading of human values in the rush toward efficient operation.

The principles developed by classical theorists are based on introspection rather than scientific observation. This casual experimental method places the entire philosophy under a cloud.

The criticisms have not gone unanswered by the advocates of the various classical theories, but many attacks have not been fully repulsed. One positive result of these critical forays has been the conduct of new and important research designed to either support or disprove various classical doctrines.

The process of analyzing, criticizing, synthesizing, and perhaps even redefining traditional areas has opened up new lines of thinking in the field of management. This probing has gone on at an increasing rate in recent years and its conclusions have become known collectively as modern management theory. Chapter 2 presents some of the more outstanding theories evolving from this research and attempts to evaluate these recent findings in the light of the more traditional doctrines. It is important to note that many of the latest research findings in this area have done more to shed light on classical doctrines than to refute them. Indeed, the questions raised by these researchers are often the same that the classicists were criticized for failing to answer fully.

Summary

Theories of management are a product of the twentieth century. In the early stages of industrial development there was little need for management theory, and little theory was apparent until Taylor popularized his "scientific management" concept. Though Taylor's teachings were accepted widely, he was criticized for his failure to give adequate attention to human resources and human motivation. Later researchers, notably Elton Mayo and the human relations school, claimed that Taylor had failed to attach adequate importance to social and group relationships in the industrial climate. Such criticisms shed serious doubt on some of the formal principles of management espoused by classical management writers, and research was initiated to investigate the validity of new and challenging hypotheses. These attacks on the classicist doctrine resulted in a body of thinking now known as modern management theory.

Study Questions

1. What conditions underlie the development of a first-rank industrial nation today? What similarities exist between these modern requirements and those

found in England during the early days of the Industrial Revolution? What about conditions in modern-day Brazil?

2. What basic premises underlie Frederick W. Taylor's theory of scientific management? Do you agree with Taylor's views? What are some present-day indications that Taylor's ideas are still with us?

3. How do Taylor's ideas on motivation contrast with those of Elton Mayo? Do you agree with either man? Explain.

4. Can you think of any current evidences of Mayo's teachings?

5. Henri Fayol was a practicing manager when he enumerated his principles. Do you feel his list would be helpful to a contemporary manager? What problems would it pose?

6. If economics and engineering are the underlying disciplines of scientific management, what disciplines are at the core of the human relations school? Can you give specific examples of how these disciplines enter into the theories developed by human relations theorists?

7. "The economic efficiency of America is the real reason why it is such a great nation." Do you agree with this statement? Why?

CHAPTER 2
Management: Modern Perspectives

Most early theories of management emphasized lists of prescriptions and sets of principles. Much validation and refinement have occurred since then and newer areas have unfolded, particularly since the advent of computer technology. Computers have allowed theorists to construct powerful and sophisticated mathematical models capable of shedding light on managing inventories, balancing assembly lines, improving production work flows, analyzing the relative profitability of various product-mix combinations, and time-activity planning techniques (for example, PERT and PERT cost [1]). Human relations researchers have also built very sophisticated and modern castles on the foundations laid initially by the Hawthorne experiments. Writings emphasizing man's role as a thinking, rational being who responds in kind to good and bad treatment have been widely read and have proven to be operationally applicable in a variety of settings.[2]

In scientific management major emphasis was placed on the job, while human relations concepts focused much more sharply on the individual and his relationships with his work group and to his work environment. Current formulations of classical management principles reflect both of these orientations, but they are primarily work- or job-oriented, a fact generating criticism from a widely divergent group of writers espousing a set of ideas known as "modern organization theory."

The viewpoints taken by theorists writing about modern organizations are so dissimilar that a small group of experts have written extensively about how to classify the various ideas making up the totality of both classical and modern organizational theory.

---

[1] PERT is discussed in Chapter 10.
[2] See, for example, Douglas McGregor, *The Human Side of Enterprise* (New York: McGraw-Hill, Inc., 1960).

Paul Gordon divides the subject into traditional, behavioral, decision theory, and ecological areas.[3] Harold Koontz classifies it into the management process school, the empirical school, the human behavior school, the social systems school, the decision theory school, and the mathematical school.[4] Haynes and Massie identify the various streams of thought as quantitative concepts, managerial economics, accounting, universals of management (principles), scientific management, human relations, and behavioral sciences.[5] Ernest Dale, on the other hand, uses the dichotomy of classicists and behaviorists.[6] Whatever breakdown is accepted, modern organization theorists have either developed new and challenging approaches and theories or have built on or sharpened traditional doctrines.

In order to fully grasp the content and scope of these new philosophies, categorization by "school," or area of emphasis, is helpful. For pedagogical purposes then, one more classification scheme is added to those in the previous paragraphs:

1. Classical management theory including Frederick W. Taylor and other writers concerned with developing formal organization structures and/or lists of principles

2. Human behavior theorists including writers in the field of individual need structures, small group theories, and interrelationships between groups

3. Social and political systems approaches such as Weber's bureaucracy, Barnard's and March and Simon's authority concepts, the political theory of power espoused by Machiavelli, and the visualization of man as a player of roles and/or decision maker

4. Ecological systems approaches including generalizations of all interactions into unified "systems" of organization or models of attitudes, sentiments and interaction which evolve into an emergent system.[7]

5. Rational decision-making concepts which focus on the decision rather than people or principles and which tend to use quantitative methods as basic tools.

CLASSICAL MANAGEMENT THEORY

Even in the most recent formulations of the classical approach, the cycle of planning, organizing, and controlling organizational activities remains as the

---

[3] "Transcend the Current Debate on Administrative Theory," *Journal of the Academy of Management,* vol. 6, no. 3 (December 1963), pp. 290–303.

[4] "The Management Theory Jungle," *Journal of the Academy of Management,* vol. 4, no. 3 (December 1961), pp. 174–188.

[5] Warren W. Haynes and Joseph L. Massie, *Management: Analysis, Concepts and Cases* (Englewood Cliffs, N.J.: Prentice-Hall, Inc., 1961).

[6] *Management: Theory and Practice* (New York: McGraw-Hill, Inc., 1965).

[7] For example, see Kenneth Boulding, "General Systems Theory—The Skeleton of Science," *Management Science,* vol. 2 (April 1965), p. 197.

key concept. Though the *P-O-C* cycle has been placed under fire by some academicians, it still provides a useful model for students and scholars and serves as a practical guide for operatory managers. Indeed, many "new" theories of organizational behavior contribute very few novel or worthwhile additions to the classical approach, in spite of strong disclaimers by their creators. The ideas of Taylor, Mayo, and others are far from dead, even though they may be less fashionable currently than other approaches. Managers *do* plan for the future, they *must* organize the work of their subordinates and units, and they *do* control results by observation, review, and corrective action. How to perform these activities more effectively is still the focus of the contemporary classical management literature. This utilitarian orientation tends to make classical writings more popular in managerial circles than in academia. Recent developments in the classical approach include more sophisticated interpretations of man and his job, more careful study of work itself, and a greater tendency to include job climate and job environment in the list of principles or variables influencing the assignment of work and the motivation of workers. In short, the most significant changes are that behavioral and decision theory have been integrated in whole or part into classical management theory. With these additions, classical concepts have shown a durability and utility that newer ideas have been unable to disprove, dislodge, or replace.

THE HUMAN BEHAVIOR SCHOOL

One of the basic reasons why behavior research has influenced classical management literature so heavily becomes obvious when one recognizes the subject matter encompassed by behavioral research. Starting with the individual, behavioral science expands in breadth to include small groups, large groups, organizations, and even larger communities. The topical coverage is so vast it is often difficult to isolate the work of different men or even different schools of thought. The method chosen to accomplish this result is to focus on the individual and then to look at small and larger group behavior as a natural extension of research on individual behavior.

Explanations of individual behavior tend to cut across the entire field of psychology, and the environmentalist reporting of individual reactions to sets of stimuli was reviewed in Chapter 1. Concepts taken from the Gestalt school of psychology appear quite clearly in the "communications" portion of organization theory and in research dealing with individual perception. Communication is influenced by how people perceive the message and its import, and a failure to communicate effectively can and does exert a critical effect on individual reactions and organizational performance. Freudian overtones are found in industrial counseling and training and in the use of modified group therapy, one version of which appears under the "T group," or "sensitivity-training," label.[8] Straightening out a man's behavior by man-to-man

---

[8] Sensitivity training is discussed in Chapter 14.

talk smacks of amateur psychiatry; and sensitivity training, though its advocates deny the fact heatedly, does bear traces of approaches first learned and practiced in group therapy sessions conducted by psychologists and psychiatrists. Various clinical and experimental findings also appear in present-day industrial settings. Industrial psychology has brought forth such ideas as Maier's frustration-aggression complex, which says a frustrated man tends to follow fixated patterns of behavior. Since there is no easy way to get into New York City from Long Island, commuters stoically drive on the Long Island Expressway day after day, frustrated but fixated. Another application is training methodologies based on Pavlov's experiments on the feeding habits and reactions of canines wherein he showed that dogs could be made to salivate by ringing a bell usually activated just before feeding time. The message learned by industrial trainers is that repetition conditions behavioral response—if a man is told something often enough (redundant training) he'll respond automatically.

For purposes of studying individual behavior, however, perhaps the most useful single framework is the need structure developed by Maslow, in which he lays out how human needs can best be classified and analyzed. A number of other approaches can be used to study individual needs, but a modification of Maslow's highly utilitarian version of the individual need structure illustrates the sets of needs he identifies as critical components of human behavior.

NEED	EXAMPLE
1. Physical or basic needs	Survival and reproduction needs such as hunger, thirst, sex, and reproduction of the species
2. Economic needs	Material goods, shelter, clothing, and economic needs which go beyond the minimum level of subsistence
3. Safety needs	The need to be safe from attack by external forces or predators
4. Social needs	The need to associate with like beings (the herding instinct) and the need for belonging to something or someone
5. Security needs	The need for security developed by the possession of knowledge or position
6. Ego or self-fulfillment needs	The need to have pride in individual accomplishment or to possess a sense of importance

These six categories, which list individual needs in what is normally considered to be an increasing order of complexity, can also be used to explain the hierarchical nature of individual need structures.

Saying that needs are hierarchical simply means that once a low-level, or primary, need is met it is replaced by another need which possesses a higher level of complexity or priority. For example, once an organism is no longer thirsty or hungry it may seek to improve its condition of life. If man is the organism in question, he might seek to improve his standard of living. Man might, once his basic aspirations develop beyond the subsistence level, attempt to provide greater security from attack and to search for companionship (man settled in walled cities after living in caves). He might then look for knowledge in institutions of learning and seek self-fulfillment in artistic, recreational, or do-it-yourself activities.

Individuals may be seeking to fulfill all these needs at the same time. The potency of a particular need at any given time thus becomes a function of the progress made toward the attainment of the entire hierarchy of needs. To put it another way, the progression of an organism through increasing levels of complexity in the need structure is not made by casting aside the conditions which met each previous, or lower-level, need, but by retaining these conditions while seeking new and higher levels of satisfaction. Thus the quest for need satisfaction involves both the retention of the status quo *and* the continual invasion of new areas of satisfaction. Psychologist Scott Myers of the Texas Instrument Company talks about "maintenance needs" and "motivational factors" to point out these differences. The former simply meet people's expectations, while the latter move them to do things, hopefully positive things. Of the two categories, the latter are the most difficult to satisfy; indeed, it is probably correct to state that within the sphere of today's level of knowledge, man's self-fulfillment, ego, and self-esteem needs cannot be met.

The portions of man's individual needs which deal with his daily work are a critical segment of his total need structure. Man at work has both on-the-job and off-the-job needs met in some part by the work he performs.[9] Work meets man's off-the-job needs for money, security, and advancement. It also provides the individual with need satisfactions derived from having some degree of autonomy over methods of performing his job, participation in decision making, knowledge of position or activities, group or social needs including friendship and teamwork, and supervisory or other related needs including the desire for fair treatment, praise, or recognition.

Needs have dimensions which must be considered, recognized, and met (if possible) by alert management. First, individual needs have several levels of complexity, as is shown by the groupings in the preceding table of needs. Next, they are hierarchical; once a need is met it is replaced by another need, usually of a higher order. Satisfaction is reached at least in partial terms for lower-order needs, but higher-order needs continually replace them in the needs hierarchy. Third, the need structure has dimensions which extend well beyond the forces controlling the organization within which the individual functions. Finally, individual needs vary at different levels in the organizational pyramid.

---

[9] For an excellent discussion of the subject, see George S. Strauss and Leonard R. Sayles, *Personnel: The Human Problems of Management,* 2nd ed. (Englewood Cliffs, N.J.: Prentice-Hall, Inc., 1967).

This final point comes into focus most sharply when a comparison is made between the needs and goals of corporate presidents and corporate floor polishers. It can be argued that needs differences are based primarily on heredity, environment, or other factors peculiar to specific occupational groupings; but the relative importance of these elements has never been established clearly. The critical thing is that differences do exist and that they must be considered carefully if corporate plans and policies are to harmonize rather than clash with individual needs. This means particular plans and approaches may have to be slanted or adapted to meet the actual and potential needs that exist at different organizational levels. A common example of such an accommodation process is the Sears Roebuck concept of decentralized store management, which allows individual store managers to exercise buying discretion within the general limits set by the long-range plans developed by central management. Similar adjustments may also be made to reflect the particular needs specifications existing within occupational categories. As a corollary to adjustment considerations, psychologists emphasizing the importance of individual needs generally advocate that managers should ponder not only what needs exist at present but also the dynamic nature of the total need structure. Then, after considering the limits imposed by organizational goals and objectives, they urge managements to develop approaches which maximize the integration of the organization's goals with those of its individual members. No one at Columbia University will ever need to be reminded again of this point after the student uprisings of 1968.

To summarize, the behaviorist treatment of individual needs holds that managers should attempt to probe what needs individuals possess, the extent to which these needs are being met, and the degree to which these needs can or will be considered in the administration of particular activities or programs. The end result of such considerations, they contend, would make work more rewarding and thus more productive.

Individual needs alone, however, cannot explain why individuals do what they do. Human behavior theorists as a group defend the proposition that group relationships are the real key to behavior. Some of these theorists have advocated theories which, though difficult to digest briefly, are so potentially useful that summarization is justified even at the risk of slighting some of the more prominent contributors[10] Keeping this risk of omission in mind. the following paragraphs attempt to pull together some of the more basic ideas which have dominated the research dealing with group theory and group dynamics.

The participative approach to management is based in the premise that people want to participate in decision making—and further that they have the

---

[10] Among the contributors here are Homans, Viteles, Lewin, Seashore, Argyris, and Haire. The writings of individuals such as McGregor, Likert, Blake, W.F. Whyte, and Barnard will be discussed more fully in upcoming chapters. No claim is made that these men exhaust the list of those who have made meaningful contributions to group research; at best this is a token listing of some of the better-known researchers in the field.

capability to help shape meaningful decisions. At least one dissenter voices the opinion that this theory is based on an oversimplified notion. Psychologist Clare Graves of Union College, Schenectady, New York, contends that many individuals need old-line authoritarian methods to meet their psychological needs.

Graves identifies seven fairly distinct stages of personality and claims that adults are at one level, moving only one or two notches at best, throughout their lifetimes. He further contends that each stage can contain individual personality types, which are bright or dull, mature or immature. Graves' seven stages and a brief commentary follow:

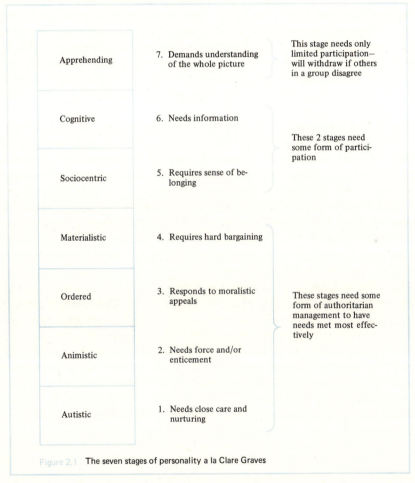

Apprehending	7. Demands understanding of the whole picture	This stage needs only limited participation— will withdraw if others in a group disagree
Cognitive	6. Needs information	These 2 stages need some form of participation
Sociocentric	5. Requires sense of belonging	
Materialistic	4. Requires hard bargaining	
Ordered	3. Responds to moralistic appeals	These stages need some form of authoritarian management to have needs met most effectively
Animistic	2. Needs force and/or enticement	
Autistic	1. Needs close care and nurturing	

Figure 2.1   The seven stages of personality a la Clare Graves

The moral Graves draws from his seven-stage model is clear: if managements wish to meet people's psychological needs most effectively they must sort out the dominant personality types and expose them to the managerial style best suited to their needs. If the Graves classification has any validity, participative management styles would apply only to a limited number of individuals.

Elton Mayo's findings have already been discussed. They point out the importance of relationships between group members in determining productivity, and other factors such as the receptivity of a given group to innovation initiated by management versus those generated by the group. These points were later expanded and developed by Homans in his far-reaching works in small-group theory.[11] Kurt Lewin conducted studies which eventually evolved into the area now known as "group dynamics." Lewin also did ground-breaking work in the relative effectiveness of various leadership patterns in small group relationships. After probing authoritarian and democratic leadership patterns, Lewin opted for democratic leadership because of its greater effectiveness. In addition, Lewin emphasized the importance of various roles that individuals play in determining which course of actions people may follow in different situations.[12] The concept of "role" thus gained exposure in management literature; and man's view of his role in particular situations became accepted as a factor shaping the individual value judgments which affect individual decision making.

A group of University of Michigan researchers headed by Rensis Likert and others such as Douglas McGregor and Arnold Tannenbaum have expanded and developed patterns and concepts of production versus person-centered leadership for achieving improved levels of morale and productivity. The famous Prudential studies conducted by the University of Michigan Survey Research Center pointed out the effect of leadership on output, and other studies of group relationships conducted in various industrial settings have given similar insights.[13] As Lewin had done, the Michigan studies advocated participative person-centered leadership as the most fulfilling and productive method of leading and supervising.

The effect of leadership on output was described more fully by McGregor when he described the effects of using authoritarian leadership (Theory X) rather than a person-oriented leadership (Theory Y).[14] In essence, McGregor said that man was treated in organizations as a nonmotivated entity rather than a noble being capable of responding positively to challenge and more demanding work. McGregor, who strongly advocated the Theory Y approach, brings to mind the old adage that it is far easier and much more effective to pull a string than to try to push it.

Tannenbaum and Schmidt also classify types of leadership but come up with a different set of classifications than McGregor.[15] They identify consulta-

---

[11] Paul Homans, *The Human Group* (New York: Harcourt, Brace & World, Inc., 1950).

[12] Kurt Lewin, *Field Theory and Social Science* (New York: Harper & Row, Publishers, 1951). See also Lewin's *A Dynamic Theory of Personality* (New York: McGraw-Hill, Inc., 1935).

[13] See Rensis Likert, *New Patterns of Management* (New York: McGraw-Hill, Inc., 1961).

[14] McGregor, *op. cit.*

[15] Arnold Tannenbaum and A. Schmidt, "How to Choose a Leadership Pattern," *Harvard Business Review,* March–April 1958, pp. 95–101.

tive, free-rein, and authoritarian techniques and set out some basic guides on how to make choices among these alternatives. Tannenbaum and Schmidt hold that the ultimate choice of an effective leadership pattern depends on the characteristics of supervisors, subordinates, and situations; but they, like Likert, McGregor, and Lewin came out with a bias for democratic, more consultative patterns of leadership.

Robert R. Blake and Jane S. Mouton, in their studies of group behavior and group decision making, advocate a more person-centered approach to leadership but focus also on the importance of production. They see production best attained through a series of group participation activities designed to enable the organization to reach its ongoing goals.[16] Communications studies conducted along with group dynamics studies showed how interaction takes place between people, how conflict can result from breakdowns in the means of transmitting information, and how harmony can be enhanced by improving flows and patterns of communication. Alex Bavelas studied these patterns and pointed out the effect of hierarchical levels on the efficiency of the information-dispensing process.[17] In general, the more levels the message passes through, the less chance it has of being understood as stated and accepted as desired by the transmitter. Such studies disclosed not only the existence of group patterns and pressures and their effect on organizational effectiveness but also the need to study how these pressures could be relieved or eliminated.[18]

This highly selective and somewhat arbitrary review indicates only a few of the thoughts that the human behavior school advocates to bring about greater knowledge and understanding of man at work. These studies, though shedding light on how and why individual and group behavior influences workers' motivations, supervision and communication patterns, and productivity, also raise some doubts and questions. To cite some of the more troublesome questions:

1. Can group findings be applied in all organizations?
2. Have the values of researchers entered into conclusions, particularly in small-group research?
3. Are the conclusions drawn by the behaviorists wholly valid, that is, is it true that adopting participative patterns actually improves both morale and output, or are individual values so subordinated to group-think that there is no net gain if group tyranny replaces management authoritarianism?

These and other problems have been raised by critics in different schools of management thought, but the most energetic attacks have been made by the individuals identified with the social and political systems school.

---

[16] Robert R. Blake and Jane S. Mouton, *The Managerial Grid* (Houston, Tex.: The Gulf Publishing Company, 1964).

[17] "Communications Patterns in Task Oriented Groups," *Journal of the Acoustical Society of America,* vol. 22 (1950), pp. 725–730.

[18] H. Leavitt, *Managerial Psychology* (Chicago, Ill.: University of Chicago Press, 1958).

SOCIAL AND POLITICAL SYSTEMS SCHOOL

Though Max Weber's work is closely associated with classical management doctrines, his basic works on bureaucratic models present a point of view that has been analyzed by modern theorists and researchers. Weber, one of the great German social scientists, developed among his many researches and writings a concept of bureaucracy that has generated a great deal of controversy and set off a flurry of research, both pro and con. Weber saw bureaucracy as one of man's major contributions to organizational efficiency and considered it far superior to the patrimonial system then in existence. Weber's ideas on rational bureaucracies run by professional managers with power springing from legal and traditional bases comprise a political-social model of organization that has undergone renaissance and rediscovery as industrial, governmental, and social institutions continue to grow in size and complexity.

One of the more far-reaching by-products of the kinds of ideas developed by Weber is the writing of Chester I. Barnard. Barnard's sophisticated ideas, which go well beyond both Weber's constructs and the outpourings of early group researchers, expound a theory of authority based not on formal or traditional power to command and expect obedience, but on the individual's decision to accept or refuse the orders given by the source or agent of authority.[19] This acceptance theory of authority, later expanded by Herbert A. Simon, made a sharp break with the traditional concepts of authority resting on such formal grounds as the rights of property owners; and it opened up an extended discussion of reasons why people do or do not follow orders. This discussion in turn gave rise to general study of the dynamics of superior-subordinate associations in one-to-one situations and in man-to-group relationships.

Many of the findings of small group theory and studies of authority have been incorporated into what is now generally known as Simon's organization theory.[20] Simon goes well beyond the scope of narrow behavioral research, since he draws on economics, the behavioral sciences, psychology, mathematics, and business and public administration to support his various points. He also moves away from the psychological and sociological slants in earlier research and brings in more of the rationality of theoretical economics. In actuality, his concepts of rational decision making hit somewhat of a midpoint between psychology and economics, since he stresses the concept of "intended" rationality as one of the critical explanations of behavior.

Simon views organizations as structures made up of decision makers. The individuals making decisions have individual preferences, given amounts of information, and certain sets of organizational goals and loyalties. Thus the decisions made are a function of the manipulation or flow of influences acting upon individual decision makers.

---

[19] Chester I. Barnard, *Functions of the Executive* (Cambridge, Mass.: Harvard University Press, 1938).

[20] The most definitive works by Simon are *Administrative Behavior* (New York: Crowell-Collier and Macmillan, Inc., 1951) and *Organizations* (New York: John Wiley & Sons, Inc., 1958), written with James G. March.

In essence, Simon's concept of organizations is an acceptance theory. It postulates that a communication is carried out only if accepted by the recipient. The final decision on what to do when a given directive is received is based on how the receiver evaluates the sanction-and-reward scheme operative in the governing organization. The decision maker, after receiving and reviewing the available alternatives, will choose the action most likely to balance all the conflicting variables rather than maximize the results which might be obtained if only a limited number of variables were considered. The key to success in Simon's approach is to recognize the factors limiting the decision maker's range of choice and to adjust them to improve the quality of decision making. Within this system the communication of information is given paramount importance, since Simon contends that the quality of the process depends on adequate and timely flows of carefully selected inputs of information.

Simon's approach expands that of the human behavior school by viewing the total context of the social system in the light of psychological, economic, sociological, political, and other key variables. It also stresses rationality and intended consequences rather than the personality and emotional factors often emphasized by the human relations school.

Another set of ideas on power and authority relationships now being revived was developed over four centuries ago by Niccolo Machiavelli in *The Prince*. Machiavelli's ideas on how the prince should run his domain have gained widespread popular exposure in two recent books, *The Secret of Santa Vittoria*, a novel by Robert Crichton,[21] and *Management and Machiavelli*, an unscholarly but thought-provoking book written by English author Anthony Jay.[22] The Machiavellian approach, now a generic term for manipulation and scheming, recognizes the impact and use of power and uses power to bring about the ends sought by the prince. People's weaknesses are seen to be as important as their strengths, and both good and bad qualities are employed as people are "managed" by the ruler (or the executive). Machiavelli also lays out principles for handling baronies and territories (analogous to divisions and firms), while pointing out the hazards of uprisings and coups and advocating means for coping with such external and internal upsets. One sample counsel he gives is to either treat heads of new territories kindly or remove them, a bit of information which Jay feels is quite valuable to firms engaged in extensive merger activities. Since Machiavelli wrote as a consultant to a ruling executive, his advice hits a responsive chord in the minds of many highly placed executives. The use of power is as familiar to many of them as it must have been to Machiavelli's prince; and Machiavelli's suggestions, unlike many theoretical postulates developed by academicians, have the ring of practicality. Power is always present in organizational relationships, but its naked use is disavowed publicly while being invoked privately. Machiavelli

---

[21] (New York: Simon and Schuster, Inc., 1966).
[22] (New York: Holt, Rinehart and Winston, Inc., 1968).

wrote the primer on the use of power and formal authority, and modern power wielders are still using his basic principles in new sophisticated guises. Machiavelli wrote, "The main foundations [of power] which all states must have ... are good laws and good armies." Substitute *policies* for *laws* and *subordinates* for *armies* and you see the power base of Machiavelli in the modern corporation.

In late 1967, the head of the giant Interpublic communications empire, Marion Harper, was ousted from the presidency in what *Fortune* termed a "coup d'etat." In words that smacked of Machiavelli, *Fortune* reported,

> In the last week of October, Harper went abroad, accompanied by Williams and Robert Durham. After he left, McNamara drew up the agenda for a special meeting of the board. Harper was then contacted in Europe and told that the banks had suggested a board meeting at which they hoped some cost reductions would be effected. When Harper agreed to call the meeting, Williams cut short his trip and came home in advance to join McNamara and Taggart, and rehearse their plan of action. During that period, Healy was told of the plan. By the time the meeting opened, Harper's fate was sealed. Spielvogel, Williams, Taggart, and McNamara formed a solid majority. When the motion to replace Harper was moved, six hands were raised to support it. Harper was stunned.[23]

The planning and execution of the coup that replaced Mr. Harper were a manifestation of the kind of corporate power play managers know and fear and yet have learned to live with, albeit uneasily. The potential exercise of power and its occasional use have established and buttressed more executives than most management authorities care to admit, and it is probably one reason why *The Prince* has remained a best seller for centuries. Rediscovered again in the 1960s, it brings a hard line out of political science into the management literature and, incidently, gives an enduring but socially sub rosa style of management a certain amount of intellectual and academic respectablility.

ECOLOGICAL, OR GENERAL, SYSTEMS

The ecological systems approach to organization suffers from neither a lack of academic acceptance nor the limitation of drawing upon only one or two behavioral disciplines. In effect, the ecological systems school of organization theory has no limits on what it can call upon to explain the hows and whys of organizational behavior and activity. Its basic idea is that groups should be studied in terms of activities, interaction, and sentiments as evolved in the development of models which attempt to evaluate what type of emergent systems may evolve from intergroup and intragroup activities relationships. It also seeks to predict how these systems may move toward stability or perhaps even greater instability. Conflict in nature, for example, has been likened to the work situation by Boulding in his recent studies of conflict in many

---

[23] "The Coup d'Etat at Interpublic," *Fortune,* (February 1968), p. 203.

forms of societies. Boulding has compared conflict between trees and grass, the sea and the land, and sharks and little fishes to oligopolistic behavior in the marketplace. Ecological studies have ranged over a wide variety of areas and activities, and they have often gone well beyond the normal limits of studies of organizational behavior.

The entire area of general systems theory developed along with the use of computer technology and it was brought to the public's attention by Nobert Weiner in his bench mark work on cybernetics.[24] Ecological systems theory approaches to organizations form a much more generalized point of view than even the social systems school; for example, findings from the social, physical, and biological sciences have been integrated into some of the analyses developed by general systems theorists.[25] These writers have widened the range of what variables may influence organizational behavior by considering factors not hitherto utilized in explanations of behavioral and developmental patterns in organizations. They have opened up new insights into relationships between organizations as well as within them, and this comparative facet has been one of their most far-reaching contributions. The other is its inclusiveness. As information-processing techniques become more sophisticated the scope of their approach may become wider, its focus may sharpen, and its teachings may become more utilitarian. Ecological and general systems concepts have already appeared in a variety of practical applications. Long-range planning models routinely consider and evaluate factors such as social climate, political influences, possible legislation, technological developments, and consumer attitudes. Military early-warning and aircraft-plotting systems utilize the findings of general systems theory to integrate recording of data and key variables into routines and programs designed to assist in deciding whether a recorded bogey is friendly or hostile; and beyond that, whether or not the button should be pushed to set off the Bomb.

The critical variable analysis model in Figure 3.3 illustrates some of the key variables and factors that might enter into the planning of strategy for a business-oriented organization. This model is still another way in which the general systems approach can be utilized to handle a complex set of interrelated problems.

RATIONAL DECISION-MAKING SCHOOL

Though certain similarities exist between the human behavior, social systems, and ecological, or general systems, schools, the rational decision-making school utilizes a somewhat different approach.[26] The focus in this school is not on

---

[24] *The Human Use of Human Beings: Cybernetics and Society,* 2nd ed. (New York: Doubleday & Company, Inc., 1956).

[25] R.A. Johnson, F.E. Kast, and J.E. Rosenzweig, *The Theory and Management of Systems* (New York: McGraw-Hill, Inc., 1963).

[26] One view of this is found in David W. Miller and Martin K. Starr, *Executive Decisions and Operations Research* (Englewood Cliffs, N.J.: Prentice-Hall, Inc., 1960).

the people or the environmental variables influencing behavior, but on the decision itself. Advocates of this school reason that decision making is the most critical function of management, thus any study of management should focus directly on the decisions themselves.[27]

Much of the thinking in this school evolves out of economic theory of consumer choice and develops in the form of choice models and maximization concepts. Mathematical decision theory, including both objective and subjective probability, has added new dimensions to the rational decision-making approach. And this development, aided by advanced computer technology, has evolved to a point where it seeks to manipulate and explain complex sets of variables in a series of decision models which specify decision guidelines under conditions of both certainty and uncertainty.

Like some of the other schools, however, the decision-making school has shortcomings. For one thing, it has never been proven that either the management job or the operation of organizations can be explained fully by focusing on the factors usually treated as variables by the decision-making school. Most decision models either cannot or do not include "soft" variables such as assessment of human potential, evaluation of political trends and pressures, and the effect of alternative decisions on the various levels of management, on customers, and on the general public. In its present state, the decision-making school is oriented much more toward technique than philosophy. It adds a great deal to the science and art of decision making, but it has not yet reached full status as a separate school of thinking. In time, with the help of better and better computer routines, it will assume new importance in the study of organizational behavior. In its short life, it has already opened up new and potentially practical avenues of exploration and development. Some of its more practical contributions to the art and practice of decision making are presented more fully in chapters 6 and 7.

Summary

The preceding discussion of modern organization theory is more a brief résumé than an inclusive cataloguing of modern organizational theories. It does, however, relate some of the more prominent ideas so that they may be compared with or added to the classical concepts described in the preceding chapter. This panorama of modern and classical doctrines dealing with management and organizations shows the kind of research and thinking underlying the ways in which managers and organizations are currently operating and will operate in years to come. The following chapter will attempt to link some of these theoretical formulations to the job of developing management strategy and tactics for use in actual organizations.

---

[27] See R. Luce and H. Raiffa, *Games and Decisions* (New York: John Wiley & Sons, Inc., 1957).

Study Questions

1. What similarities and differences exist among the classical, behavioral, and social political systems schools of management?

2. What contrasts can be drawn between the rational decision-making school and the ecological and general systems schools? Similarities?

3. What changes, if any, has the development of computer technology brought into modern organization theory?

4. Do you feel that any one theory is superior to the others? Justify your answer.

5. Do you agree that Machiavelli's ideas are widely denounced but widely used? What do you think of them in moral terms? What do you think of their practicality?

Traditional and modern management theory are the foundations of management thinking today in both academia and business. Traditional theory tends to emphasize functions and principles, while modern theories seek to explain the whys and hows of behavior in terms of decisions, systems of interacting variables, and/or human behavior. The big problem is to develop a way of organizing these approaches so that they can be useful to both students and practicing managers.

In fact, none of the schemes described in the preceding chapters are really self-supporting or independent; they overlap a great deal. Traditional approaches, if carried out carefully, use many modern concepts and theories. Modern theorists never really exclude traditional processes, no matter how carefully they avoid stating dogmatic introspective principles or hackneyed labels. The big thing is to get the job done and done well, not to bicker about terminology, technique, or research methodology.

All theories of behavior and problem solving should be designed with the eventual end of assisting managers to gain a better understanding of the hows, whats, and whys of organizational behavior. Managers should view these formulations as inputs, not as "the truth," for each man has to forge his own truth. No manager can escape his own particular truth: analytical schemes and theories can only provide guidelines, not sure solutions. This somewhat pragmatic approach is the focus of this chapter, which calls on both past and present to deal with the strategic and tactical critical problems facing management.

The models developed to bridge the gap between old and new possess

CHAPTER 3
Systems for Strategic and Tactical Analysis

many of the characteristics of both their time-honored and modern progenitors. Since the factors, variables, and theories underlying their construction are relatively well known, perhaps their main contribution lies in the attempt to blend old and new into a useful set of analytical systems.

As a generalization, all four models described are laid out in a systems format. Each column in the model's matrix relates a particular item to a corresponding item intersected in each row. Thus, in Figure 3.1, the *planning* column would be read, *planning for marketing, planning for production,* and so forth. Four models are offered because the strategic and tactical problems encountered by managers are too complex to be handled by a single approach. In order to sharpen the focus of the attack, the models illustrate application in a business orientation (titles of rows in the matrix are *marketing, finance, production,* and so forth). With very few changes, the proposed methodologies can be adapted to deal with problems of almost any kind of organization. This somewhat grandiose claim is justified by the growing number of applications that systems models now encompass. With this adaptive proviso in mind, the four models listed below are presented as general systems evaluating, analyzing, and relating theory to strategy and tactics:

Process analysis

Concept analysis

Critical variable analysis

Technique analysis

Problem / Function	Strategic and tactical emphasis varies with the nature of the specific problem				
	Planning	Organizing	Controlling	Delegating	Representing
Marketing					
Production					
Finance					
Human relations					
Research					
– – – – – – – – –					
– – – – – – – – –					
– – – – – – – – –					

Figure 3.1   Process analysis

PROCESS ANALYSIS

The first and perhaps most ubiquitous analytical scheme is based primarily on classical or traditional theories of management. It focuses on the process of management as it is practiced in solving problems inside the firm. It may also be used to handle situations in the external environment, but it is most effective in dealing with internal problems in such organization areas as production, marketing, finance, personnel, and research. It is particularly useful in handling planning problems, for example, the introduction of a new product produced by the research and development group.

Process analysis is an approach favored by many traditional management writers. The basic management functions of planning, organizing, control, and delegation are identified as the key parts of the management job. Representing the organization to its various publics such as customers, vendors, government, civic groups, and so forth has recently appeared as another basic process in much of the management literature. Problems are framed within the major areas of business or organizational operation and handled through the medium of the basic functions used to guide the managers in what should be done and how to do it. Strategies are developed in line with guiding principles, and tactics are also constructed following the basic lists of principles outlined in classical theory. The blending of strategic and tactical factors and their weighting vary with the nature of the problem, and, as always, with the practices most favored at given points in time. For example, a marketing problem may arise in terms of a competitive product cutting into sales. The strategy selected might be to develop a competing product. Plans are then set up, an organization is developed to carry them out, and controls and interim reports are instituted with appropriate feedback designed to inform management of the relative degree of progress made toward attaining desired objectives. The tactics used at various stages are determined by the specific problems faced and the particular situation where those tactics will be employed. Authors such as Newman, Koontz and O'Donnell, Terry, LeBreton, and Fox have stressed this approach in texts that have been read by large numbers of students and practicing managers. This approach to analyzing managerial duties and organizational dynamics is still advocated strongly by many able practitioners and management scholars.

LeBreton and Fox specify this approach more sharply than some of the other management process writers. Fox sets up a matrix which places the basic planning-organizing-controlling functions in columns and repeats them as headings of the rows in the systems matrix. The result is an analytical scheme which defines and analyzes problems in terms of categories such as *planning for control, planning for organizing, planning for planning,* and so on.[1] LeBreton divides the process of management into two processes: planning and implementation. He identifies fourteen steps in planning and seventeen factors in implementation.[2] He then specifies how each of the fourteen planning steps must be carried out in terms of the seventeen critical factors in the implementation phase of the model. The point-by-point development of Le-

---

[1] See W. Fox, *The Management Process* (Homewood, Ill.: Richard D. Irwin, Inc., 1963).

[2] Preston P. LeBreton, *General Administration: Planning and Implementation* (New York: Holt, Rinehart and Winston, Inc., 1965).

Breton's general administration model specifies the whats and hows of the process of administration and proceeds to detail these steps in terms of a seventeen-by-fourteen matrix. In his system, obtaining approval of the plan is one step in the planning process. A sample implementation step is "obtaining an understanding of the components of the plan." He would thus, at one of the points of intersection, specify that the planning step be implemented by providing for a procedure for explaining the technical portions of the plan.

In spite of its seeming plausibility and orderliness, process analysis has come under attack in recent years, principally because it is based on introspection rather than hard research. Perhaps the most devastating scholarly critiques of this approach have been generated by the fact that it has been expounded over and over again in different words by different authors without adding much to its content. Process analysis is no longer fashionable because it is so well known, and this familiarity has tended to breed contempt, or at least boredom. The operational value of the approach has never been disproven, as witnessed by its pervasiveness, but its theoretical triteness has placed it in a least-favored position with many management theoreticians. Managers, however, still find it to be a useful, practical model for analyzing problems and moving toward their solution. It is particularly valuable for solving problems whose parameters lie within the boundaries of the firm. Cost controls, inventory and financial control, production scheduling, quality control, sales planning, and so forth fit neatly into its confines. More complex problems involving the outside environment typically call for a slightly more sophisticated analytical model such as critical variable analysis.

CONCEPT ANALYSIS

Another so-called traditional approach to problem analysis and decision making is to base the analysis on a recognition and handling of the various concepts influencing the problem or decision under consideration. A concept, or to put it another way, a general notion or idea, can be global, intermediate, or specific in scope. For example, an organization's long-run goals are very broad concepts, while detailed operating procedures are narrower in scope. Though there are many ways to define goals, policies, and so forth, the following definitions and illustrations are offered to serve as an index to the functioning of the concept analysis model.

Goals are the organization's long-term, standing guides to action, while *objectives,* though the term is often used interchangeably with goals, are more realistically identified as organizational goals translated into individual terms. That is, objectives are the goals of the organization specified in terms of what the organization expects individuals to accomplish. *Policies* are also long-term guides to action, but they cover relatively specific areas. Policies are the operating guides set up to give direction in the day-by-day management of the going organization. Since they are less general than goals and objectives, they have flexibility that allows them to be revised with relative ease. To illustrate, a long-term organizational goal might be to seek a rate of return of an invested capital of at least 10 percent after taxes. An executive may operate within a set of objectives that are consistent with the organization's goals, that is, he may work to run his unit in such a way that it returns the desired percentage. For example, the goal of increasing long-run profitability in an enterprise might be expressed as a managerial objective for the head of division X in the following way, "Division X is expected to earn no less than 5 percent per year after taxes on a sales base expanding no less than 6 percent per year." A financial policy that helps both the organization and the individual to reach targeted quotas might set a minimum cutoff on a new capital investment. For example, this policy might state, "No new capital investments will be undertaken that yield less than 15 percent after taxes on average amounts of capital invested." In similar fashion, policies and objectives in other areas might also be tied directly into the total goals structure. Social goals have become increasingly important in recent years, as the Fairchild-Hiller Company, for one, has long recognized. President Edward G. Uhl, commenting in 1968 on Fairchild-Hiller's attempt to bring black workers and management into its Fairmicco, Inc., a joint venture with the United States government and the District of Columbia's Model Inner City Community Organization, said, "Our objective is to teach these hard-core unemployed how to work, how to get—and hold—a job, and how to be a capitalist in a capitalistic society."

Procedures are specific ways of doing things, the means by which policies are implemented and goals achieved. They are not conceptual in nature, they are the how-to-do phase of the conceptual approach. Ways to fill out order forms are often spelled out in detailed procedures manuals. *Programs* have a limited scope in time and encompass a specific set of objectives. Programs are usually set up to achieve particular results, and they contain their own objectives, procedures, and policies. And if a program is large in scope, it may even have a unique set of goals. Project Manhattan, the crash program which developed the atomic bomb during World War II, was one example of a massive program, which, like most of these efforts, was disbanded soon after achieving its desired end.

The concept analysis takes the basic points described above and relates them to the organization's functional problems. In the use of this approach, specific problems are organized in terms of *organizational goals, personal objectives, operational policies,* and *specific procedures* designed to accomplish the results set out in the goal-objective-policy stages of the analysis. In terms of strategy and tactics, goals and policies are strategic in nature, while tactics are more procedurally oriented. This relationship is shown in the upper portion of the schematic illustration in Figure 3.2. The slanting line drawn through the strategy-tactical rectangle indicates how strategic factors diminish as the diagram is read from left to right. Tactical factors, on the other hand, increase in import as the diagram moves from general to specific dimensions.

Problem \ Concept	Strategic area			Tactical area	
	Goals	Objectives	Policies	Programs	Procedures
Marketing					
Production					
Finance					
Human relations					
Research					
———————					
———————					
———————					

Figure 3.2 Concept analysis

Some traditional management writers emphasize this technique, as do many behaviorists, although the latter tend to place more emphasis on global rather than procedural aspects. The behaviorist and social and political systems groups focus more on the total social environment and the multifaceted nature of the roles played by managers. This latter group of writers are much more concerned with goals, objectives, and policies of the organization as they relate to the goals and needs of the individual in the organization. Traditional theorists also point out these relationships, but not with the same emphasis as some members of the social and political systems school.

One of the more notable illustrations of concept analysis in operation would be the bureaucracy where every person at every level in the organizational hierarchy understands the theory behind both his own duties (in terms of objectives and procedures) and the organization's expectations (in terms of goals and policies). Implicit here would be the expectation that each individual must understand his role and accept his position so that the organization operates efficiently in both economic and social terms. This would mean, for example, that every employee in the White Plains, New York office of the New York State Registry of Motor Vehicles would understand, appreciate, and accept every directive that came down the chain of command from the headquarters in Albany. In a specific instance, every clerk giving eye examinations to applicants would understand his relationship with Albany, with the County Clerk heading the local bureau, with his immediate superior, and with the flood of applicants. He would also be in accord with the need for, and the method of testing, the vision of each prospective driver. The obvious problem encountered is that such understanding is rarely achieved in practice. The ideal bureaucratic model requires that the individual either subordinate his own needs to those of the organization or equate his individual needs with those of the organization. This seldom occurs; and since most goals flow downward from top management, conflict invariably arises between individual and organizational goals.

One major criticism of the concept approach is that it espouses the potentially conflict-ridden, top-down orientation described in the previous paragraph. Another is that it relies on communications between hierarchies that may not be as effective in fact as they are on paper. A third drawback is that the concept approach usually does not encompass enough of the variables that enter into the individual's frame of reference when he is setting his personal goals. Some of the social system theorists, notably Simon, have written extensively about this latter point. He and other critics center their comments on the system's failure to consider some of the more complex variables that shape individual reaction to organizational development of goals and policies. These kinds of complexities are reflected in the generalized scheme identified as a critical variable analysis.

CRITICAL VARIABLE ANALYSIS

The critical variable approach attempts to analyze problems in terms of the most important variables influencing problem determination and decision making. It shifts the emphasis between strategic and tactical considerations depending upon the nature of the problem and/or the particular stage in time or the progress of a given problem analysis. For example, a personality variable might well be a critical one in the early stages of a collective-bargaining negotiation. But economic factors tend to be much more critical once negotiations appear to be moving toward a potential strike situation. It is thus important in this type of analysis to consider the changing weights of variables at different points in time. It is also vital to note how variables may differ at successive levels in the organizational hierarchy. For example, the possible impact of societal variables may be of much less concern to the line foreman in a steel mill than they are to the head of U.S. Steel.

It is readily evident from the kinds of variables included in Figure 3.3 that critical variable analysis is most utilitarian when applied to problems of a relatively global nature. Its design permits it to assess extraorganizational factors, and its prime value is in dealing with such variables. Critical variable analysis tends to be a top rather than a lower-level management methodology, and it handles massive unique problems that less inclusive analytical schemes are unable to evaluate properly. It is, for example, quite useful in long-range planning of facilities, product lines, and sources of funds.

The kinds of critical variables that might enter into a generalized scheme of analysis are shown in Figure 3.3. Though the variables which might be included in more specific circumstances are only suggested here, the skeleton is available for those who elect to flesh it out in particular applications. Because the labels placed on the variable listing in Figure 3.3 are rather general, further explanation is in order.

Problem \ Variable	Strategic and tactical emphasis shifts with the nature of the specific problem											
	Economic	Political	Institutional	Structural	Personality	Psychological	Ethical	Societal	Climatic	Timing	Competitive	Technological
Marketing												
Production												
Finance												
Human relations												
Research												
————————												
————————												
————————												

Figure 3.3 Critical variable analysis

Economic variables deal with matters such as costs, revenue, changes in income distribution, and consumer behavior. They include such bread-and-butter issues as profits, wages, hours, working conditions, and the cost of losing customers and/or revenues. In a long-term evaluation, they might also delve into changes in consumer tastes and preferences and the expected state of credit.

Political variables refer to the internal political problems which arise within organizations and to the general political climate in the larger society. The *institutional* entry covers the internal goals of organizations, while the *structural* factor encompasses a rather different set of considerations. Institutional factors might include company policies or union bylaws that limit or control the areas of freedom given to negotiators. A structural factor might be the restrictions appearing in the structure of the product market. Foreign competition, for example, is one factor that acts as a restraint on both the steelworkers union and U.S. Steel. Another structural factor would be the differences in individual viewpoints at varying levels in organizational hierarchies.

Personality variables are closely related to *psychological* variables, but enough difference exists to justify separate categories. A typical personality factor might be a dislike of a person or his manner, whereas a psychological designation would be used to describe the inner drive and/or the personal image one holds of his position or role in society.

Ethical factors also tend to be somewhat personal, for what people view as ethical conduct depends in part on their own judgments. Ethical issues appear most frequently where the parties have an abhorrance of corrupt practices such as bribery and fraud. Ethical factors are also influenced by the *societal* values and forces that shape the operating environment. Examples of these forces appear in public reactions to matters such as technological displacement. In our society, the "public image" and the expectations of the general public are important components of the business climate.

The *climatic* variable listed in Figure 3.3 refers to the weather, not to the general atmosphere surrounding decision making. Climatological factors, though normally unimportant, have occasionally affected the outcome of specific situations. In hot weather, in particular, a short strike may allow workers to enjoy another week or two of unpaid vacation time at nearby beaches. *Timing* factors also occupy a minor role in bargaining, but on occasion they can be critical. The imminence of a holiday such as Christmas or the proximity of a firm's busy season can be vital in bringing about the final solution to a lingering problem.

Competitive variables refer to the organizational competition in the product market. Even though it overlaps economic variables, the competitive variable is important enough in a company context to rate a separate mention.

The final set of variables in Figure 3.3 is *technological*. Technology can exert a powerful effect on operations. It is obvious, even to a layman, that an oil refinery and a supermarket face different problems.

Though some overlap occurs between the groupings in Figure 3.3, there seems to be enough variance between them to justify the classification scheme used. It should be made clear that not all the categories are prominent in every situation. It is also important to note that some situations will develop mutations of (and perhaps additions to) these basic variables. In general, however, the classes listed in Figure 3.3 provide a useful framework for analyzing and evaluating decisions.

Though this particular scheme has no direct counterpart in the literature dealing with organization theory, it reflects much of the thinking found in the social systems school and the ecological systems approach. It contains some of the factors described in the general systems writings by management authors such as Young and Suojanen.[3] And it also includes some of the kinds of variables which occur in open systems, that is, systems in which adaptations and responses to the systems' feedback are not automatic, but are taken only after evaluation and review of the inputs and factors that might be causal.

Some of the ideas developed here have enjoyed diverse applications. Dean George Kozmetsky of the University of Texas School of Business reports using a model of his school's operation to improve its functioning. In an open system such as a university environment, the variables chosen must necessarily be as broad as those described in Figure 3.3. President George Weyerhauser of the Weyerhauser Company reported in *The General Electric Forum* that

---

[3] See Stanley Young, *Management: A Systems Analysis* (Glenwood, Ill.: Scott, Foresman and Company, 1966) and Waino Suojanen, *The Dynamics of Management* (New York: Holt, Rinehart and Winston, Inc., 1966).

his firm had developed massive computer programs designed to deal with future business uncertainties. The military, notably the Strategic Air Command, has long utilized complex routines designed to identify and classify UFOs of all types. All indications point to a greater use of computers to review and analyze events before they happen or at least as close to their occurrence as possible. The kinds of data coming out of analytical schemes such as critical variable analysis undoubtedly will be the stuff from which future decisions are made. DuPont's attempt to include economic, cultural, and political influences in its capital budgeting analyses of foreign investments is one ongoing example of the use of a theoretical framework in a practical setting. This model, which takes sample groups in foreign environments and tries to translate their "group cohesiveness," that is, their ability to mobilize on a given issue, into a political influence, is now moving from hypothetical conjecture into the mathematics of risk calculation. Such applications undoubtedly will move from crude estimation to a more refined status through the process of trial, error, and retrial. In the present state of the arts, this analytical model is far from perfect and is not always well defined; but it seems certain to undergo continuing improvement and refinement.

Some of the criticisms leveled at critical variable analysis are due to poor application, while others result from more basic weaknesses. One recurring criticism is the approach's failure to allow adequately for shifts in variable weighting over time. A second is its weaknesses in identifying and selecting the variables exerting a primary influence on the problem under consideration. A final attack is that too often this method is used to evaluate or analyze decisions of insufficient complexity to justify the time and cost of its use. It is probable, however, that critical variable analysis will enjoy wider use as general systems theory undergoes evolution and as programming techniques and computer hardware capable of weighting, handling, and analyzing complex sets of variables are developed.

TECHNIQUE ANALYSIS

The final analytical scheme considered is more of a catchall than a generalized method of analysis. It tends to be more a series of problem-solving devices than a general analytical model. Perhaps because of this characteristic it is titled technique analysis. Some of the ideas of the human behavior, rational decision theory, and political-social system schools appear in this approach, although many of the researchers in these areas might not agree with their placement in such company. A goodly number of techniques here are espoused by their creators as general systems of analysis, but most fall short of that claim by a good length. Advocates of sensitivity training, specific mathematical models, and other techniques for managing things or people tend to focus on techniques and approaches not readily generalizable into overall schemes of analysis or to the development of strategic considerations that cannot be substituted for the more inclusive methodologies described previously. For example, sensitivity training is not a way to change the world as some of its advocates claim. It is a technique for developing empathy and better balance between a person, his colleagues, and his work environment. The use of this technique, even if successful, may not be particularly valuable in coping with the technical and economic factors faced in a complex problem. Perhaps such training can put a man at ease with his colleagues and himself, but it cannot give him the kinds of capabilities needed to handle factors outside the areas of personal and interpersonal competence. It works only on part of the problem and thus tends to be more of a technique than a system of handling problems, analyses, or decision making. Some of the more useful management aids fall into the kinds of categories indicated in the columns of Figure 3.4, but their utility is limited to problem situations with a fairly limited scope. Many such applications are elaborated upon in Part Three, particularly in the sections dealing with decision making, evaluation of contributions, and the various ways to improve individual and organizational performance.

Technique / Problem	Tactical and Strategic coverage										
	Engineering		Economics		Psychology		Sociology		Mathematics		...
	Time study	–	Marginal analysis	–	Person-ality testing	–	Group participa-tion	–	Queueing models	–	–	–
Marketing											
Production											
Finance											
Human relations											
Research											
————											
————											
————											

Figure 3.4   Technique analysis

Figure 3.4 shows that certain techniques taken from the various academic disciplines can be utilized in analyzing some strategic and tactical circumstances found in the kinds of problems common to most managerial decision making. For example, economics contributes marginal analysis, which is frequently applied in circumstances where strategic decisions must be made. A general strategy of technological development may be accepted or rejected on the cost and revenue projections derived after a marginal analysis conducted on a machine replacement problem. In marketing, a product strategy may be scrapped or followed depending upon the results of marginal analysis of costs and revenue projections in a particular market area. A mathematical model simulating an inventory situation or a production-scheduling model might be used either singly or in combination to develop strategies for determining an optimum mix. Employee testing procedures, engineering time and methods study, and other techniques can also be used to collect and/or analyze data which will become the basis for devising long-term strategies and shorter term tactical methods. Heuristics, the science of recognizing and establishing logical search and choice (or rejection of choice) sequences, may become the analytical method of the future, but it has not yet been developed in a form permitting its widespread use. The economic-mathematical concept of game theory also has similar potential and similar drawbacks.[4] These and other techniques will probably be made more inclusive as computers become more economical and more adaptable for general usage.

Summary

Of the four basic analytical schemes developed in this chapter, the critical variable approach is most useful in considering strategic matters, such as the determination of product-line policy for a manufacturing firm or the growth plan of an investment banking house with heavy commitments in international markets. The conceptual and process approaches are most useful for analyzing decisions in strategic areas which have a less global scope. The use of the planning-organizing-controlling approach is very helpful in dealing with such matters as manpower planning and recruitment and the establishment of financial controls to evaluate the performance of specific segments of the organization. In a sense, it is an internal approach as opposed to an external approach, although it can be adapted to deal with external matters under certain constraints. The conceptual approach can be utilized for major strategic decisions, but its greatest utility lies in managing the internal affairs of the going organization. For example, controls, objectives, policies, and procedures may be developed to assess the effectiveness of a particular operating decision; or, in another instance, a set of goals, policies, and procedures may be prepared to insure that quality or service policies will be carried out effectively. Technique analysis is useful for investigating a wide range of problems, most of which are limited in scope and internal in nature. Eventually perhaps some of these technique-oriented approaches will handle the kind of results which must be considered in a full-fledged analytical scheme, but they have not yet reached that point.

Study Questions

1. What are some aspects of traditional management theory that tie in with the process analysis model? The concept analysis model?
2. What kinds of problems are best handled by the four models? Give specific illustrations from your personal experience.

---

[4] These techniques and a series of applications are discussed in Chapter 7.

3. Contrast the applications of the critical variable analysis model with those of the techniques analysis model. Where does each seem to be most utilitarian?

4. Do modern organization theories fit neatly into any of the four models? Expand your answer in terms of your understanding of these theories.

5. Does the idea of a systems approach to problem analysis and solution offer any advantages? Any disadvantages?

6. Can you think of any nonbusiness applications of a systems approach now in use? In your opinion, are they working out well? Why or why not?

BIBLIOGRAPHY

Allen, Louis A., *The Management Profession,* New York: McGraw-Hill, Inc., 1964.

Anshen, Melvin W., and George L. Bach, eds., *Management and Corporations: 1985,* New York: McGraw-Hill, Inc., 1960.

Argyris, Chris, *Integrating the Individual and the Organization,* New York: John Wiley & Sons, Inc., 1964.

Barnard, Chester I., *Organization and Management,* Cambridge, Mass.: Harvard University Press, 1948.

Blake, Robert R., and Jane S. Mouton, *Group Dynamics—Key to Decision Making,* Houston, Tex.: The Gulf Publishing Company, 1961.

Cartwright, Dorwin, *Group Dynamics—Research and Theory,* London: Tavistock Publications, Ltd., 1954.

Carzo, Rocco, and John Yanouzas, *Formal Organizations: A Systems Approach,* Homewood, Ill.: Richard D. Irwin, Inc., 1967.

Chandler, Alfred E., Jr., *Strategy and Structure,* Cambridge, Mass.: MIT Press, 1962.

Churchman, C. West, *Prediction and Optimal Decision,* Englewood Cliffs, N.J.: Prentice-Hall, Inc., 1961.

Dale, Ernest, *Management: Theory and Practice,* New York: McGraw-Hill, Inc., 1965.

———. *Organization,* New York: American Management Association, Inc., 1967.

Dearden, John, and F. Warren McFarlan, *Management Information Systems: Text and Cases,* Homewood, Ill.: Richard D. Irwin, Inc., 1966.

Drucker, Peter F., *The Practice of Management,* New York: Harper & Row, Publishers, 1954.

Fayol, Henri, *General and Industrial Management,* New York: Pitman Publishing Corporation, 1949.

Gore, William J., *Administrative Decision Making: A Heuristic Model,* New York: John Wiley & Sons, Inc., 1964.

Haire, Mason, ed., *Modern Organization Theory,* New York: John Wiley & Sons, Inc., 1959.

_____, ed., *Organization Theory in Industrial Practice,* New York: John Wiley & Sons, Inc., 1962.

Haynes, Warren W., and Joseph L. Massie, *Management: Analysis, Concepts and Cases,* Englewood Cliffs, N.J.: Prentice-Hall, Inc., 1961.

Hutchinson, John G., *Organizations: Theory and Classical Concepts,* New York: Holt, Rinehart and Winston, Inc., 1967.

Jay, Antony, *Management and Machiavelli,* New York: Holt, Rinehart and Winston, Inc., 1968.

Koontz, Harold, ed., *Toward a Unified Theory of Management,* New York: McGraw-Hill, Inc., 1964.

_____, and Cyril O'Donnell, *Principles of Management,* 3rd ed., New York: McGraw-Hill, Inc., 1964.

Likert, Rensis, *The Human Organization,* New York: McGraw-Hill, Inc., 1967.

_____, *New Patterns of Management,* New York: McGraw-Hill, Inc., 1961.

McGregor, Douglas, *The Human Side of Enterprise,* New York: McGraw-Hill, Inc., 1960.

McGuire, Joseph W., *Theories of Business Behavior,* Englewood Cliff, N.J.: Prentice-Hall, Inc., 1964.

Machiavelli, Niccolo, *The Prince,* New York: Washington Square Press, 1963.

March, James G., and Herbert A. Simon, *Organizations,* New York: John Wiley & Sons, Inc., 1958.

Mayo, Elton, *The Human Problems of an Industrial Civilization,* Cambridge, Mass.: Harvard University Press, 1933.

Miller, David W., and Martin K. Starr, *Executive Decisions and Operations Research,* Englewood Cliffs, N.J.: Prentice-Hall, Inc., 1960.

_____, *The Structure of Human Decisions,* Englewood Cliffs, N.J.: Prentice-Hall, Inc., 1967.

Mooney, James D., and Alan Reilley, *Principles of Organization,* New York: Harper & Row, Publishers, 1939.

Newman, William H., *Administrative Action,* 2nd ed., Englewood Cliffs, N.J.: Prentice-Hall, Inc., 1963.

_____, Charles E. Summer, and E. Kirby Warren, *The Process of Management: Concepts, Behavior and Practice,* 2nd ed., Englewood Cliffs, N.J.: Prentice-Hall, Inc., 1967.

Pfiffner, John M., and Frank P. Sherwood, *Administrative Organization,* Englewood Cliffs, N.J.: Prentice-Hall, Inc. 1960.

Prince, Thomas R., *Information Systems for Management Planning and Control,* Homewood, Ill.: Richard D. Irwin, Inc., 1966.

Richards, Max, and William Nielander, *Readings in Management,* 2nd ed., Cincinnati: South-Western Publishing Company, 1964.

Roethleisberger, Fritz, and William J. Dickson, *Management and the Worker,* Cambridge, Mass.: Harvard University Press, 1939.

Rubenstein, A.H., and C.J. Haberstroh, *Some Theories of Organization,* rev. ed., Homewood, Ill.: Richard D. Irwin, Inc., 1966.

Seiler, John A., *Systems Analysis in Organizational Behavior,* Homewood, Ill.: Richard D. Irwin, Inc., 1967.

Simon, Herbert A., *Administrative Behavior,* New York: Crowell-Collier and Macmillan, Inc., 1948.

Taylor, Frederick W., *Scientific Management,* New York: Harper & Row, Publishers, 1911.

Thompson, Victor, *Organizations in Action,* New York: McGraw-Hill, Inc., 1968.

Urwick, Lyndall, *Scientific Principles of Organization,* New York: American Management Association, Inc., 1938.

Weber, Max, *Essays in Sociology,* New York: Oxford University Press, 1946.

Young, Stanley, *Management: A Systems Analysis,* Glenview, Ill.: Scott, Foresman and Company, 1966.

Part One presented a summary of traditional and modern theories of organization and a set of analytical models taken from these theoretical constructs. In Part Two these approaches and perspectives are turned into practical tools of decision making and problem solving. In spite of this operational orientation, Part Two does not put aside concepts and theories, rather it expands upon some basic ideas and even adds some concepts that fit directly in with the various theoretical formulations.

Part Two consists of five sections, all of which use the same basic approach: first, to identify the most critical areas of management; next, to describe pertinent conceptual and theoretical means of analyzing these areas; and, finally, to outline some of the most promising techniques for dealing with them. For example, in the first section, Recognition of Problems and Opportunities, organizational objectives and goals are explored and related to the organization's strengths and weaknesses. This matching process is then considered in terms of opportunities available in scanning the operating environment. The specific areas covered are growth, diversification, technological innovation, merger possibilities, and other areas where opportunities and problems may appear. Finally, detailed forecasting techniques are outlined which can be used to assist managers to make meaningful future projections in these critical areas.

The five sections of Part Two deal with the vital areas of (1) recognition of problems and opportunities, (2) decision making, (3) integration of strategy with organizational design, (4) evaluation of contribution to organizational performance, and (5) the

PART TWO
Strategy and Tactics of Management

development of improved performance at the individual and unit level. Each section devotes some attention to the methods of problem identification outlined in Part One and also delves carefully into the general concepts and broad problems encountered in each area. Each then describes successful tactics used to deal with these problems. The specifics of these tactics are illustrated in the study questions at the end of each chapter and the cases at the close of each section. Thus, concepts, analysis, and application receive explanation and elaboration in the various sections.

For managers, the problems of looking around, ahead, and within are similar to those faced by leaders of any organization. Every organization needs goals and guidelines and a way of moving toward those goals. In addition to goals, organizations also need sound strategies and tactics to foster movement along chosen paths. Some of the more critical variables in establishing goals, strategies, and tactics are growth trends, organizational forces, manpower considerations, technological changes, and the ever-present factor of timing.

Once goals and broad strategies are identified, organizations must decide upon proper techniques to analyze and forecast future events. Some of the systems models described in Chapter 3 are useful to help integrate chosen goals with the projections generated in the forecasting process. Chapter 4 describes this process in general terms, while Chapter 5 identifies specific forecasting techniques in some detail.

In *H.M.S. Pinafore* one character states, "Things are seldom as they seem. Skim milk masquerades as cream." The ability to blend goals, strategies, and forecast data into an analytical and evaluating framework capable of telling skim milk from cream is the essence of this section. Skillful recognition of problems and opportunities allows cream to be identified easier and may even offer insights on how to make more available at a better price.

SECTION I
Recognition of Problems and Opportunities

In a military sense, strategy involves the planning and direction of projects or campaigns, while tactics deal with the operational aspects of moving or handling forces or units. The same basic distinction can be used to cover the decisions and problems faced by heads of organizations. Strategic decisions encompass the development of broad directions and comprehensive plans needed to move an organization toward the achievement of its principal goals. Tactics are the specific means by which these goals can be attained. Strategies are thus expanded or contracted by internal and external factors in the organization's operating environment, while tactics are dictated predominantly by resources internal to the organization. To use military terminology again, wars are fought according to strategic plans, while battles or skirmishes involve applications of tactical plans. When wars were won in single battles, strategy and tactics were one: Ghengis Khan was a tactician, not a strategist; and though his tactics were successful in the days of walled cities, he would probably have been ineffective in planning the massive Allied attack on Fortress Europa in World War II. The military analogy is quite apt in terms of managing organizations. When the task or objective is simple, then tactics alone may achieve the desired result; but when the objective is complex and its means require careful preplanning, tactics alone cannot do the job. Moreover, when goals and directions are not clearly evident, and when strategies and tactics are dependent upon future uncertainties, the organization needs to develop a meaningful set of strategies and tactics to guide its future actions.

As Ewing W. Reilley, of the con-

CHAPTER 4
Factors in Strategy Determination

sulting firm of McKinsey and Company, writes, a successful business strategy must be based on a searching look within, a broad look around, and a long look ahead.[1] The look within includes a review of facilities and equipment, existing product lines, personnel resources, financial position, and other factors such as location, patents, existing order backlogs, and so on. The look around is relations-oriented, since it encompasses an organization's dealings with customers, suppliers, employees, competitors, and the marketplace as a whole. It also covers basic factors such as changes in the role of government, growth patterns in the economy, and the emergence of social forces such as the civil rights movement. The look ahead involves consideration of all of the previously mentioned factors plus the use of forecasting techniques to attempt to relate the realities of the present with the directions of the future. In operational terms, the critical variable approach described in Chapter 3 can provide a useful framework for conducting such an analysis.

Strategy thus attempts to relate present and future in a manner most beneficial to the total organization. In order to be most effective, strategies must spring from basic goals. Goals must be specified as clearly as possible so that strategies can be devised that accomplish what the organization sets out to achieve. One problem in this specification process arises because the general nature of goals makes them difficult to express in concrete terms. This problem is particularly pronounced in terms of how outsiders view organizational goals, since individuals who are not thoroughly conversant with a given organization often see its goals as sterile, nebulous, pious-sounding generalities. Because few outsiders ever attain close familiarity with organizational operations, general statements about goals rarely come through with meaning. Phrases such as *healthy growth, fair return on investment, being a good corporate citizen, maintaining equitable relationships with customers, suppliers, and employees,* and *diversifying into new areas* are not particularly satisfying to the manager or scholar seeking specifics. To the insider, however, these points are much more obvious, since the ambiguous phraseology in statements of organizational goals is clarified by plans and actions designed to accomplish specific results. When William Morris, president of Control Data, states, "We are now living at IBM's suffrance.... I want Control Data to be the Ford of the computer industry," his associates have more than a vague idea of what he means. They know that sharpened definitions will appear more clearly in subsequent plans, standards, and appraisals of performance. Through operational necessity, generalized goals eventually become well known to insiders, even though their meaning may remain elusive to outsiders. In most organizational settings, goals are fairly well defined or, if not sharply defined, at least generally understood. Rarely are they stated as clearly as by the Baltimore Gas and Electric Company, whose "Outlines for the Future" are listed in Table 4.1.

---

[1] "Planning the Strategy of the Business," *Advanced Management,* December 1955, pp. 8–12.

TABLE 4.1   GUIDELINES FOR THE FUTURE, BALTIMORE GAS AND ELECTRIC COMPANY

Goal No. 1	*Growth of Our Business* We must expand our business to stay healthy. Our rate of expansion should not be less than that achieved by our industry generally. Our specific targets should be higher than that. We must increase our share of the total energy requirements of our territory.
Goal No. 2	*Efficient and Effective Operation* We must develop and operate our electric, gas and steam systems to attain greater reliability of service, to be more effective, reduce costs and improve the safety of our operations.
Goal No. 3	*Rate Reductions* We must strive toward a reduction in rates charged for our service relative to other costs of living.
Goal No. 4	*Good Compensation and Improved Working Conditions* We must continue to provide wages and benefits which compare favorably with those of other local business concerns offering steady employment and with other utilities in our general area, and we must strive to enhance the working climate.
Goal No. 5	*Good Customer Service* We must strive to provide the best possible service to our customers consistent with the practices and policies of other companies and with a reasonable balance between cost and value of such services to our customers and to the company.
Goal No. 6	*Improvement in Earnings Per Share* We must strive to achieve a continuing improvement in earnings per share in order to provide a fair return to our security holders, to protect their investment, and to improve the market value of our common stock.
Goal No. 7	*Increased Public Confidence* We must strive to achieve the full confidence of the public.

SOURCE: From a company pamphlet reprinting an abridged version of a speech by Austin E. Penn, Chairman of the Board and President, Baltimore Gas and Electric Company, before participants in a management seminar, December 28, 1966.

Although goals are ill suited to definition in terms of specifics, generalized statements can be made about growth, profits, service, market share, product lines, community and social responsibility, and personal desires of owners or managers. From among such goals, frameworks can and should be forged to guide the long-term destinies of organizations. Jack Simplot, the Potato King of Idaho, whose personal fortune is estimated to be in excess of $200 million, operates his enterprises on the basis of close personal control. Says Simplot, "Sure, I know I could be a hell of a lot bigger today if I'd gone public. It is a lot easier to get a loan when you are a corporation than when you are a loner. I just never liked to work for the other guy. What I own, I built. It's mine. Nobody ever had to put a penny at risk in my rig." [2] Paul McCartney, formerly of the Beatles, and now codirector of a holding company called Apple Corps, Ltd., professes the desire to run Apple for the prime purpose of creating a "viable environment" for the performing artist. In McCartney's words, "We want to make money, of course, you understand, but it's not the end-all ... once you're totally affluent, there's beyond." In a more traditional business framework, financial wizard Charles Bluhdorn describes the aims of his Gulf and Western empire when he states, "We're like an investment company except that they just sit upstairs and watch the horses run. We get down and manage the horses." [3]

In spite of these colorful statements, goal determination is not a simple or easily defined task. It demands the ability to frame future directions in terms having meaning in the present. The Bluhdorns and Simplots seem to possess the knack of stating the general in specific terms, but not all leaders and executives have such abilities. For most managers, goal setting remains a formidable and complex task.

Though goal setting is a formidable job, it is not an insurmountable one. For example, in business a goal might be defined in terms of achieving a given profit level; or in a military situation, to win a war or major battle. Social and community relations goals might strive to "provide the opportunity for education for those students who are genuinely on the campus for that purpose," as University of Illinois Chancellor Jack W. Peltason stated following a destructive sit-in by 250 Negro students during registration week in September 1968. [4] In this situation, Chancellor Peltason found the attainment complicated by forces at work both inside and outside his organization, and an endeavor with seemingly noble goals became a tense crisis in its execution phases. The civil rights area contains numerous examples of lengthy studies which have brought forth elegantly phrased sets of goals that have fallen flat in application. Goals cannot stand alone—this is as evident in business firms as in the ghetto. In both cases, strategies and tactics are needed to reach one's goals. If strategic or tactical considerations involve a redefinition of goals to make them workable, then redefinition should be undertaken. The interplay of purpose and execution is inevitable and cannot be swept under the rug. This recognition, if handled within a framework of genuine accommodation, eventually yields to a set of goals buttressed by sound strategies and effective tactics. Because of their importance, these processes of interaction deserve much closer attention.

---

[2] Quoted by Charles J.V. Murphy, "Jack Simplot and His Private Conglomerate," *Fortune,* August 1968, p. 1220.

[3] William S. Rukeyser, "Gulf and Western's Rambunctious Conservatism," *Fortune,* March 1968, p. 123.

[4] *The New York Times* (September 15, 1968), p. 39(n).

THE DEVELOPMENT OF OPPORTUNISTIC STRATEGIES

Strategy determination is a broad process which attempts to relate goals to resources. Once the look inside and the look around are completed, the organization's strategy makers must determine their areas of competence in terms of abilities and resources and then match these strengths against available opportunities. It is not enough to find out what the organization can do; there must be an evaluation of what it can do *best*. Profits or other goals do not result from ineptitude over the long pull, they evolve from a blend of luck *and* competence. Even though luck is a fickle ingredient and hardly qualifies as a suitable cornerstone for long-term strategy determination, it can be a vital factor in success or failure. And organizations can plan to provide a climate that makes "lucky" happenings more probable. For example, the discovery of rubber is widely accepted as an accident, but the skill with which this new product was eventually introduced to the market was far from incidental. In more modern terms, IBM's decision to introduce the System/360 family of computers in the mid-sixties was a revolutionary move that could have spelled corporate disaster. Indeed, it placed the company in a risky position in a newly developing market, but helped them to retain their leadership in the dynamic data-processing and information-processing market. The magnitude of this gamble was so great at its outset that an IBM executive said, "We called this project 'You Bet Your Company.'" [5] The reason for the move was that IBM felt it had to fully utilize its skills and abilities to meet the needs of an emerging set of opportunities in the product market. When IBM leaders looked around, looked inside, and looked ahead they recognized the set of opportunities that prompted the decision to move to System/360. This decision set in motion a multimillion-dollar venture whose eventual results were in doubt for years. No one doubts that IBM used every technical and interpersonal resource available to shape its course of action, but even IBM's superb management would not deny that some small element of chance entered in at the periphery.

In the case of the 360 decision, the wishes of IBM's chairman, Thomas Watson, Jr., were continually in evidence. Other factors always in the picture were the technical know-how and managerial savvy in the executive ranks. This example, taken from one of the world's largest industrial corporations, typifies the two major dimensions of strategy determination: (1) an evaluation of the organization's tangible resources and (2) an assessment of the abilities and personal values of key people in management.

The evaluation of tangible resources calls for expert judgments by accountants, engineers, marketers, economists, financial staffers, and other skilled specialists. Buildings, inventories, equipment, good will, and liquid holdings must be assessed carefully, since the state of such assets is vital in planning

---

[5] T.A. Wise, "IBM's $500,000,000 Gamble," *Fortune,* September 1966, p. 118.

strategies. There must also be a careful evaluation of relationships with dealers, customers, and vendors and a review of future trends in products, labor and capital markets, and other key areas in which the organization operates or intends to operate. The assessment of existing and future states of tangible resources is a complex job involving the most careful technical execution. It cannot be done successfully, however, without a somewhat nontechnical look at the values and abilities of people charged with performing these critical functions.

Personal values and abilities are very important in strategy determination, and the values of individual managers vary sharply. Some have an economic orientation, while others have strong moral, religious, and esthetic values that either dominate or shape their perception of what constitutes a valid or optimum strategy. For example, the stereotype of the research chemist pictures him as having strong theoretical and esthetic convictions. If these attributes are indeed correct, then researchers may only pay lip service to an economically based strategy. "Front office" emphasis on applied research as opposed to pure research advocated by "way-out" scientists provides a familiar illustration of how value systems clash in a scientific setting. In a more complicated milieu, Dow Chemical's decision to continue manufacturing napalm after several clashes with student groups such as the revolutionary Students for a Democratic Society (SDS) was based on Dow's technical ability to make napalm in existing plants and the conviction of President Herbert Doan that it was proper for Dow to manufacture weapons of war if called on to do so by the government. In commenting on the decision to continue manufacturing napalm, Doan said, "Our critics ask if we are willing to stand judgment for our choice to support our government if history should prove this wrong. Our answer is yes." [6] In spite of the negative press Dow has received on this particular decision, the integration of technical and personal values into organizational strategies provides the kind of climate organizations need to get the best from their human resources. If Dow's policy fails, the real cause may be a lack of a sense of commitment among its employees and leadership. Personnel's belief in policies and strategies lessens the possibility of partial acceptance or subversion. Important differences exist between just doing the job and believing it is vitally important—an observation that is equally applicable to degrees of commitment to company strategy. Able people function most efficiently when they accept strategies without reservation, a fact that deserves to be evaluated with the same care as technical factors.

An interesting example of such missionary commitment appeared soon after the assassination of President Kennedy, in 1963. Within a relatively short time after his death, most of Kennedy's chief advisors left the government. Although they gave varied reasons, most observers laid their departure to

---

[6] "Why Dow Chemical Continues to Make Napalm," *Business Week*, February 10, 1968, p. 39(n).

the fact that President Johnson, after a period of adjustment, developed goals and strategies to which they could not give their wholehearted support. Once the Kennedy men lost their sense of mission and commitment, President Johnson lost their devotion and, eventually, their services.

Problem or opportunity \ Variable	Economic	Societal	Structural	Psychological	Personality	Political	Institutional	Competitive	Temporal	Climate	Technological	Ethical	....
Future trends													
Growth Existing areas Diversification Merger													
Technological innovation													
Organization planning													
Manpower													
Timing factors													
.....													

Figure 4.1 Critical variable analysis applied to key variables in strategy determination

The process of strategy determination thus constitutes a review of tangible and human factors in terms of available opportunities. Since this requires generalized handling, a critical variable analysis seems most suitable. The critical variables listed in Figure 3.3 would be relevant here. Instead of the problems shown in Figure 3.3, the range of possible opportunities which influence strategy determination might be listed. In a very elementary sense, this approach would appear much like the embryonic analysis presented in Figure 4.1. The type of analysis suggested here is one in which the problem areas and strategy determinations are considered in the light of the relevant set of critical variables. Since the variables used in this analysis have already been identified, they deserve little attention here. Areas of problem and/or opportunity, however, call for more careful review in terms of definition and in how they relate to the aforementioned variables.

KEY AREAS IN DEVELOPING OPPORTUNISTIC STRATEGIES

FORECASTING

Perhaps the most critical general problem in the process of strategy determination is the assessment of future trends. The old order constantly giveth way to the new and the ability to foresee the nature and intensity of basic shifts in such matters as consumer tastes or governmental controls is vital to the selection of an optimum strategy pattern. Thus, forecasting, since it helps to identify opportunities and to suggest actions designed to exploit these opportunities, becomes a necessity in all phases of strategy determination.

Examples are legion, but two taken from one firm might be illustrative. In the 1950s the Ford Motor Company decided to market a middle-priced automobile called the Edsel. This car was designed to meet projected market trends and consumer tastes in extremely scientific fashion. Indeed, the Edsel was tabbed "the car built by market research." Shortly after its introduction, Ford was forced to take it off the market because of disastrous sales. Post mortems on the Edsel estimated that Ford had lost over $200 million on the car's design and introduction. The fact that it failed was due more to market factors than to Ford's planning, since the middle-priced auto market dropped sharply in the years the Edsel was introduced. On the other side of the ledger, the same basic approach applied to the Mustang yielded far different results, perhaps again because of conditions beyond the control of the Ford planning staff. Ford's hope for similar success in the 1970s rests partially on the plans and forecasts made on the compact Maverick line, introduced in 1969. Thus, forecasting does not guarantee success, but it does help to identify some of the factors that may become critical ingredients of the strategy mix.[7]

GROWTH

Aside from forecasting future trends, growth is perhaps the most generally perplexing factor in strategy determination. Whether to grow at all is one critical problem in growth analysis, and the other is how growth goals can best be obtained if, indeed, growth is planned.[8] Once the organization selects

---

[7] Though made up itself principally of techniques and technical methods, the forecasting process is instrumental in bringing about a proper blending of strategic directions. Forecast methods are described in greater detail in the following chapter.

[8] A standard cliché in business is, "An organization must either grow or perish." This is sheer nonsense, for a firm can prosper by careful pruning of its product lines or by appealing to smaller but more lucrative markets. Growth offers both problems and opportunities; it is not always a blessing. *Fortune* quotes C.R. Smith, former president of American Airlines, on this point, "This [airline] industry is laboring, you might say, under the curse of growth." Other industries and firms have expressed similar feelings at various times in their life cycles.

a set of guideposts on growth, strategies must be developed and implemented. If stability or reduction (negative growth) is the goal, then product pruning, divestiture, or sale of assets may be the dominant strategies. In this situation, United States Industries might decide to sell its Educational Science Division. If increased size is the desired goal, expansion of exciting product lines, diversification, or merger are potentially feasible strategies. Here, CBS might decide to buy the publishing firm of Holt, Rinehart and Winston, Inc., and place it with Creative Playthings in an educational division that would give coverage from preschool to college.

In the case of cutting back sales volume or levels of services, the chosen strategy is influenced by many of the same factors that affect expansionary goals. Product lines may be viewed with an eye toward pruning rather than expansion or greater penetration. Diversification in a cutback sense means reduction in a number of operating units or in types and/or number of markets entered or retained. Mergers in process are usually dropped or sales are made in outright terms so that stability or reduction in size can be obtained. For example, in a horizontally integrated firm, an entire unit may be dropped as was the case when Chrysler dropped the DeSoto line in the late 1950s. In a vertically integrated firm, activities of subunits may be curtailed. For example, in some stations serving commuters primarily, the Penn Central Railroad now opens ticket windows only a limited time each day. Finally, any operating unit or company may be discontinued or sold because of market conditions or because of orders of courts or boards such as the Federal Trade Commission.

In a normal growth pattern an organization grows through both external and internal means. Expansion may occur by widening existing product lines or by penetrating deeper into markets for existing product lines or by both. Recently in the auto industry, General Motors has combined both patterns, while American Motors has gone the second route. Diversification adds to sales by acquiring new products or by increasing manufacturing operations (by acquiring new facilities or expanding old ones). For example, a firm may elect to expand either its government or its nongovernment business, move into the international area more or less extensively, or shift its marketing emphasis from consumer to industrial markets. Merger fosters growth by acquiring assets that provide a direct line to the sources of new materials (vertical merger), by gaining ownership or control of facilities standing between the acquirer and its customers (horizontal merger), or by purchasing firms or units not necessarily related to the organization's existing lines of business (conglomerate merger). These three types of mergers can be illustrated quite easily in the contemporary scene. Major oil companies such as Standard Oil are vertically integrated from crude production through retail service station outlets. Many auto companies are vertically integrated back to parts production and through dealers to the customers, while at the same time they cross the market horizontally by making autos in overlapping price ranges that compete directly with each other. Conglomerate mergers cross many industries and examples are legion. Lytton Industries, Ling-Temco-Voight, and Textron, Incorporated are several well-known firms operated as conglomerates.

The process of developing growth strategies is incomplete until all of the critical factors are given careful attention. Politics; labor problems; community feelings; economic, personal, and psychological factors; and all of the external and internal forces influencing organizational activity should be reviewed carefully before growth or cutback strategies are introduced and implemented. In particular, technology, personnel, organizational planning, and timing need to be considered with special care in the forging of a generalized strategy of growth or containment.[9]

TECHNOLOGY

Technological strategies, like growth strategies, involve a careful review of the future, the competition, and the existing state of the technological arts both within the organization and in the industry or area of operation. Although technical strategies are derived from a goal structure, they begin with a review of existing equipment within the organization and the operating environment. If the equipment is old and growth is planned, then there may be a need to institute massive modernization. For example, almost every firm in the American steel industry has increased its expenditures on both new equipment and replacement of existing assets. Bethlehem, Armco, and U.S. Steel in particular have undergone massive capital reconstruction programs to modernize their facilities. As foreign or domestic steel competitors begin to use, say, a basic oxygen process to produce goods at lower than existing prices, then the strategy selected may be to invest in new technology as opposed to replacing technologically obsolete units with new but similar equipment.

Even when the existing state of the technological arts is under review, newly developing methods and/or processes are constantly in the picture. Improvements in methods, materials, equipment, and machinery occur constantly, and significant new control devices that will bring forth still more revolutionary advances in technology are now in evidence. For example, M.W. Kellogg developed a method for producing ammonia that cut the costs of building and operating an ammonia plant in half. The Kellogg method allowed for production of one thousand tons per day at a cost of twenty dollars per ton against a previous output of three hundred tons at forty dollars per ton. The uproar caused by this new development caused President Warren L. Smith of Kellogg to say, "When the companies saw the production costs, they knew they couldn't affort not to buy the new plants." [10] In a breakthrough of potentially similar magnitude in the communications field, Columbia Broadcasting System eventually hopes to gain preeminence through its electronic video recording device (EVR), a kind of visual phonograph that allows the owner

[9] More detailed information on how to develop growth strategies appears in Chapter 5, which also gives a case history on how one product, Instant Maxwell House coffee, was viewed in Maxwell House's strategy of growth.

[10] "All that Fertilizer and No Place to Grow," *Fortune,* June 1968, p. 93.

to hear and see educational and entertainment programs by plugging pre-recorded cartridges into his own television set. CBS has probed deeply into trends in electronic broadcasting in planning the means and methods to bring this product to the market including a plan to set up a test market abroad before attempting to move into the potentially massive U.S. market.

Technology has now reached the point where devices such as EVR are much more than inventions; their impact goes well beyond engineering and economics. The critical variable approach is thus offered as a helpful model for analyzing and assessing their impact on a wide range of areas.

ORGANIZATION

The strategy underlying organizational planning is much less global than growth and technology strategies, but it, too, has very broad applications. In particular, this area covers the degree of decentralization to adopt, and the selection of an appropriate organizational structure. Decentralization of authority is not a new concept, but it has been given renewed attention because of the sophisticated reporting systems emanating from the use of computers. With such advanced systems, greater decentralization is possible because deviations from checkpoints in the control system can be detected and corrected rapidly, before drastic errors occur. This type of centralized yet decentralized system is common in large and medium-sized business organizations, and its use has fostered the recent trend toward greater decentralization of authority. Since the degree of decentralization permissible is at least partially dependent upon the state of controls, which in turn is dependent upon the people in the system and the structure in which the controls are exerted, the question, "What constitutes the *best* type of organizational structure?" has some interesting strategic overtones. Professor Alfred E. Chandler, in his penetrating work, *Strategy and Structure,* indicates that "structure follows strategy and that the most complex type of structure is the result of the concatenation [linking] of several basic strategies."[11] The sequence of events that occurs is that structure is derived from strategies, which in turn are developed in the light of organizational goal structures. Whether structures will be decentralized or centralized, whether hierarchical levels will be many or few, whether spans of control will be narrow (few subordinates per manager) or wide (many subordinates per manager), which patterns of communications are preferable, and a host of other structural matters are, in Chandler's view, dependent upon the strategies the organization chooses to reach its goals. Organizational strategies are thus derived strategies, and their ultimate form comes from a review of higher-level strategy considerations and the personal factors encountered when structural hierarchies are instituted or revised. Specific methods of structural reform are given close attention in Chapters 8 through 10, which relate the implementation of strategy to the process of constructing an organizational design.

---

[11] (Cambridge, Mass.: M.I.T. Press, 1962), p. 14.

PERSONNEL

The importance of personnel has been implied at various points in this chapter, and deservedly so. As stated previously, strategies must be accepted fully if they are to be carried out with a sense of commitment and mission. Acceptance depends both on the climate in which strategies are evolved and promulgated and on the expectations of superiors and subordinates at differing levels in the organizational structure. For example, at higher levels people expect a greater voice in strategy determination than at lower levels. Moreover, if their expectations are not met, they tend to react in a way that disrupts the grand organizational design. Student uprisings at major universities throughout the world in the late 1960s are recent indications of such disruptions. Since the nature of responses to strategic and structural changes will be treated more fully in following sections, it is mentioned here only to underscore the importance of personal reaction in strategy determination.

One other point worthy of note under the aegis of personnel matters deals with quantity and quality factors. It is patently obvious that the abilities of people already in the organization should be evaluated before major strategies are adopted. If a particular strategy demands a certain skill, that skill must be present, developed, or obtained before that strategy can be implemented successfully. A lack of specific skills in adequate quantities may cause either a shift in strategies or a delay contingent upon the organization's ability to provide needed skills in desired quantities. The attempts of the federal government to attract and retain capable, imaginative administrators has no doubt been in part hampered by the bureaucratic rules and red tape surrounding the operation of government agencies.

TIMING

The possibility of delay in developing resources brings into view the strategic problem of timing. Strategy formulation is more than just recognizing problems and opportunities—it must also generate a series of sequences which specify *when* to develop opportunities. Timing involves a long look at the forecasts of trends in product and factor markets and a blending of these long-term factors with internal considerations and the state of both present and future competitive conditions. For example, as General Electric looks into the future, it may see consumer tastes trending slowly toward more sophisticated smaller appliances. GE's strategists then would have to decide whether to tool up a production line to produce a new line of atomic-powered garbage disposals, say, in five years' time. If GE learned that Westinghouse and Sunbeam planned to produce a similar unit in three years, then the timing of GE's strategy might have to undergo revision to compete with the new entries in the field. Indeed, there might even be a product change introduced in the form of an accessory unit that would allow the industrious home owner to utilize the radioactive residual in the unit to kill off troublesome crabgrass or Japanese beetles. Timing is both a part of the strategy-making process and one of its determinants. The pervasiveness of timing, like that of personnel factors, will receive continued attention in upcoming chapters.

Summary

Even though it has its roots in the present, strategy is really a long-term concept. It comes from a look ahead, a look within, and a look around. Long-term strategy decisions require a careful, thorough analysis of factors both inside and outside the organization's operating environment, and the critical variable approach seems best suited to the type of analysis called for in strategy determination.

The major areas to consider in setting opportunistic strategy are growth patterns, technological innovations, personnel factors, organizational design, and the always present factor of timing. Forecasting, as the source of most problems and opportunities from which strategies are devised, also enters into strategy determination. Before this basic section on recognizing problems and opportunities can be concluded, it is both necessary and proper to turn to a review of the techniques and problems encountered in the art and science of forecasting, as given in Chapter 5.

Study Questions

1. Do you agree that the critical variables in the determination of opportunistic strategies are growth, organization, technology, timing, and personnel variables? What other key variables, if any, would you add?

2. Does the critical variable analysis seem to be a satisfactory model to analyze growth factors? What about the other key variables identified in question 1?

3. Can you give an example of an organization which has selected good opportunistic strategies? How about one doing a poor job? Discuss.

4. To what extent do personal values and beliefs of an organization's leadership influence strategy determination? Give examples of situations where leaders have influenced organizational goals and strategies.

5. What in your opinion are the critical societal forces and institutions which will shape the future directions of business-related organizations? Are these factors significantly different from those influencing future patterns of non-business organizations? Expound on these points in the light of your own experience.

In the previous chapter, the recognition of problems and opportunities was described in terms of a look inside, a look around, and a look ahead. Of the three, the most difficult and the most important is the look ahead—the process of forecasting the future.

Forecasting is, in an oversimplified sense, nothing more than an attempt to predict the future. A typical forecast contains elements of both past and future, but the future elements are based on estimates rather than historical facts or observations of current happenings. The difficulty of looking into the future is underscored in a now-dated, but still pertinent, incident involving Edward Stettinius and Joe Rosenthal, photographer of the famous Marine flag raising on Mount Surabachi (Iwo Jima) during World War II. While Mr. Rosenthal was photographing Mr. Stettinius at a San Francisco conference, Mr. Stettinius asked how he should pose. Mr. Rosenthal said, "Just look as if you're peering into the future." When Mr. Stettinius asked, "How do I peer into the future?" Mr. Rosenthal hesitated, then said, "Okay, so just peer." [1] How to peer into the future is the essence of forecasting.

There are two basic ways to consider forecasting. One views it in a descriptive sense, while the other concentrates on the techniques used to prepare specific forecasts. The orientation here combines a descriptive review of the steps in forecasting with a somewhat more technically oriented discussion of how forecasts are prepared at three different levels of complexity: general business conditions forecasts, industry forecasts, and the forecasts compiled for individual organizations.

CHAPTER 5
Forecasting Problems and Opportunities

[1] Reprinted from the September 24, 1955, issue of *Business Week* by special permission. Copyrighted © 1955 by McGraw-Hill, Inc., a special report on "Business Forecasting."

THE PROCESS OF FORECASTING

The word *forecasting* conjures visions of the future punctuated by cartoonist's portrayals of forecasters as Merlin-like sorcerers in pointed hats. In the 1936 presidential election, the *Literary Digest* forecast that Alf Landon would defeat Franklin D. Roosevelt, and this incredible prediction opened forecasters to ridicule.[2] When the Gallup Poll "elected" Thomas Dewey in 1948, criticisms were again raised, as they were when television's computers erred in predicting more recent results in primary elections, notably in California. In one sense, criticisms of forecasting errors are valid simply because forecasts *do* turn out wrong. Often, however, the critics, in their rush to be cleverly critical, ignore the facts that predicting the future is difficult at best and that accurate forecasts are more common now than ever before. In the 1968 presidential election, for example, Gallup forecast the final election totals within one percentage point of the actual vote. Obviously, this kind of accuracy is neither luck nor witchcraft. The art of forecasting may still be at the "Age of Merlin" in some predictions, but it never stops searching for more logical, orderly methodologies. Indeed, the processes in forecasting now use every applicable scientific method to help insure the greatest accuracy possible.

The modern forecasting process and the scientific method are similar in that both follow an orderly step-by-step approach. In the first step of forecasting, goals and hypotheses are determined and management decides exactly what information it seeks. The second step involves the collection of information. In a business organization, this would normally include a probe into company records such as sales forecasts, data on labor and materials, product line policy, and so on. It would also mean a review of any available reports on industry sales, competitor's sales, and general business practices. Going beyond industry data, the most painstaking forecasters develop and utilize pertinent data on general economic conditions by taping projections such as those prepared by the First National City Bank of New York, the National Industrial Conference Board, and the *Survey of Current Business,* published by the U.S. Department of Commerce. Supplemental information is also garnered from periodicals, newspapers, and various economic pamphlets. For example, *Fortune* frequently runs special articles on the state of the arts and the future prospects of companies in banking, petrochemicals, computers, and so on.

In the third step, the information collected is assessed, reviewed, analyzed, and perhaps synthesized into preliminary sets of projections. These predictions typically are prepared using techniques such as the extrapolation of trend lines, surveys of customers, opinions of experts, and perhaps the use of mathematical models. The weather bureau in Fort Worth has built such a model to predict the likelihood of flooding in the Texas area. This model, programmed

---

[2] The *Literary Digest* based its prediction on a sample taken from telephone books. Since telephones in the depression years were primarily in homes of high-income families, who tended to vote Republican, the sample was biased, and inaccurate results were forecast.

with the records of rainfall and river flow from over 700 participating weather stations in the area, can predict floods twelve to thirty-six hours in advance from a sample of only 20 percent (140) of the 700-plus reporting stations.

The fourth step involves the preparation of strategies, plans, and budgets. At this point, the projections and forecasts prepared in step 3 are turned into detailed guides or plans covering specific areas of operation. Divisions, departments, and geographical territories are considered in great detail and product lines and subunits are integrated into the planning and budgeting process. In the case of possible floods in Fort Worth, a less complex plan involving warnings and follow-up action by civil agencies might be an adequate first step in the action program. Step 5 refines the various forecasts as time passes. The nature of this dynamic refinement process varies a great deal in sophistication. At one end of the scale, high-powered statistical techniques such as Bayesian analysis utilize subjective (estimated) probabilities with objective (based on fact) probabilities to make better estimates of future happenings as the events of the present change the probabilities included in the original forecasts. The other kinds of techniques invoked at this time may be extremely simple ones such as revised guesses based on expert or intuitive judgment ("I know it's going to happen, I feel it in my bones.").[3]

The final step in the forecasting process is auditing and follow-up to ensure that forecasts and subplans derived from forecasts are being implemented properly. The execution stage, of course, is one that goes well beyond the forecast process, but, since feedback from execution often causes forecasts to be revised, this stage is legitimately included as part of the forecasting cycle.

The forecasting process thus has a logical sequence to follow, even though it still must rely on judgments and estimates in many steps. Though it has adopted the posture of the scientific method, forecasting remains an art, but an art that is gaining greater precision as it evolves. The wand has long since been replaced by the slide rule, and the crystal ball is now preempted by the computer. The scope of this move to greater mathematical precision is clearly evident in the kinds of techniques now used to carry out the various phases of forecasting.

TECHNIQUES OF FORECASTING

Forecasting of economic conditions usually covers three levels of activity: general economic conditions, industry or area conditions, and the individual organization. Actually, since industry or area forecasts overlap a great deal with both general economic conditions and with predictions for individual organizations, it is somewhat difficult to classify methods and techniques unique to forecasting industry conditions. There is also the frequent complica-

---

[3] The concept of probabilities and expected monetary value will be probed more carefully in Chapter 7.

tion that an industry grouping is hard to define and isolate. For example, just what kind of limits exist in the light bulb industry, if indeed there is such an industry? The approach to forecasting techniques here thus emphasizes only two levels of the forecasting job: (1) forecasting of general economic conditions and (2) projection of sales or levels of demand in individual organizations.

FORECASTING GENERAL BUSINESS CONDITIONS

Forecasts of general business conditions enter importantly into strategy determination. In order to construct optimum strategies, areas of opportunities and potential problems must be identified in current and futuristic terms. It follows rather obviously that the greater the efficiency of the forecasting process, the better the chance of achieving a given set of goals. Some care should therefore be devoted to selecting the forecast techniques that do the job most effectively.

Techniques for forecasting general business conditions can be classified in a number of ways. Gordon uses a very simple twofold classification: historical analysis and cross-section analysis.[4] Historical analysis is based on extrapolation of past trends, while cross-section analysis takes its forecasts from a look across current situations, variables, or happenings. A typical cross-section forecast might evaluate stock market trends, investment in business capital equipment, and/or housing, federal spending on defense items and other similar items before putting forth both figures or estimates. *Business Week,* in its special report on forecasting, states that forecasting can be classified as *loaded deck forecasting, the oaks from acorns method,* and the *test tube,* or systematic approach.[5] Loaded deck forecasting involves the use of inside information. A firm which *knows* it has a product that will eventually dominate a market has a marked advantage over competitors having no such knowledge. The oaks from acorns approach relies on extrapolation of past trends, much as Gordon's historical analysis. The test tube method involves the development of mathematical models or systematized techniques such as the mathematics of probability. A typical econometric model of this type appears in Figure 5.1, at the end of this chapter.

These varied classification schemes do not evaluate whether individual, group, or consensus forecasting is best, a point which has raised considerable controversy among forecasters. A study conducted by the University of Chicago and reported at the American Economic Association meetings in December 1964 tentatively concluded that individual economists or small groups do a better job of predicting general business conditions than a consensus taken from a large sample. The study also indicated that individuals or groups who historically have made close to exact projections will, in almost every instance, continue to perform at about the same level of excellence on upcoming

[4] R.J. Gordon, *Business Fluctuations* (New York: Harper & Row, Publishers, 1952).
[5] "Business Forecasting," *op. cit.*

projections. The moral here appears to be that once a man or a group starts to make accurate forecasts, he or they should be kept on the job. Though the results of this study have not been completely validated, it seems proper to surmise that in forecasting, as in other areas, a good man is hard to find and worth keeping once he comes on board.

Though classifications of forecasting techniques vary, one of the most useful breaks down techniques as historical projections, sensitive indices, survey techniques, and systematic simulation principally in the form of mathematical models.

Historical projection covers the extrapolation of past trends and very simplified techniques such as factor listing. In *extrapolating past trends,* original historical data are broken down into trend, cyclical, seasonal, and irregular data. These variations in the original data are then reviewed, analyzed, and projected into the future to make what traditional exponents of time series analysis would call accurate extrapolations of past data. Electric utilities often use such projections to predict both future rates of electrical consumption and future numbers of people who will populate their franchise area. School boards also use demographic data to plan new construction and manpower requirements. Trends such as the sagging birthrate in 1967 and further falloffs projected for 1968 through 1972 are vital inputs to school boards having only a four- or five-year lead time to meet the educational needs of this new population.

Factor listing simply shows what favorable factors exist and what unfavorable factors are expected to exist in the future environment. These unweighted factors are reviewed in subjective fashion, and tentative conclusions are made and then honed into sharper forecasts. One approach to factor listing is to seek out executive opinions on pluses and minuses influencing a projected course of action and then restate these opinions in some kind of quantitative representation for planning purposes. In new product areas, factor listing is commonly used as one of the most practical means for forecasting demand. As an alternative to factor listing, a major meat-packing firm decided on sales figures for a new packaged meat product by adding the guesses of two top executives and selecting the average of their estimates as the final sales forecast. By the way, the two executives reportedly made a five-dollar bet on whose guess would be the closest to actual sales, then canceled it because they were both so far off the mark.

The use of *sensitive indices* is a widely known and widely used forecast technique. Single indices such as railroad car loadings, stock market movements, levels of inventory, and steel ingot production are reviewed, and from these single indices projections are made about the future. Individual investors and small businesses often rely on the single index forecasting approach. Buy or sell orders in the market often follow closely the ups and downs in general activity on Wall Street, and operators of the hundreds of small metal-working shops around Pittsburgh and Detroit look to the predicted sales of the giant steel and auto companies to guide their own planning. The use of *multiple indices* is an extension of the single index method. In this approach, indices of various types are reviewed and a group of indices are selected as leading, following, or running concurrent with the economy in upturns or downturns. The National Bureau of Economic Research, paced by the pioneering work of Geoffrey Moore and Arthur Burns, developed a set of twenty-one cycles which either lead, run concurrent with, or lag behind general levels of business activity. This approach attempts to identify a group of sensitive indices which predict the behavior of the economy by relating their own known (or hoped-for) movement to movements in general economic conditions. A sample set of coincident cycles might include sales of retail stores, gross national product movements, and industrial production. Leading indicators would be new orders, stock prices, industrial materials prices, and average length of work-weeks for various groups of workers. Selected lagging series might be consumer installment debt or book value of manufacturers' inventories. Study of these groups of indicators would, according to early NBER suggestions, lead to accurate predictions of future business conditions. One problem with these indices is the confusion over which set of cycles will give the best indication of future happenings, but advocates say this drawback is removed when experience proves that selected groups of cycles are well suited to predicting areas of special interest to particular organizations. It is well known, for example, that dozens of factors influence sales of automobiles, but auto companies know from experience that the really critical factor is the projected level of consumer income, and they plan accordingly.

A third variation of the sensitive index is a *diffusion index,* in which a group of sensitive cycles are weighted and the general behavior of the group is considered to be the indicator of performance. One method uses the so-called normal distribution and attempts to predict turning points in cycles by developing statistical measures of normal dispersion of indices; that is, when certain percentages of the cycles in the normal distribution are trending upward or downward, the forecaster bases his predictions of the future on the intensity and direction of these movements. Once the number of cycles reaches a certain level of decrease or increase, the statistical evidence tells the forecaster the probability underlying the continuance of such trends. The use of sensitive indices is advocated by many sophisticated economists and forecasters, and it enjoys wide usage in forecasting stock market movements, particularly in the specialized private forecasts received by individuals and organizations investing in stock and bond portfolios. The use of diffusion indices is not nearly as widespread as single-index forecasting. Although the diffusion index is probably a more accurate technique, expense and complexity tend to limit its usage.

Survey techniques are used as both a source of information and a technique of forecasting. Surveys of experts, insiders, consumers, investors, and so on give a great deal of information to forecasters and also provide a basis for forecasting in themselves. *The McGraw-Hill Survey* of investor's plans, for example, when coupled with other economic factors, is frequently used to predict general economic conditions in both the short run and the long run. This survey interviews key businesses to determine their *actual* commitments made in future capital equipment investment. These committed expenditures are then used to predict how the critical private investment sector will influence gross national product. Given the importance of private investment in the economy, the McGraw-Hill model has a high theoretical justification for accuracy and its performance in the real world has earned it high marks.

The University of Michigan survey of consumer attitudes has long been regarded as providing a basis for projecting consumer spending patterns, which in turn have been related to other factors to develop forecasts of general economic conditions. The Michigan survey quizzes consumers about their present and future buying plans, their expectations as to future price levels, and other matters which provide current readings on future intentions. Since consumption, like investment, is a major part of the American economic scene, the Michigan studies have provided useful practical forecasts of both general economic trends and movements in attitudes toward particular groupings of products or industries. Many auto, furniture, and appliance manufacturers watch the Michigan survey closely, as do federal monetary and fiscal agencies charged with implementing the provisions of the Full Employment Act of 1946.

It is important to note that survey techniques are not always accurate, particularly if the survey is poorly designed or the sample is of inadequate size. But surveys can yield meaningful information and projections if, as in the case of the McGraw-Hill and Michigan surveys, they are carried out with knowledge of both statistical sampling and skillful interviewing techniques.

Systematic simulation involves the use of *econometric models* and variations on the "lost horse method," which asks in terms of the wanderings of the economy, "If I were a lost horse, where would I go from here?" The best and most accurate econometric models have reported projections of gross national product and various industry sales with a great deal of accuracy. The Klein-Goldberger model of the U.S. economy and its first cousin the Klein-Wharton School model, are multivariable representations of how the economy operates. In past years, the Klein-Wharton School model has developed rather good predictions of general economic activity, and it seems to be gaining greater accuracy each year as its sophistication improves. The Tinbergen model of the Dutch economy has had a similar record of achievement. One embryonic model showing future promise is the product of a joint effort of the Massachusetts Institute of Technology and the Federal Reserve System. Composed of some eighty equations, the model emphasizes the effect of monetary policy on general business conditions; and it is now being used as a tentative guide by monetary policy planners in the Federal Reserve Board. These and other econometric models start with a mathematical or logical representation of a theory and proceed to feed data in from existing and historical sources and from estimates of the future. The relationships between present and past patterns, when constructed so that many possible ranges of future behavior can be projected, give a solid basis for forecasting. Models are particularly useful when these kinds of changes or adjustments can be made to correct past mistakes or to update the variables in such a way that the model becomes a "true representation" of the economy, the industry, or whatever it is attempting to simulate.

The lost horse technique also relies on models, but many of them are less mathematically based than their econometric cousins. The lost horse is more introspective than the econometric method, but when dressed up with appropriate knowledge from the field of subjective probability, it can handle many situations which econometric models cannot handle because of time and money constraints. In other words, lost horse forecasting can be quick, economical, and, if based on sound premises, relatively high in accuracy. For example, a group of salesmen or political experts might be asked to render judgments on what products consumers would want to buy or what kind of candidate voters would support. These subjective estimates might be tried out in test markets or local elections to validate or invalidate the experts' collective judgment. With this kind of input, further deliberations might be held, from which more refined judgments would follow. Given a continual feedback of data from the field, these experts, or continually changing groups of experts, would build impressions or images that hopefully could be translated into the selection of products or candidates the market or the voter would buy. If this process were quantified and represented in some sort of simulation of reality, the lost horse method would be reasonably valid and much more sophisticated predictor than forecasts based on simple judgment.

It goes without saying that any forecasting methodology will be more or less accurate depending upon the time, effort, and knowledge which goes into it. An econometric approach poorly carried out might well yield a forecast inferior in quality to a carefully drawn historical projection. The economist's complaint that historical projections are naïve is only accurate if the historical projections are executed in naïve fashion. The same is true of carelessly structured econometric models, ill-prepared survey techniques, or any other poorly executed forecasting methodologies. Even the most elegant mathematical models of the economy failed to predict the boom following World War II; on the contrary, most forecast a depression. Perhaps the models were poorly constructed at that time, but even the more sophisticated models operative today are unable to call the future correctly 100 percent of the time. All the model maker can do is build the most accurate data available into his predictive engines and hope for the best, while he rests on the uneasy and tentative generality that extrapolation of past trends seems to show the best forecasts of general business conditions are made by the best men using the best available methods.

FORECASTING IN INDIVIDUAL ORGANIZATIONS

The same shaky generalization about the accuracy of forecasts of general economic conditions seems to hold for forecasting in individual organizations:

the better the man and his model, the better the forecast. Unfortunately, the problem of forecasting is compounded in microcosm, because few indices are available to point out exactly which variables should be studied and related to construct accurate forecasts for specific organizations. Since few guidelines are available, forecasters at the organizational level often have to generate their own inputs or amend general schemes to fit their own needs. One helpful scheme is that described in Figure 3.3. The other analytical schemes in Chapter 3 can also provide assistance in analyzing problems of lesser orders of magnitude than those calling for critical variable analysis.

Still another approach is outlined by William H. Newman and James Logan in their excellent text, *Business Policies and Management,*[6] According to them, the pertinent factors encompass not only the organization's own resources but also the forces acting on the industry in which it operates. In their opinion, the outlook for the industry depends on the demand for its products or services and on the supply of products or services available within the industry, which includes labor costs, materials costs, taxes, and other operating costs and is influenced by the goals of associated organizations, the structure of the industry, and the level of government regulation. The position of the company in the industry is also critical in an appraisal of its future outlook. This, as Newman and Logan note, includes the market position the firm may have, the relative standing of its products in the industry, the cost position of the company in terms of internal efficiencies and plant locations, and the special competitive considerations that might arise from the possession of unique strength in financial, marketing, or managerial factors.

In order to analyze the techniques that might be used to investigate the future direction of a firm, some kind of classification scheme is useful. The framework chosen here is a rough representation of one put forth by Joel Dean in his classic, *Managerial Economics.*[7] According to Dean, the best way to make individual firm forecasts is to divide the firm's products into two classes: stable and new products. Though Dean's approach deals with business organizations, it can be adapted easily to analyze and organize forecasts for almost any kind of organization.

Dean advocates a number of techniques to forecast sales of established products or product lines. He suggests that surveys of buyers' intentions and surveys of people who know (experts) are sound time-tested forecast methods. Buyers' intentions, he claims, can be gauged by directly asking customers what they intend to buy and in what quantities. People who know are defined as jobbers, wholesalers, retailers, and, perhaps, government officials and others who might know the market, including salesmen. The comments about the McGraw-Hill and Michigan surveys apply here as well. Dean's two survey methods may or may not provide useful information, depending on how they are implemented. Surveys of existing customers, potential customers, and

---

[6] 4th ed. (Cincinnati: South-Western Publishing Company, 1959).

[7] (Englewood Cliffs, N.J.: Prentice-Hall, Inc., 1951).

future customers can be especially valuable to firms in the consumer and capital goods industries. The same approach can be used by political organizations interested in voter preferences, by unions concerned about members' desires, by government bureaus interested in employee and/or public attitudes, and so forth.

Projections of past patterns are also useful, particularly when trends and cycles have been observed over long periods of time and when predictable patterns of replacement are known to exist. Appliance firms conduct lengthy studies of product life cycles to determine normal replacement times, and original equipment manufacturers such as Goodyear and Firestone Rubber perform similar studies to assist in predicting replacement sales of tires, tubes, and other accessories. Banks and financial institutions also project trends and changes in such factors as consumer credit, demand deposit growth, and their customers' investment needs. A particularly interesting factor to banks in recent years has been the increasing use of bank-issued credit cards, an opening step in the "cashless society" which may, in the near future, become a "checkless society" in which banks handle all financial transactions for customers and charge a small fee for their services.

The projection of past trends is based on a demand function with time as a single independent variable. Dean's fourth and fifth methods consider more complex interrelationships. Correlation analysis attempts to relate sales to either a single variable (simple correlation) or a series of variables (multiple correlation). Sales of automobiles, for example, might be related to how much money (discretionary income) the consumer has to spend on items other than necessities in a simple correlation analysis or to a whole series of factors including levels of general income, age of cars on the road, tax rates, styling, and so forth in a much more complicated multiple correlation analysis. Sales of motor oil can be simply correlated to gasoline sales, but gasoline sales are the product of a much more complex set of factors that seem more properly and accurately handled by multiple correlation analysis. As is the case with less powerful historical projections, correlation analysis draws most of its ability to predict from analysis of past relationships which it assumes will hold in the future.

In predicting the sales of new products, Dean describes a sixth approach. He suggests the use of evolutionary techniques, substitutes, growth curves, opinion polling, sales experience, and vicarious methods. The evolutionary approach tries to project the demand for new projects as an extension of old lines. An example might be projecting sales of a new battery-operated tape recorder from sales of nonbattery-powered tape recorders in existing markets. Another example would be the ball-point pen and the inroads it has made on the traditional fountain pen. Although such efforts are often productive, hazards abound, because new products may not follow older, more established lines. Boeing's attempts to predict sales of its proposed 747 airbus from knowledge of the industry it gained through selling its 707 and 727 passenger jets were not particularly rewarding. Boeing's failure to predict trends in the airplane market in the late 1960s cost it a great deal in both product sales and continuing market leadership.

The growth curve approach tries to guess where the market will develop, based upon existing states of growth in such matters as replacement rates. For example, projections of future vacuum cleaner sales have a great deal to do with both continued acceptance of vacuum cleaners and the existing life cycles of vacuum cleaners now in use. Opinion polling, discussed previously in stable product line prediction, may well be experts talking to experts to determine what the market may be and how it might develop. For example, IBM may send one of its engineers or hire a market research consulting firm to ask existing customers whether they might be interested in purchasing a new computerized device for measuring items with high tolerances; if, indeed, such a machine could be developed. Forecasts based on sales experience are used widely in the consumer products field, where many consumer-oriented firms give away or sell products in a test or sample market and then project sales for larger areas based upon the results obtained in the test area. Colgate-Palmolive introduced the enzyme action stain-removing product Axion in 1968 by giving away free samples in test markets and then planning a follow-up based on encouraging reports from users.

The vicarious approach is somewhat similar to opinion polling in that it uses specialized dealers and asks them to report their experiences as if they were the whole market. In the introduction of a new drug or a personal product such as lipstick, a manufacturer may go only to wholesale drug chains to test the potential marketability of his product. In another case, the "influential" citizens of a community may be sought out by the mayor to get their feelings on how the electorate would react to spending tax money on a new municipal building instead of a municipal swimming pool.

Whether forecasting techniques are used to predict sales of individual firms, entire industries, or the direction and/or intensity of general economic conditions, the basic result sought is to tie results to strategies and, ultimately, to the basic goals of the initiating organization. Poor forecasts often bring unexpected results, as Dr. Armand Hammer, president of Occidental Petroleum, discovered when he bought Mutual Broadcasting Company from General Tire for about $700,000. Hammer admits he knew only that Occidental had bought the "largest radio network." In fact, Mutual turned out to be an expensive time-consuming headache which Occidental eventually sold to Alexander Guterma, the financier who later went to prison for securities violations. Apparently Guterma's forecasting was not particularly good either, since Mutual went into a bankruptcy reorganization a few months after his takeover.

When and if forecasts bring out potential problems, such as those discovered by Dr. Hammer, plans and strategies can be adjusted to fit the situation. If it becomes necessary to adjust goals to meet conditions identified in the forecasts, then such changes are in order as long as the organization is willing to take the steps needed to chart a new course of action. The recognition of opportunities and problems through forecasting is thus a process that continually interacts with the development of dynamic strategies within the long-run goal structure of the organization.

FORECASTING AND SYSTEMS FOR STRATEGIC ANALYSIS

The relationship between forecasting techniques and the several systems for strategic and tactical analysis described in Chapter 3 are hinted at in several points in Chapters 4 and 5, but no one section brings home the point that forecasts help to fill in the kinds of factors, forces, and results that appear when preliminary systems models are forged into detailed plans backed up with appropriate commitments of resources. The systems models make sure all bases are touched, while the forecasts try to ensure that they are touched as fully as the rules of the game allow. It seems worthwhile to repeat that forecasts can change goals, strategies, and even tactics; and that changes in goals or objectives, in turn, can and do change forecasts and forecasting methods. As goals change, policies may change, and changes in policies may well alter the nature of the weighting of variables in the forecast mix. In specific terms, the items in the *problems* column of Figures 3.1, 3.2, 3.3, and 3.4 may change as conditions and requirements shift during the interaction process. In other instances, the list of variables may undergo alteration to include new critical variables (as in Figure 3.3) or to reweigh old ones. Given the dynamic nature of forecasting and the volatility of the interplay between goals and projections, it seems remarkable that organizations ever get to the point where they reach a state stable enough to allow any decisions to be made at all—never mind good and wise ones.

AN ILLUSTRATION OF THE FORECASTING PROCESS

The following discussion of forecasting by J.J. Curran, Jr., of the General Foods Corporation relates the theoretical to the practical level in very meaningful terms.

INTRODUCING A NEW PRODUCT

Forecasting and profit-planning played an important role in introducing a major postwar General Foods product and making it welcome in the American home. This product is Instant Maxwell House, which has been described as "the most marvelous merchandising success ever seen in the food business."

Instant, or soluble, coffee is a classic example of a convenience product. It's a powder obtained by brewing coffee in the factory and then extracting the water from it. It offers many advantages in that you can prepare one cup as easily as 10 cups, it keeps fresh longer than ground coffee, and it is quick—you can make a cup as quickly as water can be made to boil.

These advantages would justify a premium price over regular coffee. But instant coffee has the added advantage of economy—it is cheaper than regular coffee on a cup-for-cup basis, and it is less wasteful.

The first instants contained carbohydrate additives which gave the drink a slight off-coffee flavor. Now the instants are pure, and they make a good cup of coffee.

CREATION OF A MARKET

Instant coffee has an interesting history. Almost a hundred years ago, soldiers of our Civil War experimented with tablets of coffee powder which were dropped into hot water like Alka-Seltzer pills. The stuff was pretty bad. However, it is surprising that instant coffees were little heard of for half a century after.

Then, in 1910, a man named George Washington, who died in 1954, marketed a coffee powder in individual cup containers. The product was successful, but because of its high price it was [a] luxury or specialty item.

It was not until just before the war that the outline of a mass market for instant coffee became apparent. When the war came, production for the armed services was stimulated and civilian supplies were curtailed. The mass sampling of thousands of servicemen and civilians because regular coffee was not available undoubtedly helped create a peacetime market for instant coffees.

General Foods, as a major principal in the coffee business, realized that it must keep up with developments in the instant field. We produced instant coffee for the government during the war, and in 1946 our product appeared on grocery shelves.

Our first marketing experience was like that of some of our competitors—we were getting millions of people to buy our product once or twice, but repeat demand was weak. We knew the answer was in product acceptability and therefore directed our research toward improvement.

Research paid off in 1949 when we found ourselves with a new process which gave us 100 per cent pure coffee. We believed it was better than anything else on the market and had great promotional possibilities.

A LOOK AT PAST EXPERIENCE

What did we do with this advantage, and what part did forecasting and profit-planning play in the steps we took?

We first made a long-range forecast. To do so, we made a careful appraisal of our progress to date and took a good look at our then current situation.

Why did we look back to the past when we wanted to move forward? My answer is that business forecasting does not operate with formulas which are mathematical and infallible and for that reason must rely largely on what has happened before.

While history does not exactly repeat itself, it is nevertheless true that like causes tend to have like effects. Wise marketing and management

practice therefore normally includes a continuing effort to build a comprehensive "book of experience," so to speak.

So we examined the *sales history* of our first instant coffee. We wanted
to find out where it had sold best; through what type of outlet, chain
or independent; and in what sizes and containers.

We found that our sales had not been growing fast even though most
of the 20-odd manufacturers who had entered the business since the war
had dropped out. By 1948, four companies controlled 90 per cent of the
market, and Instant Maxwell House was a poor third in the race.

Continuing our examination, we found that our *distribution* was national
but that retailer and wholesaler stocks were low—while our competitors
seemingly had more abundant supplies.

Then we looked at our past *marketing activity*. We studied the effect
of couponing, trade dealing, and media advertising on volume, on profits,
and on our competitors. We found that our marketing had been unable
to capitalize on any outstanding *quality* or *packaging advantage*. Sales
records indicated no outstanding consumer preference for Instant Maxwell
House.

ASSESSING FUTURE POSSIBILITIES

Having looked at what had happened, we then had to forecast the future
of Instant Coffee. This is the point where we had to *assess* the *limits of
the market* and our ability to penetrate that market.

The big questions were:

1. How big was the instant coffee market?
2. How fast was the market growing?
3. How much would it grow?

We found that there was a large existing market for instant coffee and
ample evidence that there was room for great expansion. We found that
no company had yet produced an instant coffee which matched the taste
of regular brewed coffee. However, we believed that our new process gave
our instant a superiority over all our competitors.

We next projected the consumption of coffee for a period of years, taking
into account population, income, and coffee consumption trends. Then we
had to forecast how much of this coffee would be sold in instant form—and
where it would be sold.

Having made the forecast, or assumption, of the size of the instant market
and its location, we proceeded to make a *long-term profit plan*.

FACTORS IN SETTING VOLUME OBJECTIVES

The first task and the most difficult was to set *volume objectives* for our
new instant coffee for a period of years.

This first basic step in profit-planning-setting volumes is much like the first instruction in a famous English recipe for rabbit pot pie: "First catch a rabbit." Overcome that hurdle and the rest is easy.

We set volumes after checking these questions or determining factors:

1. Was our product as good as we thought it was?

2. Would the housewife share our enthusiasm?

To find out, we made many consumer surveys, one of which I shall describe.

An independent testing organization went into 3,500 homes in Washington, D.C., with a coffee pot and a pound of regular Maxwell House Coffee. The tester said he wanted to compare the brand of coffee used by the housewife and brewed in her own way with regular Maxwell House brewed in his way. So the housewife and the tester each brewed a pot of coffee. Then the housewife was asked to leave the room, but her husband or another member of the family was asked to stay.

When the woman left, the tester poured the regular Maxwell House Coffee he had brewed down the sink and quickly mixed an equal quantity of Instant Maxwell House. The husband then called his wife back into the kitchen, and she was asked to taste the two coffees—her own favorite and Instant Maxwell House. By a two-to-one vote the housewife preferred our instant to her regular!

It was a remarkable demonstration, and it convinced us *we really had something!*

MISCELLANEOUS DECISIONS

With our new product, we could now advertise 100 percent pure coffee. How effective would this claim be?

Our product was less bulky than the old one. Should we pack in two-ounce, or six-ounce sizes? We decided on two and six ounces.

Should we pack in glass jars or in tin cans? We decided the glass jar was a better selling package.

Was the name Maxwell House, which was associated with regular coffee and with our old, relatively unsuccessful "filled" instant, an asset or a liability for our new product? We decided to retain the name, but to use a distinctive redesigned label for the new instant.

After considering all these questions, we set volume goals for each of our sales regions. The cost of production at varying volume levels was then projected, using cost accounting and engineering skills.

THE MARKETING STRATEGY

The profit plan next had to set forth the marketing strategy which would be used to introduce the new product. This involved many difficult decisions.

How could we exhaust all of the old label stock and introduce the new?

Should we strive for immediate national distribution, or should we introduce the new product region by region?

What media should be used—TV, newspapers, magazines, billboards, or what combination of these?

What deals or incentives should we use to get retailers to stock, and consumers to buy, the new Instant Maxwell House?

To get answers to these questions, we set up a test market. In three cities we introduced Instant Maxwell House with one marketing approach, and in three similar cities we used a different approach. Each group of cities showed surprisingly uniform results. In both cases, consumers bought our product and remained loyal to it after they used it. The second marketing approach, however, gave the most dramatic results.

These test cities were in the East, where instant coffee was already well accepted. To check the marketing plan in an area where instant coffee was not used extensively, we tried this second marketing approach in Kansas City. The approach was even more successful there, so we planned accordingly.

PLANT CAPACITY AND LOCATION

To repeat, our volume projection was made by regions. We next made a study to determine when we would need new plant capacity and—considering freight rates, regional markets, and other factors—where new plants should be built.

As a result, plans were made to expand in New Jersey and to build in Florida, California, and Texas.[8]

AN ILLUSTRATION OF A FORECASTING TECHNIQUE

The use of models in forecasting is extremely widespread. Brennan describes a model as a complete system of structural equations including definitional and behavioral equations, both of which have systematic and random variables including indigenous and exogenous factors. He further says there are four types of models: static models, under conditions of both certainty and uncertainty; and dynamic models, also under certainty and uncertainty. Though there is frequently debate as to whether particular models are either dynamic or static or are constructed to reflect conditions of certainty or uncertainty, there is little doubt that the so-called science of econometrics is gaining greater use and acceptance in forecasting circles.[9]

To indicate how a generalized approach to model making might be used to make forecasts of economic conditions, Figure 5.1, an illustration taken from an article in *Business Week,* is both instructive and amusing.

---

[8] J.J. Curran, Jr., "Coordinating Budgets with Forecasting," *Charting the Company's Future* (New York: American Mangement Association, Inc., 1954).

[9] M. Brennan, *Preface to Econometrics* (Cincinnati: South-Western Publishing Company, 1960).

Predict the U.S. Economy for 1956.
Build Your Own Forecasting Model.

Figure 5.1

DIRECTIONS:

1. MAKE UP A THEORY.

You might theorize, for instance, that (1) next year's consumption will depend on next year's national income; (2) next year's investment will depend on this year's profits; (3) tax receipts will depend on future Gross National Product. (4) GNP is the sum of consumption, investment, and government expenditures. (5) National income equals GNP minus taxes.

SOURCE: Reprinted from the September 24, 1955, issue of *Business Week* by special permission. Copyrighted © 1955 by McGraw-Hill, Inc.

2. USE SYMBOLS FOR WORDS.

Call consumption, C; national income, Y; investment, I; preceding year's profits, P_{-1}; tax receipts, T; Gross National Product, G; government expenditures, E.

3. TRANSLATE YOUR THEORIES INTO MATHEMATICAL EQUATIONS.

(1) $C = aY + b$
(2) $I = cP_{-1} + d$
(3) $T = eG$
(4) $G = C + I + E$
(5) $Y = G - T$

This is your forecasting model. The small letters, a, b, c, d, e, are the constants that make things come out even. For instance, if horses (H) have four legs (L), then $H = aL$; or $H = 4L$. This can be important in the blacksmith business.

4. CALCULATE THE CONSTANTS.

Look up past years' statistics on consumption, income, and so on. From these find values for a, b, c, d, and e that make your equation come out fairly correct.

5. NOW YOU'RE READY TO FORECAST.

Start by forecasting investment from this year's profits. Look up the current rate of corporate profits—it's around $42-billion. The model won't tell what federal, state, and local governments will spend next year—that's politics. But we can estimate it from present budget information—it looks like around $75-billion.

6. PUT ALL AVAILABLE FIGURES INTO YOUR MODEL.

(We've put in the constants for you.)

(1) $C = .7Y + 40$
(2) $I = .9 \times 42 + 20$
(3) $T = .2G$
(4) $G = C + 1 + 75$
(5) $Y = G - T$

7. SOLVE THE EQUATIONS.

You want values of C, I, T, G, Y. Hints: Do them in this order—(2), (1), (4), (3), (5). In solving (1), remember that I and E are both part of G, $Y = G - T$, and $T = .2G$.

8. RESULTS.

(See if yours are the same.) For 1956, consumption will be $260.0-billion; investment, $57.8-billion; GNP, $392.8-billion; tax receipts, $78.6-billion; national income, $314.2-billion. The results are guaranteed—provided that the theories on which they're based are valid.

Summary

Forecasting is a technique through which problems and opportunities are recognized and turned into plans of action. Economic forecasts are made to predict general economic conditions, industry outlooks, and the sales of specific organizations. Techniques for forecasting at the general economic level include historical projections, the use of sensitive indices, survey approaches, and systematic attempts to simulate future conditions through the use of models. Many of the same techniques are used at the level of the individual firm, although perhaps greater reliance is placed upon surveys of insiders, experts, customers, and those who know something about the market. In addition, more specific variables are built into models to reflect relationships between sales and factors known to be related to sales. These correlations often assume highly mathematical and technical forms in industries where relationships are relatively stable or where projections are made for particularly long periods.

Forecast projections are related to goals and strategies in a continuing process, which yields plans of action and such operational devices as budgets and programs expressed in terms of time, dollars, and resources. Forecast data are thus used to help project long-term approaches and to provide inputs for the never-ending processes of decision making and execution of completed decisions. It is to the operational process of decision making that we turn in Section III.

Study Questions

1. What forecast techniques used to predict general business conditions seem to be most valid? Why? Do you know of other methods that may be better? If so, describe them.

2. What are some examples of survey or polling techniques not in the realm of business and economics? How valid are the results drawn from these techniques?

3. What are the potential disadvantages of using single or multiple indices to forecast the future? The potential advantages?

4. What differences and similarities appear between the lost horse and the intuitive methods of forecasting?

5. Can you think of any situation in your own experience or knowledge where goals and strategies were changed or influenced by forecast results? Do not limit yourself to businesses in answering this question.

6. Mathematical models have the advantage of yielding precise results quite rapidly. What are some of their drawbacks?

7. What relationships exist between the systems models in Chapter 3 and the factors and techniques discussed in Chapters 4 and 5? Try to be as precise as possible.

The CBS Yankees

When Douglass Wallop wrote *The Year the Yankees Lost the Pennant,* the New York Yankees were enough of a baseball legend to inspire the cry, "Break up the Yankees." In 1964, the Columbia Broadcasting System, as part of an ongoing diversification program, laid out $11.2 million for an 80-percent interest in what seemed to be a superteam. The Yankees obliged their new owners in 1964 by winning an unprecedented ninth Pennant in ten seasons.

On paper, the CBS purchase looked good. The Yankees were a winner, and CBS needed a winner to cover the high price of the club and its players. CBS television also programmed sports, and baseball's Yankees had a natural tie-in with the CBS interests. CBS executives felt that the Yankees' future was rosy and predicted a continuance of baseball's mightiest dynasty, with a consequently lucrative return for CBS. But then, the golden idols turned into mortals with feet of clay.

In 1966, when CBS invested $2 million more to gain complete control, the Yankees finished the season one game behind the Boston Red Sox. And since the Red Sox were in ninth place, the Yankees were, as the old cliché goes, the strongest team in the league: on the bottom holding all the others up. In 1967, the Yankees finished ninth, a position that gladdened neither CBS management nor the fairweather Yankee fans, who either stayed away in droves or shifted their affection to the inept but lovable New York Mets. Attendance at Yankee Stadium dropped from 1,748,000 in 1961 to 1,260,000 in 1967.

On September 15, 1968, the Yankees made a strong bid for the heights when they moved into third place in the league, but a late season slump saw them finish fifth. In the meantime, CBS's fortunes suffered a general decline. The mid-1960s were rocky years for CBS with television revenues falling off and other subsidiaries performing far below expectations. All in all, CBS faced a situation described in *Fortune* as, "Bad Days at Black Rock," Black Rock being the nickname of the modern, austere building housing CBS's corporate headquarters.

In retrospect, the purchase of the Yankees helped to make the bad days worse, even though 1968 attendance figures seemed to be a cause for future optimism.

1. Looking backwards, how could CBS have forecast what to expect from the Yankees in the first two or three seasons following their 1964 acquisition?

2. What factors, trends, variables, and so forth should CBS use to evaluate expected future contributions from the Yankees?

3. What techniques and analytical devices would be best able to forecast future Yankee finishes in the league, future contributions to revenue, and asset appreciation?

4. Forecast Yankee finishes for the next five years and specify the basis for making your predictions.

Admiral Airlines

When Samuel McDonald became president of Admiral Airlines, he was the fourth individual to hold that post in a decade. Of the three previous presidents, the first had been the founder, the second a financial expert, and the third an operating man. Sam McDonald, a former chief executive in a competitive airline, faced the job of revitalizing Admiral and bringing it up to the level of prosperity enjoyed by competing airlines. To quote a position paper prepared by Admiral's board of directors, "This airline is slowly dying, and it will die more rapidly unless it gets a transfusion of new blood. Survival depends on new men, new approaches and new techniques." The board felt that Samuel McDonald possessed the skill, experience, and judgment needed to bring about Admiral's recovery.

RECENT HISTORY

Some of the problems plaguing the new president of Admiral Airlines had deep roots. For thirty years Admiral had been under the control of Merriwether Dunlap, a former Navy pilot described by one colleague as, "a real entrepreneur in the classic sense." Dunlap was considered by many to be a strong dominant person with colossal confidence in his own skills and abilities. He was a controversial individual, respected by some colleagues and feared by others. A former Admiral executive had once called him "the last of the pure SOBs." Upon hearing this comment, Dunlap retorted, "He seems to know a lot more than he did when he worked for Admiral."

The basic philosophy guiding Admiral Airlines during Dunlap's reign was that low-cost transportation was the key to profits and success. Frills to him were extras not related to rapid economic movement of passengers. He once remarked to a gathering of his top executives, "We'll load passengers like cattle if we have to: we must never forget to keep costs down." Another of Dunlap's favorite phrases was framed on the wall of his office. It reminded everyone to "Watch the pennies and the dollars will take care of themselves."

In his final years as president of Admiral, Dunlap became more and more enamoured with the importance of cutting costs. He frequently walked around corporate headquarters flicking off lights not in use. He saved string and paper clips and personally developed a filter to strain and reuse oil formerly discarded in maintenance operations. As Dunlap grew older, even some of his most loyal followers began to feel his attitude toward cost cutting was becoming something of an obsession. One result of his continual pressure on costs was that many passenger service operations were so understaffed they were ill equipped to perform the duties necessary for a high level of customer satisfaction. Whenever priorities were issued by Dunlap, machinery and equipment rated well above customer satisfaction, and passengers began to resent their treatment at the hands of Admiral's overworked employees. In consequence, the firm's public image began to suffer, the net result of this dissatisfaction was a drop in public confidence and a deterioration of employee morale. At one point, Admiral and Eastern airlines were the two leading airlines in terms of complaints handled by the Civil Aeronautics Board. It was common for an Admiral passenger to remark, "If I had any other choice I'd take it rather than fly Admiral."

In one area, however, Admiral did have an adequate, competent staff: pilots and aircraft crews were well trained. When the jet age came to commercial aviation, Admiral moved quickly into training its pilots on commercial jets. Like Howard Hughes of TWA, Dunlap wanted good pilots, trained to fly all available aircraft. Unlike TWA, however, Admiral purchased jets long before its route structure had the volume to make their use economical. Thus, Admiral's seating capacity was far in excess of customer demand, and the company suffered losses in some seasons on even its most lucrative routes. On some routes, losses were incurred in all seasons.

ROUTE STRUCTURE

At least some of Admiral's problems could be traced to its route structure. Though Admiral had a number of long and intermediate hauls, short hauls constituted the bulk of its business. In addition to being uneconomical for jet aircraft, many of these hauls were too competitive to yield reasonable profits. Admiral was not as big as such transcontinental carriers as United Airlines, TWA, Eastern Airlines, and American Airlines, but its sales were somewhat higher than local service airlines such as Trans Texas, Lake Central, Mohawk, and Allegheny. Admiral was thus an intermediate-size carrier in the same size class as National and Delta airlines.

Admiral's main offices in Chicago were the hub of a system which fanned out in several directions. On its north-south routes, Admiral flew in competition with Delta and American airlines to cities such as St. Louis, Kansas City, Memphis, New Orleans, Dallas, and Houston. Admiral also serviced a route to Seattle via Denver in which Northwest, Continental, and United Airlines were direct competitors. Admiral's Cleveland-Detroit-New York (Newark) route also operated in the face of strong competition from United, American, TWA, and Northwest. In addition, Admiral flew directly to several Caribbean islands. These routes were largely noncompetitive, although several other airlines also serviced them to a limited extent.

In general, Admiral's routes were plagued by rather high operating costs. Terminal facilities in many cities were expensive, and waiting time for landing and takeoff was generally long and costly. Since many of its routes had spirited competition for the passenger dollar, Admiral's handling costs per passenger were above the national average. Although service to the Caribbean was profitable in season, it was run well below capacity for the remainder of the year. Like several other lines whose revenues were affected by seasonal factors, Admiral often had difficulty filling planes in the off season to the (average) break-even point of 45.8 percent of seating capacity. In the off season, for example, Admiral's planes commonly flew with only 25 to 30 percent of seating capacity filled.

Though the markets served by Admiral were potentially profitable, the line's inability to fill existing seating capacity made profits dwindle. Even with the advent of smaller, low-cost jets, Admiral had to cope with the problems of competition. On its most competitive lines, for example, Admiral's revenue per passenger mile was only 5.8 cents, one of the lowest in the industry. (see Table I.1) The route structure was thus viewed by Admiral's management as both a potential strength and an actual weakness.

RECENT MANAGEMENT CHANGES

In the mid-fifties, Admiral suffered a series of low profit years. Pressure arose from stockholders to check the downward flow of profits, but no action was taken until President Merriwether Dunlap himself decided to step down. When Dunlap resigned to become chairman of the board, his hand-picked replacement was Stanton Tillingham.

Stanton Tillingham was as much unlike Merriwether Dunlap as possible. His selection caused some surprise in the industry, since his training, temperament, and orientation were quite different from those of his predecessor. Tillingham's training had been in finance and marketing at one of the nation's better business schools. Though his basic orientation reflected his financial background, he felt the main focus of the airline should be on passenger service, not operations. He was firmly behind programs designed to improve the quality of passenger service, and he advocated such frills as champagne flights and deluxe dinner menus.

After a short time, it became apparent to insiders that Dunlap and Tillingham had too many personality problems to make an effective management team. Their personal differences were further accentuated by major clashes in philosophies, economics, and technologies. Dunlap continually second-guessed Tillingham, overruled plans he presented to the board of directors, and generally frustrated him in every possible manner. The board soon realized that either or both men would have to go before Admiral could return to profitable levels of operation. Before the board was forced to make a decision, Tillingham resigned, releasing a series of bitter public statements that caused great concern both within the company and throughout the industry.

TABLE I.1 YARDSTICKS OF PERFORMANCE: Airlines

GROWTH (Six-Year Compounded Rate)

	Sales	Common Equity Per Share	Group Ranking
Delta	16.3%	20.0%	1
Western	16.7	15.9	2
Northwest	12.6	15.1	3
National	14.9	9.8	4
Continental	18.1	9.1	5
Pan American	10.8	10.8	6
American	8.5	9.7	7
United	13.7	6.5	8
Trans World	11.5	4.7	9
			10
Eastern	7.5	−7.8	11
Industry Median	12.6	9.7	

PROFITABILITY (Five-Year Average)

	Return on Equity	Cash Flow to Equity	Oper. Profit Margin	Group Ranking
Western	11.2%	41.2	21.7%	1
Delta	12.2	39.4	22.6	2
Continental	8.4	43.1	24.0	3
Northwest	9.3	37.8	25.4	4
Pan American	9.3	41.2	20.2	5
National	10.6	35.7	20.5	6
Trans World	7.7	62.1	16.4	7
American	7.1	33.9	17.2	8
United	5.9	34.0	16.3	9
Braniff	5.1	34.9	16.1	10
Eastern	4.7	21.8	13.3	11
Industry	(d)	**	9.2	12
Median	8.4	37.8	20.2	

	Earnings Gain	Pretax Profit Margin*	Group Ranking
Eastern	†	†	1
Continental	210.3	9.0	2
Northwest	143.4	14.7	3
Braniff	156.9	6.1	4
Trans World	111.0	7.6	5
United	136.7	4.9	6
National	70.0	5.2	7
American	100.0	4.3	8
Delta	43.9	2.6	9
Pan American	37.1	0.6	10
Western	32.9	0.5	11
Industry Median	111.0	5.2	

SOURCE: *Forbes Magazine*, January 1, 1966, p. 82

* Gain or loss in percentage points
† From a deficit to a profit
** Not comparable
d Deficit

Mr. Tillingham's successor as president was Horace Leggatt, a graduate engineer who had once been interested in patents and had become an amateur authority on patent law. He had returned to school, taken his law degree, and was generally known in the Chicago area as a rather outstanding engineer-lawyer. Leggatt, who had been with Admiral some fifteen years prior to assuming the presidency, had been hired and trained by Merriwether Dunlap. The majority of the board felt, however, that Leggatt had enough of a progressive viewpoint to bring about changes needed to restore Admiral to a profitable operating position. His technical background was expected to be valuable in ironing out some of the operating difficulties Admiral faced, and the Board felt that his steady temperament would act as a balance on Dunlap's attempts to dominate operations. In short, he was considered the kind of person who could keep Admiral "on course" while instituting some much needed changes.

After Leggatt had been in office for only a few months, several board members charged that he was reluctant to make any real changes without first gaining Mr. Dunlap's concurrence. Furthermore, it became apparent to these individuals that Leggatt's strongest suit was maintenance and cost reduction, not passenger service; and, when profits continued to fall, a majority of the board began to feel the service problem had to be dealt with before the airline would obtain a satisfactory level of profits. After only one year in office, the board (with Merriwether Dunlap's lone dissenting vote) asked Leggatt to resign. Leggatt did so immediately and joined another airline as vice-president in charge of operations. Leggatt's departure caused no repetition of the furor or bitterness generated by Tillingham's resignation; in fact, those who knew him well felt certain Leggatt was happy to get back into the operations end of the business.

When Horace Leggatt resigned, several board members recognized that few, if any, substantial changes could be initiated as long as Merriwether Dunlap maintained an active influence over operating policies. These individuals asked Dunlap to resign "for the good of the company." Dunlap reacted by instituting action to have this group of directors removed. Dunlap solicited support for their ouster from several stockholders and touched off a rather flamboyant and bitter proxy fight. When news of this controversy reached the press, what had seemed to be an internal policy dispute became a public circus.

After the struggle for control had dragged on for almost a year, an outside group attempted to gain control of the board. The threat of possibly losing control to outsiders caused a consolidation of thinking among board members, and Dunlap was pressured to resign. When Dunlap realized that a majority of the board favored his resignation, he stepped down for "reasons of health." Following the announcement of his resignation Dunlap was quoted in a newspaper column as stating, "I was a victim of these damned Eastern bankers and those pussy-footing pantywaists now running Admiral." In his official public statement, however, Dunlap stated, "This airline needs new blood and new ideas. It's time for the old timers like me to step down and let the young men have a chance to run the show."

THE PRESIDENCY OF SAMUEL McDONALD

When Samuel McDonald was first approached concerning his availability for the presidency of Admiral Airlines, his reaction was guarded. But after the offer was repeated several weeks later, McDonald agreed to meet with two board members and a representative of a banking firm to discuss the terms and conditions required to attract him to Admiral Airlines. After several meetings, McDonald's set of personal and financial conditions were agreed to by the liaison group. McDonald also stressed that he had no interest in the job under any conditions if Merriwether Dunlap was to have any influence over the company. McDonald stated that he did not want Dunlap's advice as "either an operating executive or as any kind of consultant to management." In addition, he asked for a two-year contract and a clear mandate to make any changes he deemed feasible without board interference. These rigid conditions were informally agreed to by a majority of the board, and after Dunlap stepped down from the board, McDonald agreed to take over as Admiral's chief executive.

Samuel McDonald's first step as president of Admiral Airlines was to assess the current state of the company's operations and finances (see Table I.2). He spent several weeks talking to key executives and reviewing internal operating data. His initial evaluation was that Admiral needed strengthening in every major area of operation. In order to determine the extent and nature of some of the weaker areas, he hired a nationally known consulting firm to render a confidential report on passenger service and employee attitudes toward company policies. He also engaged another firm to analyze the structure and functioning of the various departments. Both reports seconded his own estimates that Admiral was in need of a major program of revitalization.

TABLE I.2   ADMIRAL AIRLINES FIVE-YEAR OPERATING DATA IN
              MILLIONS (Historical)

Year	Passenger Revenue First-Class	Coach	Total Operating Revenue	Operating Expense	Net Income
1965	33.3	29.3	68.6	74.8	(2.9)
1966	23.4	33.4	63.7	70.4	(6.9)
1967	24.0	56.1	89.8	83.4	4.3
1968	22.8	76.1	109.4	97.0	6.2
1969	25.1	85.9	121.5	104.4	7.8

As a first step in his revitalization program, McDonald hired new vice-presidents for finance, operations, and marketing. He also created a long-range planning department and brought in a member of the management consulting team to head this new group. After a brief period of orientation, McDonald asked the newly hired executives to look into the company in much the same way he had. The basic points outlined in their preliminary investigation indicated:

1. There were too few skilled or well-trained management people in the company.

2. Maintenance costs were excessively high in all phases of operation.

3. Equipment was obsolete in many cases. The greatest difficulty appeared to be in those routes where new short-range jets had not yet been purchased.

4. The company posture toward unions had left a legacy of hardship, and several of the skilled craft unions seemed to be on the verge of strike actions.

5. The company had an exceptionally poor public image, the group conceded, because of the poor service given customers in past years.

6. The route structure needed some revision and revitalization. In particular, it was recommended that the company attempt to get a Chicago-to-Miami run to strengthen its north-south route structure.

7. The airline had a reputation of not running on time. This caused additional passenger complaints, since missed connections normally resulted from late operations.

8. Sources of cash for new equipment were limited because profits had been low in years when other companies had made substantial improvement in earnings.

9. Facilities such as hangars, terminals, and so on were archaic in many cases. Even new facilities had been designed poorly and were in need of expansion and/or replacement.

10. The sales force had been trained inadequately and had not exploited all available markets. Indeed, concepts such as package deals and special promotional tie-ins had not been tried even on special flights such as those serving the Caribbean.

11. The company had no formal training programs, and personnel knew very little about the company's goals, objectives, and aims.

12. The company had an extremely low yield per passenger mile, and very little information was available on the relative profitability of the various routes.

13. The conditions outlined in points one through twelve had been in effect for a number of years and seemed destined to continue in force unless positive actions were taken.

After reviewing this list of difficulties, McDonald set about preparing an order of priority to guide the group's actions. He felt that one urgent problem revolved around whether the company should promote mass transportation at low cost or emphasize more luxurious accommodations at a higher fare. He explained that the mass transit–luxury problem should be resolved at an early date, since many of the company's future objectives and goals would be dependent upon the results of deliberations on this point. He also felt that this problem had to be solved by the group before they could make any inroads on other complex problems.

Mr. McDonald knew that Charles Kenley, vice-president of operations, and William Chaucus, vice-president of long-range planning, favored mass transportation, so he asked them to prepare a report supporting a mass-transportation, low-fare policy. Phillip Jordan, vice-president of finance, and Kendall Barth, vice-president of marketing, were asked to analyze the luxury service, higher-fare market of which they had been vocal advocates. McDonald felt that they would welcome the chance to expound their particular point of view. Because of the crucial import of the time factor, McDonald requested a preliminary report in two weeks.

All four men knew that McDonald had once coined the phrase, "Welcome aboard the world's finest airline," which was always followed by the name of McDonald's former employer. McDonald mentioned this fact to the group when he stated, "Though I've taken the quality route in the past, I'm willing to change my mind if circumstances dictate some other policy, so don't let this influence your recommendations."

THE COMMITTEE REPORTS

At the end of a two-week period, the groups met to review the mass-versus-luxury transportation options. McDonald noted that the session was principally for information and discussion and that questions and criticisms should be open and free-wheeling. He did say, however, that following this open meeting, the issue should be resolved "at the earliest possible time."

Charles Kenley spoke first for the study group reporting on the advantages of mass transportation, Kenley maintained that no basic changes in policy were needed to institute a mass-transportation concept. He reported that economy class passengers currently provided 92 percent of Admiral's annual receipts and that a change to mass transport policy would require only slight modifications designed to "pare luxuries to the bone." He emphasized that passengers should not be herded like cattle, but insisted that frills were costly and unsound. He argued that the coming of supersonic transports (ssts) would require passenger loads of several hundred people to ensure a break-even operation, since the estimated cost of each sst was in the order of $20 to $25 million. Mr. Kenley reported that domestic airlines were planning to purchase up to 400 ssts with expected delivery set for 1977. This sst delivery schedule would move back to 1972 or 1973 if the French supersonic transport, the Concorde, was developed on schedule. Kenley felt that Admiral would be forced to purchase the Concorde if competitors elected to operate the French version of the sst.

The main point in Kenley's presentation was that low fares were needed in order to increase the volume of passenger traffic.[1] He held that high cost was the main deterrent to greater public use of air travel, now that the safety issue had been resolved. He cited how volume had risen and indicated that certain airlines regularly flew over one billion passenger miles during peak months. Kenley stated that an even greater volume would be needed to operate supersonic transports profitably. He indicated that the load factor problem was even more critical on short trips, which more and more people were making by car. He felt that Admiral's profits on short hauls would remain unsatisfactory until airlines could compete directly with autos on a cost-time basis.

He cited two examples where a policy of low-cost transportation had proven to be profitable. First, he related how Mohawk Airlines had been profitable on its short-haul no-frills runs in the northeast. He next pointed out how the Eastern Airlines shuttle between New York, Boston, and Washington showed low-cost travel could generate high rates of passenger usage. He conceded that the Eastern concept of the plane waiting for the passenger, rather than the passenger waiting for the plane, had been one reason for passenger acceptance of the shuttle, but he insisted that its real success was due to its low price. In his opinion, the shuttle concept was the only way for a short-haul airline to operate profitably.

In closing, Mr. Kenley offered a series of cost-and-revenue projections showing the estimated results of his suggested policy changes (see Table I.3). These projections were described in detail by Mr. Chaucus. All data showed that substantial long-run improvements in earnings would accrue to Admiral if Kenley's recommendations were adopted.

TABLE I.3   ADMIRAL AIRLINES FIVE-YEAR FORECAST IN MILLIONS
(Mr. Kenley's data)

| Year | Passenger Revenue | | Total Operating Revenue | Operating Expense | Net Income |
	First-Class	Coach			
1970	26.3	93.7	135.9	111.8	11.8
1971	27.1	107.9	150.1	125.9	13.3
1972	28.9	120.1	163.7	132.4	15.5
1973	30.3	130.3	177.2	139.0	18.2
1974	35.4	145.2	200.1	146.0	27.1

Phillip Jordan began his presentation by stating that though Kenley's approach had been thorough, its premises were basically unsound. He made the

---

[1] Kenley did not choose to discuss the Lockheed C-5 military cargo plane which has possible use in the civilian market. This plane could be operated for 3 cents per mile as against 5 cents per mile on current planes. Some studies have projected a minimum fare on C-5 runs from New York to Los Angeles at $50 versus the current fare of $195.

point that it was far more important for Admiral to change its past image as a penny pincher than to develop the mass transport approach advocated by Kenley and Chaucus. His main thesis was that businessmen comprised a majority of airline passengers and that they knew a great deal about what to expect and what to demand in passenger service and comforts (see Table I.4). Jordan felt that businessmen were far too sophisticated to be fooled by insincere gimmicks and that the cattlecar image would have to be erased before they would fly Admiral instead of competing airlines.

TABLE I.4   ADMIRAL AIRLINES FIVE-YEAR FORECAST IN MILLIONS
              (Mr. Jordan's Data)

Year	Passenger Revenue First-Class	Coach	Total Operating Revenue	Operating Expense	Net Income
1970	30.7	93.7	140.4	115.0	17.0
1971	35.8	105.1	115.0	132.0	11.5
1972	38.5	115.0	170.5	140.0	15.3
1973	45.5	135.1	195.0	148.0	23.7
1974	50.1	150.5	220.0	156.0	33.0

One example he invoked to prove his point was the competition between Western Airlines, Pacific Southwestern Airlines, and United Airlines on the San Francisco-to-Los Angeles run. Pacific Southwest first offered a fare of $13.50 on a Lockheed Electra. Western then attempted to compete by offering a fare of $11.43 in a DC-6B piston-powered aircraft. Businessmen stayed on Pacific Southwest because they made the trip half an hour sooner on the Electras than on the DC-6Bs. United Airlines, which had been running a poor third to Pacific and Western, hopped into the lead by placing a Boeing 707 jet on the run with a fare of $14.50. Jordan reported that all three airlines eventually instituted Boeing 727 jet service at a $13.50 rate; but United Airlines, which had moved into jets first, remained in first position. The lesson, said Jordan, is quite clear: the first-place airline is the one which offers first-class service without regard to price. To back up his example, he noted that a daily United Airlines flight from Hartford to Chicago, which carried first-class passengers only, had run at close to 100-percent capacity on most days, even though its fare was considerably higher than those of its competitors. According to Jordan, the use of a Caravelle (which was considered to be a luxury aircraft by many travelers) on this run enhanced its prestige and built up its popularity. He also mentioned in passing American Airline's "red-carpet service" and indicated how specialty flights such as the "Club 21" had been very successful operations.

Jordan's basic concept was that the airlines were selling a seat in motion, not just a mass-carting operation. He agreed that economical operation was fine, but insisted that Admiral's image could not be changed by cutting costs.

Volume, he stated, could never be obtained in the future unless the company could forge a new image. It was, in his opinion, "important not to spend foolishly, but to spend on the right things—namely, passenger service." He refuted Kenley's statements about the Eastern Airline's shuttle, claiming that the shuttle had never been as prosperous as some believed. His parting shot on this point was that "Admiral has enough marginal operations without risking our future on shuttle type ventures we're not sure of." Jordan also commented that he could not see how Kenley's points about the shuttle business related to the purchase of supersonic transports, since no SSTs would be used in the short-haul operations most likely for shuttle service.

At the close of the presentations, McDonald complimented both groups on the thoroughness of their reports and suggested that a week's moratorium be declared prior to making any action decisions. At the close of the meeting, Mr. McDonald returned alone to his office. As he thought about the meeting, two phrases kept running through his mind. The first was Merriwether Dunalp's credo, "Take care of the pennies and the dollars will take care of themselves." The second was Phillip Jordan's advice "to spend on the right things—namely, passenger service."

1. What should Mr. McDonald do at this point? Suggest a step-by-step program to help him make a choice and carry it out.

The Starlight Pork Company

Harlan Wilson, general manager of the Starlight Pork Company, recently decided to introduce a new concept in the marketing of sausages. The new concept was a pancake-shaped sausage to be offered in an attractive new package. Wilson felt that this novel shape, coupled with an attractive package, would gain good consumer acceptance, and he was particularly anxious to exploit its market potential. He asked Robert Coles, director of market research, to prepare a sales forecast for the product, tentatively called the Grill 'n Grin sausage package. He also asked Harry Sanderson, his sales manager, to perform the same type of market survey.

Six months later, Coles and Sanderson reported to Wilson on the sales potential of the new product. Sanderson's estimate, which was based on customer surveys performed by his salesmen, predicted first-year sales of $400,000 based on a price of 70 cents per pound. Coles indicated that since sales possibilities were dependent upon price, there were several levels of sales to consider. At 70 cents per pound he estimated a first-year sales volume of $280,000, at 65 cents per pound $400,000, and at 60 cents per pound $560,000.

Wilson knew that with its production capacity Starlight could produce only 60,000 pounds of Grill 'n Grin sausage in the upcoming year. He also had to consider two additional facts. First, Harry Sanderson, when asked to make estimates of sales, usually developed optimistic forecasts—partly as a reflection of the optimism of Sanderson's salesmen and partly as a function of his natural expansiveness. On the other hand, Coles tended to be an excessively cautious person. His last forecast, for example, had undershot the mark by 20 percent. Some of Cole's conservatism was based upon a survey conducted by Coles's group among a varied panel of consumers, who were asked whether they used Starlight products. If their responses had been taken literally, company sales would have to have been ten times what they actually were. Such replies tended to make Coles somewhat overcautious in his estimates.

1.   Faced with such divergent forecasts, what course should Wilson take? How should he evaluate the various forecasts?

2.   How would you, given ample time and money, prepare the forecast requested by Wilson?

The Bob Gillespie Case

Bob Gillespie is treasurer-manager of the Kellerman Credit Union, a medium-sized credit union serving the employees of the S.L. Kellerman Products Company in Grand Rapids, Michigan. The company currently produces a well-diversified line of refrigeration equipment, for which there has been a steadily growing market. In the past, Kellerman had as many as seven different plants in the Grand Rapids area, though now it has only five. In 1963 and 1968, plants were closed and their operations shifted to New Jersey and southern Illinois. Despite fluctuations in total membership in Grand Rapids, the Kellerman Credit Union has shown a steady growth of assets in the last fifteen years; its loan volume has been less consistent, though it has seldom been a matter of concern. Currently the credit union has approximately $1,380,000 in total assets and $1 million total loans.

Gillespie has been active in the credit union almost from its inception in 1950. In general, his associates respect him as a steady and earnest worker, though sometimes he can become overinvolved in the mechanics of his job. Gillespie took over the post of treasurer in 1951 shortly after he was discharged from the service. Initially he operated from a desk in the stock room of one of the compressor plants, but when business became increasingly unmanageable in these quarters, Gillespie pressed the board of directors for a new building. The go-ahead was a risky decision, since assets at the time were only $100,000. But the Board assented after some lengthy discussion, and a cinderblock building with 800 square feet of floor space went up.

Although they do not mention it now, at the time two of the more conservative board members thought it "pure foolishness" to build. Gillespie has, on occasion, found it helpful to remind them of their misjudgment; but, in truth, he too had done some misjudging. As it turned out, the new building should have been at least twice its acutal size. Within eight years the number of credit union employees jumped from two to six; there are now four office girls, an assistant manager, and Gillespie, so the need for increased space became painfully obvious. The demand for privacy in handling loan applications actually squeezed Gillespie out of his own office into a back room where his privacy was marred only by the deafening clatter of the posting machines (see Table I.5).

TABLE I.5   GROWTH OF KELLERMAN CREDIT UNION ASSETS
            IN SELECTED YEARS

DATE	ASSETS
January 1, 1955	$ 82,000
January 1. 1957	101,000
January 1, 1959	131,000
January 1, 1961	190,000
January 1, 1963	230,000
January 1, 1965	810,000
January 1, 1967	997,000
January 1, 1969	1,351,000
May 31, 1969	1,384,354

In retrospect, Gillespie realizes that this move was the one which triggered his decision to push for another new building. Frankly, he had hated to give up his own office; but it was an ironically good move, whether conscious or not. When the board president, Amos Fulton, and several other sound thinkers (in Gillespie's opinion) found Gillespie hunched in the back room with the machines, they started pressing for the new building. Gillespie was, of course, 100 percent with them. He realized that he had a powerful ally in Fulton, a man who was accustomed to thinking big and not looking pained at suggested expenditures. Fulton was, for example, the driving force behind the recent $2,000 outlay for new office equipment.

However, several of the directors acted as if the Kellerman Credit Union was still a paltry $200,000 affair, instead of a continually expanding $1 million operation (see Table I.6). Gillespie and Fulton realized they would get nowhere waiting for the board to come to a decision, and they were able to persuade the members to appoint a three-man building committee. No specific powers were given or denied the committee; it was told to do as it wished, consulting the board as it saw fit. The committee thought this would mean nearly automatic, rubber-stamp approval of all its decisions.

So the committee went ahead. It recognized immediately that more land was needed, and by a stroke of luck it came upon an ideally sized plot only four miles from the main plant. What is more, this plot was for sale at a ridiculously low price. When the committee next met, they discussed the purchase for five minutes, called in the real estate dealer, and purchased the plot.

TABLE I.6 FINANCIAL AND STATISTICAL REPORT

For period Ended May 31, 1969, Charter No. 5418

Kellerman Credit Union, 2510 College Avenue East, Grand Rapids, Michigan

BALANCE SHEET

Acct. No.	Assets	Number	End of This Month Unpaid Balances
1	Loans:		
	DELINQUENT:		
(a)	2 months to 6 months	51	33,202.64
(b)	6 months to 12 months	63	21,153.36
(c)	12 months and over	82	20,947.87
	Subtotal	196	756,303.87
(d)	Current and less than 2 months delinquent	1641	975,594.55
(e)	Total loans	1837	1,050,898.42
104	Cash		14,734.34
105	Petty Cash		10.00
106	Change Fund		
107	U.S. Government Obligations		
108	Savings & Loan Shares		1,094.47
109	Loans to other Credit Unions		300,000.00
112	Furniture, Fixtures and Equipment		11,445.11
113	Unamortized Organization Cost		
114	Prepaid Insurance		1,416.00
115	Other Assets		1,227.20
	Accts. Rec.		100.00
	Bldg. Improve.		310.00
	Annual Meeting		1,248.92
	League Dues		1,870.00

STATEMENT OF INCOME AND EXPENSE

Acct. No.	Income	This Month	From To date
401	Interest on Loans	12,021.15	47,205.76
405	Income from Investments	2,500.00	12,500.00
406	Gain on Sale of Bonds		
409	Other Income		
	Total Income		59,705.76
	EXPENSES		
202-1	Treasurer's Salary	648.00	3,412.00
202-2	Other Salaries	1,557.92	8,039.22
202-3	Borrowers' Insurance	976.30	3,522.37
202-4	Life Savings Insurance	639.44	1,749.40
202-5	League Dues	270.00	1,350.89
202-6	Surety Bond Premium	51.00	253.36
202-7	Examination Fees		
202-8	Supervision Fee		324.92
202-9	Int. on Borrowed Money	728.81	2,823.62
202-10	Stationery and Supplies	59.85	413.54
202-11	Cost of Space Occupied	95.00	475.00
202-12	Educational Expense	39.56	1,562.27
202-13	Collection Expense	130.08	747.08
202-14	Depreciation Furn. Fix. and Equip.	90.00	450.00
202-15	Social Security Taxes		213.96

	Total Assets			1,384,354.46
	LIABILITIES			
101	Accounts Payable			192.97
102	Notes Payable			179,000.00
104	Withholding Taxes Payable			593.50
105	Social Security Taxes Payable			125.98
	Emp. Benefits			1,197.20
110	Shares			1,130,074.81
111	Regular Reserve			24,059.27
116	Special Reserve for Delinquent Loans			17,000.00
112	Undivided Earnings			2,559.09
113	Gain or Loss			29,551.64
	Total Liabilities			1,384,354.46

202-16	Other Insurance	183.25	695.25
202-17	Recording Fees-Chattel Lien, Ins.		709.00
202-18	Communication	247.90	532.15
202-19	Losses on Sale of Bonds		− 14.97
202-20	Cash Over and Short		
202-21	Other Losses		102.37
202-22	Bank Service Charge	43.11	251.45
	Cr. Reports	55.85	825.53
	Bldg. Maint.	129.87	532.47
	Officers Exp.	171.52	
	Bldg. Imp.	39.00	155.99
	Ann. Meeting	170.00	850.40
	Emp. Benefits	32.40	166.85
	Misc. General Expense		
	Total Expense	6,358.86	30,154.12
	Net Earnings		29,551.64
	Net Loss		

STATISTICAL INFORMATION

Item		Number	Amount
1	No. of accounts at end of period	3842	xxxxxxxx
2	No. of potential members	6000	xxxxxxxx
3	Loans made year to date	677	597,053.59

Item		Number	Amount
4	Loans made since organization	9646	5,952,797.01
5	Loans charged off since organization		12,795.90
6	Recoveries on loans charged off since organization		1,353.21

Certified correct by:

Robert Gillespie

Treasurer

The credit union's annual meeting followed shortly, and in his report to the members, Fulton made two points on the proposed expansion:

1. Additional space was badly needed because of overcrowded conditions in the present building.

2. "In view of the above, your Board of Directors has seen to the appointment of a three-man committee. It is working with as much haste as now appears consistent with a full consideration of the best fiduciary interests of the membership."

He then outlined the committee's progress to date.

Gillespie reflected on the misfortune of Fulton's tendency to use large words, which seemed to complicate everything he said; his presentation at the meeting aroused little interest. There were no questions or comments from the floor about the decision to erect a new building.

Actually, some of the board members seemed totally unaware of the facts Fulton presented. They did not see that (1) the need for space, (2) the purchase of the land, and (3) the proposal to build demanded quick action. Had Gillespie thought, he would have realized that the credit union's majority conservative flank had not coalesced; at this juncture, few board members knew what the others were thinking.

Gillespie and Fulton neglected this, however, and proceeded as they saw fit. Gillespie had another stroke of luck when he discovered that a close friend and active member of the credit union had a brother who was a partner in an engineering firm. The other partner was an architect, and Gillespie was able to spend four evenings at home with him developing a floor plan and anticipating the costs of a decent building. Both Gillespie and Fulton realized that they needed a building which would command respect and attention in the neighborhood. They were, after all, dealing with a membership long conditioned (by prevailing sales methods) to a certain level of luxury and good taste, particularly in financial or business establishment. Though Gillespie believed in the cooperative principles of credit unionism as deeply as anyone else, he also realized that many of its members thought of the Kellerman Credit Union as just another place where they could borrow and/or save money.

It did not take Gillespie long to see that the architect had an extremely clear idea of what the credit union needed, so, with the committee's assent, Gillespie hired him to prepare blueprints for the new building. The initial building estimate was $80,000, but with assorted changes and additions (suggested primarily by Gillespie and Fulton) it became obvious that the completed blueprints would bring estimates somewhat higher than the initial figure. No one was overly surprised when the five returned bids ranged from $140,000 to $170,000.

The board meeting at which the bids were presented remains terrifying and lucid in Gillespie's mind. All the members knew a decision on the bids was due, and there was a razor-sharp tension in the atmosphere throughout the meeting. When the choice of construction company came up, Gillespie (as secretary of the building committee) presented the bids, commented on each of them, and concluded with the observation that the credit union was "fortunate to have such a reputable firm as lowest bidder." In addition, he noted that this firm had worked extensively and successfully with his architect.

Immediately Dwight Underhill, a board member Gillespie had long pegged as a conservative, got up and said, "Personally, I think $140,000 is far too much to spend for any building—and particularly for this thing. It's a showcase! Frankly, I'm opposed to it all the way. Remember, we're a credit union, not a department store."

Fulton quietly pointed out that the decision to build had already been made; but another board member, insisting that no one had said anything about a $140,000 building, challenged him. Underhill followed a brief silence with "I move we reject all bids."

Two board members seconded the motion in unison, and an angry discussion followed, during which Gillespie heard a rash of negative opinions he had been utterly unaware of. Some of the counterarguments were as follows:

1. With the expense of the land and the building, the dividend rate would have to be cut.

2. The new location was too far from the main plant.

3. The new blueprints were far too plush. A stainless steel, glass, and granite building would only take money from the membership.

4. The credit union had no right to build space now which it would not need for twenty years, particularly in light of the manner in which the company was decentralizing its business east and south.

It was Underhill who applied the crusher. "I want to know," he said, "what kind of planning has been done. Or have you done any? For instance, have you talked with any Kellerman executives? What are their plans for the next five, ten, fifteen, years? Where are their operations going to be? How big are they going to get? Have you made any calculations on the impact the Globe-Wilson Compressor Patent will have on employment, even if Kellerman never moves an operation? Last month *Refrigeration Monthly* ran an article saying the machine could well cut employment by 50 percent in the compressor department. And this isn't the only innovation on the way in. How do I know that, five years from now, we won't have a $150,000 white elephant on our hands? Then what do we do? Drop back and punt?"

Gillespie still shudders when he recalls how he mumbled and hedged at that one. He felt like Underhill had steamrollered him, and what was worse was that he'd been deserted temporarily by Fulton. Gillespie did try to counter Underhill with some remarks made on the unlimited future of the refrigeration industry he'd heard a Kellerman executive make at a Kiwanis luncheon, but

Underhill had brushed that off with a "Come on now, Bob, let's get specific."
The result of the hassle was a 6:3 vote to reject all bids.

1. Where did Gillespie go wrong?
2. What should be his next step?

The Delta-Ohio
Chemical Company

The Ohio Chemical Company has long been a leader in the heavy chemical
field and a major producer of acids, brine, and a variety of solvents. In recent
years, the company has moved into a variety of special chemicals for government use and has developed its own line of insecticides. In general, operations
have been profitable, and the company is well thought of by customers and
competitors. Though the company has not had spectacular growth, it has always
paid good dividends to shareholders.

The Delta Company was started in 1960 by a group of graduates of the
California Institute of Technology in order to exploit some of the new ideas
and products coming out of some recent scientific developments in the pe-
trochemical field. The desire to develop vigorous growing product lines dominated the philosophy of this company in its early years, and all of its top
management seemed to have a compulsive need to grow in a hurry. Both
the president, Phil Harrop, and the executive vice-president, Charles Trent,
embraced the approach that change and innovation arc the keys to success,
and they regularly allocated 25 to 35 percent of their sales dollars to research
and development.

After five years of operation, Delta had built up a solid backlog of orders
and had developed a number of new products. Both Mr. Harrop and Mr.
Trent felt that some of their newly developed product lines had a high profit
potential and that the only limit on enjoying higher profits was their lack
of capital. When they looked for a source of capital, the possibility of merger
became evident immediately. One possible merger partner was the Ohio
Chemical Company, a firm with excess capital and a desire to enter some
of the fields being exploited by Delta. After extensive discussion, merger was
proposed and consummated.

The new company elected Mr. Harrop as president and Mr. Trent as
executive vice-president. Wilhelm Verworth, former president of the Ohio
Chemical Company, became the chairman of the board of directors; and
Findlay West, Ohio's financial vice-president, became financial vice-president
and controller of the Delta-Ohio Chemical Company (DOCO).

Some of the problems arising from the merger became readily apparent.
Ohio had a conservative older management and an accepted product line.
Its profit record was steady but not exciting, and it followed a conservative
approach. The Delta group was headed by dynamic young scientists who

believed in research and whose product line was new and somewhat volatile. The Delta management had a reputation for gambling and seemed to enjoy the idea of risk. Ohio's headquarters was in Dayton, Ohio, while the Delta Company had its major installation in San Jose, California. In spite of these drawbacks, both parties felt a merger was possible.

Since the merger problems and frictions have arisen. Conservatism has clashed with desire for change. Though the merger was completed in a financial sense, it failed to take place in a coordinative sense. Key management people have distrusted each other since the day of the merger. Executive offices still exist in both San Jose and Dayton. The principal source of difficulty has been the clash of the conservative financial policies of the Ohio Company with the gambler's instinct of the Delta group.

When Mr. Verworth retired last year the struggle became joined. Both Mr. West and Mr. Trent were proposed for the presidency when Mr. Harrop moved up to become Chairman of the Board. Mr. Harrop backed Mr. Trent, while Mr. Verworth advanced the candidacy of Mr. West. The bitter power struggle that resulted saw Mr. West emerge as the new president of Delta-Ohio. Mr. Trent subsequently left to join a competitor, and Mr. Harrop openly threatened to quit and set up a competing firm unless some new approaches and new philosphies were developed.

Mr. West, the new president, is faced with pulling together the torn factions of the Delta and Ohio groups. His main goal is to maintain the firm's profitability, growth, and diversification objectives. He hopes to do this without destroying the traditions of either of the merged companies.

1. What are the constraints within which Mr. West must operate? What variables are most critical?

2. What types of plans should he prepare? What scheme of analysis might he use in the planning process?

3. How should Mr. West proceed to bring about the achievement of his objectives?

BIBLIOGRAPHY

Abramson, A., and R. Mack, *Business Forecasting in Practice,* New York: John Wiley & Sons, Inc., 1956.

Ansoff, H.I., *Corporate Strategy: An Analytic Approach to Business Policy for Growth and Expansion,* New York: McGraw-Hill, Inc., 1965.

Brennan, M., *Preface to Econometrics,* Cincinnati: South-Western Publishing Company, 1960.

Chandler, Alfred E., Jr., *Strategy and Structure,* Cambridge, Mass.: MIT Press, 1962.

Dean, Joel, *Managerial Economics,* Englewood Cliffs, N.J.: Prentice-Hall, Inc., 1951.

Gordon, R.J., *Business Fluctuations,* New York: Harper & Row, Publishers, 1952.

Greenlaw, Paul, and Max Richards, *Management Decision Making,* Homewood, Ill.: Richard D. Irwin, Inc., 1966.

Guetzkow, H., ed., *Simulations in Social Science,* Englewood Cliffs, N.J.: Prentice-Hall, Inc., 1962.

Kohler, H., *Security Challenged: An Introduction to Economics,* New York: Holt, Rinehart and Winston, Inc., 1968.

Koontz, Harold, and Cyril O'Donnel, *Management: A Book of Readings,* New York: McGraw-Hill, Inc., 1964.

McDonough, A., and L. Garrett, *Management Systems,* Homewood, Ill.: Richard D. Irwin, Inc., 1965.

Manne, A., *Economic Analysis for Business Decisions,* New York: McGraw-Hill, Inc., 1961.

Miller, David W., and Martin K. Starr, *Executive Decisions and Operations Research,* Englewood Cliffs, N.J.: Prentice-Hall, Inc., 1960.

Moore, Franklin G., *Manufacturing Management,* 4th ed., Homewood, Ill.: Richard D. Irwin, Inc., 1965.

National Industrial Conference Board, *Forecasting in Industry,* New York: Author, Studies in Business Policy, no. 77, 1963.

Newman, William H., and J. Logan, *Business Policies and Management,* 4th ed., Cincinnati: South-Western Publishing Company, 1959.

Richards, Max, and William Nielander, *Readings in Management,* 2nd ed., Cincinnati, Ohio: South-Western Publishing Company, 1963.

Spencer, M., and B. Siegelman, *Managerial Economics,* Homewood, Ill.: Richard D. Irwin, Inc., 1964.

Thompson, S., *Management Creeds and Philosophies,* New York: American Management Association, Inc., Research Study, no. 32, 1958.

Warren, E.K., *Long Range Planning: The Executive Viewpoint,* Englewood Cliffs, N.J.: Prentice-Hall, Inc., 1966.

Though goals and strategies hold the key to long-term success, short-term progress depends upon the execution of tactical decisions. This section describes the factors underlying such decisions and how decision making is carried out in a variety of situations. Chapter 6 develops descriptive and illustrative materials on the process of decision making, while Chapter 7 reviews a selection of traditional and modern techniques now in use in the dynamic and expanding field of decision-making methodology.

Section II is subtitled *The Fine Art of Choice* for a very excellent reason. Decision making, even its most highly structured forms, is closer to art than science. Judgment inevitably plays a key role in decision making, even when the techniques of evaluation offer solutions arithmetically correct to the fourth decimal place. But to adopt the stance that decision making is an art does not necessarily bar decision makers from quantitative analysis. Given the rapidly advancing state of computer technology, it seems highly likely that future decision makers will turn increasingly toward more advanced techniques of information reporting, mathematical analysis, and simulation models. Judgment will not be eliminated as more precise methodologies come into the picture, but it will be exercised in a more mathematical and more knowledge-oriented environment. Though their field will become more scientific in the forseeable future, decision makers will retain many of the familiar insights and skills that characterize the practice of an art.

SECTION II
Decision Making: The Fine Art of Choice

Decisions arise out of many different conditions. Some decisions are prompted by the performance inadequacies of either people or organizational units. Some come from the need to change objectives or strategies that are unrealistic, overly static, poorly stated, too low, too high, or simply too ambiguous to be carried out. Other decisions are generated by unexpected occurrences which change normal routines, procedures, or expectations. When E.J. Korvette was a discount house, its objectives were substantially different from those embraced by the full-line merchandising house it eventually became. Korvette also underwent additional changes as its rapid expansion into new lines and new facilities stretched its finances to the danger point. When Spartan Stores joined with Korvette's faltering empire, the surviving corporation went through a metamorphosis which generated uncounted new decisions.

The *source* of decisions is only one perspective in decision making; another has to do with the *kinds* of decisions made. Ernest Dale classifies decisions under four headings: decisions which are routine, decisions which affect several areas, decisions where uncertainty is a major factor, and, finally, decisions in which uncertainty is the dominant factor.[1] An example of each type follows: a school administrator's decision to reorder paper clips is routine; selection of visual aids for classroom use affects several areas; hiring an untested assistant with little experience and questionable recommendations involves a limited amount of risk; and, finally, transferring school teachers thought to be unfit by influential members of the community may bring on massive uncertainties. Dale's classification scheme is valu-

CHAPTER 6
Perspectives on Decision Making

[1] "New Perspectives in Managerial Decision Making." *Journal of Business,* vol. 26 (January 1953), pp. 1–8.

able because it identifies decision-making situations as an aid to bringing in techniques and approaches appropriate for their solution; normally, however, recognizing why and how to classify decisions is much less important than developing solutions.[2]

Though most decision-making techniques deemphasize the importance of problem classification, most of the literature in the field does emphasize the importance of selecting proper decision-making methodology. Though these methodologies differ, they have in common a desire to identify and handle the critical variables affecting the decision according to some organized modus operandi. This central theme of logical, orderly handling of critical variables is the fulcrum around which rational decision-making processes turn.

To achieve the goal of systematic orderly analysis, it is generally desirable to develop a clear understanding of the elements affecting the decision, to study the conceptual and statistical techniques by which data and alternative solutions can be analyzed and evaluated, and to select a logical, orderly series of steps for action. These three processes are recognized universally as essential elements of sound decision making.

THE ELEMENTS OF DECISION MAKING

In a very general sense, decision making covers almost every phase of human activity. If one reached far enough, he could bring societal, cultural, economic, and political variables into the decision to get up on Monday morning or stay in bed. For most people, however, this particular decision rarely involves such comprehensive analysis, partially because it has been made many times and partly because the decision maker has routinely abstracted and weighted the variables directly influencing the decision. In business and industry, managers face decisions much like those encountered daily by housewives, doctors, and students; but they weight and abstract pertinent variables in a different value context. Thus, abstraction, weighting, and values are the stuff from which both housewives and industrial managers fashion decisions.

Abstraction occurs in every decision process; and selectivity, when applied rationally, may be carried to the level Herbert A. Simon has called "the principle of bounded rationality": settling for less than full information and for something short of a perfect solution. Thus, abstraction serves to limit the variables bounding a given decision and qualifies as one of the most critical steps in the decision process. Indeed, the famous management theoretician and practitioner Chester I. Barnard holds that abstraction involves not only bounded rationality but also the ability to select and use the strategic factor; that is, the factor that influences the decision most heavily such as the key log in a log jam.

---

[2] Problem classification is, however, extremely important in some of the newer techniques dealing with decision making, for example, in heuristic approaches. This point will be discussed more fully in Chapter 7.

Whether "the" strategic factor of a decision can be discovered by the decision maker is a moot point, but there is no doubt that the decision process involves a movement from the general to the specific. Input from all potential sources may be considered in the data-gathering stage, but only relevant variables receive permanent consideration. Forecasting and statistical inputs are both integrated carefully in the data-gathering process at a very early stage, as are daily reports of activities prepared by accounting and financial staffs. The ability to accept less than a perfect solution also comes into the decision process early, particularly in the stages of information collection. It would be unusual, for example, if the normal control and reporting systems of the typical industrial corporation provided perfect data for the decision maker. Typically, decisions are made on less than perfect information because of time and cost considerations. The decision maker's constant cry, "We don't have enough information," in time becomes, "We'll just have to decide on the information we have now." Like the consumer who shops until he is ready to buy, the decision maker analyzes until he decides to decide. Somewhere in this process abstraction ends and problems are framed and solved. It is because the results of the decision process are so important that it has undergone increasingly rigorous study in recent years.

The process of moving from general to specific boundaries of a decision has been looked at rather carefully by a number of interested authorities. Wilson and Alexis identify the key elements in decision making as

1. The state of nature
2. The decision maker himself
3. Goals or ends to be served
4. Relevant alternatives
5. The order of alternatives
6. The final choice itself[3]

The state of nature is the relationship between choices and the environment surrounding the decision maker: is he free to decide, or does he have or believe he has constraints? The decision maker may be one or part of a group, or he may be influenced by his position in the organizational, political, and/or social structure of the decision environment. Goals or ends can be personal, institutional, or some combination thereof, a condition that influences ordering and choice of final alternatives. Marcus and Alexis claim that study of just these six factors can define the scope of decision frameworks. Though this claim is debatable, it is possible to extend their viewpoint and conclude that their six elements help to classify types of decisions and to select decision-making methodologies.

Blake and Mouton see the key elements in decision making as communi-

---

[3] Charles Wilson and Marcus Alexis, "Basic Frameworks for Decision," *Academy of Management Journal,* vol. 5, no. 2 (August 1962), pp. 151–164.

cation and participation. More and better flows of data and ideas are called for in their concept of an ideal system of decision making. The key to their approach is group decision making, since these authors believe that more and better decisions are made when informed people with vital interests enter into the decision process. This viewpoint is spelled out in the title of their book *Group Dynamics—Key to Decision Making.*[4]

Decision theorists noted for their development of mathematical models, Churchman, Ackoff, and Miller and Starr visualize decision making in a series of decision models ranging in sophistication from simple problem-solving devices designed to determine sample sizes in statistical quality control to very complex schemes of analysis used to illustrate entire production flows as in the chemical industry. Still others view the key elements in the decision process as steps in a logical, rational, but not necessarily mathematical, process similar to the scientific method. The methodology of Tregoe and Kepner, which isolates causes and effects in the logical time sequence described in their treatise *The Rational Manager,* is one that focuses sharply on the problem identification phase of the decision-making process.[5]

Perhaps the most meaningful way to classify the elements in decision making is to select the best from all these approaches. Following this method, the basic elements in the decision matrix would be identified as the goals to be served, the various inputs needed from information and control systems, the means of problem recognition and classification, the creation of viable alternatives, a consideration of the ruling states of nature, the selection of a method for ordering alternatives, and the inclusion of the value systems of individual decision makers.

GOALS

Goals to be served include both individual and organizational goals. Since individual goals often conflict with those of the organization, problems occur in establishing what classical management writers call "unity of objectives," or harmony between individual and organizational goals. When conflicts exist, the concept of maximization is often replaced by a process wherein individuals or organizational units realize the necessity to settle for less than the best. The dynamic aspect of goal determination is clearly evident when one considers that goals are very rarely set in accordance with some inflexible formula. The development of goals is inevitably much more than stating a series of clichés about profits, survival, and growth. Goal determination is a dynamic process that requires tender loving care before it is understood by both decision makers and those who must live by the decisions made.

---

[4] Robert R. Blake and Jane S. Mouton, *Group Dynamics—Key to Decision Making* (Houston, Tex.: The Gulf Publishing Company, 1961).

[5] B. Tregoe and C. Kepner, *The Rational Manager* (New York: McGraw-Hill, Inc., 1965).

DATA

Another basic element in the decision process is the quality and quantity of data available from the organization's information and control systems. These inputs may exist in the form of accounting data reported in terms of cost, profits, balance sheet relationships, product reports (including quality and quantity aspects), and forecasts; such data may contain not only expected sales and product possibilities but even available opportunities. Thus, inputs may come from various sources and possess relative degrees of accuracy; that is, the validity or certainty of the information generated is always subject to interpretation and analysis. It is relatively easy, for example, to be misled by averages. A product may yield an average annual profit of $1 million over a ten-year period, but that does not mean that each year will yield a profit of $1 million. The first or the last year might produce the entire $10 million, and the results of such spacing would exert a sharp influence on the decision being considered. If cash is short, it may not be sensible to pursue a profit in the tenth year, but the reverse situation might tip the scales favorably. Thus, informational inputs should always be reviewed carefully before being integrated into the decision-making process. If not enough care is taken, what computer experts designate as "a GIGO proposition" (Garbage In—Garbage Out) may be the result.

DIAGNOSIS

A third element in decision making is problem recognition. It begins with what William H. Newman has called "felt difficulty" (a sense of trouble) and then attempts to separate causes from symptoms. Problem recognition tries to identify the relative importance of deviations and differences from accepted norms and to use these deviations to detect the strategic factors influencing the decision. Since it is a common human failing to want to reach solutions without really defining the problem, problem recognition and diagnosis is an important stage in the decision-making process.

ALTERNATIVES

The fourth basic element of the decision process is the creation and structuring of alternative solutions. Creating alternatives brings up the concept of individual and group creativity. Though an individual's inherent creativity probably cannot be improved (people are either creative or they are not), recent studies have shown that better utilization of existing levels of creativity can be obtained. Operational techniques such as brainstorming have been devised to increase one's use of his creativity, and organizations are now delving into other promising techniques which attempt to develop the depth and scope of idea generation by individuals and groups. Such methods, in essence, help a man to come up with the best he has in him: what is already there is taxed to the utmost.

Once creativity begins to function it can operate within a wide range of methodologies. Alternatives can be structured by a simple rational listing of the factors influencing the problem, by the use of mathematical probability, or by logical syllogism, in which two or more premises are made and a logical conclusion is drawn. These methods of structuring problems will be discussed more fully in the following chapter.

STATES OF NATURE

States of nature also have a basic influence on the decision process. Decisions are made under conditions of complete certainty, complete uncertainty, or some point on the continuum lying between those two boundaries. Techniques and methods used to solve problems differ according to where the problem lies (or appears to lie) on the certainty-uncertainty continuum, and the techniques chosen to solve the problem are often derived from the way in which it relates to these uncertainty boundaries. When an outcome has been preordained and is known in advance, as when a firm has inside information, then the decision and the resources employed to implement it may be quite different than those committed in a situation where the decision maker has a very sketchy knowledge of the future. General Motors commits far less money to selling its own dealers, who are really GM's customers, than it does to convincing consumers to buy GM products, even though the dealer actually sells the cars to the consumer. The captive dealer is a much more certain input in the marketing mix than the fickle buying public, and though dealers are cultivated with care, they rarely get the same cultivation as the buying public.

METHODOLOGY

The nature of the methods used to order alternatives have as much variety as those used to diagnose alternate courses of action. Simple intuitive judgment falls at one end of the range, while the highly sophisticated techniques of mathematical analysis appear at the other. A cursory listing of the kinds of techniques available might include intuition, principles of management, economic and financial techniques, statistical methods, game theory, decision models, behavioral approaches, and even heuristic programming techniques. Since some of these approaches are discussed at length in Chapter 7, it is appropriate here to note only that the selection of a particular technique depends upon the nature of the problem; the time available for solution; the availability and cost of information; the abilities, skills, and experience of the decision maker; and the characteristics of the organization in which the decision is being made.

VALUES

Values of both individuals and organizations are the final element entering the decision process. Individuals hold values fraught with moral, cultural, religious, social, economic, and esthetic overtones; and these personal values are influenced directly by the value systems and goals of the organizations in which the individuals function. Governmental welfare agencies obviously have different values guiding their activities than the profit-centered divisions of many industrial concerns. The relative utility of money is an important part of value frameworks, since a dollar in one's own pocket is rarely seen in the same way as a dollar in the organization's budget, and getting money is quite different from giving it out. Value systems are critical in decision making, since their melding with the results of the technical or procedural steps in the decision-making process generates the basic decision rule or rules which result in a particular solution to the immediate problem. If an organization values a quality product over a low-cost product, the choice of quality over cost factors is almost a foregone conclusion in the decision process. Cadillac might put low-cost vinyl into its interior trim, but this possibility is somewhat remote. The quality image of the Cadillac automobile is worth far more to General Motors than a few pennies' savings in a given model year. Thus, value systems enter directly into the ordering, recognition, and choice of alternatives.

STEPS IN DECISION MAKING

Though the subject matter of decision making constantly changes, the goals, values, methodologies, and diagnostic techniques alter very little in the short run. Preferences do shift, of course, but the other factors move slowly enough to be taken as given in a limited time span. In the short run, decision making can be visualized as a series of steps taken within an existing set of goals, values, and methods. Though such a limited view may have more pedagogical than practical value, it allows the decision-making sequence to be represented as a straight-line flow rather than as the complicated looping and feedback system it becomes in the real world.

In an effort to clarify the process of decision making, a number of leading authorities have represented it in simple steps. Peter F. Drucker, for example, lists the steps in decision making as

1. Defining the problem
2. Analyzing the problem
3. Developing alternative solutions
4. Deciding on the best solution
5. Converting decisions into effective actions[6]

Of Drucker's five points, the last has received the least attention so far in this chapter. Drucker, who is rightly concerned with follow-up on decisions, feels that implementation is absolutely necessary in any good decision process.

---

[6] Peter F. Drucker, *The Practice of Management* (New York: Harper & Row, Publishers, 1954).

Newman, Summer, and Warren spell out the four phases of decision making as

1. Making a diagnosis
2. Finding alternative solutions
3. Analyzing and comparing alternatives
4. Selecting a plan to follow[7]

In this formulation, execution is excluded from the decision-making cycle, although it does receive considerable attention in other parts of their writings.

Richards and Greenlaw, following a modification of Herbert Simon's model of decision making, describe the three key steps as

1. Determining the need for decision
2. Developing alternative strategies
3. Selecting alternative strategies[8]

Though these three sets of authors differ sharply in what steps to include in the decision process, they all attempt to systematize decision making into a logical series of steps much like those in the scientific method. Following their lead, but adding more detail, decision making can be represented as a seven-step process:

1. Recognition of problems
2. Diagnosis and definition
3. Collection and analysis of informational inputs
4. Development of alternatives
5. Evaluation of alternatives
6. Making the decision
7. Implementing the chosen course of action

The recognition stage is not always as simple to execute as it may seem at first glance. Organizations are frequently not aware of problems until some unusual or different happening occurs. A dramatic example of this occurred in 1966 in the Douglas Aircraft Corporation. In April, Board Chairman Donald Douglas, Sr., predicted that earnings would be higher than the $14.6 million logged the year before. But by the end of the third quarter, the company disclosed that it was operating at a $16,416,000 deficit for the year.[9] Douglas, which prided itself on its advanced information and control systems, thus

---

[7] William H. Newman, Charles E. Summer, and E. Kirby Warren, *The Process of Management: Concepts, Behavior and Practice,* 2nd ed. (Englewood Cliffs, N.J.: Prentice-Hall, Inc., 1967).

[8] Paul Greenlaw and Max Richards, *Management Decision Making* (Homewood, Ill.: Richard D. Irwin, Inc., 1966).

[9] John Mecklin, "Douglas Aircraft's Stormy Flight," *Fortune,* December 1966, p. 166.

became a striking example of how problems can exist without being evident to even apparently well-informed executives. The ability to recognize problems before they become crises gives any operating management an advantage expressed in the saying, "An ounce of prevention is worth a pound of cure." A failure to recognize a felt difficulty can turn it into an actual one.

Some of the best clues to potential problem areas are the organization's internal control system; its sales and revenue figures; its reports from the field sales force on dealer, customer, and public reactions to its products and policies; the relative effectiveness of its competition; the effect of technological and social change on its future operations; and the other multitudinous signs of danger or vicissitude such as union unrest. Organizations whose antennae are well attuned to detecting such harbingers of change usually have a better economic record than their less perceptive competitors, who rely on hindsight or luck before they take corrective actions.

The stage of problem definition and diagnosis seeks to perceive problems and to state them in concrete terms. The first step is definition. One must ascertain that the right problem is being attacked, lay out the critical factors that may be the potential cause of the felt difficulty, develop possible causal relationships between critical variables, and isolate causes and frame potential solutions within imposed limitations. For example, if the apparent problem is that sales have fallen, the problem definition might attempt to determine the cause of falling sales and the time period within which the decision maker would have to act so that the organization's competitive position would not be jeopardized. It might also lay out the financial boundaries limiting what can be done to solve the problem. When earnings at Texas Instrument fell off 33 percent during a mid-1960 technology shift from transistors to integrated circuitry, management decided rapid action was needed to slide smoothly into the new integrated circuit market. The problem was perceived by TI's management as a need to update management skills; and a series of tentative actions were initiated including a shake-up of top executives, a revamping of the organizational structure, and a new system of goal setting and follow-up. *Self-renewal* is one phrase which could be applied to the revitalization campaign which TI chose as the long-run solution to combat its declining profits and sales figures.

The diagnostic stage involves all of the problem-solving and problem-identifying devices to help clarify exactly what the problem is. At this point, generalities are reduced to sharply defined specifics. For example, instead of stating the problem as "To find out why sales are falling," the diagnosis would more precisely define it as "To determine why sales of product X have fallen 5.3 percent in a market which has increased 2.5 percent in the last year." The basic function of this step is to get to the truth and be precise about it, not to jump to hasty conclusions. In the TI situation described above, extensive study and review and innumerable meetings between executives and specialists throughout the organization preceded the corrective actions made.

Collection and analysis of informational inputs calls for a great deal of technical and conceptual skill. The kinds of data needed may call for a thorough analysis of historical records taken from cost accounting reports; a look at long-run forecasts; an analysis of competitive conditions and competitive actions; and/or a review of projections of costs, revenues, and profits in total rather than as individual parts. Selectivity is quite important here, for only pertinent data should be collected. Since decisions themselves have cost and time dimensions, it is important to determine what data are pertinent, how much it will cost to collect them, and how long it will take to obtain them. It follows that the collections and analysis stage involves judgments on what information to collect and what sources are best able to supply it most rapidly at the lowest cost. The cost factor in data gathering is not an inconsequential one, since information costs money. And, if outside data sources are required, costs may run into the tens of thousands. In one situation, a well-known food products firm defined its problem as a potential strike that might erupt during upcoming negotiations. In order to feel the pulse of its union and nonunion employees, the company hired a consulting firm to conduct a sample attitude survey of its work force. A preliminary survey, described by the consultants as "indicative" of employee feelings, cost the firm more than $8,000; and a more thorough job could have run upwards of $20,000. Costs should always be balanced against returns, for though this management felt it had been given good value for its money, the cost of data gathering was substantial, especially as the information supplied was inferential, not factual.

Whatever the cost in time and money, some data must be gathered before alternatives can be developed. With data in hand, the process of developing alternatives first involves creativity and then structuring. The creative parts of developing alternatives takes known facts and relates them to the problems in such a way that alternative means of solution emerge. In this step, traditional or stereotyped responses and formulations may have to be revised, and various kinds of perceptual blocks must be perceived and handled accordingly. Norman Maier, while attempting to illustrate the problem of perceptual blocks, describes a situation in which he claims that the area of a two-foot by two-foot window can be doubled without changing its dimensions.[10] In Figure 6.1 (a) the dimensions are first sketched out in a partial line diagram. The mind normally organizes two-by-two dimensions into a square as shown in Figure 6.1 (b), but a two-by-two measurement need not be a square at all; it can also be a diamond-shaped rectangle as shown in Figure 6.2 (a). If in Figure 6.2 (b) the figure with dotted-line dimensions (two-by-two) is translated into a solid-line (two-by-two) square, its area is doubled without changing its (two-by-two) dimensions. Since the mind tends to organize two-by-two dimensions into sides of squares, the diamond-shaped object with its two-by-two point-to-point measurements is not the usual perception formulated by the individual. The ability to think both squares and diamonds when confronted by a set of

[10] N. Maier, *Psychology in Industry,* 2nd ed. (Boston: Houghton Mifflin Company, 1955).

two-by-two dimensions is so unusual that the mind typically fights this formulation, rather than trying to understand it. Creativity is, of course, more than just knowledge and the ability to overcome perceptual blocks, but these factors are among the most critical in developing both the nature and quality of the creative effort. Since the number and quality of alternatives depend in large part upon imaginative handling and interpretation of data, creativity ranks high on the list of "most wanted" qualities in decision making.[11]

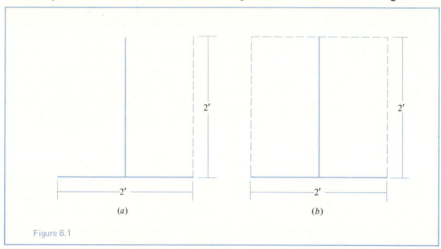

(a)   (b)

Figure 6.1

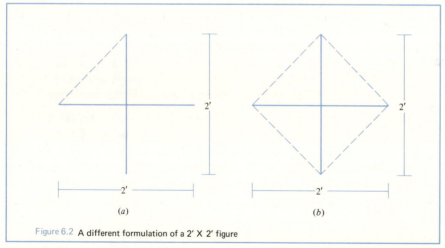

(a)   (b)

Figure 6.2 A different formulation of a 2' X 2' figure

Structuring a problem involves the mechanistic handling of critical variables in a scheme that identifies and relates them in a way that allows them to be evaluated effectively. In Part One the schemes used in critical variable analysis, process analysis, and part of tactical analysis are ways to structure

---

[11] Operational techniques designed to improve individual and group creativity receive additional attention in Chapter 17.

problems of varying scope and complexity. In the matrices in these approaches, the row subject topics are seen as the general problems for solution. The information developed in each cell sheds light on how the concept or variable relates to the problem. Analytical techniques can then be utilized to perform preliminary ranking and ordering so that choices can be made eventually among the most promising alternatives. Proper structuring is important because it provides a systematized way of organizing the masses of relatively complex variables encountered in all but the simplest decisions. Unless some orderly analytical framework is adopted, a good probability exists that one or more critical decision factors may be overlooked.

The evaluation of alternatives takes over where the structuring ends. Evaluation includes weighting the variables, their states of nature (certainty or uncertainty), the total impact of the problem being considered, the skills of those individuals charged with making the decision, and the goal structure within which the problem must be solved. The means actually chosen to evaluate the decision depends upon both the criteria themselves and the conditions surrounding the decision. For example, judgment may have to be used when cost and time limitations are quite pressing—a mathematical location model rarely is needed to determine where to place a cigarette machine. In the case of longer-term decisions calling for a major commitment of capital or resources, much more involved techniques may be brought into the decision process; for example, a simulation model may be quite useful in locating an oil refinery.

More detail on techniques of evaluation appears in Chapter 7, but the knowledge, skills, and inclinations of the decision makers themselves deserve further elaboration here. With tongue in cheek, Cyril N. Parkinson notes that very small and very large decisions often receive strikingly little attention: the former because of their lack of importance and the latter because of the inability of the decision makers to comprehend their scope and impact. After some discussion of "the point of vanishing interest," Parkinson states,

> One thing apparent, however, is that the time spent on $10,000,000 and $10 may well prove to be the same. The present indicated time of two and a half minutes is by no means exact, but there is clearly a space of time—something between two and four and a half minutes—which suffices equally for the largest and the smallest sums.[12]

If Parkinson's pseudohumorous comment is true, and there is some evidence of its veracity, the selection of alternatives has a dimension not often treated in standard approaches to decision making.

Even Parkinson would probably agree that making a decision is a balancing act which requires the individual to balance his own personal judgments and values against the results obtained in the formal evaluation of alternatives.

---

[12] C.N. Parkinson, *Parkinson's Law and Other Studies in Administration* (Boston: Houghton Mifflin Company, 1957), p. 32.

Judgment can never be taken out of the final choice, but it can be tempered by the results obtained in Steps 1 through 5. In the judgment Step 6, the decision maker earns his money—and the moment of truth is reached. Decisions may be made on whim, as when Henry Ford II purportedly decided to call a new car "Edsel" in the face of opposition from his marketers, or they may arise only after careful and painstaking reviews of facts, data, and alternatives, as in the decision to proceed with research and development of the supersonic transport in spite of pressing needs for resources in other areas; but whatever algorithm or methodology underlies the choice, the die is cast when the decision is made. This is the payoff in decision making. To quote a famous sign that once sat on the desk of President Harry S. Truman, "The buck ends here."

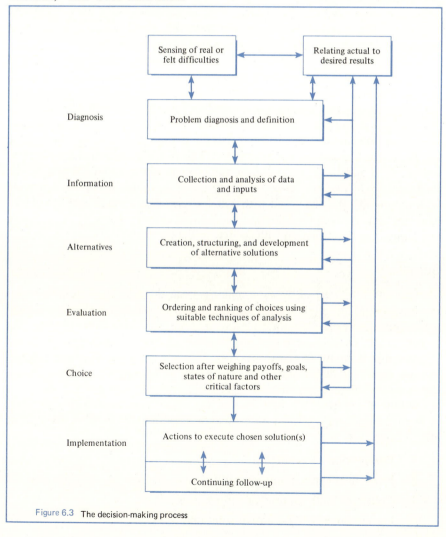

Figure 6.3 The decision-making process

Once the decision is made, implementation comes to the forefront. Implementation means taking steps to insure that a course of action is carried out in accordance with the chosen alternatives. Implementation also involves gaining acceptance of the decision by those directly influenced by it and developing controls to see whether the decision is being carried out properly. If the controls show that the decision is being subverted, circumvented, ignored, or simply not being executed satisfactorily, then some follow-up action is needed. Peter Drucker, for one, feels that implementation is one of the most important steps in the decision process and is not always executed effectively. A famous story credited to humorist Will Rogers illustrates this view. During World War I, German submarines were a threat to worldwide shipping. Rogers proposed ending the threat by raising the temperature of the water to a point where the subs would have to surface—thus becoming easy prey for Allied destroyers. When asked *how* he would heat the ocean, Rogers replied that he was a policy maker and would leave the details to others.

In spite of the range of approaches to decision making, most decision makers attempt to structure problems and develop situations in some sensible, logical, orderly sequence using the best information available. In recent years, there has been a tendency to use more advanced techniques of information gathering and analysis in the decision making process. The use of computer technology to develop information for decision makers is rapidly becoming much more widespread and much more sophisticated. This movement toward the preparation of more and better information has brought about rapid changes in the methodology of decision making. These changes apparently have upgraded both the quality and the speed with which decisions are made and has placed new emphasis on technical factors. In the next chapter, some of these newer techniques are described and illustrated in detail.

Summary

There is still a fine art of decision making, even though recent developments in decision-making methodology have scientific overtones. Relatively formal techniques now exist for gathering and handling complex flows of data, but judgment still enters into almost every phase of decision making.

The basic elements of the decision process are the goals of parent organizations, inputs from information and control systems, problem recognition, the means of creating and structuring alternatives, the ruling states of nature, the means of ordering alternatives, and the value systems of both individual and group decision makers. In the typical decision-making process, seven basic steps occur:

1. Recognition of problems
2. Problem diagnosis and definition
3. Collection and analysis of information
4. Development of alternative solutions

5. Evaluation of alternatives

6. Making a choice among alternatives

7. Implementing the chosen course of action

These seven steps are merely a description of the process of decision making. The detailed techniques used in these steps appear in Chapter 7.

Study Questions

1. Do you agree that personal values and organizational goals are important aspects of decision making? How should they be handled in the decision process?

2. Peter Drucker says that no decision is a decision. In what sense is this true? When might no decision be a rational product of a systematic decision-making process?

3. What problems exist when data are sought from internal sources? External sources?

4. Aside from perceptual blocks, what factors enter into the creation and development of alternative solutions?

5. Do any of the decision-making sequences described in this chapter make sense to you? Why or why not?

6. Do you believe the analytical models in Chapter 3 are as helpful in structuring problems as the author claims? Why or why not? Which approach do you feel is best?

7. How important is the personality of the chief executive in shaping the tone of decisions in his organization? Give specific illustrations and examples from your own experience or knowledge.

8. Is implementation a legitimate part of the decision-making process? Why or why not?

Decision making, the fine art of choice, is advancing rapidly in the direction of scientism. As the social and physical sciences have moved out of the laboratory into the millieu of the real world they have sparked innovations in every phase of the decision-making process. Diagnosis, problem formation, information collection and analysis, and approaches to improving creativity have all undergone rigorous study and improvement in recent years. But nowhere have the changes been so great as in decision-making methodology and techniques. The techniques used in evaluating alternatives are more thorough and more sophisticated than ever before, and the speed with which computers handle information is awesome. Old techniques are constantly being improved, and new approaches are developing at a rate that points to even greater changes in the future.

In view of the magnitude and variety of these ongoing developments, sorting out the wheat from the chaff is not particularly easy. Even selecting a way to classify decision-making techniques is difficult, since there is no one accepted way to categorize them. One approach is to classify them as quantitative or nonquantitative, but this is neither precise nor complete. Emphasis can also be placed on developing schools of thought or academic disciplines, but this approach is also somewhat unsatisfactory. For example, decision theory alone does not cover the whole range of decision-making methodology, and neither do behavioral science approaches, which solve problems by emphasizing better communications, group participation, or changes in group interactions. Other ways to group decision-making techniques might be to specify

CHAPTER 7
Techniques for Decision Making

the degree to which decisions are programmed or unprogrammed; to attempt to clarify how well certain methodologies cope with ruling states of nature; and to identify critical problems in areas of decision making such as market research and production planning and then to stipulate the methods that contribute most to their solution. Though each of these classification schemes has a definite utility, this chapter presents a framework which reviews both traditional methods of decision making and the more recent developments in the field. Though this kind of survey raises the risk of uneven depth of coverage and admittedly lacks the depth demanded of practitioners, it does provide a general understanding of the wide range of methodologies in current use.

Since a complete cataloguing of decision-making techniques is not intended, the chosen approaches should be considered as representative rather than all inclusive; they serve as a good starting point for more exhaustive review and analysis. The categories are

1. Judgmental techniques
2. Principles of management
3. Systems models
4. Behavioral techniques
5. Heuristic approaches
6. Economic and financial techniques
7. Statistical methods
8. Specialized decision models

Each of these methodologies is reviewed in varying degrees of detail. The illustrative materials and problems in each section indicate how these techniques may be utilized in operational situations.

JUDGMENTAL TECHNIQUES

Judgment is a time-honored methodology based on rule of thumb or the mythical best teacher, experience. Judgment is most useful in making routine decisions or decisions of limited scope, but its use is questionable in situations where large capital commitments are involved or where futurity is critical. Judgmental techniques are necessarily based on past experience, and the general observations made about the naïveté of forecasts based on historical projections are equally valid applied to decision-making techniques based only on judgment.

Some of the things favoring the judgmental approach are that it is easy to use, it costs very little, and it can be invoked rapidly. On the other hand, unless judgment is combined with other techniques, its use tends to be risky. Any methodology whose consistency varies with the user is not capable of giving consistent results. And since high-quality decision making depends upon a large number of high-quality decision makers with vast stores of experience—a condition not often found—few organizations can be assured that judgmental techniques will generate a continuing flow of top-notch decisions.

To say that the use of judgment is hazardous is not to say that it should not be used at all. It has no peer in cases where few guidelines exist and subtle distinctions must be made. In the words of Oliver Wendell Holmes, "General propositions do not decide concrete cases. The decision will depend upon the judgment or intuition more subtle than any major premise." Justice Holmes probably would not preclude the use of specific techniques to buttress judgment, but his point is still well taken. Even when the best techniques are used, judgment may be the final factor in determining what choice to make and how to carry it out. Used alone, however, it tends to be overrated.

PRINCIPLES OF MANAGEMENT

Few people believe that principles or general rules can provide specific approaches to decision making, but some executives seem to act as if they do. For example, industrial organizations set up in accordance with the chain of command principle tend to use a narrow span of control with degrees of delegation dictated by the individual's position in the organizational structure rather than by the duties of his particular job. In the development of superior-subordinate relationships based upon formal relationships at particular structural levels rather than upon the needs of the job, the principles are used in such specific fashion that they tend to lose their value; that is, they tend to become solutions rather than guides to solutions.

Principles are really guides to the total job of management—the rules of the road—they are not techniques. A number of authors in the field of management, notably Greenlaw and Richards, list principles of management as an approach to decision making and then launch a sharp criticism.[1] Such harsh words hardly seem justified, since the compilers of lists of principles make no claim that principles are specific techniques of decision making, only general guidelines. Principles of management have limited value as a decision-making technique, but they may help to shape the environment in which decisions are made. In the decision-making process they are at best peripheral, what Justice Holmes referred to as general propositions, not the essence of solution.

SYSTEMS MODELS

Systems models, like principles of management, are not in themselves techniques of decision making, but they do provide general structures and frameworks in which decisions can be evaluated; and when a system contains built-in decision rules, they actually do make decisions. For example, a cybernetic

---

[1] Paul Greenlaw and Max Richards, *Management Decision Making* (Homewood, Ill.: Richard D. Irwin, Inc., 1966).

or closed-loop system controlling oil refinery operations actually identifies critical variables, evaluates them, matches the difference between actual and desired results, and then takes effecting actions that correct deviations from desired results. In effect, the system has built-in controls that exercise judgment in the presence of detected deviations. In such a system, there are sensing units which determine what is happening in the process, a collating step which matches up desired and actual results, and an effecting step which occurs if and when undesirable deviations are detected. If no out-of-control situation occurs, then the process continues without adjustment. Most of these models attempt to induce a state of homeostasis, that is, a return to normality or a given desirable condition.

Most systems, however, do not have built-in decision-making devices. They may receive information, transmit it, or even transform it into other configurations, but the inputs and outputs are fed to a decision maker before any action is taken. For example, General Electric has used such models to prepare bids on heavy apparatus contracts. Bids are prepared after the models weigh competitors' strategies and their possible bids, and the results have been described as amazingly accurate by GE people. In advertising, many agencies use simulation models to predict sales results in test markets. The J. Walter Thompson agency, for one, feels its models are simulating actual market conditions more and more closely. In the package goods field, Pillsbury, General Foods, General Mills, and Libby, McNeill & Libby all routinely use market simulations to predict the results of price changes, promotional campaigns, and possible competitive responses to planned strategies.

The use of systems analysis has arisen concurrently with the development of computerized technology. Systems and procedures departments are now part of most major industrial corporations and almost all large organizations. Outside of a few closed-loop systems, however, no systems approaches exist as full-blown techniques for decision making. In the area of heuristics, however, some progress has been made along these lines.[2]

In the broad sense, the analytical schemes described in Chapter 3 are systems of analysis. The concept approach, the critical variable approach, and the technique approach provide a basis for the development of generalized systems for analyzing problems which then can be developed into more detailed information-decision systems. At this time, however, such systems models are more useful in diagnosis and analysis than in choosing among alternatives.

BEHAVIORAL TECHNIQUES

The use of behavioral science techniques in decision making is a somewhat fragmentary although extremely useful approach. Like the systems approach,

---

[2] The entire concept of systems theory will be reexamined in a later section dealing with control. Heuristics also will be discussed later in this chapter.

behavioral science has made major contributions in providing information on and insight into the decision-making process. It also has some specific techniques that can be utilized to evaluate decision factors directly. In Chapter 3, Figure 3.4 illustrates the framework identified as technique, or tactical, analysis. This approach covers solutions-oriented methods from such disciplines as engineering, economics, and psychology. Some of the behavioral science contributions to tactical analysis are described below as decision-making techniques. This dual role is not contradictory, since behavioral science approaches are useful in both an analytical and a prescriptive sense.

The contribution of behavioral science can be summarized best by citing how specific behavioral findings enter into decision-making methodology. One such concept is group decision making, as advocated by Robert R. Blake and Jane S. Mouton in *Group Dynamics—Key to Decision Making*.[3] In this work, they illustrate that group participation is necessary for decision making and propose a general approach to decision making which falls short of being a methodology. Research on communication, lateral and vertical nets of communication, and communications between hierarchical levels has also pointed out that wider spans of control sometimes can be utilized to gain greater individual motivation and perhaps even greater work effectiveness. This has assisted the development of "flat" organizational structures, but again, has not provided a methodology by which decision makers can solve a wide range of organizational problems. In the organization field again, the development of circular flows of production to improve output has been advocated; but again this finding provides information without being a decision-making technique. The satisfying concepts and role theory discussed earlier in this text also help the decision maker to understand what is occurring in the organizational structure, but the insights developed by these theories fail to provide specific procedural aids to the decision maker. In this respect, the behavioral science contributions described are much like the principles of organization: they provide general, not specific, assistance.

One example where behavioral science has entered directly into the decision process is selection. Psychological tests have, in many instances, replaced judgment in the selection of job applicants. Indeed, even in instances where selection tests are not the sole determinant of acceptance, they receive careful attention. In testing job applicants, behavioral science has entered into the decision process to such an extent that it often determines the decision.

Other isolated instances of behavioral approaches influence decisions directly, but most often the behavioral techniques are designed to provide insight and information rather than to actually analyze and solve specific problems. This will probably change as behavioral science methods improve; and behavioral techniques are destined to play a more important role in tomorrow's decision-making processes.

---

[3] (Houston, Tex.: The Gulf Publishing Company, 1961).

HEURISTIC APPROACHES

Heuristic decision making is a wedding of the systems and the behavioral approaches. Heuristics considers both major variables *and* the reactions, feelings, and *possible* reactions of people in the system. According to William J. Gore, it is an alternative to rational decision making in that it allows a strategy to be reached when a preferred path is blocked.[4] In other words, heuristics allows the decision maker to consider less-than-rational paths and thus preclude frustration when more preferable alternatives are somehow unavailable. Unlike rational systems of decision making, heuristic systems provide actions and routines that are not necessarily linked to rational objectives. Indeed, heuristic systems are often linked to individual emotions and objectives and thus do not have to have internal consistency in order to operate effectively. The heuristic approach has at its heart the concept that individual factors and emotions are intrinsic rather than extraneous to the decision process. Heuristic systems can thus be used to solve unstructured problems where the objectives are not clear or not quantifiable or where independent variables are symbolic rather than quantitative. Alternatively, they can assist in the solution of problems where specific algorithms are neither known nor readily available.

There are three basic problem-solving steps in the heuristic method. The first step classifies the problem as to type and tries to identify whether this basic problem type can be solved with a given routine or set of routines. Assuming no solution occurs at this point, there is then a breakdown of major problem categories into subproblems. This concept may be extremely atomistic, as in the case of the Sage Defense System, or it may attempt only to run through the first stage of subclassification. The third step is the application of problem-solving techniques to the subproblems broken down in the second step. If a given set of routines is not successful in solving the subproblem then another set is tried, until a problem-solving technique is recognized or the problem is classified as insoluble within the known parameters. That is, there is a continuing breakdown of large problems into smaller subproblems, and routines are applied and reapplied until either some solution is reached at the smallest breakdown or the problem is considered too difficult to be solved within the known set of conditions surrounding it.

There is no necessary solution to a problem fed into a heuristic system. The subproblems identified and broken down may eventually be restated in solvable form, or the state of the decision-making and problem-solving techniques available may clearly indicate that no decision is possible. There is thus a risk that no definitive decision will come out of a heuristic system; however, there will be an identification of areas that need greater definition, and then the decision-making process can continue to evolve.

In game situations such as checkers and chess, heuristic problem solving has been quite successful in analyzing moves and developing strategies. The

---

[4] *Administrative Decision Making: A Heuristic Model* (New York: John Wiley & Sons, Inc., 1964).

somewhat complicated set of patterns encountered, say, in chess can be identified by a system which has the ability to handle a large number of parameters
and routines. A given move can be analyzed in terms of alternative results,
and the steps following the move can be set into a total system to show
the ultimate effect of this move on the strategy of the player making it. The
opponents' strategies and their probable actions and reactions to a given move
also can be built into the system. This process of identifying basic problems,
breaking them down into subproblems, analyzing alternative actions and
alternative strategies in view of what an opponent might do, closely resembles
the way in which the human brain attacks problems. The random search-and-
seek pattern of heuristic systems is almost as inefficient as the brain's search-
and-seek patterns, but the bewildering speed with which computers can conduct
such search routines makes heuristics a highly feasible pattern of problem
analysis and solution.

Heuristic systems of decision making are now in their early stages of
development, but they hold great promise, particularly as computer technology
advances and as methodology of logic becomes more well developed. Though
top-level executives have at times pooh-poohed the applicability of heuristic
systems in complex decision analysis, the success of the U.S. Defense Department in using such techniques indicates that it holds real promise for the
future. In Stanley Kubick's movie "2001: A Space Odyssey," a computer
identified as HAL 9000 plays a major role. Speaking in an unemotional tone,
HAL converses with the human astronauts about their mental health, beats
them at chess (and then thanks them for a good game), and makes routine
and nonroutine decisions about the flight. When the crew decides to deprogram
HAL because he may make errors because of what they believe to be faulty
programming, HAL's reaction, in line with his programmed goal to place the
mission above all else, is to kill the entire crew—except for the one man able
to outwit HAL's massive memory and reasoning powers. HAL's almost human
reaction to being deprogrammed ("I know I've made some bad decisions lately,
but I'll improve, you'll see") is not surprising to students of heuristic decision
making, particularly since the letters in HAL also stand for heuristic algorithmic
methods of analysis and problem solving.

ECONOMIC AND FINANCIAL TECHNIQUES

Economic theories in general and marginal analysis in particular are extremely
useful decision-making techniques. In the study of pricing and relationships
between costs, revenues, prices, and profits, economists have developed frameworks which, though not always directly applicable to real situations, do
provide a means for reviewing the factors bearing upon economically oriented
decisions. Many early models in microeconomics presented a somewhat static
picture of the relationships between prices, costs, revenues, and profits in
graphic fashion. Later models adopted a more dynamic orientation, providing
a still more useful analytical framework. Perhaps the most utilitarian decision

model taken from economics is the classic relationship between price, cost, revenue, and profits presented in Figure 7.1.

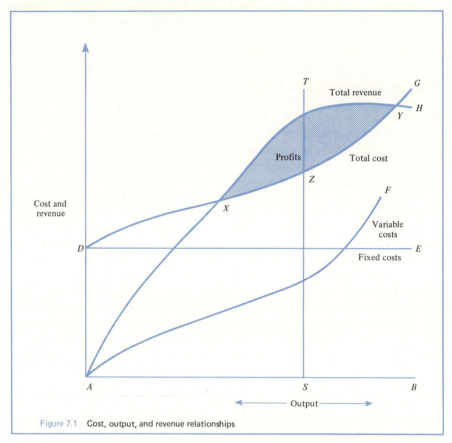

Figure 7.1   Cost, output, and revenue relationships

Figure 7.1 shows the dynamic movement of fixed costs and variable costs as production increases and shows how profit begins when the total revenue line *AH* intersects with the total cost line *DG* at point *X* and ends when these two lines cross at point *Y*, the end of the shaded profit "football." Line *TZ* in the profit section of the diagram indicates where the sides of the football are farthest apart: the point of profit maximization. Figure 7.1 shows clearly where profits are optimized (point *S*), where break-even points exist at both the upper and lower ends of the scale, (points *X* and *Y*), and how cost and revenue lines act and interact. For example, fixed costs are assumed to remain constant over all levels of volume as indicated by line *DE,* even though this assumption holds only for limited changes in volume. Variable costs (line *AF)*) shift because of factors such as increases in labor due to overtime, increases in material costs due to saturation on the market, or materials cost decreases arising from quantity discounts. The revenue curve (line *AH*) also shows a reflection of the high costs of initially getting into the market, market saturation, and, eventually, a tapering-off of demand. When the relationships outlined in graphic form in Figure 7.1 are projected for specific firms or products in terms of static break-even analysis or more complicated dynamic analysis involving a series of products or locations, pertinent variables affecting decisions are arrayed in a structural framework that helps decision makers to visualize the many relationships among these critical factors. The value of such microeconomic models is thus obvious.

Marginal analysis takes situations involving variables such as those specified in Figure 7.1 and focuses on what may happen at the margin as existing relationships change. Given a set of conditions, marginal analysis provides a framework for evaluating dynamic problems by focusing on added costs and added revenues entering directly into a decision. Thus, it has a futuristic overtone which deemphasizes averages and/or orientation to the past. For example, marginal analysis might analyze a decision in the following way. Suppose you own a business renting boats to fishermen. All of the boats are paid for; and dockage costs, maintenance of boats, and so on are paid to the owner of the marina where you moor your boats on a flat fee, seasonal basis. Your only other out-of-pocket cost is an attendant who rents boats to fisherman from 5 AM to 10 AM. Rentals are made only by the day, but many boats are returned early and tied up by the marina owner. No further rentals are made because the marina owner, who does not share in the profits, refuses to rent boats to other customers. You are considering adding a second attendant who would rent out boats between 10 AM and 4 PM. What should you do? Clearly, the added costs and added revenue considerations are paramount here, not the flat fee costs. Marginal analysis allows you to focus on the added costs, the added revenues, and other alternatives which might be still more profitable. You might then want to consider the various costs and revenues derived from adding the additional attendant or from paying the marina owner a fee for rerenting your boats. Marginal analysis provides the framework for conducting this kind of analysis. Indeed, this approach is used daily by businessmen who never realize that what they call common sense is really a modification of a formal and respectable academic methodology.

In another simple illustration, consider the case of a research project in which $4 million was allocated to develop a unique piece of machinery. At the end of a year's research and development, the engineers and scientists working on this machine indicate that an added investment of $1 million would bring the research to a conclusion. The machine eventually evolving from their efforts would, at best, bring in $4 million worth of added revenue. Should the project be continued? Looking at this proposition in normal or average cost terms the total project would cost $5 million and yield only $4 million in revenue; therefore, the decision would be to stop, not to throw good money after bad. In marginal terms, however, an added cost of $1 million would yield a revenue of $4 million. Overall, the net loss on the project would be $1 million if the decision is made to go ahead as opposed to a loss of $4 million for abandoning the project. Marginal analysis would seem to suggest going ahead with the additional investment because it makes good economic sense to lose *less money* on the project by investing the additional million. Obviously, if decision makers had known in advance that the project would cost $5 million and yield $4 million, it would not have been attempted. But once the project is started marginal analysis techniques would indicate that it makes no sense to stop at the end of the first year, even though the project's completion still will result in a loss. Since the data needed to complete such a review are not available in the organization's normal cost-reporting procedures, great care is needed in the compilation of data for marginal analysis.

There is one other factor to consider here, the degree of certainty that the additional investment of $1 million will bring in $4 million in revenue. If the engineers are not absolutely sure that the new investment will yield the added revenues (there is a degree of uncertainty in their predictions) then a careful review might have to be undertaken before the decision were made to add another million in development costs. The expected monetary value approach described later in this chapter might be invoked at this point to evaluate the probable returns from various uncertain payoffs.

Microeconomics and marginal analysis are most useful in providing frameworks in which to analyze data. Obviously, marginal analysis is a specialized technique, since it considers situations one at a time. It is not particularly fitted for use as a long-range guide to action, since in the long run considerations of average and full costs must govern enough lines so that profits can be maintained. Like the small boy with the lemonade stand who makes lemonade for three cents a cup, sells it for two cents and then tries to make up his losses in volume, businessmen quickly learn that too much marginal thinking can leave them with sound theory but no tomorrow.

Though marginal analysis is used widely, it is much less popular than its first cousin, financial analysis. Financial techniques appear in different guises throughout business and industry, and their utilization as devices for assessing capital investments and performance is spreading into government and nonprofit organizations such as churches, hospitals, and foundations. Because of their general nature, they contain a broad range of choice in terms of both degree of sophistication and type of coverage. Among the better known techniques are

1. The criteria of absolute profit
2. Rate of return on invested capital
3. Payback, or investment recovery
4. Inflow and outflow analysis using nondiscounted dollars
5. Discounting of dollar inflows and outflows

One reason for the widespread use of these classic yardsticks is their ability to perform a double duty in decision making: they serve as a method of analysis and evaluation and as a means of making choices among alternative solutions. Because of their critical role in managerial decision making, they are treated here in considerable detail.

A series of examples can be used to show how financial techniques might be applied in a practical setting. Table 7.1 exhibits how the *first three techniques* might be used to evaluate an investment in a piece of equipment with a purchase price of $300,000. The second example, Table 7.2, analyzes cash inflows and outflows in a situation involving a choice between two machines with different purchase prices and operating costs. In the second part of this example, inflows and outflows are discounted to include the time value of money in the decision analysis.

TABLE 7.1   INVESTMENT ANALYSIS USING THE CRITERIA OF ABSOLUTE PROFIT, RATE OF RETURN, AND PAYBACK

MACHINE COSTS AND REVENUES

1 Year	2 Added income before taxes	3 Depreciation	4 Taxable income	5 After-tax income (50-percent tax rate assumed)
1	$60,000	$60,000	$ 0	$ 0
2	80,000	60,000	20,000	10,000
3	80,000	60,000	20,000	10,000
4	70,000	60,000	10,000	5,000
5	70,000	60,000	10,000	5,000
			$60,000	$30,000

NOTES:
1. Investment in equipment, $300,000
2. Estimated life of equipment, 5 years
3. Straight-line depreciation per year, $60,000 (assume no scrap value)

$$\frac{\$300,000}{5 \text{ years}} = \$60,000 \text{ depreciation per year}$$

4. Desired: to find financial results yielded by absolute profit, rate of return, and payback techniques of financial analysis

Criterion 1—Calculation (absolute profit)
   Simply add column 5, the total profit after taxes.

$$\begin{array}{r} \$\quad 0 \\ 10,000 \\ 10,000 \\ 5,000 \\ \underline{5,000} \\ \$30,000 \text{ total profit after taxes} \end{array}$$

Criterion 2—Calculation (rate of return)
   Compute average cash tieup and average returns then divide average return by average tieup to get rate of return.

TABLE 7.1   (Cont.)

INVESTMENT VALUES			
Year	Start of Year	End of Year	Average tieup per year
1	$300,000	$240,000	$270,000
2	240,000	180,000	210,000
3	180,000	120,000	150,000
4	120,000	60,000	90,000
5	60,000	0	30,000
			$750,000

$$\frac{\$750,000}{5 \text{ years}} = \$150,000 \text{ average cash tieup over the 5-year period}$$

RETURNS	
Year	After-tax Profits
1	$ 0
2	10,000
3	10,000
4	5,000
5	5,000
	$30,000 total 5-year profit

$$\frac{\$30,000}{5 \text{ years}} = \$6,000 \text{ average profit per year}$$

$$\frac{\$6,000}{\$150,000} = 4\text{-percent average rate of return}$$

Criterion 3—Calculation (payback)
Compute cash recovery over time until investment has been recovered.

1 Year	2 After-tax income	3 Depreciation	4 Cash recovery per year	5 Cash recovery cumulative
1	$ 0	$60,000	$60,000	$ 60,000
2	10,000	60,000	70,000	130,000
3	10,000	60,000	70,000	200,000
4	5,000	60,000	65,000	265,000
5	5,000	60,000	65,000	330,000

Recovery occurs when after-tax income plus depreciation (noncash expenses charged to income) equal the $300,000 cost of the original investment. This occurs at 4.54 years, or slightly more than four years and six months.

Summary of results

Criterion 1   Absolute profit (after taxes) $30,000
Criterion 2   Rate of return 4 percent
Criterion 3   Payback 4½ years (app.)

Table 7.1 demonstrates the results obtained from using three different financial techniques to analyze one set of investment data. Each method uses the simplifying assumptions of straight-line depreciation over a five-year period, a 50-percent tax rate, and no scrap value on the machinery, that is, disposal and removal costs just equal payments by the purchaser.

The first criterion, absolute profit, is easy to determine, since it involves nothing more than reading off the total of column 5. Sometimes absolutes have more meaning than rates, although typically this is true only in special cases. A 20-percent yield on a one-dollar investment may be substantially less attractive than a 10-percent return on a $10,000 investment, particularly if the $9,999 remaining in the first instance has no readily available alternative investment opportunity yielding more than 10 percent.

Though exceptions abound, rate of return provides more meaningful financial data than absolute profit, since it allows comparisons between alternative uses of given sums. Accountants and financial analysts differ greatly on how to calculate rate of return, so the illustration shown in Table 7.1 should be viewed basically as a simple example of the kinds of things which might be done to determine a realistic rate of return on investment. In this example, average capital tie-up and average revenue yields are calculated over the investment life cycle. Average capital tie-up is then divided into the average yield to obtain an average rate of return. This method allows for changes in regularity of input flows, but leaves out intricacies such as imputations of added factors over the investment period. This method's popularity springs from its ability to generate comparisons, and this factor is of extreme value when decision makers are faced with a wide range of alternative uses of a limited number of dollars.

The third criterion in Table 7.1, payback (sometimes called the investment recovery period) is also quite common. It attempts to calculate the time required to recover invested funds by matching internal and external inflows of funds. Net profits and depreciation are added until their cumulative total equals the investment outlay; at that point the investment has been paid back. This method is useful in situations where rapid change makes recovery of outlays as important as rates of return. Industries with high rates of technological change and firms with potential investments in volatile political climates often prefer payback to more refined criteria better suited to measuring more stable situations. Used alone, payback is defensive, since it concentrates on the protective aspects of investment rather than on maximum financial returns over time.

None of the three methods described above considers the fact that money itself has a value. Anyone with a bank account knows he is entitled to interest for allowing any bank to use his money. If banks are paying 5-percent simple interest, $1000 in a bank account grows to $1050 at the end of one year. The $1050 then accrues to $1102.50 at the end of the second year, and this process repeats as long as the principal is untouched and the interest is allowed to accrue and compound. The concept of discounting applies this same principle when it asks, "What amount must I invest in the present (current dollars) at a given discount rate (rate of accrual) to equal a given amount of dollars at some time in the future?" For example, if interest rates are 5 percent, what amount must an individual have in the bank at the start of the year to equal $1000 at the year's end? The answer in this case, if interest accrues in uniform fashion over the year, is approximately $952.00. For an end-of-year total of $1050 at 5 percent, $1000 (current) dollars must be invested at the start of the year.

TABLE 7.2   THE CRITERION OF NONDISCOUNTED CASH FLOW

Assume the following data:

Machine A	Machine B
Cost $10,000	Cost $8,000
Life 5 years	Life 4 years
Cost to operate	Cost to operate
Year 1 $3,000	Year 1 $4,000
2 3,000	2 4,000
3 3,000	3 4,000
4 3,000	4 4,000
5 3,000	
No scrap value	No scrap value

Using a nondiscounted cash flow technique, simple cost outflows and inflows are averaged and evaluated.

OUTFLOWS

Machine A	Machine B
Year 1 $13,000	Year 1 $12,000
2 3,000	2 4,000
3 3,000	3 4,000
4 3,000	4 4,000
5 3,000	

$$\frac{\text{Total outflow}}{\text{Years}} = \frac{\$25,000}{5} = \$5,000 \text{ average cost/year for machine A}$$

$$\frac{\$24,000}{4} = \$6,000 \text{ average cost/year for machine B}$$

Therefore, if no other factors are considered, machine A is most profitable because its average cost per year is $1,000 less than machine B.

Table 7.2 involves the choice between machines A and B using nondiscounted cash flows. A discounted cash flow analysis applied to the same figures would generate the results shown in Table 7.3. The discounted cash flow approach tries to make all dollars equal by stating them in terms of current dollars. The end point in the calculation yields a result that expresses present and future commitments in terms of what it would cost in today's dollars to support an investment over its entire life cycle. Since money could be used in other investments with some sort of yield, this kind of analysis is valuable in imputing costs of lost opportunities into the evaluation mix. In Table 7.3 the total investment in machine A in current dollars would be $18,967, and for machine B, $18,348. In regular, nondiscounted dollars (absolute dollar commitment considered in terms of the face value amounts to be invested each year) the comparable figures would be $25,000 for machine A and $24,000 for machine B, as shown in Table 7.2. This difference in amounts represents the effect of discounting future cash flows to their present worth in today's dollars.

TABLE 7.3   THE CRITERION OF DISCOUNTED CASH FLOW

Data: 1. Use initial cost and operating data for machines A and B, Figure 7.3
      2. Assume the estimated discount rate for the machines listed above is 20 percent.* The discount factors for the 20-percent rate are shown below:

Time (year)	Discount rate
0 (today's rate)	1.000
1	.833
2	.694
3	.578
4	.482
5	.402

Required: Using a discounted cash flow approach, perform the following:
      1. Indicate which machine has the lowest average annual operating costs.
      2. Indicate the dollar advantage which the lowest cost machine has over the opposing machine.

		MACHINE A			MACHINE B	
1	2	3	4	5	6	
Year	Outflow	Discount factor	Discounted dollars	Outflow	Discounted dollars	
0	$10,000	1.000	$10,000	$8,000	$8,000	
1	3,000	.833	2,499	4,000	3,332	
2	3,000	.694	2,082	4,000	2,776	
3	3,000	.578	1,734	4,000	2,312	
4	3,000	.482	1,446	4,000	1,928	
5	3,000	.402	1,206		$18,348	
			$18,967			

$$\frac{\$18,967}{5 \text{ years}} = \$3,793.40 \text{ average cost per year}$$

$$\frac{\$18,348}{4 \text{ years}} = \$4,587.00 \text{ average cost per year}$$

* The 20-percent factor means that alternative uses of these same funds would have approximately the same yield (20 percent). This figure typically considers and includes all factors bearing yields of funds in alternative uses.

Comparing the calculations in Tables 7.2 and 7.3 discloses that machine A is still the best financial choice, even on a discounted cash flow basis. The difference between them is narrower, however, because of the impact of the higher initial outlay for machine A.

The examples described in Table 7.3 point out how outlays of current dollars influence the economically optimum choice. To show how discounting can be applied in a balancing of revenue inflows and cash outlays, consider the following example using the data presented in the comparison of the profit and payback criteria in Table 7.1. Table 7.4, which uses the discounted cash flow approach to analyze the data presented in Table 7.1, indicates that there would be a net outflow of $103,420, which, in terms of discounted rate of return, would be well below 20 percent, returning approximately 4.2 percent. In other words, a rate of interest that would exactly equal the return from this investment would equal 4.2 percent.[5] In this calculation, the decision maker would have to determine whether or not 4.2 percent was an adequate rate of return in a situation where a risk factor of 20 percent might be considered indicative. Given the facts in Table 7.4, it seems unlikely that this investment would be undertaken unless nonfinancial factors were given extremely heavy weightings. In practice, financial criteria would normally be the major factors underlying such decisions.

The dominant role of financial techniques in decision making arises because they provide comparative evaluations and are a custom-made way to analyze data generated by the organization's internal control system. For these and other reasons, financial criteria to evaluate capital and other investments are probably the most widely used decision-making techniques, even though other approaches, most notably the use of statistical methods, are on the ascent.

STATISTICAL METHODS

In *Design for Decision,* Irwin J.D. Bross raises the question, "If statistical decision making is such a world shaking affair, why haven't I felt some of the tremors?"[6] He answers that specialists have typically dominated the writing and thinking in the field. Bross then goes on to say statistical decision making has indeed brought new and widespread concepts into the field of decision making and proceeds to demonstrate just what changes have occurred in both theory and practice. A review of the contemporary scene seems to indicate Bross is correct in his statement that statistical decision-making methods have

---

[5] The 4.2-percent rate comes from calculating inflows at differing discount rates to find the exact point where the outflows and inflows balance ($300,000 in and $300,000 out). If an income flow represented by the dollar commitment in Table 7.4 is calculated at a 20-percent discount rate, the result is a $103,000–net outflow—below 20 percent and $103,000 short of the inflows that would approximate a yield of 20 percent on the investment. A similar calculation performed with a 10-percent discount rate would yield a net inflow of $247,880—which leaves a negative outflow of $52,200, even at the 10-percent rate. If this calculation is repeated until the net inflow is $300,000 and the net outflow is zero, the discount rate required to exactly balance the flow is 4.2 percent.

[6] (New York: Crowell-Collier and Macmillan, Inc., 1953).

TABLE 7.4   CASH INFLOWS AND OUTFLOW—DISCOUNTED DOLLAR ANALYSIS

1 Year	2 Outflow	3 Inflow	4 Discount factor*	5 Discounted dollars (Col. 3 × Col.4)
0	$300,000	$ 0	1.000	$300,000
1	0	60,000	.833	49,980
2	0	70,000	.694	48,580
3	0	70,000	.578	40,560
4	0	65,000	.482	31,330
5	0	65,000	.402	26,130
				$196,580

$300,000 outflow
— 196,580 inflow
$103,420 net outflow, representing a discounted rate
of return of 4.2 percent

* Discount factors used are the same selected to evaluate the relative desirability of machines A and B in Figure 7.3 (20 percent).

gained widespread acceptance, particularly since the development of computerized technology, which can handle some of the intricate calculations needed to manipulate variables with probabilities that shift over time.

As statistical decision-making techniques have evolved they have followed two main paths: statistical inference and statistical decision theory. Statistical inference involves point and/or interval estimation and hypothesis testing. In point or interval estimation, the decision maker tries to obtain a figure that can serve as an estimate of the unknown limit or parameter. Typically, this determination is made by using the least squares method, which either attempts to minimize the sum of the squares of the deviations from a chosen value or chooses a value that maximizes the probability a given result or example is representative of a true universe. Point estimation, though it provides what seems to be a complete answer, is far from the last word, since the result is only accurate within certain levels of confidence. The determination of confidence intervals or limits is also part of statistical inference. Confidence limits are usually calculated as a percentage within a given percentage range or value. For example, 95 percent. The 95 percent figure would typically mean that 95 percent of the cases in the true population are included. To put it another way, with a given sample, taken from a chosen universe and with a confidence limit of 95 percent, the true population represented by the sample would be excluded in only 5 percent of the cases. Thus, for example, a psychological study attempting to show the relationship between job satisfaction and morale might, within a given sample, say that the results obtained in a given structured experiment has a "p" level of 0.05, or, the statistics backing up conclusions drawn from this sample are accurate in a statistical sense 95 times out of 100. The remaining 5 percent is the statistical probability of error. Point estimation and confidence limits are used widely in the social sciences, as in the survey techniques described in Chapter 4.

Hypothesis testing, the second area of statistical inference, is really a special case of estimation in which the decision maker tries to develop some conclusions about alternatives by drafting a particular hypothesis and attempting to test its validity. In the context of a given set of data, the hypothesis being tested is usually called the null hypothesis and the one against which it is evaluated is called the alternative hypothesis. The solution of the problem comes about when the null hypothesis is evaluated against the alternative hypothesis.

Two types of errors can result in hypothesis testing. A type-1 error occurs when a hypothesis that should have been accepted is rejected. A type-2 error occurs when a false hypothesis is accepted. In a typical application of hypothesis testing, statistical quality control, the test selected is the one which tends to minimize type-two error, that is, the possible acceptance of a bad lot. Statistical sample sizes are set after determining just how vital type-one (rejecting a good lot) and type-two (accepting a bad lot) errors are in the production process. Both buyers and sellers accept some risk here, and the sample size reflects the kind of risk purchasers and vendors are willing to take. The larger the sample, the greater the chance the sample reflects the true universe (the total lot or production run); but costs of sampling also rise with increased sample size. Statistical methods help to show the sample size needed to assure a given statistical probability of accuracy, and thus statistics assist not only in making the acceptance or rejection decision but also help in keeping sampling costs under control.

Hypothesis testing and other sampling techniques are two historically tested techniques, but statistical decision-making methods are moving away from classical statistical methodologies into new and different areas. Two of the more promising recent developments have been the use of the expected value concept and the payoff matrix.

The expected value approach attempts to combine mathematics and intuition in the decision-making sequence. In this approach, probability curves are determined from empirical evidence of past occurrences as in classical statistics, but the judgments of those charged with the decision are also incorporated. For example, sales projections are reviewed by experienced executives who attach a probability of attainment to them. The resultant value is a projected sales forecast containing both past data and current judgment. To illustrate, suppose that a projected sales forecast estimates that at prices of $1.00, $1.10, and $1.20, the sales of a particular product will be $100 million, $110 million, and $120 million respectively. Executives reviewing this forecast might feel that the first figure has only a 50-percent chance of being reached, the second, 40 percent, and the third, 10 percent. If it is assumed that these three situations are the only ones that can be obtained, then the value that would be placed on the expected sales would be 0.5 times $100 million, 0.4 times $110 million, and 0.1 times $120 million, or an expected sales of $106 million. In formula fashion this would be represented as

$$EX = P_1 X_1 + P_2 X_2 + P_n^x N$$

where P values are probabilities and X values represent the reward or value expected from the weighted values of the expected outcomes and EX is the expected value of the result.

Expected value analysis combines classical probabilities with the subjective judgments of those most closely connected with the decision, and thus is a realistic way of building estimates where conditions can only be hypothesized, that is, where certainty is not possible. Essentially, this kind of analysis applies large number theory to a limited set of conditions; but if the situation is repeated often enough, then the types of judgments that would apply in a large-number situation rule in the single case.

Some of the same kinds of application of large number theory are used in the payoff matrix, which attempts to deal with decision making under uncertainty in a set of environments with varying risk characteristics. In this approach, a number of alternative strategies are recognized, and states of nature that may obtain in the face of these strategies are determined. States of nature typically are shown in the columns of the matrix, while strategies are represented in the rows. The very simple decision matrix shown in Figure 7.2 indicates how the payoff matrix might be used to make decisions with two given strategies and two postulated states of nature.[7]

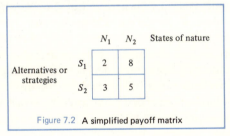

Figure 7.2   A simplified payoff matrix

In Figure 7.2 N_1 and N_2 might represent two possible states of business conditions, for example, prosperity or a recession, and S_1 and S_2 might indicate possible returns from selling a product in two different sales territories. The values in the cells of the matrix are subjective, since they depend upon estimates. The final choice of strategies is in part subjective also, since it must be made according to a criterion or rule chosen from a number of alternative decision criteria.

What decision criteria are commonly used by decision makers? Four approaches have been widely used, even though others can, and have, been

---

[7] A much more detailed application of the payoff matrix approach appears on pp. 261–267.

adopted in a variety of situations.[8] Using one popular criterion, the chosen strategy would maximize average payoff or expected value. If the probability of occurrence of each state of nature is equal, then the expected payoffs for the given matrix, since P equals one half, would be

$$S_1 = \tfrac{1}{2}(2) + \tfrac{1}{2}(8) = 5$$
$$S_2 = \tfrac{1}{2}(3) + \tfrac{1}{2}(5) = 4$$

The optimal strategy would, according to this criterion, be S_1, since it yields the greatest average payoff.

In a second approach, the biggest or most optimistic return would be chosen. Again S_1 would be selected, this time because it contains the biggest potential payoff. Since decision makers using this method know that luck or optimism is not always the best criterion for selection, they have developed a coefficient of optimism by which they discount the high payoff figure. This coefficient is calculated by determining a weighted probability of occurrences of both the highest and the lowest payoffs in the matrix. If, for example, this coefficient is considered to be 0.7 (the likelihood of the highest payoff being achieved) then the expected payoff would be

$$0.7(8) + 0.3(2) = \text{expected payoff}$$
$$5.6 \quad + 0.6 \quad = 6.2$$

The likelihood of return would be 6.2, and the choice would still be S_1 with its optimistic, highest possible payoff level.

A third criterion uses an avoidance-of-loss strategy. It attempts to choose the alternative that gives the greatest return without a possibility of loss. In our example, S_1 would yield a return of either 2 or 8, while S_2 would yield either 3 or 5. Therefore, S_2 would be chosen because its worst position (3) exceeds the worst return (2) that could result if S_1 were pursued.

The fourth criterion, that of regret, bases its decision on hindsight, since it attempts to postulate how regretful a decision maker might be if his choice differed from the alternative that did materialize. Regret is measured by the difference between what did occur and what could have occurred if the decision maker had been able to predict the future with absolute certainty. To illustrate, in this approach the maximum payoff in each column would have to be subtracted from every other payoff in the column, giving the following results:

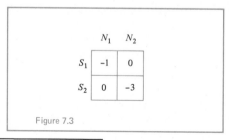

Figure 7.3

[8] See David W. Miller and Martin K. Starr, *Executive Decisions and Operations Research* (Englewood Cliffs, N.J.: Prentice-Hall, Inc., 1960).

Zero would represent an optimum in each column and the choice between columns might be selected in accordance with some other criterion such as the maximin approach. Using the maximin criterion S_1 would be selected, since it presents a maximum of the minimum regret situations.

Most statistical inference and decision theory principles are on the upswing in terms of both usage and sophistication. They have been adopted in a wide range of business situations and in nonbusiness areas such as the development of strategy and tactics in war. A more detailed and specialized application in the field of labor relations is shown in the following excerpt:

PROBABILITY CONCEPTS APPLIED TO LABOR RELATIONS-EVALUATION OF A STRIKE-SETTLEMENT STRATEGY[9]

Even though the development of value and probability systems is highly individualistic, it is possible to construct a general illustration of how such determinations might be made. Such an illustration can serve only as the starting point for the construction of more sophisticated analyses and is therefore offered as a first step rather than as a firm and final solution. After this caution, an example of the use of probability techniques to analyze a strike decision appears below, starting with the following suppositions:[10]

1. Our firm can sell its single product at either of the following prices:

    $200 per unit
    $210 per unit

2. We have one competitor who can sell his single product, which is slightly inferior to ours, at the following prices:

    $210 per unit
    $200 per unit
    $190 per unit

3. Prices, once set, will not be changed during the year, and under no circumstances will our competitor's prices exceed our price.

4. Our union is asking for a new cafeteria that will cost $150,000. If we fail to grant this demand, there is a 6 out of 10 chance that the union will call a strike (and a 4 out of 10 chance that there will be no strike). This (.6) probability of a strike is taken from the best estimates and experience of the committee of experts we set up during the data-gathering procedure.

5. Expected unit costs in the next year will be:

---

[9] From John G. Hutchinson, *Management Under Strike Conditions* (New York: Holt, Rinehart and Winston, Inc., 1966), pp. 148–154.

[10] Most of the credit for developing this illustration belongs to my able colleague, Professor E. Kirby Warren of the Columbia Graduate School of Business.

Expected unit cost	In event of strike	In event of no strike
3,000–10,000 units	$205	$175
Less than 3,000 units	$230	$200

Given the above information, we set out to combine our potential sales and profit forecasts with the probabilities of a strike. Our object is to find out just how high we can afford to go in a counteroffer to the union. That is, we want to decide at what point the cost of granting the union's demands will exceed the revenue gained by avoiding a strike. This point is really a strike's break-even point and, like all break-even points, is a helpful bench mark in the decision process. Although not the end of the trail, it is a long step along the way toward making an economically sound decision.

Suppose now that we forecast our sales and price-volume combinations on the basis of the most likely occurrences in the year's product market. Moreover, suppose that we want to consider the effect of a probable strike on these volumes. Based on the facts already presented, our committee's forecast might show the following information:

TABLE 7.5   FORECASTS OF SALES VOLUME AND STRIKE PROBABILITY

Our Price	Their Price	Our Volume	Probability of Price-Volume Combination*	Strike	No Strike
$200	$190	5000	0.6	0.6	0.4
$200	$200	9000	0.4	0.6	0.4
$210	$190	3000	0.4	0.6	0.4
$210	$200	4000	0.5	0.6	0.4
$210	$210	8000	0.1	0.6	0.4

* Based on our committee's judgment.

But we know when we look at Table 7.7 that the possibilities of gaining one profit rather than another are not equal. There is not much chance that our competitor will cut his price to $200 just because we change ours to $200. We therefore have to make adjustments in terms of the probability of making the profits shown in Table 7.7. The probability, say, of making a profit of $125,000 depends on our charging $200, our competitor charging $190, and a no strike situation. The combined probabilities, that is, the probabilities of these things happening at once, equal the product of the individual probabilities (in statistical jargon, the intersection of two sets). If the $200 (our price) and $190 (their price) figures have a .6 probability, and the probability of there not being a strike is .4, then the probability of getting a $125,000 profit is .24 (.6 × .4). In other words, we would, in the circumstances given in this example, obtain a $125,000 profit in 24 out of 100 occurrences.

TABLE 7.6   PRICE-PROBABILITY-PROFITS MATRIX

	Our Price	Their Price	Our Cost	Our Unit Profit	Our Volume	Our Total Profit	Combined Prob-ability*
	$200	$190	$175	25	4000	$125,000	0.24
(0.4)	200	200	175	25	9000	225,000	0.16
No strike	210	190	175	35	3000	105,000	0.16
Probability†	210	200	175	35	4000	140,000	0.20
	210	210	175	35	8000	280,000	0.04
	200	190	205	−5	5000	−25,000	0.36
(0.6)	200	200	295	−5	9000	−45,000	.024
Strike	210	190	205	5	3000	15,000	0.24
Probability	210	200	205	5	4000	20,000	0.30
	210	210	205	5	8000	40,000	0.06

* Probability of price-volume combination multiplied by the probability of a strike or of no strike.
† Again, the probability weightings are based on subjective evaluations of those best qualified to assess the situation. With the use of advanced calculating devices, any number of such projections might be made.

TABLE 7.7   PAYOFF MATRIX

	Their Price	Their Price	Their Price	Their Price	Their Price	Their Price
	$190 (Strike)	$200 (Strike)	$210 (Strike)	$190 No Strike	$200 No Strike	$210 No Strike
Our Price $200	$−25,000	$−45,000	$—*	$125,000	$225,000	$—
Our Price $210	$15,000	$20,000	$40,000	$105,000	$140,000	$280,000

* Remember, our competitor will never exceed our price.

In Table 7.8, this elementary example of the development of a probability prediction system reaches its final step. Table 7.8 restates the materials in the payoff matrix shown in Table 7.7 in terms of combined probability.

TABLE 7.8   COMBINED PROBABILITY-PROFIT MATRIX

	Their Price	Their Price	Their Price	Their Price	Their Price	Their Price
	$190 (Strike)	$200 (Strike)	$210 (Strike)	$190 No Strike	$200 No Strike	$210 No Strike
Our Price $200	(0.36) $—25,000	(0.24) $—45,000	(0) $—	(0.24) $125,000	(0.16) $225,000	(0) $—
Our Price $210	(0.24) $15,000	(0.30) $20,000	(0.06) $40,000	(0.16) $105,000	(0.20) $140,000	(0.04) $280,000

Suppose we were faced with deciding among the alternatives shown in Table 7.8. What would be our best choice? To put it another way, what value system can we attach to our probability system in order to establish a decision rule that will help us make a final choice among the profit alternatives outlined above? Before we go to the solution stage, we should consider some alternative methods of evaluating such a matrix. In other words, we need to review the various forms of decision criteria that we might apply to our hypothetical profit matrix in order to set up an individual value system.

Of the many approaches we might select, two are used widely. The first of these criteria is called the LaPlace (or average payoff) criteria. For the sake of simplicity let us suppose we faced the price-volume-strike *versus* the no-strike situation 100 times. On the basis of the LaPlace criterion, our best action would be reflected in the best average payoff of the various (possible) situations.

If we charge $200, our competitor can charge $190 or $200 in either a strike or a no-strike situation. Using the LaPlace criterion, the following calculation would apply:

Payoff (See Table 7.8)	Number of Occurrences	Total Payoffs
— 25,000	36	$— 900,000
— 45,000	24	$—1,080,000
+125,000	24	$ 3,000,000
+225,000	16	$ 3,600,000
	100	$ 4,620,000

$$\frac{\$4,620,000}{100} = \$46,200, \text{ average payoff for \$200 price.}$$

When a similar method is used the average payoff for the $210 price would be $68,000.

If we were to select the Wald or the Minimax criterion we would attempt to identify the best of all minimum risk payoffs available to us. Or, to put it another way, the Wald criterion seeks to adopt a strategy where the worst thing that can happen is better than the worst thing that can occur if we choose any other course of action. For example, in Table 7.8

the worst thing that could happen at the $200 price is a $45,000 loss. The worst thing that could happen at the $210 price is a $15,000 gain. In the Wald or the Minimax approach (the second approach in general use), our strategy would be to select the $210 price.

Another choice open is the use of the maximum return approach. This method dictates the selection of the greatest return available without regard to its probable outcome. We simply choose the largest absolute payoff and set our price. In Table 7.8 the $280,000 return would determine that our product be priced at $210. In cases where gambling is either necessary or feasible, this criterion may be selected.[11]

Individual degrees of conservatism, the utility curve for money, or the gambler's instinct may all affect the choice among the various decision criteria. Once the choice is made, however, the decision model has a value system to attach to its probability system, and a decision rule is ready to be formulated.

Going back to the 100 decisions for a moment, it is almost certain that the problem outlined in the illustration will not occur 100 times. But even if the decision occurs only once, the use of weighted averages still seems to be sensible as long as the same approach is used in a large number of different decisions. Continued use of weighted averages means a statistical playing of the percentages that pays off in the long run. If you cannot afford to take a loss or if you need specific sums of money to cover specific short-run obligations, you might use some other method of evaluating decisions—the Wald method, for example. In general, the average payoff approach seems to be a sensible criterion—which accounts for its widespread acceptance.

If we follow one line of reasoning and use the average payout approach as our decision criteria, how might we evaluate the relative costs and returns from a no-strike situation as opposed to one where a strike might occur?

Considering expected profits in this situation where we are certain that no strike will take place, we could derive Table 7.9.

TABLE 7.9   EXPECTED PROFIT WITH NO STRIKE A CERTAINTY

Our Price	Their Price	Our Profit	Probability of Price-Volume Combination	Probability of No Strike	Combined Probability	Expected Profit
$200	$190	$125,000	0.6	1	0.6	$165,000
$200	$200	$225,000	0.4	1	0.4	$165,000
$210	$190	$105,000	0.4	1	0.4	$140,000
$210	$200	$140,000	0.5	1	0.5	$140,000
$210	$210	$228,000	0.1	1	0.1	$140,000

[11] If an embezzler has a shortage of $100,000 and auditors are due next Tuesday, the 100 to 1 shot at the racetrack presents an inviting (but slim) probability of deliverance.

TABLE 7.10   EXPECTED PROFITS IN CONDITIONS OF CERTAINTY
AND UNCERTAINTY

Our Price	Expected Profit with Strike a Possibility	Expected Profit with No Strike a Certainty
$200	$46,200	$165,000*
$210	$68,000	$140,000

* This is determined by multiplying combined probability by profits, as in this example:

$$0.4 \times 225,000 = \$ 90,000$$
$$0.6 \times 125,000 = \underline{\$ 75,000}$$
$$\$165,000$$

The best price in a no-strike situation would be $200, since a profit of $165,000 would result. In an uncertain strike situation, a price of $210 and a $68,000 profit seems to be best. On this basis we could set our price at $200 and pay up to $97,000 ($165,000 − $68,000 = $97,000) if we were sure that no strike would result following such an offer.

Of course, other matters could affect our decision, but we have here an economic way of looking at a decision using our own probability estimates and our own value system.

No doubt the example described above seems crude to those used to more sophisticated probability techniques. But consider the refinements that could be added by more detailed analyses programmed on computers able to handle several thousands of price-volume-strike-profit probabilities. If this mass attack is combined with a technique for ascertaining the sensitivity of the affected variables, the relative accuracies of individual items in each array can be reviewed and evaluated. This sensitivity analysis (analysis of sources and magnitude of probable errors), if interpreted in terms of the validity of the subjective weightings assigned by our decision-making group, can provide useful guides to the relative validity of projected estimates of costs, profits, revenues, and prices.

During the analysis, weighting, and evaluation stages, probable outcomes of various solutions are reported and analyzed. The final choice among these alternatives depends on the decision rule or rules guiding the model. The controlling rule might be to utilize the Wald or the LaPlace (or highest absolute payoff) criterion as a guide to decision. Individual firms can, of course, develop unique criteria or utilize some variation on the themes presented in the foregoing illustration.

Many of the techniques and approaches used above have been important in the development of decision models, a classification of decision-making which seems important enough to be treated as a separate entity.

SPECIALIZED DECISION MODELS

Decision models have come to represent the basic elements of decision making in terms of some specified relationships, usually expressed in the forms of equations or structured games. The linear-programming techniques in operations research, for example, are one manifestation of a class of decision models. Another is the area known as game theory. A third widely used set of decision models are the mathematical formulae used to represent inventory and production flows.

Linear programming is a mathematical technique for determining optimum solutions to problems having linear relationships. Most economic problems attempt either to maximize a linear objective such as profit or to minimize a linear function such as cost. Linear programming in this case becomes a way of representing relationships between cost and profit variables as a system of equations. With a given mix of resources, with given limitations on what can be done, and with linear relationships existing between variables, an operating situation can be represented or simulated in systems of linear inequalities. These systems of equations can then be solved through a series of trial-and-error steps called iterations, which eventually indicate an optimizing or minimizing condition. For example, in an auto company there may be limitations on motors, stampings, and body styles, and also restriction on what models in the line can be sold in various markets. In order to maximize profit, the company must determine which product mix will yield the greatest profit within the limits placed on output by the existing equipment and machinery. If the relationships between these variables are linear, then this particular program can be set up as a system of linear inequalities. This has been done in many auto firms. In oil refineries, the quality of the output depends on the nature of the crude oil being fed into the product, the processing steps, and the various products that can be cracked off at different temperatures with differences in resultant yields. These yields are related to the profitability of marketing the different profit lines, and they can be represented in a matrix that simulates refinery operations in terms of costs and profits. Still a third example of linear programming would be a firm which has scarce resources, say, limitations on metals available to them, and a series of products that can be made from these materials. The relationships between the raw materials (metal) inputs, and the product lines resulting from the combination of these metals can be set up in linear-programming form to determine the product mix which would be most profitable. Because many business situations do have straight-line relationships between variables, linear-programming techniques are used widely.

Game theory is another decision-making technique that utilizes a model of reality in which choices are not only available but opponents also have a strategy and can decide their actions on the basis of what they think their opponent will do. In contrast to linear programming, game theory assumes there is a conscious opponent who has his own objective-seeking strategy.

Game theory concepts seek to guide decision makers to a selection of strategy that has the best probability of success, given an opponent with a strategy of his own. Most game theory assumes a rational opponent who is seeking to optimize something, usually economic gain. It further visualizes an environment in which the gains of one person are losses to his opponent. This type of situation is called a two-person, zero-sum game.

Game theory uses the payoff matrix approach to determine which strategy is superior within a given set of assumptions. In the matrix, strategies, states of nature, and possible payoffs are similar to those shown earlier in this chapter in the section on statistical methods. If the two opponents in a game situation are intelligent besinessmen, for example, each will choose an objective in the light of what is best for him, but will not forget that his opponent is acting similarly. If the first man assumes some rational behavior pattern on his opponent's part, he can guess what choices his competitor will make and select his own best course of action accordingly. Given his opponent's postulated course of actions, he will be able to assess alternative payoffs, and build a strategy that gives himself the highest *probable* yield. Since the game situation allows the decision maker to calculate potential payoffs for any number of possible actions and reactions of both parties in a set of conditions, a real competitive environment can be simulated almost completely with the game theory model. With the range of payoffs from these sets of circumstances available, the decision maker is able to determine those strategies holding out the best chance of success from all strategies available to him at a given time. Unfortunately, if the opponent is not rational, the results are not quite as deterministic as in situations where the rationality assumption holds true. Under conditions of nonrationality a whole new set of possibilities opens up, which makes game theory analysis much more complicated and far less definitive. As more and more information on market behavior develops, however, game theory becomes an increasingly utilitarian aid to the decision maker.

INVENTORY DECISION MODELS

Inventory models are decision models covering situations different from those represented in game theory. Among inventory models the economic lot size, or economic order quantity (EOQ), model is perhaps the best known. In this particular model, an attempt is made to determine purchase lot sizes that will minimize both order and carrying costs, the two chief cost components of inventory management. As a generalization, the fewer the number of orders written, the lower the order cost; that is, order cost declines directly with increases in lot size. On the other hand, carrying charges increase because interest costs, rental on storage space, property taxes and insurance, obsolescence of inventories, and deterioration begin to appear as larger lots of inventory sit in storage. Economic lot size models try to detect the point where total costs are lowest by balancing the difference between carrying costs per unit and setup costs per unit. One simple formula showing this relationship is:

$$Q = \frac{2RS}{I}$$

in which Q equals the economic lot size, R equals annual usage of the item in units per year, S equals the setup cost each time a new order is placed, and I equals the carrying costs per unit per year. This is shown in graphic form in Figure 7.4. Point Q is where the total of order costs and carrying costs are at a minimum, that is, the optimum lot size. It would thus pay in this example to order approximately once every four months.

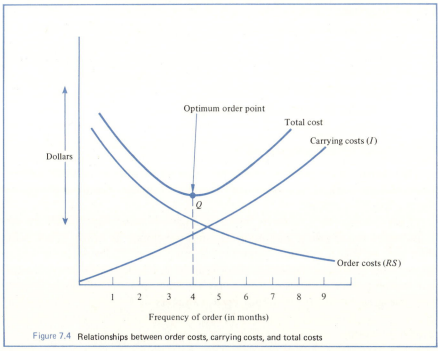

Figure 7.4 Relationships between order costs, carrying costs, and total costs

This generalized model of the economic lot size can be adapted to reflect the number of other factors and to apply the specific facts and specific areas or plants. In short, in order for this model to work effectively, it must be adapted to meet specific circumstances—conditions should not be adapted to fit the model. This particular formulation is extremely simplistic, but when allowances are made for multiproduct lines and for factors such as discounts and out-of-stock costs, the models become much more complex. They are nonetheless useful for decision making in many facets of purchasing and inventory control.

The use of Linear programming, game theory, and economic lot size models are techniques now enjoying growing popularity. They offer assistance in solving both general and specific problems, and their use seems destined to increase in the near future.

Summary

This chapter has not attempted to chronicle every decision-making technique; rather it has attempted to develop an overview of those methods which are in widespread use and which hold promise of continuing usage in the future. Some of the techniques in this chapter are complete in themselves. Others are much more fragmentary in their development or their ability to carry out a complete set of steps leading to a final decision.

Though classification of decision-making techniques is difficult, the following listing indicates the range of methods now in use:

1. Judgmental techniques
2. Principles of management
3. Systems models
4. Behavioral techniques
5. Heuristic approaches
6. Economical and financial techniques
7. Statistical methods
8. Specialized decision models

This classification is in no particular order of excellence or development, since decision making involves using the most suitable techniques available for the specific problem.

Great changes are now taking place in information handling which are sure to influence the decision-making techniques developed in future years. More than ever before, it is vitally important to keep up with developments, techniques, and methodologies in the field of decision making. This chapter points out contemporary aids to decision making and indicates which techniques hold the greatest utility for tomorrow's managers.

Study Questions

1. For what kinds of decisions are judgmental techniques most appropriate? Give examples from your experience.
2. What role do principles of management play in the decision-making process?
3. How does marginal analysis differ from other evaluation techniques? What are its advantages and disadvantages?
4. Why is rate of return used so widely as a financial yardstick? Is payback ever better than rate of return? Why or why not?
5. What does discounting of cash flows mean? What does discounting show the decision maker above and beyond calculations made with nondiscounted cash flows?
6. What principles underlie the industrial use of statistical quality control? How does statistics enter into forecasting? Give examples of statistical methods used in decision making.

7. What is expected value, and how does it relate to traditional methods of statistical decision making?

8. What is a payoff matrix? Describe the kinds of criteria which may be invoked to forge decision rules from stated payoffs. Which of these criteria seem to you most meaningful? Justify your choice. What qualifications enter into your justification?

9. What are the chief problems connected with the use of game theory? What contributions can game theory make to decision making? Develop a mathematical example illustrating how game theory relates strategy determination to decision making.

10. What is an economic order quantity (EOQ), sometimes called economic lot size? What is the nature of the theory underlying the calculation of an EOQ?

11. What are some behavioral techniques entering into decison making? Do you agree that these techniques will be used more extensively in the future?

12. Does group participation improve the quality and quantity of decisions? Try to justify your answer with factual information gleaned at work or in classroom activity.

13. How might the decision-making techniques and approaches described in this chapter be related to the four analytical frameworks presented in Chapter 3?

Hurry Up and Wait

Ed Phillips, office manager in the Washington State Education Department's Seattle office, noticed that clerical and professional employees constantly had to wait in line at the central supply office to obtain the books, supplies, forms, and equipment needed to perform their jobs. Since some of the materials distributed were costly, setting up several loosely controlled supply centers was ruled out as a practical solution. Phillips wondered if putting another service person on the supply center window would be feasible, and he called upon his recent experience in an office methods course at a local university to provide the answer. He came upon an approach which seemed ideally suited to his purpose: a queueing formula in the form

$$W = \frac{S^2 + G^2}{2(a - s)}$$

The notation, which was based on a Poisson distribution, showed the following relationship:

W = expected waiting time (the probable wait time)

S = time taken to service each arrival

A = average arrival time interval

G = standard variation from average service time

2 = a constant

After deciding to give the formula a try, Mr. Phillips collected the following data on the arrivals and departures at the central supply office:

One attendant serviced the clerical and professional people coming to the office.

The average time to serve each person was four minutes, with a one-minute variation.

On the average, 96 persons came to the central supply each day in a 480-minute work day.

$$\frac{480}{96} = 5 \text{ minutes per arrival}$$

Plugging these results into the formula, Mr. Phillips calculated an 8½-minute average wait (W):

$$W = \frac{(4)^2 + (1)^2}{2\,(5-4)} = \frac{17}{2} = 8\frac{1}{2} \text{ minutes}$$

He further calculated that adding one more man at the supply window would cut service time by a minute, an act which the formula showed would reduce the wait time to 2½ minutes:

$$W = \frac{(3)^2 + (1)^2}{2\,(5-3)} = \frac{10}{4} = 2\frac{1}{2} \text{ minutes}$$

1.   How many hours of professional and clerical employees time would be saved by adding the second man?

2.   What circumstances would make it economical to add the second man?

Zandski Machine Tool Company

Herman Dorshin, chief order clerk for Zandski's manufacturing department, received a note from President Bill Zandski, inquiring whether Herman was using techniques designed to keep inventory costs at their lowest possible point. In fact, Herman was not, since his ordering was based more on past experience than on careful analysis. To study and improve his procedures he picked out two products and tried to calculate order quantities that would keep costs to a minimum (the economic order quantity). Herman's preliminary data on the two selected products are shown in Table II.1.

TABLE II.1   COST AND USAGE INFORMATION

	Product A	Product B
Monthly use rate	$20.00	$50.00
Average safety stock (minimum level desired)	1 month	1 month
Carrying charge on inventory	10 percent	10 percent
Cost per order	$1.00	$2.00

Herman further determined he ordered product A every four months and product B every six months.

1.   In order to keep costs at a minimum, should Herman order these products more often, less often, or with the same frequency? Justify your answer.

The Webster Company

Scientists at the Webster Company (WEBCO) have developed a new personal product, a deodorant, which, because of a newly discovered chemical, offers substantial cost and use advantages. According to WEBCO's marketing and production staff, the new discovery will allow longer periods of protection for users at about half the current cost of competitive products. Financial projections on the new product's cost and revenue flows indicate the company can, for a total outlay of $120,000 over four years, gain a ten-year income flow of $850,000 (see Table II.2). WEBCO management expects that competitors will not be able to catch up for at least three years; after that they can only guess how competition may affect sales.

Assuming that a discount rate of 20 percent is valid, and after reviewing the following figures, would you recommend that WEBCO undertake this investment?

TABLE II.2   FINANCIAL PROJECTION FOR THE NEW PRODUCT

Year	Added costs in current dollars	Projected net income	20-percent discount factor (end of year)	Liklihood of reaching income projection
1	$50,000	$ 10,000	.833	1.00
2	30,000	30,000	.694	1.00
3	20,000	60,000	.578	1.00
4	20,000	150,000	.482	.90
5	....	100,000	.402	.80
6	....	100,000	.335	.60
7	....	100,000	.279	.40
8	....	100,000	.233	.30
9	....	100,000	.194	.25
10	....	100,000	.162	.20

1. How strongly do you feel about your recommendation? What basis do you have for your stand? What reservations?

Shediac Company[1]

DECISION WHETHER TO MEET COMPETITIVE PRICE

The executives of the Shediac Company, a manufacturer of rubber footwear, were confronted with a pricing problem. They learned that on a highly competitive item of footwear, which had accounted for 10 percent of the company's physical volume of sales last year, other manufacturers planned to reduce their prices substantially for the next selling season. It was proposed that the Shediac Company either make some price reduction or discontinue manufacture of this item of footwear for the season. The Shediac Company had fairly steady sales and production throughout the year on its business in the aggregate; but this particular item was produced and sold only during five months in the fall and winter, when activity in some of the company's other

---

[1] From *Problems in Business Economics* by M.P. McNair and R.S. Merviam. Copyright 1941 by McGraw-Hill, Inc., pp. 197–199. Used with permission of McGraw-Hill Book Company.

product groups was relatively low. The item was trademarked, but it was very similar in quality and service to several competing articles. It was advertised only as part of the company's general line.

From past experience, the Shediac Company had learned that attempts to sell this product at prices much above those of competitors resulted in large losses of sales. The sales manager estimated that if competing prices were lower than the Shediac Company's, unit sales would be as follows:[2]

Shediac Company's Price	Expected Competitive Price	Estimated Units to be sold by Shediac Company
65¢	55¢	150,000
60	55	275,000
55	55	470,000

In the last fiscal year, 470,000 units of the product under discussion had been sold to retailers at a net price of 65 cents per unit; retailers had secured a gross margin ranging from 30% to 35%. Previously, the price had been maintained at 65 cents net, and all producers had enjoyed steady sales. The sales manager was confident that for the next selling season the competitive price would be cut to 55 cents net per unit. The company had no lower-price items which it could effectively substitute in sales to retailers, because the latter were unwilling to attempt substitution of inferior goods. Retailers had found in the past that inferior goods of the Shediac line were not well received, since there were on the market products of approximately similar character that could be had at prices somewhat below the prices charged for the Shediac Company products. Superior quality of the product made by the Shediac Company and its competitors, so long as maintained, apparently was conducive to ready sales.

The sales manager of the Shediac Company did not expect that the volume lost by discounting the item under consideration would be replaced by any resulting increase in the sales of other Shediac articles. At the same time, he did not anticipate a general increase in the sales of other products to such an extent that there would be any production difficulties in turning out the product if the company decided to keep it in the line. On the infrequent occasions in the past when the company had refused to meet competitive prices and had temporarily discontinued manufacturing certain items, the sales of such products had been easily regained when, at a later time, the company resumed manufacture of the discontinued items in the line and offered them at competitive prices.

All of the company's products were sold direct to retailers by the same force of salesmen. Salesmen were paid a salary and a commission of one cent a unit. Frequency of call and number of customers called on would

---

[2] Throughout this case, the "unit" is one pair.

not be affected, executives concluded, by the decision reached on the product under discussion.

The products manufactured by the Shediac Company all were made by nearly the same processing procedure. Each item in the line went through the eight departments of the plant and required almost the same proportion of the total manufacturing time in each department. According to the company's usual method of cost calculation, the cost per unit for the next selling season would be 61.22 cents, made up as shown in Table II.3.

TABLE II.3   SHEDIAC COMPANY COST SCHEDULE

Department	Burden Rate (Percentage of Direct Labor)	Direct Labor	Burden*	Direct Labor Plus Burden
1	150%	$0.0020	$0.0030	$0.0050
2	200	0.0083	0.0166	0.0249
3	135	0.0099	0.0134	0.0233
4	143	0.0314	0.0449	0.0763
5	83	0.0431	0.0358	0.0789
6	92	0.0261	0.0240	0.0501
7	85	0.0328	0.0279	0.0607
8	110	0.0085	0.0094	0.0179

Total direct labor and department burden	$0.3371
Materials	0.2000
Supplies	0.0152
Packages	0.0175
Spoilage	0.0331
Royalty	0.0115†
Total	$0.5844
Sales expense	0.0278
Total cost	$0.6122

* Burden charges based on assumed volume of 470,000 units. $50,000 of the total annual burden is fixed expense; the balance varies with volume.

† On actual production only; no minimum.

1. Restate the cost schedule to reflect costs which are pertinent to a decision on whether to stay in the market and, if so, at what price.

2. Indicate how you would decide on a best price if you decide not to discontinue this product line.

American Circle Company (A)

In September 1966, Mr. John A. Arthur, president of the American Circle Company (ACCO), presented to ACCO's nine-man board of directors a recommendation that ACCO merge with the Stenco Corporation. Mr. Arthur's proposal stemmed from two sources: (1) his desire to diversify and expand ACCO's product lines and (2) his belief that ACCO's management could turn Stenco's operating losses into profits within a reasonable time period. Though the board was expected to scrutinize his recommendations quite closely, he felt that any opposition would disappear once the board recognized the long-run potential offered by the acquisition of Stenco's production facilities and product line. Mr. Arthur was naturally concerned about a recent deterioration of Stenco's market position, but he felt that ACCO's management was experienced enough to reverse this trend in short order. On balance, Mr. Arthur viewed the recommended merger in a very optimistic light.[1]

At the same time that John Arthur presented his merger proposal to ACCO's Board of Directors, John Stenco, the president of Stenco Incorporated, made a similar presentation to his board. William Bartholdy, an influential Stenco board member, asked for time to study the merger in detail. Several board members shared Mr. Bartholdy's concern, and approval was delayed until the November fifteenth meeting of the board.

In the past two years, Mr. Bartholdy, a major shareholder (20,000 shares), had lost confidence in John Stenco because of the losses suffered by the firm under Mr. Stenco's leadership and because he believed that Mr. Stenco had devoted too little time to his duties as chief operating officer. Though Mr. Bartholdy had never said so publicly, he felt that Mr. Stenco had deliberately tried to build up Stenco's losses to make the corporation more attractive (in terms of tax writeoffs) to firms seeking a merger. His suspicions along this line were reinforced by a provision in the ACCO proposal which guaranteed Mr. Stenco a salary of $1,500 per month for sixty months as a consultant to the surviving firm. Bartholdy was uncertain whether Mr. Stenco was recommending merger for his own personal gain or for the good of all stockholders.

In order to gain an outside viewpoint, he hired the firm of Peters, Kelly, Hanson, & Kelly Associates to analyze the merger. Though he engaged the firm as a private individual, he intended to use the consultant's report to block a merger if merger seemed unwise.[2]

On November tenth, Mr. Bartholdy received the consultant's final report. What he saw there convinced him that the analysis was quite thorough and factual. He was, however, quite concerned with the tenor of a key recommendation. The report and covering letter appear on p. 158.

---

[1] The impact of the merger on ACCO's Chairman of the Board, Herbert Kennedy, is described in ACCO (B) in the cases for Section III. Though the financial data in the two cases are similar, the issues and variables facing Mr. Kennedy and Mr. Bartholdy are not. Thus, the two ACCO cases, (A) and (B), can be used separately or assigned in sequence without a great deal of redundancy.

[2] In this, his position was similar to that taken by Mr. Herbert Kennedy, Board Chairman of the American Circle Company in ACCO (B).

Peters, Kelly, Hanson, & Kelly Associates
New York, New York
November 10, 1966

Mr. William Bartholdy
Banks Building
East 72nd Street
New York, New York

Dear Mr. Bartholdy:

This letter and the attached report contain an analysis of the pending merger between the American Circle Company and the Stenco Corporation.

The information offered is confidential and personal. If you discuss our recommendations with anyone, you will lessen the value of the suggestions and you may embarrass those who helped us to gather some of the more sensitive material.

The report outlines several courses of action which you could conceivably pursue. You can approve and support the merger, fight the merger, sell your stock on the open market, or vote your 20,000 shares against the merger and ask for fair value of your shares. We suggest that you follow the latter plan for reasons contained in the body of the report.

If you have any questions or desire clarification of specific suggestions, I will be in my office throughout the next two weeks.

Sincerely yours,

John Ringer Kelly
President

TO: Mr. William Bartholdy
FROM: Mr. John Ringer Kelly
SUBJECT: Pending merger between the American Circle Company and the Stenco Corporation

SUMMARY OF FINDINGS

We believe that there are four possible positions you might choose to take in regard to the pending ACCO-Stenco merger:

Approve and support the merger. This is desirable under certain circumstances detailed later in this report.

Fight the merger. We do not believe that this course of action is desirable. Continuing in business or fighting the merger to gain better terms are less favorable than other courses of action.

Sell your stock on the open market. This we do not advise, since there are market and tax gains which can be realized from the ACCO merger.

Vote against the merger and ask for fair cash value of your shares. If less than 6 percent of Stenco stockholders vote against merger and ask for fair cash value of their shares, the merger will stilll be consummated as long as a majority of shareholders vote approval. Since fair cash value is greater than market value of Stenco stock upon which the 7.5:1 exchange ratio is derived, you stand to gain the difference between fair cash value and market value of your shares. We estimate that for your 20,000 shares this gain would be approximately $15,000. This would be a net gain in that no tax would have to be paid on Stenco shares, since they would have been purchased by you at a market value higher than their present cash value. An analysis of these choices indicates that number 4 is the most desirable from a personal point of view. A detailed review of each choice appears below.

APPROVE AND SUPPORT THE MERGER

To show why approval and support of the pending merger is advisable under certain conditions it is necessary to examine the structures of the two merging companies.

THE AMERICAN CIRCLE COMPANY

Products and employment. ACCO has 1,500 employees who make machined parts and die castings for automotive, electrical, appliance, plumbing, and replacement markets. ACCO has a reputation for making good quality products.

Property. ACCO property is located in both Michigan and Alabama. In Detroit, Michigan, ACCO owns some relatively outmoded production facilities which will be taken over by the American Stackpile Corporation on March 31, 1968. The sale price is $827,500 against a book value of $202,086. In Andersonville, Michigan, the Bartol division is housed in a one-story brick structure of 80,000 sq. ft. This building and additions were all built in the last six years. In Pontiac, Michigan, the die-casting division holdings are largely brick and steel structures with 95,000 sq. ft. of production and administrative facilities and 15,000 sq. ft. of warehouse space. Built in the last eight years, the die-casting division's modern buildings house new efficient die-casting and plating equipment. In Burnside, Alabama, ACCO has an option to buy 30,000 sq. ft. of modern buildings and fairly new die-casting equipment.

Management. ACCO is headed by Herbert Kennedy and John A. Arthur. Both men are vigorous, proven managers leading a capable management team. They appear to have the ability to provide good leadership for any future ventures undertaken by the American Circle Company.

General economic position. ACCO has been a successful operator in a highly competitive business for over forty years. ACCO holds only a small percentage of total sales in the machined parts and die-casting market, but it is highly regarded because of its quality products. The company is not dependent upon one large customer. One flaw in the ACCO picture is its occasional lack of dependability on delivery time. A summary of ACCO's recent sales and earnings figures appears below:

Year	Sales	Earnings	Earnings on Common Stock
1966 (7 mos.)	$ 9,100,697	$424,765	$1.05
1965	17,430,573	827,696	2.05
1964	6,484,578	176,541	1.01
1963	6,972,628	252,191	1.45
1962	6,502,888	335,653	1.93
1961	6,906,959	435,569	2.50

Note: Additional forecast data appear in Table II.

Capitalization and funded debt. ACCO has 500,000 authorized shares of common stock with a par value of $10.00. Issued and outstanding are 402,947.3 shares which include 46.3 shares of fractional scrip.

On September 11, 1966, ACCO had $625,000 in funded debt repayable at $37,500 per quarter starting on November 30, 1966. The last payment on this amount ($137,500) is due on February 28, 1970. The overall rate of interest payable is 4 percent. The loan requires that ACCO maintain a net working capital of $2,500,000 during the tenure of the loan. This limitation could restrict dividend payments, but similar arrangements in the past have not tended to do so.

THE STENCO CORPORATION

Sales, earnings, dividends, and working capital. The very difficult position of Stenco is shown by a listing of selected financial data.

Year	Sales	Earnings	Working Capital*	Dividends on Common Stock
1966	$11,895,531	($1,184,068)†	$ 352,222	(1.56)
1965	14,645,072	(705,881)	1,558,000	(0.92)
1964	11,950,558	(605,842)	1,651,000	(0.79)
1963	19,019,720	303,440	2,169,000	0.40
1962	15,540,258	41,535	1,757,000	0.05
1961	17,428,760	800,732	2,692,000	1.04

* Last three digits rounded for 1961–1965
† ( ) = Loss

These figures show a gradual decline in sales, a sharp drop in earnings, a marked deficit per share in dividends paid, and a working capital that had declined to $164,000 by September 1, 1966. Future indications are that working capital will be almost nonexistent by the end of the (1966) calendar year. No future improvement in sales and earnings is anticipated under existing operation conditions.

Management. The management of Stenco has become a liability to the corporation. Effective control over production and administration costs has been lost. Little management drive or imagination is evident. Instead of actively planning to counteract the operating losses of the past three years, management has adopted a relaxed and seemingly indifferent attitude toward these losses. When action was taken, it proved to be haphazard or ineffectual.

Stenco management has also lost some of its reputation because of a situation which finally resulted in the loss of a large Stenco customer. No chance remains of ever getting back this business unless ACCO is able to rectify the problems of the past.[1]

Favorable Aspects of Stenco. Stenco, in spite of its poor management and deteriorating market position, is still a salable commodity because of its good physical assets and the operating and capital loss tax credits which it offers to buyers. Stenco has modern plants and equipment in Hamtramck, Michigan, which include five new die-casting machines and modern plating equipment. These physical facilities are excellent, and there is reason to believe that ACCO can operate them at a profit. Stenco also has an operating and capital loss carry-over which could add up to $2.60 on each new share of stock if merger occurs. The details of this tax advantage are discussed more fully in subsequent paragraphs.

REASONS FOR SUPPORTING THE MERGER

There are several obvious reasons why you might want to support the merger.

First, you would obtain the stock of a going profitable concern for the stock of a failing, unprofitable company.

Second, you would gain ownership in a concern with an excellent management and good future growth prospects. This would enhance your chances of receiving dividends in future years. It should be noted that ACCO has paid dividends in all but two of its forty-four years of operation.

Third, you stand to gain $2.60 per share in terms of tax gains on the outstanding shares in the new corporation. The arithmetic of this tax advantage is as follows:

$1,734,000	Operating losses to June 30, 1966*
342,000	Capital loss carry-over to June 30, 1966*
224,000	Operating loss July 1, 1966, to August 31, 1966
400,000	Estimated operating loss to December 31, 1966†
$2,700,000	Estimated total tax credit

---

[1] To be more specific, the loss of this customer is allegedly due to personal problems existing between Mr. Stenco and key representatives of the customer's organization.

$2,358,000	Total operating loss carry-over
.52	Tax savings percentage
$1,266,160	Total operating carry-over tax saving
$ 342,000	Capital carry-over
.25	Tax savings percentage
$ 85,500	Total capital carry-over saving
$1,311,660	Actual tax credit gain to ACCO
$ 504,974	Total shares new company = $2.60
$2.60	Tax gain per new share

---

* Estimate.

† This is a conservative figure which projects the July–August loss forward to the end of the year.

This means a total gain for older ACCO shareholders of 402,947 times $2.60, or approximately $1,047,600, and a gain for new ACCO shareholders of 101,026 times $2.60, or approximately $264,000.

This means a total gain for older ACCO shareholders of 402,947 times $2.60, or approximately $1,047,600, and a gain for new ACCO shareholders of 101,026 times $2.60, or approximately $264,000. In addition, if ACCO is able to write off existing Stenco assets against ACCO profits there may be further credit available which would tend to lower the purchase price.

Fourth, there is a strong possibility that the market value of ACCO shares will not decline in value (in the long run) if the companies merge. Present value (November, 1966) of the outstanding shares of the two companies ($9,763,771) divided by the new shares outstanding after merger (503,947) shows an estimated new company market value of $19.40 per share. The exchange ratio of 7.5:1 would mean Stenco shareholders would gain the difference between the actual rate of exchange value of their holdings and the market value of the new securities. For your 20,000 shares this would work out in the following manner:

$$\frac{10}{75} \times 20,000 = \frac{200,000}{75} = 2,666 \; 2/3 \text{ shares of new ACCO stock}$$

$19.40 Potential new market value
 16.75 (7.5:1 ratio @ $2.25 market price on November 1, 1966)
$ 2.65 Potential gain per share

2,666 2/3 Number of shares of ACCO
    2.65 Potential gain per share
$7,086.66 2/3, or approximately $7,000 potential total gain

Adjustment may not take place as predicted here, but there is a strong possibility that such a movement will occur.

If we look at the book value figures for the merger, the picture does not appear to be as rosy as previously indicated. ACCO book value per share is currently $14.06, while Stenco is $2.98. The new corporation would have an estimated book value of $15.28 per share. Since book value is a somewhat nebulous concept, we suggest that the figures showing a potential loss here are almost meaningless. ACCO property, for instance, has a market value well above its book value. This is shown by the sale of one ACCO property for a figure 252 percent above its book value. In any case, book value figures are overbalanced by potential market and tax considerations.

FIGHT THE MERGER

The second general course of action you may take is to fight the merger. Here, there are three choices you may wish to consider.

One, you can urge liquidation of the company. This would be costly to you because of gains (already discussed) which the ACCO merger can bring. Another big objection here is that selling assets piecemeal might bring a lower total return than the proceeds from selling the business as a unit.

Two, you can urge that Stenco continue in business. This would be dangerous because of the state of Stenco's operations (principally, a loss of control over costs). Since Stenco's future is at best uncertain, your support of continuing operations would almost certainly mean forfeiting any chance to collect dividends for a long period of time. A final caution is the condition of Stenco's working capital. Our projections indicate that Stenco will be insolvent by the end of the calendar year (1966). Continuance in business could mean bankruptcy and a subsequent settlement at (most likely) a fractional value of your present holdings.

Finally, you could hold out for better merger terms. The difficulty here is that Stenco probably cannot avoid bankruptcy long enough to find another buyer if ACCO balks at more stringent terms of the merger. Again you would tend to take a chance on a large personal loss for what would amount to only slightly more favorable terms.

It is our opinion that fighting this merger would be both unwise and unprofitable. We believe that merger must occur, and rapidly, or Stenco will become bankrupt.

SELL YOUR STOCK ON THE OPEN MARKET

The sale of your Stenco stock on the open market would lose the tax credit value which Stenco offers as well as potential appreciation in the new ACCO issue you will receive at the time of merger. Perhaps the only thing in favor of selling is its simplicity. No other advantages are readily apparent.

VOTE AGAINST MERGER AND ASK FOR FAIR CASH VALUE OF YOUR SHARES

Section 44 of the General Corporation Laws of Michigan is presented in your proxy statement. The law deals with the rights of dissenting shareholders. In brief, the law provides that dissenters wishing to come under its provisions must vote against the merger, object to the merger and demand the fair cash value of affected shares (in writing) within twenty days after closing. This fair value is to be determined on shares as of the day prior to the merger. If no figure for fair value is reached by agreement between shareholders and the corporation, a three-member board will decide such value without consideration of appreciation or depreciation due to the merger. A final provision states that objectors lose voting rights and that only the corporation board of directors can approve withdrawal of objections to the sale.

We believe that this law offers you, as an individual shareholder, the most profitable course of action in regard to the pending merger. We suggest you vote your 20,000 shares against the merger and request the fair cash value of your holdings. With the proceeds from your settlement, you may then repurchase ACCO shares on the market. We believe that this will bring you a gain of approximately $15,000 in excess of what you would realize from simply approving the merger action. This statement is based upon the following reasoning:

1. Current value of Stenco shares on market $ 2.25
                   Your holdings in Stenco   20,000
                                             $45,000

Since Stenco's position does not appear to be improving, the $2.25 valuation probably will not be increased by the time the merger takes place.

2. The "fair cash value" of Stenco shares will not drop below the book value of $2.98. The impartial board cannot ignore the fact that the value of the relatively new Stenco plant and equipment is represented quite closely by the book value figures. The fair value of shares will probably be listed as $3.00 per share, since current book value per share is $2.98.

Fair value $ 3.00
Your Holdings   20,000
Total value $60,000

3. You will gain the difference ($0.75 per share) between market value on which Stenco-ACCO 7.5:1 ratio is based ($2.25) and the fair cash value of your shares ($3.00) if you follow the provisions of Section 44 as outlined above. This means net gain to you of $15,000. If you reinvest in ACCO at an estimated market price of $17 (shortly after the merger) you will

gain 882 added shares of ACCO with no additional cash investment. Even with ACCO at $20 you could gain 750 additional shares. These approximate figures would be somewhat reduced if brokerage and other fees are considered, but the overall gain would still be substantial.

4. Since you purchased Stenco shares originally at a price greater than $3.00 per share you have no capital gains tax to pay.

The one difficulty with the plan outlined is that your vote against the merger could cause its demise because of the clause invalidating merger negotiations if over 6 percent of Stenco shareholders dissent and ask for fair value. You now own 2.6 percent of Stenco. This allows only 3.4 percent of all other shareholders the right to dissent and ask for fair value and still have the merger take place. Though a failure to merge can mean substantial loss to you, the chance you take here is a calculated one. If your action causes the 6-percent figure to be exceeded, you can probably convince the board of directors to permit you to withdraw your objections. This would then allow the companies to merge but tend to cost you the $15,000 previously described, which would still be better than bankruptcy. There is little doubt that the board would object to withdrawal of your negating vote because the board wants the merger to occur.

If the 6-percent figure is not exceeded by your request for payment of fair value, you stand to gain all the tax and market advantages presented by the merger plus the added number of ACCO shares previously described.

Conclusion

Of all the courses of action open to you, we suggest the latter one as being most advantageous. We realize that if all the shareholders follow such a plan no merger can take place, but we feel that well under 6 percent of current Stenco shareholders will request the fair value of their holdings. If you intend to follow our advice, it is obvious that you should disclose to no one that you intend to vote against the merger. In addition to the need for secrecy you should also consider the (unlikely) possibility that your actions here could be considered illegal under SEC regulations dealing with "insider" use of privileged information. In any case, the merger must be approved if you are to obtain maximum personal gain, since failure to merge would result in bankruptcy for Stenco in the near future.

You should therefore make every effort to promote the merger. Since *only a majority vote* is needed to approve the merger, we predict that it will take place. It should be clearly understood that merger negotiations will not collapse if over 6 percent of shareholders cast dissenting votes, but only if 6 percent dissent *and ask for fair value*. To repeat, if your request for fair value does cause the merger to collapse you should withdraw your claim rather than risk bankruptcy.

Though the course of action we outline may be somewhat compromised by the fact that you hold a seat on Stenco's board, our recommendation is quite legal and quite advantageous to you personally. Since there is such a clear financial gain involved in our proposal, we believe that any other course of action would be far less desirable.

TABLE II.   FORECAST AND HISTORICAL DATA—Stenco Sales

Year	Sales (Millions)	Profits (Thousands)
1972*	21.5	170
1971*	20.9	150
1970*	17.0	(57)
1969*	14.5	(200)
1968*	14.2	(1,100)
1967*	13.2	(1,200)
1966†	15.5	(1,184)
1965	19.0	(705)
1964	10.1	(605)
1963	19.1	303
1962	15.5	41

* 1967–1971 Forecast estimates

† 1962–1966 Historical records

Study Questions

1. Do you agree with Mr. Bartholdy that the consultants' report is both thorough and accurate? Do you agree with the consultants' recommendations?

2. If Mr. Bartholdy chooses to oppose the merger, how should he proceed? What steps (if any) should he take following the declaration of his intent to oppose merger?

3. If the board of directors acts in opposition to a major proposal or program offered by operating management, what does this mean in terms of future relationships between the board and the management? What types of situations or conditions are likely to follow such opposition?

4. What should Mr. Bartholdy decide in this case? How should his fiduciary relationship as a board member be balanced against his economic interests as a shareholder? Calculate the specific financial gains from the various alternatives in the long and short run and indicate whether or not their magnitude would and/or should influence Mr. Bartholdy's choice among alternatives.

BIBLIOGRAPHY

Ansoff, H.I., *Corporate Strategy: An Analytic Approach to Business Policy for Growth and Expansion,* New York: McGraw-Hill, Inc., 1965.

Blake, Robert R., and Jane S. Mouton, *Group Dynamics—Key to Decision Making,* Houston, Tex.: The Gulf Publishing Company, 1961.

Bross, Irwin J.D., *Design for Decision,* New York: Crowell-Collier and Macmillan, Inc., 1953.

Churchman, C.W., R. Ackoff, and E. Arnoff, *Introduction to Operations Research,* New York: John Wiley & Sons, Inc., 1957.

Computers and Management: 1967 Leatherbee Lectures, Cambridge, Mass.: Harvard University Press, Graduate School of Business Administration, 1967.

Dearden, John, and F. Warren McFarlan, *Management Information Systems: Text and Cases,* Homewood, Ill.: Richard D. Irwin, Inc., 1966.

Folsom, M., *Executive Decision Making: McKinsey Lectures,* Columbia University, Graduate School of Business, New York: McGraw-Hill, Inc., 1962.

Gore, William J., *Administrative Decision Making: A Heuristic Model,* New York: John Wiley & Sons, Inc., 1964.

Greenlaw, Paul, and Max Richards, *Management Decision Making,* Homewood, Ill.: Richard D. Irwin, Inc., 1966.

Jones, Manley, *Executive Decision Making,* rev. ed., Homewood, Ill.: Richard D. Irwin, Inc., 1962.

Holt, C., F. Modigliani, J. Muth, and H. Simon, *Planning, Production, Inventories and Work Force,* Englewood Cliffs, N.J.: Prentice-Hall, Inc., 1960.

Hutchinson, John G., *Management Under Strike Conditions,* New York: Holt, Rinehart and Winston, Inc., 1966.

————, *Organizations: Theory and Classical Concepts,* New York: Holt, Rinehart and Winston, Inc., 1967.

McDonough, A., and L. Garrett, *Management Systems,* Homewood, Ill.: Richard D. Irwin, Inc., 1965.

Maier, N.R.F., *Psychology in Industry,* 2nd ed., Boston: Houghton Mifflin Company, 1955.

Miller, David W., and Martin K. Starr, *Executive Decisions and Operations Research,* Englewood Cliffs, N.J.: Prentice-Hall, Inc., 1960.

————, *Inventory Control, Theory and Practice,* Englewood Cliffs, N.J.: Prentice-Hall, Inc., 1962.

————, *The Structure of Human Decisions,* Englewood Cliffs, N.J.: Prentice-Hall, Inc., 1967.

Moore, Franklin G., *Manufacturing Management,* 4th ed., Homewood, Ill.: Richard D. Irwin, Inc., 1965.

Porter, A., and P. Applewhite, eds., *Studies in Organization Behavior and Management,* Scranton, Pa.: International Textbook Company, 1964.

Prince, Thomas R., *Information Systems for Management Planning and Control,* Homewood, Ill.: Richard D. Irwin, Inc., 1966.

167

Schlaifer, P., *Probability and Statistics for Business Decisions,* New York: McGraw-Hill, Inc., 1959.

Schlender, W., W. Scott, and A. Filley, eds., *Management in Perspective: Selected Readings,* Boston: Houghton Mifflin Company, 1965.

Schuchman, A., ed., *Scientific Decision Making in Business,* New York: Holt, Rinehart and Winston, Inc., 1963.

Seiler, John A., *Systems Analysis in Organizational Behavior,* Homewood, Ill.: Richard D. Irwin, Inc., 1967.

Shubik, Martin, "The Use of Game Theory in Management Science," *Management Science,* October 1955, pp. 40–54.

Simon, Herbert A., *The New Science of Management Decision Making,* New York: Harper & Row, Publishers, 1960.

Spencer, M., and B. Siegelman, *Managerial Economics,* Homewood, Ill.: Richard D. Irwin, Inc., 1964.

Stockton, R.S., *Introduction to Linear Programming,* 2nd ed., Boston: Allyn and Bacon, Inc., 1963.

Young, Stanley, *Management: A Systems Analysis,* Glenview, Ill.: Scott, Foresman and Company, 1966.

The integration of strategy and organizational design requires careful consideration of three major questions: first, how can the objectives of the organization be developed in terms of specific organizational structures; second, how can the organization staff these structures with appropriate personnel; and finally, what specific techniques can be designed to assist the process of integrating strategy and structure.

Once basic opportunities and problems are recognized and decisions are made about goals, objectives, and strategies, organization structures must be designed and staffed. Section III covers selected concepts, problems, and techniques proven by experience to be theoretically or operationally feasible in bridging the gap between goal determination and goal attainment. Chapter 8 describes some of the formal and informal structures used to organize work in organizations having extremely diverse goals and functions. Chapter 9 discusses the theories and practical devices governing the delicate art of delegation. Chapter 10, the last in the section, specifies which techniques have proven to be most useful in integrating strategy and structure. This final chapter delves into decentralization, line-staff relationships, the problems of introducing change, and the means of establishing organizational control over structures and information flows.

SECTION III
Strategy and Organizational Design

As organizations grow they pass through a series of evolutionary stages. In his classic work *Strategy and Structure,* Professor Alfred E. Chandler, Jr., identifies four chapters in the history of organizational growth: (1) initial expansion and accumulation of resources; (2) rationalization of the use of resources; (3) expansion into new lines and markets to ensure continuing use of resources; and (4) development of new structures to allow continuing mobilization of resources to meet changes in both short-run and long-run demands and trends in markets.[1] In each of Chandler's four stages, strategies are developed and organizational structures are designed and staffed with suitable personnel. It is Chandler's contention that as organizations mature they continually forge new sets of goals whose attainment depends on the development of appropriate organization structures. Robert Hersey seconds Chandler's views about the important relationship between strategies and organizational design, but adds that obtaining good people to shape objectives and structures is of prime importance.[2]

Both Hersey and Chandler underscore the importance of proper organizational design in both long-term and short-term goal attainment. This view is shared by classical management writers and most executives charged with operating a going concern. In an appropriate and not understated comment on the importance of effective organizational design, professors Harold Koontz and Cyril O'Donnell state, "Organizing is, then, the process by which the manager brings order out of chaos, removes conflicts between people over work or responsibility, and establishes an environment suitable for teamwork."[3]

CHAPTER 8
Integrating Strategy with Organizational Design

---

[1] *Strategy and Structure* (Cambridge, Mass.: MIT Press, 1962).
[2] "Organizational Planning," *Business Topics,* vol. 10, no. 1 (Winter 1962), pp. 29–40.
[3] *Principles of Management,* 3rd ed. (New York: McGraw-Hill, Inc., 1964), p. 214.

ORGANIZATIONAL DESIGN

Like most areas where judgment plays an important role, the various means of developing organizational designs are the subject of ongoing debate. Classical management writings in this area have emphasized structures and relationships between structural levels, while the works of modern management theorists have tended to lean more heavily on the importance of interpersonal factors. Peter F. Drucker, striking a middle ground, summarizes three ways to determine the kinds of structures necessary to achieve the objectives of a given organization: (1) activities analysis, which includes a determination of typical functions, (2) decision analysis, which is essentially a cataloguing of the kinds of decisions made in the organization and the levels at which they are made, and (3) relations analysis, which investigates who will have to work with whom and at what horizontal and vertical levels in the organizational structure.[4] Newman and Summer frame the problem in much more specific terms by asking four questions, the answers to which govern organizational design:

1. What kinds of balance and influence should be given to various departments?

2. How can limits to the effective span of control of each executive be overcome?

3. What provisions can be made for dynamic changes?

4. How can organizing be integrated with the other management functions of planning, control, and direction? [5]

Management professors Haynes and Massie describe the following seven approaches to organizational design, but their categories, as they admit, overlap a great deal:

1. *Formalism* relies on everyone knowing what he is to do based on such things as job descriptions; the use of the principle of unit of command; and individual knowledge or functions, duties, and activities.

2. *Spontaneity* structures organizations on informal groups within the organization. This approach is flexible and follows good information flows, but has overlapping functions and gaps in the total process.

3. *Participation* structures organization by utilizing committees, conferences, suggestion systems, and so on. There are joint efforts and presumably better decisions, but there are evidences of buck-passing, fuzzy areas of responsibility, and a tendency toward watered-down decisions.

---

[4] *The Practice of Management* (New York: Harper & Row, Publishers, 1954).

[5] William H. Newman and Charles E. Summer, *The Process of Management* (Englewood Cliffs, N.J.: Prentice-Hall, Inc., 1961).

4. *Challenge and response* constructs organization structures on competitive principles. Wide spans of control are used in decentralized organizations, and individuals are given broad grants of authority. Men presumably develop well in this kind or organization, but tight controls are frequently needed to make it work in operating situations.

5. *Specialization* provides detailed allocations of duties and responsibilities through an analysis and breakdown of the structure, from general descriptions of executive jobs to the details of particular jobs. This system, though it provides efficiency in the short run, has a tendency to overspecialize certain jobs so that boredom and monotony often result.

6. *Directiveness* stresses reports, controls of higher levels over lower ones, and a series of interlocking command structures based on bureaucratic information flows. Obviously, there is inflexibility in this system, but routine decisions can be handled with relative ease.

7. *Checks and balances* utilize the constitutional organization setup. Multiheaded units such as boards of directors make decisions or check on decisions made by other parts of the unit. It is very difficult to get good balance in such systems, and thus duplication is difficult to avoid.[6]

The differences in these systems are a matter of degree according to Haynes and Massie, who advocate a synthesis of these approaches as having the greatest hope of building an effective organization.

Though the seven-point classification developed by Haynes and Massie is quite comprehensive, the range of approaches to contemporary organizational design can be categorized much more simply as threefold:

1. The building-block approach
2. The information flow approach
3. The people-make-the-organization approach

THE BUILDING-BLOCK APPROACH

Based on the classical principles of specialization, the building-block approach relies on the fact that greater efficiency occurs if tasks are broken down into specialized functions. Specialization, the core of this approach, occurs at all levels in the organization. The critical question is not what to specialize or whether to specialize, but to what degree to specialize.

Division of labor is a basic principle underlying modern industrial society. Specialization of work, for example, was a major factor in the destruction of local patterns and customs of feudal society. Later it caused newly emerging industrial nations to seek markets and raw materials through the medium

---

[6] Warren, W. Haynes and Joseph L. Massie, *Management: Analysis, Concepts and Cases* (Englewood Cliffs, N.J.: Prentice-Hall, Inc., 1961).

of international trade. Specialization on the international level gave rise to interdependence between nations and forced a continuing reaction, which has exerted, and still exerts, an important influence on the structure and organization of society. For example, the flow of trade between the United States and the United Kingdom is one powerful reason why the two countries have been long-time allies.

In a practical sense, division of work extends well beyond the boundaries of tasks, jobs, and industries. The products associated with certain nations are pointed evidence of the principles of specialization at work on a supranational scale. Brazil is not an auto-making country, but it produces fine coffee. Switzerland produces little steel, but it makes fine clocks and watches. These examples indicate the extent to which the critical concept of specialization permeates the structure of modern society. But it is not at the international level that the advantages and drawbacks associated with the division of labor receive the most attention: the highest degrees of utilization, and also the greatest amount of criticism, are found at the level of the individual organization, particularly the business firm. This statement is not much of a revelation to people living in a world where up to five tradesmen or technicians must be called in to install a single electrical appliance.

Division of labor developed in the historical sequence shown in Figure 8.1.

Though most of the arrows move in the same general direction, there was, and is, a two-way flow of activity that reinforces the various stages of development. For example, high-volume production for mass markets also fosters the rise of mass production technology and an increasing use of task and job specialization. These same circular and redundant effects can be observed in most of the steps in the diagram.

Within the structure of an organization, specialization appears at several different levels of complexity. It can first be viewed in terms of the total organization structure. Next, it may be applied in overseeing how the work to be done will be assigned to particular units or departments. It also helps to develop methods of assigning jobs within various departmental groupings. Finally, it helps to determine how the total work flow will be divided into specific jobs or operations. The importance of doing this step well is pointed out by the French pundit J.J. Servan-Schreiber in his influential report *The American Challenge,* which spells out why American industry has surpassed its European competition.[7] Servan-Schreiber holds that the secret of American industrial superiority lies in the "art of organization,"—the mobilization of resources and intelligence to construct a more effective, higher-order society.

The determination of a basic organizational structure is the first step in the process of specialization at the level of the operating organization. A number of choices exist, ranging from a pure line organization to the line-staff approach. Of these, the line-staff hierarchy enjoys almost universal usage,

---

[7] (New York: Atheneum Publishers, 1968).

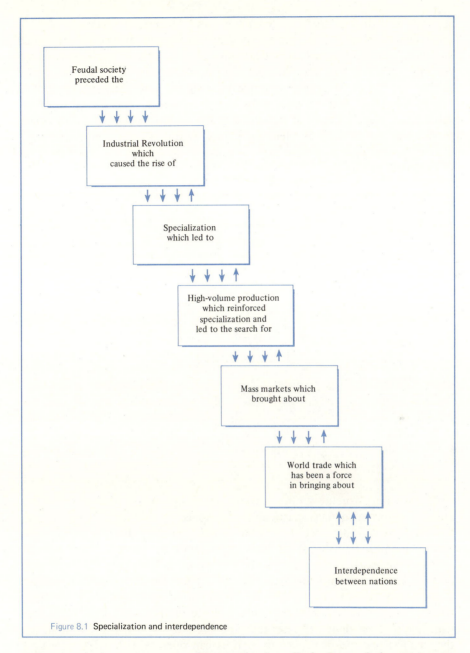

Figure 8.1 Specialization and interdependence

although other structures may be superior in a limited set of circumstances.

In a relatively small organization or one having a simple set of goals, the pure line approach has a valid raison d'être. In the pure line organization each superior is directly responsible for his immediate subordinates, who are in turn accountable only to their immediate superior. Each department is separate and distinct from all other units and, since staff specialists are not in evidence, there is little diffusion of accountability. In such a simplified structure, communications are not complicated, discipline is easy to administer, reporting relationships are clear-cut, and boss-subordinate relationships are simple and direct. A typical example of a simple line structure appears in Figure 8.2. Note that no staff units are in evidence, and direct superior-subordinate relations exist at each level in the organizational structure. Small service businesses such as cleaning plants, barber shops, "mom-and-pop" grocery stores, and local law firms are likely candidates for the line form of organization.

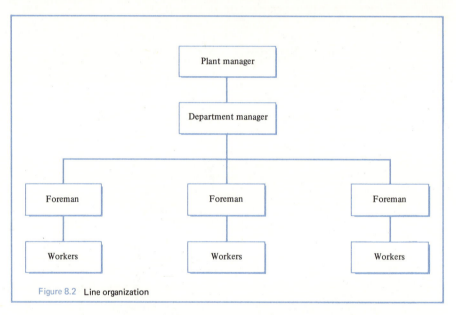

Figure 8.2   Line organization

Though line structures offer certain advantages, they also suffer from a number of serious defects, particularly if applied in medium-to large organizations. First and foremost, they fail to provide the specialized skills so necessary in modern industry. They also rely heavily on the talents of workers and supervisors. If these abilities are lacking or as is usually the case, exist only in limited amounts, the organization suffers. Another serious drawback is the heavy burden of paper work thrust on supervisors, which normally reduces their efficiency. The net balance of plus and minus factors connected with line organizations indicates that line structures are ineffective in all but the smallest organizations. Beauty parlors can operate with a line structure, but General Telephone and Electronics cannot.

Frederick W. Taylor, of scientific management fame, attempted to solve the problem of the line organization's lack of specialization by introducing a functional concept of organization. Taylor set up a structure combining line and staff activities by recognizing areas of specialization which encompassed certain functions. Taylor's approach is shown in Figure 8.3, which singles out the areas of expertise Taylor considered the chief contributors to efficient operation.

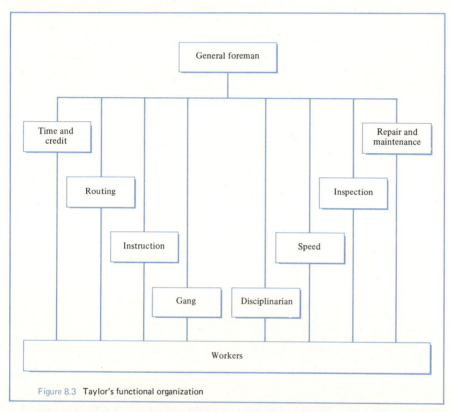

Figure 8.3 Taylor's functional organization

Though Taylor's system brought specialization to the organization structure, it also brought the problem of dual subordination (one man reporting to more than one boss). Moreover, since the system was only applicable at shop level, it was not a universal form of organization. Able to cope with a quality control problem, this system broke down when applied to central areas such as new product development which cut across both functional areas and levels in the structure.

For all practical purposes, the line-staff structure is the only organization form capable of meeting the diverse requirements of modern organizations. The line-staff structure attempts to combine the speed of decision and the excellence of communications found in the line organization with the expert knowledge needed to direct complex or widespread activities. It provides for expert staffs to assist operating units and tries to establish an optimum level of efficiency without losing the concentrated decision authority found in the line structure. Figure 8.4 provides an elementary breakdown of the reporting relationships in a typical line-staff structure.

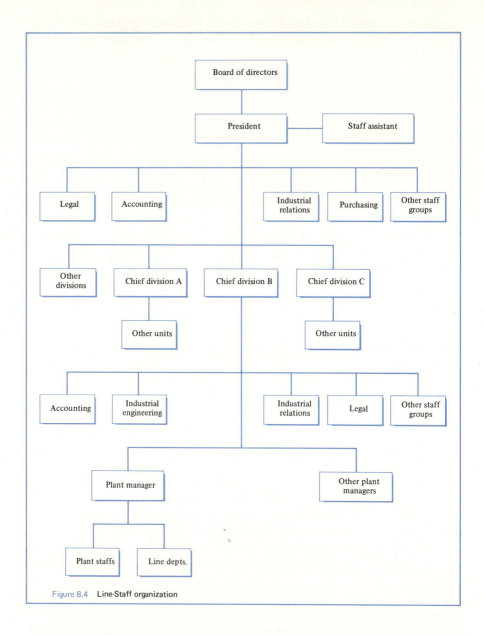

Figure 8.4   Line-Staff organization

The line positions shown in the figure are the president, the division chiefs, and the plant managers. The board of directors has line authority, too, but usually exercises this authority only to oversee, review, or set outer limits on the activities of those officials responsible for day-to-day operations. All other positions in the chart are in the staff category. The staff assistant performs special duties for top management, in this case, the president. Staff assistants fall into the category of personal staff, since they typically work for a particular person or committee. The other staffs in Figure 8.4 can be called general staffs, since they perform duties in a particular functional area. Their orientation is to a subject, not to a specific person, and their services may be made available to any individual or area in need of assistance. The research staff is the classic example of a staff with more allegiance to science than to the parent organization. Staff and line relationships may be repeated down to the worker level. Except in large plants, staff units are not commonly found below the plant manager level.

The difficulties in running line-staff organizations come primarily from the relationships that occur when line authority overlaps or conflicts with staff activities. If the amount of authority possessed by a particular staff is unclear, or an overzealous line or staff man tries to usurp another's area of responsibility, serious problems can develop. "Why ask me," says the foreman, "when the industrial engineers run my department?" Discipline is also difficult when accountability cannot be identified easily, and this confusion undermines the operation of the entire organization. Unclear delegation is another damper on the effective use of responsibility and authority concepts, and the old army game of passing the buck is common when delegation is fuzzy: witness the salesman who blames his high travel costs on routings determined by his sales manager. One final disadvantage inherent in the use of line-staff structures is that the specialized knowledge of the staff may remain within the staff unit if its relations with other departments are not smooth or cooperative. When this happens, friction is retained, the gains from specialization are lost, and the organization suffers the worst features of both worlds. In the period when General Dynamics lost over $400 million on their Convair aircraft line, much of the blame for this fantastically large loss was placed on poor line-to-line and line-to-staff communications. No doubt exists that this was one of the most costly misunderstandings in business history.

The board of directors in the line-staff structure is one example of a more specialized organizational form known as committee organization, or "the plural executive." In this setup, the form is the same as in the line-staff organization, but at each level decisions are made by more than one person. One executive is replaced by the plural executive; and thus committees, not individuals, make decisions. The committee does not perform its usual function of giving advice, but instead has decision authority. This structure is common at the board-of-directors level, but it is rarely found at other levels. It may be used temporarily to meet emergencies, for example, when a three-man junta takes over decision authority until a new man is appointed to fill a position vacated by an unexpected death in the executive ranks. In recent years, however, the "office of the president" concept, as used in General Electric and Boise Cascade, has come into prominence. In this form, several men close to the president can, alone or in concert, act as if they were the president in solving certain problems or in making particular decisions. As organizations grow in size and complexity, the office of the president may be the answer to one man's inability to grasp all of the facts and factors needed to run the organization effectively.

Departmentation, or the grouping of functions within an organization structure, is the second level of structuring in the building-block approach. Since the groupings may cover a wide variety of circumstances, organizations usually select one of several approaches. The final choice depends on the activity performed, its ultimate objectives, and the relationship of each department to the organization's overall goals. The most generally accepted methods of grouping work into departments are described briefly in the following paragraphs. Each approach is a working example of how the process of specialization is, in part, carried out at the operating level.

Functional departmentation places a particular activity in a specific department. For example, all financial activities might be centralized in a finance department, which might have the responsibility for handling short-term cash flows and the long-run financial dealings necessary to expedite both the internal and external aspects of corporate financial policy. The basic rationale underlying this approach is that special skills should be grouped together for easy access and coordination.

The basic functions of a business organization are to make goods, to sell them, and to finance their production and sale. The functional approach applied to a business firm usually results in the establishment of marketing, finance, and production departments (similar titles may serve to identify these key activities). Functional departmentation is most commonly found at higher levels in business organizations, but it also appears at other levels.

Territorial or geographical departmentation divides work into departments representing localities or geographic areas. It is used when activities, because of their dispersion, are not susceptible to grouping by function or other means. Sales territories set up by states or metropolitan areas are geographic departments; for example, Allstate Insurance Company (auto) divides its sales and claim adjustment activities into regional groupings. This technique is commonly invoked at intermediate levels in an organization's structure.

Product departmentation organizes departments around particular products or product lines. Its principal value is that it can, when combined with an effective control system, provide a basis for evaluating the performance of specialized asset groupings. Found in decentralized organizations such as automobile and can companies, this type of departmentation seems to be effective when applied at intermediate levels in the organizational structure. The Maxwell House division of the General Foods Corporation is one example of product departmentation.

Equipment or process departmentation is a variation of product departmentation. Here the unit upon which departmentation is based is typically a single machine or a complex of associated pieces of equipment. The price of an IBM System/360 computer installation or an expensive special purpose machine such as a large electrical generator might justify the establishment of a separate department. This approach is usually adopted at low levels in the structure, though the equipment may be used by the entire organization.

Customer service or customer expectation is a variation of departmentation that has its form dictated by factors in the external environment. If customers expect certain departments to exist, organizations may departmentize to accommodate these expectations. Macy's or Gimbel's store with its departments for women's budget dresses, women's better dresses, and women's original or high-fashion dresses, provide an example of customer departmentation. When customers demand special treatment, groupings such as retail and wholesale trade departments may be set up to meet the ends or expectations of the various clients. Do-it-yourself lumber sales outlets in the traditional lumberyard illustrate this condition.

Clean-break departmentation may also exist in department stores. When special functions are difficult to separate, they may be grouped together and evaluated in total rather than individually. In a women's shoe department, the buying and selling functions are difficult to separate. Skill in buying products that match customer demands and the ability of sales people to move the product may both contribute substantially to the success or failure of the department. Since the buyer in charge of the department performs or directs both the sales and buying functions, he is held responsible for the entire department's performance. Thus, the department is separated from other areas; and both it and the buyer are evaluated as an entity. Actually, this technique might well be called the principle of "no clean break," since it avoids the pitfalls connected with differentiating between overlapping or interrelated functions.

Alphabetical and numerical departmentations usually appear at low levels in the organization structure. They are most useful when applied to organizing relatively simple tasks. Fruit pickers in a cherry orchard are set up in work teams by counting off so many men needed to pick the fruit. All skills are considered to be homogeneous; and thus numerical or alphabetical selection (for example, choosing people whose names begin with the letters *A* through *H*) determines a department within the context of this simple agricultural task. Persons with past military service no doubt recall how this technique is used to count off work parties for a "clean sweep fore and aft" or an enlightening session of "policing the area."

Once work is grouped into departments, it must be assigned within the departments; this is usually done in one of two ways: (1) like functions are grouped together or (2) work is assigned to the areas or persons most likely to ensure its completion. Thus, grouping is the third step in the building-block structure.

The process type of grouping is common in job-lot manufacturing and in repetitive clerical activities. All punch-press activity may be grouped in a single punch press section of the metal fabrication department, or all routine typing may be done by the members of a central typing pool. The underlying idea in this approach is that all like work should be performed at a central location or a series of locally centralized work stations.

For unlike activities, assignment of work may be based on such considerations as degree of use, personal interest, or desire to exercise control. A supervisor may want to control an activity simply because it catches his fancy or arouses his interest. In this case, and if empire building is not in the picture, it may make good sense to give the man his way until he either loses interest or the function is performed poorly. If an activity can be better coordinated or can be controlled more effectively under an interested person's direction, that may be sufficient reason to assign the work to him. The same reasoning holds in regard to spatial relationships. If a particular function is performed in a given location, the area supervisor may be the best person to oversee its operation, at least until this is proven otherwise.

The critical reasons for assigning work within departments should stem from the nature of the job being done (functional specialization) and the concern that particular people have about the execution of the work (executive interest). The choice of how to group activities within departments should depend upon a careful analysis of the work to be done and the people who will assume responsibility for its completion.

The determination of what jobs to do and how to do them is the final variation and one of the most technical steps in the building-block approach. The methods used to identify, combine, and group such tasks range from simple judgment to advanced mathematics. In jobs where conceptual and planning activities are important, duties are normally assigned on the basis of judgments made by top-level executives. Judgment and experience are also used to define the limits of many other managerial or staff jobs. Some attempts have been made to assign work in such jobs after a careful review of time and duty studies, but these efforts have generally been incomplete both in coverage and depth. Time and duty analysis is currently little better than expert judgment, even though statistical work sampling is beginning to provide more accurate information on job content at a relatively low cost.

Operational analysis is used at the lowest level of specialization. Within a given operation the intimate details of how to do the job must eventually be laid out in sequence. Various kinds of charts can be used to analyze low-level productive activities. One such device, commonly used by industrial engineers, is a *simo-chart,* which details what the left and right hands are doing in a given time interval. If idle time appears, the motion pattern is changed to provide for more effective utilization of the operator's motions. Another is a *man-machine chart,* which relates a man's movements to the cycling of a single machine or multiple machines. Again, adjustments are made if idle time is detected. Still other methods employ various combinations of men and machines and men and materials in both time and space dimensions. Some charts, for example, plot activities, while others relate activities to a time scale. *Flow charts* and *flow-process charts* respectively perform these functions. After the spatial relationships between worker and product have been identified, the next step is to combine them in optimum fashion. The guiding principle is to minimize operator time while maximizing operator output. Figure 8.5 illustrates one form of a flow process chart.

Standard Symbols	Present Method*
◯ Operation	Operation: Process Pricing Invoice
→ Transportation	Department(s): Order and Billing
☐ Inspection	Date: 1/5/70 Analyst: J. H. Johnston
△ Temporary storage	Notes:
D Delay	Sequence of Activities
◯ → ☐ △ D	Remove invoice from envelope at order processing desk
◯ → ☐ △ D	Place order in clerk's work folder
◯ → ☐ △ D	Move work folder to delivery cart
◯ → ☐ △ D	Wait for mail delivery clerk
◯ → ☐ △ D	Move work folder to clerk's desk
◯ → ☐ △ D	Remove folder from cart, remove invoices and place in clerk's basket
◯ → ☐ △ D	Invoice stored in basket
◯ → ☐ △ D	Wait for clerk to process invoice
◯ → ☐ △ D	Clerk reads invoice and prices items
◯ → ☐ △ D	Invoice placed in clerk's out basket (upper level)
◯ → ☐ △ D	Wait for supervisory check of invoice
◯ → ☐ △ D	Supervisor checks invoice for accuracy (inspection and operation combined)
◯ → ☐ △ D	Invoice placed in clerk's out basket (lower level)
◯ → ☐ △ D	Await arrival of delivery cart
⋯	⋯
◯ → ☐ △ D	Place completed billing in envelope
◯ → ☐ △ D	Move to mailroom for mailing

*A similar form and charting procedure would be used to compare any proposed method with the present method.

Figure 8.5 Sample flow-process chart (partial representation)

Charts may be only one part of operations analysis. Stopwatch time study can be used to show the content and quantity of work performed in a given time period. Micromotion analysis can analyze work patterns with motion pictures or through the use of so-called synthetic motion time systems. In this particular technique, all human motions are identified, and various lengths of time are determined for each set of basic motions. Based on Frank Gilbreth's "therbligs," these systems attach a time value to a motion sequence by identifying every motion in the sequence and then giving each a time value (from a table). A given percentage is added for personal and delay factors, and the results are added to get the total elapsed time for the observed motion sequence. Several synthetic measurement systems are in use, the most common being methods-time-measurement (MTM).

The basic measurement tools used in time and motion study have recently been supplemented by mathematical and statistical approaches that often carry the title "operations research," or "systems analysis." Methods now exist that can determine when to order certain inventory items and how many to order. Order programs maintain records of costs and prices of the units used in given manufacturing lots. Techniques that select the best production routings in terms of time, cost, machine capacities, and other critical factors are also used. Generally, these analytical approaches shape the outer limits of jobs, not the specific methods of motions actually used to perform tasks. They have, however, changed the nature of many factory jobs by replacing individual judgment with sets of carefully drawn rules and procedures.

It seems somewhat ironic that the most technical and sophisticated work measurement and assignment techniques are used to analyze the least complicated jobs. Perhaps as techniques become more sophisticated, they will be used more widely to analyze complex jobs.

To summarize, the building-block approach recognizes functions; groups them into structures, departments, jobs, tasks, and procedures; and establishes formal relations between these blocks, or units. Its basic efficiency springs from its use of the principles of division of labor to obtain economic, efficient operation. It appears principally within the context of the line-staff structure and utilizes formal reporting relationships which follow chains of command up and down the hierarchy. It normally has relatively tight systems of controls, reports, and checks on the performance of units, groups, and even specific individuals. It is the heart of the classical analysis for organizational design, and much has been written about it both pro and con.

Some critics have bitterly attacked its end results. Chris Argyris notably describes it as a system that has generated psychological failure, frustration, short-term perspectives, and conflict.[8] Others have attacked it because it lacks effectiveness; for example, Herbert A. Simon says it generates debilitating rigidities. These criticisms have been the basis for the other two basic approaches to constructing organizational design, namely, the information flow concept and the people-make-the-organization approach.

THE INFORMATION FLOW APPROACH

The information flow approach views organizations as a series of large information networks connected by various processing and decision centers. These centers determine, collect, analyze, transform, transmit, and use data inputs

---

[8] *Personality and Organization* (New York: Harper & Row, Publishers, 1957), p. 233.

to administer the going concern. According to Prince, the traditional information flow approach performs the following functions:

1. Identifies tasks
2. Coordinates tasks to avoid conflict
3. Specifies the extent to which each task is to be performed
4. Assigns personnel to tasks
5. Allocates the resources and materials for the accomplishment of each task[9]

Once these functions are performed, decisions can be made concerning which raw materials to use, which finished goods to produce, which machines to use, and which employees to assign to these machines. Prince's basic attack identifies, plans, and relates activities, and is particularly suited to managing activities which can be programmed into a computerized model simulating the operating system.

The structures in this organizational construct are a cousin to, but not a twin of, those used in the line-staff hierarchy. Special groups are set up, and mixtures of functions may appear in each group. Each subgroup has a purpose and a set of functions based on company objectives rather than on task or specialization. A systems research group, for example, might be a pool of talent containing diverse functional specialities drawn from different portions of the organization. Where it would report, however, would be determined by information flows: what it needed to know, what information it utilized in its day-by-day duties, and where it should be placed to best relate to pertinent information flows.

The ruling models would still be line-staff in terms of special units supported by operating units, but within departments there would be less emphasis on functional groupings and more concern with constructing organizations to meet particular purposes. Horizontal slices might be made across hierarchical structures to bring skills and people together into particular units designed to reach sets of objectives. An example might be the project organization used by Boeing to set up bids on the supersonic transport. In some aircraft firms, special units were set up on a project basis and talent was assembled with the specific objective of obtaining the SST bid. These units or task forces were kept intact until after the prime contractors (the Boeing Company for airframes and General Electric for engines) were announced. In the winning firms these bidding units were then reshuffled to meet the new objectives connected with development and production. Among the losers, more drastic reassignment procedures went into effect.

Another example is the kind of organizational scheme which might be set up to elect candidates to political office. The program grouping used in such organizations draws upon skills available in many disciplines and areas

---

[9] Thomas R. Prince, *Information Systems for Management Planning and Control* (Homewood, Ill.: Richard D. Irwin, Inc., 1966).

of expertise, but all people involved in the campaign's development have one object in mind: the election of the candidate. Obviously, the organization undergoes modification following election day; and in the losing party serious revisions may be made in operating personnel, platforms, and leadership.

The grouping of diverse skills within one group with a specific objective makes unity of direction (one group with one central set of goals) more attainable and also realizes some of the benefits of product-line organization.[10] Indeed, the use of product-line decentralization where organizations are set up on the basis of operationally autonomous profit centers closely resembles the ideas advocated in the information flow approach.

Lower-level task orientation in this method is usually developed through a mission or project approach. Skills and information needed to do jobs are grouped into projects or subprojects, and detailed job and task analysis spring from the "need to know about" or the "need to use" the results of the information generated by pertinent data flows. To refer again to the SST example, draftsmen and technicians would be grouped into units with a mission directly related to building a prototype or drafting a component part of the total package included in the final bid. They would not be involved in say, the pricing phase of the bidding activity.

In the information flow approach, data flows are structured to furnish rapid inputs of pertinent information to appropriate decision makers. Structural design is based on a recognition of what the organization wants and what decision makers need to reach decisions advancing the attainment of those wants. Thus, organizational hierarchies are generated from analysis of objectives and the data needed to make decisions to reach those objectives, not from a principle calling for grouping according to functional specialization or task.

Some firms have adopted a "matrix" or "task force" type of organizational structure in which special groups are set up as a task force to achieve particular results. These units draw on resources and people found in the regular line-staff structure and use them to achieve specific goals or to complete specific programs. If the normal flow of communication and delegation runs up and down the structure, the matrix organization could be considered as possessing upward and downward flows with special projects or programs set up across the normal structure. Traditional line and staff units would remain intact on a going basis, while the special task force units would be set up on an ad hoc basis. In a firm making defense hardware on a regular basis, the production organization would be the column of the organizational matrix (vertical flows), while bids on special projects or relatively short-term research and job-lot contracts might be set up to draw resources from across the various levels in the structure (the horizontal rows of the matrix). Personnel could be drawn from any part of the permanent organization to perform special tasks and then returned at the close of the special assignment.

---

[10] Rensis Likert, *New Patterns of Management* (New York: McGraw-Hill, Inc., 1961).

Critics of the information flow approach to organizational design score it as being overly manipulative, since individuals are given only data that someone decides they "need to know." This "Big-Brother" supervision causes a resentment in some people that may tend to overcome the flexibility and control advantages it offers, but, on balance, more people seem to favor the system than oppose it. Since Big Brother is constantly second-guessed, corrected, and reviled when *he* makes mistakes, this system, as all others, contains within itself a continuing process of accommodation. Since, as its advocates claim, manipulation occurs in all systems, the advantage here is that it is done openly with the intent of benefiting the entire organization, not one privileged person or group.

This approach, which is a relatively recent development in the field of organizational design, is gaining ground principally because of the impetus given to its use in research in the fields of communications, information theory, information processing, industrial sociology, and general systems theory. Though it differs little in its end point from line-staff structures, which also utilize both upwards and downwards flow of ideas and data, it does place enough importance on feedback and communications principles to differ substantially from the traditional line-staff structure. Its flexibility and its emphasis on goals and objectives rather than on performance of tasks make it well suited for use in organizations whose final products are idea-oriented or service-oriented rather than production-oriented. Thus, it has gained acceptance in organizations manufacturing job-lot quantities of complex products such as the electronics firms engaged in making components for NASA and rocketry programs. It has also been adopted by research laboratories whose major functions are turning out new products and new scientific discoveries. Its success in these applications indicates it will enjoy wider use in the future.

THE PEOPLE-MAKE-THE-ORGANIZATION APPROACH

The final organizational design in use today is based on a variation of the labor theory of value, and it states that people generate all value in the organization and organization structures must reflect this fact. Structural patterns are thus based on actions, interactions, sentiments, and activities of the people in the organization. Work activities are grouped to conform with interactions between people and are constructed to reflect the needs of people, as individuals and in groups.

An illustration of this approach is setting up an assembly line using a U-shaped rather than traditional straight-line layout. The major purpose of the horseshoe-shaped layout is to provide a higher degree of social interaction between workers on the line. In the U-shaped layout, tasks might not be assigned to individuals but rather to the entire group spaced along the U. Group decisions might determine who would do what job or task instead of the rigid work assignments commonly imposed on workers in assembly lines designed on a straight line. According to its advocates, the people-oriented, U-shaped assembly line improves both worker morale and total output and thus is the most desirable form of organization.

The person-structured organization focuses on the individual and his feelings and on the group and its collective reactions. In this approach, studies of individual needs, group goals, intergroup relations, and group solidarity are some of the major components considered during the design of organizational structure. Person-centered approaches reject specialization and informational flow analysis as the keys to setting up organizational structures and substitute instead an emphasis on people. Improved information flows and high levels of efficiency are not downgraded completely; rather they are given less emphasis than human factors. Results are not obtained through delegation and tight controls, but through group participation and meeting individual needs. Efficiency is obtained through greater personal commitment and a lessening of friction and nonproductive conflict.

Structures evolving from this approach often take the form of interlocking groups, each of which theoretically strives to have goals coincident with those of the organization. Information is fed back to group members, and individuals are allowed to participate in decisions affecting their areas of expertise and/or concern. This approach uses concepts taken from classical organizational formulations such as line-staff departments, but bases departmentation on studies of what work groups do and how they react to work assignments, not on analyses of specific tasks and duties.

Though the theory underlying this approach seems reasonable, its application is difficult and time-consuming. What groups want and what people want is not particularly obvious, and identifying such needs and aspirations is not a job for the insecure. Even in the best run organizations with scores of skilled social scientists, the information underlying the people-oriented approach to structures comes to light only after painstaking probing and a series of informed but nonscientific guesses.

One well-publicized example of the kind of organization structure existent in the people-make-the-organization framework is the "linking pin" theory developed by Rensis Likert, in which each supervisor is a leader of the group reporting to him and a member of the group reporting at a level above him in the organizational pyramid. The supervisor thus links the ideas of the group above with those below, in his immediate group (he is the linking pin between levels). Group-to-group supervision is emphasized here, not person-to-person supervision, and organizational rewards are meted out on the basis of an individual's cooperation with others, not on his ability to compete with them in what Likert calls "destructive fashion." Some of Likert's ideas that reflect the kind of thinking in this particular approach can be found in his popular *New Patterns of Management* and in his more recent *The Human Organization*.[11]

The person-centered approach to organizational design seems to have won many supporters because of its success in low-level applications, but how

---

[11] *Ibid.* and *The Human Organization* (New York: McGraw-Hill, Inc., 1967).

it can be used to organize the top levels of complex organizations is not clear. It is not a complete structural approach in its present form because it does not deal effectively with factors outside the organization's control. It does, however, give new insights into techniques and methodology that may become more widespread as technology becomes more idea-oriented and less production-oriented. According to Waino Suojanen, this change is already taking place.[12] If his contention is true, then the people-oriented approaches to structure may, along with information flow approaches, enjoy wider use in research and development activities and in project-oriented industries such as aerospace and electronics. Further applications of this promising approach are developed in Chapters 13 and 17, dealing with the revitalization of organizational units, and the management of research and development.

Summary

The approaches to organizational design described in the preceding pages are the skeleton on which the organization hangs its attempts to carry out various strategies. The choice of one does not preclude the use of some portion of the others, since each approach contains theoretical truth and operational utility. The three constructs underlying contemporary structural design are

1. The building-block approach
2. The information flow approach
3. The people-make-the-organization approach

Any effective structure should help to mitigate the ubiquitous difficulties encountered in developing organizational designs. It should also be the vehicle by which both the organization and its individual members reach their desired levels of objectives. Since no single approach can meet all of these requirements, it seems likely that management must blend portions of all three into the design of organizational structures.

Study Questions

1. In *The Good Society,* Walter Lippman describes the division of labor as the foremost revolutionary principle of our society. Do you agree? Why or why not?

2. What problems exist in Frederick W. Taylor's functional organization structure?

3. What are the major advantages and disadvantages arising from the use of line-staff organizations?

4. What are the various forms of departmentation? At what levels are they commonly found?

5. Should all units in a multiunit organization have a parallel organizational form? What are the advantages and disadvantages of parallel departmentation?

---

[12] *The Dynamics of Management* (New York: Holt, Rinehart and Winston, Inc., 1966).

6. Give examples of process grouping, executive interest and executive control. What factors determine how activities should be grouped?

7. How do the means for evaluating executive jobs differ from those measuring relatively routine factory jobs?

8. What are the main differences among the building-block, information flow, and people-make-the-organization approaches? What similarities exist?

9. Which of the three approaches in question 8 make the most sense to you? Elaborate.

10. How do the three approaches in question 8 relate to the various schools of management thought outlined in Chapters 1 and 2? Discuss.

CHAPTER 9
The Delicate Art of Delegation

When decisions have been made about objectives and tentative conclusions have been drawn about organizational design, organization structures must be fleshed out with people. Departments, tasks, and duties built into the ideal structure must be staffed with people who can make them function smoothly. When ideal structures have ideal people no problems exist, but such a perfect match is so rare that, inevitably, adjustments must be made. People must be added, transferred, trained, or assigned to positions calling for more or less ability than they possess. In this situation structures must be reassessed and realigned to fit the not-so-round pegs already on hand into as many round holes as possible. This basic process of adjustment, including the assignment and reallocation of duties to fit available personnel into the existing structure, is the core of the difficult and delicate art of delegation.

Delegation of authority in a practical sense is an art performed in a three-act sequence: (1) assigning tasks to specific people, (2) granting them authority to perform the tasks assigned, and (3) exacting an obligation from them to complete the assigned tasks. Delegation is thus the process of creating obligations and exacting authority within the organization structure and among the people staffing its various levels. As Chester I. Barnard points out in *The Theory of Authority,* personal decisions cannot be delegated, but organizational decisions always must be delegated.[1] Delegation thus becomes not only a delicate art, but also an unavoidable one.

---

[1] (Cambridge, Mass.: Harvard University Press, 1900).

191

THE BASES OF AUTHORITY

The delegation process has its roots in the legal and social bases of authority. Authority, in a legal sense, is the power to command others or to perform certain acts. In democratic societies, legal authority is difficult to utilize effectively. If those over whom authority is to be exercised resist, it may become unenforceable. Authority then possesses at least two bases: (1) the structure of formal authority and (2) the concept of acceptance.

Formal authority is made up of the legal and other power bases found in the social structure. The underpinnings of formal authority may reach as far back in time as the divine right of kings, when the ruler-god held absolute sway over his domain. The ruler's absolute control over the life and death of his subjects was an extreme but clear-cut example of such divine authority.

Though the bases of formal authority may have started with or even before the pharaohs, the master-servant relationship in English common law is a much more recognizable predecessor of modern authority concepts. In England, the lord of the manor set the terms and conditions of work, and his servants and tenants either accepted them or left. As industry developed, owner-managers established similar understandings with their workers. The concept of divine right of kings was modified over time, and more importance was attached to the widely accepted right of property owners to set the rules and terms under which workers came to toil on their property. The concept of property rights is still one of the basic foundations of formal authority. Others are found in legislative acts and judicial decisions which set rules of behavior, conduct, and relations between individuals and society.

Acceptance theories of authority state that the basis of authority lies in customs, mores, restrictions, and limits placed on the use of authority in particular societies at particular points in time. Barnard summarizes this concept as "The decision as to whether an order has authority or not lies with the person or persons to whom it is addressed, and does not reside in those who issue the orders."[2] In these circumstances, proprietary rights and other formal, legal bases of authority are valid only insofar as people are willing to accept them. Thus, formal authority exists only when it is accepted by the individuals subject to its directives.

Some advocates of acceptance theories of authority use a modification of hedonistic concepts to explain why man does what he does. These theorists state that individuals weight the relative degrees of pleasure and pain before obeying a particular indication of authority such as an order to perform a specific task; their decision whether or not to obey is based on their evaluations of the consequences (good or bad) of obeying. This model of authority is based on the assumption that individuals are continually striving to maximize pleasure or to minimize pain. In this approach, the net balance of these

---

[2] Chester I. Barnard, *Functions of the Executive* (Cambridge, Mass.: Harvard University Press, 1938), p. 163.

weightings of pain and pleasure is considered to be the determinant of the strength of a given authority relationship. Authority thus depends on the reactions of the recipient of an order, not on the formal or legal rights held by the person giving the order. To place this concept in a familiar business setting, if a boss asks a man to write a report, the man can decide the job he'll do on the basis of the benefits he feels he'll receive from doing the report well, poorly, moderately well, or perhaps not at all. His personal evaluation forges the decision, not the formal power of his boss.

In practice, both formal and acceptance theories of authority have some validity. Formal authority covers the entire structure of society, while acceptance theories are generally limited to superior-subordinate relationships. Social institutions such as private property and long-accepted laws and customs do influence person-to-person relations, but the willingness of people to accept direction in particular situations depends upon much more than formal customs, expectations, and traditions. The truth, as usual, seems to lie somewhere between the extremes of formal and acceptance theories of authority.

Individuals may accept authority because of fear of the power held by the superior in the authority hierarchy. Fear of sanction, reprisal, withholding of some desirable goal, or even physical pain may bring about obedience to a command or acceptance of some obligation. Many authority relations are based on fear of either latent or actual power. In dictatorial societies, power is the keystone of the command structure. Power is commonly used in such societies in both its overt and implied forms to ensure acceptance of authority. But power tends to lose its effectiveness if overused. In democratic societies in particular, it is most useful in its latent form. Power is thus most effective in the short run, and its continual use generally is not justified in terms of either morality or effectiveness.

Another reason why people accept authority is that they believe certain commands are legitimate and should be followed. They may have confidence in the person giving the order, or they may feel they owe a certain obligation to the organization or the institution commanding obedience. A layman usually follows his doctor's advice in what medication to take to relieve a stomachache; and most citizens feel that a call to serve the country during wartime is a legitimate demand, even though it may infringe upon individual freedom. On the other side of the coin, there may be a failure to comply when the opposite is true; that is, if the recipient of the prescription lacks confidence in his physician, or the inductee feels deep opposition for either religious or moral reasons to bearing arms. Antidraft riots from the Civil War to Vietnam indicate that failure to accept formal orders can cause explosive and divisive consequences.

Many of the authority relationships developed in democratic societies are based on influence rather than power. Influence is the attempt to gain acceptance of authority through voluntary means. These means may take the form of pay, status, titles, office location, or other economic and noneconomic rewards.[3] In addition to these rewards, the status of key men may be enhanced by channeling information through them or by backing them. Influence-building devices in this latter instance are paying attention to advice given by subordinates, using chains of command to reinforce subordinates' authority and confirming decisions made by subordinates so that face is saved or prestige built up. In group situations, pressures are used by group members to bring deviates into line with the group's norms. These same pressures may be used to bring nonconformists' ideas back into harmony with organizational goals embraced by the group. Influence can be used to gain both individual and group acceptance of authority, and it is particularly effective in maintaining authority relationships over long periods of time.

The limits of powers and influence depend upon a number of widely varying factors. These factors, which cover economic, social, political, psychological, and other areas, set constraints on the use of power and identify conditions where the use of influence is most likely to bring the best results. People tend to react differently to authority within this wide range of factors, and their responses to specific directives vary with the nature of the command and the structure of the originating environment. One man may accept orders from his boss about how to do a job, but may choose to ignore his boss's advice on how to woo and win a mate. Another man might be an unwilling listener to his boss's directives on both wooing and working, and a third might follow the supervisor's advice on these and other matters. Cultural factors bring about similar results. In France, which has long had a tradition of paternalistic-authoritarian supervisory styles, American methods of management have run into stiff opposition. In the words of a deputy general manager of the Machines Bull–General Electric complex, "The hardest thing here is to get middle and even top management to act and take responsibility rather than just ask questions. They want authority and status without responsibility and accountability."[4] Obviously, the acceptance theory of authority has supranational overtones.

The relationship between superior and subordinate can be replete with all sorts of factors that serve to influence acceptance of authority. People have certain zones of acceptance within which they consider commands to be reasonable. Outside these zones, they are unwilling to follow commands. A boss can order a man to set up a machine and expect the subordinate to obey him, but the boss should not expect obedience if he tells the same man to jump off the Empire State Building. A classic example of the problems of authority relationships at the top level occurred when Wheeling Steel was taken over by Norton Simon's financial empire. Steel men resented Simon's takeover and Simon's hand-picked president, Robert A. Morriss, ran into opposition within his own managerial ranks and in the industry. Morriss

---

[3] See William H. Newman and Charles E. Summer, *The Process of Management* (Englewood Cliffs, N.J.: Prentice-Hall, 1961) for an excellent discussion of the power of influence and authority in the delegation process.

[4] Gregory H. Wierzynski, "G.E.'s $200 Million Ticket to France," *Fortune,* June 1967, p. 92.

summarized his problems inside Wheeling when he said, "My problem is that there was no one to listen." His relations problem in the industry was focused on at a dinner when an executive from a competing company blasted him with, "We don't like you or Simon because we don't want outsiders in this industry. You won't get any help from us in any way. Even a magician can't lick Wheeling's problems in less than five years and you won't get five years to try."[5] The authority that can be exercised with some expectation of compliance is thus limited to certain zones or areas. These areas may depend upon the closeness of the relationships between boss and worker or other factors such as organizational distance. An assembly line worker in Flint, Michigan, does not really fall under the direct authority of the president of General Motors, even though the formal organization chart indicates he does.

Authority relationships reflect a complex blend of organizational levels, zones of individual acceptance, and the influence of environmental factors. To generalize on this point, consider the relationships existing within the various levels in the typical organization. Top-level managers have the greatest amounts of authority and control over people at higher levels in the organization. The effectiveness of their personal control is lessened sharply at the lowest levels in the structure. Not only is the amount of authority less pronounced at lower levels but the scope of authority is reduced. Managers hold only a limited amount of authority over the work done by foremen because of organizational "distance"; but at the same time they may exert a great deal of control over both the work and the personal lives of their immediate subordinates. William Whyte's charges that corporations have tried to make individuals into organization men is one critical view of what could happen if and when corporations and other organizations attempt to widen their scope of control over the personal lives of their employees.

PROBLEMS IN DELEGATION OF AUTHORITY

Once the bases explaining why individuals accept authority are understood, managers must undertake the difficult and challenging problem of delegating specific tasks. In almost every delegation situation, the problems of parity, consistency, and clarity appear. Each of these problems is in turn complicated by the interactions of various factors in the dynamic environment of the delegation process.

How to give the proper amount of authority needed to exact the desired level of accountability is the trickiest art in delegating authority, since granting either too much or too little authority can be extremely difficult to correct. Furthermore, when authority has been delegated improperly, objectives may be difficult to reach or attainable only at the expense of other objectives.

---

[5] Dan Cordtz, "Antidisestablishmentarianism at Wheeling Steel," *Fortune,* June 1967, p. 105.

The sales manager cannot go out and sell another hundred thousand automobiles unless he has the funds to promote customer interest. Neither can he bring customers flocking into the salerooms without an adequate advertising and promotion budget. On the other hand, a division head with authority to make unlimited capital expenditures could make such costly mistakes that the entire firm would suffer as a result of his miscalculations. Thus, delegation of excessive amounts of authority can have unfortunate and detrimental effects on the organization's total goal structure. Capital budgets prepared for divisions could, for example, exceed the financial resources available to meet the organization's total obligations. Whenever legal authority exceeds the reasonable bounds of operating authority, the organization is placed in an awkward position. If authority relationships are revised to prevent financial chaos, internal power struggles result; individuals seek to retain or expand their empires, and only a strong top executive can keep order.

A classic example of this situation recently occurred in a major manufacturing company where unit managers had the power to make annual expenditures on capital equipment in amounts up to $500,000 without obtaining home office approval. The firm moved to reduce the $500,000 limit when it became apparent that its financial resources could not support such a high degree of financial freedom. This move to exert closer control over capital expenditures was met with grumbling, but a strong executive helped to make the changeover relatively easy. In another firm, such a move might have triggered a power struggle of massive proportions.

A witty, delightful, but nevertheless pointed, view of the delegation process appears in a satirical volume by Cyril N. Parkinson, appropriately enough titled *Parkinson's Law and Other Studies in Administration.*[6] On the way to describing his "law," which states that the number of people increases at a rate somewhere between 5.17 percent and 6.56 percent per year irrespective of any variation in the amount of work, if any, to be done, Mr. Parkinson describes the delegation process in this way:

> The fact is that the number of the officials and the quantity of the work are not related to each other at all. The rise in the total of those employed is governed by Parkinson's Law and would be much the same whether the volume of the work were to increase, diminish, or even to disappear. The importance of Parkinson's Law lies in the fact that it is a law of growth based upon an analysis of the factors by which that growth is controlled.
>
> The validity of this recently discovered law must rest mainly on statistical proofs, which will follow. Of more interest to the general reader is the explanation of the factors underlying the general tendency to which this law gives definition. Omitting technicalities (which are numerous) we may distinguish at the outset two motive forces. They can be represented for the present purpose by two almost axiomatic statements, thus: (1) "An official wants to multiply subordinates, not rivals" and (2) "Officials make work for each other."

---

[6] 2nd ed. (Boston: Houghton Mifflin Company, 1957).

To comprehend Factor 1, we must picture a civil servant, called A, who finds himself overworked. Whether this overwork is real or imaginary is immaterial, but we should observe, in passing, that A's sensation (or illusion) might easily result from his own decreasing energy: a normal symptom of middle age. For this real or imagined overwork there are, broadly speaking, three possible remedies. He may resign; he may ask to halve the work with a colleague called B; he may demand the assistance of two subordinates, to be called C and D. There is probably no instance in history, however, of A choosing any but the third alternative. By resignation he would lose his pension rights. By having B appointed, on his own level in the hierarchy, he would merely bring in a rival for promotion to W's vacancy when W (at long last) retires. So A would rather have C and D, junior men, below him. They will add to his consequence and, by dividing the work into two categories, as between C and D, he will have the merit of being the only man who comprehends them both. It is essential to realize at this point that C and D are, as it were, inseparable. To appoint C alone would have been impossible. Why? Because C, if by himself, would divide the work with A and so assume almost the equal status that has been refused in the first instance to B; a status the more emphasized if C is A's only possible successor. Subordinates must thus number two or more, each being thus kept in order by fear of the other's promotion. When C complains in turn of being overworked (as he certainly will) A will, with the concurrence of C, advise the appointment of two assistans to help C. But he can then avert internal friction only by advising the appointment of two more assistants to help D, whose position is much the same. With this recruitment of E, F, G, and H the promotion of A is now practically certain.

Seven officials are now doing what one did before. This is where Factor 2 comes into the operation. For these seven men make so much work for each other that all are fully occupied and A is actually working harder than ever. An incoming document may well come before each of them in turn. Official E decides that it falls within the province of F, who places a draft reply before C, who amends it drastically before consulting D, who asks G to deal with it. But G goes on leave at this point, handing the file over to H, who drafts a minute that is signed by D and returned to C, who revises his draft accordingly and lays the new version before A.

What does A do? He would have every excuse for signing the thing unread, for he has many other matters on his mind. Knowing now that he is to succeed W next year, he has to decide whether C or D should succeed to his own office. He had to agree to G's going on leave even if not yet strictly entitled to it. He is worried whether H should not have gone instead, for reasons of health. He has looked pale recently—partly but not solely because of his domestic troubles. Then there is the business of F's special increment of salary for the period of the conference and E's application for transfer to the Ministry of Pensions. A has heard that D is in love with a married typist and that G and F are no longer on speaking terms—no one seems to know why. So A might be tempted to sign C's draft and have done with it. But A is a conscientious man. Beset as he is with problems created by his colleagues for themselves and for him—created by the mere fact of these officials' existence—he is not the man to shirk his duty. He reads through the draft with care, deletes the fussy paragraphs added by C and H, and restores the thing back to the form preferred in the first instance by the able (if quarrelsome) F. He corrects the English—none of these young men can write grammatically—and finally produces the same reply he would have written if officials C to H had never been born. Far more people have taken far longer to produce the same result. No one has been idle. All have done their best. And it is late in the evening before A finally quits his office and begins the return journey to Ealing. The last of the office lights are being turned off in the gathering dusk that marks the end of another day's administrative toil. Among the last to leave, A reflects with bowed shoulders and a wry smile that late hours, like gray hairs, are among the penalities of success.[7]

Parkinson's satirical description of delegation and assignment is realistic enough to strike uncomfortably close to home in more than a few large organizations, and it has surprising validity even in some smaller companies.

In addition to the assignment problems so wittily described by Parkinson, another difficulty in delegation is the inconsistent use of delegated authority. If managers are confused about their individual areas of freedom or discretion, or if they use their authority inconsistently, subordinates may be demoralized. When a boss makes polite suggestions one week and shouts orders the next, subordinates become bewildered, perhaps even frightened. If a boss reprimands a man for being late one week and fires another the following week for the same offense, his inconsistency causes subordinates to be continually uneasy. But suppose an arbitrator reinstates the discharged man. What effect will this have on the boss? Will his insecurity be compounded? If so, what form will his insecurity take? Will the authority relationships after the reinstatement be those that existed before?

The problems raised by inconsistent use of authority or by ambiguous delegation of authority go well beyond those raised in the hiring, firing, and reinstatement example. Violation of the unity-of-command principle (one man–one boss) is one of the most common, and one of the most frustrating, problems in organizational structures; and such a violation stems directly from a lack of clarity in the delegation and use of authority Ambiguous delegation of authority and muddled use of legally delegated authority are critical problems in the process of delegation and raise the questions of *what* authority is involved and *by whom it should be possessed.* The question of implied versus actual authority is also a critical one, particularly in line-staff relations. Does a staff man have the authority to make a change? Is he acting for the line man or simply implying that he is? Finally, there is the relative degree of willingness to delegate. The supervisor who must delegate is in quite a different

---

[7] *Ibid.,* pp. 4–7.

relationship to his subordinate than the one who chooses to delegate. Grudgingly granted authority must be viewed in quite a different light than that which is delegated freely. Any person who has been responsible to several masters at the same time is well aware of the seriousness of these problems.

The process of delegating authority shelters many of the common mistakes encountered in the design of organization structure. When improperly executed, delegation can result in confusions of line and staff authority and corresponding problems in information flows. It can also cause a misuse of staffs and service departments and unnecessary conflicts between units in the organizational hierarchy. In addition, it can generate a lack of parity between authority and responsibility, and this imbalance causes goals to be subverted. Failure to establish proper control relationships between portions of multiunit, decentralized operations can result from poorly executed delegation, as can the tendency toward rigidity or overorganization. And underorganization can occur if excessively unstructured associations are allowed to develop. It is thus important to consider delegation carefully and to give it its just due in the design of operating organizations. In particular, delegations should be planned in advance with proper consideration given objectives, personnel, and duties to be performed. Even with planning, problems will continue to exist; but their incidence will be less if delegation is done with skill *and* a great deal of preplanning.

A certain amount of progress can be made toward clarifying authority relationships by developing effective ways and means of specifying exactly which matters are to be delegated and which are not. The degree of specificity required in delegation, the nature of the matter being delegated, the degree of repetitiveness of the assigned duties, and other concerns such as the level of performance demanded are the critical points encountered in laying out authority relationships. In general, written delegation is good when relatively long time periods are involved or when the written word is needed to legitimize individual action. In some cases, a document or a job description must be prepared to assure certain individuals that express authority has been granted to allow a particular person to perform specified deeds or to make particular decisions. For example, specific limits on capital expenditures almost always appear in written form. On the other hand, oral directives are most expeditious when the duration of delegation is short, when an extremely complex matter is being delegated, when delegation is related to the performance of minor or infrequently performed tasks, or when other factors make the preparation of written instructions either unnecessary or cumbersome; for example, there is little need to write out a request to answer the telephone or to answer the door.

FUNCTIONAL AUTHORITY

One aspect of delegation of authority that causes a great deal of conflict is the area know as functional authority. Chandler's "chapters in the growth of business" (described in the previous chapter) point out how goals are continually reshuffled as business firms pass through stages in their growth cycles.[8] In the earliest phases of growth, the one-man business sees all authority held by the owner-manager. As growth occurs, one man can no longer do it all; he must, as he reaches limits on his time, energy, and expertise, delegate duties to various specialists. Thus, growth involves not only an ongoing reassessment of goals and objectives but also a shifting pattern of delegation. Of all of the areas of delegation, the shifting of pure line authority to specialized staff units is perhaps the most important.

If authority could be represented on a continuum as "pure line authority," any staff or functional authority that might be delegated would have to be visualized as "taking over" a segment of the continuum. As firms grow in size and complexity and the need for expertise grows, greater authority over various functions is entrusted to specialists. Accounting and legal functions typically are delegated initially on a part-time basis or subcontracted to outside consultants. Accounting services or public accounting firms receive a part-time delegation of authority in the record-keeping function. Later, as demands for specialized services grow, full-time staff units take over these functions. As the need for still more specialization and/or technical expertise arises, the line organization gives up more and more authority to functional staffs. The authority which special staffs gain by encroachment on existing line authority is called "functional authority," because its legitimacy is rooted in knowledge of specialized functions. Since the exercise of functional authority is a major source of line-staff conflict, it requires further elaboration.

FUNCTIONAL AUTHORITY IN STAFF UNITS

Functional authority is the ability to exercise control or command over a given functional area across departmental lines. It can be strong or weak, depending upon the extent to which command authority is delegated. A classification scheme for staffs outlined by Holden, Fish, and Smith specifies four varieties of staffs holding functional authority:[9] control staffs, coordinative staffs, advisory staffs, and service staffs. The *control staff* exercises a considerable amount of authority over special functions and therefore has a strong functional authority. A corporate accounting staff with the power to dictate methods of recording and reporting inventory data would fall into this category. *Coordinative staffs* also possess command authority, but the scope of their authority is narrower than that of control staffs. A typical coordinative staff might direct the flow of materials, parts, or products between several producing departments. Theoretically *advisory staffs* have no functional authority, but most do have implied authority. When an advisory staff reporting to a top manager makes a pointed suggestion, the burden of proof of why the recommendation should not be accepted rests on the person receiving the suggestion; and the higher the level to which the staff unit reports, the greater the authority

[8] Alfred E. Chandler, Jr., *Strategy and Structure* (Cambridge, Mass.: MIT Press, 1962).

[9] See P. Holden, L. Fish, and G. Smith, *Top Management Organization and Control* (New York: McGraw-Hill, Inc., 1951), pp. 36–58.

imputed to its suggestions. *Service staffs,* on the other hand, have little functional authority, either assigned or implied. A staff charged with operating
a cafeteria, for instance, has almost no authority to require the purchase or
consumption of meals by those who may use its services. It does, however,
retain line authority over its own functions such as purchasing food.

As Figure 9.1 indicates, degrees of functional authority can vary quite
sharply in different classes of staff units. Within a single organization, any
and all classes of staffs can exist and within the classes differences in functional
authority held can appear: some control staffs are far less in control than
others. Obviously, the concept of functional authority is not an easy one to
put into use, and for this reason it remains a source of conflict and confusion.

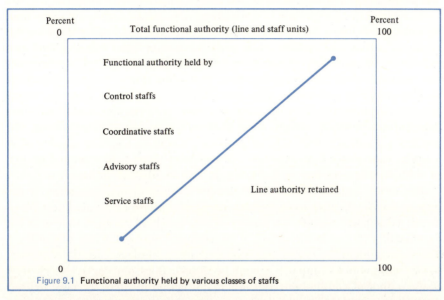

Figure 9.1 Functional authority held by various classes of staffs

In order to clarify relationships between line authority and functional staff
authority more fully, consider the following situation: when Zeron Products
selected a new president, the chairman of the board decided to help the
president ease into his new duties by retaining control of staff activities for
a period of one year. Accordingly, Zeron began to reorganize its activities
so that line departments would report to the president and staff departments
would report to the chairman of the board. The following departments were
the principal ones affected by the change:

Finance department
Legal department
Production department
Sales department
Research and development group
Industrial relations department

Assuming that their names reflect their major activities, how should the departments be divided to fulfill the chairman's wishes?

Suppose the departments were listed in these categories:

Line	Staff
Finance	Legal
Sales	Industrial relations
Production	Research and development

What reasoning might be used to justify this particular grouping?

To begin with, designation of a department as line or staff is not dependent upon title, but upon the *type of authority* possessed. The ability to command or direct actions designates a line activity; on the other hand, a staff has "advisory authority." In practice, most supervisors of staff groups exercise line authority in hiring and firing their own subordinates. A line department such as production typically has line authority over these same personnel functions, and it may hold action authority over operating decisions. Production departments, however, rarely have authority over the actions of, say, the finance department. The type of authority possessed and exercised is thus a major determinant of whether a department should be classified as line or staff. Action authority is line authority, while advisory authority is not.

The other major criterion used to identify line or staff authority is the relationship of the unit to the organization's purposes or product lines. When a unit is engaged directly in producing the goods or services that give the organization its reason for being, it is usually considered a line department. There is a tendency to classify units by title; for example, the legal department in one automobile company is staff because it does not contribute directly to the output of automobiles. But in a major law firm where the legal department does general as opposed to special legal work and contributes a large part of the firm's total billings, it is invariably a line department.

Clearly, the use of titles to classify departments can be misleading. The distinctions between line and staff departments can only be determined after a review of both the main functions of the business *and* its component parts *and* the authority possessed by the unit being classified. Thus, in the case of Zeron Products, categorization of the six departments as either line or staff would depend on both the main flow of the company's business *and* the actual authority possessed by each department. Finance, for example, might be placed in the line category because it has a considerable amount of action authority. This assumption is certainly reasonable in industries where financial resources must be carefully conserved and rigidly controlled, that is, where they must be handled in line fashion. It is obvious, but not often noted, that line departments often advise each other on certain matters, for example, sales advises production about expected volume requirements. These line-to-line relationships perform more of a staff advisory function than one involving line authority.

This discussion of how Zeron might attempt to classify certain departments as line or staff may seem to be artificially contrived to prove a point. It makes no difference that the Zeron illustration is taken from reality; the main point is that delegation of authority in line-staff organizations often generates serious conflicts over the control or coordination of given areas or activities. Line personnel tend to be suspicious of staff personnel who suggest changes but do not have to live with them after they go into effect. Staff specialists, if they really know their areas of specialization, often tend to be overzealous; and they frequently push their ideas, convictions, and conclusions well beyond the normal limits of their duly constituted authority. When the zeal of staff specialists usurps or infringes on line authority, the natural reaction is either inner resentment or open opposition. This can take the form of passive or overt resistance to any change suggested by the staffs. ("If you want to know who thinks he runs this shop, see the time-study man.") Such an attitude not only hinders the efficiency of operations but also builds mistrust and conflict. This friction has a generally adverse effect on the organization's long-run goals.

The question of who should do what is extremely important in line-staff relationships. If line supervisors do not know how to use staff effectively, they too can cause much confusion. It is perfectly natural for line personnel to downgrade staff assistance if they do not know what a staff unit does or *can* do for them. On the other hand, line officials who overwork staffs by requesting services beyond the staff's normal scope of duties are depriving themselves of a source of special knowledge and skill. If frequent requests for such "make work" projects generate an increase in staff size, staff activities may proliferate to maintain the size and influence of the expanded staff unit. This in turn causes still more confusion and additional conflicts in authority. The persistent misuse of staff talent can bring about a nightmare of bureaucracy and empire building. Examples of such situations have often appeared in large business firms and in government.

The line between persuasion and functional authority is rarely clear in line-staff dealings. Since confusion exists, buck passing is common and there is a tendency for both line and staff personnel to claim credit for good ideas and to disavow responsibility for bad ones. "Suggestions" that are really veiled threats complicate line-staff interactions, and threats phrased as seemingly innocuous suggestions can cause similar difficulties.

Summary

Delegation involves assigning tasks, granting authority, and exacting responsibility. The critical problem lies not in recognizing the structure of delegation, but in actually doing the job. Delegation is truly an art, but an art that is practiced with increasing complexity as the organization grows and patterns of development shift. As degrees of line authority are delegated to functional staff units, the depth and scope of delegation widens even within given functional specialties. The problems encountered in delegation are vital ones, and the long-run goals and the short-run efficiency of the organization depend upon effective delegation patterns.

The remaining chapter in this section turns to the approaches and techniques which have been utilized to bring about improved practice in the difficult art of delegation.

Study Questions

1. How can staff departments be classified? What kinds of staffs are most common in industrial organizations?

2. What is functional authority? How does it evolve in the organization's life cycle?

3. Contrast the concepts of formal authority and acceptance authority. Which of these concepts seems to have the greatest validity?

4. Contrast the nature of power and influence. Under what conditions is each most effective?

5. What is a zone of acceptance (of an order)? How might you define it in terms of a student-professor relationship?

6. Under what conditions should authority be delegated in writing? Orally?

7. What kinds of subordinates prefer loose control? Authoritarian control?

8. Is there any evidence of the "divine right of kings" type of authority in modern times? Under what conditions does it exist?

9. What problems arise when legal authority and operating authority are not identified clearly?

10. How can the definition of "line" and "staff" authority be clarified? Give an example of line-staff confusion over authority relationships.

The process of building effective organizations involves innumerable activities, but none are more important at the outset than the relationship between strategies, structures, and delegation. Strategies, once devised, must be carried out in some structural framework; and no matter what organizational design is chosen, delegation takes place within it. Whether the organization structure is based on building blocks, information flows, or people-oriented concepts is immaterial; what really matters is that work must be assigned and executed in accordance with strategic plans and organizational goals. It follows logically that organizational planning and delegation procedures are important segments of the integration of strategic goals and organizational designs.

Clarification of the kinds of authority relationships in the organization is one of the most productive approaches used to relate strategy to organizational design. Delegation is invariably a dynamic process which calls for continuing revision of assignments based on planning, but tempered by judgment and pragmatism. If a person can handle more authority, he usually gets it; but if he fails to make the grade, he may find himself the victim of a shuffling of assignments designed to lighten his work load and reduce his scope of authority. It is highly doubtful that techniques will ever be developed to handle the process of delegation scientifically, but better approaches are being developed constantly. New concepts based on analysis of information flows and communications patterns are under continual study. Program Evaluation Review Techniques (PERT), a series of devices primarily for planning and allocating work, are also making a

CHAPTER 10

Planning to Integrate Strategy with Organizational Design

contribution to better delegation by pointing out interrelationships between the tasks which must be accomplished to meet given sets of objectives. Though PERT and the various means of improving delegation are not directly related to the development of organizational design, they do help to forge the links which integrate strategic and structural considerations. Along this same line, the reshaping of structure or hierarchical relationships in existing organizational designs requires techniques that are often used in addition to or in conjunction with the techniques advocated to improve the planning and integration of delegation. Three approaches have made particularly valuable contributions to the linking of strategy and structure through the process of delegation: (1) techniques for improving relationships between line and staff departments; (2) studies of interaction patterns to identify possible points of conflict which can then be reduced by changing interactions in existing structures; and (3) delegation of authority to decentralized decision-making centers.

PLANNING FOR IMPROVED DELEGATION

Better delegation begins with careful preplanning of organizational design. Planning provides inputs of materials, human resources, and information flows; and the implementation process carries out the chosen courses of action. Planning attempts to deal with potential problems before they arise, and careful planning helps the organization to reach its objectives within the constraints of available material and human resources. It is almost self-evident that planning, organizational design, and delegation interact constantly and that any designs or techniques utilized are subject to the dynamics of an ongoing fluid set of factors and constraints. As much flexibility as possible must thus be built into plans; and conflict should be minimized by careful clarification of duties and assignments and the development of appropriate information flows.[1] The key factor in this process is preplanning; and the real trick is not to make revolutionary moves, but to do what has to be done with as little uproar as possible. Though authorities differ on the specific means to this result, they generally agree that preplanning is a necessary ingredient in sound delegation.

Management writers as far apart in theoretical constructs as LeBreton and March and Simon stress the importance of specificity in laying out the steps needed to achieve effective delegation.[2] LeBreton's approach is noted briefly in Chapter 3. March and Simon in their most important work, *Organizations,* also lay out a series of rational approaches to recognizing authority relationships and the perceptions and cognitions of persons in the system.[3] Though

---

[1] George S. Odiorne, *How Managers Make Things Happen* (Englewood Cliffs, N.J.: Prentice-Hall, Inc., 1961).

[2] Preston P. LeBreton, *General Administration, Planning and Implementation* (New York: Holt, Rinehart and Winston, Inc., 1965).

[3] James G. March and Herbert A. Simon, *Organizations* (New York: John Wiley & Sons, Inc., 1958).

this latter approach seems to be less cookbook-oriented than the former, it, too, specifies limits in rational and irrational behavior patterns so that specific steps can be developed to improve planning and delegation activities in given organizational designs.

A group of professors at the Harvard Business School have developed a dozen critical steps that contain all phases of planning and implementation.[4] In this twelve-step approach, a number of steps directly assist the kind of planning effort needed to improve the integration of strategy and structure. For example, the first two steps specify the need to find potential problems in a given set of strategic choices and to decide how to and to whom to delegate authority. The third and the fourth steps set up formal means of coordinating objectives and strategies in some sort of hierarchy and indicates that information systems must be devised to coordinate various units to prevent divided accountability. The fifth, sixth, and seventh steps relate tasks clearly to objectives and provide for comparisons of actual to projected performance and the assignment of tasks to existing skills with some preparation of people possessing the right skills for the future. The remaining steps deal with evaluating performance, developing motivation and controls, and providing managerial direction and leadership style. In each of these steps there are specific details on how to go about improving the clarification of objectives, duties, information flows, and other activities that serve to integrate strategy with structure in the overall attainment of organizational goals.

In his classic work *Administrative Action,* William H. Newman outlines what he calls a tool for analysis and integration of broad management problems.[5] Beginning with a discussion of the basic foundations of administration, Newman describes the processes of planning, organizing, assembling resources, supervising, and controlling. Though each of these processes has some pertinence in the integrating of strategy and structure, a selective look at the detailed implementation plan he presents in each of these areas shows that one of the most critical aspects of planning is the development of an integrated and comprehensive organizational design. In the organization category, Newman stresses the need to establish departments, to provide adequate staff, and to clarify relationships between units and men within a sound structural framework. Under the assembly of resources he states that selection and development of executives are the most pertinent points. One of the critical portions of supervising, according to Newman, is the establishment of the necessary direction and delegation to obtain desired results in general supervisory areas and to improve coordination of the various factors of production. Finally, he identifies checks on performance and standards, and the development of balance in the control structure as the most pertinent variables influencing the integration of organizational objectives with the control processes in the hierarchy. Newman's extremely thorough and inclusive approach

[4] E.P. Learned, C.R. Christianson, K.R. Andrews, W.D. Guth, *Business Policy Text and Cases* (Homewood, Ill.: Richard D. Irwin, Inc., 1965).

[5] 2nd ed. (Englewood Cliffs, N.J.: Prentice-Hall, Inc., 1963), pp. 475.

ranks high on the list of explanations of how to bridge the gap between objectives and their implementation. Ralph Cordiner, former head of General Electric and the architect of its massive internal reorganization in the 1950's, has outlined an approach to organizational planning. Based on his extensive practical experience, the following program indicates how to deal with the technical and human problems encountered in organization and delegation:

1. Determine the goals, objectives, programs, and plans best designed to meet objectives—for the company as a whole and for each division.

2. Determine the work to be done to achieve the results expected within these general guidelines.

3. Divide, group, and relate work in a simple, logical, understandable, and comprehensive organizational structure.

4. Assign essential work clearly and definitely to the various departments and groups in the organization structure.

5. Determine the requirements and qualifications of the required personnel.

6. Staff the organization with people needed to meet these qualifications.

7. Establish policies and procedures designed to help achieve the organization's goals.[6]

Cordiner starts with the determination of goals and assignments of work to specific units and then develops some of the human dimensions of organization. His generalized list contains few specific details, but it is common knowledge that General Electric has made many accommodations and adjustments in its production and service operations in an attempt to increase productivity without adversely affecting morale or motivation. These attempts, though not always successful, have been defended as honest efforts to effect a meaningful compromise between individual needs and organizational goals. Cordiner's listing is one practical view of how the theory and practice of organizational planning and delegation can be welded together to meet the realities of competitive operation. It is interesting to note in passing that Cordiner's approach to improving delegation differs little from those proposed by Newman and the Harvard group.

PROGRAM EVALUATION REPORT TECHNIQUES

Another basic approach currently being utilized to assist in the planning of work loads to be delegated is the technique known as PERT, or critical path analysis. PERT attempts to relate work assignments to plans and goals in terms of events and activities networks. Events are points in the network which are reached when activities, usually represented in terms of time of completion

---

[6] Ralph Cordiner, *New Frontiers for Professional Managers, McKinsey Lecture,* Columbia University Graduate School of Business (New York: McGraw-Hill, Inc., 1956).

(days, weeks, or months), are ended. Suppose it takes two weeks to dig a foundation for a new apartment building in a PERT representation of the entire construction project. The activity of digging would be represented in terms of a two-week period and the event (the completed foundation) would be shown in the network as the completion of the excavating job.

In a PERT diagram, all paths needed to reach a goal are shown as events and all activities are usually given three possible values: (1) most likely time of completion, (2) most optimistic time of completion, and (3) most pessimistic time of completion. The paths of various activity-events chains are shown in the diagram and the most likely times (T_E) are calculated for each possible chain. The longest chain is called the critical, or limiting, path, since the project's completion is dependent upon its length rather than on the time it takes to complete other, shorter paths. To illustrate the concept of the critical path, if four people take four routes of unknown length to a common end point, and all travel at the same basic speed with no delays, their arrival times will vary directly with the length of the routes they travel (assuming equal difficulty in traversing the four paths). If all must arrive before the travel plan is complete, then the latest arrival has traveled the critical path. The time the others have had to wait for the last man to arrive in order to reach the desired objective in the system is labeled "slack time."[7] If slack time is known in advance, the other three trips could be started at varying times after the critical-path wayfarer has begun his journey, and thus the other travelers could be either resting or performing other activities without holding up the collective time of final arrival. One obvious advantage of knowing about such slack time is that resources can be diverted to cut down the time span of the critical path if speed of completion is the desired goal. The latter use is especially important in defense and aerospace industries, where lead time is vital.

PERT analysis allows controls over projects by making checks available at each event and each path in the total network. Estimated times can be checked against actual times, and in a PERT/cost network, similar calculations can be made for costs of individual events or entire projects. Tradeoffs can be instituted to move resources from one area to another to cut costs, to reduce lead times, to shorten critical paths in selected subareas, or to achieve other desired goals or subgoals. The ability to identify and make tradeoffs is particularly valuable in industries under intense competitive pressures or where lead time is extremely important. The Boeing Company, for example, used PERT in the early stages of development of the Minuteman and Bombarc missiles. Thus, PERT helped the United States to reduce the missile gap, and it has also seen countless applications in new product development. General Foods even uses PERT in routine fashion to plan and analyze policy changes which partially affect several areas of operation.

---

[7] Two key assumptions here are that all four people must complete this event before the next event can be undertaken, and there can be no looping back in the diagram. If there is no such relationship, the conclusions taken from this illustration are invalid.

The chief value of PERT is that it can simulate what would happen further along the event-activities network if tradeoffs are made at any earlier stage. If the PERT system is programmed on computers, simulation of alternative actions is readily available (in seconds or minutes) with little commitment of men, money, or physical resources. Potential dangers and problem areas are thus identified in advance, and prescriptive or preventative actions can be instituted before the fact.

The PERT system presents the total planning network within critical times based on expert estimates and then compares its results with the latest allowable times of completion imposed by external limits such as competitive conditions or contractual stipulations. Once estimates of completion are made for the critical path (stated in latest allowable times), the estimated probability of completing projects on time can also be determined by manipulation of the PERT system. If the probability of completion is either too low or too high, resources may be shown as too ample or too limited; and adjustments can then be made to provide the optimum blend of productive inputs.[8]

PERT thus has a number of advantages that make it uniquely useful in planning and integrating strategy and structure. The construction of the PERT system forces analysts to spell out the work in units and the tasks in quantifiable terms; these quantitative terms are then used to predict where problems are likely to occur. PERT can help in scheduling the start of potentially slack paths after activities and events are undertaken in the critical path. It can also point out what specific resources need to be allocated or can be reallocated without lengthening the time taken to reach various points in the network. It can give specific cost and time estimates for each event and thus help to avoid overlap or delays in succeeding points in the diagram; and it can do this long before the problem arises, thus minimizing costly delays. A typical PERT diagram is shown in Figure 10.1. The amount of preplanning that goes into the development of PERT systems is in itself valuable, since managers with project responsibilities are forced to take a good hard look at what may occur before the happening actually takes place. Simulation is particularly helpful here, since any number of potential situations can be analyzed in terms of their probability of occurrence and their probable outcomes.[9]

On the other hand, PERT has some technical and negative aspects. On the technical side, experts point out that certain projects are just not economically feasible for network-type analysis. Other technical complaints center on the fact that estimates and judgments underlying the PERT system are subjective or take too long to prepare properly. Finally, unless projects included in the PERT network are specifically interrelated, there are some difficulties in using the technique. If projects are not related, then PERT networks fail to generate

---

[8] The appendix to the SUNY—Wilshire Campus case at the end of this chapter explains the technical calculations used in a PERT network in greater detail.

[9] For a somewhat dated, but nonetheless worthwhile, view, see Ivar Avots, "The Management Side of PERT," *California Management Review,* vol. 4, no. 24 (Winter 1962) or R.W. Miller, "How to Plan and Control with PERT," *Harvard Business Review,* vol. 4, no. 2 (March–April 1962), pp. 93–104.

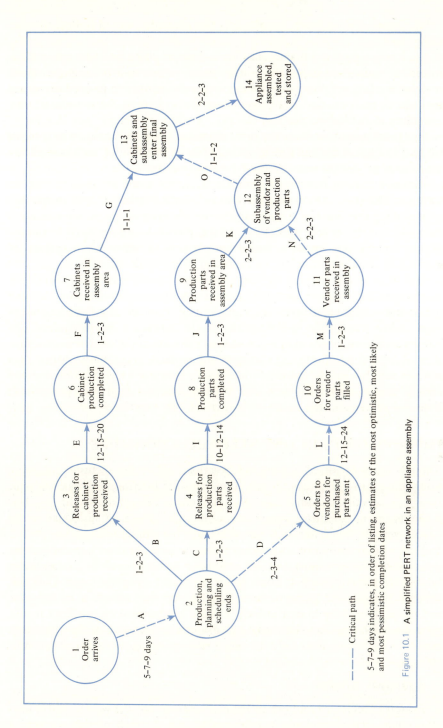

5–7–9 days indicates, in order of listing, estimates of the most optimistic, most likely and most pessimistic completion dates

– – – Critical path

Figure 10.1 A simplified PERT network in an appliance assembly

valid results. Projects run in parallel, for example, are ill suited to PERT techniques.

On a more personal plane, PERT faces human objections because it tends to replace individual judgment. Furthermore, estimates are sometimes made in defensive fashion; that is, they may be pessimistic or even padded to conceal inadequate performance. If a project does last as long as the pessimistic time estimates, individuals concerned can say, "I told you it might take that long." If the completion date is sooner than estimated, they can shrug their forecast off as a bad guess and not lose anything because the flush of early completion tends to wipe out the onus of the incorrect forecast.

Actually, a good number of complaints against PERT are centered not on technical critiques, but on the fact that it has not worked as well in practice as it should theoretically. On balance, though, PERT seems to have made a valuable contribution to allocating human, physical, and financial resources. It has, for example, made a major contribution to improved delegation by helping to integrate strategic and structural planning activities. It has also served most successfully in defense and construction industries where time is important and slack resources can typically be diverted to other uses. Another area where PERT has proven its worth is new product development, where adjustments are legion and mistakes or changes must be recognized and corrected before costly errors are made. PERT has one final disadvantage: it must be carried out by top management, since its coordinative aspects are not yet suitable for delegation to low-level operating units. Staffers can and should prepare PERT diagrams and calculations, but final veto power over their use remains in the hands of higher-echelon executives.

IMPROVEMENTS IN LINE-STAFF RELATIONSHIPS

Though the generalized approaches described above are inclusive means of integrating strategy and structure, the line-staff interface in organizational design is so critically important and influences delegation so directly that it merits special attention. Numerous techniques have been advocated as the "sure" way to foster line-staff harmony, but no panacea has yet appeared. Indeed, a combination of approaches seems to hold the most hope of success, a fact some organizations discover only after being burned by the teachings of some ill-starred prophet. Looking for the "right" solution is not foolhardy though, because the game, if won, can be very rewarding; it is, however, not particularly wise to cast out all possible solutions to embrace what may be a disappointing "one best way." Consideration of some of the alternative means of improving line-staff relations is one way to help avoid such potential myopia.

ADVISORY STAFFS

Douglas McGregor and others have advocated that the way to better line-staff relations is to structure interactions so that the staff performs a strictly advisory function. Staff never comes to the aid of the line unless specifically asked to do so. On request, staffers will give advice or technical guidance, but under no conditions will they usurp line authority. The main job of the staff is assistance, and it functions as a resource or a consulting department, not as a command unit.

In practice, this approach does tend to cut down conflict between line and staff units, but it needs care and feeding to be carried out successfully. Unless the line feels the need to use staff help, much of the specialized talent available in the staff organization is not called upon, and the advantages gained from its special skills are not fully utilized. If the staff is just a think tank, its usefulness is limited; and if the line seeks advice for show and then casts it aside without careful appraisal, the advisory staff concept has limited utility. A mature viewpoint is needed before this approach can work, and developing such an outlook requires considerable training and an understanding of the benefits available from the use of staff experts to help solve specialized problems.

COMPULSORY STAFF SERVICE

A variation on the theme of a strictly advisory staff is the concept of compulsory review of completed staff work. Widely used in military operations during World War II and now found throughout the business community, this concept sees managers outlining problems and broad limitations to staff people and then awaiting a final report. Staffs present only complete work; and the line manager either acts upon, modifies, or rejects the report, or returns it for additional work or modification. Decisions are made by the line, and the staff report's actions, dates, schedules, and so on become line management directives only if adopted by the appropriate level of line management.

Some confusion appears in this approach over the implied authority used by staffers when they prepare plans. This results in the ghost-writer syndrome: the staff presents such a mass of detail that the line manager cannot really refute the plan and so adopts it in his own name. In effect, the staff man makes the decision, not the line manager, and the staffer thus assumes authority not rightfully his. When this situation is repeated over and over again, the organization tends to impute authority to the staff, and the distinction between line and staff is blurred sharply. In fact, the completed staff work approach helps to improve the delegation process, but it is not unique.[10] It reflects an extension of some of the techniques described in other parts of this chapter.

GENERAL PRINCIPLES

Generalized approaches to improving line-staff delegations have been proposed by many writers, two of whom are selected as representative of this particular point of view. One of these authors is Melville Dalton; the other is Louis A. Allen.

[10] J. Lewis Powell, "Completed Staff Work—Key to Effective Delegation," *Management Review,* June 1956.

Dalton, basing his suggestions on an extensive study of operating environments, offers the following guidelines for reducing line-staff conflict.

1. Set up a separate staff unit to cut down line-staff conflicts in coordination.
2. Increase promotion and rewards available within staff units.
3. Create more of a responsibility for project workability within staff units. (In effect, make them more accountable for results.)
4. Require staff people to have supervisory experience before transfering them to line positions.
5. Remove fear of reprisal in both line and staff units if ideas or approaches fail to work out.
6. Place more emphasis on the social sciences in education for industrial careers.[11]

These six suggestions contain both specific and general aids to the reduction of line-staff conflicts, and they reflect a modern research-based orientation that contains clear overtones of neoclassical writings derived from introspection and practitioners' summaries of experience. The first principle, for example, has found widespread application in defense contracting where one spectacularly phrased job title, "internal project interface coordination engineer," reflects how Dalton's coordinative orientation has made inroads. Other, less direct illustration is found in the increasing use of social scientists in industry, even though not all of them are being utilized in their chosen fields of specialization. Dalton's remaining guidelines call for little elaboration because of their coverage elsewhere in this chapter.

Louis Allen, a noted management consultant, presents the idea that successful line-staff interaction must be based on a clear definition of roles and relationships and then offers these prescriptive suggestions:

HOW THE STAFF CAN DO A BETTER JOB

1. Operate in terms of the objectives of the company as a whole rather than as a specialized unit.
2. Encourage and educate the line on how to use staff help effectively.
3. Recognize all aspects of resistance to change and plan to overcome it by considering relationships, personnel effects of given changes, and so on.
4. Develop and acquire technical proficiency in order to do assigned jobs more effectively.

---

[11] Melville Dalton, "Conflicts Between Staff and Line, Managerial Officers," *American Sociological Review,* vol. 15 (June 1950), pp. 342–351.

HOW THE LINE CAN DO A BETTER JOB

1. Make maximum use of staff—make the staff do its job.

2. Make proper use of staff—use them for special and technical problems in which they can contribute some positive assistance.

3. Keep the staff informed of changes and happenings in line operations in which they have some connection.

4. Line officials should not abdicate line responsibility in favor of the staff—there is no reason to believe that the staff can do the operations job better than line people.[12]

Allen's suggestions reflect the view of a management consultant who has had considerable experience in helping to soothe difficult problems in line-staff relationships. Their practicality is somewhat diminished by their generality; but Allen's prescription, when implemented fully, is well regarded by many operating executives.

All the means of improving line-staff relationships stress the need for clear direction, and their common bond is their attempt to develop practical guidelines for improvement. The key emphasis in many of these approaches is on personnel relations and on the possession and use of authority rather than on structural factors. The nature and use of authority is the key factor, not the hierarchy within which it is exercised.

ANALYSIS OF INTERACTION PATTERNS

In contrast to the emphasis on authority in setting up "principles" to improve line-staff relationships, interaction analysis concentrates on structures to identify and reduce possible sources of friction, conflict, or delay in assignment and delegation. William F. Whyte's classic portrayal of work activity problems in barrel manufacturing and his even more famous study involving the crying waitress in a study of restaurant operations are examples of this approach.[13] While studying work relationships in a barrel-manufacturing department, Whyte determined that the growing friction in the department was rooted in the supervisor's inability to cope with the changing nature of his interactions with workers brought about by changes in the size and nature of the barrel-manufacturing operation. In the case of the "crying waitress," Whyte hypothesized that similar pressures in work flows and work relationships brought on the flood of tears that converted hidden tensions into a visible crisis. Whyte, and later Chapple and Sayles, developed methods for analyzing work flows and interactions as a means of improving assignments and delegation activi-

---

[12] Louis A. Allen, *Developing Sound Line and Staff Relationships,* Studies in Personnel Policies (New York: National Industrial Conference Board, no. 153, 1956), pp. 70–80.

[13] *Human Relations in the Restaurant Industry* (New York: McGraw-Hill, Inc., 1948), pp. 47–60.

ties.[14] He also advocated interaction analysis as one of the basic ways to bring about better implementation of strategic plans within existing organizational designs or within structures revised after interaction analysis has identified sources of potential difficulty and causes of nonproductive conflict.

Interaction analysis traces flows of work in the organizational structure and, after an analysis of activities, interactions, and observer-perceived sentiments, tries to determine what problems exist. Turbulence in the system is identified, and possible causes are postulated. Solutions are then framed by recommending changes in interaction patterns between individuals, jobs, and/or the structures supporting the work flow.

Suggested changes may take several forms. For example, work flows may be redesigned to prevent or reduce the impact of physical problems such as delay in the arrival of materials to the workplace or other evidences of poor scheduling. Another example of how conflict in the system might be removed is the adoption of training programs to improve the performance of supervisors or workers trained insufficiently for their jobs. When defective equipment causes conflicts, either it can be replaced or maintained more effectively to avoid irritating imbalances in the work flow. Machinery and equipment problems are relatively easy to solve, but human problems are generally more complex. The interactionist solution to human problems commonly invokes transfers, training, removal, promotion, or some variation of group or individual counseling.

This approach focuses on work flows and interactions at the point where friction seems to occur and typically recommends adapting structural hierarchies to lessen the observed conflict. According to its advocates, it tries to change the changeable rather than changing people or stressing more rigidly defined areas of authority. It thus concentrates on continued high levels of output without attempting to bring about changes in individual personalities.

One of the chief drawbacks found in applying this approach is that the analytical techniques it utilizes are subjective, especially in measuring attitudes and sentiments. In the final analysis, results depend directly upon the wisdom, judgment, and experience of the observer. Another drawback is that it has limited applicability in capital intensive industries. The problem is seen quite clearly in an auto assembly line, where monotony results from specialization, but basic changes cannot be made easily because of the inefficiencies of scale suffered in a transformation of technology. In its present state, however, interaction analysis adds new dimensions to the problem of structuring organization. As social science techniques and measurement become sharper, it undoubtedly will play a bigger role in organizational design activities.

DECENTRALIZATION OF AUTHORITY

The problems encountered in line-staff authority relationships have a close kinship to problems appearing when organizations attempt to adopt decen-

---

[14] Elliot Chapple and Leonard R. Sayles, *The Measure of Management* (New York: Crowell-Collier and Macmillan, Inc., 1961).

tralized decision making. Decentralization calls for the exercise of authority as near as possible to the point where problems originate. The concept of decentralization is an authority concept, however, it is not a geographical one. Decentralization attempts to make use of the economic advantages springing from knowledge of local conditions; the location of these decision points is immaterial. Decentralized decision making can thus occur in an organization with only one location, even though it is more usually associated with multi-unit operations.

As organizations grow, the volume of decisions also rises, and the sheer crush of size increases pressures to shift decisions to lower levels in the structure. The total number of decisions made is not necessarily related to organizational size, but size is one critical variable in determining the totality of the decisions to be made. Other factors are the geographical dispersion of operating units, the extent of merger and acquisition activity, the degree of closeness of control desired by top management, the level of sophistication of decision makers, the pressures of competition, and cost factors in the external environment.

A number of well-regarded management process scholars hold that managerial talents can be observed and developed more readily in operating environments where decision making is decentralized.[15] Testing the man on the job is considered to be the best means of identifying this managerial talent *and* a practical way of developing it in the most expeditious fashion. Since decentralization allows goals to be set and results to be measured close to the point of decision, it purportedly stimulates and motivates performance. It also tends to overcome the dilutions and distortions that occur when approval must be gained from the "top" before a decision can be made. Norton Simon of the Hunt Foods empire is one industrialist noted for his devotion to decentralization. He believes that management is best performed when an outstanding man is given his head and then held accountable for results. In the Simon organization, though, the failure to achieve expected results has sometimes been dealt with harshly.

Though the advantages accruing when decentralization is successful are impressive, certain negative aspects enter into any decision to decentralize. The initial cost of establishing a decentralized organization structure may be high, and mistakes made in the various operating units may not be detected until relatively large costs have been incurred. If such situations are to be avoided, meaningful standards of measurement must be set. Without them, the organization may incur tremendous losses before top management recognizes the gravity of the problem.

In areas less technical than finance and accounting, decentralization poses problems when shifts in power or prestige change existing relationships between individuals. As a practical matter, executives (and subordinates) frequently oppose changes in the nature of their responsibilities. Some individuals resent reductions in their personal power, while others resist any attempt to expand their duties. Changes in the status quo are met invariably by human

---

[15] See, as one example, the works of Peter F. Drucker, including *The Practice of Management* (New York: Harper & Row Publishers, 1954).

resistance; and such opposition, whether open or hidden, can be a serious deterrent to the successful completion of any move toward decentralized decision making. When Defense Secretary Robert MacNamara reorganized military procurement and decision-making powers to allow for greater civilian participation and more decentralization of authority, he set in motion a chain of resentment and resignations that outlasted his stay in the Pentagon.

One of the most troublesome problems of decentralization is the question of balance. Balancing the degree of looseness and closeness of control is an extremely difficult feat. Once decentralization becomes the goal of the organization, the question "How much authority should be delegated?" demands an immediate answer. Harlow Curtice, former president of the General Motors Corporation, when testifying before a congressional committee, cited the problem of balance as the real key to understanding GM's well-known policy of decentralization. Mr. Curtice described centralized policy and decentralized administration as the basic GM formula and emphasized the continuing kinds of efforts GM management expends in getting cooperative action to maintain this balance.[16] According to Mr. Curtice, a balance between centralization and decentralization of control should be established only after a careful analysis of the total operating environment, a condition Peter Drucker calls "Federal decentralization."[17] Most attempts to establish decentralized decision making undergo a considerable amount of review and revision of authority relationships before a satisfactory balance is established between organizational desires and the realities of the world. In General Motors, for example, it is recognized that all available facts and figures must be marshalled before final decisions are made on organization relationships. Some of the more difficult problems in this balancing sequence arise in the areas of levels of command and spans of managerial control.

Developing a meaningful span of control at the various organizational levels is one of the most troublesome aspects of achieving organizational balance. The span of control, or, as it is also called, the span of management, is the number of people reporting directly to a superior. If six subordinates report to a boss directly, his span of control is six. This would be true whether those six men were in one department, two departments, or in six separate departments. The span of control is a person-to-person concept, not a person-to-department relationship. Spans can be "flat" and "wide" (many people) or "narrow" (few people). Although the general tendency is to have narrow spans at high levels in the organization and flat ones at lower echelons, there are numerous variations. The width of the span depends upon a number of factors, which range from the nature and severity of contact needed to get the work done up to and including the organization's existing philosophy of management. Other factors affecting spans are the variety of work done, the time

---

[16] Harlow Curtice, "GM Organization and Structure," Statement before the subcommittee on anti-trust and monopoly of the United States Senate Committee in the Judiciary, December 2, 1955, pp. 5–12.

[17] Drucker, *op. cit.*

spent on supervision, the abilities of subordinates, the repetitiveness of work done, and the degree of staff assistance provided.[18] In firms with decentralized operations, spans can be either narrow or flat, but tend to be flat. For example, Sears Roebuck, which advocates decentralized decision making, has a wide span of control philosophy. Tightly centralized firms normally have narrow spans of control, as is the case in several major public utilities.

To summarize briefly, the more levels in a firm of a given size, the narrower the span of control. The upper levels in an organization with a narrow span philosophy might have from three to six people in each span, the middle levels might have four to ten people, and the lower ranks might consist of from five to thirty individuals. In a flat-span organization, the following subordinate-superior ratios might be in effect: upper ranks, about fifteen-to-one; middle levels, up to forty-to-one; and lower levels; twenty-five to one hundred or more subordinates reporting to each superior. More levels usually mean tighter control over performance, but proliferation of levels brings added problems in communications. Each level tends to create blocks that increase the complexity of communications flows in direct proportion to their numbers. As the number of levels increases, communications problems grow at a rate faster than the increase in numbers of levels. This same phenomenon occurs when spans of management increase. As the span of management increases arithmetically, the complexity of relationships increases geometrically.[19]

Individual organizations must decide which span is most appropriate at each level and whether managements should embrace narrow or flat spans. Each organization must view its own needs, determine its own objectives, and draw up a philosophy and a plan of attack reflecting its needs. The establishment of a proper span of control and operationally effective degrees of decentralization demands both human relations skills and knowledge of organization structures. Similar abilities are also required to carry out many of the basic duties connected with the more general task of developing the organization's total structure. Some of the aspects of decentralization overlap with the clarification-of-delegation approach, particularly when managers have profit responsibilities over decentralized units. In this situation, duties, responsibilities, and performance standards are set up in rather rigid form; and performance of units is judged on the basis of actual versus expected showing. Since profit decentralization is usually considered in the context of control of performance, detailed analysis of its operation will be treated in the sections dealing with control and organizational performance.[20]

---

[18] See William H. Newman and Charles E. Summer, *The Process of Management* (Englewood Cliffs, N.J.: Prentice-Hall, Inc., 1961).

[19] This relationship is demonstrated by Graicunas's formula, $n(2^n-(n-1))$, where n equals the number of subordinates. This formula calculates the total number of direct and cross relationships that can exist with a given number of subordinates.

[20] PERT is also thought of as a control device but it is included here because of its importance in organizational design and delegation. Budgets, cost standards, and other control devices are described in Chapter 13. Planning for profit, another variation, appears in Chapter 14.

Summary

Though many techniques are used to bring about the integration of strategy and structural hierarchies, five techniques have enjoyed widespread use. The first utilizes the classic principles of organization to improve organizational design and delegation through careful planning of duties, information flows, and the human, physical, and financial resources that make up the total of organizational activities. The second; PERT; utilizes programming techniques to prepare mathematical simulations of networks designed to optimize the blending of resources needed to reach given sets of objectives. The third method, which is a variation on the first, tries to improve relationships between line and staff units by minimizing conflicts and maximizing cooperation and coordination between specialized staffs and operating, or line, management. The fourth approach utilizes interaction analysis to minimize frictions and blockages in the going organization. This technique focuses on analysis of work flows to identify causes of friction, and then deals with perceived conflicts by removing or adjusting observed sources of interference. The final technique, decentralization of authority, utilizes broad delegation of authority and (usually) wide, or flat, spans of control to allow administrative decisions to be made at low levels in the organization structure. Since these decisions usually fall within a given policy framework, the system has built-in controls, which are most stringent when managers have profit responsibility over operating units. Because of the nature of decentralized structures, careful coordination is an essential condition for successful operation.

Overlap exists between these five approaches to the integration of strategy and structure, and even within one organization any or all may be invoked to solve problems. Moreover, the five categories are merely representative of the range of techniques available for converting broad goals into desired results. Selected aspects of these systems will be reviewed in a slightly different context in the following sections dealing with control and motivation.

Study Questions

1. What are the advantages and disadvantages of decentralized decision making?
2. Has the development of high-powered computers tended to encourage or discourage the movement toward decentralized decision making?
3. Does Mr. Cordiner's approach to delegation differ sharply from that espoused by Professor Newman? Compare and discuss.
4. What are the chief advantages and drawbacks encountered in the use of PERT to help construct organizational designs?
5. Is PERT a technique that the Harvard group might use to improve the process of implementing strategic goals? Explain and discuss.
6. How do Dalton and Allen propose to reduce line-staff conflict? In what ways are their ideas similar? Different?
7. How does Allen's approach compare with that espoused by Whyte? Do you feel the interaction approach is superior to Allen's? Why or why not?

8. What types of standards of performance are needed to allow decentralization to function effectively?

9. What happens when spans of control are widened in an organization? Discuss in terms of information flows, personal reactions, decision making, and numbers of supervisors affected.

10. Do you favor wide or narrow spans of control? Qualify and justify your answer.

The Winslow Products Company

The Winslow Products Company has a single plant employing 550 people. The main product is a metal fitting produced through a series of machining and assembly operations. The company also makes other parts similar to the one described, principally for the steel industry. The president received a degree in law, but he has had considerable experience in the sales field. He can also perform basic design work, and he holds several patents. The vice-president and general manager has engineering training, and he is well versed in manufacturing techniques and processes. He also has had long and intimate association with cost controls and cost accounting techniques and is considered to be an expert in this field.

The board of directors performs the normal duties of developing policies and passing on long-range plans. The board has some expertise in financial planning, since it is heavily loaded with individuals from investment houses and banking firms. The company treasurer works on a part-time basis and holds a partnership in a local law firm. The secretary of the company is a former salesman who is within one year of retirement. For the past two years the secretary has been afflicted with an illness that has limited his overall effectiveness.

The union in the plant is newly organized, but labor relations have been very good to date. The initial stages of unionization were accomplished with only minor problems, and the manager of industrial relations feels that the local union (United Steelworkers of America), which is now bargaining with the company, has very responsible leadership. The volume of purchased parts is somewhat small, although raw materials are critical to the company in terms of total profitability. The general manager in particular likes to keep a close control over purchasing because he feels that it is a key area in cost control.

The engineering department is headed by a relatively inept manager. Most of the creative ideas and planning in engineering originate with the general manager. Without the general manager's guidance, this department would be woefully inadequate.

Winslow Products operates in a very competitive industry. Because of this, cost controls are extremely important. Moreover, the sales effort must be kept at a vigorous and continuous pace. In recent years, the company has seen its profits fall steadily. This decline has worried the president and has caused some anxiety among members of the board of directors. In general, company profits have not dipped below levels considered acceptable by the board. The president, however, feels that if present trends continue, the company will be unable to maintain its position in the industry.

1. What departments, if any, should be added, liquidated, or combined in the future to make this organization operate more efficiently? Give the reasons for your decision.

2. Draw up an organization chart showing how this company should be organized.

The Michigan Transport Company

In 1965 the Michigan Transport Company (MTC) bought a small chemical plant which produced heavy chemicals. Though MTC had never owned or operated any chemical installations, company officials thought that diversification was necessary if the company was to remain profitable and keep growing. The decision to enter chemicals turned out to be initially successful, as certain phases of the cold war created a demand for the product of the acquired property.

Encouraged by this early success, the company decided to enter the chemical industry in a big way. The board of directors began to investigate companies with the idea of either outright purchase or merger. None of the board members had much knowledge of the chemical industry, although the chairman of the board felt that their combined business wisdom would enable them to make wise purchase decisions. After surveying several dozen companies over a period of several years, the board decided, in 1967, to try to merge with a medium-sized chemical producer with a narrow but profitable line of heavy chemicals. Negotiations began in late 1967, but because of the death of the chairman of the board of MTC, no final decisions were made by the middle of 1968.

In June of 1967, the grandson of MTC's founder became president. He believed in rapid diversification and continued expansion of the company. He felt, however, that the board had not been careful in carrying out policies of diversification. For instance, all merger or purchase decisions were made by the board alone. He believed that the current organization was not well suited to investigate possibilities of expansion or diversification (see Figure III.1). The major departments of traffic, maintenance, export and domestic sales, insurance, dock and warehouse facilities, and finance were cumbersome and suited only for adequate handling of the old shipping business of the company. This organization was particularly outmoded, according to the new president, because it failed to allow for industrial development and because insurance now accounted for almost half of the company's current revenue.

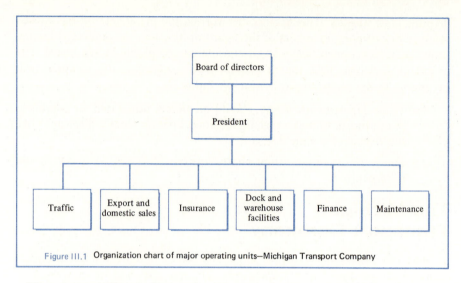

Figure III.1 Organization chart of major operating units—Michigan Transport Company

The new president believed that his first job was to reorganize for growth and efficiency. He wanted to

1. Streamline the current organization to reflect the true needs of the company
2. Provide for adequate analysis and decision making on expansion
3. Maintain a good organization operating at a profit
4. Establish central staffs in order to use the existing talent and experience of organization members in the most profitable manner

Though MTC was still profitable, revenues had been falling steadily. By the end of 1968, profits were expected to fall to 5 percent of sales. In view of this forecast, the new president planned to take strong steps to keep the company prosperous and profitable.

1. What do you think of MTC's approach to diversification?
2. Prepare a new organization chart to help the president meet his goals. Add, delete, or combine departments as necessary.

Haynes Manufacturing Company

The Haynes Manufacturing Company has seventeen plants located in nine states. These plants make a wide variety of products including textiles and cloth, hardware, sheet metal products, automobile parts, food and plastic products, missile components, transistors, and a line of aeronautical stabilizers. The most recent addition to company holdings has been an extensive mineral deposit in the Province of Ontario. The tremendous diversity of the Haynes product line calls for a skilled sales force with a wide degree of background and interests and a considerable amount of technical knowledge.

The company product line is divided into eight groups, each headed by a sales manager responsible to the executive vice-president of marketing management. Each sales manager has an assistant who handles field work, advertising, and various other aspects of the company marketing effort. Though some of these assistants will move eventually into sales managers' jobs, many will be shifted into other jobs as the competitive situation demands.

Over the past ten years the company has brought all of its sales personnel to New York City for a Christmas meeting. Last year, however, the company president decided that the sales managers should retire to a lodge in northern Canada where they would be free of some of the pleasures and pressures of the city. As part of the total program for the meeting, a company plane was to fly all the sales managers, their assistants, the executive vice-president in charge of marketing, and two other company vice-presidents (engineering and research) to Ontario to view the company's new mining interest. During this flight the plane developed engine trouble and crashed, killing all on board. In effect, this terrible accident wiped out Haynes's entire corps of marketing and sales executives.

After the funerals of the seventeen sales executives and the two other vice-presidents, the president took stock of his position. According to his director of salaried personnel, there were few experienced sales or marketing executives currently on the company payroll. With an estimated annual sales of $700 million projected for the following year, the company faced a troubled future.

1. What immediate steps should the president take? Specify those steps in order of priority.

2. How might his actions affect spans and/or levels in the organization's structure?

3. What steps could be taken to prevent a recurrence of the personal and corporate problems arising from this tragedy?

The Mooney Generator Group

The generator group of Mooney Switchgear Limited is divided into five operating divisions: (1) electrical parts and supplies, (2) assembly, (3) tool shops and equipment, (4) machine shops, and (5) accessories and supplies. Each of the five divisions is headed by a general supervisor.

The general supervisor of the tool shops and equipment division has under him an assistant general supervisor in charge of the tool room; under the assistant general supervisor are five foremen who direct the work force.

The machine shops division has three sections: (1) milling and boring, (2) piping, and (3) wheels. Each of these sections is headed by a general foreman who has five foremen reporting directly to him.

The accessories and supplies division is led by a general supervisor, who is assisted by an assistant general supervisor. Six foremen, reporting to the assistant general supervisor, supervise the workers in this division.

The assembly division is run by a general supervisor, who has an assistant general supervisor, to whom six supervisory foremen are subordinates.

The general supervisor of the electrical parts and supplies division does not have an assistant general supervisor, but he does have seven foremen under his immediate direction.

The top man in the generator group has the title of superintendent. He has access to five staff advisors: (1) supervisor of tests, (2) supervisor of inspection, (3) supervisor of costs, (4) supervisor of production, and (5) supervisor of wage rates and planning. Although these staff men are not part of the line organization, they provide staff services to the group.

1. Draw a chart of the generator group showing the organization from the superintendent down to the workers.

Roper Appliances, Inc.

The appliance industry is a fiercely competitive industry in which both major and small-sized companies battle for the consumers' dollars. Roper Appliances, Inc., is one of the giants in the industry. Roper has had a generally well-accepted product line and is looked upon as one of the better companies in the field. Yet Roper has had its troubles. In 1963, Roper sales were $430 million. By 1966 they had fallen to $357 million. In 1967 sales recovered, only to fall again sharply in 1968. Part of this fall was due to general competitive conditions, but Roper's share was declining relative to other companies as well as absolutely. The profit picture was even worse. Operating profits of $13 million in 1963 dwindled to $567,000 in 1966. In 1967, profits rose to $4.4 million, but losses of $300,000 occurred in 1968. In 1969, however, profits were expected to rise again.

Roper management felt that the decline in sales and profits was based on factors other than competition in the market. Products were sound, yet the company appeared to be failing badly.

Prior to 1968, Roper had eight consumer products divisions. Each operated on a decentralized basis and had responsibility for making its own profits. Each time Roper had added a new line of products, it had added a new division. In 1966 the divisions were TV, radio, phonographs, freezers, laundry equipment, electric ranges, room air conditioners, and refrigerators. Superimposed over all these divisions was the marketing department, which had authority over the sales force, but no authority over operating divisions and no profit responsibility. The divisions competed with one another and tried vigorously to show as much profit as possible. Each division called on distributors separately and used its own promotional and advertising campaigns. Distributors frequently were able to gain better price deals for themselves by bypassing marketing salesmen and getting price quotations from division executives. Confusion was compounded when divisional sales campaigns tended to conflict with sales programs and promotions planned by the marketing department.

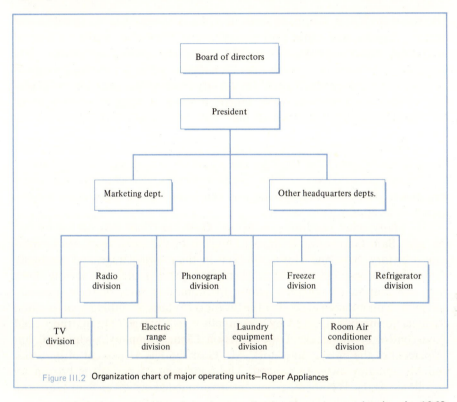

Figure III.2 Organization chart of major operating units—Roper Appliances

Some other general points in existence in the Roper organization in 1968 were

1. Division research budgets were based on percent of sales by the divisions.

2. Little central control and training of distributors was present.

3. Long-range planning was hindered by the pressure of gaining short-term profits.

4. There was no valid system of intracompany transfer pricing.

5. Many layers of control existed in spite of a seemingly decentralized organization.

1. Assuming that you are a consultant called in to correct the problems of the Roper Appliances, Inc., what course of action would you recommend? Indicate organizational, managerial, marketing, and other changes which might be advisable for Roper.

The Garrison Chair Company

The Garrison Chair Company manufactures a special line of furniture for doctors, dentists, and other professional users. They also produce a line of specialized office furniture for beauty shops and similar operations. The company is located in a small city in western North Carolina. Though it has only five hundred employees, it is the largest manufacturer of its particular type of specialty furniture. Thus, Garrison Chair is large in relation to its own market, though it is much smaller than other major furniture manufacturers.

The Garrison company has long made its own stampings and wooden parts. It also manufactures some forgings and a number of specialty hardware items. It purchases plastic covers, padding, and other materials including cloth, foam, and plastic parts. In addition, surgical items and special equipment are obtained from appropriate vendors.

Like many small furniture companies, Garrison Chair was started by two partners, Sam Garrison and Harold Quigley. In the early years of the company's history, Sam and Harold worked in their own garage and gradually expanded the business as their markets grew. After building a factory, both Sam and Harold turned their efforts to promoting sales of their furniture and left the manufacturing end of the business to Hank Weinberg, a production engineer formerly employed by a competitor in Chicago. The partners hold close control of the stock of the Garrison Chair Company, owning all but 25 percent of the outstanding stock. Mr. Garrison has 41 percent of the stock and Mr. Quigley owns 34 percent. The remaining 25 percent is broken up as follows: Hank Weinberg, 5 percent; two married sisters of Sam Garrison, 5 percent each; and Alice Garrison, Sam's only daughter, 10 percent.

Each of the stockholders is a member of the board of directors, but meetings are called and generally dominated by Sam Garrison, who, in spite of being seventy years old, still monitors the operations of the business. Neither he nor Mr. Quigley are around the plant very often, but they do feel that they play an important management role as advisors to Mr. Weinberg.

Hank Weinberg has run Garrison Chair in his own way for the past ten years. He has shown a continual profit and has made a number of product and manufacturing changes. Garrison and Quigley feel that he has done a good job, but tend to think of him (as Sam puts it), "as a hired manager, not an owner."

In the past five years, Sam Garrison has been an active booster of North

Carolina's attempt to revitalize its industry and its image as a vacation and resort area. He has become interested in local politics and belongs to a number of civic committees. The most important of these is the Better City Committee, which has as its major purpose the beautification and preservation of cities in a five-county area in western North Carolina. Among its principal duties are vigorous attempts to reduce the level of air pollution and stream pollution in the area. Sam has been very proud of his participation on this committee and has vigorously pursued its aims and objectives.

At a recent meeting of this civic betterment committee, another member asked Garrison about a new addition being built on the Garrison factory. Sam, who had not heard about the addition, called Hank Weinberg that evening and demanded an explanation. Weinberg discussed how he had begun the manufacture of a new product line which he believed would be a very profitable one with an excellent potential. Weinberg indicated to Mr. Garrison that the profitability of this particular activity was no longer in doubt, since development costs had now been expended and the product was well mounted in the market. The addition to plant capacity was, Weinberg felt, justified by the results of a market research study on the new product's market potential.

Mr. Weinberg was somewhat surprised that Sam Garrison was so disturbed by the new facilities construction. He had told Mr. Garrison a year ago that he was going to try out some new products "on a small scale." When he mentioned this, Garrison asked Hank the extent of the investment to date. Weinberg replied that over $60,000 had already been expended on the project, but that sales of over $300,000 and gross profits up to $18,000 could be expected over the next year. Sam exploded with the comment, "You call that small scale? How can you start a project like this without checking with me?" Weinberg's immediate reply was that he thought he was in charge of manufacturing activities. Sam, in a burst of anger, replied, "Well, I'll see about that."

1. What basic problems exist in the Garrison Chair Company?

2. What do you think Hank Weinberg should do to handle the problems you specified in your answer to Question 1?

3. What might Sam Garrison choose to do to protect and preserve his proprietary interests?

State University of New York—Wilshire Campus[1]

The fact that Dr. Edward Antoine held a Ph.D. in Industrial Engineering made him somewhat unique among his colleagues in educational administration. Though technical training is common on university faculties, university

---

[1] Though data referring to educational trends in the nation and in New York State are based on fact, the Wilshire Campus has no real-life counterpart.

administrators trained in engineering are seldom found outside of schools of engineering. Dr. Antoine was unusual in one other respect too: few people held his intense commitment to the task of educating the country's youth. This conviction had caused him to leave a lucrative post in industry to join the faculty of a graduate school of engineering.

During his tenure as a professor of engineering, Dr. Antoine had built up an excellent reputation as a teacher, scholar, and consultant. Though he devoted his full energies to this triple role, Dr. Antoine felt he could do more for education in general by entering educational administration. He believed there was a great dearth of skill and talent in this field, and he felt his technical skills in the planning area could make a significant contribution to the improvement of the education process.

When Professor Antoine read a 1965 report issued by the Department of Health, Education and Welfare outlining the tremendous growth projected in school age populations during the 1970s and 1980s, he decided to leave teaching and devote all his energies to meeting the expected influx. He contacted a friend in New York City who was chairman of a committee seeking a vice-president for administration and planning at the yet-to-be constructed Wilshire Campus of the State University of New York. After several weeks of interviews and discussion, Dr. Antoine decided to accept this position. Though he knew he would receive a substantial cut in income, he felt that this financial loss would be more than offset by the psychic gains from fulfilling his sense of devotion to the education process.

THE CHALLENGE TO EDUCATORS

The statistics underlying Dr. Antoine's decision to leave teaching were thoroughly documented in the previously mentioned HEW report. According to this report, total college enrollment was expected to rise from 3 million in 1960 to 8 million in 1975. In that same period, tuition was projected to increase from $100 to $300 in public schools and from $600 to $1,100 in private institutions. Living costs were expected to double during the 1960s and then double again by 1980. Also, student population figures for 1985 were projected at twice the 1970 estimates. Dr. Logan Williams, president of the American Council of Education, stated early in 1965 that it would be necessary to double the size of all existing colleges and set up a thousand more new schools with an enrollment of 2,500 each to meet the needs of 1980.

The challenge in 1985, according to Commissioner of Education Francis Keppel, would be one of numbers, knowledge, and cost. The price of college educations was scheduled to rise from $3 billion in 1960 to $12 billion in 1970. California, which had 632,000 students in 1965, expected 30 percent more in 1970. According to every forecast, better planning was needed in all areas—and this is what interested and attracted Dr. Antoine. His knowledge of planning, scheduling, and controlling industrial and civic activities could, he felt, contribute much toward helping to counter the challenges raised by burgeoning college enrollments.

As he reviewed the HEW figures, Dr. Antoine recognized that planning was particularly vital in the following areas: faculty manpower, construction of facilities, maintenance of academic excellence during periods of rapid growth, development of curricula to provide graduate education beyond the bachelor's degree level, and the adoption of new techniques to lick the problems of numbers, cost, and knowledge by adopting modern teaching methods such as TV, computerized learning processes, electronic tapes, mass lectures, and programmed learning. Dr. Antoine felt that many of these problems could be analyzed using techniques commonly invoked by engineers to solve a range of technical (but related) problems.

NEW YORK'S ANSWER TO THE CHALLENGE

New York had no state university until 1948, when eleven teachers colleges, six agricultural and technical units, a maritime and forestry college, and five contract colleges were fused into the State University of New York (SUNY). These colleges had a minimum number of libraries and science buildings, few special classrooms, and limited recreational facilities. As late as 1962, New York ranked forty-ninth out of the fifty states in per capita expenditures on higher education; and until 1964, SUNY was little more than a state department reporting to both the state government and the state board of regents. Since then, it has grown both in size and stature.

In 1964, SUNY was allowed to present its budget to the state in a lump sum. This departure from a line-item budget was viewed as a major step forward by SUNY's officials, since it deprived the legislature of the power to control or delete specific items. In addition, many jobs in SUNY were declassified from civil service, giving the university more power over its internal staffing procedures. SUNY's operational independence was further increased by the establishment of an agency especially created to handle SUNY purchases. Finally, the state government created the State University Construction Fund (SUCF) which, shortly after its inception, authorized expenditures in excess of $1 billion for facilities expansion. SUCF has been empowered to issue bonds by a somewhat complicated process not requiring approval by voters: the state lends money to the fund, which is financed by bonds and notes; these bonds and notes are then paid by rental fees, since SUNY leases all its buildings in amounts sufficient to cover principal and interest payments. SUCF can also contract a single bid for a single job; there is no need to let out contracts separately. Architects can thus coordinate and supervise building programs with a relatively high degree of efficiency.

In 1965, SUNY consisted of two medical centers, three university centers, eighteen four-year colleges, six two-year agricultural and technical institutes, twenty-eight locally sponsored community colleges, and one graduate school of public affairs. At the time Dr. Antoine became interested in SUNY the fifty-eight units had over 88,000 students. When he joined the staff in 1965, about 108,000 students were enrolled. Projections of student population for 1970 showed some 167,000 students expected, a total exceeding every state except California. Indeed, if junior colleges were excluded from the California forecast, the State University of New York could claim to be the largest system of higher education in the nation.

In 1964, 56 percent of New York State's 291,000 college students were enrolled in private institutions. By 1970, when total student population was projected at 440,000, the private school percentage was expected to drop to about 50 percent. Such shifts prompted President Samuel Gould of the State University of New York to make the statement, "By 1985, 80 percent of the state's college kids will be in public institutions." SUNY thus expected to expand its facilities 78 percent from 1964 to 1970—a rate far greater than that projected by the state's private institutions.

The massive planning job facing SUNY had an irresistible appeal to Edward Antoine. He saw the visions of the future as a challenge to the present. He felt that his new job as vice-president of the Wilshire Campus was the right vehicle to carry him to his goal of melding his training and technical skills with his lifetime commitment to education.

The Wilshire Campus. When Dr. Antoine took over as vice-president of administration and planning, he set about determining the limits of his planning horizons. To accomplish this result he initiated a series of discussions with the top officials at the Wilshire Campus. From President Alvin Binckley he obtained a sweeping mandate to plan the buildings and other facilities needed to support first-rate academic programs in the fields of engineering, business administration, and liberal arts. Since the Wilshire Campus was a grass-roots operation, that is, a full-blown university started from scratch, President Binckley indicated that he expected to be directing a first-rate, stable university center in at most ten years. Since the first class was scheduled to enter in two years, Dr. Antoine was given the power to decide what facilities to build and when. He thus had some control over which type of degree-seeking students would be given priority in the admissions procedure. Construction of all facilities, however, was expected to be completed by the end of five years, at which time enrollment was scheduled to include 7,500 undergraduate students.

From Vice-President Nelson Forsythe, Dr. Antoine received a green light to go ahead with any and all projects needed to house and educate the 8,000 students expected in the upcoming five-year period (ending in 1973). Financial support for expansion was quite adequate; and, although it was never stated, Mr. Forsythe indicated that cost was much less of a problem than providing needed facilities.

From Dean Robert Rosetti Dr. Antoine received a promise to provide the faculty and staff needed to meet the explosive rate of growth in facilities. Rosetti stated confidently, "Staffing is my problem. You get the mortar and I'll see to it that your buildings house academic excellence. As soon as you determine which school will be completed first, I'll develop the proper lines of faculty recruiting."

Though Dr. Antoine had some doubt about Rosetti's ability to provide staff, he felt confident that Forsythe's views on the availability of funds were correct. He determined that his first job was to concentrate on building construction. Once facilities were planned, he then hoped to work with Dean Rosetti to fill faculty positions.

In planning for buildings and facilities construction, Dr. Antoine elected to use a technique commonly known as PERT. Though PERT had been widely used in engineering applications, it had seen only limited use in planning educational facilities. Dr. Antoine felt that this technique was readily adaptable for use in educational planning and development, and he hoped to organize the bulk of Wilshire's facilities planning around a series of integrated PERT diagrams.

The building plan. One of the goals which Dr. Antoine set for himself was to guarantee construction of all buildings on the Wilshire Campus by September 1975. Since the first class was scheduled to enter in September 1970, Dr. Antoine knew that he had exactly two years to carry out the initial phases of his construction plan. According to President Binckley, 2,500 students would be in the first entering class (September 1970) and 2,500 more were expected each year for at least the next five years. Antoine knew that close coordination was called for if all these students were to be housed and educated. To develop the scope of his program fully, Antoine realized that he had to establish a schedule of both building construction times and priorities of starting times of construction on the various buildings. To accomplish this result he set up five basic classes of buildings to be constructed: classrooms and faculty offices; physical educational facilities; laboratories; dormitories; and support buildings such as cafeterias, administrative services, libraries, recreational facilities, and general maintenance.

Through extensive discussion with contractors, architects, and state government experts on construction, Dr. Antoine was able to formulate Table III.1, showing time estimates for construction of major facilities.

With these estimates in mind, Dr. Antoine began to consider what priorities to establish in order to meet the onrush of students. After some discussion with the university executive council and the board of trustees, he gathered information from which to forge a set of working priorities. This information included the following (critical) sets of data: classrooms and dormitories for at least 2,500 students were needed in two years; physical education was scheduled to be introduced as soon as possible; laboratories were not necessary for the first-year students in languages and engineering, but were needed in the first term in the biological sciences, statistics, chemistry, and other physical sciences; the use of engineering and language labs could be postponed until the fall of 1971, but maintenance and repair facilities and the administrative services building were needed as soon as possible; cafeterias, since they were needed in dormitories, had the same priority as housing units; a general library was desirable as soon as possible; finally, engineering and business library construction could be delayed by as much as one year, but these libraries were needed by the term beginning in September 1971.

Since money was no problem, Dr. Antoine proposed to use a simple PERT time technique to develop the facilities construction program for the Wilshire Campus.[2] In late August 1968, he began to prepare such a plan.

TABLE III.1   BUILDING CONSTRUCTION TIME ESTIMATES

Facilities to be constructed	Range (months)	Most Likely Completion Time (months)
Dormitories	18–24	22
Classroom and faculty office buildings	18–22	20
Physical education buildings	30–36	32
Laboratories		
Language	10–14	12
Chemical	18–30	24
Engineering-test	18–24	22
Engineering-machine shop	15–24	18
Engineering-experimental	18–30	24
Statistical	10–15	12
Biological sciences	18–24	20
Physical sciences	18–24	20
Administrative and support buildings		
Cafeteria	18–30	20
Maintenance and repair	18–30	20
Libraries		
General	30–36	34
Engineering	27–36	28
Business	18–21	20
Recreation (Student Union)	24–30	27
Administration	16–24	18

1. What factors must Dr. Antoine consider in construction of a PERT diagram of the Wilshire Campus construction program? What areas would be critical in the diagram? What would be the critical path in a PERT diagram of the Wilshire Campus' development plan?

2. What are some of the obstacles that might influence the achievement of desired completion dates for each event?

3. What should Dr. Antoine do to insure the achievement of both his short-run and long-term objectives?

A SIMPLIFIED NOTE ON THE USE OF PERT AT THE WILSHIRE CAMPUS

The PERT method Dr. Antoine intended to use at the Wilshire Campus emphasizes time factors in the planning process. PERT identifies the events needed to reach a set of objectives and lays out the kinds of activities needed to complete these events in logical, organized fashion. In a typical PERT diagram,

---

[2] A simplified note on the PERT time technique appears at the end of this case study.

events are shown as circles and *activities* appear as the lines joining these circles. Events use no resources and have no time dimension, but activities use both time and resources. Events are usually shown by letters, while activities carry a numerical designation.

In almost all PERT networks three estimates are made of time use: optimistic, most likely, and pessimistic. These estimates are made for each activity and are entered in PERT diagrams as numbers, for example, the 20–25–30 line for activity I indicates the most optimistic, most likely, and most pessimistic completion times estimated (in days) for activity I:

$$A \quad \overset{\text{20–25–30}}{\underset{\text{I}}{\longrightarrow}} \quad B$$

If a weighted time is used (as is common) the notation t_e replaces the set of times. The value of t_e is calculated using the formula

$$t_e = \frac{a + 4m + b}{6}$$

(This uses a statistical distribution known as the beta distribution.)

where a = most optimistic time
b = most likely time
c = most pessimistic time

For the 20–25–30 time set, the value t_e would thus be

$$\frac{20 + 4(25) + 30}{6} = 25 \text{ days (the weighted-expected time)}$$

The wider the range between the most optimistic and most pessimistic time estimates, the greater the uncertainty associated with the activity. This degree of uncertainty is determined by calculating the *variance* associated with each activity. Using the statistical convention that the standard deviation can be estimated at one sixth the range, the variance of a given activity is represented by the following formula:

$$\sigma 2 = \left(\frac{(b - a)}{6}\right)^2$$

σ^2 = the variance of the activity
b = most pessimistic time
a = most optimistic time

The variance associated with the example above is

$$\sigma^2 = \left(\frac{(30 - 20)}{6}\right)^2 = (1.67)^2 = 2.79$$

When more than one activity is undertaken, the activity with the greatest (largest) variance will reflect the most uncertainty about the reliability of its estimate time of completion (t_e).

Shifting from activities to events, the expected time for an event to be

reached is commonly labeled T_E and is the sum of the small t_e values leading
to that event. Using the prior example, the

$$T_E \text{ for } \textcircled{B} = t_e = 25 \text{ days}$$

If several paths exist between $\textcircled{A}$ and $\textcircled{B}$ the T_E for $\textcircled{B}$ would vary.

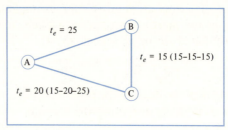

If T_E $\textcircled{B}$ cannot be finished until all activities preceding it have been completed, then T_E $\textcircled{B}$ in the above diagram would be the sum of the t_e values,
along the path $\textcircled{A}$ — $\textcircled{B}$ — $\textcircled{C}$, or 35 days $(20 + 15)$.

Two other notations are used in connection with events: T_S equals scheduled
time; T_L equals the latest allowable time. To complete T_L, you must work
backwards by subtracting the t_e value for each activity from the T_L value of
the succeeding event. In the example above, T_L $\textcircled{B}$ equals 35 days $(T_S$ would
also be 35 days, since event $\textcircled{B}$ is the last event in the network). T_L $\textcircled{C}$ would
be 20 days $(35 - 15)$ and T_L $\textcircled{A}$ would be zero days $(35 - 35)$. The zero
value means you must begin $\textcircled{A}$ by a particular date or be behind schedule
at the start of the project.

By using PERT for planning and control purposes, Dr. Antoine hoped to
utilize the concept of the *critical path* to assign resources to areas where they
were most needed. In the critical path concept, slack time is defined as the
excess of the latest allowable time over the time expected to reach a particular
event $(T_L - T_E)$. Slack times can thus have zero, plus, or minus values depending upon whether or not a planned project is on schedule. The less slack
time associated with an event, the more critical the event. Negative scores, of
course, indicate events of an extremely critical nature.

The critical path of events needed to reach a final event (or objective)
has the least slack time of any path leading to that event. To put it in terms
of a simple diagram, the critical path from event $\textcircled{A}$ to event $\textcircled{B}$ is $\textcircled{A}$—$\textcircled{C}$—$\textcircled{B}$,
which represents a time of 35 days. The critical path is *always* the path which
consumes the most time. Any delay in movement along the critical path means
delay in reaching the desired objective. Critical path analysis thus focuses on
those activities and events most likely to stand between the planner and his
stated objectives.

Another useful concept in PERT analysis is the probability of meeting a
scheduled completion date for a given project (P_R). This probability is usually
calculated for an entire network using the statistical concept of *standard scores*
(Z scores). The process of completing a P_R for a given network begins with

the calculation of a Z score for the entire network. Z scores are calculated using the following formula:

$$Z = \frac{T_S - T_E}{\sqrt{\Sigma \sigma^2 -}}$$

where σ^2 = the variance
  Z = the standard score
  T_S = scheduuued time
  T_E = expected time for an event

$T_S - T_E$ is computed for the final event in the network. The summation of $\Sigma \sigma^2$ is the *sum of the variances in the critical path of the event*. In our simplified example:

$$Z = \frac{35 - 35}{\sqrt{2.79} = 0} = 0$$
(only critical path variances are used in this calculation)

By checking the computed Z score in the Table of Values for the standard distribution of areas under the normal bell-shaped curve, a Z value can be translated directly into a P_R value (the probability of reaching an event in the time expected).

In the normal curve tables, a Z score of 0 is equivalent to a P_R of 0.5 or a 50-percent probability of meeting expected dates. When T_S and T_E coincide, P_R equals 0.5[3]. If the P_R value falls at 0.5, the project or event is considered to have a relatively desirable probability level. If P_R values are as low (say) as 0.20, then the probability of completing a project on time is quite remote. If P_R estimates run as high as 0.65 or higher, perhaps too many resources are in use, and costs may be excessive. What the P_R value shows is how and where people, materials, and so on, can (or must) be diverted to insure the attainment of certain goals.

Projects needing the most attention are usually those having the greatest variance associated with them. The absolute size of network variances helps to point out where effort or resources seem to be either relatively adequate or lacking. The PERT network thus assists in both planning and control activities. To Dr. Antoine, it promised to be an ideal technique for planning the construction of educational facilities.

---

[3] Other sample Z scores are:

Z Value	P_R
0.5	.692
1.0	.841
1.5	.933
−0.5	.308
−1.0	.159
−1.5	.067

American Circle
Company (B)

When John A. Arthur took over the presidency of the American Circle Company (ACCO) in 1964, he launched a series of internal reforms. He first developed a vigorous program of modernization of facilities and equipment. He then went through a series of reorganizing steps designed to streamline the company's organizational structure and product lines. He also initiated innovations such as a research laboratory and a customer relations department.

When Mr. Arthur thought that his most pressing internal problems were well under control, he turned his attention to external affairs. After an extensive survey of ACCO's marketing activities, he decided to embark on a program of merger and acquisition. He believed that ACCO could improve its sales, profits, and long-run market position by gaining greater penetration in existing markets and by moving into new allied product lines.

Under Mr. Arthur's direction, ACCO moved rapidly through a series of relatively small mergers. In addition, several other potential mergers came under study by Mr. Arthur and Peter Van Hiesen, his chief financial officer. Of these merger possibilities, the most promising seemed to be a fusion of ACCO and the Stenco Corporation.[1]

In September 1966, Mr. Arthur presented to ACCO's nine-man board of directors a recommendation that ACCO merge with the Stenco Corporation. Mr. Arthur outlined the advantages and disadvantages of the merger to the board and asked it to approve merger before the end of the year. Though several board members expressed concern about the merger, others gave what seemed to be tentative approval of Mr. Arthur's proposal.

Chairman of the Board, Herbert Kennedy, expressed no opinion in either direction on the possible merger. He did, however, suggest that the board be given time to study the merger before taking any definitive action. Mr. Arthur voiced opposition to any delay because of time pressures, but Mr. Kennedy's motion to postpone the final decision until the next board meeting on November twentieth was passed by a vote of 5 to 4.

Though Mr. Kennedy had not expressed his feelings openly at the board meeting, he felt that Mr. Arthur was moving much too rapidly into the area of merger and acquisition. He had developed a growing uneasiness about the scope and direction of the merger program. His own belief was that certain mergers should have been studied more carefully before their consummation, perhaps by an ad hoc study group or a long-range planning department. In particular, he felt that the marketing aspects of the Stenco merger had been overemphasized, while its financial and managerial impact had been

---

[1] American Circle Company (A) in the cases for Section II, describes this potential merger from the viewpoint of William Bartholdy, a major stockholder in the Stenco Corporation. Though the financial data in the two cases and the two consultants' reports are similar, the issues facing Mr. Bartholdy and Mr. Arthur involve different sets of considerations. The cases can be used alone or assigned in sequence without excessive repetition.

largely ignored. His reasoning was based on the premise that the chief duty of the Board of Directors is to protect the stockholders' interests. His concern with these matters was further heightened by the fact that he was a major stockholder in ACCO and in both his roles he felt that the ACCO-Stenco merger should be reviewed carefully and objectively.

In order to obtain an objective appraisal, he requested the firm of Barney, Ross, and Jonas Associates to provide him with a thorough and confidential analysis of the pending merger. If the BRJ report recommended going ahead with the merger, he was prepared to vote his approval. On the other hand, if the outside analysis opposed a union of the two firms, he planned to release the report to selected board members and seek their support in blocking the merger. The report of BRJ Associates is reproduced below in its entirety.

> Barney, Ross, and Jonas Associates
> 17 File Street
> New York, New York
> November 15, 1966

Mr. Herbert Kennedy
Chairman, Board of Directors
American Circle Company
Detroit, Michigan

Dear Mr. Kennedy:

This letter and the attached report are submitted in answer to your request of October 18 asking us to investigate the pending merger between the American Circle Company and the Stenco Corporation. We will of course, follow your directive to keep this information confidential and we trust that you will do the same, since certain facts presented are controversial and their release could cause embarrassment to those who supplied them to us.

Of several possible courses of action you may take in regard to the merger, it appears your best course of action is to vote approval. The possibility of selling your personal holdings is also discussed below, but this would occur after voting to approve the merger.

Detailed analysis of these and other factors are discussed in the body of the attached report. If you require any additional information we will be happy to furnish it as soon as possible.

Working with and for you has been a great pleasure. We hope that any future contacts will be as pleasant as those in the past.

> Sincerely yours,
>
> Bradford K. Ross
> Senior Partner

TO: Mr. Herbert Kennedy
FROM: Mr. Bradford K. Ross
SUBJECT: Confidential report on the pending merger of American Circle
           Company (ACCO) and the Stenco Corporation.

SUMMARY OF FINDINGS

It is our opinion that you should vote to approve the pending merger
between the American Circle Company (ACCO) and the Stenco Corporation.
We believe this action would be advantageous to you for the following
reasons:

1. Issuance of new stock in payment for Stenco will (in a short period
    of time) probably leave ACCO stock at substantially the same market
    value as on the date of this report.

2. Stenco has a modern plant and facilities which can be profitably
    integrated into existing ACCO operations.

3. Larger sales volume and a somewhat greater diversification of products
    will result from the merger.

4. Volume purchasing can be utilized, and the Stenco die-casting opera-
    tions will tie in well with ACCO's needs for castings.

5. If ACCO can operate Stenco at a profit, tax loss carry-over provisions
    may pay for almost the entire Stenco acquisition.

6. It appears that in the case of possible loss, Stenco's physical plant
    could be sold on the market for a price which would be greater than
    its actual cost to ACCO.

7. Acquisition of Stenco assets will not weaken ACCO's working capital
    position because payment can be made by issuing new stock. This
    will mean dividend payments need not be lessened because of problems
    in working capital flows.

8. ACCO management can take steps to overcome certain deficiencies
    in Stenco management which have caused operating losses and some
    ill will toward the Stenco Corporation.

9. ACCO's management appears to have the skills and experience needed
    to run the Stenco operation at a profit.

BACKGROUND

The proxy statement you received lists certain facts pertinent to the pending
merger. A brief summary of these facts appears below:

Property. Stenco owns the following pieces of property:

1. The Softwash Corporation makes water-softening chemicals in a small
    plant in Dayton, Ohio.

2. The Stenco Metals Company operates in a portion of the Jonquil Avenue plant.

3. The Jonquil Avenue property in Hamtramck, Michigan, is a group of modern buildings (1950, 1955, 1961, and 1962) of aluminum or concrete-block construction. These one-story buildings cover 161,930 square feet.

4. The Milligan Street property in Hamtramck is a one-story brick structure with an area of 35,820 square feet. Built in 1935, this building is also in good condition.

5. The Wintergreen Street holdings in Troy, Michigan, are over forty-five years old. Of the six buildings, three are brick two-story structures and three are one-story brick and frame structures. This group of assets is only in fair condition.

Products and Employment. Stenco has six hundred employees who make a variety of plated parts (such as grills, bumpers, and hood ornaments) for the auto industry and bathroom accessories for the plumbing industry.

Competition. Stenco operates in a highly competitive industry with low profit margins. A large volume of business is required to ensure adequate profit margins. In this particular industry, customers such as the major auto companies can actually make or break a company by granting or withholding business.

General Information on Stenco Management. John Stenco and his wife own 11 percent of Stenco shares. Note that the merger agreement provides that Mr. Stenco will receive $1,500 per month for sixty months upon consummation of the merger. This $90,000 is in payment for duties as a consultant to the American Circle Company.

Financial Data. Those statements directly pertinent to the merger are reproduced for your convenience at the end of the report. Two significant facts not found in the delivered statement are the state of Stenco's assets in terms of market value and the factors underlying the merger.

ANALYSIS OF THE MERGER

REASONS FOR THE MERGER

Stated. The proxy statement lists the obvious reasons for the merger in rather straightforward fashion. Stenco was operating at a loss even with new production equipment. ACCO management saw a chance to diversify its operations. In addition, ACCO believed it could operate Stenco at a profit by making certain changes such as integrating Stenco's plating operations into ACCO's Die-Casting Division.

Actual. Though the obvious reasons favoring merger are both valid and pertinent, certain other factors tended to enter into merger negotiations.

First, sales and earnings of Stenco were sagging badly, as indicated in Table III.2.

TABLE III.2 STENCO SALES AND EARNINGS, 1962–1966

Year	Sales	Earnings
1962	$15,540,258	$ 41,535
1963	19,019,720	303,440
1964	10,132,468	(605,842)*
1965	14,645,072	(705,881)*
1966	11,895,531	(1,184,068)*

* Loss

In fiscal 1963, Stenco lost a large customer with little or no hope of ever regaining this business.[2] Investigation shows that Stenco has lost control of its manufacturing and operating costs due to an inefficient, indolent management. In addition, there is insufficient working capital to keep Stenco solvent for even a few more weeks. The future appears to hold little hope for solution of Stenco's problems, and merger or dissolution are all Stenco can expect to achieve.

In spite of the poor record of Stenco sales and earnings, operations and working capital, Stenco's purchase may be a real bargain. Stenco has excellent production facilities. These facilities can help ACCO to meet delivery dates in more expedient fashion. ACCO also has the opportunity to gain the kind of integration and diversification stated in the proxy. Then, too, ACCO management's knowledge of the manufacturing process used at Stenco will increase the chances of operating Stenco's facilities profitably. Of course, the really important factor from the ACCO point of view is the tax advantage, which reduces the actual cost of the merger substantially.

A final reason for merger is the apparent desire of John Stenco to merge with ACCO as long as personally favorable terms can be reached. If the merger is completed, Mr. Stenco will receive 11,080 shares of ACCO stock and, as noted, a sixty-month $90,000 consultant's fee. ACCO will use him sparingly in his capacity as a consultant and will probably take steps to ease him out of its board of directors as soon as it is contractually feasible. Mr. Stenco and his salary should be regarded as a necessary but not exorbitant cost of the merger.

CAPITALIZATION AND FUNDED DEBT

The capitalization of ACCO, Stenco, and the surviving corporation are summarized in Table III.3.

---

[2] Though our investigation was unable to document the reason for this lost customer, several sources traced the cause to a personal indiscretion on the part of a top-level Stenco official.

TABLE III.3   CAPITALIZATION OF ACCO, STENCO, AND THE SURVIVOR

	ACCO	Stenco	Survivor
Shares common stock outstanding	402,947.3	767,500	503,974
Shares common stock unissued		−9,800 = 757,700	
Book value issued stock (August 31, 1966)	$14.06	$2.98	$15.28
Market value stocks (November 1, 1966)	20	2.25	—
Market value new corporation (estimated)			
Date of merger	—	—	17.00
After market adjustment	—	—	19.40*

* Based on our analysis of trends in the market and the financial data bearing on the merger

The common stock outstanding and unissued and the respective book values are taken directly from the proxy statement. The surviving corporation's shares are the original ACCO shares added to 10/75 of the listed Stenco shares (402,947 1/3 + 101.026 2/3 = 503,974). The ratio used is the one stated in the merger agreement (7.5:1).

Market values listed for ACCO and Stenco are closing prices as stated in *Barron's Magazine* on November 1, 1966.

The values estimated for the new corporation were calculated as in Table III.4.

TABLE III.4   VALUES ESTIMATED FOR ACCO-STENCO

1. As of the date of the merger:

$ 2.25	Est. value Stenco stock on market
7.5	Exchange ratio
$16.875	Est. market value or
$17.00	Rounded market value estimate

2. After adjustment:

402,947.3	ACCO shares
$ 20	Market price of ACCO shares
$8,058,946	Total market value of ACCO shares

767,500	Authorized Stenco shares
9,800	Unissued shares
757,700	Outstanding Stenco shares

757,700	Outstanding Stenco shares
$ 2.25	Market price of Stenco shares
$1,704,825	Total market value of Stenco shares

$$\frac{\$9,763,771 \text{ Value Stenco and ACCO shares}}{503,974 \text{ New shares Stenco outstanding}} = \$19.40$$

$19.40	New market value (in time) of each share in the new corporation

MERGER TERMS AND PRICE

Merger Terms. A copy of the merger agreement is found attached to your proxy statement. The most important points in the merger agreement are

1. ACCO will give up 101,026 50/75 shares (less 10/75 times the number of Stenco shares dissenting) to Stenco stockholders.
2. Stenco will retain $100,000 to pay dissenting stockholders and other outstanding indebtedness not assumed by ACCO.
3. John Stenco will receive $1,500 per month for sixty months and will be elected to the ACCO Board of Directors.
4. The merger is automatically canceled if the Internal Revenue Bureau disallows tax carry-overs; or if over 6 percent of Stenco shareholders dissent (this latter provision is subject to certain modifications) and ask for fair market value of their holdings.

Price. The actual price which ACCO will pay for Stenco can be viewed in terms of book value, market value, or actual cost.

Book value comparisons are not really meaningful to analyze this merger. Book value has a tendency to be little more than an accounting convenience. Attempts to use such figures in accurate cost calculations are nebulous. Illustrating this point is the fact that ACCO sold one of its Detroit properties on January 23, 1966 for a price which was 252 percent in excess of book value. No further analysis is presented with respect to book value cost.

Comparison of market value of ACCO stock before and after merger indicates that the current ACCO listing of $20 will be regained shortly after the merger takes place. A temporary price of about $17 may occur until investors realize the value of the merged companies is much greater than that shown in the exchange ratio. This opens up a possibility that you may wish to explore further.

If ACCO shares are to fall after merger occurs, it may be advantageous to you personally to first vote for the merger and then sell at least some of your ACCO holdings at a price of approximately $20. After the merger, ACCO stock may drop to approximately the exchange ratio valuation set by ACCO and Stenco. A prior calculation shows this to be about $17. If you repurchase ACCO shares shortly after the merger, you may be able to gain a greater number of shares in the new company without increasing your monetary investment. This, of course, would have to be balanced against the 25-percent capital gains tax you would have to pay on any long-term gains from the transaction. We do not advise this course of action strongly because it is not certain that ACCO shares will fall as low as $17. There is also the possibility that such action may be illegal under SEC regulations dealing with stock transactions based on "inside" information. It is, however, a speculation which holds some possibility of personal gain.

The real price of Stenco is not found in a comparison of book or market values, but in the tax carry-over which Stenco has accrued (and is accruing) due to operating and capital losses. If ACCO can operate Stenco at a profit, substantially all of the cost of Stenco can be written off against ACCO profits. This, of course, assumes that ACCO will continue to show operating profits in the future. Since projected ACCO sales for 1967 are $22 million; for 1968 $26 million; and for 1969 $35 million; and since we expect past profit margins (1963–1965 average 9.6 percent before taxes) to continue, such future profit expectations seem reasonably valid. (see Table III.5 for added details).

TABLE III.5 ACCO SALES FORECAST AND HISTORICAL DATA

Year	Sales (Millions)	Net Profit (Thousands)
1972*	43	2,200
1971*	42	2,100
1970*	38	1,900
1969*	35	1,750
1968	26	1,310
1967	22	1,100
1966	18.2	942
1965	17.4	827
1964	6.5	176
1963	6.9	252
1962	6.5	335

* Forecast estimates

The arithmetic of the tax credit carry-over is as follows:

TABLE III.6

$1,734,000	Past operating loss carry-over to June 1966 (Rounded)
342,000	Capital loss carry-over (Estimate)
224,000	Operating loss July and August 1966 (Rounded)
400,000	Estimated operating loss carry-over Sept. 1 to Dec. 31, 1966 (Estimated at $100,000/month)*
$2,700,000	Estimated total tax loss carry-over
$2,358,000	Tax operating loss carry-over
0.52	Tax savings percentage
$1,226,160	Actual operating tax credit gain to ACCO
$ 342,000	Capital carry-over
0.25	Tax savings percentage
$ 85,500	Total capital carry-over saving
$1,311,660	Actual tax credit gain to ACCO
503,974	Total new shares = $2.60
	$2.60 tax gain per share

* This is a conservative figure which projects the July–August loss forward to the end of the year.

This means that if the value of Stenco assets is as represented in the proxy statement, tax credits will add a value of $2.60 to each current ACCO share. Total gain to the 402,947 currently outstanding ACCO shares would be approximately $1,047,600. If existing Stenco assets can be depreciated by approved methods against future ACCO earnings, the entire cost of Stenco could be recouped through tax and reserve allowances. ACCO would thus obtain a corporation with over $2 million in fairly modern assets at substantially no cost.

Another favorable feature here is that ACCO's working capital is not substantially diminished by the merger because of limitations placed upon dividend payment by working capital restrictions in long-term debt agreements. No change in dividend payment is anticipated from this merger because of diminutions in working capital.

CONCLUSION

Because of the existing tax carry-over provisions it is suggested that you vote for the merger. If consolidated operations continue to make a profit, and if ACCO can operate Stenco's facilities at better than a break-even level, you can gain much from a merger.

In addition to tax benefits, this merger offers such things as diversification of products, better delivery, fuller utilization of management skills and the chance to make the American Circle Company more profitable. These factors tend to overbalance the difficulties which may have cropped up during the last few years of Stenco operation.

1. Do you agree with the recommendations of BRJ Associates?

2. In your judgment, are the BRJ financial calculations and estimates valid ones?

3. How does Mr. Kennedy's role as Board Chairman differ from that as a major stockholder? What should he do if these roles conflict?

4. If Mr. Kennedy decides to oppose the merger (for either financial or other reasons) how should he proceed?

5. What organizational changes might Mr. Kennedy propose to guarantee more careful analysis of future merger or diversification activities by ACCO management?

BIBLIOGRAPHY

Allen, Louis A., *Management and Organization,* New York: McGraw-Hill, Inc., 1958.

Ansoff, H.I., *Corporate Strategy: An Analytic Approach to Business Policy for Growth and Expansion,* New York: McGraw-Hill, Inc. 1965

Argyris, Chris, *Personality and Organization,* New York: Harper & Row, Publishers, 1957.

Barnard, Chester I., *Functions of the Executive,* Cambridge, Mass.: Harvard University Press, 1938.

Blake, Robert R., and Jane S. Mouton, *The Managerial Grid,* Houston, Tex.: The Gulf Publishing Company, 1964.

Carzo, Rocco, and John Yanouzas, *Formal Organizations: A Systems Approach,* Homewood, Ill.: Richard D. Irwin, Inc., 1967.

Chandler, Alfred E., Jr., *Strategy and Structure,* Cambridge, Mass.: MIT Press, 1962.

Chapple, E., and Leonard R. Sayles, *The Measure of Management,* rev. ed., New York: Crowell-Collier and Macmillan, Inc., 1961.

Cordiner, Ralph, *New Frontiers for Professional Managers: McKinsey Lectures,* Columbia University, Graduate School of Business, New York: McGraw-Hill, Inc., 1956.

Dale, Ernest, *Management: Theory and Practice,* New York: McGraw-Hill, Inc., 1965.

————, *Organization,* New York: American Management Association, Inc., 1967.

Dalton, Melville, *Men Who Manage,* New York: John Wiley & Sons, Inc., 1959.

Drucker, Peter F., *Concept of the Corporation,* New York: John Hay Company, Inc., 1946.

————, *The Practice of Management,* New York: Harper & Row, Publishers, 1954.

Fox, W., *The Management Process,* Homewood, Ill.: Richard D. Irwin, Inc., 1963.

Goldberg, S., *Probability: An Introduction,* Englewood Cliffs, N.J.: Prentice-Hall, Inc., 1960.

Haynes, Warren W., and Joseph L. Massie, *Management: Analysis, Concepts and Cases,* Englewood Cliffs, N.J.: Prentice-Hall, Inc., 1961.

Holden, P.E., L.S. Fish, and H.L. Smith, *Top Management Organization and Control,* New York: McGraw-Hill, Inc., 1951.

Hutchinson, John G., *Organizations: Theory and Classical Concepts,* New York: Holt, Rinehart and Winston, Inc., 1967.

Kazmier, L., *Principles of Management: A Program for Self Instruction,* New York: McGraw-Hill, Inc., 1964.

Koontz, Harold, ed., *Toward a Unified Theory of Management,* New York: McGraw-Hill, Inc., 1964.

————, and Cyril O'Donnell, *Principles of Management,* 3rd ed., New York: McGraw-Hill, Inc., 1964.

Learned, E., C.R. Christianson, K.R. Andrews, and W.D. Guth, *Business Policy: Text and Cases,* Homewood, Ill.: Richard D. Irwin, Inc., 1965.

Likert, Rensis, *The Human Organization*, New York: McGraw-Hill, Inc., 1967.

_____, *New Patterns of Management*, New York: McGraw-Hill, Inc., 1961.

Litterer, J., ed., *The Analysis of Organizations*, New York: John Wiley & Sons, Inc., 1965.

McGuire, Joseph W., *Theories of Business Behavior*, Englewood Cliffs, N.J.: Prentice-Hall, Inc., 1964.

Mailik, S., and E. Van Ness, eds., *Concepts and Issues in Administrative Behavior*, Englewood Cliffs, N.J.: Prentice-Hall, Inc., 1962.

March, James G., and Herbert A. Simon, *Organizations*, New York: John Wiley & Sons, Inc., 1958.

Moore, Franklin G., *Manufacturing Management*, 4th ed., Homewood, Ill.: Richard D. Irwin, Inc, 1965.

Newman, William H., *Administrative Action*, 2nd ed., Englewood Cliffs, N.J.: Prentice-Hall, Inc., 1963.

_____, Charles E. Summer, and E. Kirby Warren, *The Process of Management: Concepts, Behavior and Practice*, 2nd ed., Englewood Cliffs, N.J.: Prentice-Hall, Inc., 1967.

Odiorne, George S., *How Managers Make Things Happen*, Englewood Cliffs, N.J.: Prentice-Hall, Inc., 1961.

Parkinson, Cyril N., *Parkinson's Law and Other Studies in Administration*, Boston: Houghton Mifflin Company, 1957.

Prince, Thomas R., *Information Systems for Management Planning and Control*, Homewood, Ill.: Richard D. Irwin, Inc., 1966.

Rubenstein, A.H., and C.J. Haberstroh, *Some Theories of Organization*, rev. ed., Homewood, Ill.: Richard D. Irwin, Inc., 1966.

Scott, W., *Organization Theory*, Homewood, Ill.: Richard D. Irwin, Inc., 1967.

Servan-Schreiber, J.J., *The American Challenge*, New York: Atheneum Publishers, 1968.

Simon, Herbert A., *Administrative Behavior*, 2nd ed., New York: Crowell-Collier and Macmillan, Inc., 1957.

Smith, R.A., *Corporations in Crisis*, New York: Doubleday & Company, Inc., Anchor Books, 1963.

Summer, Charles E., and J. O'Connell, *The Managerial Mind*, Homewood, Ill.: Richard D. Irwin, Inc., 1964.

Soujanen, Waino, *The Dynamics of Management*, New York: Holt, Rinehart and Winston, Inc., 1966.

Thompson, V., *Organizations in Action*, New York: McGraw-Hill, Inc., 1967.

Urwick, L.F., *The Pattern of Management*, Minneapolis: University of Minnesota Press, 1956.

Whyte, William F., *Men at Work*, Homewood, Ill.: Richard D. Irwin, Inc., 1961.

Whyte, William H., *The Organization Man*, New York: Simon and Schuster, Inc., 1956.

Wolf, W.B., *How to Understand Management: An Introduction to Chester Barnard*, Los Angeles: Lucas Brothers, 1968.

All forecasts of future business conditions indicate that today's technical, human, social, political, and economic problems seem almost certain to become more complex tomorrow. As a result, solutions will demand astute and sophisticated decision making based on all available factual inputs. Goals will need to be sharpened so proper attention can be paid to strategy determination and implementation. Plans of action will, of necessity, be focused on progress toward those goals as measured against set standards of performance. These reports of progress in turn will have to be transmitted rapidly to decision makers so appropriate adjustments and corrections can be executed. This process of evaluating and reviewing contribution will call for the most modern and well-designed management information systems.

Fortunately for tomorrow's decision makers, the use of carefully structured management information systems is already on the upswing, principally because recent developments in computer technology make their use efficient and economical. Computers, with their fantastic speeds and infallible memories, have revolutionized the handling and reporting of information for planning and control and have widened the coverage and effectiveness of traditional measures of performance. In just two decades, computers have made such inroads into managerial control practices that the control function will never be the same again.

In spite of their incredible technological additions to the control process, computers have done little to change some of the reservations people hold about controls. For one thing, individuals take some time to adjust

SECTION IV
Evaluation and Review of Contribution

to the major technological innovation represented by computerized information processing. For another, human reactions against controls may be even more pronounced in the computer age, since rapid feedback frustrates the inefficient performer's desire to remain anonymous. Though this "Big Brother" aspect of computerized control systems gets wide publicity, an often ignored built-in plus is that competent and outstanding performers are also identified rapidly. Notwithstanding their contribution to pointing up good performance, computerized control systems are more often seen as threatening rather than supportive factors in the work environment. Because of this negative image, many organizations have invested considerable time and care designing management information systems that reflect the opinions, ideas, and thoughts of individuals affected by their operation.

In most classic management writings, control is usually represented as the final step in the planning, organizing, and control cycle. Feedback appears in these formulations, but most historical writings view the time gap between recognition and use of control information as relatively lengthy. In recent years, the tremendous strides made in recording, reporting, and transmitting information have obsoleted some of the classical theories so completely they have been dubbed an "information revolution." Information flows and feedback are frequently reported almost as soon as they occur, and rapid action is becoming more the rule than the exception. Hand tabulation and recording has passed very quickly from the punchcard era into the computer era, and now the computer age is entering the world of real time. In the real-time dimension, results of information flows are available to decision makers almost immediately, and the absence of time lags turns historical records into instant facts (real time). In short, decision makers receive information at the time the information is being generated. In the Owen-Illinois Company, the Toledo data-processing headquarters is connected by direct wire with one hundred different sales and manufacturing locations. Orders feed into Toledo where the computer matches them up with products in stock, places orders, and sends releases to warehouses or directs plants to make the products ordered by the customer.

In addition to more rapid data transmission, modern real-time information systems can handle bigger, newer, and more complex problems.[1] The Sabre system of reservations and scheduling used by American Airlines involves a multimillion dollar inven-

CHAPTER 11
Management Information and Control Systems

---

[1] See Robert V. Head, *Real Time Business Systems* (New York: Holt, Rinehart and Winston, Inc., 1964), which limits real-time systems to those in which data are available in less than one day. More typically, knowledge is made available almost instantaneously.

tory, hundreds of programming hours, and hundreds of thousands of instructions. The upshot of this complex system is that now an individual can call from a New York suburb and get a reservation to Detroit or San Francisco in seconds. He can also learn of cancellations on any of several hundred flights in the same small time interval.

Writing in *European Business,* A.E. Amstutz of MIT notes how management information systems have evolved in terms of both speed of information handling and reporting, and increasing levels of analytic sophistication. His findings, summarized in Figures 11.1 and 11.2, show that inventory reporting is now at less than the one-day processing and reporting stage, while custodial accounting on corporationwide matters has reached the fortnight stage. According to Amstutz, all signs point to greater aggregates of information being recorded and reported more and more rapidly. In terms of problem complexity, Amstutz claims that information systems now have moved into a prediction and learning phase, which means they can ingest behavioral simulations and handle adaptive heuristics. Such systems are fully capable of analyzing data, learning from experience, and remembering never to make the same mistake twice. In short, management information systems are now capable of simulating thinking and decision making—and so qualify as ersatz alter egos of managerial decision makers.

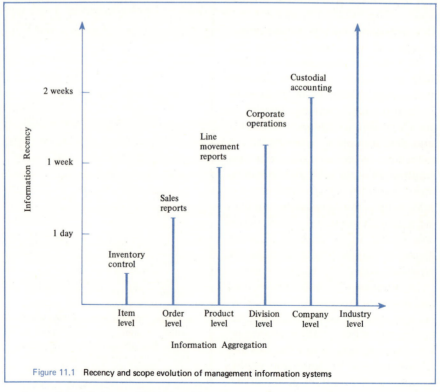

Figure 11.1 Recency and scope evolution of management information systems

Source: From A. E. Amstutz, "Management Information Systems," *European Business,* July 1968, p. 26.

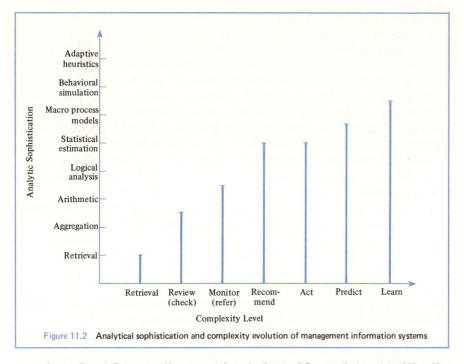

Figure 11.2   Analytical sophistication and complexity evolution of management information systems

Source: From A. E. Amstutz, "Management Information Systems," *European Business,* July 1968, p. 27.

The name *management information system* is now firmly etched into the literature and practice of management, but the primacy of the concept is a recent phenomenon, a product of the computer age. Using the computer as their basic instrument, systems analysts have tried to develop management systems utilizing rules and techniques of measurement which seek to maximize objective-seeking activities and minimize wasted time and effort. Their objectives have rarely been achieved with ease, since technical factors in management information systems come into conflict with human values and reactions.

DESIGN OF MANAGEMENT INFORMATION AND CONTROL SYSTEMS

Organizational goals are the genesis of management information systems. In determining its objectives, the organization may want to look at such matters as profitability, market position, productivity, product leadership, personnel development, employee attitudes, public responsibilities, and any number of institutional or personal values. A well-designed management information system should furnish management with the reports needed to evaluate progress toward their goals. Though normally much more detailed than the type of information used in the planning function, control information should (except in rare exceptions dictated by management) be structured to report, group, and process data to reflect progress toward or movement away from the organization's goals. The first step in constructing a management information system thus involves setting broad goals similar in nature to those discussed in Chapter 4. In textiles, the Deering-Milliken Company established a "total information" center to centralize all vital corporation data in the hands of a single staff. Roger Milliken, Deering-Milliken president, has indicated the goals of the system are to provide executives with more time for decision making and planning and to help them base decisions "on fact, rather than intuition." To bring about these goals, the company has routinized billing, payroll, purchasing, and record-keeping procedures in the hope that reductions in paper work will give executives more time for "management," while better reporting and control techniques will provide the factual inputs for improved decision making.[2]

Once basic goals have been determined, the structure of the information system itself must be formulated. In addition to the organization's objectives, the structure of the management information system must rely on economically and technically feasible measurement, labor relations factors, the state of the competition's use of management information and processing systems, the timeliness of the data needed, the comprehensiveness of data needed, the importance of balancing results in the system against external standards of performance, and the technological processes available for handling and processing information. Figure 11.3 indicates how these various components interrelate in a representative management information system.

In addition to the rather specific points shown in Figure 11.3, the basic philosophies of the corporation on such matters as closeness of control and extent of decentralization exert an important effect on how the system will be constructed. For example, organizations may choose what Arnold Emch calls the Captain Queeg approach or the Will Rogers approach to control. The Captain Queeg approach, named after the famous captain in the *Caine Mutiny,* is extremely close, detailed control; whereas the Will Rogers approach is a much looser structure.[3] Emch characterizes the close control approach in the words of Lt. Keefer, character in the *Caine Mutiny,* who describes the Navy system as one devised by excellent brains near the top who use the basic assumption that morons will be responsible for each activity at the bottom of the chain of command. This system is control "by the book," whereas the Will Rogers approach is more judgment-oriented and leaves control to the discretion of the individual. Both of these systems tend to be "open-loop systems" in that judgment is a built-in factor; but the Queeg, or tight-control, philosophy is close to being a self-regulating, or closed-loop system.

Closed-loop control systems have a built-in self-adjustment feature that reacts automatically when deviations occur. The cybernetic (machine) system

[2] "Meshing Managers and Computers," *Business Week,* July 3, 1965, p. 82ff.
[3] Arnold Emch, "Control Means Action," *Harvard Business Review,* vol. 32, no. 4 (July–August 1954), pp. 92–98.

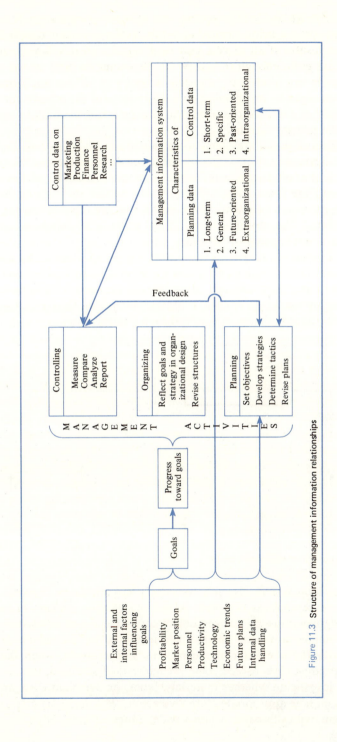

Figure 11.3 Structure of management information relationships

is a typical example. In this system, the process or operation is measured by a gauge or a sensing device, and the results are then checked against the desired results. If all is well, that is, if actual and standard performance measures are close enough to satisfy the requirements built into the system, the process is not altered or adjusted in any way. If deviation occurs, the process is changed by an effecting unit. The nature of the adjustment depends on the extent of the deviation from the standard and the built-in limitations on what the process can do.

In a perfect closed-loop system, no outside judgment enters into the decision to correct deviations. For example, the electrical contact needed to power a furnace is shut off as the metal in the thermostat expands; and the furnace goes off until the room cools sufficiently to generate the impetus needed to restart the furnace. These actions are automatic and recur unless the furnace is disconnected, the power is shut off, or some other situation arises that the system is not capable of handling.

When oil refineries are run by computer programs, the automatic combining of flows and blends of elements follows a similar pattern of action-reaction-action. Computer programs can direct operations until conditions arise that are not programmed into or anticipated by the system. Figure 11.4 pictures a simple, generalized version of a closed-loop control system.

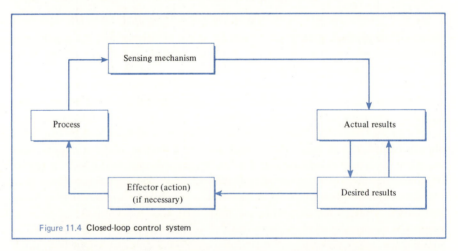

Figure 11.4 Closed-loop control system

An open-loop system also follows the pattern shown in Figure 11.4 with one major exception: at the point where the effector appears in the cycle, human judgment must be invoked before corrective action is initiated. Adjustments are made only after changes are instituted by individuals or groups familiar with the operation of the process. For example, when the system indicates product costs exceed some predetermined standard, the plant manager may investigate whether materials, labor, or overhead costs are out of line and then take appropriate corrective action. The decisions made in open-loop systems typically cover a much wider range of knowledge than can be conveniently or economically built into fully automatic systems. Open-loop controls are used to control sophisticated processes or ones that are not repetitive enough to justify the construction of elaborate closed-loop control procedures. Figure 11.5 illustrates the processes that comprise a rudimentary system of open-loop controls.

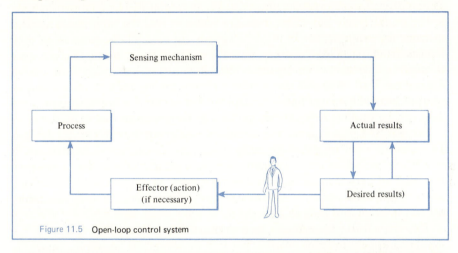

Figure 11.5   Open-loop control system

In the open-loop system, judgment becomes a critical variable. Not only *what* will be done but *whether* it will be done is determined by judgmental factors, not by built-in programs. Adjustments to correct deviations from expected standards or results are thus made on an individual basis.

It is obvious from this discussion of structure and objectives that management information systems must begin with clear objectives, must have a rather detailed way of structuring these objectives, and must have some system of gathering and reporting information. Processes or activities must be identified clearly, standards of desired performance must be set, measurements must be taken of actual conditions, and adjustments must be made after a review of disparities between actual and desired results. The major components of the management information system are thus identified as sensing units, standards of measurement, collating units, and the development of decision rules. Decision rules derived from objectives have already been discussed in Chapter 6, and calculation methodology will be described with computer operations. At this point, a discussion of sensing units and standards is in order.

The selection of sensing units depends in part upon what the organization wants to measure. If quality is the key to manufacturing, the organization may stand or fall on the ability of its sensing devices to measure the quality level required in the various production operations. The units to be sensed in this case might be attributes such as color or smoothness or variables such as length, width, and thickness. Reports from such a system might take the form of statistical quality control charts comparing performance with a set of upper and lower control limits constructed with due consideration of engineering tolerances. The sensors themselves might be scales, calipers, gauges, light-sensitive cells, or any number of chemical sensors which might report such factors as acidity or viscosity. If dollars are critical, sensing devices might measure actual cost of materials, labor, and overhead utilized in given cost centers against some predetermined set of cost standards. The quality of sensing devices is extremely important to good control. In many computerized control systems, for example, the input data (which are basically nothing more than reports from particular sensing units) are often the limiting factor, since calculating devices can handle informational inputs more rapidly than sensing devices can feed them into the system. In the chemical industry, for example, computers are capable of handling data far more voluminous and sophisticated than can be provided by existing process instrumentation.

Standards of performance are much more judgmental than sensing devices. They reflect a set of values on what the organization wants to accomplish in a given period of time. Though they vary greatly in specifics, almost all standards of performance fall into five categories: (1) time standards; (2) cost and revenue standards; (3) capital standards; (4) physical or unit standards; and (5) intangible standards.

Time standards are normally used to measure production operations. Time standards appear in terms of time per unit of output, for example, "machine time per piece" or "minutes (of labor) per piece." Eastman Kodak uses such a system in its giant Kodak Park works in Rochester, New York. Time standards can also be constructed by relating time to groupings of activities. For example, military orders are frequently stated in the following terms: "This unit must complete Phase Two by 30 November 1969 or the enemy will move his reserves in Section Three and impede or stop our advance to objective M."

The form and coverage of time standards is a continuing source of controversy in industrial circles. The quest for a fair day's work has focused considerable attention on the setting and administering of time standards. In firms using incentive payment plans based on time standards, the fair day's work phase is expanded into "A fair day's work for a fair day's pay." When time standards are related to both work and pay, the resultant problems are far more complex than those existing when work alone is being evaluated.[4]

Cost and revenue standards are used to report both individual and unit performance levels. They may be absolute (total dollars spent), or they may appear in the form of ratios. Some commonly used ratios are *dollars per unit produced, sales to cost of sales,* and *profits per unit per order produced.* Cost-accounting systems normally use cost and revenue standards to report information to higher levels of management. According to Joel Dean, "Standards for measuring profit should cover only those items in operating costs that managers have some control over. Their effectiveness should be measured

---

[4] For an expanded discussion of work standards, see John Hutchinson, *Managing a Fair Day's Work* (Ann Arbor, Mich.: University of Michigan, Bureau of Industrial Relations, 1963).

on these points, not on other noncontrollable items."[5] This focus is both sensible and necessary in the preparation of revenue-cost standard reporting systems, which issue daily, weekly, monthly, quarterly, or annual reports, depending on the nature of the items. Cost and revenue standards are used extensively in industry. Perhaps all of the firms in *Fortune*'s five hundred largest industrials listing use them in some form or other.

Capital standards are more general than either time or cost-ratio standards. They appear frequently as ratios, but the areas to which they relate have a wide degree of coverage and significance. The absolute dimensions of current liabilities may be viewed as an upper limit, or standard, against which future liabilities may be compared, unless some other standard of comparison is agreed upon. Balance sheet items are the basic figures that underlie most capital standards. One illustration of this type of standard is the rough rule of thumb that the current ratio $\left(\dfrac{\text{current assets}}{\text{current liabilities}} \right)$ should be no less than 1:1. Ratios falling below this proportion usually indicate a financial condition that calls for careful review. Financial and brokerage houses such as Merrill, Lynch, Pierce, Fenner and Smith commonly use these ratios to furnish clients with a quick set of evaluations of profitability and performance.

Physical or quantitative standards (other than time standards) measure performance in terms of tangible output. Examples are units of produce (tons, pounds, and so on), square feet of floor used, percentages of scrap or reject materials, sales related to the total number of sales calls, and customer attitudes as measured by surveys. Physical standards are used whenever possible because their very measurability seems to give them validity. Quite frequently, however, they measure the wrong thing well and thus have little real utility in assessing overall performance. For example, a low reject or scrap ratio may also mean low production, which could be disastrous in a period when production is needed to meet customer demands. On the other hand, total output may be great (tons and tons), but the reject level may be so high that all profit is wiped out. Physical standards are rarely used alone, but are normally combined with other qualitative and quantitative factors in judging total performance.

Intangible standards are used less commonly than other types, probably because they are difficult to measure and evaluate correctly. Intangibles are by their nature somewhat vague; and when they can be defined well enough to satisfy the needs of measurement, they may not report exactly what is desired. For example, a measured change in a company's public image may be due to almost any number of real or implied happenings, including errors in the means of measuring the change. Even if the change does exist, the reason why may not be readily apparent. The underlying complexity of intan-

---

[5] *Managerial Economics* (Englewood Cliffs, N.J.: Prentice-Hall, Inc., 1951).

gible factors tends to make them ill suited to measurement and evaluation by quantitative means. Thus, intangibles such as morale, image, and attitude are generally assessed in more subjective fashion that the physically countable units encountered in production and service operations. One form of evaluation is the "employee attitude survey," an attempt to find out how employees feel about a number of points related to their employment. Firms such as Burlington Industries conduct these surveys regularly, and the results often uncover shifts and trends which call for changes in policies, procedures, and/or supervisory practices. Though such surveys do not always measure cause and effect accurately, they do provide a fever chart which senses employee thoughts and feelings.

In the control process, standards state what is expected, while measurement calculates how closely that expectation is being met. When poor information is fed into the control process, adjustments have little chance of correcting deviations from standard performance levels. Consistent and accurate standards are thus at the heart of every well-conceived control process.

In summary, a management information system is composed of objectives and decision rules; a sensing apparatus which performs the measurement function; a set of standards; and an apparatus which provides the basis for collecting, comparing, processing, analyzing, and reporting information. Though many management information systems have inputs prepared and processed manually or mechanically, more and more systems are utilizing electronic data-processing equipment. Management information and control systems in most large organizations have already entered what Gilbert Burke calls the "Age of the Computer."[6]

THE COMPUTER'S ROLE IN MANAGEMENT INFORMATION SYSTEMS

Whenever computers are mentioned, dramatic visions typically come to mind. Computers can operate at speeds beyond man's ability to understand—during a ten-minute coffee break, one computer can perform a decade of human computation. One six-inch-by-six-inch memory unit can now record and read back on call the entire contents of the *Encyclopaedia Britannica*. A picture drawn on a special "light screen" with a "light pen" can direct a computer to punch a tape which, when fed into a numerical control machine, will actually cut a metal part; the design to finished part cycle occurs without blueprints, dies, or human intervention. And this is not Buck Rogers in the twenty-fifth century—thousands of people operated light pens in an industrial exhibit at Expo 67 in Montreal, Canada.

Computers can perform calculations not only with bewildering speed but

---

[6] *The Computer Age and Its Potential for Management* (New York: Harper & Row, Publishers, 1965).

also with more efficiency and more accuracy than man. A computer needs only to be programmed properly, and it can turn out thousands and tens of thousands of calculations in errorfree fashion. If heuristic programming techniques are sufficiently advanced, computers can simulate man's thinking process and actually reason through a series of calculations without the built-in emotional factors encountered when people perform the same job. In performing calculations computers can do much of what man can do, and they have no emotional drawbacks and never get tired—even when adding 250,000 sixteen-digit characters in one second. In time, according to Herbert Simon, relative costs will decide whether men or computers will do a job, since the technology for handling both structured and unstructured problems is now in existence.[7] Computers *can* direct even menial pick-and-shovel jobs today; but it is not yet economical for them to do so.

Though the calculating speeds and potential uses of computers have some exotic overtones, the computer's role in most management information systems is much less fanciful. Computers act as the muscles, nerves, and hands of the system; and they collect, array, pile, sort, analyze, rearrange, and report data at high speeds with great accuracy and tirelessness. Once programmed, they perform data-processing chores with the greatest efficiency ever known. Masses of input are handled with an ease that truly can be classified as an information revolution. Areas in scientific problem solving and information handling never before available now can be reached through computer technology; and these advances have opened new opportunities for management, particulary in the areas of planning and control.

COMPUTERIZED INFORMATION PROCESSING

Like most computational devices, computers are more effective in some applications than others. They have been particularly useful in handling large masses of information requiring fairly simple processing. Such information usually has the following characteristics:

1. The variables involved are interacting ones.
2. The values reported are reasonably accurate.
3. Speed is important in terms of final results.
4. The preparations are repetitive.
5. Accuracy in reporting is required.
6. The information masses are large.

In a general sense, any routine function is a prime target for control through the use of data-processing equipment.[8] Specific examples of computer applications are legion. Computers now help to process business data, to solve mathe-

---

[7] *Ibid.*

[8] John Dearden and F. Warren McFarlan, *Management Information Systems: Text and Cases* (Homewood, Ill.: Richard D. Irwin, Inc., 1966).

matical problems, to control manufacturing operations, to simulate activities, to store and retrieve knowledge, to control communication flows, to translate languages, and to relate information sources to various predetermined standards. According to an article in *Fortune,* the Lockheed Corporation forecasts that in the 1970s computer usage will move rapidly into medicine, education, and government record keeping.[9] This is in addition to further expansion in business, industry, government, and other current applications.

Even though the computer is rather awesome to the layman, understanding its form of operation is not complicated, since the computer utilizes the kind of thinking patterns that a man might follow in solving the same problem. First, the computer analyzes the problem; second, a program is written which lays out the steps and the instructions needed to calculate a solution. The program is then punched into cards and read on to magnetic tape or some other input device. The steps in the program are fed into a central processing unit memory, and the computer then begins to calculate. The facts and directions then move in and out of the calculating unit until all the necessary arithmetic is completed and the result is reported "read out" at the output unit, typically a typewriter or printer. Thus, the basic steps in computer processing are

1. *Compilation,* gathering inputs so that they may be fed into the system
2. *Storage,* or putting data into the computer so it is ready for immediate use
3. *Calculation,* or adding and subtracting facts as directed by the program
4. *Output,* or recording of results
5. *Control,* or developing a set of processing steps so that the sequence occurs in a logical order

Human beings do these things in calculating and solving problems, but, obviously, they perform them less rapidly than computers. On the other hand, the human mind can handle a wide variety of functions, something computers have not yet been able to do very well or very economically.

To illustrate the specifics of how a computer handles a typical problem, the General Electric Company has prepared a booklet for student use. The core of the computer's computational activities appears in the following passage from the GE pamphlet.

> You're paymaster of the Supersonic Hubcap Company. You want to figure out how much to pay one employee, George Geargrinder, for last week's work. You ask your secretary to check the pay records and bring you certain information: how many hours Mr. Geargrinder worked last week, how much he earns an hour, and his payroll deductions. She checks the records and reports that Mr. Geargrinder worked 35 hours. His rate of

---

[9] Lawrence Lessing, "Where the Industries of the Seventies Will Come From," *Fortune,* January 1967, p. 96.

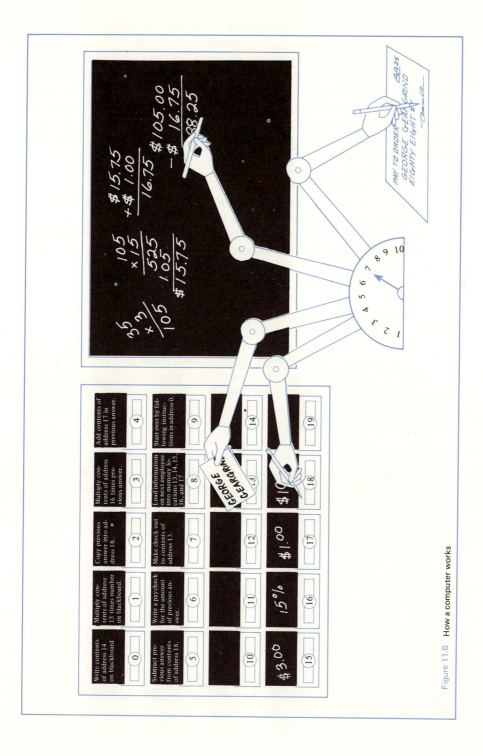

Figure 11.6　How a computer works

pay is $3 per hour. His deductions are 15 percent for income tax and $1 for insurance.

With these facts you can easily figure out George Geargrinder's wages. First, find gross pay by multiplying the hours he worked by his rate of pay. This comes to $105. Now figure the deductions: income tax is 15 percent of $105 or $15.75; add $1 for health insurance and you get a total of $16.75. Subtract these deductions from $105 gross pay, and you end up with $88.25, which is Mr. Geargrinder's take-home pay. Write him a check for this amount.

"BASIC" COMPUTER AT WORK

The heart of the computer's ability to work automatically is its ability to remember instructions as well as facts.

The computer's memory can be compared to a block of post-office boxes, where each box holds one person's mail. In the computer's memory each "box" holds one item of information, either a fact or an instruction. In the computer these "boxes" are called memory locations.

With some post-office boxes as the memory, a blackboard as the calculating section, and a mechanical hand to control the movement of data and instruction, we have a basic computer.

Let's see if we can have our computer calculate the wages of Supersonic Hubcap Company's 10,000 employees and issue their checks.

First, we need input, which in this case is payroll facts. Previously prepared time cards—one for each employee—will provide such facts. We place these cards in an input machine that loads payroll facts on one employee at a time into the computer's memory.

We must decide in which memory locations to store each fact. Each memory location has its own identifying number called an address. Let's put the employee's name in address 13; hours worked in address 14, rate of pay in address 15, percentage of income tax deduction in address 16; and health insurance deduction in address 17.

(In the boxes illustrated above we have used George Geargrinder's pay information—35 hours worked, $3 an hour, 15 percent tax deduction, and $1 for health insurance.)

Now we can write a series of instructions that will automatically figure the pay of George Geargrinder, or any other person whose pay facts are loaded into the computer.

We will store the instructions in the computer's memory in exactly the same way we stored the pay facts. It doesn't make any difference which boxes we use, as all are equally accessible. Let's put the first instruction in box number 0.

To get our computer started on the payroll, we can "set" it at address number 0, just as we might set the hands of a clock. After following the instruction in address 0, the computer will automatically move forward, one address at a time, carrying out each instruction as it goes. The last instruction—stored in address 9—resets the computer at address 0, thus automatically starting the operation all over again.

ADDRESS	INSTRUCTION
0	Write contents of address 14 (hours worked) on the blackboard.
1	Multiply contents of address 15 (rate of pay) times number on blackboard.
2	Copy previous answer into address 18 (but don't erase it from blackboard).
3	Multiply contents of address 16 (percentage of income tax deduction) times previous answer.
4	Add contents of address 17 to previous answer.
5	Subtract previous answer from contents of address 18 (gross pay).
6	Write a paycheck for the amount of previous answer.
7	Make check out to contents of address 13 (name of employee).
8	Load information about next employee into memory locations 13, 14, 15, 16, and 17. (Loading new data into memory automatically erases information previously there.)
9	Start over by following instructions in address 0.

A real computer doesn't have mechanical hands. Instead it has electronic connections that carry information at nearly the speed of light (186,000 miles per second). Thus, you can see how the computer could easily figure out a payroll thousands of times faster than you could, working by hand.

When all 10,000 employees have been paid, we remove payroll instructions from the computer's memory and store them for future use on coded form on cards or tape. Then we can put in a different set of instructions and do a different job. For instance, we might put in a program that decides how many hubcaps we should manufacture next month. Along with this new program, we would put into the computer all the required data—sales reports from regional offices, number of hubcaps already on hand, etc.—and start the machine. In the same methodical, step-by-step way, the computer would come up with the month's manufacturing requirements.[10]

This simple example, further elaborated in Figure 11.7, gives the basics of how the computer calculates the facts and figures generated in management information systems. The hardware and software configurations differ in

---

[10] *You and the Computer* (New York: General Electric Company, 1965), pp. 5ff. Reprinted with the permission of General Electric.

computer systems, so speeds of calculations, degrees of data, and types of inputs and storage which can be handled are quite varied. This means that the kinds of information generated in a given system also vary.[11] All computer components, however, should be designed to further the aims and goals of the organization, and the various phases of the management information system should reflect these objectives and future directions.

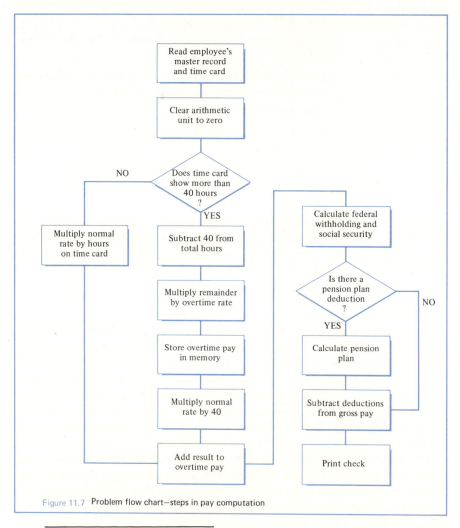

Figure 11.7 Problem flow chart—steps in pay computation

---

[11] Salesmen from IBM, Univac, Honeywell, RCA, SMC, Control Data, and AT&T and other information technology companies are happy to expand on this point at length with very little encouragement. Most of these firms sell both hardware, the actual devices that do the calculating, and software, the planning and system approaches that go into the development of management information systems.

HUMAN PROBLEMS IN MANAGEMENT INFORMATION AND CONTROL SYSTEMS

Even though the organization attempts to use all the "best" ways to establish a system of information reporting and control, the imposition of controls usually brings a spate of resistance. In some cases, opposition may be open; for instance, union members may stage a walkout to protest the installation of a system of production standards. In other situations, opposition may be much more subtle and far more difficult to detect. In a hospital, physicians simply may fail to remember to fill out a form through which the hospital administrator is attempting to pinpoint the source of rising medical costs. Even after control systems have been in operation for years, objections and misunderstandings are common. Part of this reaction springs from personal inadequacies, but much of the difficulty is due to a lack of clarity in explaining the objectives of the system or in harmonizing personal objectives with those of the organization. When the American Can Company decided to recentralize activities using a new tighter control system in mid-1964, Canco's president resigned in protest. Commenting on the new centralized setup Board Chairman William May stated, "We lost some good people, but fewer than we anticipated."[12]

Individuals may dislike controls for many reasons. They may have a moral abhorrence of controls, or they may fear that control activities will uncover poor performance. In some cases, controls bring on a feeling of uneasiness that eventually develops into a sense of inadequacy. Such a condition apparently affected Tom Rath, Sloan Wilson's protagonist in the widely read novel *The Man in the Gray Flannel Suit*. Some people with outstanding records of performance feel that having systems report or check on their activities has distasteful totalitarian overtones. They dislike pressure from "outside" sources and feel that freedom of action is a better motivating device than the "Big Brother" approach. In speaking of one such control, budgets, Professor Chris Argyris of Yale University states that budgets generate obvious pressures that are a focal point for opposition: groups spring up with the express purpose of opposing company goals as represented in budgets. He also points out that pressures arise between line officers and budget makers which help to build additional fences between finance and factory.[13]

The main objections raised against controls by productive individuals are that standards are often arbitrary or inaccurate, that the system is being applied unfairly or inconsistently by particular supervisors, that the objectives of the system are frequently unclear, and that existing controls are not meeting the goals they purport to. Indeed, controls may become goals in themselves, and the resultant inflexibilities may defeat the purpose for which the standards

---

[12] "The New Package at American Can," *Business Week,* September 17, 1966, p. 94.

[13] "Human Problems with Budgets," *Harvard Business Review,* vol. 31, no. 1, pp. 97–110.

were originally intended. Poor performers may complain of a lack of clarity in objectives and of feelings of unfairness, but their reactions may be colored by fear of having their personal inadequacies brought to the attention of supervision. Inability to meet organizational norms becomes, in their minds, a justification for attacking the use of controls. This motivation, though based on insecurity, is equally as strong as the desire to maintain autonomy or freedom of action.

Though reasons for criticizing control systems may spring from different motivations, administrators charged with implementing the control system must deal with them all. No matter what objections are raised, actions must be initiated to overcome resistance without undermining the original reason for establishing the system. One step an administrator can take to overcome resistance is to review the soundness of the technical aspects of the system. Another is to encourage positive responses to controls by expending careful and systematic thought on ways to develop and improve acceptance of control systems.

The organizational structure itself can be a vehicle which helps to obtain better acceptance of both new and existing control systems. Interdepartmental coordination committees can be set up at all levels and can meet to insure a thorough dissemination and sharing of information. These meetings can be utilized in addition to or in conjunction with some of the participative and consultative approaches suggested in earlier chapters. In nonparticipative organizations, the normal chain of command can be used to initiate superior-subordinate discussions of the need for, and the makeup of, control systems. Such meetings will be most productive if criticisms and suggestions are not only allowed but encouraged. It is important that everyone concerned realize that control standards are only estimates and that since estimates fail to cover all possible outcomes, control standards cannot include every possible exception. Participation can help to temper rigid controls, but it must be viewed in light of the requirements of the total system. Performance standards that are set too high may have to be revised to prevent frustration or conflict; but too frequent revision may subvert the stabilizing influence of a given bench mark. Comparisons between actual and standard performance estimates are rather meaningless if the basis for comparison undergoes frequent revision. Balance and flexibility are prime considerations in this readjustment process, but excessive ambiguity breeds insecurity and opposition.

The most important personal factor in the control effort is a sense of restraint. Restraint is necessary because personal feelings about particular individuals often influence the actions taken to correct deviations from expected levels of performance. Corrective actions should be instituted with a minimum of emotion and without fear or favor. Consistent, unemotional, calm behavior is the key to superior control. Judgments are best when based on relevant facts, not on the personalities responsible for shaping those facts. When personality differences do exist, personal restraint must be invoked to balance personal dislikes against the rational adjustments needed to maintain an effective control system. The obvious reaction to irrational or discriminatory treatment is summed up in the age-old Indian proverb, "If you do good, good will be done to you; but if you do evil, the same will be measured back to you again."

Empathy is another personal attribute that makes control more palatable in the short run and more enduring in the long run. The administrator should try to understand how his subordinates will react to the pressures of control and be flexible in his interpretation of factual inflows of control data. He should always give his subordinates a certain amount of leeway in using their skills and talents; but too much flexibility can interfere with the corrections needed when substandard performance continues beyond a reasonable time. Empathy can make the superior appreciate why deviations occur, and it can give him a basis for allowing exceptional circumstances to subvert the system for short periods. It should not be used to release one individual from accountability while others are held to the mark. Such discrimination, even if practiced for the noblest of purposes, eventually places the humane discriminator in a bad light with his less charitable subordinates. Pity poor Mr. X, who, after he lets pretty Miss Jones off early to take care of her mother, finds the office up in arms. And when he charitably pays her rent for the month because he knows she has medical expenses, Mr. X's good-hearted actions become the potential breath of scandal. Empathy, though it gives a wonderful assist to the implementation of control systems, must obviously be exercised with considerable restraint. Indian lore has another ancient and relevant proverb dealing with this situation, "There is no gathering the rose without being pinched by the thorns."

IMPROVING MANAGEMENT INFORMATION AND CONTROL SYSTEMS

The basic postulates underlying the implementation of successful management information and control systems have a deceptively simple appearance. These basic rules state that all good systems should possess the following characteristics:

1. They should generate returns in excess of their cost.
2. They should be set up in such a way that undesirable side effects are kept to a minimum and a consideration of whether controls are too extensive or too restrictive is made. (They should be neither Captain Queeg nor Will Rogers controls.)
3. They should be constructed to point out causes of weakness so that preventative action can be taken as soon as possible.

In the words of Emch, "control means action."[14] And, simple as these three

---

[14] *Op. cit.,* pp. 11–25.

objectives may seem, they cannot be attained without concerted and vigorous effort.

Some of the difficulties in management information systems applications come from a lack of the expertise needed to translate objectives into an operational system. Others result from the fact that individuals fail to view controls as a means of meeting organizational objectives. In many cases, the human problems in implementing the management information and control system are every bit as critical as the technical ones.

Design of the management information and control system can be improved almost always if two fundamental suggestions are followed: (1) develop a set of rules or guides defining the limits of a good system, (2) provide a staff specializing in control.

Five basic points might be included in the general principles developed. First, control techniques should attempt to pinpoint critical factors. In other words, systems should be tailored to meet specific consequences. The selection of strategic factors is important in separating symptoms from causes and in showing the way to appropriate corrective actions. Cost and time are two common criteria by which such factors are selected.

Second, control systems, whenever possible, should be oriented to the future rather than the past. Emphasis must be given to preventing the recurrence of past mistakes. Prevention is the key here, not the placement of responsibility for past actions. Continuing systems of control should be built on corrective, not punitive, bases. Planning-for-profit programs now in use in many business firms are evidences of control activities with futuristic overtones. Such plans have been in use in such industrial firms as Olin-Mathieson, the Friden Company, Westinghouse, and the American Can Company.

Third, techniques should be devised so that reported information can be analyzed and acted upon with a minimum delay. The time lapse between recognition of an actual or potential deviation and appropriate adjusting actions should be kept as short as possible. Delay in reporting or delay in taking necessary action can undermine the workings of the entire control procedure. In retailing, J.C. Penney now has its response time for use and reorder on staple items down to two weeks, while response time in the Washington, D.C., planned traffic control system will be measured in minutes.

Fourth, control systems should have enough built-in flexibility to meet changes in the organization's operating environment without having to undergo serious revision. Adjustment of poorly constructed controls is vital, and rapid changes should be made when techniques become obsolete. The retention of inappropriate sensing mechanisms is a common fault in control, and such inflexibility generates vast amounts of information—but on the wrong subject matter. This brings to mind the character in *Alice in Wonderland* who tried to fix a watch by covering it with butter and then bemoaned the fact that it didn't work, even though he had used "the very best butter." The moral for control systems is clear: the best techniques are only useful if they meet the needs of a given situation. This means that flexibility must be built into the system.

Finally, the plans and objectives of the organization must be considered carefully when controls are formulated. Balance between desired and actual objectives must be obtained without disrupting coordination between operating units. Reports should reflect the needs of plans and planners; and when such needs are not being met, control techniques should be adjusted. Herbert Simon in particular stresses the importance of having the right information in the right amount at the right time to help managers make decisions as expeditiously as possible. In his eyes, too much data can be as bad as too little.

The second major consideration in developing a good control system is to hire or train a staff specializing in control activities. In order to turn generalities into specifics, skilled, trained people are indispensable. Since they possess the special training and experience needed to make intricate technical measurements, industrial engineering staffs are perhaps best prepared to measure and devise time standards and physical unit standards. It is probably accurate to state that consistent time standards cannot be set without drawing upon their skills and knowledge.

The accounting staff is another source of expertise in the development of meaningful control systems. Accountants, particularly cost accountants, have the know-how necessary to set up standard cost systems. They can also develop financial ratios, budget standards, and prepare the information needed to control inventories, production flows, and cost-profit relationships. Accounting staffs with well-defined roles in carefully structured systems can be the catalysts that make management information and control systems operate with a high degree of success.

In recent years, systems and procedure specialists have entered the control area. These specialists, whose functions cut across traditional lines of authority, are rapidly assuming a dominant role in the development and implementation of control systems. Systems analysts, with the aid of computerized programs, are now helping to set up improved data-processing techniques, faster and more complete information flows, highly sophisticated reporting techniques, and more fully integrated planning, organization, and control cycles. They also have established methods of improving the quality and speed of corrective actions. Systems and procedures groups are a relatively new breed in the control area, but their comparative youth in no way detracts from their current importance. In future years, their role will probably be expanded to the point where they will take prime responsibility for designing, installing, and monitoring management information systems.

Summary

The basic steps in designing management information systems include a review of organizational objectives, development of appropriate sensing and collating units, preparing standards and decision rules, integrating the system with the data-processing setup, developing appropriate output in the form of reports, and overseeing changes in the system as it relates to the dynamic human factors in the organization. Management information systems help management to recognize basic contributions to organizational goals. These systems relate reported output to predetermined standards of output performance and point out both superior and substandard performance, thus allowing management to recognize superior achievement and to take steps to improve performance that is below expected levels.

Management information systems contain both technical and human variables, and the design of a successful system calls for expertise in both areas. The following chapter treats the technical aspects of management information systems and outlines approaches that have been used with varying degrees of success.

Study Questions

1. How does the concept of "real time" differ from traditional control and reporting systems?

2. How important are electronic computers in modern control systems? What advantages and problems arise when computers are used to record and analyze data?

3. What levels of evolution in computerized information systems do you think will be reached in the next ten to twenty years?

4. What kinds of information typically enter into an MIS (management information system)? How do planning and control data differ?

5. Contrast closed-loop and open-loop control systems. Do you believe closed-loop systems will become more widespread? Why or why not?

6. Describe some of the better known units by which performance is measured. Which are most common? In your view which are most useful?

7. What kinds of information are best suited for computerized data processing?

8. What are the basic steps in computerized data processing? Describe them in terms of the normal human thinking process.

9. What are the typical human reactions to control? Outline an approach to help overcome the negative reactions.

10. What general rules, or principles, can be invoked to improve management information systems?

11. What relationships exist between goals, policies, procedures, and the design and operation of a well-constructed management information system?

The factors that guide the construction and development of management information systems also carry over into the implementation and execution phase. The role of the management information system is to help executives turn general guidelines into operational controls over costs, time, performance, and quality and quantity of output. Each component of the management information system (MIS) should be chosen because it assists in the generation of information needed by managers to achieve their objectives and should reflect an effort to optimize the effectiveness of the system in terms of cost and timeliness of data. One of the more critical aspects of this selection process is whether to use general or specific controls. This particular choice is not an either-or proposition, but the emphasis decided on can determine the eventual shape of the system and the kinds of decisions it will tend to produce. General controls usually measure performance of either the organization or relatively large subunits, while specific controls attempt to evaluate particular product lines, processes, areas, or, in some cases, even departments as large as plants or branch offices. Some overlap exists between these two types of controls, but an artificial dichotomy helps to focus attention on the nature of particular systems in use. This chapter concentrates on control systems designed to measure organizational or unit performance, while the following section deals with both the recognition of individual contributions and selected methods of developing superior performance.

CHAPTER 12
Techniques of Control

GENERAL SYSTEMS OF CONTROL

No single classification scheme can adequately encompass all general controls, but a fairly comprehensive overview of the state of the arts can be provided by delving into a number of techniques now in widespread use. These techniques, which have been employed successfully in many leading companies and institutions, are

Personal observation

Analysis of statistical data

Financial controls

Audits

Industrial dynamics

Real-time simulation

Time-network analysis

Planning for profit

PERSONAL OBSERVATION

Control by personal observation is often the rule in small or medium-sized organizations, since managers of such firms may feel that no other controls are necessary. It is also relatively common in nonprofit organizations, where there is much less pressure to show results on a time-cost basis. Personal observation may involve nothing more than a walk through a factory area to see if machines are running and workers are manning them. If machines are operating and workers seem to be busy, then performance is typically rated as satisfactory. Another type of personalized control is to simply check payouts and inflows. If the inflow is greater than the outflow, potential problems are simply ignored. This system was purportedly the one the original Henry Ford used to manage his gigantic auto empire.

In the typical personal control system, standards are set subjectively. If a man running a small business betters the break-even mark, he may feel he is doing well; but what "doing well" means varies very sharply. While studying new small businesses in the Michigan area, a team of researchers encountered many owner-proprietors who thought that a return on sales *after taxes* of 50 to 100 percent was "reasonable." In much larger firms—notably many of those listed as the five hundred largest by *Fortune* (the *Fortune 500*)—a return on sales of 5 percent after taxes is generally rated as acceptable.

In most personal systems of control there is little continuity, and standards shift continually or tend to be imprecise. There is very little record keeping and thus no way to compare present or future performance against the past. Personal control is invariably less effective than more carefully structured systems; and though it can be workable in small organizations, it is rarely effective in larger ones. Personal controls provide no basis to compare what is with what could be—and hidden problems stay hidden. When Henry Ford manufactured a product the public bought, his Tin Lizzies sold at a profit. But his back-pocket control sputtered and died in the fire of post–World War II competition. The Ford Motor Company reportedly was losing millions per month shortly after World War II and corrective actions were hindered by lack of available information on production, distribution, and marketing costs. The net result was a massive reorganization characterized by a marked emphasis on tight financial and cost controls.

Personal control is efficient only if used in conjunction with some of the other approaches below. If used alone, personal control invariably leads to poor decisions and lowered effectiveness. Though this point has been demonstrated time and time again, intuitive or judgmental control systems are still an article of faith in many organizations.

ANALYSIS OF STATISTICAL DATA

Statistical data dealing with changes, trends, cyclical movements, sales, business conditions, shifts in consumer preferences, interest rates, or other vital matters provide useful inputs for control. Comparisons of relative performances of internal units against competitors can also serve as inputs for control systems, but they can be viewed as a control in themselves. For example, trends in competitors' sales versus in-house sales may be a good indicator of market movements which are particularly helpful when broken down into sales of products or product lines. Similar data can also be used to point out developments in technology, energy sources, materials, consumer preferences, or other areas calling for review and/or action.

Statistical information is also handy in pointing out internal problems such as imbalance in orders and shipments; shifts in inventories of raw materials; semi-finished goods and finished products; movements in layoffs or hirings; or changes in costs, revenues, sales or profits. Statistical inputs thus can serve not only as general indexes of performance but, when used as parts of other control systems, can become effective general controls over performance. For example, population statistics in New York City might show that the percentage of teen-agers in the total population will grow sharply over a five-year span. For the city's school board, these figures provide a basis for future planning and an index against which to judge progress on a building program designed to meet the needs of the expected increase in teen-age school attendees.

FINANCIAL DATA

One major use of statistical data is in the compilation of financial controls, particularly ratio analysis. Ratio analysis attempts to evaluate the health of an organization by looking at various relationships in its financial statements. Since these relationships are an index of performance, they can easily be classed as standards rather than controls. They appear in the control techniques section primarily because they are often tied in closely with corrective control systems.

One of the most commonly used financial ratios is the *current ratio,* the ratio of current assets to current liabilities. "Current" is generally defined as being payable or receivable within a period of one year. The current ratio is particularly useful in determining the relative liquidity of a firm.

The *quick ratio* tends to provide a rigid test of organizational liquidity by relating assets with an immediate cash realization to current liabilities. This ratio shows the relationship between cash flows immediately available and immediate drains against the available flows. Inventories are the items in the current ratio category that are often difficult to turn into cash, and the quick ratio recognizes this fact by subtracting inventories from current liabilities before making its acid test of liquidity. A quick ratio in excess of 1.0 means that an organization has enough cash and liquid assets to pay off its obligations coming due within a year.

Debt-equity ratios attempt to relate long-term or fixed debt to the total capital employed in the organization's financial structure. When debt-equity ratios are high, the obligations incurred may be in the form of charges that cannot be escaped. The organization thus experiences strains on its current cash position, and an overpoweringly heavy debt-equity ratio may tend to bring on the specter of illiquidity or bankruptcy.

Rate-of-return ratios attempt to measure performance by dividing total capital employed into the net income for a period. This method is widely used to evaluate performance of projects, products, subunits, and even total organizations. The typical rate-of-return calculation divides average income for the investment period by average capital committed. Rate-of-return ratios are particularly widespread because they allow comparisons between alternative uses of capital commitments, as described in Chapter 7.

Another general ratio is *capital turnover,* or net sales divided by total capital employed. This ratio can also take the form of comparing net sales to specific dollar values of operating units or asset groupings.[1]

Net sales–to–working capital ratios indicate how much working capital is available to take advantage of opportunities arising because of increased demand. This is another form of liquidity ratio, since working capital is normally defined as the difference between current assets and current liabilities.

---

[1] To show another method of how return on investment might be calculated, the diagram on p. 277 outlines how the DuPont organization measures return on investment: "How the DuPont Organization Appraises its Performance," by T.C. Davis, appearing in *American Management Association Financial Management Series,* no. 94, New York: 1950. Also reprinted in Harold Koontz and Cyril O'Donnell, eds., *Management: A Book of Readings* (New York: McGraw-Hill, Inc., 1964).

Cost-to-sales ratios measure performance or various aspects of operations against sales volume. Cost of sales to total sales, and administrative expense to total sales are commonly used forms of the cost-to-sales ratio.

Acccounts receivable–aging ratios measure how rapidly customers are paying their bills. These ratios are computed by taking sales for the year and dividing them by twelve to get a monthly sales figure. Monthly sales are then divided into average receivables to give an average time of payment of accounts receivable. If the aging of receivables is high, the organization may have liquidity problems or even be in danger of a high bad-debt percentage. If the aging period is short, customers are paying their bills in time and the organization's liquidity position is strengthened.

To illustrate how ratios are compiled, consider the following balance sheets and income statements and the kind of ratios that might be generated for review and control purposes and the ways in which these ratios may serve as guides to corrective actions.

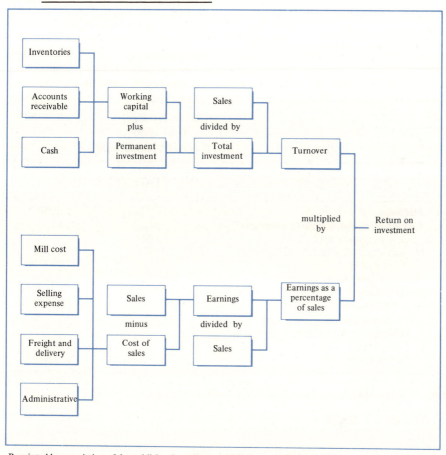

Reprinted by permission of the publisher from Financial Management Series No. 94, *How Dupont Organization Appraises Its Performance*, by T. C. Davis © 1950 by the American Management Association, Inc.

TABLE 12.1   MST CORPORATION BALANCE SHEET,
             DECEMBER 31, 197–

Assets		Liabilities	
Current assets		Current liabilities	
Cash	$ 4,750	Accounts payable	$ 5,000
Marketable securities	7,750	Notes payable	4,250
Accounts receivable	10,000	Accrued expenses payable	1,500
Inventories	7,500	Federal taxes payable	1,750
Total	$30,000	Total	$12,500
Property, plant and equipment		Long-term liabilities	
Land	$ 750	First mortgage bonds 5%	
Buildings	19,000	due 1980	13,500
Machinery and equipment	5,250	Total	$26,000
	25,000	Equity	
Less depreciation	9,000	Capital stock	
Net	$16,000	Preferred stock	$ 1,500
Prepayments and deferred charges	$ 500	$1 par, 5% cumulative	
Patents, goodwill, other	500	authorized issued and out-	
Total assets	$47,000	standing 1,500 shares	
		Common stock	7,500
		$1 par, authorized issued and	
		outstanding 7,500 shares	
		Capital surplus	3,500
		Retained earnings	8,500
		Total equity	$21,000
		Total liabilities and equity	$47,000

TABLE 12.2   MST CORPORATION INCOME STATEMENT, 197–

Net Sales		$32,500
Cost of sales and operating expenses		
Cost of goods sold	$22,000	
Selling and administrative expenses	2,500	
Depreciation	4,500	29,000
Profit on operations		$ 3,500
Other income		550
Total income		$ 4,050
Less bond interest		675
Profit before federal tax		$ 3,375
Federal tax provision		1,750
Net profit after taxes		$ 1,625

Given these statements the following ratios can be calculated:

CURRENT RATIO:

$$\frac{\text{Current assets (30,000)}}{\text{Current liabilities (12,500)}} = 2.4{:}1$$

A rather healthy ratio in most circumstances. The firm seems able to meet its current obligations and still have funds left over to meet various operational needs.

QUICK RATIO:

$$\frac{\text{Current assets-inventories}}{\text{Current liabilities}} = \frac{30,000 - 7,500}{12,500} = 11:8:1$$

Again, this is an acceptable ratio for liquidity, but not an excellent one. The firm could pay off all its current obligations and still have some margin left over for financial flexibility.

LONG-TERM DEBT RATIO:

$$\frac{\text{Long-term debt (13,500)}}{\text{Equity (47,000)}} = 28.7\%$$

Since a ratio of one-third debt to equity is generally considered acceptable for a manufacturing firm, the MST Corporation seems to be in a relatively good position vis-à-vis long-term debt. This, of course, would differ from company to company and industry to industry, depending upon industry conditions, the organization's objectives, and other factors.

RATE OF RETURN ON EQUITY AND RATE OF RETURN ON SALES:

$$\frac{\text{Net profit (1,625)}}{\text{Total equity (21,000)}} = 7.7\% \text{ on equity}$$

$$\frac{\text{Net profit (1,625)}}{\text{Net sales (32,500)}} = 5\% \text{ on sales}$$

What constitutes an acceptable figure for a given firm depends on many factors including cost of capital, alternative returns from other uses of money, industry profit figures, and so on; but, on an after-tax basis, this performance is about average for the typical manufacturing firm.

CAPITAL TURNOVER RATIO:

$$\frac{\text{Net sales (32,500)}}{\text{Total capital (47,000)}} = 0:7:1$$

This is a relatively low figure, but its importance must be weighed in terms of profitability figures before the result becomes really meaningful. It is quite possible, for example, for high profits to accrue in a high-margin industry, even though the capital turnover ratio is low.

WORKING CAPITAL TO NET SALES: Since working capital equals current assets minus current liabilities, this ratio would be calculated in the following way:

$$\frac{\text{Working capital } (30,000 - 12,500)}{\text{Net sales } (32,500)} = 0:54:1$$

This result seems to be quite adequate, since a 0:15:1 ratio is considered by most financial analysts to be satisfactory for manufacturing firms. Another figure showing the relative financial liquidity of the firm is the net working capital position. This is calculated by subtracting current liabilities from current assets; in the case of MST, $30,000 minus 12,500, or $17,500, a figure indicating MST is relatively liquid by this measure too.

ADMINISTRATIVE COST TO SALES RATIO:

$$\frac{\text{Administrative costs } (2,500)}{\text{Net sales } (32,500)} = 7.7\%$$

This is close to what analysts consider to be a normal percentage. Any higher cost might bear further review.

ACCOUNTS RECEIVABLE–AGING RATIO:

$$\frac{\text{Accounts receivable (current) } (10,000)}{\text{Average receivables calculated } (2,708)} = 3.7 \text{ months, or 112 days (approximate).}$$
$$(30,000 \div 12)$$

This result indicates receivables are not in as good a position as they might be. The state of existing accounts no doubt bears further investigation. Customers are not paying their bills within 30 days, and this can cause liquidity problems. It may even mean that some customers are poor credit risks, since good credit risks usually pay their bills quickly to keep their credit rating high and to take advantage of any discounts available.

Financial ratios are indicative of how the organization stands at a given time, but for more demanding measures of performance over time, they must be viewed on a more long-term basis than the ones shown above. Since they represent an instant picture of an organization, they fail to show directions of trends and movements over time—a marked weakness in a device measuring performance of a dynamic organization. In a control system, longer-term perspectives and trends usually need to be studied before proper causality can be recognized and corrective actions undertaken. A short-run cash shortage at the end of the year caused by financing Christmas inventories might generate excessive borrowing if not seen in the proper time perspective. A fast write-off of obsolete facilities might cause panic if the reason for the poor rate of return ratio were not seen in its true light. Financial ratios thus play the role of indicators in control systems, and the feedback they report must be tempered by the judgment of control agents and the effect of other forces in the control system.

Other financial techniques to evaluate organizations or to control a specific performance are analyses of long-term assets and sales growth trends, and studies of ratios such as price earnings ratios and earnings per share. Of these the price earnings ratio and the earnings-per-share calculations are particularly important in evaluating a firm over the long pull for investment purposes.

The *earnings-per-share ratio* would be calculated in the following way:

Net income less preferred stock payment yields the amount available for dividends and common stock. This amount divided by the number of common shares outstanding yields earnings per share, or

$$\$1,625 - \$75 = \$1,550$$

$$\frac{\$1,550}{\$7,500} = 20.7 ¢[2]$$

The *price earnings ratio* would be determined by dividing assumed market price by earnings per share, or

$$\frac{\$2.50}{20.7¢} = 14:1$$

Given the assumption that the market price of MST is $2.50 the company's stock is selling at fourteen times earnings, a figure that would have to be evaluated in light of both present conditions and future expectations. If, for example, forecasts of future earnings per share showed an upward trend, the stock might be a bargain. If, on the other hand, future expectations were down, the investment might not be parlicularly attractive.

Ratios and other financial controls are helpful in evaluating firms and often decide how a firm is viewed by outsiders. Take for example the case of Litton Industries. When earnings per share dropped from 63 cents to 21 cents early in 1968, Litton stock fell to almost one half of its 1967–1968 high of $120. Litton stock plummetted eighteen points in one week following the reported drop in earnings per share, even though the company's basic strengths had undergone little or no diminution.

---

[2] The 1,500 shares of outstanding 5-percent cumulative preferred stock must be paid $75 (5-percent of $1,500) before common stockholders receive their share of the proceeds of operation.

Financial ratios and controls are widely used because of their versatility and because dollar ratios are often more readily understood than other units of measurement. Figures such as 10 percent on sales after taxes are relatively easy to grasp, and they cover a wide range of activities. Because of their general nature, however, financial measures leave much to be desired in the identification and control of individual contributions to output. In spite of such shortcomings, their importance cannot be denied; as Litton's management, for one, is acutely aware.

AUDITS AS CONTROL DEVICES

Audits also constitute a useful type of general control. Whether done by inside specialists (internal audits) or outside agencies (external audits), they provide an overall check or review of preselected sets of variables. Public accounting firms conduct the best known of all auditing procedures. Their audits typically certify that an organization's fiscal reports are made in accordance with accepted financial practice and seem to represent a true picture of the organization's financial health and well-being. Price Waterhouse or Ernst and Ernst cannot guarantee that a given organization will stay solvent, but they can certify that the organization *seems to be in fact* what it *claims to be* in its financial reporting.

Certain specialized agencies other than certified public accounting (CPA) firms also perform an outside audit function. One such organization is the American Institute of Management (AIM), which gives a rating for excellent management if a firm scores high on the criteria AIM uses to evaluate performance. The AIM criteria are economic function, corporate structure, health of earnings growth, fairness to stockholders, research and development activities, directorate analysis, fiscal policies, production efficiency, sales analysis, and evaluation of executives. These factors are weighed by AIM staffers and reported in the *Manual of Excellent Managements.*[3] Since the AIM's method of gathering information tends to invite error, its audit process has come under sharp attack in management circles.

Internal audits go well beyond a generalized scrutiny of financial accounts. A good internal audit delves into what is being done, how well it is being done, and the means of improving techniques and approaches currently in use. Recommendations often cover more than financial areas, which gives an internal audit report an impact similar to one prepared by an outside consultant. Suggestions coming out of an internal financial audit might, for example, lead to the development of a management appraisal system or the installation of a better way to handle disbursements. Internal audits act as checks on performance and often serve as a moving force behind the initiation of new and better methods. Because of these initiation and consultation activities, internal audits have generated valuable and useful contributions

---

[3] See Jackson Martindell, *The Appraisal of Management* (New York: Harper & Row, Publishers, 1962).

to the control process. In many firms, systems and procedures departments have evolved directly out of internal audit activities.

INDUSTRIAL DYNAMICS

Industrial dynamics is a system of evaluating organizational performance by developing simulations of activities based on actual observation of flows of factors critical to effective operation. Flows analyzed under this system include manpower, money, materials, orders, communications, and data inputs entering into the decision-making network. Decisions lie at the heart of the industrial dynamics analysis, since they control the vital flows governing operations. In this system, the information fed to decision makers holds the key to the objectives of the organization.[4]

According to students of industrial dynamics, the basic activities of ordering, production, and shipment of goods normally occur in cyclical or fluctuating patterns. Time lags built into the order-shipment system cause decisions to be made on what types of products to make, what size labor force to employ, and how best to utilize resources. When time lags are great and when information processing is delayed, decisions made may fall short of the organization's objectives. Because of a lack of good information, the decision maker hires when he should be laying off, builds inventory when he should be selling out of stock, and generally performs inefficiently.

In traditional management control systems, fluctuations occurring in uncontrolled situations are dampened somewhat, but not as much as they should be. Industrial dynamics advocates contend that sales, production, and other vital flows should be investigated thoroughly both inside and outside the firm. The information obtained in these studies is then used to "dampen" fluctuations to a point where ordering, hiring, and other normal functions of the business follow a stable pattern.

One of the really major contributions of the industrial dynamics approach is that it cuts down the time lag typically found in information processing. Its second major achievement is its ability to view the organization as a unit, not as a series of separate departments. Each department is considered as part of a total entity, and actions taken to correct fluctuations often move across departmental lines or even across environmental factors outside the firm. For example, a typical way to dampen order fluctuations is to go directly to customers and attempt to control the timing and volume of their orders by a variety of policies including added discounts for large orders or extra services offered at no charge for a limited time only. In short, industrial dynamics recognizes that the effective components of control may lie beyond the boundaries of normal departmental control systems or outside of the firm's organizational structure.

Three charts taken from a study of an uncontrolled firm, a traditionally

---

[4] Jay Forrester, *Industrial Dynamics* (Cambridge, Mass.: MIT Press, 1961) is responsible for the theoretical formulation of industrial dynamics.

controlled firm, and a firm controlled by industrial dynamics principles appear as Figures 12.1, 12.2, and 12.3. According to Professor Jay Forrester, who developed industrial dynamics, these charts indicate how fluctuations are dampened in the industrial dynamics approach to bring about the positive advantages of employment stability, smoother sales, lower inventories, and a much better ability to predict future trends and directions in sales and costs.[5]

As localized computer terminals become more available, applications of industrial dynamics stand to gain wider acceptance. Since the cost of localized terminals as inputs for central computer units falls every year, industrial dynamics may soon reach the point where its economic costs are low enough to allow for expanded applications.

REAL-TIME SIMULATION MODELS

Real-time systems of control attempt to represent reality through the medium of simulation models. These models, usually set up in mathematical form on computers, attempt to direct decision making by recording and reporting actual occurrences as they take place. In real-time systems, decisions are programmed into the system (closed-loop controls) or require judgmental action (open-loop controls). The industrial dynamics approach is a modified real-time system, since it typically involves a greater time lag than true real-time systems.

One specific example of a real-time system is the cybernetic (machine) control described later in this chapter. Another is the system now in use to control traffic flows in Toronto, Canada. In the Toronto system, hundreds of traffic directors located on major street segments report traffic volumes and speeds and send them directly to a computer installation. The computer analyzes the patterns of movement and sets sequences of traffic light changes to best coordinate traffic signals and traffic flows. The Toronto system is set up so that operators can request information on activities at various points or intersections in the system and receive an answer almost instantaneously. If blockages, congestion, or accidents occur, the computer reports them to the operator who then can alert police or fire units to move to the area of difficulty. Since *actual* traffic flows are recorded and analyzed by the computer as they *actually occur,* the computer program simulates the real-time flow of traffic through key arteries of the city. According to Toronto officials, the results of this control system have been sharp reductions in accidents and a more rapid movement of traffic over a limited number of streets. It has also reduced the necessity of constructing additional roads to handle greater traffic volume.

The greatest advantage of real-time simulation is the speed with which action can be taken, but its biggest drawback is the cost. In Toronto, the scales seem to be balanced favorably because of better use of street capacity

---

[5] Much of this discussion is taken from Edward B. Roberts, "Industrial Dynamics and the Design of Management Control Systems," *Management Technology,* December 1963.

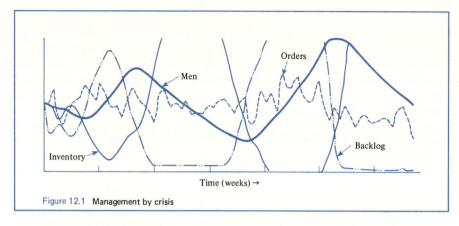

Figure 12.1   Management by crisis

Source: From Edward B. Roberts, "Industrial Dynamics and the Design of Management Control Systems," *Management Technology,* December 1963.

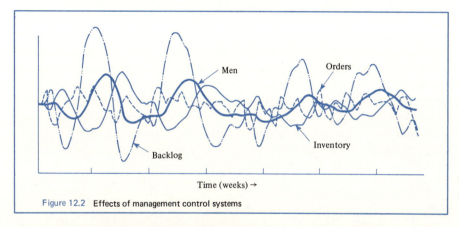

Figure 12.2   Effects of management control systems

Source: From Edward B. Roberts, "Industrial Dynamics and the Design of Management Control Systems," *Management Technology,* December 1963.

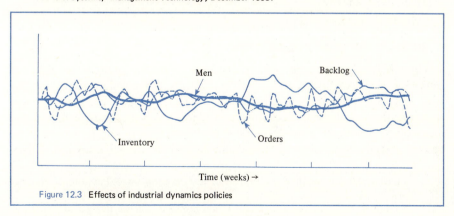

Figure 12.3   Effects of industrial dynamics policies

Source: From Edward B. Roberts, "Industrial Dynamics and the Design of Management Control Systems," *Management Technology,* December 1963.

and reductions in delay, accidents, and property damage. In similar situations, real-time simulation has been a revolutionary approach to control. Business applications of simulation are now on the ascent due to lowered costs of computer operations and the increasing size of memory units. Business organizations are now using real-time simulations of production flows, inventory warehousing, traffic planning, and other critical functions. It seems inevitable that this trend will continue.

TIME-ACTIVITY NETWORKS AND PLANNING-FOR-PROFIT APPROACHES

Time-activity networks such as the Critical Path Method (CPM) and PERT cost are often used as both planning and control devices. PERT has been used to control or to reduce lead time in aircraft, missile, submarine, and electronics systems.[6] Since PERT is described in Chapter 10, it will not be discussed at this point. This same comment applies to integrated planning for profit, which receives detailed attention in Chapter 14.

SPECIFIC SYSTEMS OF CONTROL

Though many general systems of control are also adaptable for use in specific areas, certain control systems are best fitted to use in specific areas or in particular sets of circumstances. To identify the difference between general and specific control systems is difficult, but certain techniques seem to possess the characteristics needed to control specific operations rather than those which appear in general systems of control.[7] A selected sample of some of the most widely used specific controls shows

Budgets, both fixed and variable

Standard-cost and direct-cost techniques

Project control

Break-even analysis

Cybernetic models

BUDGETS AS CONTROL DEVICES

Though break-even point analysis, statistical indexes, analysis of flows of activities, PERT techniques, and other control devices are widely used to record and analyze projected or actual results, financial budgets remain the most widespread of all control mechanisms. Budgets are a financial profile of the planning and control process. Once a dollar budget is set, it becomes the desired objective against which actual and desired results are compared. When

---

[6] For examples of CPM techniques, see Thomas R. Prince, *Information Systems for Management Planning and Control* (Homewood, Ill.: Richard D. Irwin, Inc., 1966), pp. 108–112.

[7] No attempt will be made here to delve into inventory control, production control, or quality control, since these matters are treated elsewhere.

planning increases in scope and coverage, budgeting becomes much more involved and more difficult to coordinate effectively. Budgets are prepared for master plans, subplans, and units within subplans. As the various phases of planning go into effect, budgets become part of control activities. As information is reported back through the organization's control system, variations in expenditures made may dictate further planning or adjustments in existing budgets. The dollar variance between actual and budgeted results is the basic index by which the need for corrective action is weighed and evaluated. Budgets thus serve as plans, controls, and standards against which performance is judged. Budgets are so widely used that they have almost infinite variety. They can cover expense and revenue flows, short-term cash requirements, capital outlays, man-hour costs, and time-cost relationships. For example, a series of budgets may be prepared to represent different states of expectations or different volumes of output. Either a fixed budget, which has one set of projected outlays based on a given level or expected volume of activity, or a flexible budget, which attempts to predict standard outlays for several different levels of activity, might be used. *Fixed budgets* are often set on expenditures for advertising projects. A firm might decide to expend $100,000 for advertising in a particular year. This sum would be allotted to various media for promotional campaigns, but the budget would not be changed or expanded if advertising needs changed during the year. The actual outlay might either exceed or fall below this figure, but deviations would be analyzed only from this bench mark. This does not mean that good reasons for change might not appear, it simply means that actual expenditures on advertising would be compared to the $100,000 projected at the start of the budget period. Incidentally, advertising costs, because they are relatively easy to postpone or eliminate, are often singled out for cuts when cost pressures mount. General Steel Industries followed this path early in 1968 to obtain temporary cost savings.

Flexible budgets may show expected costs of producing products, say, in volumes of 10,000, 15,000, and 7,000 units. If output were 10,000 units, then costs of production would be estimated at $50,000, but if output were to rise to 15,000 units, costs might increase to $70,000. On the other hand, if output were to fall to 7,000 units, then costs might be forecast at $40,000. The use of several bench marks thus allows comparisons to be made with estimates closest to actual volume; and interpolating between projected figures gives accurate representation of budgeted forecasts for any specified volume of output. Such estimates can be made well in advance of actual production, and one basic reference set covers many possible levels of output.

Budgets not only state the component parts of plans in dollar terms but also help to coordinate the various subplans into an integrated whole. They provide bench marks against which actual results may be evaluated and furnish the information needed to guide corrective actions if and when such actions seem advisable. When budgeted figures went out of line in Philco-Ford, the company laid off four hundred workers in its color television plant in Lansdowne, Pennsylvania. In another industry; Consolidated Foods of Chicago realized an eight-month saving of $4 million after a budget review and cutback, mostly in advertising and travel budgets.[8]

The budget, since it is a plan of action laid out in dollar terms, is an attempt to influence dollar outlays by actions taken in the present. This means both a comparison of actual expenditures to budgeted ones and a series of action steps when actual and budgeted expenditures are at variance.

To trace how these steps might occur in a large multiunit organization, consider this hypothetical case: At the end of the fiscal year, the Armada Company finds that budgeted expenditures for the entire organization exceeded planned expenditures by $300,000. Assuming the budget to be a realistic one, what might top management do to seek an explanation of this excess?

First, division managers might be asked to explain the part of the budget variances charged to their respective divisions. Division managers would then request the same kind of information from their plant managers. Each plant manager would then ask his superintendents to detail the nature of departmental variations, and the superintendents in turn might obtain similar variance data from individual foremen. At this point, problem areas would be pinpointed, and specific reasons for deviation could be identified. Once the apparent causes (if detectable at all) became evident, changes could be initiated to bring about desired, or budgeted, results. The report system underlying this hypothetical case might appear in the form of Figure 12.4.

The actions dictated by these reports may be widespread, but they call at least for review of division C's budget procedure and expenditure patterns. Within division C, plants 1 and 2 need to be looked at carefully. Plant 2 has three departments that seem well over budget expenditures, but sections 1 and 2 in department A and section 3 in department C seem to be more out of line than other units. The latter section shows well over budgeted expenses on direct labor and direct materials. The reasons for this overage seem to call for further analysis and review. The results of similar analysis of variances at all levels in the Armada organization would develop a line of attack to bring budget estimates into line with actual expenditures.

This illustration shows how budgets can identify sources of variance in which adjustments may be long overdue. They can also provide assistance in making constructive changes. If, for example, section 3 of department C has an overtime problem causing excessive labor and material costs or has been forced to use untrained workers, the budget procedure can help to spot the trouble so that corrective action can begin at an early stage. Thus, budget variance analysis points up areas of difficulty and acts as a basis for corrective action.

STANDARD COSTS AND DIRECT COSTING

Standard costs are determined by estimating the costs of materials and labor going into each unit and adding a standard amount of overhead. Over-

[8] "Putting Costs Through the Wringer," *Business Week,* March 2, 1968, p. 72.

head rates are calculated after all nondirect costs are determined and related to a preestimated volume of output, measured typically in terms of labor hours utilized in a selected accounting period. The overhead rate per unit of output is generally calculated by dividing the total pool of overhead costs by the total labor hours estimated for the period. Thus, if total overhead charged to a product was projected at $50,000 for a given year, and esti-

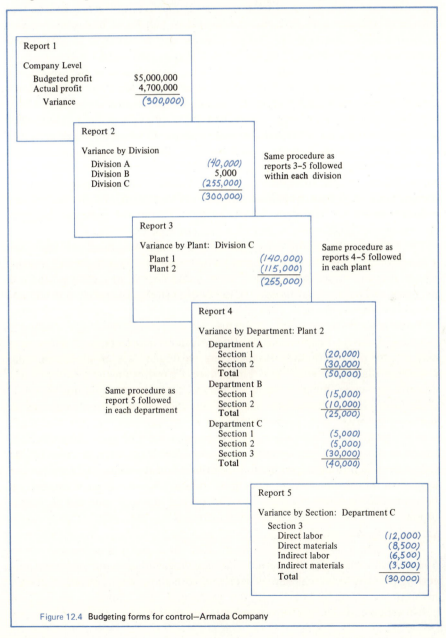

Report 1

Company Level

Budgeted profit	$5,000,000
Actual profit	4,700,000
Variance	(300,000)

Report 2

Variance by Division

Division A	(40,000)
Division B	5,000
Division C	(255,000)
	(300,000)

Same procedure as reports 3–5 followed within each division

Report 3

Variance by Plant: Division C

Plant 1	(140,000)
Plant 2	(115,000)
	(255,000)

Same procedure as reports 4–5 followed in each plant

Report 4

Variance by Department: Plant 2

Department A	
Section 1	(20,000)
Section 2	(30,000)
Total	(50,000)
Department B	
Section 1	(15,000)
Section 2	(10,000)
Total	(25,000)
Department C	
Section 1	(5,000)
Section 2	(5,000)
Section 3	(30,000)
Total	(40,000)

Same procedure as report 5 followed in each department

Report 5

Variance by Section: Department C

Section 3	
Direct labor	(12,000)
Direct materials	(8,500)
Indirect labor	(6,500)
Indirect materials	(3,500)
Total	(30,000)

Figure 12.4 Budgeting forms for control—Armada Company

mated annual labor hours were 20,000, the standard amount of overhead charged to the product for each labor hour used in its manufacture would be $2.50 = \left(\dfrac{\$50,000}{20,000}\right)$.

The key to standard costing lies in analysis of variance figures. Rarely do standard costs equal actual costs, and the amount and nature of the variances point out where adjustment may be needed in much the same way that profit variances provide clues to corrective actions in budgets.

Variances in standard labor costs may be due to changes in labor rates or excessive use of labor. Material variances may also arise because of price changes, misuse of materials, or poor quality of output. Overhead variances typically occur because production either exceeds or falls short of the volume used to allocate overhead charges. If volume is high, burden is "overabsorbed" because an overhead charge is attached to more units than the forecasted level upon which the standard overhead charge was based. If, for example, one unit produced uses one hour of labor and 30,000 units are manufactured, the amount charged out of overhead is 30,000 times $2.50, or $75,000, which means burden is overabsorbed by $25,000. If volume is low, "underabsorption" occurs, since less than budgeted amounts of overhead are charged to the products produced. Using the overhead figures from the previous example, production of 15,000 units would see overhead charged at 15,000 times $2.50, or $37,500; an underabsorption of $12,500. Overhead variances can also occur if the pool of overhead costs rises or falls during the budget period, causing actual costs to deviate from planned or standard cost figures. If property taxes are raised during the year by $5,000, the pool of overhead rises to $55,000 and the $50,000 bench mark is changed.

Principally because of the problems arising out of arbitrary allocation of overhead costs to output, standard-cost systems have come in for a great deal of criticism. Volume variances, in particular, are troublesome, since periods of high production show a high rate of absorption—and thus a "good" cost picture—even though production may be for inventory and not for immediate sales. Thus, high profits may be reported, even though sales are not particularly brisk. This causes confusion in management circles, for profits can be reported as high in periods where sales are low and vice versa. This situation is especially pronounced in seasonal industries such as the container company which in peak production months found itself reporting profits that topped monthly sales totals. The result of such apparent inconsistency has been the development of a standard-cost system that does not allocate cost to product but applies it directly to the profit and loss statement. This system is known as direct costing.

Direct costing charges the overhead cost for a given time directly to the operating statement for that period. This contrasts with the standard absorption costing procedure, which charges overhead costs to product inventory; product inventory costs then enter into the profit-and-loss statement through the cost-to-sales and the underabsorbed burden entries. Over the long run, both methods work out to the same end point; but in the short run, very different cost and profit figures may be reported. These differences can be critical to the control process and thus deserve further discussion.

Using the same set of data, the absorption-costing and direct-cost systems could show contrasting pictures of operations for two operating periods; as in Table 12.3.

TABLE 12.3   OPERATIONS REPORTS—MST COMPANY

Operating Data	Period 1	Period 2
Sales (units)	1000	1500
Production (units)	2000	500
Selling price	$ 5.00	$ 5.00
Direct cost (materials and labor at standard)	$ 2.50	$ 2.50
Overhead cost (at standard)	$ 1.50	$ 1.50
Actual overhead for each period	$3000	$3000
Other expenses	$1000	$1000

Reporting using standard absorption costing (inventory based on estimates)

	Period 1	Period 2
Sales @ $5.00	$5000	$7500
Cost of sales (units @ $4.00 standard cost)	4000	6000
Unabsorbed burden ($3000 less $1.50 per unit produced)	—0—	2250
Gross profit	$1000	$(750)*
Other expenses	1000	1000
Net operating profit	$ 0	$(1750)*

Reporting using direct costing

	Period 1	Period 2
Sales @ $5.00	$5000	$7500
Direct cost of sales (@ $2.50)	2500	3750
Gross profit	$2500	$3750
Overhead expenses	3000	3000
Other expenses	1000	1000
Net operating profit	$(1500)	$(250)*

* Loss

These two operating statements represent quite different situations, which a sophisticated absorption-costing system could reconcile. But many managers would not really appreciate or understand such explanations. Direct costing eliminates the need for explanation of volume variances and thus is relatively easy to understand. Because costs incurred in each period are charged to the period, not to inventory (and then to profit and loss), this method seems easier for managers to follow. Though direct costing is not generally approved by the Internal Revenue Service for external reporting purposes, it has some real value for internal reporting and cost control analysis. In fact, standard absorption cost systems which explain volume variances in great detail may provide better action data for informed managers than direct-costing approaches, but the mysticism surrounding absorption costing has helped to spread acceptance of direct-costing techniques. Though direct costing is gaining greater acceptance, standard absorption costing is still dominant.

PROJECT CONTROL

The basic difference between project control and other control activities is the identification of a given project as a special unit for evaluation. Budgets, standard or direct cost systems, financial ratios and other controls may still be used, but the project is viewed and evaluated as a separate and distinct entity rather than in the context of other segments of the organization. Project control calls for a different view of an organization structure since it cuts a cross-section of an organization rather than following the normal, vertical chain of command. Projects are viewed as microcosmic organizations, and a special organization for control is set up to handle each separately.

Special controls in this approach might include task differentiation, organization of work into control units, development of report forms, preparation of specific budgets, and all of the other things done to tighten or sharpen controls in larger organizational units. One added contribution here is that changes and improvements can start with a given project, without having to wait for the entire organization to revamp its management practices or its planning and control activities. Much has been written about project control, including claims that it is a revolutionary new approach to organizational design and profitability. But like the story Mark Twain read about his own death, these claims seem to be somewhat exaggerated.

Project control does provide a means of looking at the contributions of particular projects and does give some flexibility to the organization structure, but it is neither revolutionary nor new. Special task forces have always been set up within organizations to handle special projects, and these units invariably have been given special handling and special controls. Perhaps the most novel aspect of project control is that it is now being introduced into production and manufacturing organizations. The advertising industry, for example, has used project control for many years and would consider it not as particularly revolutionary, but merely as a special case of some of the other approaches described.[9]

BREAK-EVEN ANALYSIS

Break-even analysis is another way to analyze data for specific planning and/or control purposes. It attempts to determine what volume of sales (or profit level) must be attained to just cover the fixed and variable costs as-

---

[9] For a detailed explanation of how project control works in practice, see E.L. Williams and G.A. Wilson, "Project Cost Control at Raytheon's Wayland Laboratory," IEEE Transactions in *Engineering Management*, September 1963, pp. 138–149.

sociated with a particular product or product line. This technique can also be used to evaluate expenditures for items such as advertising costs. The most simplified form of break-even analysis separates fixed and variable costs and tries to calculate at what volume fixed costs are covered by "contribution to fixed costs."[10] This contribution comes from a simple subtraction of variable costs from the unit sales price. If fixed costs are $20,000 and the sales price of a product is $1.00 per unit, and if variable costs total $0.60 per unit, then the unit contribution to fixed costs is $0.40. The break-even point is calculated by dividing the amount of contribution into the total of fixed costs. To illustrate:

Selling price	$1.00
Variable costs	0.60
Amount of contribution to overhead	$0.40

$$\frac{\text{Fixed costs (overhead)}}{\text{Contribution to overhead}} = \text{Break-even volume}$$

$$\frac{\$20,000}{\$0.40} = 50,000 \text{ (or the fifty-thousandth unit at the \$1.00 per unit price)}$$

This means that with a given cost structure and a known selling price in the market, the product will cover its entire fixed cost outlay with the sale of the fifty-thousandth unit. When the next unit is sold, the unit contribution is pure profit, above and beyond any profits that may have been included in the variable costs figure.

The example shown above is highly oversimplified, since it covers only a single product, not a complex product line or lines. In addition, changes in variable and fixed costs may occur as volume changes. Prices may rise or fall, discounts may be given or taken, or market saturation may be reached with subsequent price adjustments. Other assumptions underlying break-even analysis undergo similar alterations when time factors enter into the analysis. For example, consumer preferences might change and the resultant inventory accumulations could confuse the issue of whether or not a true break-even point had been achieved. Since key variables can be altered in time, the value of break-even analysis is limited. But if suitable adjustments are made and time and complexity factors are allowed for, break-even analysis can be a

---

[10] Variable costs vary directly with the volume of output; examples are labor and direct material costs. Fixed costs theoretically remain constant for all ranges of output; for example, property taxes on factory buildings. In practice, variable costs may vary with factors other than output levels; for example, labor costs may increase per unit because of overtime, and materials costs may be altered by quantity discounts. Fixed costs tend not to be truly fixed when large changes in production volume take place. If production rises sharply, heat, light, supervisory, and indirect materials costs may change the amount of fixed overhead incurred: the "fixed" cost is not fixed for all ranges of output.

valuable control device, particularly in situations where funds must be committed in lump form before any revenues are realized.

CYBERNETIC CONTROL SYSTEMS

Cybernetics, or closed-loop systems, are true decision-making devices when they reach operational form, and along with real-time simulation and detailed mathematical models, they form a self-regulating system which recognizes deviations and makes corrective adjustments. Since these devices are tailored for specific uses, they are inflexible and expensive. In many newly emerging uses, however, their cost and use limitations are subordinated to the results obtained.

Cybernetic systems exist in a variety of situations. Oil refineries have closed-loop controls over flows and feeds of inputs as they move through various steps in the refining process. Numerical control machines cut machine parts with great precision following a program having its own built-in adjustments. Automobile assembly lines utilize transfer and integration machines with tools and gauges that adjust themselves automatically to changing conditions. Cement is mixed on a continuous basis by computers that analyze and adjust flows of materials to predetermined specification. Students are given questions, answers, remedial subcourses of study, and automatic progress reports in some of the programmed instruction devices now in use in the classroom. The word, "cybernetics," which means "steersman," is in itself indicative of the guidance and control aspects of the cybernetic systems already in use. In spite of their inflexible nature, there is every reason to believe that the proven utility of cybernetic controls will result in their being used much more extensively in the foreseeable future, particularly in the process industries.

Summary

Control techniques vary very widely in both sophistication and coverage. Simple judgment at one end of the spectrum contrasts with the mathematics of industrial dynamics at the other. To be effective, any control technique must work with, rather than against, individuals in the organization and must point out areas where adjustments or improvements are needed. Control is truly a steering function, and its major payoff lies in its remedial or corrective aspects.

Two types of controls exist: general and specific. Some of the more widely used general controls are personal observation, analysis of statistical data, financial and ratio analysis, audits, real-time simulation, time-network analysis, and planning-for-profit techniques. Among the more accepted specific controls are budgets, standard-costing and direct-costing techniques, project control, break-even analysis, and cybernetic models. Whichever controls are used in the future, it seems likely that computerized information processing will lessen reporting time and speed corrective adjustments.

Study Questions

1. What are the key similarities and differences between open-loop and closed-loop systems of control?

2. How might you describe driving along a highway in terms of open-loop and closed-loop systems?

3. Contrast the scope and nature of internal and external audits. What similarities appear between the work of internal audit groups and outside consultants?

4. What is a flexible budget? What are its advantages? In what kinds of industries might it be most useful?

5. What are some of the various kinds of performance standards? Discuss them.

6. What are the more commonly used financial measures and ratios? What areas or activities do they measure most effectively? What accounts for their widespread use?

7. Contrast the relative flexibility of budgetary controls and cybernetic controls. Why are budgets used so extensively?

8. How would you explain the differences between absorption costing using standard costs and direct costing?

9. Contrast "fixed" and "variable" costs. Are fixed costs ever variable on a unit basis? Explain.

10. What are the advantages and disadvantages of personal judgments as a control methodology? What about the use of statistical analysis of trends and so forth?

11. What distinctions, if any, exist between general and specific controls? Can you provide some examples from personal experience?

Rooster-Crow
Alarm Clocks, Inc.

The Rooster-Crow Alarm Clock company makes a line of high-quality alarm clocks that sell in the $8 to $10 price range. One of the reasons for the high quality of the Rooster-Crow clock has been the rigid inspection procedures insisted upon by company management. Indeed, inspectors on the final assembly operation of the Rooster-Crow line go through a six-month training period before they are certified for the top rate on the job. These inspectors are well-paid, highly skilled individuals who have a special wage incentive plan that allows them to earn 25 percent above their base rates, assuming they apply themselves diligently. The management feels that this money is well spent in terms of guaranteed excellence of the product line.

The inspection performed on each clock is quite intricate. It includes fifteen separate checks of a visual and mechanical nature. There is no way, however, of telling whether any of these checks has been performed, since no markings or other visible changes are made on the product. Inspectors take a box of twelve clocks, complete the fifteen inspections on each clock, put their number in the box, and record the total number inspected for inventory and control purposes. This inventory control slip also serves as the basic document in the calculation of incentive pay. Every one of the inspectors is a long-service, skilled employee. Exclusive of fringe benefits, the group averages $3.85 per hour.

In the past year, labor efficiency reports on the inspection group have shown that the inspectors averaged 125-percent efficiency (that is, 25 percent above expected output). Bob Heinz, production superintendent over the alarm clock line, has been concerned with two irregularities in this figure. First, three of the ten men on the job have sported percentages as high as 150 percent every other week. This has increased their earnings above those of other members of the group. Moreover, in the two weeks before Christmas and before the annual vacation shutdown in August, the percentage of the entire group rose to 160 percent. The net effect of these increases was that for four weeks' production, the entire group earned 35 percent more than its usual average. Heinz considered the 150-percent figures posted by the three men and the group increase before vacation and Christmas as serious problems both in terms of pay and quality.

Heinz felt that the achievement of 150-percent efficiency was almost impossible if the inspection was done properly. He believed that the standards were tight in the inspections operation and that they had been maintained in such a way that they were not inaccurate. Heinz felt that the three inspectors were cheating every other week, and the whole group was reporting production figures incorrectly for four weeks of every year. Though this cheating was serious because of the wage inequities, Heinz was particularly concerned that a failure to perform the required amount of inspection might mean that defective clocks would be sent to the market. He proposed to do something about it.

1. Do you believe that there is cheating going on in the inspection operation? How would you verify your belief?

2. If Heinz concludes that cheating is going on, how should he proceed to stop it or at least reduce its incidence?

3. Should he handle the group problem first or the problem of the three men first? Should they be treated in the same way?

4. If Heinz believes that cheating is taking place, should he attempt to talk the problem over with the groups before he initiates actions or controls. Why or why not? What advantages and disadvantages exist in both courses of action?

5. What controls might be established to prevent cheating in the future?

The Dispensomat Company

The Dispensomat Company, a coin-vending machine corporation, recently purchased a coin-operated, self-service car-wash firm. The self-service feature allowed the customer to put a coin in a slot and receive a hose, a brush, and a metered amount of hot and cold water for twenty-five cents. This low price was possible because the customer supplied his own labor. No attendant was required at the installation, since it was completely automatic. Some minor maintenance was required at each installation, but this was done by part-time help such as service-station attendants from nearby areas, who were paid a flat fee to check the equipment from time to time.

The company's board of directors expected a high rate of return on the new acquisition, since it seemed to have a good potential market. In order to determine what rate of return to expect, they checked their own records of other vending operations, and they asked a small business investment company to supply estimates of returns in firms having similar installations. After some discussion and review, the board determined that a minimum

25-percent rate of return on sales after taxes should be obtained from each new installation.

The investment in the three new stations operated by the subsidiary was $60,000. The company expected to write off the cost of these installations over a ten-year period. Annual costs of depreciation, labor, maintenance, and other variable and overhead costs were expected to total $20,000 for the three units. The annual cost figures for the installations appear below:

Depreciation: $6,000

Maintenance: $4,000

Labor: $4,000

Materials: $3,500

Overhead (including interest, leases, and insurance): $2,500

Annual cost total: $20,000

Though a projection of expected sales was somewhat difficult, the directors estimated that the annual sales of the three units would be $40,000. They calculated the annual rate of return in the following way:

$40,000 Sales
−20,000 Cost

$20,000 Gross profit
−10,000 Taxes (estimated at 50 percent)

$10,000 Net profit after taxes
$40,000 Sales

25-Percent rate of return on sales

After one year, the actual results were somewhat disappointing. Net profit after taxes on the three units was only $5,000 on sales of $30,000. Costs, however, were as originally forecast. The rate of return on sales was thus only 16⅔ percent calculated in the following way:

$30,000 Sales
−20,000 Cost

$10,000 Gross profit
− 5,000 Taxes

$ 5,000 Net profit
$30,000 Sales

16⅔-percent rate of return on sales

After two years sales increased, but so did costs, and the rate-of-return figure rose to only 20 percent. At the end of three years the same rate-of-return figure, 20 percent, appeared. Sales were up in the third year, but, again, so were costs. The board was concerned by the fact that sales goals had not been met by the end of the third year, but no particular action was contemplated at that time. This situation was changed instantly when the board received an offer to sell the car-wash facilities at what it considered a good price.

Two of the members of the board wanted to sell the washing units outright. Two others thought the rate of return was acceptable and moving in the right direction. One member of the board was in doubt. At the beginning of the fourth year, the board met to decide what to do with the three self-service units.

1. What criteria should the board use to decide whether or not to sell the automatic car-wash units?

2. What do you think of the board's forecast procedures?

3. How should rate-of-return figures be set?

4. Is the board correct in feeling its 25-percent figure should be met? What criteria determine whether or not this figure is a reasonable one?

5. Suppose the board elects not to sell. What should it do to increase the rate of return?

6. What kinds of standards should be used to evaluate the performance of the three units? How would you go about setting such standards?

The Grimes Axle and Hubcap Company

Recently, the Grimes Axle and Hubcap Company introduced a new inventory control reporting procedure in all of its fifteen plants. The plant accountants were directed to follow a procedure which required the reporting of inventory values on the fifteenth of each month. In the Kansas City plant of the axle division it was common practice to ship out inventories on the third and seventeenth of each month. Inventory was thus near a peak on the fifteenth of the month.

Shortly after the new system was announced, Hollis Warner, the general manager of the Kansas City operation, called William Mossback, the head of his plant accounting department, into his office and pointedly suggested that Mossback list inventory figures on his reports of the fifteenth as they would actually be on the eighteenth. The net effect of this procedure, Mossback realized, would be to reduce the value of inventory figures reported. Warner emphasized to Mossback that his "suggestion" was not an order, it was only a "request." Mossback was told by Warner that precise dates of reporting did not make any difference to anyone except company headquarters and himself, since his bonus was determined in part by inventory performance—the higher the inventory, the lower the bonus, and vice versa. Mossback reported directly to Mr. Warner in terms of promotion, pay, merit increases, an so on; but he was under the functional guidance and control of the corporate staff accountant in technical matters such as reporting procedures.

When Mossback mentioned the "suggestion" of his boss to an accountant friend in another firm, his friend made two comments. First, he discussed the ethics of the accounting profession and the importance of following certain stated principles and guides to obtain truthful reporting. On the other hand, he reminded Mossback, "You have an obligation to your four kids and your wife."

1. If you were Mossback, what would you do? Defend your position.

2. Assuming Mr. Mossback chooses to follow company directives, how do you suggest he handle the process of explaining his actions to the plant manager?

Lake Charles Industries

The dispute between Larry Bitgood and Homer Dando first came to the attention of Division Manager Lorne Sundsmith at the monthly staff meeting of the electrochemical division of Lake Charles Industries (LCI). In a routine budget variation report Division Controller Dando noted that Mr. Bitgood's manufacturing development section was substantially in excess of budgeted costs. Mr. Bitgood, in commenting on this variance, pointed out that the high costs could be traced to the unexpectedly numerous changes in design, processes, and manufacturing methods demanded by the biggest, and as yet the only, customer for a new product now occupying all but a small percentage of the time of Mr. Bitgood's department. Bitgood himself noted that development costs were always hard to estimate accurately and stated that many of the costs incurred were beyond his control. He then asked for a revision of his unit's budget to adjust for the large numbers of changes, claiming that the efficiency of the section was represented incorrectly by existing budgets. He also jokingly noted that his own bonus was in danger of reduction because of the inflexible way the controller's group had interpreted his budget.

Mr. Dando responded quickly to Bitgood's final remark. He stated, "Budgets are bench marks, not absolute figures, and you yourself gave us the figures for probable development costs. These estimates were then discussed and approved by the new-product development committee, of which you are a member. Further, the controller's group revised the original estimates upward six months after the project started at your request, even though we felt that such changes were not justified thoroughly. In my opinion and in the opinion of one or two members of the new-product development committee, there's no reason why your group shouldn't be meeting budgeted costs."

Mr. Bitgood, who had listened angrily to Mr. Dando's comments, responded quickly. Tensely, he replied, "You damned graphite engineers are all alike. Just because you push the pencil on engineering design figures you think you know all about engineering. Budgets are estimates, not final figures, and engineering has to be done in the lab, not in the accounting office. Theory is just fine, but your controller's staff has never understood the fact that this company has a philosophy of giving the customer what he wants, not what the accountants say will be the best just because it's cheaper. Sure, you updated our figures six months ago, but we've had several hundred changes since then—and no adjustments were made to cover them. If you and your boys would get out of the office once in a while, you'd find out what's going on around here. There's more to this company than sheets of figures. Ask Lorne [Sundsmith] here; he appreciates the value of what we're doing."

Before Mr. Sundsmith could answer, Mr. Dando snapped, "I still say if you were doing your job properly your costs wouldn't be out of line. Not all of our design and development problems come from customers—plenty are caused by failures within your group. I believe you're just trying to avoid responsibility."

At this point, Mr. Sundsmith quickly cut in to prevent further recriminations. "I'm surprised to hear you two going at each other like this," he said, "Let's calm down and talk this over on its merits."

1. How should Mr. Sundsmith conduct the meeting from this point?
2. What purposes do budgets serve? Are they being served well in LCI?
3. What *step-by-step* program would you recommend to improve relations between Mr. Dando and Mr. Bitgood?

National Motor Parts Company

The National Motor Parts Company is one of the five largest firms in the basic auto industry. It has nine operating divisions and a total work force of over fifty thousand employees. Its extensive staff organization provides specialized skills at the corporate, divisional, and plant levels. At each of these levels, the cost-accounting and industrial-engineering groups exert a considerable amount of influence over the development and execution of corporate policy. Though individual divisions are operationally autonomous, division officials generally follow the policy suggestions made by the cost-accounting and industrial-engineering staffs. A partial organization chart for the National Motor Parts Company appears in Figure IV.1.

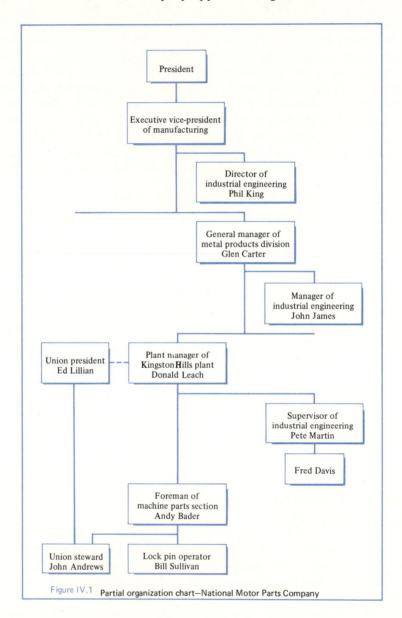

Figure IV.1   Partial organization chart—National Motor Parts Company

One program recently advocated by Phil King, corporate director of industrial engineering, was a review of work standards on all jobs which had not been checked or audited within the previous two years. King's request arose from the fact that during a tour of plants in several of National's operating divisions, he had seen several instances of what appeared to be goldbricking. Upon his return to the central office, Mr. King met with two of his staff engineers and, after careful deliberation, an audit plan was drawn up. This plan was subsequently approved by the executive vice-president in charge of manufacturing operations.

The basic plan suggested by King used a technique known as work sampling to check on the idle time present in individual job standards. In essence, this approach relied on the fact that a series of short random observations, if taken often enough over an appropriate time period, could give an accurate picture of the operations performed in each job. The work sampling results would be used to determine which jobs were not requiring the employees to work for an entire day to meet their output standards. By the same token, those jobs which were demanding a full day's work to meet existing standards would also be recognized. Though work sampling was to be used to identify standards which were loose (that is, standards which did not require a full day's work to meet daily standard output requirements), King's proposal included the further suggestion that looseness in a job, when detected, should be checked in detail by a stopwatch time study and a thorough motion study.

To launch his program, Mr. King held a series of meetings with the heads of divisional industrial engineering groups. Though objections were raised about the cost and time considerations inherent in the proposal, the division engineering managers agreed that the plan was technically sound and they decided to put it into effect as soon as possible.

One of the receptive listeners to Mr. King's standards audit procedure was John James, manager of industrial engineering in National's metal products division. James, who held degrees in both industrial engineering and mathematics, enthusiastically returned to division headquarters in Kingston, Michigan, and drew up procedures to utilize the plan in the metal products division's five plants.

Within a month after the corporate staff meeting, James offered his version of the audit plan to Glenn Carter, the division manager. Carter, who had come to respect James' technical ability and practical know-how, accepted the plan readily and agreed to present it at the next weekly meeting of his plant managers. Carter suggested that he should merely outline the plan to his plant managers and that James should be available to fill in details and to answer questions.

In the subsequent meeting, each of the plant managers agreed that such an audit was sound, and each, in turn, suggested that James contact the heads of their plant industrial-engineering departments to explain the details of his plan. Three plant managers who had formerly been in charge of industrial-engineering groups in the National hierarchy offered to provide additional clerical and engineering help on a temporary basis in order to get the program moving quickly.

After gaining the support of Mr. Carter and the five plant managers, James met with the heads of industrial engineering in each of the division's five plants. Though the familiar objections were raised about the time and cost of such a program, all five men stated that the audit procedure was practical and agreed to put it into effect immediately. Within the group, the plan was embraced most enthusiastically by Pete Martin, the industrial engineer in charge of the Kingston Hills plant.

The Kingston Hills plant shared the same plot of land as the headquarters of the metal-stamping division. It employed more than five thousand workers and was generally considered to be the most modern and most efficient of the division's plants. Donald Leach, the plant manager, was one of the three men in the division who rose to his present position from a supervisory job in the industrial-engineering hierarchy. Leach's plant was equipped with the latest automated equipment and was, according to division records, the most profitable plant in the division. Leach prided himself on his ability to attract and retain good managerial talent, and he was particularly proud of the work done by Pete Martin in developing new methods of work and in adapting mathematical techniques and procedures to fit the needs of the operations at the Kingston Hills plant. Thus, when Martin suggested the adoption of an audit program, Leach readily agreed and offered Martin additional clerical help to work on the details of setting up the program.

Pete Martin went to work on the program immediately, and within a week, the first audit reports were completed. After one month, audits had been completed on seventeen operations. These audits indicated that very little idle time was evident in sixteen of the operations, but one job, the production of a tiny metal lock pin used in automatic transmission units, seemed to show an unusual amount of idle time. The job in question was performed by Bill Sullivan, an experienced, long-service employee. Sullivan set up, tended, and performed certain minor maintenance tasks on an automatic screw machine. Because the products he worked on were varied, the original standards had been measured quite carefully. Since the original standards had been set, changes had occurred which caused the standards to become loose. Changes in materials, tolerance limits on the various runs, and the actual length of machine runs as well as the adoption of a more standardized parts line had all occurred in recent years. And since several of these changes apparently had not caused adjustments in the affected output standards, it was a rare day when Sullivan failed to obtain his expected or standard output.[1]

The looseness of Sullivan's standards was no revelation to several of his immediate coworkers. One worker, for example, when conversing with Pete Martin about the audit, stated, "If your audit doesn't pick up that soft touch Sullivan's got, you'd better toss the whole thing down the drain." Few of his fellow workers were bitter about Sullivan's gravy train, however, since the looseness of his standards gave him no wage advantages over them. In other National plants, where payment was tied directly to output through

---

[1] Sullivan's standard at this time was 0.33734 minutes per piece or approximately 180 units per hour. This is shown in Table I in Martin's memo.

the use of incentive plans, the relative looseness of standards frequently caused bitter disputes because of the wage inequities it generated. In the Kingston Hills plant, a loose standard meant that workers accrued leisure time benefits, not higher wages. Though workers objected to "unfair" work loads, few grievances had ever been filed to ask management to correct such inequities.

The second phase of the audit procedure entailed a review of Sullivan's job by Fred Davis, one of Martin's most competent engineers. In his study, Davis compared the previously set standard (see Table IV.1, in Martin's memo) with the newly calculated time required to perform the operation *under changed conditions* (see Table IV. 2, in Martin's memo). This, in turn, showed an idle time of four hours per shift.[2] Davis's stopwatch time study of the screw machine operation confirmed the results of the initial audit, and a detailed methods study of the job turned up changes in materials and methods of operation. Mr. Leach, when confronted with this information by Martin and Davis, ordered them to take steps to correct what he believed was an inequity in the basic work load structure.

After several weeks of study, Davis devised a plan where, with certain layout changes and some methods improvements, Sullivan would operate not one, but two, machines. Davis's methods study showed that the time allowances were enough to allow Sullivan to complete the requirements of the revised job if he worked a full, eight-hour day. Davis showed his plan to Martin, and together they presented it to Mr. Leach. Leach approved the plan and directed the purchasing department to acquire another automatic screw machine. He then called in Andy Bauer, Sullivan's immediate supervisor, and informed him that Sullivan should be told of the impending change.[3] Bauer, who had worked with Mr. Davis on the methods study, agreed to tell Sullivan that management intended to exercise its contractual right "to make changes in methods, equipment, materials, and conditions of work in order to obtain greater efficiency and to adjust existing work standards to reflect such changes." The labor contract further stated that "in case of such methods change, only those elements of the standard will be changed which are affected by the changes in methods, etc." Another section of the contract stipulated that "standards will be set on the basis of fairness and equity and that they shall be consistent with the quality of workmanship, efficiency of operation, and reasonable working capacities of normal operations." In the National Motors contract, as in most others in the basic auto industry, the resolution of work standards disputes can be solved only by dealings between management and the labor union. Arbitration is specifically prohibited as a means of settling disputes over work standards.

---

[2] Though a four-hour idle time may seem so high as to be almost unbelievable, engineering studies performed elsewhere in National Motors uncovered similar looseness. Experts in the industrial-engineering field concede that this situation can arise even in the best managed plants.

[3] The new standard called for a time of 0.1664 minutes per piece, or approximately 360 units per hour.

Two months later, the new machine was installed at the workplace along with several minor changes in layout and work flow. Foreman Bauer instructed Sullivan in his new duties; and Sullivan, though he was unhappy about the new layout, started to work with the two machines. During the day, John Andrews, the union steward, stopped by to check on the new job.[4] Sullivan complained violently that he was the victim of a speedup. Andrews, after listening to the details of the shift from one to two machines, suggested that Sullivan file a grievance.

That evening Sullivan wrote a grievance; and shortly before starting work the next morning, he turned it over to Andrews. Following the normal procedure for processing such grievances, Andrews presented it to Andy Bauer for discussion and possible solution. Because of the technical nature of the grievance, Bauer called upon Pete Martin and Fred Davis to explain the change to Andrews. When Martin and Davis showed their detailed methods studies to Andrews, he stated, "What you guys have done here is to blow up a big smoke screen to hide the fact that you're pulling a speedup on Sullivan's job." The net result of the meeting was that the grievance, still unsettled, moved to the second step in the grievance procedure. This step involved discussion between the head of the local union, Ed Lillian, and Donald Leach, the plant manager.

Mr. Leach, when presented with Bill Sullivan's grievance, immediately called Pete Martin into his office to discuss the problem. Together they reviewed the methods study and the subsequent standards revisions. The approaches and the figures shown by Martin seemed correct and reasonable to Mr. Leach, and he believed that the contractual clause allowing him "to make changes in methods, equipment, materials, and conditions of work in order to obtain greater efficiency and to adjust existing work standards to reflect such changes" justified the introduction of the second machine. He stated, "It's my duty to my work force to maintain an efficient operation so that the job security of all the workers will be protected"; he also said, "The only way we can continue to grow and prosper and provide steady employment for our workers is to push for more efficiency in all of our plant activities." In his upcoming meeting with Ed Lillian, Leach planned to use this reasoning as the basis for his insistence on the introduction of the second machine. He also intended to allow Lillian to review any and all of the data used as the basis for changes made on the disputed job.

Ed Lillian, on the other hand, expected to rely heavily on John Andrews to present the union side of the dispute. Lillian told Andrews that he would support him fully if the company's actions were in violation of the labor contract.

---

[4] One of the main duties of a union steward is to represent the worker in presenting grievances to management. He is usually elected to this office by fellow workers. Stewards hold regular jobs in the plant where they perform their duties, and they receive no extra pay for their union activities.

The feelings of the parties prior to the grievance meeting are summarized below:

Bill Sullivan: "All of a sudden I'm expected to turn out three thousand pieces a day where I used to have to do fourteen hundred.[5] If this isn't a speedup I don't know what the hell it is. I've got rights and I expect the union to protect them."

John Andrews: "The company hasn't done a thing to change methods here. They've just come in and made changes to correct their mistakes from the past. Their actions violate the fairness and equity clauses relating to revisions of work standards which exist in the labor contract."

Pete Martin: "We've made good studies of Sullivan's job and we know that the lock pin standard is loose. It's not unfair to ask him to put in a fair day's work in order to earn a fair day's pay."

Ed Lillian: "Even though Don Leach is sometimes tough in his dealings with us, he's been fair and consistent. On this issue, however, I'm not sure he's really in the right."

Donald Leach: "I believe that I'm both contractually and economically correct when I take the stand that the second machine should be maintained on this operation. After all, if we don't have efficiency in this plant the workers won't have any job security."

Glenn Carter: "The real issue here is whether or not managers have the right to run their own plants. If we have to subsidize inefficiency in our operations we won't be in business very long."

The grievance meeting scheduled to resolve this dispute was affected by at least two other factors:

1. Strikes over production standards were legal during the life of the labor contract. Though other issues (wages, hours, working conditions, and so on) could be grieved, no legal strikes could be called on these matters until the existing contract expired.

2. Though one more step remained in the division's grievance procedure, Mr. Carter had written a note to Ed Lillian which stated that, "I will not, under any circumstances, alter the stand taken by Mr. Leach in the plant level negotiations." Since the dispute cannot be arbitrated, the parties are faced with the problem of devising some other strategy to solve (or to "win") the disagreement.

In a front-page editorial on the day before the grievance meeting, the local *Kingston Daily Record* asked the disputants to act with "caution and care."

---

[5] In actuality Sullivan was required to turn out 1440 pieces per day before the audit. After the methods and subsequent standards revision, Sullivan's quota rose to 2880 (see Martin's memo).

The *Record's* editorial recalls that "the steel industry in 1959 and 1960 became embroiled in a similar issue which evolved into a strike lasting six months."

TO: Andy Bauer, Foreman, Machined Parts Section
FROM: Peter Martin, Plant Industrial Engineer
SUBJECT: Standards on lock pin operation performed by William Sullivan, Clock # 45716

In reponse to your request during our recent standards grievance meeting with Bill Sullivan and John Andrews, I have described both the general procedure for setting machine standards and the specific calculations performed to set a standard on Sullivan's lock pin operation. Though you may feel that some parts of the explanation are overly detailed, I have included them so that your records on this matter will be complete and accurate.

A production standard for a machine operation is determined by measuring two things: (1) the time used by the operator to complete a unit of output and (2) the machine time needed to produce each unit. The operator's time might consist of the following items: setting up the necessary tooling, jigs, and fixtures to produce the part; feeding materials into the machine; inspection activities; some minor maintenance activities such as oiling the machine and keeping it clean; and other factors which could vary widely depending upon the nature of the job and/or the equipment in use. Machine time represents the time when the machine is performing some operation on the unit being produced.

A simple addition of the operator's time and the machine time rarely produces an accurate work standard, however, since workers can perform certain of their activities during the run time of the machine. It is also true that machines don't always operate perfectly, and to compensate for such a contingency it may be necessary to determine an allowance (commonly called a "down-time allowance") in the final standard. Such complicating factors make a rather knotty problem out of what seems to be at first glance nothing more than a simple job of measurement.

Take, for example, the standards on Bill Sullivan's job at National Motors. Prior to the industrial engineering audit, Sullivan was operating one machine. When a machine is operated by one man a good deal of overlap generally occurs between operator time and machine-run time. In order to illustrate the setting of a work standard on this operation, we would first determine which of the operator's activities can be performed during the machine's run time. We would then have to adjust the total elapsed time observed during our study of the lock pin operation to reflect such overlap. If we can grasp the relationship between operator time and machine time on a one-machine job, we can, if we desire, expand the concept to illustrate the methods used to measure standards on more complicated multimachine operations.

The first step in setting a standard is to identify the unit by which we intend to measure output. Sullivan's machine is turning out a metal part called a lock pin. The lock pin, then, is the unit of output upon which our standard is based.

The next task we face is to thoroughly analyze the job, to determine a standard method of performing the job, and to measure the various elements of this standard operating method. One procedure used to determine the most efficient way to do the job involves the use of a flow chart. Flow charts trace the path of materials and men as they relate to the machines needed to make the product under observation. Another attack uses detailed studies of the motions made by the operator in setting up and running a machine. This latter approach may be performed in very detailed fashion and may even utilize motion pictures of the operation to enable the industrial engineer to study the most refined and intricate motion patterns practiced by the operator.

Though a number of methods are used to set work standards, stopwatch time study is used most widely. In time study, a trained observer records the time taken to manufacture, say, a lock pin. He then rates these observed times to reflect a so-called normal output expectation on the job. A normal, or average, rating is generally assigned a value of 100 percent. A below-average, or less-than-normal, performance is given a rating less than 100 percent, while a better-than-average operator would be rated over 100 percent. The rating factor multiplied by the observed time yields the normal time for performing the portion of the job under observation.

If, for example, a rating of 110 percent was given to a time value of 0.2000 (two tenths of a minute), the normal time to perform this task would be 0.2200 (1.10 × 0.2000). This shows us how a faster man's time (0.2000) would be adjusted to reflect the pace expected of an average operator (0.2200). If a rating of 90 percent was placed on an observed time of 0.2444 for the same task, the normal time for the operation would be (still) 0.22 (0.90 × 0.244). It is no accident that both of these normal (0.22) times are identical. If the rating process is done correctly, the observed times multiplied by the rating *will always yield an identical normal time.* Since human errors invariably crop up in the rating procedure, there is always some variance in so-called normal times. Skilled industrial engineers, however, claim that such variance will not exceed the true normal by more than ± 5 percent. Though the veracity of this claim is often disputed, the rating process is still the most common method of evaluating the elapsed times recorded during a stopwatch time study.

Once the times are recorded and rated, adjustments must be made to reflect the number of times each element occurs during the production of one lock pin. Setup time, for example, occurs only once per production run, but each run may result in thousands of lock pins. This adjustment occurs in the final standard as a setup time per unit allowance. Similar adjustments are made for all other items which occur more or less frequently than the cycle needed to produce one lock pin.

As a final step in the standard-setting procedure, allowances are added for personal time, delay beyond the control of the operator, and, in some cases, for fatigue. Where particularly unusual job conditions exist, other allowances are sometimes added to the standard. As you know, many of the allowances in use in our plant are set by collective bargaining rather than by work measurement.

The actual calculations of the original standard on the basic lock pin portion of Bill Sullivan's job appear in Table IV.1.

TABLE IV.1   TIME STUDY SUMMARY SHEET FOR ORIGINAL STANDARD

1 Task or Element	2 Average Time	3 Rating	(col. 2 × col. 3) 4 Leveled Time	5 Occurrence per Cycle	(col. 4 × col. 5) 6 Standard Minutes
1. Set up machine to run lock nuts*	5.00	100(1.00)	5.00	1/2000	0.00250
2. Feed first metal bars into machine†	1.50	90(0.90)	1.35	1/2000	0.00067
3. Machine run time per unit‡	0.30	100(1.00)	0.30	1/1	0.30000
4. Inspection time (sample basis at end of each run)§	6.00	80(0.80)	4.80	1/2000	0.00240
5. Oiling and cleaning machine‖	6.60	100(1.00)	6.60	1/6000	0.00110
			Total time per unit		0.30667
			Add allowances (10-percent for rest and delay taken from local labor contract		0.03067
			Standard Minutes per unit		0.33734

* All times recorded in decimal minutes, that is, 0.20 is two tenths of a minute

† Average production run per setup—2000 units.

‡ Standard metal bars of a particular hardness are specified for this product by the general foreman.

§ Based on average run time for varying grades of materials utilized. Also contains allowances for unavoidable down time.

‖ Based on tolerances specified by general foreman acting under the direction of the statistical quality control group.

The time of 0.33734 minutes per unit means that the standard time allowed to produce one lock pin is approximately one third of a minute. Thus a standard output of three lock pins per minute, or 180 lock pins per hour, is expected. If we could assume an eight-hour work day for Sullivan, his daily output quota on this standard would be 1440 units.

To illustrate how standards can become loose, we can take Bill Sullivan's job as a prime example. Let us first assume that the setup operation became easier for Bill as he developed skill. Then, longer production runs were planned and changes were made in the materials used to manufacture the lock pin. Now let us assume that Bill performs his inspection operations during the run time of the machine and also manages to cut his oiling and cleanup time in half.

The big item to consider is the machine run time. Suppose now that the new materials allow a more rapid machining cycle and that the machines on the job, after an initial break-in period, operate faster and with less down time than the same machines measured in the original job time study.

The new time study by Fred Davis detected the changes described above and Table IV.2, another time study summary sheet, shows the results of Davis's study:

TABLE IV.2   DAVIS'S TIME STUDY SUMMARY SHEET

1 Task or Element	2 Average Time	3 Rating	(col. 2 × col. 3) Leveled Time	5 Occurrence per Cycle	(col. 4 × col. 5) 6 Standard Minutes
1. Set up machine to run lock nuts*	3.00	100	3.00	1/6000	0.0005
2. Feed first metal bars into machine†	1.50	90	1.35	1/6000	0.0002
3. Machine run time per unit‡	0.150	100	0.150	1/1	0.1500
4. Inspection time (sample basis during each run)§	6.00	100	x	x	x
5. Oiling and cleaning machine	3.30	100	3.30	1/6000	0.0006
			Total time per unit		0.1513
			Add 10-percent allowances (from labor contract)		0.0151
			Standard Minutes per unit		0.1664

* Average production run per setup—6000 units.

† Standard metal bars of a particular hardness are specified for this product by the general foreman.

‡ Based on average run time for varying grades of materials utilized. Also contains unavoidable down time allowances.

§ Based on tolerances and procedures specified by the statistical quality control group.

The 0.1664-minutes-per-unit figure means that the standard time allowed to produce one lock pin is approximately one sixth of a minute. This rate of 6 per minute calls for an hourly quota of 360 units. Again assuming an eight-hour day, Sullivan's new standard output requirement would be 2880 units per day.

The problems of undetected methods changes are quite common, although they are usually not as obvious as they appear to be in this case. Though the numerical calculations shown above are quite simple, the problems they illustrate are not.

I hope that this memo answers the questions you raised last week. If I can be of any further help, do not hesitate to call me. By the way, I am now in 408 Engineering, but my extension number is still 4193.

Pete

BIBLIOGRAPHY

Anshen, Melvin W., and George L. Bach, eds., *Management and Corporations: 1985,* New York: McGraw-Hill, Inc., 1960.

Argyris, Chris, *Personality and Organization,* New York: Harper & Row, Publishers, 1957.

Boulding, K., *Economic Analysis,* 3rd ed., New York: Harper & Row, Publishers, 1955.

Bower, James, and William Wilke, eds., *Financial Information Systems,* Boston: Houghton Mifflin Company, 1968.

Brummet, L., *Overhead Costing,* Ann Arbor, Mich.: University of Michigan, Bureau of Business Research, 1957.

Burke, G., *The Computer Age and its Potential for Management,* New York: Harper & Row, Publishers, 1965.

Carzo, Rocco, and John Yanouzas, *Formal Organizations: A Systems Approach,* Homewood, Ill.: Richard D. Irwin, Inc., 1967.

Dale, Ernest, *Management: Theory and Practice,* New York: McGraw-Hill, Inc., 1965.

Dean, Joel, *Managerial Economics,* Englewood Cliffs, N.J.: Prentice-Hall, Inc., 1951.

Dearden, John, and F. Warren McFarlan, *Management Information Systems,* Homewood, Ill.: Richard D. Irwin, Inc., 1966.

Forrester, Jay, *Industrial Dynamics,* Cambridge, Mass.: MIT Press, 1961.

Haynes, Warren W., and Joseph L. Massie, *Management: Analysis, Concepts and Cases,* Englewood Cliffs, N.J.: Prentice-Hall, Inc., 1961.

Head, Robert V., *Real Time Business Systems,* New York: Holt, Rinehart and Winston, Inc., 1964.

Hill, T., and M. Gordon, *Accounting: A Management Approach,* rev. ed., Homewood, Ill.: Richard D. Irwin, Inc., 1959.

Horngren, C., *Accounting for Management Control: An Introduction,* Englewood Cliffs, N.J.: Prentice-Hall, Inc., 1965.

How to Read a Financial Report, New York: Merrill, Lynch, Pierce, Fenner and Smith, Inc., 1962.

Hutchinson, John G., *Managing a Fair Day's Work,* Ann Arbor, Mich.: University of Michigan, Bureau of Industrial Relations, 1963.

Jerome, W., *Executive Control,* New York: John Wiley & Sons, Inc., 1961.

Koontz, Harold, and Cyril O'Donnell, *Principles of Management,* 3rd ed., New York: McGraw-Hill, Inc., 1964.

McFarlan, D., and F. Wickert, eds., *Measuring Executive Effectiveness,* New York: Appleton-Century-Crofts, 1967.

Martindell, Jackson, *The Appraisal of Management,* New York: Harper & Row, Publishers, 1962.

Measuring Productivity in Federal Government Organizations, Washington, D.C.: U.S. Government Printing Office, Executive Office of the President, Bureau of the Budget, 1964.

Moore, Franklin G., *Manufacturing Management,* 4th ed., Homewood, Ill.: Richard D. Irwin, Inc., 1965.

National Industrial Conference Board, *Administration of Cost Reduction Programs,* New York: Author, Studies in Business Policy, no. 117, 1965.

Newman, William H., Charles E. Summer, and E. Kirby Warren, *The Process of Management: Concepts, Behavior and Practice,* 2nd ed., Englewood Cliffs, N.J.: Prentice-Hall, Inc., 1967.

Parkinson, Cyril N., *Parkinson's Law and Other Studies in Administration,* Boston: Houghton Mifflin Company, 1957.

Paton, W.A., and R. Dixon, *Essentials of Accounting,* New York: Crowell-Collier and Macmillan, Inc., 1958.

Prince, Thomas R., *Information Systems for Management Planning and Control,* Homewood, Ill.: Richard D. Irwin, Inc., 1969.

Schleh, E.C., *Management by Results,* New York: McGraw-Hill, Inc., 1961.

Schlender, W., W. Scott, and A. Filley, eds., *Management Perspectives,* Boston: Houghton Mifflin Company, 1965.

Seiler, John A., *Systems Analysis in Organizational Behavior,* Homewood, Ill.: Richard D. Irwin, Inc., 1967.

Spencer, M., and B. Siegelman, *Managerial Economics,* rev. ed., Homewood, Ill.: Richard D. Irwin, Inc., 1964.

Staley, J.D., *The Cost Minded Manager,* New York: American Management Association, Inc., 1961.

Strong, E., and D. Smith, *Management Control Models,* New York: Holt, Rinehart and Winston, Inc., 1968.

Taggart, H., *Cost Justification,* Ann Arbor, Mich.: University of Michigan, Bureau of Business Research, 1959.

Wadia, Manek, ed., *The Nature and Scope of Management,* Glenview, Ill.: Scott, Foresman and Company, 1966.

Wilson, Sloan, *The Man in the Gray Flannel Suit,* New York: Simon and Schuster, Inc., 1955.

You and the Computer, General Electric Company, 1965.

Young, Stanley, *Management: A Systems Analysis,* Glenview, Ill.: Scott, Foresman and Company, 1966.

In his thoughtful book, *Self Renewal*, John W. Gardner stresses the fact that societies and individuals must safeguard their vigor and growth by conscious attempts to develop programs of self-renewal. In other words, their survival depends upon their continued regeneration of ideas and approaches and a striving for higher levels of excellence in performance.

Developing superior performance is an aspect of the regeneration process affecting organizations and individuals. No one person or unit in an organization holds the key to total self-renewal; it is and must be a collective effort. But this is not to say that the seeds of self-renewal germinate equally well in all climates. Some grounds are more fertile than others, and revitalization invariably proceeds at differing rates of speed.

Though Gardner does not give a specific solution to the problem of advancing decay, he does offer the following general description: "We must discover how to design organizations and technological systems in such a way that individuals' talents are used to the maximum and human satisfaction and dignity are preserved. We must learn to make technology serve man, not only in the end product but in the doing."[1]

Gardner's emphasis on the individual is in general accord with many recent writings in the field of organizational development. In the past, most attempts to revitalize organizations were geared to formal structural changes or to a restructuring of economic or financial controls. Even formal approaches to revitalization have begun to investigate individual and group factors more carefully, usually to the ultimate benefit of the initiating organization.

SECTION V
Moving People to Action

[1] John W. Gardner, *Self Renewal* (New York: Harper & Row, Publishers, 1964), p.57.

315

This section describes how both formal and modern approaches to organization have been used as means of developing superior performance. Chapter 13 treats the acquisition and leadership of human resources, while Chapter 14 describes the utilization and revitalization process. This artificial division is defensible on the grounds that certain approaches are designed for total revitalization, while other methods have greater applicability in more limited sets of conditions.

For centuries, the means of achieving superior performance have remained a mystique. The Crusaders called upon God to give them the strength and will to conquer the infidel defilers of the Holy Sepulcher. Machiavelli urged his ruler to obtain both obedience and excellence of performance through the judicious exercise of power. Recently, social scientists have called for the liberation of the individual, no doubt recalling Shakespeare's Cassius, who, in *Julius Caesar,* stated, "The fault, dear Brutus, lies not in our stars, but in ourselves, that we are underlings."

Some of the ancient mysticism about means and methods lingers in contemporary theories dealing with improving individual and group performance in organizations. Formal organization theories emphasize structural approaches to efficiency, but leave the critical human variable in operational limbo. Human relations advocates point out the importance of individual needs and group interactions, but do not always relate solutions to the pressures of a competitive marketplace. Newer theories emphasize rational decision making, role differentiation, and concepts such as settling for less than best (satisficing) rather than best (maximizing); but these theories invariably stop short of integrating their contentions into practical methods of implementation. Given such inconsistencies in theory and application, pragmatism seems to be a justifiable factor in rating one above others; and executives probably are exerting a certain amount of rationality themselves if they first experiment with many approaches and then stick with the one or ones that seem to work best in their own bailiwicks.

CHAPTER 13
Acquisition and Leadership of Human Resources

Though attempts to generalize about techniques for improving performance can lead to conceptual errors or logical inconsistencies, there is little doubt that some relate directly to formal theories of organization, while others bear the stamp of human relations theories. For example, certain techniques visualize man as a productive factor requiring close and constant control, while others are based on the premise that man is self-motivated.[1] All of these theories attempt to improve performance, even though their means may differ. They seek what John Gardner might describe as devices designed to make possible the account of individual identity.[2] Most techniques attempt to bring about this result without making great changes in organizational structure or goals—perhaps because most leaders believe that no drastic changes are needed to bring about improved motivation and efficiency. As Roger Blough, former head of U.S. Steel, states:

> I believe that working in a corporation can contribute greatly to the freedom and growth of the employee; that an individual is not a machine, but a warm, changeable, unique person who—partly because of his membership in a corporation group—is free and encouraged to grow as a personality and can do so in a reasonable relation to his abilities and ambitions.

Unfortunately, this set of beliefs is not always evident in industrial organization, and changes must be instituted to go from reality to the kind of world Blough visualizes.[3]

How to improve individual and group motivation is a complex subject covering a far wider range of theories and implementing devices than can be described here; but two broad classes of actions can be examined with their means of execution. The first basic means of achieving better performance is manpower planning, which occurs before the man is on the job. Once the man is hired, the second set of techniques—which attempts to obtain better performance through appraisal, counseling, and training—is used.

Manpower planning is a well-established practice which recently has shifted its emphasis from the short term to much longer time horizons. The appraisal, counseling, and training method is also a widely used technique, especially in industrial circles—where its familiarity has not served to lessen its value.

MANPOWER PLANNING: IMPROVING PERFORMANCE BEFORE THE FACT

Many of the pitfalls and problems encountered as a result of inferior performance can be mitigated by careful manpower planning. An ounce of prevention here *does* provide the proverbial pound of cure, and manpower planning

---

[1] Douglas McGregor, "The Human Side of Enterprise," *Management Review,* November 1957, p. 22, presents the latter view.

[2] *Self Renewal* (New York: Harper & Row, Publishers, 1964), p. 57.

[3] *Free Man and the Corporation: McKinsey Lectures,* Columbia University, Graduate School of Business (New York: McGraw-Hill, Inc., 1959), p. 44.

designed to place future goals in harmony with the actions needed to achieve them is one of the best time-tested ways to improve organizational performance over the long pull. Long-run efforts must be related to short-term endeavors on a master priority list, and the manpower requirements of each subplan should be drawn in concrete form. This calls for a determination of the number, type, and quality of people needed to perform specific duties at particular points in time. The final form of such specific requirements might appear as a table of manpower needs projected over periods ranging from one to twenty years. Clerical, technical, white-collar, blue-collar, and managerial skills need to be laid out in terms of when and where they are needed. Actual and available resources should then be plotted against future requirements to indicate areas where shortages are most acute and where the greatest efforts should be concentrated.

Once the total organization's manpower requirements are determined, sources of supply must be considered. Two basic sources of manpower are available: internal and external. Internal sources of manpower must first be recognized; then, assuming that the present employees' preparation is adequate, they can move into new positions when the proper time arises. If added skill is needed, the chosen employees can move into their new duties after the completion of a specified training program. When external sources of manpower are tapped, personnel can be recruited from other organizations, from among the unemployed, or from the new faces entering the labor market each year.

THE HIRING SEQUENCE

Whenever an organization seeks to fill its manpower needs from external sources, it usually follows some variation of a standard hiring sequence. Though the degree of formality would be somewhat dependent upon structural factors such as organization size, almost every hiring sequence covers six steps:

Requisition

Recruiting

Selection

Hiring

Placement

Follow-up

Requisition is the process whereby manpower needs are identified and specified. Detailed manpower quotas may be generated from long-range or short-range manpower plans, current budgetary allocations, growth patterns, shifts in goals or objectives, changes in technology, or any number of initiating circumstances. Requisition is only the first step in the hiring sequence, but it helps to clarify the directions and dimensions of the entire short-term staffing effort.

Recruiting locates and contacts the markets capable of providing the manpower potential suited to the organization's needs. Managerial positions are typically filled from white-collar and blue-collar ranks, competitors' work forces, colleges, military retirements and separations, and other sources such as the government. Sears Roebuck, for example, typically promotes from within, which means that recruiting efforts are subordinated to identifying promotable individuals already with Sears. But when new blood is sought on the outside, Sears goes to colleges and other traditional sources of supply. At the very top level, vacancies are often filled from outside company ranks, usually by employing the services of executive recruitment firms ("head-hunters"). Simon Knudsen went from General Motors to Ford's presidency via the outsider route, as did Harold S. Geneen in his move from Bell and Howell to International Telephone & Telegraph. Recruiting to fill middle management and lower-skilled jobs is carried out in high schools, trade schools, among the relatives and friends of employees, and also through newspaper advertisements, employment agencies, union sources, and numerous other means. Recruiting can be costly; one major electronics manufacturer estimates the cost of locating, hiring, and getting an engineer on site at $1700, but its success is tied directly to the future fortunes of the organization. In the words of billionaire J. Paul Getty:

> Business management is largely a matter of decision, and there are few decisions more critical than those involved in hiring or promoting executive personnel, for the men ultimately picked will themselves be required to make decisions that can quite literally make or break the company that employs them.[4]

Selection of potential employees may start with interviews, the preparation of an employment application blank, or both. Next, the credentials of prospective employees may be investigated through reference checks; reviews of elementary school, high school, or university grade records; inquiries to previous employers; or more extensive procedures. Certain tests of skill, dexterity, aptitudes, personality, and intelligence may be an integral part of the selection process.[5] The importance attached to the results of such tests varies, but almost every organization using a testing procedure has some minimum cutoff score below which applicants are rejected. Certain divisions in IBM and Proctor & Gamble routinely subject prospective management candidates to batteries of tests whose results are weighed by recruiters. If tests are used and results are favorable, or if first impressions call for further discussion, the prospective candidate may be asked to fill out a detailed personal history and sit through a final interview or interviews. Though most personal history forms run to three or four pages of what-have-you-done data, some probe deeply into the

---

[4] "How to Pick the Right Man," *Playboy,* April 1968, p. 121.

[5] In lower-skilled occupations, formal evaluation programs can provide helpful data on the factors needed to perform particular jobs. For managerial positions, formal evaluation data are much less valuable, principally because the factors in such systems are usually imprecise.

candidate's personality. In Humble Oil, younger managers (but not prospective hirees) are asked to fill out a 292-question personal history form which attempts to identify patterns of behavior which Humble feels are needed in its top executive ranks.[6]

Up to this point, a personnel department or personnel executive may have been in control of the selection procedure, but at the time of the final interview, the personnel function takes a back seat. The final decision to hire or reject an applicant is normally made by the person who will serve as his immediate superior. Interviews usually are given great weight when managerial talent is being sought, but they are less critical in lower-level jobs, where physical skills are more vital, and tests can measure these skills fairly well. Performance tests leave little room for supervisors to reject prospective employees because of inability to do the job well. On the other hand, managerial skills are less tangible, and interviews are highly valued as a device to determine whether or not a man possesses managerial skills to any marked degree. Unfortunately for the supervisor, a nonobjective reason for rejecting an employment application may be viewed as evidence of an inadequacy on his part by personnel officials, a factor that he may weight too heavily in making his final selection. When personnel is a strong staff department, this situation is all too common; and supervisory interviews with job applicants may be perfunctory and ceremonial.

When and if a prospective job candidate completes his final interviews satisfactorily, he is required to take a physical examination. If he passes his physical exam, and if he clears any final hurdles such as the preliminary security checks required in defense industries, he reaches the end of the selection procedure. He is now worthy of the hire, and all that remains is the tricky job of turning courtship into marriage.

Hiring is the manpower-management version of offer and acceptance. Since starting rates for lower-level jobs in the blue-collar, clerical, and management categories are set by labor contracts and local market conditions, little wage bargaining takes place. In jobs where higher-level skills are required, the range of bargaining widens, but not to any appreciable degree. Rates set on such jobs are principally dependent upon the applicant's experience and the going rates paid for his occupation in the appropriate labor market. In cases where personnel are lured away from competitors, the range of bargaining is much more flexible and, thus, more sensitive to manipulation. What the traffic will bear is important here, and personal demands for special concessions often enter into final negotiations. When C. Lester Hogan left Motorola to become president of Fairchild-Hiller, he reportedly received a $30,000-increase in salary, an interest-free loan of $5.4 million to buy 90,000 shares of Fairchild-Hiller (expected to net him a profit of $1.8 million), and an additional 10,000 shares of stock with a paper profit of $700,000.[7] After an offer is made and accepted, however, the hiring procedure involves little more than the new

---

[6] Robert C. Albrook, "How to Spot Top Executives," *Fortune,* July 1968, p. 110.

[7] "The Fight that Fairchild Won," *Business Week,* October 5, 1968, p. 106.

employee's routine completion of a multitude of employment forms and records and his physical appearance at work.

Placement means matching man to job, both prior to and following hiring. Screening occurs before a person is hired, and those who actually come to work are assumed to possess at least the minimum qualifications or experience needed. In organizations where induction training is given, initial placement may involve a formal orientation program covering company policies, practices, procedures, and, perhaps, even product lines. Certain jobs require more extensive special training before the new man functions as a full-time employee.[8] Placement is not really over until the training period is completed and the individual is actually working full time. At this point, the job and the man arc matcd, and the requisition that started the hiring sequence finally is filled.

Follow-up is a post-hiring step that can be performed formally or informally. In less-structured circumstances, follow-up may be little more than a quick chat with a boss who inquires, "How are things going?" In more formal situations, the employee is interviewed after a stated length of time to determine how he feels about his placement. Follow-up is probably the least organized step in the hiring process. In many firms, it is omitted entirely, much to the detriment of the staffing process. Even a good apple can rot quickly if placed in the wrong barrel.

Programs attempting to meet the organization's manpower needs from external sources depend upon successful execution of the steps in the hiring sequence. The sequence suggested above tends toward the ideal: in practice, only giant industrial companies and large government agencies adopt such elaborate and formal procedures. Internal programs, on the other hand, count their degree of success or failure in terms of the vigor with which manager development is pursued. Really talented managers often develop with little formal training, but most men progress more rapidly and grow more quickly in organizations where planned development programs exist. The adoption of formal training programs to improve technical, analytical, conceptual, and perceptual abilities invariably improves the quality of skills available to meet the organization's manpower requirements.

Management training is closely related to manpower planning. This relationship takes the form of comparing the future needs of the organization with existing supplies of managerial manpower. The normal method used to obtain such information is the appraisal process, which provides for a systematic evaluation of actual against expected performance. "Counseling" is the term used for the method by which performance is discussed; this method usually takes the form of an interview between a subordinate and his immediate supervisor. One of the natural results of counseling interviews is the preparation of a personal development program designed to improve the

---

[8] Interestingly enough, new men placed in top-level management jobs are often given little or no special training. The top man frequently says, "This job will be what you make it— no more, no less." Such ambiguity is not always welcomed by the neophyte, but the "code of the newly promoted" forces him to remain silent.

subordinate's level of performance. The formal methods for attaining self-improvement goals go under the wide-ranging title "manpower development."

The various manpower plans prepared in the organization may start with a series of management audits. The typical management audit reviews how well personnel are performing their present jobs and measures the potential they may have for more responsible jobs. Management audits provide the information needed to prepare a table showing which men are available at a given time, how well they are performing existing jobs, and what management responsibilities they may eventually aspire to before reaching the limits of their potential. This table, commonly known as the replacement table, shows the organization's current strengths and weaknesses and indicates areas of surpluses and shortages of managerial talent. A sample replacement table for a personnel department appears in Figure 13.1.

The replacement table is a rather sensitive document, since it names names and places limits on the level of advancement that those persons can expect

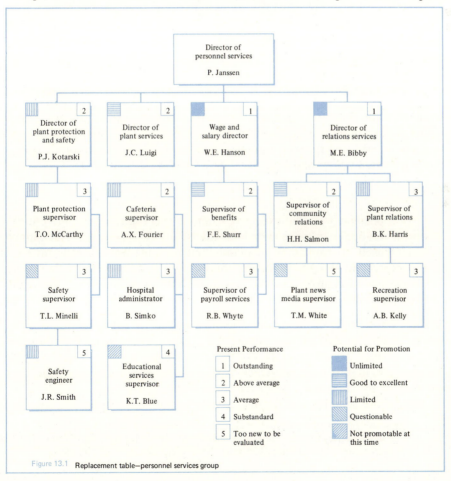

Figure 13.1   Replacement table—personnel services group

to achieve. It also shows who may have to be moved where to meet future manpower needs. It is obvious that widespread distribution of replacement tables might lower the morale of all but the most outstanding performers. Needless to say, they usually have limited circulation and highly restricted access.

A management audit shows the stock of managerial talent and potential on hand; a manpower plan lists total manpower needs. After a thorough personnel audit is made, the organization becomes aware of which jobs can be staffed with existing personnel and the kind of men it must recruit.

Manpower planning does not stop with the execution of hiring and placement or even with the preparation of replacement tables. It also attempts to develop broad guidelines to train, motivate, and develop people to meet the needs of dynamic organizations. It might seek, for example, to outline recommended actions in such traditional personnel management areas as wage and salary administration, merit rating, training methods, and performance evaluation. All of these items can affect the numbers of people needed and the types of skills that might be required or necessary to develop. Manpower planning can only set broad guidelines; execution must wait until individuals are actually on the job.

ON-THE-JOB APPROACHES TO IMPROVING PERFORMANCE

Traditional on-the-job approaches designed to improve individual and group performance emphasize the evaluation of present and potential performance and some structured form of training. To illustrate, a time study of an executive's job might show that he is wasting a great deal of time. He might not have a sense of purpose or the ability to put first things first. To quote Peter F. Drucker,

> In a peculiar way, the executive's time is everybody else's time but his own. Everybody can move in on him and usually everybody does. He cannot shut himself off from these demands, but he must use the little time he can control to do the important things. This is the secret of those few people who accomplish so much with so little apparent effort. They put first things first.[9]

Using a traditional evaluation and training approach, a typical remedy might be to have the executive take a course or read a book on how to improve his use of time. The training department or a senior executive might suggest, for example, that he use a self-teaching device such as a programmed-instruction course on "Effective Use of Executive Time."[10]

Much more complex and detailed are the performance, appraisal, counsel-

---

[9] "How the Effective Executive Does It," *Fortune,* February 1967, p. 140.

[10] For an elementary treatment in a programmed text, see Neeley Gardner, *Effective Use of Executive Time,* United States Industries, Educational Science Division, 1964.

ing, and training activities used by organizations to motivate and train their employees. These techniques deserve careful review because of their widespread use. Appraisal in particular needs elaboration because of the role it plays in recognizing potential abilities in both traditional and more behavior-oriented methods of obtaining improved performance.

METHODS OF APPRAISAL

There are several well-known methods of appraising managerial performance. The most commonly used are

Forced distribution

Forced choice

Subjective appraisal

Results appraisal

Critical incident review

Forced distribution is rating of performance based on percentage rankings. The rater *must* rate people in percentage classes such as deciles, quartiles, or upper and lower halves. Thus, a rater may place Mr. A in either the top or the lowest 10 percent, or he might place a person in the highest performance quarter or the second quarter. This system forces a distribution of percentages among a given group of people. Thus, if one man in ten is placed in the upper 10 percent, no other man can be given that ranking. The other nine men *must* be distributed among the nine remaining categories. This causes a real problem when several exceptional men appear in a single group. If a poor man in a low-rated group is ranked higher percentagewise than a good man in a good group, frustration or resentment usually arises. Even if cross-rankings are not generally available, the problems in trying to compare cross-group performances are still quite formidable.

Forced choice occurs when the choice of ratings in various performance categories are set up in advance of the individual's performance. Classifications might include "best to worst," "excellent to unsatisfactory," or even a choice of various phrases or sentences—"most like" or "least like" the individual's abilities, aptitudes, or output. The *A, B, C, D, F* system used to grade performance in school is a variant of forced-choice rating. This system tends to take free choice away from the appraiser by limiting him to specific choice classes, but it does assist the process of comparing performance across departmental lines.

Subjective appraisal may use varying techniques, but the general approach is the same: traits, behavior patterns, and performances are ranked or compared to obtain an index of achievement. Actually, forced choice or forced distribution may be used in conjunction with subjective rating, but the latter also can be quite unstructured. It may be carried out by having each rater write a paragraph or a few sentences summarizing the degree to which he has experienced or observed a criterion. Hazy comparability between ratings is a problem here, as is the choice of traits or items to rate. Subjective rating causes difficulties because it is subjective, and it tends to be overused in situations where other systems would be much more effective.

All *results appraisal* methods attempt to evaluate performance in terms of how well job duties are executed. Traits, characteristics, or other general behavior patterns are used only if they relate directly to performance. Appraisal methods here vary a great deal, but they all focus on the job and how effectively the individual does it. One popular method of results appraisal is to compare employee performance against measured standards of output. Ratings can then be expressed as a percentage of achievement related to standards, or some relative measure such as "less than" or "more than" standard performance.

The *critical incident* method is one variation of the results-appraisal method. A job is defined in detail, and each day the supervisor enters outstanding or unusual items—both favorable and unfavorable—in each individual's performance record. On some days, no entries are made; on others, more than one entry is recorded. At the end of a given time period, perhaps six months, the totals of "bad" and "good" entries are discussed with each individual. This system has been embraced enthusiastically by several organizations because it bases appraisals on reports of observed activities, not on subjective recollections. Government units in particular have adopted it rather widely.[11]

Whatever method is chosen, the appraisal process is usually performed by the subordinate's immediate boss. When group appraisal is used, the ratee's boss, his boss's boss, and an outsider may be on the rating committee. When appraisal systems have been used for some time, the third man may be a supervisor from another department. In newly installed systems, or when consistency of rating is not yet achieved, the outsider is most often a representative of the industrial relations department.

Appraisal processes are not all milk and honey by any stretch of the imagination. Used unwisely, they can be quite damaging to morale and individual confidence. Since they also tend to be somewhat subjective, they may measure either the wrong things or the right things poorly. In the absence of systematic appraisal, hit-or-miss guesswork takes over; and this compounds the difficulties in recognizing both good and bad performance. Because every organization must evaluate performance and potential, appraisal systems should be constructed to reflect the results desired within the context of a given set of environment conditions. Results appraisals seem to provide the most promising overall outcomes, but even here the exceptions are almost as numerous as the cases proving the rule.[12]

[11] J.C. Flanagan, "A New Approach to Evaluating Personnel," *Personnel,* July 1959, p. 35.

[12] For an extremely thorough and thoughtful review of the appraisal process see the classic work by John Reigel, *Executive Development* (Ann Arbor, Mich.: University of Michigan Bureau of Industrial Relations, 1952).

COUNSELING

Counseling is an interchange of opinions or ideas that typically takes the form of an interview or interviews between superior and subordinate. Counseling attempts to develop internal manpower resources by helping individuals to recognize personal strengths and weaknesses and by assisting them to develop the means to overcome areas of deficiency. One of the best approaches to counseling is to review past achievements and to suggest how future performance may be improved. Almost without exception, the best way to start this process is to review a man's appraisal form. Expert counselors strongly urge that this review be focused on facts, not generalizations, and that it explain why the standards used to arrive at the results listed on the form were or were not met. One means of studying counseling is to study the planning, conduct, and structure of appraisal and counseling interviews.

Counseling interviews may be conducted using directive or nondirective techniques. In directive interviews, the counselor points out strengths and weaknesses in performance and suggests methods by which improvement can be made. Such interviews are quick and to the point, but they can be too quick and too authoritarian. The basic difficulty is that the rater is always in control, and two-way communication is absent. This lack of participation often has a detrimental effect on the subordinate's acceptance of his boss's suggestions. With little or no feedback, neither party gets his complete message across to the other.

Nondirective interviews place major emphasis on the subordinate, not on the superior doing the interviewing. The expectation is that the subordinate will realize his own deficiencies and suggest methods to improve his performance. This technique requires skill, since the interviewer must draw the discussion into productive channels without seeming to do so. He cannot admonish, advise, censure, or argue with the interviewee, and he must be able to listen without falling prey to the temptation to take control of the session. The skills needed to listen to digressions without losing sight of the ultimate purpose of the counseling interview are quite rare: more people think they possess these skills than actually do.

If nondirective interviews are conducted successfully, the end product is a self-improvement plan constructed by the man himself. Such a plan brings with it the benefits of acceptance through participation and the release of a certain amount of psychological pressure. An emotional catharsis is a positive aspect of nondirective counseling if handled well; but, when and if emotional outpourings are blocked or misunderstood, ill will and strained relationships result. For these reasons, it is vitally important to plan interviews carefully.

A well-planned counseling interview usually starts with a review of individual performance appraisals. The counselor should review each appraisal form carefully to check its accuracy and to assure himself that its evaluations and conclusions are well grounded and carefully formulated. Objective facts should be separated from subjective judgments, and the counselor should be reasonably certain that the man is being judged on how well he has done the job, not on his personality or on some peripheral activity. Preplanning should also include a review of the man's past history and a determination of whether or not to discuss his performance ratings with another experienced counselor prior to the first interview. This type of consultation often suggests what factors to emphasize, how the man's ratings compare with those given to men on similar jobs, and how much the organization should be willing to commit to his future.

The main reasons for preplanning the counseling interview are to be certain that appraisal information is accurate and to decide what training might be beneficial to the man's development. The supervisor needs to determine what *he can do* to assist the man and what *he cannot do*. Since the supervisor may have only a limited ability to help his men enter specific training programs or may be strictly limited in the time he can allow them for training purposes, he should be realistic about his capability to deliver results. Unattainable goals should not be included in the counseling process simply to prove to higher authorities that the counselor is thinking big. If anything, he should be thinking small and making sure that less elaborate goals are met fairly.

One quick device to check results of individual interviews is the simple technique for plotting interviews shown in Figure 13.2. The diagram shows the start of the interview as a neutral point. Even if the subject is angry, frustrated, or cool, the interview starts with his opening attitude as a neutral "given." Then, as the interview progresses, the interviewer tries to move toward an objective, which initially may be an attempt to achieve an emotional cartharsis or a release of pent-up frustrations. An ideal interview would follow the dotted line shown in Figure 13.2. Plotting interviews in a detached fashion can serve the twin functions of helping the counselor to appraise his own deficiencies and strengths and to assess the relative degree of success in reaching the goals sought in the interview. This information is also helpful in planning future sessions.

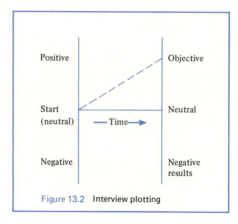

Figure 13.2   Interview plotting

TRAINING

Though generalized training programs cover a wide range of subject areas, training is largely an individual matter. What type of training to recommend depends upon the man, his needs, the skills of the trainer, and the costs and returns expected from various training alternatives. When training programs are already set up and working, they may be better than no training at all; an imperfect fit may yield results greater than the perfect programs that never get off the ground. Though time and cost considerations may cause their elimination, programs tailored to meet individual needs are eminently superior to blanket programs. Training is the final phase of most formal development programs, but manager training is emphasized here because of its critical importance to the organization.

A natural time to initiate manager training is immediately after the appraisal and counseling sequence. Training suggestions fit in quite naturally with the total scheme of evaluation, discussion, and follow-up of managerial performance ratings. Specific training plans can be developed by supervisors alone or can be drawn up with the help of appropriate staff specialists. The responsibility for training always lies with the supervisor, but staff specialists can advise him on costs and relative effectiveness of alternative training methods. Now even the Roman Catholic Archdiocese of New York has a personnel committee to assist in the transfer, assessment, and management of benefits for its priests and administrators.[13]

The need for specialized help in developing training programs is particularly pressing when the line manager is not able to keep up with the latest developments in training techniques and methods. Training staffs can assess the value of various methods and provide information on the costs, time duration, and degree of repetition needed to achieve given results. Training specialists can also estimate the potential value of training methods such as job rotation, job enlargement, problem-solving conferences, cadet or junior executive training, and coaching by the immediate superior. In addition, training staffs can estimate the potential returns to be derived from formal off-the-job programs such as university sponsored executive programs, lectures, film series, or information-sharing conferences.

The training department also can perform an auditing function for the nonexpert and can provide guidance on which teaching methods are best suited to meet particular needs. Experts in the training area can recommend whether case discussion; role playing; assigned reading in books, pamphlets, or company manuals; or sensitivity training should be used to achieve a given set of training objectives. Though final decisions must be made eventually by supervisors, the training department can provide the information needed to make each supervisor aware of the latest developments in training techniques and educational methods. Consulting firms such as Science Research Associates also can offer expert help in specialized areas.

---

[13] *The New York Times Magazine,* October 13, 1698.

The appraisal-counseling-training cycle in Figure 13.3 is basic in traditional personnel management approaches to obtaining improved performance. Both supervisory management and subordinates relate continually in the cycle; and the industrial relations staff, by providing expert assistance and guidance, helps the process to function smoothly. Some of the more modern approaches use scientific and mathematical methodology and utilize the findings of psychological, sociological, anthropological, and other social science research. One illustration of the use of a social science approach to personnel development is the sophisticated Careers Planning Program developed by IBM.[14]

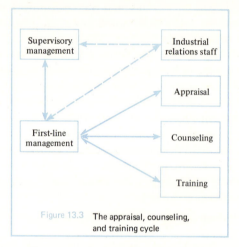

Figure 13.3   The appraisal, counseling, and training cycle

What sets the counseling-appraisal-training cycle off from more behaviorally oriented approaches is its reliance on measurement and on changes in interactions or personality characteristics. According to its critics, this is its fatal flaw; the pressure generated by measurements and controls undermines the system, which stops the system from reaching its stated objectives. Advocates, of course, deny that the pressures generated by the system wipe out its basic advantages.

LEADERSHIP STYLES

Inherent in all systems of improving performance are the problems of supervisor-subordinate relationships and the lively and continuing debate over which pattern of leadership is the "right one" in a given set of circumstances. Good leadership itself is a prime requisite of effective organizational performance, and particular leadership patterns can spur individuals and groups to higher and more rewarding levels of achievement. In this context, choice of a proper leadership pattern can be viewed as a legitimate means of improving individual or group performance.

Although alternative patterns of leadership range from authoritarian control

---

[14] Saul Gellerman, *The Management of Human Relations* (New York: Holt, Rinehart and Winston, Inc., 1966).

to completely group-centered decision making, the leader normally chooses a pattern which reflects a blending of currently popular theories of organization and the objectives of the parent organization. Usually, individuals have some discretion over their choice of leadership patterns, and they can and do press for approaches best suited to their own qualifications.

In the early days, authoritarian approaches to leadership dominated industrial organizations. The Carnegies and Fricks were succeeded by the Henry Fords, and the influence of such powerful personalities was pervasive. In the 1930s, and particularly during the labor shortages of World War II, participative management came to the forefront. More emphasis was given to human relations factors, and the authoritarian image faded. The postwar period saw the revival of more restrictive controls over costs and freedom of action. Greater emphasis was placed on profits and costs, and human factors received somewhat less weight, even though they were under more sophisticated observation than ever before. Recent years have seen the development of a mixed approach to leadership, but the primary emphasis—in spite of much criticism by both academic and business leaders—remains on economic performance rather than on the development of abilities, skills, and individual initiative. Leadership patterns still tend to be somewhat autocratic, although human values are receiving increasing attention, particularly in industries and occupations where highly skilled workers perform nonrepetitive duties requiring a substantial amount of initiative and creativity.[15]

ALTERNATIVE APPROACHES TO LEADERSHIP

If all possible leadership patterns could be placed along a continuum, authoritarian leadership would constitute one boundary, and a completely free-rein pattern of control would rest at the other extreme. Between these two limits various degrees of consultative supervision would hold sway. Faced with such alternatives, leaders have to decide which patterns are best suited to particular situations.

If the leader looks to research findings for an answer, he can find support for almost any approach he might care to choose. The findings derived from the classic human relations experiments at the Hawthorne plant of the Western Electric Company emphasize the importance of participation and social interaction patterns.[16] The indication of the findings is that consultative leadership yields the best results. Studies conducted for the armed forces indicate that the organizational structure and leadership climate, or the situation surrounding the choice, may exert important effects on behavior and morale. The choice here would evolve from an evaluation of formal and informal factors. Pushed to conclusions well beyond those postulated in the original experiments, these studies could be used to provide justification for the use of authoritarian techniques in given situations. Other studies offer a still greater range of

[15] For an excellent summary of differing views of leadership patterns, see Warren Bennis, "A Revisionist Theory of Leadership," *Harvard Business Review,* January–February 1961, p. 26.
[16] See Chapter 1.

support for particular leadership patterns. For example, research done in a large utility firm reported that the nature of the job itself was more important in determining job satisfaction (and by inference, output) than the type of leadership in use. If the results of this research were taken at face value, good leadership clearly would call for job enrichment activities on the part of supervisory management.

Since research studies on leadership offer limited guidance on which patterns are most effective in restricted sets of circumstances, generalizations are always dangerous. Certain general comments can be made, however, which express a consensus of findings rather than unanimous agreement.

Autocratic leadership patterns offer the advantages of clear-cut power relationships and rapid decision making. They can, in certain short-run situations, be the best or the only choices to adopt. When the brakes fail to hold and the hill is short and steep, the driver does not have time to consult the passengers about what to do. Given time, the riders might be able to pool ideas on how to avoid a malfunction, or they might devise a scheme that would soften the force of a crash; but, unfortunately, the luxury of extended discussion is out.

In general, autocratic leadership patterns cause long-run dependencies that stifle individual initiative and generate organizational friction.[17] A former Control Data executive, when accusing CDC President William Norris of running a one-man show stated, "People learn what he wants to hear and then they play it back to him."[18] When time is not a critical factor, autocratic control breeds friction between the leader and his men. Work completion depends on the leader, and output slackens when he is absent. Furthermore, weak men functioning under a strong leader are ill equipped to take over the burdens of leadership. When the leader passes from the scene, the resulting power vacuum is a source of continuing conflict and inefficiency. Perhaps the most damaging result of autocratic leadership is the negative effect it has on the development of subordinates. The leadership vacuum in the Ford Motor Company following Henry Ford, Sr.'s fall from power illustrates this situation at its worst.

Consultative supervisory patterns possess all the advantages gained by group deliberation—and also all the disadvantages. On the plus side of the ledger, consultative management helps a leader to gain acceptance of his objectives; it encourages the development of diverse viewpoints; it helps to obtain better coordination; and it creates a climate designed to develop better leaders. In the words of President Robert Hansberger of Boise Cascade, "People can contribute more if they're treated as individuals and permitted to work in a corporate environment which is relatively free of restrictions and policies or regulations."[19] On the minus side, consultative management is time-consum-

---

[17] An interesting dissent from this viewpoint is Robert McMurray, "The Case for Benevolent Autocracy," *Harvard Business Review,* January–February 1958, p. 82.

[18] Gregory Wierzynski, "Control Data's Newest Cliffhanger," *Fortune,* February 1968, p. 126.

[19] "Building a Case for Youth," *Business Week,* February 24, 1968, p. 150.

ing; it calls for great tact and patience on the part of the leader; and it can be costly in the short run.

When a group possesses decision authority, the time horizon of decision making is typically extended. There is also a tendency to develop decisions that smack of compromise. Individual needs to participate are realized, however, and other self-actualization needs are at least partially gratified. But again, all is not perfect. Though individuals may improve their skills while participating in group decision making, they can develop other less desirable traits. When decisions go wrong, there is a strong tendency to pass the buck. There is, in addition, a tendency to engage in overlong discussion of insignificant proposals that should require only brief discussion before they come up for a final decision. This is not so in the Ford Foundation, where acerbic head McGeorge Bundy commented on an overlong rejection of a proposal not in line with the foundation's programs, "Program, schmogram. What are the merits of the case?"[20]

In most forms of consultative management, decision authority is retained by the superior. Even in this situation, however, the group members must understand how and why decisions are made, or their relationship with the supervisor becomes somewhat tenuous. If the leader chooses to ignore the group's suggestions, he must either explain and justify his actions or risk a possible loss of support and confidence. If consultative leadership patterns encourage pseudoparticipation rather than real participation, they eventually degenerate into meetings resembling casual bull sessions.

If the leader of the group is weak or unskilled, unproductive discussion can be prolonged far beyond the point of diminishing returns. When supervision is poor or if the group functions without a definite superior, quarrels can develop over who should take the reins. The ensuing power struggles can diminish the effectiveness of the group and, eventually, undermine the goals of the parent organization. Free-rein techniques thus have some serious disadvantages. They flourish best in environments where freedom of action is expected, demanded, or made necessary by pressures upon the organization and its members.

CHOOSING A LEADERSHIP PATTERN

The choice among alternative patterns depends upon three sets of factors. The first set deals with the leader himself; the second, with his subordinates; and the third, with the situation or environment surrounding the decision.[21]

The leader should try to choose leadership patterns that reinforce and reflect his own attitudes and aptitudes. Some bosses are extremely uncomfortable in an authoritarian setting, but others flourish in it. One who believes in man's democratic right to shape his own destiny might flounder in the midst of

---

[20] Irwin Ross, "McGeorge Bundy and the New Foundation Style," *Fortune,* April 1968, p. 104.

[21] The structure of this analysis is taken from the article, "How to Choose a Leadership Pattern," by Robert Tannenbaum and Warren H. Schmidt as reported in *Harvard Business Review,* March–April 1958, p. 95.

an autocratic system. Similarly, the stereotyped authoritarian ex-general might find his effectiveness reduced if he were suddenly asked to supervise a group of scientists doing pure research in a government laboratory. In both cases, the leaders' personal inclinations would undoubtedly clash with the beliefs, ideas, and expectations of their subordinates. Thus, the eventual choice of a leadership pattern is seen to be influenced by the leader's own preferences, by the way his subordinates see themselves, and by the manner in which the leader sees and evaluates them.

One other vital factor influencing the leader is his perception of his position in the organization. If he feels secure, his choice may differ from one he would make in a less sure circumstance. Moreover, he may make another selection if he harbors a great deal of personal insecurity. A scientist would probably be somewhat autocratic in choosing research projects in his own area of specialization, but he might be more than willing to accept the advice of his secretary on what to give his wife or mother for a birthday present.

The second set of forces influencing the choice of a leadership pattern relates to subordinates. To understand the reaction of subordinates to various leadership patterns, one must understand their training and their personal levels of expectation. Some decisions can be made only by people who possess special skills, knowledge, training, or competence. Thus, even though a large number of people may want to participate in certain decisions, they may not have the qualifications to do the job well. A clerk at company headquarters might well feel that she should be consulted on where to locate a new factory, but she would have to be disqualified on technical grounds. In a situation closer to reality, a draftsman may claim he can design new parts more effectively than a graduate engineer, but unless he has training in mathematics, metallurgy, fluid mechanics, or thermodynamics, he may quickly reach the limit of his capabilities. Desire to participate is not sufficient to be the dominant force in dictating what pattern a leader should adopt, but desire *is* important in particular situations.

Subordinates who expect to participate in decisions may be rudely disappointed and downright uncooperative if their expectations are thwarted. Certain people thrive on involvement, and they desperately want to have their opinions heard. They willingly share the burdens of added work and added responsibility in order to identify themselves with particular ideas and decisions. They want to make decisions, are willing to tolerate ambiguous directives, and are eager to exercise initiative and to carry out independent actions. Such people demand participative leadership. They react violently to authoritarian control, and they seldom last long in autocratic environments. On the other hand, certain individuals and groups do not want authority, cannot tolerate ambiguity, and are willing to keep things just the way they are. The status quo is the standard for such people, and rocking the boat is frowned on and usually opposed.

The great majority of subordinates populates the area within the boundaries set by these aggressive and lethargic groups. Most subordinates want to be consulted on some matters, but not on others. They expect to contribute their ideas in specified areas of specialization, but they do not feel frustrated if they are not invited to participate in decisions in unrelated areas. Each supervisor must look at his own group closely and try to determine how it thinks, what it expects, what knowledge it possesses, and what matters it believes to be within the framework of his personal inclinations; he must then choose a leadership pattern that balances these findings with the factors in the external environment.

The forces active in the organization's operating environment are the last set of factors influencing the supervisor's choice of a leadership pattern. These factors are partly shaped by the goals, objectives, and policies of the organization and partly by structural variables such as organizational size, states of technology, direct and indirect cost structures, and competitive markets for products and services. Past experience and traditions also influence expectations of reasonable performance, as does the critical factor of timing. Though it may be generally desirable to allow leadership to develop through participative means, time pressures may call for much faster action. In such a case, external pressures may exert the greatest effect on the process of choosing a leadership pattern.

The final choice of a pattern of leadership is based on an analysis of the leader, his subordinates, and the situation existing at the time the pattern is chosen.[22] If he subscribes to a concept such as Douglas McGregor's Theory X, the leader may choose an authoritarian pattern; but if he thinks in terms of McGregor's Theory Y, which sees man as capable of self-motivation, he may decide to utilize a consultative or participative form of leadership.[23] These choices might be reversed or revised if the leader were more comfortable in either an autocratic or a consultative pattern, or if the situation develops pressures that dictate a particular choice. Though the weightings of the variables may change in time or in each new choice situation, the three sets of factors described above are valid guides to the selection of the leadership pattern most likely to yield particular, or desirable, returns.

Studies of leadership still leave many vital areas unexplored or explored incompletely. Leadership takes place in a dynamic environment, and the volatile nature of the pertinent structural and personality variables leaves some of the following questions unanswered:

1. What patterns should be adopted in specific circumstances?

2. When should an approach be changed to insure optimum motivation?

3. Should subordinates be shifted to strengthen weak leaders?

4. Should good leaders be used in various roles, or will shifting them around hinder their effectiveness?

---

[22] John M. Pfiffner and Frank P. Sherwood, *Administrative Organization* (Englewood Cliffs, N.J.: Prentice-Hall, Inc., 1960) would add the importance of differences in organizations and their structures to this list.

[23] Douglas McGregor, *The Human Side of Enterprise* (New York: McGraw-Hill, Inc., 1960).

5. If a man becomes ineffective simply because he is moved from job to job, is he really a good leader?

Until researchers devise meaningful answers to these questions, the concept of leadership will remain full of paradox and subjective judgment.

A final note on leadership should include the comment that leadership, though important, is only one of the many variables that contribute to the success of an organization. Even a good leader can fail if the other ingredients necessary for success are missing. Leadership is, however, a vital part of the mix of people and things that make the going organization go. Though certain writers dispute the importance of leadership in our society,[24] the great weight of research supports the argument that leaders and leadership patterns do exert an influence on both productivity and levels of individual and group performance.

Summary

Improving the performance of individuals and groups is a complex task. Preliminary manpower planning occurs in one part of the cycle, and on-the-job training follows the execution phase. One widely used approach tries to bring about improvements in behavior through additional training and better basic personnel policies. A second approach attempts to reduce conflict and eliminate friction in interaction patterns; while a third approach attempts to improve performance by bringing about changes or adaptations in basic personality variables. In all of these techniques the impact of leadership seems to be great; and studies of leadership patterns and variables are important ingredients in any attempt to improve individual or group performance.

These techniques will never bring a man to the point where "nothing matters to him but the job—not the clock, not your personal life, nothing," a description applied to Mr. Harold Geneen, the head of the giant IT&T combine,[25] but perhaps this is not a too desirable goal in any case. All of the techniques, however, do help individuals and groups to make more meaningful contributions to both individual and organizational goal attainment. When mobilized, the efforts of people can be formidable and productive. In the words of former Cadillac General Manager Harold Warner, "This continuity of people is its most important asset—the one real competititve advantage—that Cadillac has."[26]

Study Questions

1. Trace the hiring sequence from the awareness of need to its end point. What are the major problems encountered in the sequence?

---

[24] See E. Jennings, *An Anatomy of Leadership* (New York: Harper & Row, Publishers, 1960)

[25] "One Man's Billion Dollar Company," *Business Week,* May 4, 1963, p. 80.

[26] "A Cadillac is a Cadillac is a Cadillac," *Fortune,* April 1968, p. 161.

2. Should job specifications be drawn to fit the job or the man? Should a man be changed to fit a job? How about the reverse?

3. How does "manager development" differ from "management training," if at all?

4. Counseling interviews have been criticized as watered-down psychiatric interviews. Do you agree? What is the basis for your answer?

5. How should a counseling interview be planned? What does interview plotting show? What are the elements of a sound interview procedure?

6. Can a man learn by going to classes or must he learn by doing? Expand and qualify your answer.

7. What can be done to improve appraisal? Counseling? Develop your answer into a set of guidelines.

8. Draw a leadership continuum. How would you distinguish between the various kinds of leadership patterns? Give an example of consultative leadership and one showing a free-rein pattern.

9. What factors should influence the choice of a leadership pattern?

10. Leadership patterns today are a blending of consultative and authoritarian techniques. What patterns do you expect to be prevalent in the future? Why?

Revitalization begins where so many important managerial activities begin: with a review of the organization's goals and objectives. Renewal attempts almost always follow a review showing that the organization's current goals are not being met fully or that futuristic goals are short of total fulfillment. For example, the economic picture may be good in the short run, but long-term social goals may not appear to be fairly met. When actual and desired results are not in accord, revitalization can proceed in many directions. It may include a thorough appraisal of the existing goal structure or go beyond the existing goal hierarchy to include Barnard's elements of organization, communication, and common purpose.[1] It may even review the organization's basic philosophies of leadership, understanding, and structure, which Worthy describes as being the keys to effective management and good morale.[2] In most cases, revitalization calls for a thorough review of all current activities, how well they are being performed, what could have been done more effectively, and what may be expected in the future. In effect, all of the possibilities determined during the recognition of problems and opportunities and the evaluation of performance are analyzed, and all existing and potential resources are considered in the light of long-range goals, operating policies, and observed results.

In the revitalization process, some areas are more critical than others. Organization structures, for example, are particularly important, since they provide the framework which relates day-to-day operations to the organization's goals. Following the 1968 restructuring and reshaping of Cutler-

CHAPTER 14
Revitalization of Organizational Resources

[1] Chester I. Barnard, *Functions of the Executive,* Cambridge, Mass.: Harvard University Press, 1938.
[2] James C. Worthy, "Organization Structure and Employee Morale," *American Sociological Review,* vol. 15, no. 2 (April 1950).

Hammer, Inc., President Edmund Fitzgerald underscored this point: "We had good people, but the method we had used to organize them didn't bring it out."[3] Reviews of organizational structures and functioning also brought about significant changes in Standard Oil and the American Can Company. Production policies and facilities are also critical areas. A review of the existing state of the arts in scheduling, automation, data control, machinery, methods, and so on often brings about the kind of changes that recently caused an updating of Scripto's production operations and modernization of Olivetti-Underwood's facilities in Hartford, Connecticut. Information flows for decision making also require careful analysis including the amount and type of information needed at various points, the means of its distribution, and whether electronic data-processing equipment should be used to speed information flows. After such studies, RCA and Western Electric made significant changes in a number of operating procedures. Western Electric in particular has been influenced by information technology, with its Kansas City plant being one of the most up-to-date examples of a factory run by computerized information processes and controls.

Development of innovation is also critical in terms of marketing old products and developing new ones. In new product development, research and acquisition activities receive equal billing along with discovering new uses for old products, new marketing techniques, and, in some cases, the need to undertake product-pruning activities. Douglas Aircraft, IBM, Litton Industries, and the SCM Corporation—after conducting extensive reviews of their product lines— have all made substantial moves toward revitalization.

Profit planning is still another area that deserves careful attention. Profit planning can be considered on the organizational level, on the divisional level, or even on the basis of individual products or product lines. General Motors and General Foods have, for example, organized on several of these bases.

Utilization of human resources is another area that is somewhat intangible, but extremely vital. The commitment of people and their ideas is important in any revitalization effort. This fact has been recognized by many corporations, notably the TRW Corporation, Eastman Kodak, and Standard Oil of New Jersey.

All of these points appear in most revitalization efforts, but they receive different emphasis. The basic point is that continual renewal is needed for survival and growth. To quote Gardner in his *Self Renewal,* "Exploration of the full range of his own potentialities is not something that the self-renewing man leaves to the chances of life. It is something that he pursues systematically or at least avidly to the end of his days."[4] This basic truth also applies to self-renewal in organizations.

---

[3] "Can a New Broom Sweep too Clean?" *Business Week,* October 5, 1968, p. 78

[4] John W. Gardner, *Self Renewal* (New York: Harper & Row, Publishers, 1965).

ACHIEVING SUPERIOR PERFORMANCE IN ORGANIZATIONS: SELECTED APPROACHES.

Some approaches to achieving superior performance in organizations emphasize economic and financial matters, while others stress the importance of restructuring the content and scope of informational flows or changing formal organization structures. Another set of methods underscores the importance of individuals in the revitalization process and bases its solutions in effecting improvements in morale and individual behavior. Still other techniques utilize a blending of some or all of the above, but emphasize the importance of some particular economic or human factor.

No one approach to organizational regeneration has been universally successful, and management experts insist that any program must be individually tailored to the particular situation. When Xerox decided to move into a new era, it chose merger with the giant CIT Financial Corporation as its most desirable alternative. Westinghouse decided to tighten its internal controls and strive for greater profits. The Baltimore Gas and Electric Company entered into a massive reorganization and management training program. And the Defense Department under Secretary MacNamara changed its entire approach to goal setting, decision making, and control. Obviously, no one method fits all organizations, but some methods do appear to be more operationally successful than others. Some of the more promising of these methods are included below. Their selection rests in both their success in use and their ability to illustrate how economic, financial, and human relations factors interact in the revitalization process.

PLANNING FOR PROFIT

Basic goals in planning-for-profit approaches place heavy emphasis on the need to increase or maintain high profits and to utilize resources more profitably. These goals are not particularly different from those embraced by most businesses, but they are set out clearly so that specific results can be met by proceeding in a logical, orderly way.[5] A typical planning-for-profit approach would include the following:

1. Integrating future plans with present resources and developing plans designed to fill in gaps between desired and actual results. Such plans would have specific profit targets at several different levels in the organizational structure.

2. Fixing the responsibilities of key people and defining performance expected in key operating areas in terms of both financial and other criteria, but with the former receiving the greatest weight.

---

[5] Planning for profit is sometimes called MPC or IPC for Management Planning and Control or Integrated Planning and Control.

3. Setting up action programs and reporting systems to detect and correct for variances from plans or planned activities.

The exponents of planning for profit hail it as a "modern" approach, while in fact it is little more than an old technique executed in much more thorough and logical fashion.[6] It is difficult to believe that Ernest Weir of National Steel was not profit-centered or futuristically oriented when he planned the building of Weirton, West Virginia. Weir was reported to have walked through a wheat field, seen the city in his mind's eye, and then proceeded to plan the factory and community to make his dreams come true.[7] Thoroughness, not novelty, is the prime characteristic of the planning-for-profit approach, and the critical ingredient in the mix is the relationship of activities and achievements to profits.

The specific steps in a planning-for-profit approach can be summarized as:

1. Review the objectives and goals of top management.

2. Evaluate existing resources and match these with organizational goals.

3. Consider available opportunities in both current and potential markets.

4. Develop action plans from the matching process in steps 1, 2, and 3.

5. Prepare general budgets with detailed cost, volume, and profit figures for each major operation for stated time periods.

6. Develop a system of controls and a means of correcting variances using regular rather than periodic checks.

7. Establish areas of coordination and communication, including decisions on whom should be given results, the timing of reporting, and how coordination can best be obtained.

8. Determine where additional plans and resources are needed to bridge the gap between desired and actual results and take appropriate action.

9. Implement and execute the various steps in the planned approach, including revision in the total procedure, if called for.

The advantages of this step-by-step approach is that it builds profit and cost consciousness and makes people aware of the importance of profits. In a sense, emphasizing the concept of profitability is a logical extension of the planning process. This approach helps managers to become more effective by showing how their performance stacks up against determined profitability standards at particular points in time or at particular stages of development; and it also helps them to avoid pitfalls that might occur without careful preplanning. The futuristic orientation of planning-for-profit techniques also tends to force the organization to review its goals and to chart its path with

---

[6] John O. Tomb, "A New Way to Manage: Integrated Planning and Control," *California Management Review,* vol. 5, no. 1 (Fall 1962).

[7] Ernest Dale, *The Great Organizers* (New York: McGraw-Hill, Inc., 1960), ch. on "Ernest T. Weir, "iconoclast of management.""

extreme care. The National Cash Register Company and other leading business organizations claim that its adoption has brought about significant gains in effectiveness and profitability.[8]

The area of product planning and development provides a number of illustrations of how one particular facet of planning for profit can be executed within a business organization. In this phase of the total planning-for-profit picture, an analysis of product lines might be framed in terms of these questions:

1. What are the objectives of new product activities?

2. How similar are new products to existing ones?

3. Is planning set up from the factory to the consumer or the reverse?

4. Have all basic assumptions been tested?

5. How often are marketing plans reviewed and updated?

6. Have all the marketing differences of new and existing product lines been carefully considered?

7. Is the scheduling of product development set up on a reasonable basis?

8. Is new-product testing done routinely on a test-market basis?

9. Has the buildup of inventory time been considered carefully in the light of past experience and other factors?

10. Has sales volume and prebudgetary activity been compared with after-the-fact budget data?[9]

These ten questions might next be considered in terms of how market strategies relate to product line in a profit sense. If studies show that segmentation is potentially profitable, the Ford Motor Company might choose to bring out the Maverick to compete with Volkswagen and Renault in the U.S. market. Strategy considerations might then call for a detailed review of organizational resources in terms of plant finances, personnel, marketing advantages, special skills, and so forth.[10] All of these analyses would be studied to determine what product lines and policies should be integrated into the total planning-for-profit program. When similar activities are completed for each area of the organization's activities the total planning-for-profit plan can then be finalized. Cutler-Hammer did this in reorganizing its electrical divisions.

Though the detailed steps in planning for profit seem relatively easy, they are often difficult to implement in practical situations. The planning process is costly, and the successful integration of the various parts is difficult. Furthermore, actual results do not always match those in the plan. Variations can occur because of poor control, inadequate selling, difficulties in the market,

---

[8] See R.S. Lange, "MPC: Key to Profit Growth." *Financial Executive*, February 1963.

[9] These questions are based on an article by Robert D. Crisp, "Product Planning for Future Profit," *Dunn's Review in Modern Industry*, March 1958, p. 34.

[10] Charles Klein, "The Strategy of Product Line Policy," *Harvard Business Review*, July-August 1955, p. 91.

human opposition in the organization, or technical flaws in the planning process. American Motors, in spite of clear planning-for-profit goals, foundered in the mid-1960s because of competitive and market factors.

In spite of such difficulties, purposeful profit planning still has much to recommend it. Even though optimum results may not be achieved, planning for profit provides a better means for reaching goals than haphazard management by crisis or drift. Perhaps the biggest difficulty encountered in planning for profit lies in the hands of financial men who develop techniques that build up pressures on the individuals connected with the plan. The result is often conflict between human pressures and financial controls. The most obvious advantage is that planning for profit provides concrete standards and goals based on a careful step-by-step review of problems, opportunities, and methods of implementation. Often attacked by social scientists as being too hard-nosed in its attitude toward people, planning for profit remains in wide use because of its ability to deliver results (profits) in a wide variety of applications.

MANAGEMENT BY OBJECTIVES

One approach which seeks to lessen personal objections to tight controls without losing an integrated planning methodology is "management by objectives." Management-by-objectives methods seek to specify profit and performance goals in advance, but they rely more heavily on the participation process than most planning-for-profit approaches. Objectives are set in joint discussion between supervisors and subordinates at each level in the organization, with only rather general standards set by top management or members of the financial staff. Peter Drucker, an advocate of this approach, indicates that one of its strong points is the setting of objectives by discussion between subordinates and their immediate superiors.[11] Drucker suggests that organizational objectives and economic efficiency objectives be integrated with individual needs and desires and that participation and communication provide the means to such integration. Dean George S. Odiorne also champions the management-by-objectives approach and emphasizes a strong personal goal orientation as a key factor in successful programs.[12]

One of the more detailed plans of action describing management by objectives is outlined by consultant Edward Schleh, who says management by objectives must be framed in terms of the individual's desires, reactions, and other personal variables.[13] According to Schleh, an objective should

1.   Be set in the light of all known conditions

---

[11] Peter F. Drucker, *The Practice of Management* (New York: Harper & Row, Publishers, 1954).

[12] *How Managers Make Things Happen* (Englewood Cliffs, N.J.: Prentice-Hall, Inc., 1961).

[13] This paragraph is based on E.C. Schleh, *Management by Results* (New York: McGraw-Hill, Inc., 1961).

2. Indicate both basic and outstanding performance objectives for each individual

3. Be developed in light of a man's experience, especially for newer men

4. Be set in sequence, with line objectives established first and staff objectives following

5. Be blended with other's objectives

6. Be fair in the individual's eyes

7. Be prepared in joint discussion with the individual so that he agrees that objectives are sound

8. Be believed in by the superior who participated in the objective-setting procedure

9. Be set so the minimum is required in all basic areas

In Schleh's method, getting the program into action should be a somewhat exploratory procedure, starting with rough standards and then gradually establishing more meaningful objectives as the program progresses through its first years of operation.

In practice, establishing individual goals is usually accomplished in a series of negotiations which, if they do generate meaningful objectives, are tough face-to-face confrontations. Objectives dictated by supervisors are seldom embraced wholeheartedly by subordinates, and objectives set too high or too low by the subordinate may be incompatible with an individual's ability or too distant from organizational realities dictated by company policies, competition, and/or forces in the external environment. Odiorne recognizes flaws in goal-setting procedures, but believes that management by objectives can succeed if supervisors are trained to work with subordinates to establish goals reflecting what the subordinate *can* do within the organizational limits placed upon him and his superior. In Odiorne's view, the errors most commonly encountered in goal setting are committed by supervisors, and he holds that the success of the system depends on supervisory training in management-by-objectives philosophies and the effective conduct of goal-setting sessions.[14]

Management by objectives has a sound economic orientation, but it also considers the human equation by establishing individual goals through a process of joint determination. Theoretically, this develops commitment and allows a reward and feedback system to be tied into the determination of objectives. In theory, at least, management by objectives seems to fit human needs better than more economically oriented methods.

On the negative side, critics of management by objectives say it is too pressure-oriented, that objectives are set only for one year and thus fail

---

[14] George S. Odiorne, "Twenty Common Errors in Goal Setting," a handout for Management of Management Seminars, University of Michigan, Ann Arbor, Mich., April 1966.

to give it a long-run orientation. Further, they hold, because it is geared to the individual, it may prevent cooperation between individuals and tend to subvert teamwork and block innovations calling for cooperative effort. In short, management by objectives has a limited-time horizon in a divisive context which tends to prevent the unlocking of full human potential. Therefore, it is felt to be relatively ineffective by management experts who emphasize a much more human relations–oriented approach to revitalization. On the other hand, many operating managers accept management by objectives as an article of faith, seeing it as one of the few really practical ways to achieve improved performance.

THE NEW PATTERNS OF RENSIS LIKERT

One critic of planning for profit and management by objectives is Rensis Likert, a social scientist whose "new patterns of management" are designed to guide organizations of the future.[15] Likert emphasizes that human resources are a vital and necessary ingredient in good, profitable management and holds that human relations factors and leadership styles are central, not peripheral, components of economic operation. Disavowing the viewpoint that human relations is simply do-goodism, he bases his ideas on the proposition that profits depend upon the establishment and maintenance of sound human relations policies. Research conducted by Likert's Survey Research Center at the University of Michigan indicates that productivity increases and costs decline when supervisors are personnel-oriented rather than production-oriented. The best supervisors thus achieve both high levels of output and lowered costs, while still developing the human potential of their subordinates by using "person-centered" leadership styles. Likert stresses sustained productivity over time. He believes that management-by-objectives and planning-for-profit approaches are pressure-oriented to bring about production in spurts rather than sustained productivity. He claims that production can rise in the short run with or without good morale; but, for the long pull, he contends that pressure must be reduced, or sustained levels of productivity will not be maintained.

Likert also indicates that a responsible attitude toward work is important and should be emphasized by supervisors. The poorest supervisors, he claims, cause production "pegging" and he holds that supervisors must, by their actions, show that management attitude toward workers is indeed one of encouragement and support.[16] In Likert's approach, workers would be given greater participation in the setting of realistic standards of output and a somewhat freer hand in making decisions involving their jobs and work environment. In his mind, American industry has followed an opposite approach. He sees most organizations in the United States as falling into one

---

[15] For a detailed presentation, see his *New Patterns of Management* (New York: McGraw-Hill, Inc., 1961).

[16] "Pegging" or restriction of production by workers is a common occurrence, particularly when output is measured against measured work standards.

of four supervisory patterns: System 1, an authoritarian style with little delegation; System 2, a paternalistic approach with little real delegation and minimum commitment on the part of subordinates; System 3, with a substantial amount of delegation and confidence, but failure to fully utilize the subordinates' potential; and System 4, a truly participative form of management involving genuine delegation and full confidence in subordinates, an attitude which brings full commitment and capacity use of human resources.[17] In Likert's opinion, industry tends to lean most heavily on System 1 and System 2, which bring low commitment, low group loyalty, undesirable conflict and pressure, and low motivation. These variables in turn generate lower profits, higher costs, and less total effectiveness. System 4 management, though identified by most managers as the system in which they themselves perform best, is not put into effect except in unusual circumstances, even though it brings loyalty, motivation, cooperation, reduction in unconstructive conflict, and resultant increases in profits and output.[18] Likert's approach is thus geared to group participation and loose control over operations, two ideas that he espouses as the keys to successful management in tomorrow's idea-oriented technology.

One specific piece of research supporting Likert's ideas involved a study of the leadership and supervisory patterns used in both high-production and low-production groups in a major insurance company. In this study, the following conclusions were obtained:

1. Less responsibility was felt in hierarchically controlled groups than in participative groups.

2. There was a better attitude toward higher levels of output in groups having participative decision making.

3. More interaction and good feeling existed between management levels in participative groups.

4. Better attitude toward supervision and their support appeared in participative groups.

5. A generally better attitude was found in participative groups.

6. Productivity was higher in groups with person-centered supervisors.

7. Nonparticipative groups had a reduction in productivity when people saw themselves as "cogs in a machine." Pressures only build up productivity in the short run; in the long run stresses tended to increase costs.

In an article showing how his system might be implemented, Likert states that the existing management structures and systems of measurement are ill suited to carry out a true performance appraisal. To correct this deficiency he suggests new standards to measure performance and indicates that trained social scientists need to develop and apply such systems within a given organi-

---

[17] Rensis Likert, *The Human Organization* (New York: McGraw-Hill, Inc., 1967).
[18] *Ibid.*

zational context. Some of the indexes of measure Likert proposes are the extent of loyalty to the organization and its goals; the extent of feeling that individual and company goals are in concert; the level of motivation individuals feel to cut costs, increase output, improve methods, and so on; the amount of teamwork existing between units; the degree to which people feel delegation is well done; the consideration given to ideas, and so on by supervision; the levels of skills of groups in the organization; and the effectiveness of organizational communications. Other measures are also proposed by Likert, who stresses that organizations need new and better methods to evaluate contributions and that social scientists are best fitted to perform this vital job. Such measures, Likert feels, are the only true ways to evaluate productivity over the long pull. Several major firms have begun exploratory research on the compilation and reporting of the conservation and development of human resources, or "Human Asset Accounting."

Likert's basic idea is to utilize human relations principles fully, even to subordinating short-run profits to achieve the full utilization of the human resources necessary for continued future operation at high levels of profitability.[19] In stressing the use of participative management, he seeks to allocate decision authority to subordinates and advocates the development of supervisory leadership styles designed to allow maximum freedom to members of work groups. Participation, not competition, is one of Likert's basic commandments; and his formulation of the world of work sees men and managers linked in search of common goals—goals understood *and* embraced by supervisors and subordinates at all levels in the organizational hierarchy. In Likert's outlook, these common goals are attainable through participative means; and progress is assessed by social scientists able to measure the organization's relative ability to utilize its human resources.

Likert's System 4 is not easy to describe briefly, but its essence lies in the ability of management to coordinate and communicate across and between levels in the structure. Likert visualizes a group-to-group supervisory pattern rather than a man-to-man approach. In his system, each supervisor serves as a link ("linking pin") between levels in the hierarchy and acts to make the goals of the group he leads one with the higher authority group of which he is a member. Groups, not individuals, are charged with meeting goals; and groups are interlocked with each other so that unity of objective is achieved throughout the organization. Individual supervisors are appraised on their management and development of human assets—not by the traditional measures of profits, costs, and quality—and they serve more to coordinate, inform, and lead than to direct and control. As in the traditional approaches of System 1 and System 2, the supervisor is the key man, but he serves more as a democratic leader than an autocratic director. The superior remains responsible for decisions in the System 4 approach, but his means of achieving results are very different and, in Likert's view, more effective in the long run.[20] Figure

---

[19] Rensis Likert, "Measuring Organizational Performance," *Harvard Business Review,* March–April, 1958, p. 41.

[20] Likert, *op. cit., The Human Organization,* p. 5.

14.1 shows how supervisors A, B, C, and D serve both as leaders and members of groups and shows the kind of structure Likert suggests to implement his ideas.

The shaded areas below show overlap between supervisory leadership and membership functions, arrows show Supervisors B, C, and D acting as "linking pins" between groups at various levels in the structural hierarchy. Similar "linking pin" relationships appear at the level directly below B, C, and D.

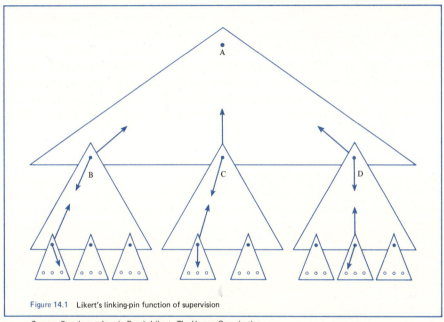

Figure 14.1   Likert's linking-pin function of supervision

Source: Based on a chart in Rensis Likert, *The Human Organization* (New York: McGraw-Hill, Inc., 1967), p. 50.

One of the basic difficulties in Likert's approach is that his theoretical formulations are not currently backed up by adequate methods of implementation. Developing greater degrees of cooperation between individuals and groups is a lofty and worthwhile objective, but how to do the job is much more difficult than simply stating that it must be done. What Likert says is interesting and has given him widespread publicity, but the means of achieving his goals are not always clear. In particular, his measures of contribution are not well defined, a fact that has caused skepticism in some circles and rejection in others. Until personal contributions to group goals are clarified, it seems likely that resistance will remain the handmaiden of imprecision. A similar lack of clarity exists when Likert's loose patterns of supervision are applied in industries having high levels of technology. In machine-controlled operations, for example, there is some question about the salutory effect of free-rein supervision on worker output. Indeed, there is reason to believe that just the opposite is true; that loose supervision brings about reductions in operating efficiency.

In high-labor or idea-oriented industries, however, Likert's ideas seem to have a great deal of applicability. Since idea-oriented industries are growing in size and importance, his approach may well be, as he claims, the wave of the future. Though a continuing underestimation of technological factors and capital investment considerations tends to undermine the force of Likert's arguments, his concept of new patterns of management has already influenced management practices in areas such as research and development. It seems likely that his ideas will have a growing impact in areas where technology is not a controlling factor in the achievement of high levels of output.

THE MANAGERIAL GRID APPROACH

The "managerial grid" approach developed by Blake and Mouton is much more comprehensive in scope and coverage than almost any other human relations approach to organization revitalization. According to Blake and Mouton, the use of the managerial grid yields the following results:

1. Contributes to increases in profitability
2. Gets better intragroup relations between plant and company head-quarters and management and unions
3. Promotes a fuller awareness of the importance of group relationships
4. Reduces interpersonal friction in the organization
5. Produces better effort, increases creativity and generates higher levels of satisfaction
6. Creates job security for the individual[21]

What sets this approach apart from others is that it offers a complete plan for organizational redevelopment. It is not a limited type of training device. The managerial grid approach not only states what objectives it hopes to achieve but also lays out a specific, detailed, step-by-step sequence for reaching these objectives. Blake and Mouton describe how to accomplish this end in the following excerpt:

HOW THE GRID PROGRAM SHOULD WORK

The Managerial Grid identifies five theories of managerial behavior, based on two key variables found in organizations. One variable reflects concern for production or output; the other variable, concern for people. In this instance the term "concern for" refers to the degree of concern, not the actual results. That is, it does *not* represent real production or the extent to which human relationship needs are actually met. It *does* indicate managerial concern for production and/or people and for how these influence each other.

---

[21] Robert R. Blake and Jane S. Mouton, *The Managerial Grid* (Houston, Tex.: The Gulf Publishing Company, 1964).

MANAGERIAL GRID

These two variables and some of their possible combinations are shown in Figure 14.2. The horizontal axis indicates concern for production, and the vertical axis indicates concern for people. Each is expressed on a scale ranging from 1, which represents minimal concern, to 9, which represents maximal concern.

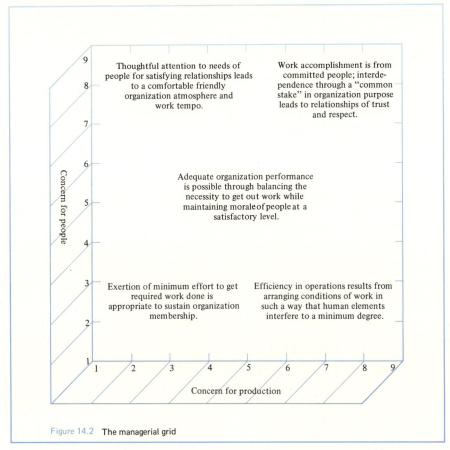

Figure 14.2   The managerial grid

Briefly, the lower left corner of the Grid diagram in Exhibit 1 shows a 1, 1 style. This represents minimal concern for production and minimal concern for people. The 1, 9 style in the upper left corner depicts maximal concern for people but minimal concern for production. The 9, 1 style in the lower right corner portrays maximal concern for production and minimal concern for human relationships. The 9, 9 style in the upper right-hand corner represents maximal concern for both human relationships and production. The 5, 5 style in the center of the diagram is "middle of the road" in both areas of concern.

Once managers have studied the classroom material accompanying the

Grid, it is possible for them to revise practices and procedures so as to work toward a 9, 9 organizational climate. These efforts use an educational program as the core, in contrast to more conventional ways of getting better organizational results (e.g., changing organizational structure, leadership replacement, tightened accounting controls, or simple pressuring for more output).

EDUCATIONAL STEPS

The educational steps are simple in concept, though complex in execution. They include the following:

An investigation by each man of his own managerial style, using certain Managerial Grid forms of analysis. These include self-evaluation instruments, self-administered learning quizzes, in-basket procedures, and organizational simulations.

A detailed and repeated evaluation of team effectiveness by groups which work with each other.

Diagnosis of major organization problem areas; e.g., long-range planning, profitability of operation, union-management relations, promotion policies, incentive awards, new-product development, absenteeism, utilities conservation, and safety.

We should emphasize that this entire approach to organization development is self-administered by management except for occasional consultation regarding major issues. As of now, the Managerial Grid approach has been used in both industry and government. Changes in the near future will be in degree rather than in basic approach.

SIX-PHASE PROGRAM

At the present time, we describe these organization development programs in terms of six overlapping phases. Taken sequentially, these phases can cover from three to five years, but they can also be compressed into a shorter period of time within a company.

MANAGER DEVELOPMENT

The six phases can be divided realistically into two major parts. The first two phases involve *management* development so that the other four phases can help managers work toward the 9, 9 goals of *organization* development. Here are two management development phases:

1. *Laboratory-Seminar Training.* This is a one-week conference designed to introduce the manager to Grid concepts and material. From 12 to 48 individuals are assigned as members of problem-solving teams during each Laboratory-Seminar. These Seminars are conducted by line managers who

already have been through the Seminar and thus know its material and schedules.

The Seminar begins with the study and review of one's own Managerial Grid style of behavior as outlined in a series of questionnaire booklets completed by each manager. It continues with 50 hours of intensive problem solving, evaluation of individual and team results, and critiques of team performance. The problems typically simulate organizational situations in which inter-personal behavior affects task performance. Each team regularly evaluates its own behavior and problem-solving capabilities. A team which performs poorly on one problem exercise is able to assess and adjust its problem-solving style in time for the next exercise. In addition, one exercise involves an attempted 9, 9 "feedback" from team members to each individual concerning *team* impressions of his managerial styles.

Though Grid Seminars are sometimes compared with "T-Group" or "Sensitivity" training, the two training experiences are quite different. The strongest similarity comes in the face-to-face feedback experience of Phase #1. Even here, however, the Managerial Grid Seminars take a more structured approach by focusing on managerial styles rather than on personal behavior characteristics which may or may not be related to management.

Phase #1 is not intended to produce immediate organization improvement. It serves more as the trigger which creates a readiness to really work on human problems of production. Participation in a Grid Seminar is set up so as to include a "diagonal slice" of the organization chart. No man is in the same group as his boss or immediate work colleagues. At the same time, this diagonal slice arrangement permits many organizational levels and departments to be represented in each session.

2. *Team Development.* This represents an on-the-job extension of Phase #1. The general 9, 9 concepts and personal learning of the Grid Seminars are transferred to the job situation after each work group or department decides on its own 9, 9 ground rules and relationships. Team development usually starts with the boss and his immediate subordinates exploring their managerial styles and operating practices as a work team. The ground rules of openness and candor which were established in Phase #1 can now become the daily operating style of Phase #2.[22]

Taken together, Phases #1 and #2 provide management development conditions which are designed to—

... enable managers to learn Managerial Grid concepts as an organizing framework for thinking about management practices;

... increase the self-examination of personal performance characteristics;

---

[22] See R.R. Blake, J.S. Mouton and M.G. Blansfield, "How Executive Team Training Can Help You and Your Organization," *Journal of the American Society of Training Directors* (now called *Training Directors Journal*), January 1962, p. 3.

... increase a manager's willingness to listen, to face and appreciate work-related conflict, to reduce and work out inter-personal frictions, and to reject compromise as a basis for organizational decision making;

... build improved relationships between groups, among colleagues at the same level, and between superiors and subordinates;

... make managers more critical of outworn practices and precedents while extending their problem-solving capacities in interdependent situations. Words like "involvement" and "commitment" become real in terms of day-to-day tasks.

ORGANIZATION DEVELOPMENT

The last four phases build on this management development and help managers work toward the more complex goals of organization development.

3. *Inter-group Development.* This involves group-to-group working relationships and focuses on building 9, 9 ground rules and norms beyond the single work group. Situations are established whereby operating tensions that happen to exist between groups are identified and explored by group members and/or their representatives.

The goal is to move from the appallingly common "win-lose" pattern to a joint problem-solving activity. This seems to be possible when competing groups work their problems through to resolution using inter-group procedures developed in behavioral science studies.

A second type of inter-group development helps to link managers who are at the same level but belong to different work units (e.g., foremen, district sales managers, department managers, and so forth). Their competitiveness may increase organizational productiveness, but it may also result in departmental goals being placed ahead of more important organizational goals. Here, the problem is again met using joint problem-solving efforts which confront inter-personal issues according to 9, 9 ground rules and norms.

4. *Organizational Goal Setting.* This involves issues of major importance to all managers. Organization development moves beyond team areas into problems that require commitment at all levels. Such broad problems include: cost control, union-management relations, safety, promotion policies, and over-all profit improvement. These problems are identified by special task groups which may again come from a "diagonal slice" of the organization chart. Departmental groups may also help to define goals and assign roles. The goals prove to be "practical" when managers who must implement them also establish responsibilities for implementation. Commitment gained from the goal-setting procedures of this phase also avoids those negative responses now grouped under "resistance to change."

5. *Goal Attainment.* This uses some of the same educational procedures

used in Phase #1, but here the issues are major organizational concerns and the stakes are real.

For example, when problem areas are defined by the special task groups, other teams are set up throughout the organization. These teams are given a written "task paragraph" which describes the problem and the goal. Team members are also given packets of information on the issue under discussion. This information is usually studied overnight, after which individual managers check themselves on a true-false test designed by the special task group. Once individuals have studied the information and the test, the teams begin discussion on the same items, checking their agreed-on answers against an answer key. This way, agreement is reached on the nature of the problem and its key dimensions. From this point on, the team members work toward a better statement of the problem and toward corrective steps. They also begin to assign responsibility for these corrective action steps.

Phase #5 also relies on a manager serving as a coordinator during Phases #4 and #5. His primary goal is to help achieve the goals set during Phase #4. His secondary aim is to help identify previously unrecognized problems. He should have neither line nor staff responsibility in the conventional sense, but should hold a position similar to an industrial medical officer. He would be a specialist in organization development and intervene at those times when proposed steps seem inconsistent with 9, 9 theory. He would seek action based on understanding and agreement, not because of any formal authority he holds. This approach, though more difficult than access through authority, reduces resistance. It also improves the quality of joint effort.

6. *Stabilization.* This final phase is designed to support the changes brought about in the earlier phases. These changes are assessed and reinforced so as to withstand pressures toward "slip back" and regression. This also gives management an opportunity to evaluate its gains and mistakes under the organization development program.[23] [End excerpt.]

The managerial grid approach has been tried with mixed degrees of success in a wide variety of organizations. Oil companies, insurance companies, food-processing firms, several firms in mass-production industries, and a number of government organizations have applied it in operational settings. Perhaps the basic difficulty encountered is that results concerning later steps in the sequence have not been widely disseminated, although some of the earlier steps in the grid approach seem to have been executed successfully. In particular, conflicts seem to have arisen when lower-level units in the hierarchy have attempted to extend their suggestions on policy changes to higher-level units.

One of the chief advantages of the managerial grid approach is its holistic nature: it brings a total-change concept into the organization. Others are that supervisors actually perform the training function and that changes are derived

---

[23] Robert R. Blake, Jane S. Mouton, Louis B. Barnes, and Larry E. Greiner, "Break-through in Organizational Development," *Harvard Business Review,* November–December 1964. © 1964 by the President and Fellows of Harvard College; all rights reserved.

from discussion and participation between employees at different levels in the organization structure and thus generate what Blake and Mouton feel is true commitment, not psuedocommitment.

Like Likert's linking-pin approach, the managerial grid concept bases its success on execution by and for the people who believe in group decision making and who are trained in it. Training and commitment are especially critical in the early steps of the method, for unless positive results show up then, skepticism tends to wash out attempts to apply the grid at higher levels in the structural pyramid. Since people trained in installing managerial grid principles are in short supply, it may be some time before the method's full potential is tested thoroughly. In its present form, the grid stands as one of the more promising contemporary methods for revitalizing organizational performance and for developing human resources.

CHANGES IN PERSONALITY

The final technique selected to illustrate methods for improving the utilization of human resources uses psychological or psychiatric means to bring about changes in personality. This approach attempts to obtain changes in individual or group behavior by modifying or altering basic personality characteristics. Two of the most widespread methods used in this approach are individual counseling interviews and sensitivity training.

Individual counseling interviews designed to change behavior by changing personality traits are analogous to sessions on a psychiatrist's couch. The interviewee is the patient and the interviewer is the analyst. Changes evolve during a series of nondirective interviews designed to follow a sequence of catharsis, analysis, and synthesis. In this series, the person first sees his defects and then acts to correct them. Though similar in format to job counseling these sessions differ in content, since their aim is to change personality traits. The prescription chosen to effect these changes may be as mild as a training course in human relations or as strong as a series of intensive probings of personality traits by a psychiatrist or psychologist.

The key problem here is the same as in any other approach; most of the interviews are conducted by amateurs, that is, people not trained in the techniques of psychology and psychiatry. The net result is that the sessions are often bungled, leaving the subject worse off than before. One other problem is that there is a real question of whether or not an organization has the right to change an individual's personality. Both of these matters have caused concern in organizations using individual counseling interviews, but the second point seems to be less troublesome than the first. Most organizations appear to be more concerned that counseling sessions are ineffective than troubled by the morality of probing into areas where they have no legitimate concern.

Sensitivity training differs from individual counseling methods in its means of execution, but it is not singularly different in intent. In the words of one observer, "The techniques and procedures of the T group [training group] resemble closely those that are used in group psychotherapy." Almost all trainers stress that there is also a difference, although they disagree on how closely sensitivity training must approach psychotherapy in order to be effective.[24]

The basic intent of sensitivity training is to impart greater awareness of the self and the impact of one's behavior on others. In the training sessions, the individual develops an awareness of his effect on others as well as a sensitivity to the impact of his personality traits. In most sessions, he also is given an opportunity to see how new patterns of activity influence and affect others. Sensitivity training develops a sense of self, a feeling for the way in which different behavior patterns are perceived by others (empathy), and an understanding of how different means of dealing with people can bring different results.

The characteristics of sensitivity lab sessions differ somewhat, but most utilize a somewhat unstructured situation wherein no one controls the group and titles and status are not evident. No agenda is set, and no particular goals are established and no prescriptive way of proceeding is laid out by the trainer; indeed, the instructor does not teach the participants—he simply moves them in certain directions. For example, when one person says another is doing something for a particular reason, the trainer might say, "Yes, he did something, but you cannot *infer why he did it,* since this is an assumption rather than factual knowledge." Here, the trainer separates fact from inference and tries to develop the important distinction between them.

In the typical training session, the participants have some initial difficulty deciding what to do.[25] Eventually someone asks where they are going and what they should be doing and shows some minor irritation that nothing is being done. After discussion flounders for a time, individuals begin to raise questions about why particular people set forth their views in particular ways. They may then state their feelings about why he did what he did, and what effect his actions or words had on them. The group continues to grope for some sort of orderly progression, and frustration usually sets in as various group members attempt to develop goals and directions, what should be done, and how to go about doing it. Some of this frustration and concern is directed toward the instructor and some is pointed toward other members of the group. Eventually, the group begins to analyze its own behavior and this brings an airing of particular points of view. The recognition of different approaches and opinions typically brings a discussion of procedures and eventually personal interactions and impressions are described and discussed. Individuals who know little of each other's status or qualifications enter into face-to-face confrontations with interesting results. The lack of formally defined status

---

[24] Walter S. Wikstrom, "Sensitivity Training in Developing Managerial Competence," *Changing Concepts and Emerging Practices* (New York: National Industrial Conference Board, Studies in Personnel Policy, no. 189, 1964), p. 90.

[25] The training groups may meet twice a day for several hours in laboratory sessions with the number of participants ranging from a few to two or three dozen.

symbols tends to point up how positioning in the structure of authority may be more important than the force of an individual's personality. This condition may be framed in the context of the question, "Do subordinates follow your orders because you're a superior person or because you happen to be the division manager?" Obviously, this kind of challenge can cause anxiety, insecurity, and concern. Following a series of sensitivity-training sessions, one group of government officials were so defensive they refused to discuss any part of their experience with a hired consultant.

The value of sensitivity training seems to be that it *does* tend to develop a sense of empathy and an understanding of what happens both within and between groups. The ultimate value of the T group is somewhat questionable, however, because the understandings developed in sensitivity-training sessions may not be particularly useful when transferred to the operating organization. The advocates of sensitivity training say that it helps people to work together with a sense of purpose. The ability to understand group interactions and to cultivate a sense of self and empathy is rated highly by proponents of the system. Firms such as Gulf Oil believe this to the extent that they have scheduled sessions for key management people at a university training facility.

On the other hand, its opponents say that sensitivity training can harm the executive who has developed a particular supervisory style because it may cause him to change the kind of patterns that have made him effective. Some object to it on moral grounds, feeling that it either violates the privacy of the individual or causes destructive conflict. A final and serious objection to sensitivity training is that it is medically and morally unethical to "practice medicine without a license." One extreme point of view on invasion of privacy is described by William H. Whyte, the author of *The Organization Man,* in an article on personality testing: "The Bill of Rights did not stop at the corporation's edge. In return for the salary the organization gives the individual, it can ask for superlative work from him, but it should not ask for his psyche as well."[26] Sensitivity training does look into a man's psyche, and many people feel sensitivity training fits Whyte's negative description to a "T."

On balance, sensitivity training seems to help individuals to develop heightened empathy, improved interaction skills, and greater introspection, even though its use raises moral and ethical questions. It is doubtful, however, that the positive effects are long-lasting or that the current mode of sensitivity training will bring about significant changes in overall organizational performance.

Summary

The development of superior performance in organizations can be achieved through a variety of approaches. But whatever approach is used, it is important to tailor solutions to individual organizations. It is equally important to have the method executed in such a way that individuals visualize it as a meaningful

---

[26] "The Fallacies of Personality Testing," *Fortune,* September, 1954, p. 117.

way to revitalize the organization. No approach can be successful if it fails to meld company objectives with the way in which individuals view them.

Alternative approaches to revitalization can be based on financial factors, person-oriented techniques, or some combination thereof. The execution of the plan obviously differs in terms of techniques, time periods, and philosophies. No one approach seems to be universally applicable in all situations, even though most approaches claim universality. In this chapter, five selected means of revitalizing organizations were discussed:

Planning for profit

Management-by-objectives

Likert's new patterns of management

The managerial grid concept developed by Blake and Mouton

Sensitivity training

Short-run pressures may dictate the use of one approach while longer-term developments may suggest the use of another. Achieving a balance between these different philosophies is truly an exercise in the managerial art of judgment. Since revitalization is such a critical matter, the choice among alternatives may directly influence the future welfare of the organization.

Study Questions

1. What is planning for profit? In what ways, if any, does it differ from traditional planning concepts? Describe how specific steps differ in the two approaches.

2. What role can diversification and merger play in planning-for-profit methods? Product pruning? Reorganization?

3. What is management by objectives? In what ways is it similar to, and different from, planning-for-profit approaches?

4. What are the critical pitfalls in implementing a management-by-objectives system?

5. What are the four systems of management described by Rensis Likert? Which patterns does he deem most and least desirable? Why?

6. What are the advantages inherent in Likert's approach? What problems and disadvantages appear?

7. What is Likert's "linking pin" concept? What role does the linking-pin function serve in his system?

8. What is the managerial grid? How does this approach seek to improve organizational performance?

9. What similarities exist between Likert and Blake and Mouton's approaches to organizational effectiveness?

10. Of the selected means of revitalizing organizational performance described in this chapter, which one seems to have the greatest applicability? What qualifications do you place on your answer? Why do you feel as you do?

11. What other approaches to organizational renewal do you know about that

are not reported in this chapter? Describe them in some detail to spark discussion and contrast with the selected approaches discussed above.

12. What does sensitivity training seek to accomplish? In your opinion, can it succeed?

13. What are your beliefs about the morality of sensitivity training methods? Their effectiveness?

Carter-Brine
Company

Faced with the problem of selecting three new foremen, Joe Holden, Carter-Brine's manager of industrial relations, decided to use psychological testing to facilitate the procedure. A colleague in another company recommended a test entitled "How Supervise" published by the Psychological Corporation.

"How Supervise" required a man to state his feelings and judgment on three classes of items: supervisory practice, company policies, and supervisor opinions. The test asked him to respond with what he believed to be the opinions of other supervisors holding positions similar to his own. Answers were in the form of a forced choice between "desirable," "undesirable," and "uncertain." The test purported to measure supervisory ability based on reactions to its questions. Specific variables tested were knowledge and insight into human relations, but the general purpose of the test was to obtain better supervisors.

The test had several forms with comparable reliability. One form asked about seventy questions, and another asked roughly one hundred. The author of the test claimed that the two forms had equal power to discriminate between good and bad supervisors.

Holden tried the test on sixteen men using the one-hundred question version. Four men scored over 80 percent and thus were selected as possible candidates. One of these men was slated for transfer in the next work period, so he was dropped from consideration. The other three men were placed on jobs as assistant foremen for a period of one month and then promoted to foremen.

Six months after the three foremen took over their new jobs, Holden conducted an evaluation and appraisal of their performance. One man, Jerry Williams, had really worked out well. He had done everything that the company expected of its foremen. Another man, Mike DiJula, had done an adequate, but not outstanding, job. The third man, Morgan Flowers, had not performed well at all. He seemed to know his job and company policy, but his men disliked and distrusted him. Moreover, there was some threat of a wildcat strike in his department due to the tremendous backlog of grievances that had built up since he had taken over.

With another plant expansion coming up in the next year, Holden wondered whether or not it was worthwhile to continue using the "How Supervise" test to assist him in the foreman selection process.

1. What do you think of the test's ability to select foremen? Is this test a good predictor of performance?
2. What is a good percentage of success in foreman selection?
3. What criteria make a "good" foreman?
4. How would you go about selecting a foreman from a group of candidates?

The Henry Johnston Talent Agency

The Henry Johnston Talent Agency received the following request from a small machine-tool firm: "We would like you to send us a receptionist who has a pleasing personality and makes a good appearance. This receptionist would be expected to meet the public and represent the organization to the public by greeting any and all people who come to our plant for visits. She should also be able to type, since we want her to perform some relatively routine clerical chores when there are no visitors in the lobby."

1. How could the agency attempt to fill the position if the specification remains as it stands?
2. On what basis would the machine-tool company be able to reject any applicants sent by the agency?
3. How could the specification be redrawn to more clearly define the agency's job?

Monroe Welding, Inc.

Charlie Jenkins works in the machine shop of Monroe Welding, Inc. Jenkins is a high school graduate who up until recently has been hardworking, ambitious, bright, conscientious, and interested in moving into a supervisory job. Don Murphy, his supervisor, has continually given Jenkins superior ratings. After a series of such ratings, Murphy nominated Jenkins for a set of company-sponsored courses covering such areas as cost control, work methods, production scheduling, statistical work sampling, inventory control, and product design. Jenkins was very excited over the possibility of taking such courses, and he thanked Murphy profusely for giving him the chance to enter the program.

When Murphy's proposal to enroll Jenkins in the next series of classes was received by the training department, he was informed that the next two groups were already filled. Murphy explained the situation to Jenkins, indicating that he was sorry, "but we can try again later on." Jenkins stared at him blankly for a moment and then mumbled, "Thanks, anyway."

During the next six weeks, Jenkins's performance dropped sharply. At the end of the next appraisal period, Murphy expressed surprise that Jenkins had not performed up to expectations. Jenkins denied that his work had fallen off in any way and appeared to be quite upset.

Toward the end of the appraisal session, Murphy asked Jenkins to suggest how he might improve his performance during the next appraisal period. Jenkins looked up and said, "What's the difference whether I put out or not, I don't have any chance to get ahead around here anyway. Why should I bust my tail?"

1. What would you do if you were Murphy and you felt that Jenkins really had outstanding potential as a worker and as a supervisor?

2. Should Murphy try to change Jenkins's attitudes? How should he proceed? Describe your approach step by step.

The Light Tight
Products Company

In February, Bill McMurray, technical sales manager of the Light Tight Products Company of Albany, New York, sent a requisition to the personnel department for a "bright, alert man to act as a sales engineer and customer representative." He indicated as a minimum requirement a degree in marketing from a "good" university. The duties of a sales engineer included developing customer contacts and assisting customers in installing equipment manufactured by Light Tight. The area to be served by the new man covered the southeast and middle south.

The personnel department went into the college placement market immediately and came up with several names. After reviewing the qualifications and test scores of several candidates, McMurray felt that one had the most promising credentials and invited him to Albany for interviews. After two days of interviewing the man, McMurray was convinced that he was not the man for the job. The candidate had the required bachelor's degree from the right kind of school and excellent scores on his intelligence tests. He was also bright and alert. Unfortunately, he seemed far too aggressive to suit McMurray, who feared that he would intimidate customers. There were no specific grounds other than this uneasiness upon which he could reject the applicant; however, since the man was a Negro, McMurray did feel he would not be the best representative for Light Tight in its southeastern area. McMurray would not have asked the man to visit the Albany plant if he had known the man's race; but since New York is a Fair Employment Practice state, the employment application did not indicate the man's race, religion, or creed.

1. Assuming McMurray honestly feels that the man is not qualified for the job, how can he explain his position without opening himself to accusations of discrimination?

2. How can McMurray avoid wasting the time, money, and energy devoted to interviewing candidates who do not meet his immediate needs?

3. How would you draw the specifications and the requisition for the sales engineer's job if you were McMurray?

The Worldwide Construction Company

Bill Johnson was a self-taught, seat-of-the-pants-type individual who headed the engineering, construction, and maintenance division of the Worldwide Construction Company. Bill believed that experience was the best teacher and that young men needed to be "yanked out of their diapers" before they could be valuable to the company. Though Johnson's personal approach was somewhat rough and tough, he had been a successful, competent executive in the Worldwide organization.

Charles DePew had been working in Johnson's department for six months when his first performance appraisal interview was scheduled. DePew had made a number of minor mistakes in design projects during his break-in period; but he felt that these errors, which he attributed to his lack of experience, were now behind him. Johnson felt that DePew might become "a good engineer if he could be dried out a bit behind the ears" and that by going over DePew's appraisal in great detail he could point out corrections which would help DePew to develop his potential. He telephoned DePew and asked him to "stop by at one o'clock to have a talk about your performance appraisal."

At the appointed time, DePew came into Johnson's office and sat stunned while Johnson spent a full hour going over the mistakes DePew had made in the previous six months. At the end of his harangue, Johnson looked at DePew and said, "You've been just adequate around here and you're going to have to improve before you can expect to come up to the level of performance we expect of our top engineers." He then closed the interview by telling DePew that he would appraise him again in six months.

DePew was crestfallen. He felt that his first six months at Worldwide had been little short of catastrophic. He told one of his coworkers about the interview and indicated that he had about decided to quit his job. He was amazed when this colleague turned to him and said, "Quit? Hell, you got a good appraisal. Old Johnson never says anything good about anybody unless he thinks the man's really on his way. If I got that kind of appraisal, I'd be looking for a raise next month."

1. Do you agree with his colleague's estimate of DePew's appraisal?

2. What can DePew do to try to convince Johnson that he is doing a good job?

3.   Would you try to change Johnson's approach to appraisal? If so, how?

Steelcraft Novelty, Inc.

The Steelcraft Novelty, Inc., uses a modified management-by-objective approach to set sales objectives for its salesmen. Each year the salesmen determine their own objectives in a joint consultation with the sales manager, Howard Harrison. The typical goals set by and for each salesman include (1) gross sales, (2) new customer accounts, and (3) sales expenses.

Jim Winters covers a five-state territory including Nevada, Arizona, New Mexico, Colorado, and Utah. Winters's sales performance for a five-year period is shown in Tables V.1, V.2, and V.3.

TABLE V.1   GROSS SALES

Year	Actual Sales	Minimum Goals	Maximum Goals
1966	$110,000	$100,000	$120,000
1967	115,000	110,000	130,000
1968	117.000	120,000	140,000
1969	111,000	120,000	130,000
1970	121,000	140,000	150,000

TABLE V.2   NEW CUSTOMERS

Year	Actual	Objective
1966	6	10
1967	7	10
1968	7	10
1969	9	10
1970	9	15

TABLE V.3   SALES EXPENSES

Year	Actual	Minimum	Maximum
1966	$14,000	$ 9,000	$14,000
1967	15,000	10,000	15,000
1968	16,000	10,000	15,000
1969	17,000	12,000	15,000
1970	18,500	12,000	15,000

Winters has been an eager, ambitious salesman with a great deal of drive. His sales territory is widespread, has few customers, and requires a considerable amount of energy to cover adequately. The profit margins on Winters's line average about 25 percent.

Mr. Harrison has been concerned recently with Winters's high costs of performance, his continued desire to set objectives he seems unable to reach, and his frustration whenever he does not achieve his objectives. In spite of these problems Mr. Harrison considers Winters an outstanding salesman.

In January, the new goals for the coming year came up for review. Winters, after consulting with Harrison, set the following goals:

Sales: minimum, $140,000; maximum, $150,000

New customers: 15

Sales expenses: $15,000 to $20,000

Harrison felt that all three figures were too high. He believed that the territory couldn't absorb much over $130,000 in sales, and ten new customers seemed to be a much more realistic goal than the fifteen insisted upon by Winters. He also felt that Winters, in view of the size and profit makeup of his territory, should not spend over $15,000 on expenses in the coming year.

1. Should Harrison try to get Winters to reconsider his first two goals?

2. How can Harrison try to get Winters to accept a low expense figure without destroying his motivation to meet those goals?

The Oxford Valve Company

The Oxford Valve Company is a multiplant organization which sells a variety of auto parts to Ford, Chrysler, General Motors, and American Motors. One of its high-volume items is the auto valve line housed in a plant outside Detroit, Michigan. This line runs at a speed of about four thousand valves per hour. Much of the inspection of valve tolerances is performed on the line, but a visual inspection for surface defects is done at the end of the line by female operators. Though the automated valve line has been set up for over a year, some difficulties still exist in the final inspection operation. The girls performing the job have a high rate of turnover; they complain of frequent nervousness; and at least one operator has had to have psychiatric help.

The production supervisor, Harry Jackson, is concerned with both the technical and human problems connected with the final inspection of valves. He attempted to rotate the girls every two hours, but problems continued. When Jackson called in the production engineers to seek their assistance, they concluded that there was no economic way to mechanize the final inspection operation. One engineer commented that the girls were simply goofing off and that Jackson could solve the problem by "pinning down the goof-offs."

The chief industrial engineer suggested that the solution was to install a wage incentive plan on the final inspection operation. His opinion was that wage incentives would improve the level of worker satisfaction and thus the total performance of the operators. The industrial relations representative indicated that the best solution was to increase the number of rest periods and to convince the girls, in formal and informal meetings, about the importance of cost consciousness in factory operations.

When Jackson sought the operators' opinions, they stated the job was far too hard, required too much attention time, demanded too much responsibility, generally made them nervous, and was monotonous. Four of the six operators complained that the final inspection operation was so isolated that they had no chance to socialize with other girls.

Jackson weighed all the alternatives; and, after careful thought, he decided to follow the advice of the chief industrial engineer. He felt that the pay increase associated with placing the job on a wage incentive basis would make the job more attractive and would overcome some of the discontent expressed by the female operators.

1. What do you think of Jackson's choice? Why?
2. If you were in Jackson's place, what would you do? Why?

Consolidated Insurance Company

When Arnold Kaplan, vice-president of personnel and executive development of the Consolidated Insurance Company read a flyer announcing a seminar dealing with a new training concept, the managerial grid, he almost threw it in his wastebasket. Before he reached that point, however, he linked the name "managerial grid" with a training program alleged to have been quite successful in a firm in another industry. As he reread the brochure, he wondered about the validity of the method. He called in Richard Sunderland, director of training, to inquire what Sunderland knew about this new approach to training. Sunderland indicated that he had read an article or two, but otherwise, his information was quite sketchy. After further discussion, Mr. Kaplan asked Sunderland to look more fully into the grid concept.

Mr. Kaplan's reason for expressing interest in the managerial grid was part of his continuing search for new and meaningful training concepts that might be useful to the Consolidated organization. When Kaplan had joined Consolidated fifteen years ago, little formal training had been in effect. Training of executive and sales personnel had been quite limited in scope; and even low-level introductory training was handled in a very casual, almost haphazard, manner.

One of Mr. Kaplan's initial steps was to introduce a series of courses in basic supervisory practices. He then introduced a rather structured training program for salesmen. His next step was to work with supervisors in the various branch offices. When this phase was completed, he started training sales supervisors in slightly more advanced managerial techniques.

When supervisory training became more widely accepted, he introduced programs for middle-management personnel in both branches and home office operations. These general supervisory training courses ran some eight to ten sessions and were well regarded by the people involved. Kaplan knew, however, that they were only a start toward more sophisticated training programs.

As part of his upgrading of the training function, Mr. Kaplan introduced technical and human relations training for upper-middle management. The technical training programs covered financial analysis, accounting techniques, the use of statistics to measure performance, and a package of courses dealing with operating and programming computers. The human relations courses emphasized people's contributions to effective operations and an understanding of how supervisory activities influence subordinate motivation. At this point, a limited number of people were sent to universities to attend middle-management training programs.

Recently, training programs finally began to enter Consolidated's executive suite. A number of vice-presidents and divisional managers attended university sponsored executive programs such as those at Arden House under the direction of Columbia University, Graduate School of Business. Executives at other levels left the company for periods from two to six weeks for so-called sensitivity training in the various training laboratories.

Though diverse programs had thus been introduced at all levels of the Consolidated organization, no single approach had proven to be entirely satisfactory in Kaplan's eyes. All methods had some good points, but each contained a number of rather glaring weaknesses. Evaluation of these programs had been made in terms of costs, but as yet Consolidated had no really firm data on their relative effectiveness in terms of results. Consolidated was not alone in its failure to obtain results-oriented data, since no competitors had such data available either. Another big difficulty encountered in all training programs was that individuals tended to revert to old patterns of behavior once they returned to their particular work environment. Mr. Kaplan felt that a new approach was needed before the benefits of individual training programs could be made to stick in any given operating environment. According to the write-up in the managerial grid pamphlet, this problem was met and solved. Though Mr. Kaplan felt that the brochure made some overly enthusiastic claims, he believed that the managerial grid approach might help to enhance creativity, productivity, commitment, and communications. He also felt it might reduce certain conflicts plaguing the internal hierarchy of the corporation.

After a great deal of thought and discussion, Mr. Kaplan asked Richard Sunderland to attend a managerial grid seminar being held near Consolidated's home office. Sunderland agreed to enroll in the seminar and indicated he would report back to Mr. Kaplan shortly after completing the course.

THE MANAGERIAL GRID CONCEPT

When Richard Sunderland returned from his two-week seminar, he was extremely optimistic about the use of the managerial grid at Consolidated. He felt that it was sound in concept and practical in application. In his report to Mr. Kaplan, he included the first part of an article published in the *Harvard Business Review* by Robert R. Blake and Jane S. Mouton, the developers of the managerial grid. This excerpt describes the ideal application of the managerial grid in an operating situation, and appears in Chapter 14 in the same form as in Mr. Sunderland's report.

The approaches and the action steps outlined in the article seemed promising to Mr. Kaplan, but he was not prepared to enter a managerial grid program without further investigation. He asked Mr. Sunderland to prepare an additional report on the feasibility of using managerial grid concepts in Consolidated.

Mr. Sunderland began his investigation by contacting a consultant versed in the use of managerial grid techniques. Though Sunderland learned a great deal from this consultant, he was disappointed because the consultant knew of no insurance company comparable to Consolidated that had used managerial grid training on a large scale. Upon further investigation, Mr. Sunderland came across the second half of the *Harvard Business Review* article from which he had obtained his summary of the managerial grid concept.[1] The latter part of this article evaluated a manufacturing company which had used the managerial grid approach extensively.

Mr. Sunderland studied this article carefully and got what he felt was a valuable insight on the use of managerial grid techniques to improve organizational effectiveness. He was particularly impressed because this study had been done by an impartial group of researchers, and he felt that its conclusions on productivity increases, changes in practices and behavior, improved intergroup and intragroup relations, and apparently improved attitudes toward company goals and company policies were stated objectively. In general, he felt confident these results would be repeated if the approach was used within the framework of the Consolidated Insurance Company. For one thing, he felt that employees in the Consolidated organization were more pliable than those studied by the Harvard group. He also felt the chance for costs savings was greater in his company, since controllable costs were a higher percentage of total expenses in insurance companies than in manufacturing operations.

When Mr. Kaplan heard Mr. Sunderland's report, he was impressed by its optimistic tone. However, he knew that the Consolidated Insurance Company had a number of rigidities that might affect the implementation of a managerial grid approach. Thus, his reaction was more cautious than Sunderland's, and he decided to introduce the managerial grid on a small scale until it could be proved within the framework of the insurance business. As he said to Mr. Sunderland, "Suppose we try it out in a branch office and

[1] Part ii, "How the Grid Program Did Work," is reprinted at the end of this case study.

see what happens. I'm not really sure that the grid technique is as good as it seems, but I'm willing to give it a try. Suppose you go down to the Atlanta office and start a modified grid program there. You can kick it off as the training instructor and stay there until the program gets under way. I expect you can get it going in about a month. By then it should run itself as long as you make yourself available to help over any rough spots. If you think this is sensible, I'll call Jim Byrnes in Atlanta and try to set it up."

Sunderland agreed with Mr. Kaplan's basic approach and, after several calls to Atlanta, the program was agreed upon. Since the starting date was scheduled two weeks after the final phone call, Mr. Sunderland immediately began to make plans to install managerial grid training in the Atlanta branch. After a short planning period, the grid program went into effect at Atlanta.

At the end of one year, the first two phases of the managerial grid approach had been successfully completed in the Atlanta branch. Job-training seminars had been conducted by branch supervisors trained by Mr. Sunderland. These six individuals were enthusiastic about the training and its potential. They had worked diligently to master the various concepts and techniques used in the managerial grid approach, and, in turn, had tried hard to communicate the techniques and approaches to their own subordinates.

The team development phase (Phase 2) had also been performed with enthusiasm and apparent success. The group rules of openness and candor had been established and seemed to be in effect at most levels in the Atlanta branch. Though a few people had held back, both Mr. Byrnes and Mr. Sunderland felt that Phase 2 had been executed according to the best grid principles.

Phases 3, 4, and 5 were not completed at the end of the first year, and for a variety of reasons, Mr. Sunderland felt they might never be executed fully in the Atlanta branch. The basis of his feeling was that the entire set of grid results could never be achieved unless the basic managerial approach was extended beyond the confines of the Atlanta branch to other parts of the Consolidated organization. Some intergroup relations had improved during Phase 3, but company policies and procedures continually stymied attempts to improve intragroup relations at the branch-division level. This blockage in Phase 3 was even more critical in Phase 4 where organizational goal setting was to take place. Sunderland knew that unless Phases 3 and 4 could be executed, Phases 5 and 6 would not be attainable. He also believed that the achievement of Phases 3 and 4 required a greater acceptance of grid concepts at all levels of the Consolidated organization. This acceptance, he felt, would have to begin at the top and filter down through all levels of management.

At the year's end, Mr. Sunderland reported the results of the training program to Mr. Kaplan. Unfortunately, Sunderland was not able to quantify many of his results because they were somewhat intangible. Sunderland felt that costs had been lowered, but not by amounts sufficient to trace them directly to grid concepts. Morale was better, he felt, but he had insufficient data to relate morale at the end of the year to previous morale ratings in the Atlanta branch. Productivity also seemed to be up, but the units of measure in the insurance business were too imprecise for Sunderland to make positive claims about gains traceable to the training program.

Mr. Kaplan was extremely interested in the Sunderland report, but he was concerned about its obvious lack of tangible results. He still felt the managerial grid approach held promise for Consolidated, but he knew Sunderland's report was not strong enough to justify the adoption of managerial grid training throughout the entire company. When Kaplan openly stated his doubts, Sunderland expressed deep disappointment. There was no doubt in Sunderland's mind that the managerial grid concept was perfectly suited for use in branches and in the home office. He wondered how he could make his convictions felt throughout the Consolidated organization.

In order to sell a more extensive grid program to Consolidated management, Sunderland knew he would have to devise some means of evaluating the grid program in tangible terms. Further, he knew he would have to come up with some measure of its intangible benefits. His thoughts turned to the article on the grid that had attracted his attention in the first place, and he wondered whether he could use the findings reported to help implement and evaluate a grid program in Consolidated.*

1. If you were Mr. Sunderland, what specific approaches and techniques would you advocate to help support your belief in the managerial grid approach to organizational development? What specific action steps would you suggest to reach your various objectives?

2. If you were Mr. Kaplan, what kinds of informational inputs would you require before you decided to extend or curtail training programs using the managerial grid approach?

3. What types of controls should Mr. Kaplan exercise over the development of managerial grid programs if he decides to extend the concept beyond the Atlanta branch? What units of measure should he use?

HOW THE GRID PROGRAM DID WORK[1]

This part describes the early findings and conclusions of a research study which evaluated the Sigma plant's program in organization development. The evaluation was suggested by the research manager in Piedmont's employee relations department. Those responsible for the program at the Sigma plant gave the idea immediate support. A research design was presented to the Sigma management and accepted. On-site field work began in June 1963 and ended in November 1963.

---

* The second half of the article referred to by Mr. Sunderland is reproduced below in partial form. The remainder of the article (except for introductory material) is reprinted in Chapter 14.

[1] The authors of Part II are Louis B. Barnes and Larry E. Grenier.

EVALUATION GOALS

The evaluation of this large-scale organization development program seemed important for a number of reasons:

As noted at the start of this article, corporate managements have had trouble in transferring behavioral science concepts into organizational action. The Sigma program represented a deliberate effort to move these concepts from the classroom into the mainstream of organization life.

The Sigma program was run by *line* managers. Even Phase #1, which introduced Managerial Grid concepts, was directed by rotating pairs of line managers. Staff experts and outside consultants played peripheral roles only. Typically, programs of this kind and scope involve considerable outside guidance and/or teaching.

Any management development program which focuses on self-introspection and self-other relationships runs some risk of psychiatric disturbances. The question was whether the Managerial Grid program at Sigma was able to avoid such problems by using exercises involving managerial styles rather than depending on the deeper exploration of personal characteristics. Altogether about 800 managers and technical men experienced Phase #1 at Sigma. These men were of varying ages and educational backgrounds. They came from all areas and levels of the organization.

The program at Sigma sought collective group changes, not just individual changes in attitudes and behavior. Most management development programs treat the individual as the learning unit. The six phases of the Grid program were explicitly aimed at group and cross-group shifts in attitudes and behavior.

Consequently, a "successful" program at Sigma might have important implications for business and the behavioral sciences alike. Sigma's experience might help answer the following questions implied in the above reasons for an outside evaluation:

Can a program based on behavioral science concepts be translated into meaningful organization action?

Can management take primary responsibility for such a program?

Can important attitude and behavior changes be accomplished without their being psychologically threatening?

Can a change of focus from the individual to the group aid collective learning and behavior change?

MEASUREMENT PROBLEMS

Given the possibility of Sigma's running a "successful" program, how were we to determine whether it was *really* successful? How was organization development to be adequately identified and measured? Such questions involve major issues in behavioral science methodology, and the answers are complex.

Put bluntly, there is no really satisfactory way of identifying and measuring organizational change and development. Too many variables are beyond control and cannot be isolated. An investigator never knows when "extraneous" factors are just as responsible for an important finding as are the "key" factors identified in his research.

Yet this complexity provides no excuse for not attempting to evaluate such programs. The important thing is to approach the project with some qualms and to apply caution. On this basis, we hope to show how different "measures" of Sigma's program furnish enough evidence for readers to piece together what happened before and during the program. These measures include productivity and profit indexes, results of opinion and attitude surveys from members of management, and evidence of behavioral changes taken from interviews and conversations.

None of these indexes is satisfactory by itself, and even when used jointly, they require cautious application. Each finding can only be treated as a piece in the over-all puzzle. It is the consistency and direction of the many different findings which lead us to believe that something important was happening at the Sigma plant.

DECISION ON PROGRAM

Historically, a number of factors influenced the management of the Sigma plant in making its decision to undertake the organization development program.

NEW POLICIES

The first significant factor occurred early in 1960. At that time, Piedmont was merged with another company. This merger disrupted a long-standing relationship between the Sigma plant and its parent organization. Among other things, the merger ended a prior contract that for over 25 years had assured Sigma of a cost-plus profit. It also brought with it a new headquarters management that stressed plant autonomy. Henceforth important decisions, which previously had been made almost exclusively by headquarters management, were to be delegated to the plant level.

However, complications arose when headquarters adopted its new policy of "hands-off" management. Headquarters hoped that the Sigma management would use its autonomy to solve chronic problems which had carried over from the more directive previous management. The most serious problem involved the use of Sigma manpower on construction work of new units. One headquarters manager described the situation as follows:

"We had heard from higher level people that Sigma had too much manpower. Our reaction, I suppose, was that this should have been reduced before the merger.

But we were faced with it. And the Sigma plant was telling us that they were
in balance. We got long memos from them, and finally the issue began to center
on using manpower for construction work. This practice was typical of several
plants in our organization, but Sigma appeared to be defensive, implying that
they could do *all* the construction work better than contractors. This was the summer
of 1961. We weren't sure about the true answer either, although I guess we thought
they had a lot of people. Also, the vice president in charge of our group isn't
one to go out and directly tell someone to do something. He would rather let
them find out for themselves and then seek help. I believe in this. So we'd prod
Sigma and ask questions. But I guess we weren't always too subtle. They became
defensive, and some of our later sessions became emotional."

IN-PLANT RELATIONSHIPS

A second major factor which helped to set the stage for the Sigma
program involved the strained relationships between different departments
and levels within the plant. Major operating and engineering departments
were on the defensive. Accusations of "empire building" were not uncom-
mon. Lower level supervisors still felt somewhat alienated because upper
level management had frequently overruled them on union grievance decisions in the past. In short, while Piedmont was concerned about Sigma's
major decisions, Sigma management worried more about day-to-day
operating problems.

This factor was all the more crucial because of the complex technology
of Sigma's plant, a technology that required constant interdepartment
cooperation. Mistakes were costly and even dangerous. As a result, Sigma's
management felt considerable pressure to resolve departmental differences
and improve coordination. Yet these differences persisted, much to the
frustration of many people.

THE PLANT MANAGER

Another key factor in setting the stage for the development program
was the attitude and reputation of the Sigma plant manager. Prior to
assuming operating control of the plant in 1959, he had worked at Piedmont
headquarters on a reorganization study committee, and before that he had
been research director at Sigma. Because of many important technical
contributions he had made to the company, he was held in high regard
within the Sigma plant. In his newer role as plant manager, he had tried
to identify and correct the problems facing the plant. But he had experienced
some difficulty in gaining full acceptance and cooperation on these desired
improvements. One of the plant manager's key subordinates described his
reaction to the plant manager's methods as follows:

"The plant manager would go around and ask people, 'What would you think
if I made such and such a decision?' Actually, he already had his mind made

up, but he was just testing people to see if they would accept it. He always wanted people to agree with him."

And a first-level supervisor made this specific comment:

"The plant manager came down and gave us a lot of company philosophy. We started out with his 'Black Book'—he wrote it. It was pretty positive. It told the men to make decisions. But a new union had just come in, and a lot of people were suspicious that he only wanted us to make tough decisions rather than fair decisions."

The plant manager reported a cautious and circumspect reaction to the 1960 merger. This attitude was shared by most of the Sigma management. When Piedmont representatives asked the plant manager what he considered to be prying questions, he reacted rather strongly—"like Horatio defending the bridge," as he later described it.

PRIOR PLANT EXPERIENCE

Still another factor encompassed past efforts by Sigma's management to meet the production requirements. The plant was noted for its management and worker training. Like all of Piedmont's plants, Sigma had sent managers to university training programs, as well as running in-plant training programs with and without outside assistance. These efforts were intended to supplement an already high educational level in the plant, where over 48% of 800 managers and supervisors at all levels held college degrees, including 80 with graduate degrees. In addition, Sigma was frequently characterized as a "family" and "meeting" plant where cooperation was considered important.

However, like many organizations, Sigma lacked a consistent way of fitting these concerns for productivity and people together. Instead, Sigma seemed to have emphasized one or the other, depending on headquarters directives and the other pressures on it at various times.

CONSULTANT'S ENTRY

Finally, the consultant, Dr. Blake, must be considered as a key factor. Blake had an impressive reputation as an organization analyst with management in other parts of Piedmont. Headquarters management had asked him to visit the Sigma plant, provided the plant manager approved. The plant manager described the entry of Blake as follows:

"I guess we decided on some sort of trial marriage with Blake. . . . I said, 'Why don't you look us over and we'll look you over.' In this trial period he began to look into our headquarters relations and concluded there were real problems. Then he asked if we wanted to explore these problems in a joint session with headquarters. I was impressed by that meeting. It did some real good. I guess headquarters at the end of the first day was ready to call off the dogs. We had a lot of misconceptions on the manpower problem—a lot of people in headquarters thought we weren't coming to grips with it. I guess one of the most enlightening things—when we started to let our hair down on the second day of these sessions—was when the vice president of manufacturing said, 'How should I know what Sigma is doing about manpower when they haven't told me?' I would have asked the same thing if I had been in his situation. But it shocked us.

"I'm not too clear on what happened from here on. But I feel we began to establish a rapport that we didn't have before. We ironed out a lot of misunderstandings on both sides. There was no longer a feeling of a lack of trust between us. This session convinced me and the whole group that Blake's methods had helped us—at least on this problem. He got us to see that conflict is something you get out on the table. Then four of us went to an outside Grid Seminar. We invited one manager from the headquarters group to come with us—and he did. All of these decisions to go ahead were made here at Sigma—mainly by a group of sixteen. It was a group decision to send the four of us to the Grid Seminar. We came back and reported—then we had some more discussions—and finally we evolved the development program."

SIGNIFICANT CHANGES

Phase #1 of Sigma's organization development program began in November 1962 with 40 managers participating in a one-week Managerial Grid Seminar. This phase continued until the summer of 1963, by which time 800 managers and technical men had completed it. Meanwhile, the earlier participants began to embark on later phases of the organization development program.

Our data collecting began about the same time. These data, accumulated over the next four months in the field and by reports thereafter, show significant changes in Sigma's operations. Both plant operations and internal-external relationships were influenced. In this section we shall describe these changes and attempt to show how the organization development program affected them. The data include changes in:

Productivity and profits.

Practices and behavior.

Perceptions, attitudes, and values.

The analysis of these data moves from "hard," relatively objective material involving profits to "softer," more subjective data such as attitudes. The important things for readers to ask are: Do the different findings seem consistent? Do they reinforce each other? And do they suggest that the development program played an important role in Sigma's own development?

A. PRODUCTIVITY & PROFITS

There were significant increases in productivity and profits during 1963, when the organization development program was in effect. EXHIBIT II indicates that total production rose somewhat (with fewer employees), and profits more than doubled. At first glance, it would seem that Sigma had struck gold, that its worries were over, and that the development program had been highly effective. But this in itself would be a gross oversimplification.

To begin with, Sigma's business involves widely fluctuating market prices, raw-material costs, and other noncontrollable factors. Possibly higher revenues or lower materials costs would explain profit increases. In addition, new automatic machinery and new plant equipment investments might be sufficient cause for the reduced labor force and increased profit picture. Finally, an over-all manpower reduction had occurred (involving over 600 employees), and this in itself might account for the increased profit picture in 1963, particularly if the increased overtime costs (at time-and-a-half) had been spread over the remaining work force. These possibilities make it difficult to draw simple cause-effect conclusions about Sigma's development program and operating performance.

CONTROLLABLE FACTORS

At the same time, some of these noncontrollable factors can be identified and assessed for their contributions to profit. For example, noncontrollable factors can be separated from controllable factors. At Sigma, changes in certain of the noncontrollable factors—revenues, depreciation, taxes, and raw materials—accounted for about 56% of the increase in profits, despite the fact that noncontrollable costs as a whole had increased.

The remaining 44% of the profit increase was due to reductions in controllable costs—i.e., wages, maintenance materials, utilities, and fixed overhead—over which plant management had decision-making control. These reductions in controllable costs led to a profit contribution amounting to millions of dollars. Meanwhile, net investment had *not* increased appreciably (1.5% during 1963), and overtime had increased only slightly (5% over a small base) during the same time.

Consequently, it appears that a sizable part of the 1963 increase in Sigma's productivity and profit came from controllable factors. Futhermore, the explanation for this increase was not due to the addition of more efficient machinery or longer work hours. The next question, therefore, is: How much of this increase in profits was due to the manpower reduction, and how much to increased productivity on the part of remaining employees?

Company records show that 69% of the controllable cost savings came from the manpower reduction. The remaining 31%, amounting to several million dollars, came from improved operating procedures and higher productivity per man-hour. EXHIBIT III shows how these productivity and controllable cost measures for 1963 compared with previous years. (Productivity, in this case, is represented by dividing the number of employees for each year into the number of total production units.) The only really comparable year in terms of profit increase, according to EXHIBIT II, was 1961. However, the profit increase in 1961 was due more to factors outside of the Sigma management's control than in 1963. EXHIBIT III shows that the 1961 increase in productivity and decrease in controllable costs were very small compared with 1963. Most impressive, EXHIBIT III shows that the productivity index per employee increased from a high in 1962 of 103.9 to a new high of 131.3 in 1963 without the aid of substantial investments in plant and equipment, as shown earlier.

TABLE V.4   RELEVANT OPERATING FIGURES, 1960–1963

	1960*	1961	1962	1963
Gross revenue	100	101.6	98.2	106.6
Raw material costs	100	98.8	97.2	103.2
Noncontrollable operating costs	100	97.5	101.8	104.6
Controllable operating costs	100	95.0	94.1	86.2
Net profits before taxes	100	229.0	118.0	266.0
Number of employees	100	95.5	94.1	79.5
Total production units	100	98.5	98.2	102.2

* 1960 used as a base year, since it was the first year that Sigma's records could be compared with post-merger years.

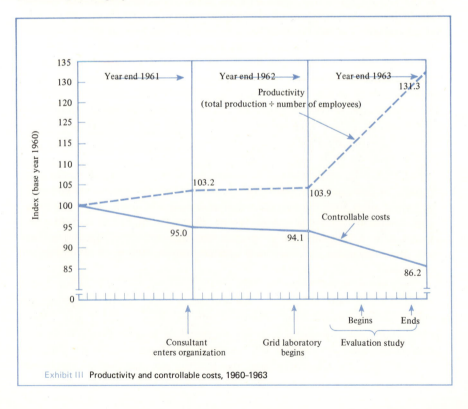

Exhibit III Productivity and controllable costs, 1960–1963

EFFECTS ON PROFITS

The difficult problem now is to assess the role played by the organization development program in Sigma's improved productivity and profit picture. Concerning ourselves only with the controllable cost savings and productivity increases, how did the Sigma management account for these?

MANPOWER SAVINGS. The largest saving was due to the manpower reduction. On this issue, consider the following comments from a talk given by the Sigma plant manager at a Piedmont conference:

"The group's decision-making process on the manpower question drew heavily on the approaches that had been developed in our development program. The approaches used stimulated a high degree of interplay of ideas and suggestions advanced by the various members of the group. It is believed that this permitted development of group answers that were better than the sum of the individual contributions. In the final analysis, it was evident that everyone involved was deeply committed to using methods and procedures that each had helped devise to accomplish or surpass goals that each had helped establish.

"One of the key decisions made on a team basis involved the timing of the announcement. At the start of the discussions, most of the group favored the conventional approach, namely, that of deferring the announcement of the voluntary retirement program as long as possible and of delaying the announcement of the layoff until the completion of the voluntary program. However, a small minority took the reverse position and finally were able to convince the majority of the soundness of this position. We are convinced that this decision was a major factor contributing to the success of the manpower reduction. . . .

"It was particularly gratifying that 520 of our employees accepted early retirement or termination voluntarily in comparison with an expected loss of only 196 employees by these measures. As a result, only 84 employees were laid off versus 260 that we had projected originally. The fact that the total reduction in forces was 160 employees greater than anticipated is particularly significant, since we foresee a continuing need to operate our plant with a fewer number of employees.

"In addition to these numerical results, the program was successful in other important ways. Little bitterness or resentment toward the company has been evidenced by the relatively few employees involved in the forced layoff. Many employees expressed appreciation of the length of the advance notice and of the assistance given by the placement office. None of the unions took a stand against management's actions, nor did any union try to impede the implementation of the program. Community and press reactions were gratifying. There is some evidence of a trend that the community is moving in the direction of becoming more self-reliant and less dependent on Sigma.

"The Sigma management feels very strongly that the quality of the decisions made in connection with setting manpower goals and the implementation of the reduction program was largely responsible for the success of the program. It feels equally as strongly that the quality of the decisions made was profoundly influenced by the application of organization development principles."

Comments by other Sigma managers indicate that they also give high credit to the program for the quality of the manpower reduction decision.

At the same time, it appears that some such decision was inevitable under any circumstances. The plant manager had decided to reduce manpower before the organization development program began. However, he had not yet communicated this to headquarters (he did this during the joint headquarters-Sigma meeting suggested by Blake), nor had any official implementation plan been worked out. But here is one of those difficult points where observers will argue whether or not the quality and the implementation of this difficult decision were as important as the decision itself was. The Sigma management apparently believes that they were.

WORK-GROUP PERFORMANCE. Another measure of improved performance and profit consciousness is shown in EXHIBIT IV. A voluntary-response, anonymous questionnaire was sent to those men who had participated in Phase #1 of the Managerial Grid program. Each man was asked to compare several performance indexes of one year ago with those of the present time. The responses were marked on an eight-point scale and returned by 606 of these men. EXHIBIT IV shows perceived improvement on all of the performance-related items, including an increase of 30.5% in the profit-and-loss consciousness of the work group. The least improvement is reported in "Boss's work effort," which was the only one of the six items *not* explicitly addressed in the Phase #1 training. Apparently the Sigma respondents saw greater performance-productivity improvement in areas which had been stressed in Phase #1 than in areas not stressed.

TABLE V.5   PERCEIVED CHANGES IN GROUP PERFORMANCE, 1962–1963

| | PERCENT OF MANAGERS RATING DIMENSIONS OF PERFORMANCE "HIGH"* | | |
	In 1962	In 1963	Increase or decrease
"Boss's work effort"	67.1%	78.5%	+11.4%
"Leveling with other group members"	45.9	67.7	21.8
"Group's work effort"	50.2	74.2	24.0
"Problem liveliness in group discussions"	27.2	53.0	25.8
"Quality of decisions made in group"	38.8	64.6	25.8
"Profit-and-loss consciousness in group"	41.2	71.7	30.5
Average	45.1%	68.3%	+23.2%

* Refers to the per cent of 606 questionaire respondents rating their managers either "7" ir "8" on an eight-point scale.

FOLLOW-UP PROJECTS. A final indicator of the program's contribution to the productivity-controllable cost picture is reflected in some of the follow-up projects which were part of Phases #4 and #5 of the

Managerial Grid program. These activities were intended to solve specific organizational problems using 9,9 concepts and methods, and in this sense they also represent changes in actual behavior (to be examined more closely in the next section). They include some projects which are directly related to productivity and cost improvement, as well as other projects less directly related. For example:

During the period of contract negotiations with the union, a management team used problem-solving approaches learned in the Grid Seminar to keep all levels of management informed as to management's position.

An organization development coordinator was appointed to keep track of different follow-up projects.

A management team was established to work out a program for reducing utility costs. This team used Managerial Grid concepts to create awareness of the problem and to introduce the program to other managers.

Another management team began work on reducing the costs of maintenance materials and supplies, again using Managerial Grid principles.

A new series of Grid programs was extended beyond lower level supervisors in the plant. These men included sliding supervisors who moved back and forth between worker and supervisor positions. In addition, an effort was made to extend Grid concepts to the labor force. Consequently, union officers were invited (and many accepted the invitation) to participate in these sessions.

A series of half-day sessions was held for second-level supervisors to discuss and determine guidelines which would help improve supervisor-subordinate relationships. These sessions were based on the Grid Seminar format, with both supervisors and subordinates participating in the discussions.

A safety program, based on Grid methods, was designed to increase awareness of safety problems and to get new ideas for improvements. This program was to include all plant employees.

The plant manager initiated a plan whereby supervisors would encourage subordinates to set personal goals for the coming year. This was intended to replace previous performance appraisal methods wherein the supervisor set the goals and told the subordinate how he was measuring up to them.

An example of how one of these follow-up efforts, the utilities improvement program, was affecting profit consciousness is shown below in a conversation among two members of the program committee and the field researcher:

Researcher: How is the utilities improvement project coming along?

Manager A: Real well. This morning we attended a meeting of the project committee that has been created. They have a long way to go, but they're enthusiastic.

Manager B: They've set up a committee with a full-time project head, John J. They've put some real important people on the committee—all at the department head level.

Researcher: Management took Jim P. away from his line job on a full-time basis?

Manager A: Yes, he's off for at least a year. This shows the importance management is giving to utilities conservation.

Researcher: Have there been any noticeable P & L effects yet?

Manager A: Yes, just this morning I got the fuel bill for last month, and it dropped to such an extent that, if it keeps up, we could save over a million dollars for the year.

Manager B: And the best we can figure is that this was due to motivational reasons, as little else could account for the drop.

B. PRACTICES & BEHAVIOR

Because the research was begun after the beginning of Sigma's organization development program, we have only a few accurate indexes of changes in practices and behavior. However, the ones available are important indicators of the changes taking place in the plant. They include:

Increased frequency of meetings.

Changing criteria for management appraisals.

Increased transfers within the plant and to other parts of the organization.

MORE MEETINGS

EXHIBIT V shows the increase in meeting schedules from a representative sample of 30 Sigma managers. The calendars of these men showed a 31% increase in formal meetings scheduled during a summer week in 1963 as compared with a year before. Questionnaire data also showed managers reporting an average of 12.4% more time in "team problem-solving" meetings.

The fact that the character as well as the frequency of these meetings was changing is shown by the following statement made by a Piedmont headquarters representative, formerly quite negative toward Sigma's management:

EXHIBIT V.   MEETING ATTENDANCE BY MANAGERS

	AVERAGE NUMBER OF FORMALLY SCHEDULED MEETINGS ATTENDED PER MGR. PER WEEK		
Number and Category	1962	1963	Per Cent Change
21 Administrative managers	5.5	7.5	+36%
9 Technical managers	2.7	3.2	+19%
Average	4.6	6.1	+31%

"I think the recent change in the way that Sigma is being managed is the most drastic thing. You just go to a meeting now and you see it. I sat in on a recent meeting. People talk as though they are making decisions, and they are. This didn't happen before. A meeting would usually conclude with the plant manager's reaction. You knew damn well that he made the final decision. There wasn't a meeting he wasn't in. You could never get hold of him. Now he is the most available guy in the place."

EXHIBIT V also shows a discrepancy between the findings for administrative managers and those for technical managers. (Administrative managers are line and staff people whose work is concerned mainly with daily operating matters; technical managers are staff people dealing primarily with long-range technical problems. It should be pointed out, however, that almost all administrative managers at Sigma had technical backgrounds.) Administrative managers showed more frequent meetings and a greater increase over the year than technical managers did. Similar tendencies persist throughout these findings. Administrative managers consistently report behavior that is "in line" with Sigma's change trends and more positively oriented toward the organization development program.

PROMOTION CRITERIA

One reason for this difference appears in EXHIBIT VI, which shows a second indicator of actual behavior change. This suggests that promotion criteria are changing at Sigma, as shown by the profile of the 50 most highly evaluated managers. Youth and a line position (largely held by administrative managers) now seem to be better predictors of success than higher age, company seniority, and position in the staff organization (largely populated by technical personnel).

These figures suggest shifting qualifications for promotion in a changing organization. They also suggest a shift in the power structure of the plant, with administrative-line managers becoming more highly rewarded than technical-staff managers. We therefore begin to understand one possible reason for the greater acceptance of organization development by the administrative managers. For them, the reward potential was relatively high.

MANAGER MOBILITY

EXHIBIT VII shows the third indicator of actual change. Manager transfers, while not increasing sharply in total numbers, rose 52% over 1962 transfers within and outside of the plant. The number of transfers in 1962 tended to be typical of previous years. The increase in internal movement suggests greater flexibility within the plant, and the increase in transfers to outside units suggests stronger ties with headquarters and the other operating plants. Company records also show that managers typically spent (and wanted to spend) their careers within the plant. More recently, however, managers have been promoted out of Sigma. In support of the conclusion that the plant has developed stronger outside ties, we find that in 1962 only 18%

of the men transferred out were rated among the top 50 managers at Sigma. In 1963, 38% of those transferred out were rated among the top 50.

EXHIBIT VI.   ATTRIBUTES OF FIFTY MOST HIGHLY RATED MANAGERS

Attribute	1962	1963
Average age (years)	42.2	39.4
Average length of service (years)	18.4	15.6
Per cent in line jobs	42%	64%
Per cent in staff jobs	58%	36%
Per cent in high-level jobs	64%	50%
Per cent in middle-level jobs	34%	36%
Per cent in low-level jobs	2%	14%

EFFECTS ON BEHAVIOR

In the previous section on productivity and profits, we saw evidence that follow-up project savings were credited largely to the organization development program. The same was true of the new emphasis on teamwork and problem solving. Again and again, specific behavioral changes were ascribed to effects of the program by Sigma personnel. For example, one higher level manager noted:

"We had a pretty good example of group action here last Friday evening. We had a personnel problem; and if that problem had come up a couple of years ago, they would have used a 9,1 on it—told the complainer to go back to work—and that would have been the end of it. I was involved myself and still am. My two supervisors brought me and the other man together and used the Grid ideas. They gave us an opportunity to talk. Anybody could say what he wanted to. We got a little personal, but it works. It works because each of us got some things off his chest. I made a mistake a long time ago in not reporting the trouble I was having. When they cut the other man in, he was able to tell us what he thought was wrong."

EXHIBIT VII.   CHANGE IN MOBILITY OF MANAGEMENT PERSONNEL

Transfers	1962	1963	Per Cent Change
Within plant	21	39	+86%
Out of plant	33	43	+31%
Total movement	54	82	+52%

A lower level supervisor described the effects of Phase #1 in this fashion:

"The way I see it, we had an old philosophy that we had to get away from ... this being a country club atmosphere, of doing nothing and just having a good time. Well, there are two ways you can change: One is that you can do it by attrition, but this takes too long. The other is that you can do it like the Chinese do it—by brainwashing. Now this may sound critical and I don't mean it this way, but this is how the Grid training program was done. You were under conditions of pressure and you kept getting those theories repeated to you over and over, and it has worked.

"I don't think it's so much that individuals have changed, but the philosophy has definitely changed. Why, there is one department where it used to be dog eat dog with them. But since March we have been able to work together much better. And I attribute this change to the program because the change is so uniform in that department. It couldn't have been done by one man in the department because then the difference would be more inconsistent."

Finally, a first-level supervisor and former union member commented:

"It's just here in the last year or so that company officials have branched out and let lower level people have a say in things. I guess I'd say, and all us working foremen do things differently, that I make 90% more decisions now compared to ten years ago. Routinely, we have a lot more responsibility now. It used to be that decisions came down from the top—it was all cut and dried—and you did it. In the last year particularly, the supervisors are giving us a lot more authority and getting better cooperation. They give a man a chance to do a job. It seems like they keep bringing things out and getting us to do more."

With regard to the increase in meetings, managers tended to have mixed feelings. Their time was precious, and some of their new problem-solving meetings failed to provide the answers. Furthermore, they, like so many managers today, felt sensitive to "committeeitis" and "group think" criticism. At the same time, there was wide support for the "team" and "problem solving" approaches stressed in the Managerial Grid Seminar, because they provided opportunities to confront problems that had been avoided or unrecognized earlier.

C. ATTITUDES & VALUES

The anonymous survey questionnaires asked each manager to report on his views of organizational relationships during the fall of 1963 as compared with a year earlier. EXHIBIT VIII shows that improvements had occurred in boss-subordinate relationships, within departments, and between work groups.

Perceived improvement was highest in intergroup and interdepartmental relationships, although impressively high in the other areas too. Improvement was again seen as higher in administrative-line than in technical-staff areas, as shown in EXHIBIT VIII-B.

CHANGING GROUND RULES

These perceived improvements, theoretically, came from more basic changes in values and attitudes among managers and the technical people. In order to test this, we devised a game whereby each member of a top-management committee (N = 19) chose from a deck of 132 cards those statements which best described managerial ground rules and values as they were "five years ago," "today," and "preferred for future" in the Sigma plant. The 19 managers' choices indicated a 26% shift from "either-or" and "compromise" card statements to statements representing an integrative synthesis (as shown in EXHIBIT IX). They hoped to see an even greater shift (17%) toward integrative values and ground rules in the future.

To the extent that "either-or" values still existed (as shown in the smaller circles), they had reversed direction from where they were five years ago. Current polarized values tended to emphasize stronger management. Five-year-ago values tended to emphasize weaker management direction. This weakness was apparently due to headquarters management's strong hand and the lack of incentive provided by the cost-plus contract. After the 1960 merger, a "tougher" line was followed by the plant manager, although this was not enthusiastically received by suspicious lower level managers, as we saw earlier. By 1963, however, there had emerged an integrative value system that was backed up by "tougher" task-oriented values.

This exhibit suggests that the changes in management ground rules were both rapid and extreme. "Soft" practices were condemned in the 1963 value system by Sigma's top management. Integrative values were preferred; but where these were not currently practiced, management saw "hard" values as being preferable to the "soft" ones of five years ago.

EXHIBIT VIII. CHANGES IN WORKING RELATIONSHIPS, 1962–1963

	PER CENT OF MANAGER RESPONDENTS REPORTING IMPROVEMENT IN:		
	The Way They Work Together With Their Boss	The Way Their Work Groups Work Together	The Way Their Work Group Works With Other Groups
A. Over-all improvement (N = 598)	49%	55%	61%
B. Departmental improvement Most improvement			
Administrative services (N = 67)	59%	68%	65%
Plastics (N = 106)	55%	60%	68%
Least improvement Research and development			
(N = 43)	36%	41%	59%
Engineering (N = 90)	37%	35%	55%

Note: Based on a questionnaire that asked each respondent to compare in three separate questions: (a) the way he works together with his boss, (b) the way his work group works together, and (c) the way his work group works with other groups.

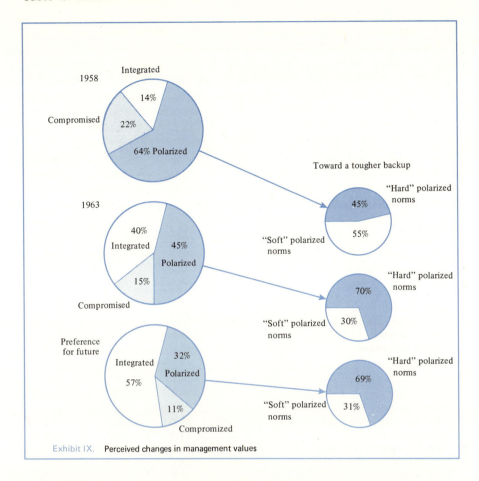

Exhibit IX. Perceived changes in management values

EFFECTS ON ATTITUDES

How were these perceived changes influenced by the organization development program? The evidence from the survey builds up some impressive links.

To begin with, the changes were directly in line with the 9,9 concepts introduced in Phase #1 of the Sigma program. "Integrative" values were disguised but consistent examples of 9,9 ground rules and norms. The "polarized" examples were analogous to 9,1 and 1,9 procedures and beliefs. The "compromise" statements, of course, were akin to 5,5 practices and values. The Phase #1 Grid sessions had tended to reward 9,9 and 9,1 behavior over and above the other styles of management. These same two patterns seem to have been most widely practiced in 1963, according to the management group that sorted the 132 cards in the game described earlier.

BOSS BEHAVIOR. Still further evidence of change directly in line with Phase #1 concepts is shown in EXHIBIT X and XI.

EXHIBIT X.   PERCEIVED CHANGES IN BOSS BEHAVIOR, 1962–1963

	PER CENT OF SUB-ORDINATES RATING MANAGER "HIGH"*		
	In 1962	In 1963	Increase or decrease
Dimensions stressed *in positive direction in Grid Seminar*			
"Keeps me informed"	45.3%	62.6%	+17.3%
"Aware of others"	42.9	55.3	12.4
"Plans ahead with me"	45.5	57.6	12.1
"Encourages suggestions"	53.1	64.7	11.6
"Sets goals with me"	48.1	59.5	11.4
"Helps me to learn"	44.7	56.1	11.4
"Gets me to have high goals"	54.4	65.8	11.4
"Follows up with me on action"	53.8	64.5	10.7
"Listens carefully to me"	60.6	71.3	10.7
"Aware of himself"	63.9	72.8	8.9
Average	51.2%	63.0%	+11.8%
Dimensions not stressed *either positively or negatively in Grid Seminar*			
"States his views clearly"	58.2%	69.3%	+11.1%
"Rewards me for good job"	48.5	56.6	8.1
"Stands behind me"	65.9	72.8	6.9
"Has management's backing"	62.3	68.4	6.1
"Controls his emotions"	76.0	82.0	6.0
"Acts self-confident"	72.8	78.7	5.9
"Acts at ease"	78.6	83.4	4.8
Average	66.0%	73.0%	+ 7.0%

* Refers to the per cent of 606 questionnaire respondents rating their managers either "7" or "8" on an eight-point scale.

EXHIBIT X is tabulated from the reports of 606 participants on 17 specific changes in their boss's and work group's behavior in 1962 as compared with more recent behavior in 1963. The questionnaire used for this purpose included some items which were consistent with and important to Phase #1 training and others which were "equally good" but not emphasized in the Grid sessions. EXHIBIT X shows that 10 out of the 11 items depicting greatest boss improvement reflected ideas taken up explicitly in the Phase #1 training. Only one high-scoring item ("States his views clearly") had not been emphasized at that time. As for the other six items not stressed in the training, all show only moderate increases. Bosses had improved somewhat on these items, according to subordinates, but not as much as on the items addressed during the Phase #1 training.

EXHIBIT XI also suggests a cause-effect relationship between the Sigma program and changes in work-group behavior over the year. This time, negative rejection of some items (rather than positive reaction) was examined. We asked which items describing work-group practices were least accepted by managers in 1963, compared with those least accepted in 1962. Some of the items included were highly at odds with Phase #1 9,9 concepts, though not identified as such. Others were simply less relevant to the Phase

EXHIBIT XI.   PERCEIVED CHANGES IN WORK-GROUP NORMS, 1962–1963

	PER CENT OF MANAGERS RATING DIMENSIONS OF GROUP BEHAVIOR "RELATIVELY NEGATIVE"*		
	In 1962	In 1963	Increase or Decrease
Dimensions stressed *negatively in Grid Seminar*			
"Group's attitude toward a member who gives more importance to maintaining friendly relations than to solving work problems."	40.1%	65.2%	−25.1%
"Group's attitude toward a member who prefers to keep his own opinions to himself rather than to lay his cards on the table."	44.5	66.8	−22.3
"Group's attitude toward a member who prefers to do a job by himself rather than with other members of the group."	29.0	50.3	−21.3
"Group's attitude toward a member who often compromises when disagreement arises."	25.3	42.0	−16.7
Average	34.7%	56.1%	−21.4%
Dimensions not stressed *either positively or negatively in Grid Seminar*			
'Group's attitude toward a member who doesn't make up his mind until others have expressed their opinions."	40.4%	51.3%	−10.9%
"Group's attitude toward a member who prefers to spend his career at the plant rather than go elsewhere in the organization."	10.3	16.2	− 5.9
"Group's attitude toward a member who maintains a close friendly relationship with his boss."	59.1	51.2	+ 7.9
"Group's attitude toward a member who greatly outproduces other members of the group."	35.9	23.9	+12.0
Average	36.4%	35.7%	+ 0.8%

* Refers to the per cent of 606 questionnaire respondents rating dimensions of group behavior toward the negative end of an eight-point scale.

#1 training. EXHIBIT XI shows that the most strongly rejected practices in 1963 were those at odds with 9,9 beliefs. The "irrelevant" practices were less strongly rejected or were positively accepted.

EXHIBIT XII.   RATING OF MANAGERIAL GRID SEMINAR

| | PER CENT RATING GRID LABORATORY AS: | | | |
	High Very	High Somewhat	Low Somewhat	Low Very
A. Total respondents (N = 580)	37%	47%	10%	6%
B. Highest and lowest departments				
Highest rating				
Administrative services (N = 67)	51%	39%	8%	2%
Plastics (N = 106)	46%	35%	12%	7%
Lowest rating				
Engineering (N = 90)	33%	51%	9%	7%
Research and development (N = 43)	26%	51%	14%	9%

Note: Based on data from questionnaire asking respondents to evaluate the Grid Seminar for its job-related usefulness. An eight-point scale was provided. The results were later combined into four categories, 7 to 8 for "very high," 5 to 6 for "somewhat high," 3 to 4 for "somewhat low," and 1 to 2 for "very low."

POSITIVE RESPONSES. Favorable attitudes toward Phase #1 also appear in EXHIBIT XII. Participants were asked to evaluate their experience in the Grid Seminar. The results were generally favorable. The most positive responses came from the members of two administrative departments. The least enthusiastic responses (and even these were generally positive) came from the members of two technical departments.

These differences might reflect the fact that administrative men were currently receiving a larger share of evaluation and promotion rewards than before. They might also reflect the classic value differences associated with business, on the one hand, and science, on the other. Some interview data suggested that members of technical departments valued individualism over the team strategies of the organization development program. Although many of Sigma's managers (including the plant manager) were engineers or scientists by training and early work, our evidence suggests that they adopted managerial values when they left the technical departments. At any rate, administrative department managers were somewhat more enthusiastic about Sigma's program than were men from the technical departments.

Generally speaking, the changes reported in the behavior of bosses and work groups, as well as the changes in work practices (shown in EXHIBIT

IV), are right in line with the 9,9 values and ground rules designed into the Phase #1 training. Taken together with the enthusiasm for the Grid as a training experience, it is clear that most Sigma participants valued the on-the-job results of their organization development program.

SOME UNDERLYING FACTORS

The material discussed so far suggests that Sigma's program made an important contribution to: (a) productivity and profits, (b) changes in practices and behavior, and (c) at least some changes in attitudes and values among managers.

Although the underlying motivation may have existed long before this program, Sigma's program seemed to provide the specific vehicles for mobilizing and directing managerial energy. Perhaps other programs or methods would have worked just as well, though, as already stated, Sigma and other Piedmont plants had earnestly engaged in a number of them without comparable results in the past. In addition, the "hands-off" policy of the new headquarters group had not gained widespread improvement at Sigma any more than the more directive line taken by the previous headquarters group had. Furthermore, the plant manager's early managerial toughness had gained resistance as well as slow results.

Therefore, what were the causal factors in and around the organization development program that permitted it to make a contribution to Sigma's improved position? To examine these (and to gain even further understanding of the program's influence), we turn our attention next to a review of evidence and opinion that describes the underlying factors which seem crucial to Sigma's program and its contributions.

HEADQUARTERS ROLE

Earlier, we described the events which led Piedmont to exert pressures on the Sigma plant management for improved performance. In some respects, the pressures may have been overly subtle. Sigma's management did not fully appreciate just how important certain issues were to headquarters until these issues emerged in open discussion. This occurred for the first time during the three-day meeting suggested by Blake. As a result of this meeting, headquarters personnel became the source of help they sought to be, rather than the ambiguous threat they had been. At the same time, headquarters left implementation, including the organization development program, in the hands of the Sigma plant management.

The results of this new relationship seemed to satisfy headquarters management. The verdict late in 1963 was that Sigma had made considerable progress and that headquarters-plant relationships had improved. After the first year of Sigma's program, Piedmont's management expressed strong pleasure and partial surprise at Sigma's improved position.

CONSULTANTS' CONTRIBUTION

At this point the work and reputation of Blake and Mouton provided the specific departure point for an organization development effort. Their prior design of the Grid Seminar and their six-phase concept of organization development represented a significant contribution, even though they themselves spent little time at the plant.

PLANT MANAGER'S SUPPORT

An early and especially important factor was the support and subsequent involvement of the plant manager. His enthusiasm became a strong stimulus and model for the rest of the plant. He remained in the middle of the program rather than on the outside where he might have guided the effort with impersonal mechanisms. More important, he made some significant modifications in his own behavior.

These changes in the plant manager's behavior could not be called major personality changes. Instead, they seemed to reflect changes in his concept of working with others on management problems. Most of the changes were consistent with behavior he had long practiced within the organization. He had a reputation for being a creator and advocate of new projects. He had always disliked being second to others. He had a profound respect for science and extended some of this respect to the behavioral sciences. Finally, he had always explained and shown his ideas to others before implementing them. During the program, the plant manager found that although the ground rules of management relationships had changed, none of them violated his basic beliefs. One of his top subordinates made the following comments:

"He has certainly taken a hard look at the way he runs his business and is trying to change. I think he is trying to involve more people and is more considerate of others. It is not so much a change, though, as it is a recognition that others once misunderstood him. I think he found that others saw him as intolerant because of his enthusiasm. I've always seen him as a pretty strong '9,9,' but no one else seemed to recognize it. He has a real strong '9,1' backup theory though. I think his experience in the Managerial Grid session made him stop and think; being a real intelligent man, he's made a change. He has learned to listen and to be more patient. Also, we have learned to talk better and insist on having a say. It's a two-way street."

TOP-MANAGEMENT INVOLVEMENT

The Sigma top-management group became involved at an early date in discussions of the program. More important, they chose to become involved not only as students in the Phase #1 training but as rotating instructors for two-week periods. Our material shows this group to be among the key supporters of the program and instrumental in the follow-up projects.

Moreover, the teaching-learning role provided further evidence of the program's impact. Using questionnaire data, we derived "most improved" and "least improved" categories from weighted scores taken from subordinates' ratings of superiors' improvement. As many as 16 of the 22 "instructors" were among the ‹87 "most improved" bosses as evaluated by their own managerial subordinates. Only one "instructor" was included in the 35 "least improved" superiors.

This finding suggests that being an instructor in Phase #1 served to reinforce a man's understanding of 9,9 principles as well as to aid his on-the-job practice.

The 9,9 commitment of this group had apparently been strengthened by their early success in reducing manpower under delicate community and union conditions. When 9,9 problem-solving methods helped them to accomplish the difficult manpower reduction task, the top-management group became strong supporters of the organization development program.

Considering their involvement and support, what did this group look like in action? Were they now a collection of 9,9 supermen? Had each made significant changes in his behavior? These questions are important, and the answers are "no." Instead, the top-management group had agreed collectively (and continued to reinforce) a set of 9,9 ground rules among themselves. The balance was precarious, however. Two or three key individuals seemed to be most highly respected as 9,9 interpreters and proponents. Several others were "take-charge" and "task-oriented" members who still demonstrated respect for the 9,9 ground rules. Still others helped to formulate issues in nonthreatening ways. The tie that bound the group together was its shared commitment to 9,9 concepts and practices. As long as this tie held, the members seemed to feel that they could continue their pacesetting role within the organization.

LEARNING READINESS

The factors identified above did seem to influence men at or near the top of Sigma's organization. But these factors were not sufficient to explain the diverse attitudes found among the managers. There were less-evident forces which affected each manager in the plant. One of these was the attitude of some managers which made them more ready than others to learn in the Phase #1 training and thereafter. EXHIBITS V, VII-B and XII-B have already shown that technical-staff men were generally less involved and enthusiastic than administrative-line managers. EXHIBIT XIII shows that the technical managers were seen as less improved by their subordinates also. In general, technical managers from R & D, engineering, and production planning received fewer "improvement" ratings from subordinates than others managers.

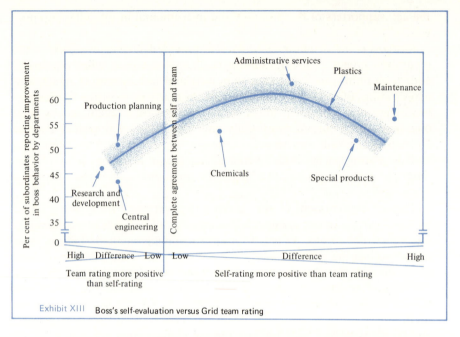

Exhibit XIII   Boss's self-evaluation versus Grid team rating

EXHIBIT XIII also shows how these on-the-job "improvement" ratings correspond with a boss's self-evaluation *before* Phase #1 training, and his team's evaluation of him *during* Phase #1 training. (These two evaluations were done with the assistance of Grid teaching material made available to us.)

An analysis of this material shows that:

Technical managers and staff tended to rate themselves as less 9,9 *before* Phase #1 than their colleagues did *during* Phase #1 training. In other words, technical men tended to be "overrewarded" by their colleagues.

Administrative managers tended to rate themselves as more 9,9 *before* Phase #1 than their colleagues did *during* Phase #1 training. In other words, administrative men were "underrewarded" by their colleagues.

According to EXHIBIT XIII, it is the administrative managers, "under-rewarded" by their teams, who showed more improvement than technical managers, who were "overrewarded." Why? One explanation is that administrative managers, rating themselves as 9,9 to begin with, were given an incentive to improve by the sobering comments of their Seminar team-mates. Technical managers, who tended not to see themselves as 9,9 to begin with, were given little incentive to improve because their teams told them they were "better" than they thought they were. However, there is apparently such a thing as too much "underrewarding" (note the downturn of the curve to the right in EXHIBIT XIII). If the administrative manager's 9,9 self-rating was too much higher than the evaluation given him by his Seminar team, his subordinates would tend to find him less improved than those managers (at the peak of the curve) who were slightly "underrewarded" in the Seminar.

In other words, some Phase #1 participants seem to have been more ready and receptive to Managerial Grid learning than others (although even these were seen as improved by subordinates, according to EXHIBIT XIII.) The higher-readiness learners described themselves as 9,9 managers before training and received team impetus toward further steps in that direction. The lower-readiness learners, with little team impetus toward improvement, tended to be technically (not managerially) oriented. In a later interview, one of these technical men talked as follows:

"I see no point in having scientific personnel take this training course. We believe the results of reproducible experiments and can be informed and convinced without [personal] experience. The data from other experiments will do the job. . . . The program gives a much better understanding of people who can discuss Shakespeare endlessly, or who can enjoy baseball without paying attention to any other sport. One can get into the habit of enjoying a single activity to the exclusion of all else. Give the program enough time on the present tack, and we can become so interested in interpretation of management action that we can play happily at this for years and forget all about the realities of management."

REINFORCED EFFORTS

The final factor underlying the plant changes at Sigma occurred after Phase #1 training. This involved the extent to which boss and colleagues reinforced a manager's efforts to change his behavior. To show the importance of this reinforcement, we can examine its presence among the "most improved" and the "least improved" managers (according to their subordinates' weighted ratings).

EXHIBIT XIV shows that 77% of the 87 "most improved" managers had bosses who were also "most improved." This suggests that a man's superior is a major force in his learning and improvement, until we note that 55% of the 35 "least improved" managers *also* had bosses who were "most improved." Apparently the boss's improvement wasn't the most important reinforcing agent, although it does seem to have exerted some influence.

EXHIBIT XIV. RELATIONSHIP BETWEEN MANAGER IMPROVEMENT AND SUPERIOR-COLLEAGUE SUPPORT
(Evaluations by subordinates)

	Superior also rated among "most improved"	Setting where "most improved" colleagues outnumbered "least improved" colleagues
Managers rated as "most improved" (N = 87)	77%	92%
Managers rated as "least improved" (N = 35)	55%	26%

EXHIBIT XIV also shows that colleague reinforcement may have been a more important key than boss reinforcement. Of the "most improved" managers, 92% worked in settings where "most improved" colleagues outnumbered "least improved," while only 26% of the "least improved" managers worked in similar settings.

A closer analysis of these 26% "least improved" managers in "most improved" groups shows they were outnumbered by "most improved" colleagues by only a 2.55 to 1 ratio. In contrast, the 92% "most improved" managers worked in settings where "most" outnumbered "least" by a ratio of 3.41 to .33. This suggests that the chances for manager improvement in the eyes of subordinates were greatest when a manager worked with larger numbers of others who also sought improvement. Or put another way, possibly one "least improved" cynic was enough to dampen his fellows' enthusiasm and therefore their chances of being among the "most improved." This possibility is supported by the fact that 60% of the "most improved" managers worked in settings where there were *no* "least improved" colleagues to disillusion the 9,9 atmosphere being built.

These data suggest that Phase #1, the plant manager, and a man's boss all played secondary roles when it came to making the lessons of Phase #1 "stick." The most important reinforcers were a manager's own colleagues who either encouraged and supported, or discouraged, his improvement efforts.

CONCLUSION

We can return now to the reasons for studying the Sigma program which were given at the start of Part II. To begin with, we wished to know whether the program had been successful in transferring behavioral science concepts into organizational action. Now, after reviewing the program and its consequences, even a conservative answer to this question would seem to be "yes." The program had become a part of day-to-day managerial activities at Sigma. Both in opinion and behavior, most managers endorsed the work patterns presented in the Phase #1 Grid Seminar.

A second reason for studying the Sigma program was the unusual teaching-learning role adopted by line management. The evidence shows that not only did senior line managers take the key "instructor" roles during Phase #1, but they later stood out as among the "most improved" managers in the eyes of their subordinates. It seems likely that the "instructor" roles helped to reinforce their attempted 9,9 behavior back on the job.

With regard to psychiatric difficulties, which was another concern in studying the Sigma program, there was, to the best of our knowledge, no evidence of any such issue among the 800 men who participated in the program. This suggests that the Phase #1 Grid training was relatively "safe" in this company setting because of its emphasis on managerial styles rather than on personal introspection.

The final reason given for studying the Sigma program involved the question of groups as units of learning versus individuals. As we have seen, learning (improvement in the eyes of subordinates) was greatest when supported strongly by colleague values and norms. Where this reinforcement was weak or not present, managers were far more likely to be evaluated as among the "least improved" by their own subordinates. Consequently, colleague groups apparently were crucial in helping individual learning become organization development.

The chances are fairly strong that this crucial factor has been missing in countless would-be organization development programs—including previous efforts within Sigma and Piedmont. In all of these cases, the supporting groundwork of shared values was most likely neglected or made too abstract to be implemented.

MANAGEMENT IMPLICATIONS

The lessons from this study also involve a number of implications for businessmen. Initially, it *does* appear that behavioral science and human relations education can assist with large-scale organization development under certain conditions. These conditions, as suggested by our data, include:

Demanding but tolerant headquarters.

An enthusiastic and involved top-manager and senior management group.

Educational strategy that effectively and continuously builds team problem solving and mutual support into work-related issues.

An organization whose work requires some interdependent effort and common values.

This study suggests that managerial and team effectiveness *can* be taught by managers with outside assistance. Furthermore, it appears that this type of educational strategy can help to make significant contributions to organizational effectiveness. This in itself seems to be an important lesson for management to recognize and use in its future efforts to build stronger organizations.

BIBLIOGRAPHY

Argyris, Chris, *Personality and Organization,* New York: Harper & Row, Publishers, 1957.

Barnard, Chester, *Functions of the Executive,* Cambridge, Mass.: Harvard University Press, 1938.

Beach, D.S., *Personnel: The Management of People at Work,* New York: Crowell-Collier and Macmillan, Inc., 1965.

Bennis, W., and E. Shein, *Personnel and Organizational Change Through Group Methods: Laboratory Training,* New York: John Wiley & Sons, Inc., 1965.

Blake, Robert R., and Jane S. Mouton, *The Managerial Grid,* Houston, Tex.: The Gulf Publishing Company, 1964.

Blough, Roger, *Free Man and the Corporation: McKinsey Lectures,* Columbia University, Graduate School of Business, New York: McGraw-Hill, Inc., 1959.

Chapple, Elliot, and Leonard R. Sayles, *The Measure of Management,* rev. ed., New York: Crowell-Collier and Macmillan, Inc., 1961.

Collins, B., and H. Guetzkow, *A Social Psychology of Group Processes for Decision Making,* New York: John Wiley & Sons, Inc., 1964.

Dale, Ernest, *The Great Organizers,* New York: McGraw-Hill, Inc., 1960.

Dalton, Melville, *Men Who Manage,* New York: John Wiley & Sons, Inc., 1959.

Dill, W., T. Hilton, and W. Reitman, *The New Managers,* Englewood Cliffs, N.J.: Prentice-Hall, Inc., 1962.

Drucker, Peter F., *Managing For Results,* New York: Harper & Row, Publishers, 1964.

———, *The Practice of Management,* New York: Harper & Row, Publishers, 1954.

French, W., *The Personnel Management Process,* Boston: Houghton Mifflin Company, 1954.

Gardner, John W., *Self Renewal,* New York: Harper & Row, Publishers, 1964.

Gellerman, Saul, *The Management of Human Relations,* New York: Holt, Rinehart and Winston, Inc., 1966.

Ginsberg, E., ed., *What Makes an Executive—A Columbia Roundtable,* New York: Columbia University Press, 1955.

Haire, Mason, *Psychology in Management,* New York: McGraw-Hill, Inc., 1956.

Hampton, D., Charles E. Summer, and R. Webber, eds., *Organizational Behavior and the Practice of Management,* Glenview, Ill.: Scott, Foresman and Company, 1968.

Homans, Paul, *The Human Group,* New York: Harcourt, Brace & World, Inc., 1950.

Houston, G.C., *Manager Development: Principles and Perspectives,* Homewood, Ill.: Richard D. Irwin, Inc., 1961.

Hutchinson, John G., *Managing a Fair Day's Work,* Ann Arbor, Mich.: University of Michigan, Bureau of Industrial Relations, 1963.

———, *Organizations: Theory and Classical Concepts,* New York: Holt, Rinehart and Winston, 1967.

Jay, Anthony, *Management and Machiavelli,* New York: Holt, Rinehart and Winston, Inc., 1968.

Jennings, E., *An Anatomy of Leadership,* New York: Harper & Row, Publishers, 1960.

Jerome, W., *Executive Control—The Catalyst,* New York: John Wiley & Sons, Inc., 1961.

Knudsen, H.R. *Human Elements of Administration,* New York: Holt, Rinehart and Winston, Inc., 1963.

Koontz, Harold, and Cyril O'Donnell, *Management: A Book of Readings,* New York, McGraw-Hill, Inc., 1964.

Lawrence, P., and John A. Seiler, *Organizational Behavior and Administration,* rev. ed., Homewood, Ill.: Richard D. Irwin, Inc., 1965.

Likert, Rensis, *The Human Organization,* New York: McGraw-Hill, Inc., 1967.

Lynton, R., and U. Pareck, *Training for Development,* Homewood, Ill.: Richard D. Irwin, Inc., 1967.

MacFarland, D., and F. Wickert, eds., *Measuring Executive Effectiveness,* New York: Appleton-Century-Crofts, 1967.

McGregor, Douglas, *The Human Side of Enterprise,* New York: McGraw-Hill, Inc., 1960.

McGuire, Joseph W., *Theories of Human Behavior,* Englewood Cliffs, N.J.: Prentice-Hall, Inc., 1964.

Moment, D., and A. Zalesnik, *The Dynamics of Interpersonal Behavior,* New York: John Wiley & Sons, Inc., 1964.

Newman, William H., Charles E. Summer, and E. Kirby Warren, *The Process of Management,* rev. ed., Englewood Cliffs, N.J.: Prentice-Hall, Inc., 1967.

O'Connell, J., *Managing Organizational Innovation,* Homewood, Ill.: Richard D. Irwin, Inc., 1967.

Odiorne, George S., *How Managers Make Things Happen,* New York: McGraw-Hill, Inc., 1961.

————, *Personnel Policy: Issues and Practices,* Columbus, Ohio: Merrill, 1963.

Piffner, John M., and Frank P. Sherwood, *Administrative Organization,* Englewood Cliffs, N.J.: Prentice-Hall, Inc., 1960.

Pigors, P., and C. Meyers, *Personnel Administration,* 4th ed., New York: McGraw-Hill, Inc., 1961.

Porter, D., and P. Applewhite, eds., *Studies in Organizational Behavior and Management,* Scranton, Pa.: International Textbook Company, 1964.

Riegel, John W., *Executive Development,* Ann Arbor, Mich.: University of Michigan, Bureau of Industrial Relations, 1952.

Roethleisberger, Fritz, and William J. Dickson, *Management and the Worker,* Cambridge, Mass.: Harvard University Press, 1939.

Schleh, E.C., *Management by Results,* New York: McGraw-Hill, Inc., 1961.

Strauss, G., and Leonard R. Sayles, *Personnel: The Human Problems of Management,* 2nd ed., Englewood Cliffs, N.J.: Prentice-Hall, Inc., 1967.

Stryker, P., *The Characteristics of the Executive,* New York: Harper & Row, Publishers, Harper Torchbooks, 1960.

Tanenbaum, A.S., *Social Psychology and the Work Organization,* Belmont, Calif.: Wadsworth Publishing Company, 1966.

Tyler, L., *The Psychology of Human Differences,* 2nd ed., New York: Appleton-Century-Crofts, 1956.

Whyte, William F., *Human Relations in the Restaurant Industry,* New York: McGraw-Hill, Inc., 1948.

Though all phases of managerial activity pose difficult challenges in the future, some areas will place greater demands on management than others. This part identifies four areas where special degrees of skill and knowledge will be required: international operations, government relations, labor relations, and research and development. These areas are growing in import and complexity, and, from all indications, they will continue to do so in the future. As business moves closer and closer to a "one-world" concept, new and different problems will enter the executive suite. The role of government agencies as competitors, customers, regulators, and partners undoubtedly will continue to expand, and new approaches and philosophies will be needed to cope with this institutional evolution. Labor relations has always posed troublesome problems for managers, partially because general managers have allowed it to drift out of their hands. The future may allow no such luxury, so management of labor relations is emphasized more strongly here than in most management texts. Finally, management of research and development activities, one of the most publicized phases of business activity, is singled out for still more exposure. Creativity and project control are given major emphasis in this area, but other vital factors also receive close attention.

The wide coverage offered in Part Three necessarily means that scope is achieved at the expense of depth, but even an overview can provide meaningful insights if presented in terms of strategic and tactical overtones. The case-studies at the end of each chapter provide a limited number of realistic experiences to help fill out each

PART THREE
Critical Areas for Tomorrow's Managers

The past is but the beginning of a beginning, and all that is and all that has been is but the twilight of the dawn. . . . A day will come when beings . . . shall laugh and reach out their hands amid the stars.

H.G. Wells, *The Discovery of the Future*

401

chapter's coverage. Though the interested reader will undoubtedly have to probe more deeply into life and literature before he masters the details of the four special areas of management covered in this final part, he will have a guide to where the action is and some guidelines on how to handle it.

There is no doubt that government-business relations exert a powerful influence over modern management activities; a look at government hearings on auto safety and the resultant industry controls clearly show government's direct impact on business operations. Taxes and special investment credits influence private investment decisions. Government agency rulings have delayed mergers such as the one joining United and Capital airlines into today's massive United Airlines system and the courts have dissolved the marriage of Chlorox and Proctor & Gamble. In activities more far reaching than direct, selective controls, government has entered into joint ventures such as Telstar, and government agencies such as the Tennessee Valley Authority compete directly with private enterprise. In its many guises, government relates to business as customer, partner, regulator, and competitor; and from all indications, the scope and variety of its activities will undergo progressive expansion in the foreseeable future.

Active alert managements have long recognized the pervasive influence of government, but in spite of this awareness, their success in dealing with government has been much less pronounced than their relationships with other publics. Some of the failures in government-business relations are due to differences of opinion about hard-core economic facts, but a surprising amount of discord still seems traceable to ideological conflict.

Too often, old-time ideologies control the actions and the images of government-business relations and the outmoded stereotype of the business executive as a robber baron confuses the issue still further. In the words of former Dean Courtney Brown, of the Columbia University Graduate School of Business,

CHAPTER 15
Management of Government-Business Relations

... the intermingling of government and business activities that has occurred in the past century is but a prelude to even greater intermingling in the years ahead. One contemplating the respective roles of business and government in the middle of the nineteenth century could never have envisaged that business might make this kind of service available to mankind. Yet it has happened, and the fact of its happening serves to give emphasis to the thought that as the world moves toward greater abundance, and as technology and understanding bring to bear the full impact of their subtle benefits, the opportunities and range of instances of collaboration between government and business cannot fail to develop in ways that we do not now foresee nor could we anticipate. It is a healthy and encouraging thing, however, that we have finally emerged from the restrictions of rigid, ideological interpretations of their respective roles. No longer can we resort to the simple concept of nineteenth-century formulation and hold the businessman in one image, not too flattering, and the government man in a different and perhaps more attractive role. The old ideologies described in the top roles of government and business will have to be replaced, for they have been so faded by the march of time as to become little more than ancient incantations of little relevance.[1]

Dean Brown's point about images being no longer valid is all too true in the contemporary scene, and though the stereotype of the entrepreneur may live in the minds of certain businessmen, it is more valid there than in fact. There is scant evidence that government controls over business will dry up and wither away: controls will persist and grow. This fact is as inescapable as the old saying about death and taxes, which itself indicates the pervasiveness of government action.

Even though managements have recognized the important impact of government controls over business activities, few managers have handled relationships with government bodies with the skill they show in conducting other critical operations. Some of this ineffectiveness may have developed because of commitment to outmoded economic ideologies, but most difficulties seem to be rooted in misunderstandings of how government relates to business. Though ideological convictions change slowly, fairly rapid changes can be made in techniques and approaches. Thus, ideological factors are deemphasized in the following sections, while emphasis is placed on sketching approaches designed to bring about improvements in government-manager relations.

Some of the difficulties in business-government relations have come from the failure of business managers to recognize that government is not a monolithic structure. Government performs different functions in dealing with various portions of the business community: at times it assumes the guise of lender, policeman, nursemaid, servant, dictator, and protector; and these

---

[1] From a speech by Dean Courtney C. Brown, Conference on Government-Business Relations, American University, Washington, D.C., April 17, 1967.

postures can exist in varying permutations and combinations at any level of federal, state, or local government. In spite of the diversity of these roles, it is possible to identify those having the greatest effect on business operations.

While any grouping of complex relationships is hazardous, governmental units seem to influence business most directly as its customers, partners, regulators, or competitors. In order to deal most effectively with government, managers must first identify its roles and then develop the best means available to handle them. This chapter attempts to provide some insight into how this end may be accomplished.

GOVERNMENT AS A CUSTOMER

No other customer is as large as the United States government. One need only look at the Federal budget for any fiscal year to grasp the enormity and impact of federal spending. For example, in 1968 total expenditures, estimated in terms of payments to the public, were $172.4 billion, while total receipts from the public were estimated at $168.1 billion. National defense expenditures swelled to $76.8 billion and health, education and welfare expenditures totaled $47.6 billion. Veterans cost another $6.7 billion, interest on the national debt was $10.5 billion, and civilian and military pay increases fell into the $1 billion range. These massive expenditures, when added to the burgeoning expenditures of state and local units, make government a customer of almost unbelievable size. To put it another way, one fifth of the outlay in the United States is accounted for by government spending.

What are the characteristics of the massive market that is government? Actually, "government" is not one customer, but a broad and complex market. The purchasing policies of many of the thirty thousand school boards in the United States are light years away from those the Pentagon uses to select a prime contractor for a major weapons system. Business has recognized this difference at the federal level, but has done a much less successful job in dealing with state and local governments. Sales efforts at state and local levels have been somewhat haphazard in past years and market research in these markets has been neither extensive nor effective. Any large complex market calls for market research which tells what products can best be sold and the kinds of special treatment demanded by major customers. All of these considerations apply to government selling, and better research is needed to bring about a successful sales effort. Very few firms have recognized the full potential of government sales, and so the Boeings, Lockheeds, General Electrics, and dozens of other smaller firms with savvy have done well in dealing with the government.

Some of the arguments used against entering the government market are that it is fraught with low margins, red tape, and the frustration of dealing with bureaucrats.[2] In addition, complaints are often lodged about difficulties

---

[2] See for example, the Avion Aircraft case at the end of this chapter and the International Mineral and Chemical Company case after Chapter 18.

in finding out whom to contact, where to go, and what to do. But these objections differ little from those encountered in reaching any market. The profits are there for successful firms and so is the volume, and the skills and expertise needed to tap the government market are no more difficult to come by than those needed to reach any other major market area.

The role of government as a customer is easy to recognize, even though businessmen are often uneasy in dealings with governmental units. At least part of the problem exists in the internal organization of government units, but much of the difficulty lies in the fact that business has failed to cultivate the skills needed to deal with this complex, massive, and potentially profitable market.

GOVERNMENT AS A PARTNER

In recent years, the number of government-business partnerships has increased sharply, partly because of the high cost of research and partly because of the scientific advances springing from areas with either military or quasimilitary potential. Government and business have joined in partnership to develop a series of recent scientific and technical breakthroughs including rocket and missile development, earth satellites and space vehicles, underwater research, borings into the earth's crust, and dozens of other activities. These efforts provide dramatic evidence of how a joining together of government and industrial specialists can forge massive advances. Though many government-business ventures have military overtones, commercial applications often follow. And the firms participating in the government development and research phases have typically been allowed to introduce these products into appropriate civilian markets. Boeing, for example, has profited greatly from the sale of 707 jet liners whose forerunner was the military KC135 jet tanker. The Telstar satellite is another endeavor that has now, in a joint government-business effort, entered the commercial phases of its development. In housing, many cities have set up boards to work with private firms to develop low-cost housing and solve the financial problems which tend to bog down housing improvements in slum areas. In education, state governments have long set standards and controls over education and worked out curriculum changes with local school boards and private agencies interested in bringing new techniques such as programmed learning into the schools.

In many countries, public transportation and communication systems are in the hands of the government. Such has not been the case in the United States, but this may change as Telstar, the introduction of high-speed trains, and the government's control and financing of supersonic transport (SST) herald the coming of increasing governmental control. For example, the SST is a joint venture between the Federal Aviation Authority, airframe and engine manufacturers, and the various airlines—all of whom will share in the plane's development costs and will benefit from its use. Since the massive R&D effort needed to develop the SST could not be borne by private industry, government support was imperative, and government controls inevitably followed government commitments.

As research projects grow in size and complexity, government funding increases sharply, as do concomitant controls. Managements are more and more aware of government's expanding role as a partner in many activities formerly reserved to business, and this change has fostered the development of a changing ideology. Assuming that a firm does not wish to be a partner of government, it is almost forced to choose directions away from high-cost technology and/or areas that might bring about voluntary or involuntary connection with government research or matters involving national security. To stay in these areas, managements must be willing to cooperate with governmental units and to accept government as both a partner and a regulator.

If the choice is made to work with the government, then firms seem well advised to set up offices whose main function is to deal with the special needs and problems encountered in government-business transactions. For example, a firm must be prepared to deal with security restrictions, it must develop ways of handling governmental reporting and disclosure procedures, and it must build a tolerance for the frustrations that result when profit-oriented mentalities clash with value frameworks shaped by public-service motives. For larger firms in particular, it seems important to initiate and develop improvements in government relations, for whether business likes it or not, government-business unions, for better or worse, are becoming more common.

GOVERNMENT AS A REGULATOR

Though government's roles as customer and partner are growing in importance, governmental regulatory activities still generate the lion's share of attention. One doesn't have to be a student of business to know how many businessmen feel about government controls and constraints. Some of these constraints come from government's position as a partner or as a customer, for example, whether government grants contracts or withholds technical developments can be a life-or-death matter in some businesses. These growing pressures and restraints arise mostly in the executive branch of government, as presidents, governors, mayors, and other government administrators trade on economic power to influence, restrain, coerce, or cajole businesses to move in particular directions. One example of how the President of the United States can influence business practice is the way President Kennedy and President Johnson fought price increases in the steel industry. At the state level, governors Romney of Michigan and Rockefeller of New York have been prominent in settling labor disputes. The role of local officials is illustrated by Mayor John Lindsay's efforts to attract new industry into New York City and his attempts to induce established firms to remain there in the face of transportation, labor, school, and tax problems.

Quasi-judicial bodies also can exert important influences over business activities. The famous "television is a vast wasteland" speech by Newton Minow of the FCC is one example of a government regulatory body exercising influence over private enterprise. Another is the manner in which the policies of Federal Reserve Board chairmen William Martin and Arthur Burns have periodically tended to influence the financial community. Executive and quasi-executive boards thus have an important influence on business activity, but even more important restraints are imposed by the other two branches of government.

Legislative and judicial interpretations and limitations arising therefrom are the government's formal means of constraining business activities. Any number of schemes might be used to classify the kinds of legislative acts and decisions influencing business, but five general classes contain the core of restrictive limitations:

1. "General welfare" legislation
2. Tax laws
3. Labor laws
4. Antitrust laws
5. International regulations

GENERAL WELFARE LEGISLATION

This class of legislation is widespread in scope and coverage. It includes matters such as fair employment practice acts at the state level, civil rights legislation, social security statutes, fair labor standards acts, state and federal unemployment compensation statutes, medical insurance coverage (including Medicare), public-housing legislation, aid to education, workmen's compensation, accident and insurance laws, and safety and health codes. All of these rules or legislative acts place constraints and levy financial burdens on the business community and individual firms.

Though many of these laws are seen as beneficial by businessmen, they tend to add another cost burden to the going business. Since there is every reason to believe that general welfare legislation will expand in the near future, and since business will have to help finance such programs, planning to meet expected new levies seems to be in order.

TAX LAWS

No law-abiding citizen having an annual income over the minimum allowance for exemption needs to be told how income taxes affect individual finances. Federal income taxes and their first cousin, the state income tax (and now a third cousin, the city income tax) have a painfully evident effect on practically every American. Income taxes are only one form of the tax burden, which includes almost every shape and color. Taxes can be levied on income, transactions, sales, property, and even, in some cases, on suspicion of being included under any of these or other labels. There will probably be few changes in future tax structures, but it seems highly possible that state and local taxes will increase in amount and nature. In addition, it seems likely that the tax power will be used much more selectively to control business activities.

From the business point of view, taxes can influence decisions covering a wide range of areas. In 1967, the prospect of a 6-percent (tax) surcharge on individual income tended to cause a stutter in the economy and influenced the consumer expectations that businessmen watch so closely in building up or drawing down inventories. The possible reinstatement of a sudden investment tax credit, on the other hand, tended to cause business to think more about its long- and short-run expenditure policies and to reconsider capital budgeting decisions. In economic circles, it is currently fashionable to consider raising or lowering business or personal taxes to bring about changes in the level of economic activity. If the tax power is eventually used in such flexible fashion, it will assume a still more important role in determining management strategies and tactics.

LABOR LAWS

Labor laws have a direct influence on the organization of workers and the relationship of management and employees. The Clayton Act of 1914 and the Norris-LaGuardia Anti-injunction Act of 1932 tried to free labor unions from restrictive controls by the courts. Injunctions had been widely used to limit union activities, and the Norris-LaGuardia Act in particular attempted to restrict the conditions under which injunctions could be utilized to stop labor disputes. With the passage of the National Labor Relations Act (NLRA) in 1935, the government established a national policy of recognizing and supporting unions and set up a National Labor Relations Board to help carry out this policy. Included in the NLRA was a list of unfair labor practices designed to limit managerial action against attempts to organize American workers. The Taft-Hartley Act in 1948 added balance to the somewhat one-sided picture by listing unfair labor practices for both management *and* labor and by including a "national emergency" provision to limit strike actions in industries affecting the national interest. This act also established the Federal Mediation and Conciliation Service to assist in reducing industrial conflict. One added proposal here was the establishment of the right to sue to collect financial damages caused by labor disputes (Section 301). The Landrum-Griffin Act of 1959 placed greater restraints on the activities of the unions and their leaders and set up rules for reporting union finances, with stipulations for stiff penalties when its reporting and disclosure provisions were violated.

Since labor legislation receives additional attention in Chapter 16, the only comment called for here is that all of the aforementioned acts have served to establish additional constraints under which governments regulate dealings between organizations and their employees.

ANTITRUST LEGISLATION

The list of antitrust laws in the United States is not long, but judicial interpretation of these acts has made their effect pervasive. The basis for many court rulings appears in the grandfather of all antitrust legislation, the Sherman Act of 1890. The Sherman Act made contracts, combinations, and conspiracies to restrain trade among the several states and with foreign nations illegal, and it set up sanctions in the form of fines and divestitures. The Clayton Act of 1914 was a fairly major amendment to the Sherman Act in that it forbade companies from acquiring stock in other companies if their aim was to restrain trade or lessen competition. It also included prohibitions against price discrimination (except when made in good faith to meet competition), the formation of exclusive dealing and tying arrangements that would tend to restrain competition, and the establishment of interlocking directorates between firms having competitive interests in a market. The Robinson-Patman Act of 1938 was another law which prohibited the use of price discrimination to restrain competition including the granting of discriminatory discounts. The Celler-Kefauver Act of 1950 prohibited the acquisition of stock or assets of other corporations where the effect might be to lessen competition substantially or to tend to create a monopoly.

These acts have been expanded and interpreted quite liberally in many different court decisions. One classic decision broke up the Standard Oil Company in 1913, and another in 1957 forced DuPont to divest its interest in General Motors. Other rulings have delayed or prevented mergers prior to their consummation. A proposed (1967) merger between the International Telegraph & Telephone Corporation and the American Broadcasting Company was delayed by court decision as was a then-pending merger between the New York Central System and the Pennsylvania Railroad, which was eventually approved.

A brief history of the more famous antitrust cases show the kinds of problems and inconsistencies which have arisen from various court decisions. The U.S. Steel Case in 1920 created a ruling that monopoly was in evidence only where its intent was illegal. This good-intent motive held for many years, but in the Alcoa Case in 1945, price fixing was declared to be illegal whether or not it was accomplished by collusion or size. In effect, what the decision said was that size per se *did* constitute monopoly and was therefore illegal regardless of intent. There have also been some extremely confusing interpretations of the discriminatory pricing sections of the Robinson-Patman Act. The only conclusion an impartial observer can draw from these interpretations is that the law means that *competitors,* not competition, should be protected. The confusion over this act is so extensive that *any* pricing decisions stands a high probability of being illegal, even when the firm fixing the price has tried to obey the law. If a firm sets its prices *at the same level* as competitors *or at different levels,* it can, under existing rulings, be performing an illegal act.

Antitrust rulings have created a seething mass of frustration for business.

Since few real guidelines exist, the only certainty seems to be uncertainty, a highly tentative and undesirable state. Since reforms are not likely in the foreseeable future, antitrust regulations will probably continue to be a sore point in government-business relations.

INTERNATIONAL REGULATIONS

Tariffs have long been part of the regulatory scene. Often backed by particular businesses, tariffs and other regulations covering international trade have generated considerable concern, but the criticisms are no worse than those leveled at other governmental restraints. One constraint on worldwide business activity appears in treaties or international agreements wherein businesses are prohibited from trading in certain areas or selling goods in specific countries. Following the rise of the Castro regime, Cuban goods were not allowed to enter the United States and American businesses were forbidden to export goods to Cuban ports. Even Cuban cigars purchased by U.S. citizens at Canada's Expo 67 were not allowed across the border. On the other hand, certain nations are given favored treatment in trade with the United States under the "most favored nation" clause in trade regulations.

Government controls over international trade are both negative and positive: subsidies may be granted in the form of fast tax write-offs; embargoes and shipments of arms may be set up to constrain movements of goods across certain borders; American restrictions on sales of goods to Communist countries are widespread; and constraints and quotas are levied on imports such as oil and Japanese goods. All of these artificial rules influencing free trade or trade-related matters such as currency blockages are becoming more critical to the United States, since American business is now moving rapidly into worldwide markets. As world trade increases, such limitations will call for closer study by thoughtful businessmen, and programs designed to deal with restrictions and controls will become part of the planning activities of almost every firm with international commitments. In the present state of the arts, this means that every major firm has a stake in suggesting changes designed to enhance the free movement of goods across national boundaries.

GOVERNMENT AS A COMPETITOR

Of all the relationships between government and business, government's role as a competitor is perhaps the most distasteful to the business community. Most businessmen probably never will agree that government should compete directly with business in the product market, particularly since government groups are partially financed by tax dollars supplied by businesses and, worse still, are exempt from taxation themselves. Clearly, this line of thinking has some validity, but, as is so often the case, there is another side to the coin. Government does serve a useful function in many areas where its role is clearly noncompetitive. Business leaders do not want to run unprofitable city transit systems, but they do object to governments running potentially profitable transportation operations. Businessmen typically are not interested in such unprofitable things as rural electrification programs, but they do complain about the Tennessee Valley Authority. Apparently, there is a great difference between profitable and unprofitable situations: government can enter an area of loss and business remains quiet, but a clamor rises when the government contemplates entering a market where profits are available. The question here is who should do what in which area, and this conflict undoubtedly will persist until clear limits are drawn, a solution unlikely to occur in the near future. Fortunately, government's role as a competitor has less impact on the business scene than its other areas of regulatory constraint. Indeed, a forward look indicates that government-business competition will not increase substantially, particularly since government has now taken the tack of emphasizing partnerships with business above competitive relationships.

DEALING WITH GOVERNMENT: MANAGERIAL ACTION PROGRAMS

All of the general government activities constraining business have tended to create or perpetuate conflict, misunderstanding, mistrust, and general concern in government-business dealings. As a consequence, both sides have now begun to devote greater efforts to lessening the nature and degree of existing differences. It seems unlikely, however, that differences of opinion will disappear entirely; and, for this reason, management might be well advised to develop positive forward-looking programs for dealing with all levels of government.

Two kinds of action programs can be identified in the area of managerial dealings with government: direct and indirect. Even though the emphasis in the past has focused on the federal government, these programs should be designed to deal with varying levels of government. The growing size and influence of state and local governments justifies the same level of planning and preparation called for in dealing with units of the federal government.

DIRECT ACTION PROGRAMS

Direct and indirect action programs are not mutually exclusive because any combination of activities can, in differing situations, provide the most meaningful relationship with government. Nor do all programs have equal appeal, since economic, moral, ideological, or esthetic values may exert disproportionate influence over the course a given management group deems most advantageous. Because of situational and value considerations, the choice process in this area is intricate, and the many nuances encountered are difficult to deal with fully within the limits constraining this text. For this reason, the coverage and depth of the direct action programs presented below are not exhaustive. Only the better-known programs appear, and space prohibits a complete discussion of how these programs might operate. They are thus presented in abbreviated form with only passing attempts to evaluate their efficacy.

One of the best known and most discussed aspects of government-business relations is the power of financial *contributions to political campaign funds.* Such contributions have never been studied exhaustively, but a great deal of folklore exists about "king making," "buying" legislators, and various other practices of the so-called business establishment. This controversial issue arose sharply in the 1964 presidential campaign, in which the Goldwater forces adamantly opposed the influence and control allegedly exerted by the "Eastern Establishment." In *The Making of the President 1964,* Theodore H. Whyte commented, "Wall Street can no longer command, yet it still leads. The Wall Street men do not meet collectively at the Banker's Club, nor can they be gathered any longer in a cozy group in J.P. Morgan's study to turn on or off the spigots of credit, yet they set the climate." Indeed, the granting of support by certain wealthy individuals and industrialists is alleged to have turned many elections in the direction of a favored candidate. In a day and age when political contributions by corporations are not tax deductible, contributions by individual executives who are allowed to pad loosely audited expense accounts accomplish the same purpose. Certainly, the power of the political contribution is great, even though its exact influence and extent is hard to determine.

In addition to direct political contributions by individuals, many organizations have developed other methods designed for *support of candidates.* For example, candidates have been given time off to campaign. Certain firms have provided individuals with leaves (paid and unpaid) and have given them access to the time and skills of key staff people. As a generalization, business organizations have begun more overtly to encourage political action. For example, the Ford Motor Company has openly encouraged its people to enter politics and Henry Ford, II, has spoken vigorously on the importance of people taking on more political responsibility as democratic citizens of the community.

The "Washington office" is simply one of the pseudonyms given to lobbying activities. Hiring a lobbyist or two or hiring an "influential" Washington law firm is a long-standing practice designed to gain favor or to present positions in a favorable light at the proper level of government. This approach is widely used at the state level, too; and in some firms the Sacramento or Albany office is becoming as important as that in Washington. All sorts of organizations indulge in lobbying; one need only note the location of the central headquarters of the AFL-CIO (just across the mall from the White House) to see how the labor movement competes with its industrial counterparts. Indeed, in both the scope and effectiveness of its lobbying activities, the labor movement has often been ahead of the industrial community.

Lobbying has come in for considerable attention, most of it unfavorable. The Bobby Baker scandal during the Johnson administration, the "five percenters" of the Truman years, and the famous vicuna coat of President Eisenhower's aide Sherman Adams have given lobbying and "influence peddling" a sinister public image. But not all lobbying is negative; shades of good and bad exist. Congress and other legislative and judicial bodies are far from perfect, and lobbies can inform as well as pressure. The five thousand lobbyists in Washington, D.C. alone are a formidable group, but they can help to protect the voter as well as hurt him simply because all lobbyists rarely wind up on the same side of an issue, and countervailing power is generated. Writing about lobbies, Senator Stephen Young of Ohio states, "More than 50 years of public life have taught me that lobbying can be good or bad, constructive or corrosive. It's all in the eyes of the beholder and the hands of the practitioner."[3] Reputable organizations should have no doubt about where they stand in the range of behavior implied by Senator Young. Even disregarding morality, long-term survival and growth must be based on forceful presentations of meritorious proposals, not on shabby unethical propositions clandestinely offered by underhanded sharpies and assorted shysters. In a speech before the Financial Executives Institute. Chase Manhattan President David Rockefeller suggested the formation of the business committee for social progress which would lobby for better social laws. This particular brand of lobbying is the kind business might well adopt and embrace to put forth its beliefs in the right places in the most effective manner.[4]

Somewhat related to lobbying activities, but of a distinctly different nature, is the *hiring of "influential" executives,* people who have served as military officers, Congressmen, or members of appointive boards or who simply possess some other connection with government activities, or simply have a great deal of savvy in dealing with government. Though these individuals may be top-drawer executives in their own right, they usually also have the prime additional benefit of being familiar with or able to influence particular units or people in the governmental establishment.

In its most moral form, the hiring of influential executives is simply an attempt to use well-qualified men to present a company's position in its most favorable light. In its more reprehensible form, it may be an attempt to bring pressure on people or a device to "buy" people able and willing to provide privileged information or tip-offs on such matters as stock offerings, and so on—activities which may not be illegal, but which may be either unethical or on the edge of legality. Used ethically, this activity is simply another means business has used to "get a fair hearing at the proper point in the government hierarchy." Used as a device to exert undue influence or to obtain "inside [unethical] information," it is both morally reprehensible and politically dangerous to a firm's hard-earned corporate image.

Loaning executives or services to the government is another possibility. Loaning executives is much more common than loaning services. Examples of this are abundant, particularly at the federal level. John Connor of Merck and

---

[3] "The Case for Lobbies," *Playboy,* January 1968, p. 65.
[4] *New York Times,* October 27, 1968, p. 37.

Company served as Secretary of Commerce. Defense secretaries Robert S. McNamara and Clark Clifford came from industry and law respectively; and innumerable other instances appear of business executives having been granted leaves or given special permission to serve on advisory boards or to work in various government bureaus. In 1968, Ford Foundation funds set in motion a program among thirty industrial firms which would allow younger executives in the $18,000 to $24,000 per year category to spend up to two years in government jobs on a lend-lease basis. In return, government officials would serve a similar time in an industrial organization.

In addition to swapping people, assets can be interchanged. Government agencies often use private laboratory facilities for research, particularly in the scientific area. This has been especially useful when scarce equipment or talents were needed in a hurry by the defense establishment. Interchanges of executives have proven to be particularly beneficial to both government and business. The talents of business people have been extremely useful in the management of governmental operations. In return, businessmen serving with governmental bureaus have gained an insider's knowledge of government practices that have been invaluable to them in subsequent dealings with government agencies. On balance, loaning of key executives has been a particularly fruitful form of government-business cooperation.

The use of *joint advisory boards* has provided a forum for an interchange of ideas between business interests and government agencies. Some of these advisory boards have been set up at the behest of business, while others have been initiated by the government. One of the best known examples is the President's Advisory Board on Labor-Management Relations. Another ad hoc example is the Special Committee to Study the Effects of Automation. These committees and boards have become more widespread at the federal level and have, in recent years, also appeared more commonly on the state and local scene. The establishment of joint boards is in part a reflection on the increasing degree of cooperation between government and business organizations, and it seems to be showing good results. Again, as in the case of interchanging executives, it tends to bring about an improved ability to communicate and a greater degree of understanding between the public and private sectors. Participation in these boards is advantageous because it provides business with an opportunity to influence policy without any real commitment of resources except time and travel expenses.

One of the most recent means business has used to attempt to influence or deal with government agencies is *direct appeal to the public*. A dramatic example of such appeal saw airframe manufacturers go directly to the public to gain support for their designs of a supersonic transport. The major competitors in the SST bidding took out full-page ads in the *New York Times* to convince the public that their particular approach to designing and building the SST was superior to the other's. Another example is the continual advertising of investor-owned utility companies which proclaim their superiority over government-run utilities.

Going to the consumer directly to attempt to influence government actions is a questionable procedure, principally because its effects are problematical. It is extremely doubtful that the public *does* exert much direct influence over government boards and agencies in matters of this kind. The practice itself may not be completely ineffective, however, because benefits may occur in the public relations and advertising areas when such campaigns are used. If a firm becomes better known because of this kind of institutional advertising, it may be better able to sell its securities in the open market.

Very little is known about the extent of *bribery and illegal practices* in government-business relationships. When a scandal breaks, the public gets alarmed and concern is expressed about how rampant corruption and bribery are. Illegal practices typically receive intensive coverage in the newspapers and when issues appear such as the massive road scandal in Massachusetts or sanitation department irregularities in New York, the public becomes both aroused and concerned. No moral individual can endorse bribery and corruption, and any business encouraging or condoning bribery of federal officials should suffer every available sanction. This discussion of illegal practices indicates no approval whatsoever, it simply points out the existence of such reprehensible practices.

INDIRECT ACTION PROGRAMS

Several forms of indirect activity have been undertaken by businesses to improve their relations with government or to gain a favored position. Most of these activities involve support of some kind for institutions or associations. A discussion of the best known approaches follows.

The National Association of Manufacturers is basically a *trade association,* while the Council for Economic Development (CED) is basically a *special interest association.* These associations are developed to try to promote the interests of business or business groups and they have become associated with sets of policies or statements of position. Though the benefits of membership in such associations is difficult to trace, individual firms may have benefited indirectly from better representation in hearings held by government bureaus or legislative bodies.

An example of an *independent or semiindependent foundation or board* is the National Industrial Conference Board (NICB), which is business-supported, but independent; while the Ford and Carnegie foundations are autonomous agencies founded by business contributors. The NICB publishes studies of the activities of its member firms and also delves into areas of general interest to members of the business community. Ford, Carnegie, and other foundations are quite independent and deal only in selected activities with the business community. Though these organizations support direct-action programs in some cases, their basic influence on government-business relations is exerted on both businessmen and government officials by the results of sponsored projects and research studies.

Internally controlled, or closely held foundations are independent in operation, but run on contributions donated by a particular sponsor or group of sponsors. The General Electric Foundation and the Ford Motor Company Fund belong to this general classification. With captive foundations, the focus of the foundation's activities can be influenced in the direction of the sponsoring organizations. Both direct-action programs and research studies can be utilized by internal foundations, and this enhances their effectiveness in bringing about better relationships with government. Though the activities of foundations are not limited to government solutions, they can (and have been) used to bring about improvements in government dealings with the business community.

Independent organizations and institutions of learning such as colleges, universities, and nonprofit laboratories like the Battelle Institute also provide ways of indirect action. Here, particular projects can be proposed, and if the independent organization feels that the project has some merit, it can proceed to do an "impartial study." Though the results are not usually controllable, the sponsoring institution does have some choice over what will be studied and perhaps even over the method of study.

At the other end of the scale from subordination of public employees are the laudatory concepts of the *junior achievement program*. Here, the business community attempts to work with youth to develop an understanding of how business operates and how the free enterprise system can provide incentives for individuals to better both themselves and their communities in which they live. Although the benefits to businesses are not as direct as from, say, the establishment of a Washington office, the long-term effects of junior achievement programs may be much more beneficial, since the favorable attitudes developed by participating youngsters tend to be carried with them for the rest of their lives. As a side benefit, the executives participating in these programs themselves gain a great deal from association with the young participants.

At the state and particularly the local level, business is moving more forcefully to develop *job opportunities and improvements in neighborhoods* in the central city. Usually managed jointly by business and government officials, these programs open communication lines between business and government that stay operative long after the completion of specific projects. The dual benefits of such relationships make them doubly rewarding for both participating executives and their parent organizations.

The basic rationale in indirect action is to force the development of studies, inquiries, and other investigations that will give more and better information on how business operates. Hopefully, the results will present business in a favorable light; but if not, the studies can be used to start corrective or, in some cases, evasive action. It is often hard to control the activities of the direct-action groups, but supporting them typically pays off for business in the long run. On the other hand, it can also cause problems. For example, studies of smoking by impartial laboratories have had a far-reaching negative effect on the cigarette industry. Generally, business can profit from being involved in research activities, since they provide useful information and may support business attempts to have a say in important issues. The CED, for example, has had a major voice in establishing business policies related to particular areas, and its research has been well accepted by nonbusiness interests, primarily because of the thoughtful preparation underlying most of its statements.

It seems apparent that business must take steps to represent itself to the government in a realistic light. This has particular importance today, since the representing function of business has been done poorly in the past. When William H. Whyte probed business's ability to present its views by asking the question. "Is anybody listening?" the answer was an emphatic "No!"[5] Business's ability to present its views still needs to be improved, and the methods outlined here can help to bring about that result.

AN OVERVIEW OF GOVERNMENT-BUSINESS RELATIONS

The concern of businessmen for improving government-business relationships arises because of several reasons: (1) they are forced to be concerned; (2) they have been persuaded that they should be concerned; and (3) changes in organizational leadership and direction have been favorable to the development of concern. The separation of ownership and control and the growth of businesses are two major reasons underlying improvements in government-business relationships.[6]

Aldolph A. Berle, Jr., has said that changes will occur in corporate-state relationships and that these changes will either come by common sense or struggle.[7] His claim that change is inevitable indicates that he believes businesses should prepare for it in advance. He also states that the profit system cannot handle everything, but what it should handle will be a cause for debate. In view of the fact that businessmen may be involved in conflicts over who should do what, they are well advised to develop a philosophy for dealing with the various levels of government.

One approach business might take vis-à-vis its government relations is the fatalistic view espoused by the great economist Joseph Schumpeter, who said, "Since the capitalistic enterprise by its very achievements tends to automate progress, we conclude that it tends to make itself superfluous—to break to pieces under the pressure of its own success."[8] This view, however, seems neither appropriate nor progressive.

A much more reasonable and seemingly workable view is to accept society

---

[5] "Is Anybody Listening?" *Fortune,* September 1950.

[6] Harold R. Bowen, "Why Businessmen Are Concerned about Their Social Responsibility." *Social Responsibilities of the Businessman* (New York: Harper & Row, Publishers, 1953), pp. 103–107.

[7] "The Corporation in a Democratic Society," in Melvin Anshen and George L. Bach, eds., *Management and Corporations; 1985,* (New York: McGraw-Hill, Inc., 1960).

[8] *Capitalism, Socialism and Democracy,* 3rd ed. (New York: Harper & Row, Publishers, 1942), p. 134.

as pluralistic and to consider the business corporation as a constellation of interests, not a single special interest group. Eels and Walton identify direct and indirect claimants in the business enterprise.[9] They list direct claimants as security holders, employees, customers, and suppliers; and indirect claimants as competitors, the local community, the general public, and government. In their view, all these factors enter the corporate goal structure, bringing considerations of "corporate image" and "social responsibility." In effect, they feel, profitability and survival goals must be tempered by service and social responsibility factors.

Indeed, the pluralistic concept of society tends to be the one adopted by many major business firms today. Their attempts to develop cooperation and understanding with government units and their desire to promote free capitalism in a framework which protects the rights of individuals is becoming more of a reality than an ideal.

The need to develop broad philosophies patterned on this line is pressing, and the cost of failure may be high. In the words of Clare E. Griffin, "We now stand as the last great industrial country that avows the principles of our system of liberal democratic capitalism. If the torch of the liberal tradition, with all that it implies for human dignity and freedom, is extinguished here, it may be a long time before it is relighted anywhere."[10] This statement might well serve as the basis for a really meaningful philosophy of business in its relations with the government and its many other publics.

Study Questions

1. Can you give examples of how government influence has increased in recent years at the federal level? The state level? The local level?

2. What are some of the key acts in the area of general welfare legislation? Antitrust legislation?

3. What acts have been the key determinants of collective-bargaining relationships between unions and management?

4. What effect does international legislation have on the size, nature, and direction of world trade? Give specific examples.

5. What are the major roles played by government in its relations with business? Which of these roles do you consider most critical to business?

6. In what activities does the government compete directly with business? What rationale underlies these activities?

7. What is the future of government-business partnerships? Again, what rationale underlies the use of such joint activities?

8. Which direct-action programs seem to you to be most rewarding? Do you know of any programs not listed which seem effective in government-business relationships?

---

[9] Richard Eels and Clarence Walton, *Conceptual Foundations of Business* (Homewood, Ill.: Richard D. Irwin, Inc., 1961).

[10] *Enterprise in a Free Society* (Homewood, Ill.: Richard D. Irwin, Inc., 1949).

9. Which of the indirect programs appear to offer the greatest chance of success? What other approaches could be added to the list in the text?

10. What is your personal opinion of lobbying? Do you believe individual firms should support lobbying? Should they join trade associations committed to lobbying activities?

11. Is the philosophy of pluralism meaningful for a business firm, or should it adopt a primarily profit-motivated approach? How extensively can a profit-making organization embrace a philosophy of "social responsibility"?

CASES
for Chapter 15

Tritono Electronics

Tritono Electronics, a firm located in New York City, hired eight new workers in one of their three technical drafting departments. After a sixty-day trial, four of these workers were judged "unsatisfactory performers" by the head of the drafting section. In accordance with the labor contract, the union bargaining committee was notified of the company's intent to release the workers; and a meeting to discuss the situation was held by the local union committee, the head of the drafting section, the company industrial relations representative, the head of engineering (the drafting supervisor's boss) and the division manager. During the meeting, there was unanimous agreement that the four individuals be dismissed for failure to meet required standards. They were subsequently given the usual two-week notice and dismissed. The four men who had shown satisfactory effort were retained on the payroll.

Two weeks after the four men were discharged, the division received a formal notice from the New York City Human Rights Commission stating that the company had been accused of a violation of city and state fair employment practice laws by "exercising discrimination against employees because of their color." The notice explained that of the eight men hired, the four retained were white, while the four dismissed were Negro. A formal reply was requested.

The division manager flatly denied the charge, stating that the dismissals were on the grounds of capability and performance alone, not on color. One week later, the commission notified the company that hearings would be held on the matter and specified the time and place. The following day a letter arrived from the Pentagon requesting information on the firings and formally notifying the company that it was in the preliminary step of an inquiry procedure designed to determine whether or not it had violated antidiscrimination laws covering employees working on government work now under contract to the company. On the same date the president of the local chapter of the Congress of Racial Equality demanded that the company prove its claims of no discrimination by "hiring and training fifty black people immediately . . . an action that would place black men on the payroll in proportion to their numbers in the community."

The division manager felt that the dismissals had been justified by the facts of the situation, but had some doubts that outsiders could understand the nature of the company's measuring process and the way in which it was applied to individuals who had not yet achieved high levels of skill.

The division manager's call to headquarters provided very little help in handling his dilemma. In response to his plea for advice, the executive vice-president, his immediate boss, stated, "Stick to your guns, but don't let this thing get out of hand. You know how sensitive this civil rights area is right now."

1. What should the division manager do to handle this situation?

2. How can he avoid recurrence of such problems in the future?

The Associated Motel, Hotel, and Tavern Owners of Vermont, Ltd.

In spring 1968, the Vermont legislature passed a law prohibiting the erection of billboards on all highways after January 1, 1970. This law covered small and large billboards except for signs on property owned by the advertiser. Vermont thus became the second state to pass legislation controlling billboards, the other being Hawaii, whose laws have existed since prestatehood days of 1927.

Governor Phillip Hoff pushed the bill hard in the legislature and other groups supported it with equal vigor. The newspapers supported its passage, as did the Stowe Area Association, a group of property owners in the plush ski areas around Stowe, Vermont.

The major groups opposing the legislation were the outdoor advertising interests and the Associated Motel, Hotel, and Tavern Owners of Vermont, Ltd.,[1] a group formed to "assure adequate representation of the travelling public's interest." The AMHTOV opposed the bill claiming that (1) it would prevent adequate notice to the traveling public concerning places to stay, eat, and vacation; (2) it would tend to hurt individuals who had already made investments in Vermont and had shown faith in the state in concrete terms; (3) it would prevent the right of individual businessmen to advertise—a concept that this group felt to be vital to the continuance of small business in particular and free enterprise in general; (4) it would circumscribe billboard advertising, an area in which no abuses had been perpetrated, unlike other media such as television; (5) it would lessen additional investment by outsiders in the Vermont economy and would tend to divert money into competing areas such as the Massachusetts Berkshires, the New Hampshire White Mountains, and the New York Adirondacks, where investments could be protected through adequate advertising; (6) it was favored by people who, though

---

[1] This association is fictitious, even though the legislation described is real.

obviously concerned about Vermont, had no particular stake in Vermont business and thus could afford to be irresponsible; (7) it would weaken Vermont, which as a tourist state was in a position of attempting to satisfy travelers, for the removal of notices of accommodations would frustrate tourists who came without advance reservations.

Though the state agreed to provide a series of sign plazas with controlled sign boards and a book of accommodations that would "get wider distribution than the Gideon Bible," the AMHTOV was convinced such devices would be inadequate. It planned to test the constitutionality of the law in state and federal courts if necessary. Its general contention was that travelers in Vermont deserved much better treatment than they were receiving and that the removal of billboards would hinder the state's attempt to develop tourist trade.

1. What is your reaction to AMHTOV's stand?
2. What should AMHTOV do to try to achieve its objectives?

Norfamco Fabrics, Inc.

Though only about 2 percent of Norfamco's $20 million annual sales are to government, the company has made above-average profits on government contracts. Norfamco's sales to the government have been in "exotic" fabrics, used in space and high-altitude research projects, an area in which few firms have expertise. As a consequence, almost all contracts on government-purchased items are negotiated on a fixed-fee basis rather than being offered to the lowest competitive bidder. Several of Norfamco's competitors have shown interest in the exotic fabrics area in recent months, but a lack of knowledge of costs and possible returns have caused them to hold back from direct competition. Recently, the federal General Accounting Office requested that Norfamco submit complete data on costs and profits in connection with a current contract negotiation. The GAO cited a federal court ruling in a GAO suit against Hewlett-Packard to justify its claim to data that previously had been confidential. It was further noted that legislation was pending which would result in the GAO's being privy to confidential cost data on all negotiated contracts.

Charles Hewson, Norfamco's president, was quite concerned about the GAO request. He knew that GAO records were available to Congressmen and he believed that the inevitable result of full disclosure would be leakage of internal cost data to competitors. Mr. Hewson felt such disclosure would put Norfamco at a disadvantage in both its government and nongovernment markets and might thus endanger future profitability. He also knew that the auto companies had voiced similar concern about disclosure of cost data, as did other industries with large sales to the government. In some firms with a high percentage of government business, disclosure meant real problems vis-à-vis competitors who, armed with full knowledge of their competitors' costs, could shave bids to a point where they took business away from the firm having to air its costs publicly. Since Norfamco had only 2 percent of its business in government contracts, Mr. Hewson felt the government was overstepping its bounds in making requests for internal cost data unless the possibility of fraud existed. Still, he did not want to forego the profits available on government contracts and he honestly believed Norfamco had an obligation to produce products important to the space program.

1. If you were Mr. Hewson, what would you do?

Avion Aircraft, Inc.

As soon as William Rosen, Avion Aircraft's director of engineering design, completed his call with the Pentagon, he called Phil Torkelson, Avion's vice-president of manufacturing, to tell him that Avion had lost in its bid to manufacture the (military) C5A cargo plane. His opening comment to Mr. Torkelson was, "Well, Lockheed got the C5A—all $1.4 billion of it. The hell of it is, we don't really know why we lost out, and yet we've got to try it all over again on the SST. If we miss that one, we're cooked." Mr. Rosen's concern sprung from the fact that Avion had been a prime contractor on both the TFX military fighter plane and C5A transport and had lost them to General Dynamics and Lockheed respectively.

After some discussion of the lost C5A contract, Mr. Torkelson said, "Look, Bill, why don't you take a few days off and relax. Go up to the mountains and let this thing simmer down a bit. Check with me on Monday and we'll try to sort the wheat from the chaff on this contract business. Perhaps while you're gone your staff can summarize the results of our last two bidding efforts. Maybe in the middle of next week, we can pull this material together and hash out some of the angles to guide us in our bidding on the SST."

Mr. Rosen called the key people who had worked with him on the previous two contracts and told them the bad news about the C5A. After some general discussion, he explained the need to pull together information describing exactly what Avion had done during the various phases of the bidding on the TFX and C5A contracts. Since bids on the C5A had been submitted under a new "one-step" purchasing procedure initiated by the Pentagon, he also felt that there should be a careful study of how this information was to be used to guide Avion in its attempt to win the SST contract. In addition, loss of the C5A contract did not necessarily mean that Avion should leave the civilian market exclusively to Lockheed. Indeed, he felt that it might be worthwhile for Avion to invest some of its own money in development of a modified C5A design for industrial users. He hoped that this group would gather data to help shed some light on whether it would be possible or even feasible for Avion to enter the non-military market. In his opinion, Boeing would probably design a civilian version of the C5A, a point which would bear heavily on Avion's deliberations.

Mr. Rosen asked Sam Griffin, director of government contract procurement, to prepare a summary report on the new Defense Department purchasing procedure. Ed Lombardi, the head of engineering and tests, was requested to draw a detailed analysis of the bidding procedure used on the TFX contract. Jack Morris, the manager of engineering design and development, was asked to construct a similar report on the procedures used in the recently completed C5A round. So that a Wednesday meeting could be set up with Mr. Torkelson, Mr. Rosen indicated that the reports should be ready on Monday morning, leaving Tuesday for Griffin, Lombardi, Morris, and himself to hash over the details of the three reports before discussing them with Mr. Torkelson.

As Rosen closed the meeting, he remarked, "It may seem that the game we've been playing with the government has been a crooked one so far, but it's the only game in town and we've got to play. Do your best and I'll see you on Monday."

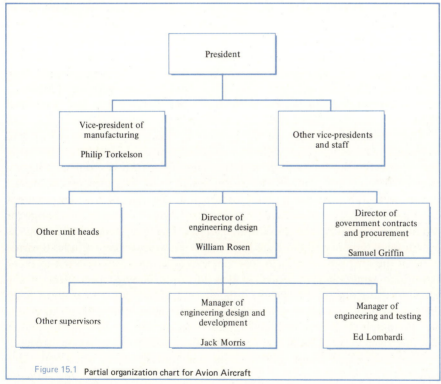

Figure 15.1 Partial organization chart for Avion Aircraft

THE REPORTS

Each man set about preparing his report in his own way, but all three knew that time was of the essence. When Mr. Rosen returned on Monday, two reports were already on his desk. The third, according to a note from Mr. Lombardi, would be available by 1:00 PM. Rosen had copies of the reports made early in the afternoon and sent them to each man. He asked them to read the reports written by the other two, and to prepare a list of key policies that Avion had used to guide their bid efforts. In addition, he requested that they think about why these policies had been either valid or invalid and to prepare a list of the policies most likely to be effective in guiding bidding on the SST.

Mr. Rosen, though familiar with some of the details of the C5A and the TFX bids, read the reports with great interest. He was particularly interested in the one-stop bidding summary prepared by Mr. Griffin, since this was relatively new and since it seemed as though Secretary McNamara of the Defense Department and Assistant Air Secretary Charles would be likely to adopt it to evaluate future contract proposals. He also strongly suspected that the Federal Aviation Authority would use the one-stop procedure to select a contractor when the SST contract was finally awarded.

THE TFX CONTRACT   Mr. Lombardi's report on the TFX contract contained a summary of competitive strategies used in bidding on the aircraft, a discussion of the announced military selection criteria, a review of Secretary McNamara's interpretation of the various bids and his process of selection, and finally, a brief analysis of the effect of politics on contractor's selection. There were also three supplementary schedules providing additional information on certain parts of the bid procedure. (See Tables 15.1, 15.2, 15.3, and 15.4).

The competitive strategy of the bidders in the TFX case revolved around technical, economic, good will, and political considerations. The technical aspects covered the extent of private financing before the race officially began, engines to be chosen, and, of course, the design itself. The principal economic factors were the absolute amount of the bid, the size of the development contract, the chance to recover development outlays on design change or production contracts, and the attitude of the Defense Department on costs overrunning the original bid. Good will had to do with service attitudes towards some of the airframe manufacturers. For example, the Navy was felt to favor Grumman while the Air Force tended to favor Boeing. The effect of the *good will* category was, however, difficult to evaluate prior to or even after the TFX bidding procedure. Political factors were even more difficult to evaluate. Politics in this case included interservice politics as well as the efforts of Congressmen to channel contracts into their particular states or districts.

Given these four factors and some of their ramifications, Mr. Lombardi's report indicated that Avion had weighted them approximately the same as their chief competitors.

The military selection criteria identified in the Lombardi report included four main points: operational performance, technical design, logistics and production management, and cost factors. Secretary McNamara, in explaining why he awarded the contract to General Dynamics, paralleled these major points with his own criteria. McNamara's first criterion was service acceptance. According to his comments, the major competitors had little to differentiate

TABLE 15.1   CHRONOLOGY OF TFX PROCUREMENT

1959	Commander of Air Force TAC, General Everest, originated idea.
October 1, 1961	McNamara approved opening of bidding. Work statement, 250 pages of requirements; designs to be submitted by December 6, 1961.
January 19, 1962	First evaluation unanimously selected Boeing design, but the Air Council rejected it.
May 1, 1962	Deadline for new submissions by Boeing and General Dynamics. Second evaluation voted Boeing and Air Council now agreed—Navy dissatisfied with designs. Navy and Air Force secretaries, with McNamara's concurrence, set June 1, 1962 as new deadline.
June. 1962	Third evaluation voted Boeing and Air Council agreed, but Navy disagreed and a few admirals "retired." Civilians were against Boeing on grounds of cost and commonality, while the services were for Boeing for operational reasons.
September 11, 1962	Fourth evaluation commenced.
October 15, 1962	Both designs were now acceptable to Navy.
November 10, 1962	Secretaries discussed the bids alone and later with McNamara.
November 13, 1962	McNamara told President Kenndy, "looks like General Dynamics," with no public comment from the President.
November 14, 1962	Air Force secretary Zuckert volunteered to write a memo to Secretary McNamara.
November 14–21, 1962	Fourth evaluation, which did not choose source, received and studied (summary available before).
November 17, 1962	Memo costs prepared by Assistant to Deputy Assistant Secretary of the Air Force.
November 20, 1962	Source Selection Board made its unanimous selection.
November 21, 1962	McNamara approved award to General Dynamics.
November 24, 1962	(Saturday) Public announcement of decision.
February 26, 1963	Senate subcommittee on commenced hearings.
November 20, 1963	Senate subcommittee after 2,740 pages of testimony recessed, subject to recall
December 21, 1964	First flight—ten days ahead of date specified in the contract.
1970	Controversy continued through 1970. With TFX design flaws causing crashes, public controversy, and curtailment of production.

them on this point. In terms of design, General Dynamics had a very high degree of identical structure and a large number of identical parts. Boeing had fewer common parts; but, according to experts, an accurate comparison was difficult, since many of Boeing's parts were grouped differently and reported

TABLE 15.2 AVION AND MAJOR COMPETITORS' PROFIT AND LOSS,—1959–1967

	1967	1966	1965	1964	1963	1962	1961	1960	1959
Lockheed									
Sales	2335	2084	1814	1801	1930	1753	1445	1332	1301
Net Income	100	107	98	83	85	81	56	80	16
Net Income After Tax	54	58	51	45	43	37	26	42	8
Boeing									
Sales	2879	2356	2023	1969	1771	1769	1801	1555	1612
Operating Profit	160	138	146	92	49	56	74	52	26
Net Income After Tax	84	76	78	45	22	27	36	24	13
Grumman									
Sales	968	1059	852	598	468	357	316	326	289
Net Income After Tax	21	27	21	11	8	6	6	7	5
General Dynamics									
Sales	2253	1796	1472	1579	1415	1898	2062	1988	1812
Operating Profit	89	92	85	66	66	58	(168)	(62)	54
Net Income After Tax	57	58	49	50	50	53	(143)	(27)	31
Avion									
Sales	1070	1108	1289	1207	1107	1093	897	1321	898
Income Before Tax	40	45	50	48	44	38	35	62	37
Net Income After Tax	22	24	23	21	20	17	14	29	15

Notes: Brackets ( ) signify loss.
On November 2, 1961, the financial vice-president of General Dynamics told legal advisors of the very serious situation possibly involving bankruptcy or reorganization.

TABLE 15.3   AVION'S FORECASTS 1968–1970, WITH AND WITHOUT NEW BUSINESS

	1968		1969		1970	
	Present	New Added	Present	New Added	Present	New Added
Sales	1055	1125	685	698	207	1100
Operating Profit	37	48	(117)	10	(485)	45
Net Income After Taxes	20	24	(110)	4	(460)	21

TABLE 15.4 COMPARISONS OF BOEING, AVION, AND GENERAL DYNAMICS PROPOSALS ON TFX SPECIFICATIONS

	Boeing	General Dynamics	Avion
(a) "Selection" of Secretary of Navy Korth			
e.g. Hours on station—fleet air defense	requirement + 6 percent	Requirement	Requirement + 3 per cent
—beach head support	60 per cent Reqt. with internal fuel	Reqt. + 50 per cent	Requirement + 5 per cent
Max. speed—sea level	Reqt. (before improvement)	Reqt. + 20 per cent	Requirement + 10 per cent
—altitude	Reqt.	Reqt. + 25 per cent	Requirement + 12 per cent
Take-off weights	12 per cent more than desired	15 per cent more than desired	10 per cent more than desired
Height	Acceptable	9″ less than Boeing	Acceptable
Length	Acceptable	3′ less than Boeing	Acceptable
Carrier handling and accommodation	Acceptable	Easier, carry 5 more	Acceptable
Wind over deck—take off	Reqt. + 10 Knot	Reqt. + 10 Knot	Requirement
—landing	Reqt. + 14 Knot	Reqt. + 6 Knot	Requirement
(b) "Selection" of Senate Subcommittee			
Cost—Contractor's proposal— $ millions	5,364.2	5,455.5	5,410.2
Air Force estimate	6,983.0	7,083.2	7,019.2
Air Force estimate (adjusted)	5,387.5	5,803.0	5,680.1
Ferry range	* x + 450 or 1,100 miles	x	Requirement
Landing distance	x	x + 590 feet	Requirement
Navy weight	x	x + 2,208 lbs.	Requirement
Loiter	x + 30 or 5½ (x)	x	Requirement
Number carrier can carry	x	x + 5	Requirement + 5 per cent
Intercept radius, nautical miles	x + 177 miles	x	Requirement
Bomb loading	x + 11 per cent or 69 per cent	x	Requirement + 3 per cent
Contractor's proposed ordinance load	x + 44 per cent to 250 per cent	x	Requirement + 40 per cent

* x = requirement

differently than those of General Dynamics. In the early evaluation process, Boeing was considered to be equated with General Dynamics in the commonality factors; but McNamara indicated that this situation changed as the evaluation neared its end. The third point mentioned by the Secretary was realistic costs. McNamara felt that the cost estimates submitted by General Dynamics were substantially lower than Boeing even though Boeing originally submitted a lower bid. According to the Secretary and others in the Pentagon, Boeing estimates in many areas were too low and not realistic.

On these three major points, there was no clear-cut decision as to which of the two main competitors was superior. Indeed, many of Boeing's estimates which were questioned inside the Defense Department were supported by outside experts. There thus seems to have been some question that the Defense Department thinking was justified or could be validated in the light of the technical knowledge in the airframe industry at the time the contract was awarded. In spite of this, Secretary McNamara stated he felt he had made the right decision when he chose the General Dynamics design.

The final section of the TFX report dealt with politics. According to some quotations from *Fortune* magazine, the political forces seemed to be fairly evenly disposed between the two final contenders, Boeing and General Dynamics. Mr. Lombardi felt, contrary to *Fortune*, that General Dynamics had a little more solid foothold in Washington than Boeing. People such as Secretary of the Navy Korth, Vice-President Lyndon Johnson, and former Secretary of the Navy Connelly, were known to have favored giving the contract to the General Dynamics facility in Texas. In addition, Deputy Secretary of Defense Gilpatrick had been a partner in the law firm of Cravath, Swain, and Moore, which had a professional relationship with General Dynamics. Mr. Gilpatrick also admitted to a close friendship with Mr. Frank Pace, who, at the time, was head of General Dynamics. Though Mr. Lombardi offered no proof that any undue influence had been exerted by Mr. Gilpatrick or by any political figures, he did note that the final evaluation procedures contained an instruction that information should be exchanged between contractors. The effect of this directive was to cut down on some of the lead Boeing held at that point.

Mr. McNamara's final statement was that he had made the choice on a rough judgment, but he thought it was the best one. Mr. Lombardi concluded that the Secretary himself had not made his final decision on political grounds. He was, however, concerned with the fact that "rough judgment" was used after a bidding procedure that involved the submission of literally thousands of pages of specifications and testimony.

Mr. Lombardi felt that the publicly announced criteria were ones on which Avion had made careful bids and done careful preparation. The unpublicized selection criteria such as politics, military and civilian feuding, and so on in the Pentagon were factors that Avion had not handled carefully enough. Lombardi felt that Avion's technical designs were as good or better than competitors (see Table 15.2). He also felt that criticisms of Avion's figures were as invalid as those raised against Boeing. It was his firm belief that some kind of general welfare or internal rivalry considerations were critical in the final selection process.

The set of tables accompanying Mr. Lombardi's report showed the sequence of bidding, comparative information on the sales of competitors, and information dealing with the concepts of commonality as submitted by General Dynamics and Boeing. The last exhibit was used to support the point that an apparently superior technical design was overruled by hazy, undefined criteria hastily contrived by the Defense Department.

THE C5A REPORT   Jack Morris's report on the C5A bidding procedure began with the story of how the military officer in charge of the bidding sent each company a wooden hara-kari sword with each bid and a note reading, "Why wait?" Indeed, this sentiment seemed appropriate, since Douglas and Boeing had each spent close to $20 million of their own funds and Lockheed about $16 million (on top of $6 million each had received from the Air Force), before any decision was made by the Pentagon team. In all, Boeing. Lockheed, and Douglas, who along with Avion were the three main competitors in this bidding, committed almost four thousand engineers to the job of preparing bids on the C5A. Douglas, for example, in its final bidding procedure, submitted 60,000 pages in 625 volumes, and these bids were in turn evaluated by over five hundred officers and civilian technicians in the evaluation phase at Wright-Patterson Field.

What these monumental documents were attempting to justify were a series of evaluation criteria which were in essence quite similar to those drawn on the TFX. Morris boiled these criteria down to three questions: (1) What design should our airframe be? (2) What engine should be used? (3) What would be the total cost of the end product? In essence, the report summarized the equation determining the criteria for evaluation in the following way:

$$\text{Cost effectiveness} = \frac{(UE) \times U \times V_p \times P \times C_p}{\text{Cost}}$$

In this equation, UE stands for unit equippage, the number of planes for six squadrons; U is utilization rate, hours in the air per day; V_p is block speed, the time between two given points at most efficient cruising speed plus fifteen minutes; P is payload, C_p is correction of payload for terminal effectiveness, meaning maximum landing runway length required; this latter capability determines how many airstrips the plane can use in various areas. Cost is the price of six squadrons plus the operating expenses for a ten-year period.

Though Avion's main concern was not with engines, Morris's report noted that a General Electric design was the victor fairly early in the game over a Pratt & Whitney engine. The airframe problem, however, as Mr. Rosen knew all too well, probably would not be determined until much later.

One of the interesting things in the C5A bidding was that the source selection board initially selected Boeing, as it had in the TFX contract. Boeing's design was the most sophisticated according to the source selection board, and it seemed to present a faster plane which could land on shorter runways.

The Pentagon reacted to the source selection board's evaluations in much the same way that it would to antiwar demonstrations on various campuses. Secretary of the Air Force Zuckert was quoted in *Fortune* as saying, "You don't need a wet towel like the TFX slapped in your face more than once to get the idea."

Secretary Zuckert set up a review group of senior officers and asked them to review existing proposals and to submit ways to improve the existing designs. The issue then proceeded to the Air Council, an advisory group composed of the vice-chief of staff, seven three-star generals, the commanders of the three interested commands (Air Transport, Systems, and Logistics), the three Air Force assistant secretaries, and the chief of staff, General John McConnell.

Finally, Secretary Zuckert made a recommendation to Secretary of Defense McNamara, who then announced that Lockheed had been selected the prime contractor. Lockheed was naturally pleased with its selection, while President William Allen of Boeing said, "We are disappointed, of course, but we are not complaining. I have no doubt that price was the determining factor."

From the point of view of Avion's bidding procedure, Morris raised the question that price might not have been the determining factor. His own feeling was that other factors were paramount. Lockheed, he noted, had a facility in Marietta, Georgia, which employed some 22,000 workers, making it the biggest plant in the southeastern United States. Without the C5A contract, at least 10,000 jobs would have been lost. In contrast, the loss of the C5A contract cost no jobs at Boeing, since Boeing had a backlog of some $2.4 billion in orders for 707 jet airliners. Morris felt that the Air Force had given great weight to the maintenance of a national asset such as the Marietta plant. His feeling was that general welfare considerations had over-ruled the criteria of cost, design, performance, and know-how that should have been the key factors in awarding the contract. He noted that Douglas in particular had suffered from this selection and that Avion itself had been hurt because of its failure to receive the award. The C5A was a major contract loss in terms not only of utilization of existing capacity but of capacity utilization for many years to come.

In closing, Morris stated quite strongly that he felt that the announced criteria seemed to have been given little importance in the final selection, especially when bids and specifications were relatively close or similar. His feeling was that nontechnical factors should be considered much more carefully in Avion's attempts to secure the SST contract.

THE NEW PENTAGON DEFENSE PROCUREMENT PROCEDURE

Sam Griffin's report on the new Pentagon defense procedure focused on the C5A contract, since this was Avion's most recent and most painful experience with the new procedure. Griffin described the concept as being "total package procurement" and identified its main objective as an attempt to tie in all the parts of the total cost of procuring aircraft into one package rather than seeking bids on separate components. For example, it had been common practice for development contracts, engine contracts, airframe contracts, and other contracts to be submitted separately. In the C5A bidding all costs, maintenance, prices for spare parts, loading facilities, training, and expenses such as engine overhaul, were included in the initial bid. Each bid also contained an option for the Air Force to purchase fifty-seven more planes at a fixed price and eighty-five more under a rigid price formula calculated on a declining scale to compensate for the manufacturer's "learning curve." On top of this, there was a flexible incentive pricing formula that allowed a contractor to make additional profits if he produced planes at a price below the bid costs and imposed a penalty if he was unable to meet the costs submitted in his estimates. In effect, it made the contractor put his money where his mouth was. This new bid procedure was called "the Charles plan," after its initiator, Assistant Secretary of the Air Force Robert Charles. Though the contract procedure seemed to call for a blizzard of paper work on the C5A it was considered to be acceptable by Mr. Griffin. Griffin felt that Avion would not be hurt by this procedure and could live with it better than most direct competitors.

The new procurement procedure contained an ingenious pricing formula that rewards efficient production and penalizes overruns, that is, costs in excess of original estimates. Broadly, it works by having the contractor fix a target price plus 10-percent profit for the contractor. If costs rise above the target, 15 percent of the excess comes out of the contractor's profits, while the Air Force pays the other 85 percent. If costs fall below the target, the contractor receives 15 percent of the savings and the government gets the rest. The contract states, however, that the government will in no case pay more than 130 percent of the target costs. Thereafter, all additional costs accrue to the manufacturer, and his profit declines to zero if costs reach 135.5 percent of the target.

For example, assuming a target price of $1 million, the contractor's profit would be $100,000 and total contract cost would be $1.1 million. If the contractor holds costs to $900,000, his profit would be $100,000 plus 15 percent of the savings, or $15,000. If, however, costs mount to $1.1 million, his profit would be only $85,000 and would disappear entirely if costs reached $1.35 million.

Another innovation in the Charles plan is the flexible incentive which gives the company the opportunity to increase savings and profits while risking possible loss. At particular points, the company can choose to gamble for a share of cost savings above the initial 15 percent and up to a maximum 50 percent on the work still remaining. If the contractor, for example, could see the economies ahead, he might elect to boost his share to 50 percent of savings after half the work had been done. If he then did the job for

$900,000, his profit would be $132,000: the original $100,000 plus 15 percent ($7,500) of the savings on the first half of the $100,000 additional cost savings plus 50 percent ($25,000) of the savings on the second half. If, however, costs exceed the target, 50 percent of the difference comes out of the contractor's profit.

In the case of the engine contract on the C5A, General Electric's initial target price was $417 million plus $41.7 million profit. The company stands to make an additional 15 cents on every dollar its actual costs fall below $417 million, and the company can increase profits by up to 50 percent on added cost savings if it chooses to elect the flexible incentive approach. The most, however, the government can pay GE is $542 million. Any further costs would be borne entirely by the company.

The new method tends to stop low-contract bidding on development costs in the hope that a high-cost production contract would follow enabling the bidder to "get well." Griffin felt this approach would force greater initial risks on bidders, but fewer controls would be installed at a later date. In the words of Air Force Secretary Charles, the object of the new procedure is to "rediscover in defense industry the law of supply and demand. We seemed to have mesmerized ourselves into believing that there is a nonmarket in the weapons acquisition process."

Griffin's report was extremely helpful to Mr. Rosen, since it filled him in on some of the confusing details of the new defense procurement procedure. In particular, he was interested in the flexible pricing formula because he felt that it could mean real bidding advantages to Avion on upcoming contracts.

After reading the reports, Mr. Rosen jotted down a few questions and compiled a set of guidelines on how to conduct the meeting the following day. On Tuesday morning, he brought forth some of the questions raised by the reports, and the group reviewed and answered these questions. The three men submitted their lists of policies so that Mr. Rosen could review them for the Wednesday meeting. Rosen noted that he would prepare a joint list of policies to submit to Mr. Torkelson on the following day.

THE WEDNESDAY MEETING

When Rosen and his three subordinates met in the conference room on Wednesday with Mr. Torkelson, he opened the meeting with a summation of a report that had just crossed his desk. This report, prepared by the consulting firm of Arthur D. Little, Inc., Cambridge, Massachusetts, dealt with some of the ongoing and expected changes in the aircraft and aerospace industries. The report was entitled, "Strategies for Survival in the Aerospace Industry." Mr. Torkelson summarized several selected excerpts to the group. One quotation in particular caught the group's attention: "At least some of the 21 hard-core firms that form the nucleus of the industry must suffer major shrinkages and changes in the size of operations or face disaster." This section of the report went on to say that production of airframes would be down 30 percent by 1970 and that research, development, engineering, and test funds would fall 15 percent. The Little researchers concluded that the aerospace industry was no longer a growth industry and that contracts were now primarily of the job-shop variety rather than long production runs. The industry, it went on to say, was suffering in every technical area from excess capacity, which was no longer considered an asset by the Defense Department. On the contrary, the report claimed the government had developed a new concept about the aerospace industry (it was no longer a mobilization base because future wars would be fought from weapons stockpiles) leaving no incentive to keep existing firms in business. The Little report anticipated that in 1969 the government research and development budget would be 60 percent greater than the budget devoted to production needs and hardware.

The Little report suggested that specialization should be reviewed by certain firms. It indicated that some companies should pull out of areas where performance was not proven and that these organizations should stay in areas where they had "proven market position." It cited the example of Ryan Aircraft, a company that had specialized and also prospered, and concluded that the aerospace industry had become a research industry which could not afford excess investments in facilities, personnel, and useless diversification.

As a final statistic on this last point, it showed how, in 1963, 40 percent of Lockheed's sales had come from Pentagon R&D contracts while Boeing, United Aircraft, and Republic had 67, 72, and 90 percent of sales credited to production contracts. In 1963, North American had 25 percent of sales in NASA research and development contracts. These percentages showed how some firms were heavily dependent upon areas in danger of not being maintained or increased in either absolute or relative terms. The airframe manufacturers were particularly vulnerable according to the report.

To show how the shifting approach to defense procurement had already begun to affect the major defense contractors, Mr. Torkelson passed out a list of the top defense contractors in 1963, 1964, and 1965, including Avion. The indication here was that firms which had failed to diversify or recognize this shifting type of demand were losing and would continue to lose their place in the shifting environment of the defense business.

After referring to the Little document, Mr. Torkelson asked why Avion had failed to secure the last two major contracts on which it had submitted bids. He asked, "If our policies are good, why did they fail in these contracts? If they are poor, how should we change our approach? Remember, gentlemen, if we fail again, we may be out of the aircraft industry completely. As you know, we're in the market now for the SST. This plane may well be the last major aircraft that the government sends out for bids in the next ten years. We can't make a mistake here. We've two strikes against us: one more and we're out. I want to know how to go about bidding on the SST, and I want to know whether or not we should proceed with our own research and development activities on a plane similar to the C5A. I know that we're not prepared at this time to do much on the C5A matter, but I would like to have your basic thinking on how we should handle our approach to bidding on what well may be our last chance to be a major firm in the airframe business."

DECISIONS FOLLOWING THE WEDNESDAY MEETING

The discussion with Mr. Torkelson, though informative, was not conclusive. Further meetings were held to discuss alternative courses of action, and various specialists were asked to evaluate their plus and minus aspects. After a three-month study, Torkelson's group decided to make the following proposals to Avion's top management:

1. Avion should not enter directly into bidding for the SST contract because Boeing apparently had the inside track because of its superior design and because it was "owed" the contract following awards to General Dynamics and Lockheed on the TFX and C5A. (This recommendation was given credence when Boeing was chosen as the major airframe contractor for the SST.)

2. Avion should invest substantial funds in developing its own version of an air bus based on the know-how gained while working on the losing C5A bid. This action was recommended in spite of the lead already enjoyed by Lockheed, Boeing, and Douglas, whose knowledge of airframe manufacturing was at least equal to that possessed by Avion.

3. Avion should revise its bidding procedures on government contracts to give more muscle to intangible and political factors. The specific means to this result was to come from a study of the weighting of all factors (including technical design) and an assessment of the "reality of this company's relations with government, the public, and other groups or agencies connected with government contracting procedures."

4. Long-term study of diversification should begin at once, with the Little report offering data on why such action seemed advisable. In view of lost C5A and TFX contracts and the recommendation to withdraw from SST bidding, this project was given high priority.

Mr. Torkelson felt that in principle, top management would adopt the four proposals, but he believed that their far-reaching effects would set off a great deal of discussion and conflict. He knew that the uneasy heads currently wearing the Avion crown would be looking at past achievements and failures with the same cold and clinical eyes they would use to view the future.

1. What policies did Avion use in the past to guide its bidding?
2. Should any policies be added to or deleted from the above lists? Indicate the reasoning underlying your recommendation.

3. What are the pertinent considerations management should investigate if it decides to go into further development work on a privately financed version of the C5A?

4. What specific steps should Avion take to sharpen its bidding procedures on any future government contracts?

5. What considerations does Avion management face if it decides that the Little report is applicable and seeks to diversify in the aerospace industry or in other areas?

Of all the publics managements deal with, labor unions are perhaps the largest and most influential. Labor's more than 17 million members exert obvious and direct influence on managerial activity through the collective-bargaining process. Indirectly, labor has the ability to invoke its social and political power to constrain or direct management actions. Because of labor's political influence and economic power, it is important for management to develop philosophies, strategies, and tactics designed to promote more effective relations with labor leaders and their constituencies. It is also critical for management to realize how labor relations are similar to and different from their dealings with other publics. And finally it is vital for management to recognize that the key to an improved labor-management relationship lies in the means of handling these differences.

In many ways, labor unions resemble the groups and institutions regularly dealt with by management. For example, managements buy parts, supplies, raw materials, services, and components from all sorts of vendors. Labor unions, too, are vendors who bargain for the services of a valuable and scarce resource. Here, as in dealings with other sellers, managements typically try to minimize their long-term costs and maximize their long-range returns. Relations with the various levels of government also have overtones similar to labor relations, because governments, like labor unions, have objectives and goals which go well beyond the realm of economics. Indeed, management frequently complains that government units and labor unions emphasize political factors so heavily that their actions are motivated more often by

CHAPTER 16
Management of Union Relations

politics than economics. Management's dealings with shareholders and with labor unions bear some resemblance in that a common desire exists to promote the economic well-being of the firm, but differences of opinion appear over how to distribute the profits. Customers, too, are another public that has a great deal in common with labor unions, since each is trying to maximize its own interests. In the sense that they constantly seek to gain satisfaction from management by improving their own positions, unions are customers. Obviously, similarities exist between relations with unions and with other publics; but differences do appear, which, since they point the way toward better relations, deserve special attention.

POLITICS

Perhaps the most unique aspect of labor-management relations occurs in the political, legislative, social, and ideological areas. The extent of union control over politics is the subject of open dispute, but there is no doubt that unions are political bodies, particularly in their internal functioning. Labor certainly had a say in the nomination of Hubert Humphrey as the Democratic presidential candidate in 1968, but labor's ability to get members to vote for Mr. Humphrey was nowhere near as potent. On the other hand, there was no uncertainty about the force of internal politics in bringing about rejections of leader-recommended contracts in United Auto Workers (UAW) local unions dealing with the various auto companies. Obviously, management needs to know a good deal about the internal and external aspects of political unionism before labor unions can be dealt with effectively.

LEGISLATION

Special legislation and rules governing labor-management relations must also be considered carefully before a firm adopts a set of labor policies. At the federal level, the most important laws are the Sherman Anti-Trust Act of 1890; the Norris-LaGuardia Anti-injunction Act; the Railway Labor Act; the National Labor Relations Act of 1935, which served to legalize collective bargaining; the Fair Labor Standards Act of 1938, which laid out certain rules covering wages and hours; the Taft-Hartley Act of 1947, which established a degree of balance between labor and management; the Landrum-Griffin Act which set controls over internal reporting procedures; and other less critical acts such as the Walsh-Healy Act, which set limits on wages paid by contractors working on public contracts. At state and local levels, right-to-work laws, fair employment practices acts, and safety and building code regulations have developed rules governing how parties must conduct themselves in specific circumstances and relationships. At the federal level, discriminatory actions against union membership drives may generate an unfair labor practice, which, if upheld by the National Labor Relations Board and (if necessary) the courts, can result in sanctions that might overturn a representation election, reinstate a discharged worker, or decertify an established local union. At the state level, violation of legislation such as New York State's Taylor law governing strikes by public employees sent United Federation of Teachers' President Albert Shanker to jail. At the local level, antidiscrimination statutes can force employers or unions to show just cause why Negroes, Puerto Ricans, or other minority members are barred from employment or membership in union locals.

Administrative rulings have also set important limits on labor-management relations. Agencies such as the National Labor Relations Board, the National Mediation Board, and the various state labor relations boards have set constraints and precedents on what the parties can do and cannot do according to the terms of various rulings and statutes. Arbitration, too, has tended to set certain precedents by interpreting contracts to specify what parties must do until a particular labor-management contract reaches expiration. The complex and continuing disputes between the railroads and their unions have been notable examples of the importance of boards and arbitration in handling labor-management differences. Though compulsory arbitration is universally condemned by labor and management alike, unions at least seem more inclined to be susceptible to allowing disputes involving public employees to be solved by voluntary arbitration.[1]

SOCIAL GOALS

Social goals of unions have sometimes exerted almost as important an effect on bargaining as economic goals. Unions such as the International Ladies Garment Workers' Union (ILGWU), the United Auto Workers, and various foreign unions have espoused goals such as "social betterment of the worker" or "more equitable or egalitarian distribution of income" between the various social classes. The business-oriented unionism of the Teamsters and the United Steelworkers of America has been in contrast with some of the more ideological goals established by other unions. This does not mean that the UAW and the ILGWU have disavowed interest in economic goals, but only that many of their goals have gone well beyond the economic arena.

The political, social, ideological, and economic differences in labor union philosophies can help direct managers toward better approaches to labor relations. Once these differences are recognized and assessed, more realistic labor policies can be developed. Too often the labor relationship is seen by management as strictly economic or as paternalistic; even worse, it may be visualized as a kind of class warfare. Most relationships defy such simplistic classification, being instead a mixture of many subtle factors and forces. Before any workable climate for enduring and mutually rewarding relationships can exist, these forces need to be viewed realistically by both managers and labor leaders.

---

[1] "A Cure for Public Employee Strikes," *Business Week,* March 2, 1968.

UNION PHILOSOPHY AND MANAGEMENT POLICY

Some of the more interesting leads toward better understanding of management-union relations appear in attempts to answer the question, "Why do workers join unions?" This has been the subject of many studies, some of the better known being by Joel Seidman, Jack Barbash, and Morris Viteles. Viteles sets out a three-fold classification to explain why workers join unions; he talks about economic needs, compulsion, and social norm adherence as being three critical categories.[2] Professors Strauss and Sayles embrace the categories developed by Viteles but add a need for communication with management and a desire for self-expression and recognition.[3] Generally, workers seem to join unions primarily to protect their interests, not because they are compelled to—a belief that seems to be almost a fixation with some managers. Whether workers are required to join unions because of some closed-shop arrangement is almost an academic point, since workers join with or without compulsion. A summary of the studies attempting to explain why workers join unions would show the following reasons:

1.   Desire to share the profit pie with management
2.   Greater control over the share workers obtain
3.   Nonarbitrary treatment by managements
4.   Social recognition, or treatment as peers rather than as underlings
5.   Developing an outlet for the talents of the performer who has not been recognized by management or, worse, has been classed as a troublemaker
6.   Establishing a mass-action power base to help control their own economic lot and the general climate of how they are treated

An understanding of these reasons can help managements to establish a much more viable set of labor relations strategies.

Though union objectives partly reflect why workers join unions, objectives quickly outgrow such simplistic listings once workers are organized and the union becomes an entity with an outlook and philosophy of its own. Some of the obvious factors in understanding union activities spring from the reasons why workers join unions, but a thorough grasp of the total picture calls for more intense study. In the United States, union-management relations are conducted in a milieu of economic conflict, political maneuvering, court decisions, rulings of quasi-political boards, and the personal beliefs held by a wide range of businessmen, individual union members and union leaders.

In unionism's early years, the courts were the arena in which labor battles were fought. Though it is not appropriate to outline every important court

---

[2] Morris Viteles, *Motivation and Morale in Industry* (New York: W.W. Norton & Company, Inc., 1953).

[3] Leonard R. Sayles and George Strauss, *Personnel: The Human Problems of Management*, 2nd ed. (Englewood Cliffs, N.J.: Prentice-Hall, Inc., 1967).

decision influencing union development at this point, a few landmark decisions can give the flavor of how judicial rulings have influenced labor relations. In 1806, in the Philadelphia Cordwainers Case, labor combinations were declared to be prima facie illegal. In 1842, in the Massachusetts case of Commonwealth versus Hunt, association of workers were considered to be illegal only if "their powers are abused." Combinations were not construed to be illegal per se, but only if their intent was illegal. The Danbury Hatters Case in 1908 indicated that strikes against any business involved in interstate commerce were illegal if they stopped the flow of interstate trade, but the Hutcheson decision in 1941 reversed this ruling when the courts recognized the legality of primary boycotts directed against interstate trade.

While these and other decisions were being made, legislative actions were influencing the development of the American labor movement. The Sherman Act of 1890 prohibited combinations in restraint of trade, and labor unions, at first thought to be exempt from its provisions, came under the act's jurisdiction following the Supreme Court ruling in the Danbury Hatters Case. Section 20 of the Clayton Act of 1914 ostensibly freed labor from monopolistic status, but several court rulings, notably the Duplex Case (1921) muddied the water in spite of a general belief among union leaders that this provision exempted labor organizations from the antitrust laws. Even as late as 1964, the Supreme Court ruling in United Mine Workers versus Pennington et al. (381 U.S. 657, 1964) again cast labor's exempt status in doubt, since it declared that unions were covered by the Sherman Act's provisions when involved in price-fixing arrangements restraining trade. By and large, though, modern American unions are for all practical purposes exempt from antitrust statutes.

Though labor had its ups and downs prior to the 1920s, the movement grew fantastically during the Great Depression of the 1930s. Following the passage of the National Labor Relations Act of 1935, which made collective bargaining an approved government policy, unions grew rapidly both in size and power. The Taft-Hartley Act of 1947 and the Landrum-Griffin Act of 1959 tended to balance the power held by labor by establishing more orderly processes for worker organization and by placing constraints on the actions and activities of both managements and unions. By the 1960s, labor unions had passed through their early growth pains and had become an extremely powerful and well-established institution on the American scene.

The philosophy of the American labor movement is both a product of and a contributor to the economic, political, social, and judicial factors found in democratic societies. American unionism is a product of conflict and strife, but its ideology has never been based in the bitterness and class struggles that characterized union development in Europe. This rejection of a class-oriented goal structure seems to have evolved at least partially because of the Protestant ethic, which guided American economic and educational systems, and partially because of beliefs held by some of the strong early leaders of the American labor movement. In Hoxie's classic breakdown of ideologies, there can be either business unions, uplift unions, revolutionary unions, or predatory unions.[4] In fact, American unionism has never seemed to fall into the third and fourth categories, but has embraced a combination of the first two. In discussing labor unions, Eels and Walton describe the philosophical categories espoused by Tannenbaum and Perlman.[5] They relate Perlman's concept that union activity is based on control of scarce job opportunities (job scarcity) and Tannenbaum's statement that man's loss of dignity to technology and the realities of the industrial world as the two factors underlying the rise of unionism.

Whatever categorization is used to describe the theoretical rationale underlying unionism, the economic orientation of American unions is clear, especially when contrasted with the socialistic and communistic philosophies of unions in Europe. In France, for example, when the Communists want to embarrass the government, labor unions may embark on a politically motivated general strike. In the United States, unions are much more prone to embrace the dictates of Samuel Gompers, founder and long-time leader of the AFL. Two colorful excerpts from Gomper's speeches express his philosophy in very pointed terms:

> I want to tell you Socialists that I have studied your philosophy, read your works on economics and not the meanest of them; studied your standard works, both in English and German—have not only read, but studied them. I have heard your orators and watched the work of your movement the world over. I have kept close watch upon your doctrines for thirty years; have been closely associated with many of you, and known how you think and what you propose. I know, too, what you have up your sleeve. And I want to say that I am entirely at variance with your philosophy. I declare it to you, I am not only at variance with your doctrines, but with your philosophy. Economically, you are unsound; socially, you are wrong; industrially, you are an impossibility.[6]

> I ask any delegate in this convention whether he knows any trade where the union has recognized a machine or improved tool where the conditions of working people were made worse. It is not in the order and nature of things. The better we organize, the more thoroughly we will be in a position to defend, not only what we have, but to move onward and forward to those things which ought to be ours and which we can obtain.[7]

---

[4] R.F. Hoxie, *Trade Unionism in the Labor Movement* (New York: Appleton-Century-Crofts, 1923).

[5] Richard Eels and Clarence Walton, *Conceptual Foundations of Business,* rev. ed. (Homewood, Ill.: Richard D. Irwin, Inc., 1969).

[6] American Federation of Labor, *Report of Proceedings of the Twenty-third Annual Convention,* 1903, pp. 196–198.

[7] From a speech at the convention of the Cigar Makers International Union, Chicago, August 14, 1923.

These two statements, when added to Gompers' famous declaration that unionism's demand is for "More, now!" are the basic core of the business-oriented philosophy of contemporary American unionism.

One updated summary of union philosophies and objectives outlined in 1950 by Solomon Barkin. Barkin, then research director of the textile workers union, indicated that the objectives of trade unions were to minimize the costs exacted by the process of production and to maximize human advancement in terms of economic gains, security, industrial citizenship, and the strengthening of the union.[8] Though his view is less business-oriented than that held by Gompers, it seems to be fairly representative of union objectives in the late 1960s—a blend of economic desire and a need for recognition and social betterment.

Gaining an understanding of the ideals and philosophies of unions is important in determining their impact on management. When a union organizes a firm, management normally feels both uneasy and apprehensive. In effect, union organization is a rejection of managerial stewardship and this rejection may leave a legacy of bitterness, concern, or fear. According to Professor Lloyd G. Reynolds of Yale University, the effect of union policy influences eight areas:

1. Structure of labor and product markets
2. Level of money wages and prices
3. Level of real wages
4. Relative wage rates for different industries and occupations
5. Nonmonetary terms of employment
6. Social structure of the plant
7. The status of the individual worker
8. The balance of political power in the community[9]

This generalized list is narrowed by Professor E. Wight Bakke to the industrial relations area in his often quoted "guideposts" to management's idea of workable industrial relations. According to Bakke, management feels that unionization influences industrial relations four ways:

1. Industrial relations is no longer a matter between management and its own employees once a labor union has entered the picture.
2. The economic welfare of the company is no longer the only and primary objective of the company's industrial relations policies, since unions are competing for a share of the pie.

---

[8] Solomon Barkin, "A Trade Union Appraises Management Personnel Philosophy," *Harvard Business Review,* September 1950, pp. 59–64.

[9] Lloyd G. Reynolds, *Labor Economics and Labor Relations,* 4th ed. (Englewood Cliffs, N.J.: Prentice-Hall, Inc., 1964).

3. Industrial relations no longer can be conducted in an aura of unilateral management rights, since the union has set checks and controls on these rights.

4. All parties to industrial relations are, in management's eyes, at least, no longer businesslike and responsible, since union democracy frequently prevents ratification or full acceptance of agreements negotiated by leaders. In the case where individual members reject their leaders' bargaining solutions to problems, management feels that there has been irresponsibility rather than what union leaders would call democracy.[10]

Sayles and Strauss indicate that the impact of the union on management challenges management decisions, competes for worker loyalty, causes review of personnel policies, threatens efficiency, decentralizes decision making, and introduces outsiders into labor relations.[11]

A more comprehensive managerial view of union organization is that it limits areas of control, curtails flexibility, particularly in costs of labor which are unknown until after collective bargaining is completed, reduces the speed of decision, infringes on many management prerogatives, lessens managerial arbitrariness, reduces the ease of movement between jobs, increases costs in terms of greater time spent on grievances, and so forth. It also introduces a rather personal dimension into bargaining negotiations, since the union's gains tend to reflect on a manager's performance ratings. There are thus economic, psychological, and organizational reasons for management's concern over the coming of the union. The net result of these far-reaching effects is that management needs to develop ways and means to deal with unions so that the most beneficial mutual relationships can develop and prosper.

MANAGEMENT OF UNION RELATIONS

Management of union relations covers a much more narrow area than the political, social, and cultural philosophies shaping union goals. It centers on the pragmatic issue of maintaining and improving relations with particular unions, not the raison d'être of the entire labor movement. It is important to note that this section has no antiunion bias, even though its orientation is the management of union relations rather than the broader topic of labor-management relations. The focus here continues to be, as it has been throughout, on the manager and his role in dealing with critical problem areas. It is equally critical to remember that management-union relations draw heavily on the goals, policies, and philosophies of both union and management organization, and look to institutions such as government and the community to set the rules of the road. Pragmatism, not philosophy, is the usual ruling

---

[10] E. Wight Bakke, *Mutual Survival: The Goal of Unions and Management* (New Haven, Conn.: Yale University, Labor and Management Center, 1946).

[11] *Op. cit.*

force, and results-oriented policies are normally rated above elegant but unworkable theories. In the light of developments in the contemporary business environment, most current manifestations of such policies are based on the realistic foundation of equitable treatment and mutual survival.

A LABOR RELATIONS CREDO

Though any generalized statement of labor-management philosophies can offer little more than a series of broad guidelines, a mature approach to a viable labor relations credo well might include the following:

1. There should be full acceptance of collective bargaining by both parties.[12]

2. Unions should accept the concept of private property, and management should try to set prices and develop products or services to keep the organization strong and to insure workers' job security.

3. Union and managements should not espouse ideological goals, but should work together to develop mutually beneficial policies and relationships.

4. Managements should not tamper with union politics and should accept the fact that unions must be responsible, strong, and democratic to maintain effective working relationships.

5. Widespread consultation and information sharing between the parties should be put into practice, including sharing of financial performance records, information on competition for contracts, and backup data on work standards.

6. Bargaining should not be legalistic, but solution-oriented. Thus, the parties to bargaining should not be outsiders, but should be well versed in labor relations matters.

7. The issues to be bargained over should be highly practical rather than theoretical.

8. A good grievance procedure should be set up and made to work. Arbitration seems desirable to help bring about workable settlements in areas where no mutually satisfactory agreement can be reached by the parties.

The adoption of such a credo lays the basic groundwork for labor-management relations, but it is only the beginning. Philosophies are needed before collective bargaining and day-by-day contract administration can be implemented effectively. The results of a particular negotiation can be far-reaching, so basic bargaining strategies should be developed in advance of

---

[12] In a seminar at Columbia University's Arden House Campus, the benefits of collective bargaining were discussed in some detail. The results of this conference are reported in "Challenges to Collective Bargaining" in Lloyd Ullman, ed., *The American Assembly* (Englewood Cliffs, N.J.: Prentice-Hall, Inc., 1967).

negotiations following a careful appraisal of the factors and variables likely to influence the bargaining process. The key variables must be weighed, evaluated, and merged into a plan of action specifying what postures to adopt and what settlements to accept. The development of such a model allows alternatives to be weighed and gives management a chance to consider the probable results of pursuing various strategies or tactics. The key factors to include in this evaluation model are presented in Figure 3.3, the critical variable analysis model. The general nature of these variables is obvious, but they can be adapted to analyze the specific conditions and circumstances influencing a particular labor negotiation.[13] This generalized model is especially valuable in shaping broad strategies and forecasts of possible long-term results of various strategic and tactical decisions.

TACTICAL BARGAINING

Once the variables influencing bargaining are weighed and appropriate strategies are developed, the tactical phases of bargaining must be planned. Professor George Brooks of the Cornell University School of Labor and Industrial Relations, a former union official, sees collective bargaining as a sort of tribal rite. He indicates that all that happens during bargaining is ritualistic mumbo jumbo which justifies and authenticates decisions already determined by negotiations already completed in other parts of the economy. In actual practice, there may be some truth to his proposition, but power forces shape the settlements upon which other ritualistic processes are based; and bargaining, which pits force against force, is more aptly described as a power process than a ritual. All the basic steps in bargaining involve give and take: the more one side takes, the less the other retains. Given this condition, the tactical steps of bargaining must be planned with the utmost care and clarity. One of the more utilitarian descriptions of bargaining tactics is put forth by Meyer Ryder of the University of Michigan. Professor Ryder, who is a noted labor arbitrator, describes nine steps used by the parties as they move from the prebargaining stage through the final contract settlement.

Step 1 Ryder calls "the probing," since each party tries to determine what the other wants, what it will take, and what its preliminary public position will be. At this point, the union typically outlines demands far in excess of its ultimate expectations. This list, generally known as "the laundry list" because of its length and detail, is rarely the final set of union proposals, but placates certain groups within the union and allows the parties to indulge in what Professor Brooks might describe as "ritualistic chest beating." Little serious bargaining occurs at this point, and management usually chooses to remain silent or to express shock and/or horror at the magnitude of the union's "exorbitant and irresponsible demands."

---

[13] This discussion of variables is based on the author's book *Management Under Strike Conditions* (New York: Holt, Rinehart and Winston, Inc., 1966); chapters 1, 2 and 9 are particularly helpful in developing a strategy to handle bargaining under strike conditions, which is a special case of the general outline described above.

Step 2 is "the dressing," where each side backs up its position with facts, figures, and public utterances. Here, gains made by other unions are cited by union officials, while corporate negotiators disclaim ability to pay. Ritual is still important in this step, since union and company bargainers rarely reveal their true positions. A notable exception to this rule is the General Electric Company, which specifies detailed positions and presents data designed to justify the specific contract settlement terms it plans to offer during negotiations.

In step 3, the "simulated-real position," or the stated position of the parties comes to bear. To give a numerical example, the union's real position might be to get eight cents, but its simulated position is fifteen cents. The "bargaining cushion" is thus seven cents. The company's simulated position might be that no wage increase is possible, whereas it *really* could give five cents. The company's bargaining cushion is five cents. Each party, then, tries to gain part of the other's bargaining cushion, and the extent to which it succeeds is a real test of the bargainer's skill. This is where carefully prepared tactics can give one party a pronounced advantage. What to emphasize and avoid, what to grant and withhold, and what to say and not say are factors which can make or break success in negotiations. If the simulated real position is considered carefully in advance and presented according to a planned tactical approach, then mistatements and unproductive side steps can be avoided or reduced.

Once the simulated real position is established, the parties may proceed to step 4, an initial breakoff in negotiations that Ryder calls the "false breaking-off point." This is a threatened, not a real, intent to stop bargaining, but it can become a real break-down if one party miscalculates the other's position. In this step, bargaining is approaching the critical stage, so tactical planning is again called for to avoid undesirable or unforeseen consequences. Since this phase is a continuance of the information presentation and public-airing stages of steps 1 through 3, it demands similar tactics and methodologies. For management, a defensive position is usually most rewarding, as it avoids errors in form while presenting what are seen as substantive proposals by the public, outsiders, and the union rank and file.

Following this false breaking-off point, the parties then engage in step 5, known as "painting the picture of loss." They try to show hardships the public and the other party will endure if negotiations collapse. In these activities all forms of media may be used including flyers to homes, newspaper advertisements, and public announcements on radio and television. Only funds and ingenuity limit the use of media to propagandize both the public and other party. The importance of message and media choice need not be emphasized in this communications-conscious day, but the need to plan for their proper use deserves considerable stress. Management in particular has often been guilty of poor planning and execution of this vital phase of bargaining. The silence and caution which characterize the most effective tactics early in negotiations need to be replaced at this stage by well-publicized statements outlining the merits of "our stand" and the hardships the public will face because of "their position."

In step 6, the "area of bargaining expectancy" is reached. Here, serious negotiations begin and a real breakoff of negotiations may occur. In the bargaining-cushion example described in step 3, or the simulated real position, the difference between the eight cents the union feels it has to get and the five cents the management sees as its maximum allowable concession is only three cents. This amount is the real marrow of collective-bargaining differences as the parties begin to hone in on a settlement. The tactical expertise needed in step 6 revolves around providing the negotiators with the data required to state their positions authoritatively. The smokescreen of publicity for public consumption is now replaced by the cold clear daylight of factual data, and negotiations move into the realm of power bargaining.

Step 7, the "trading position" is where nonmonetary issues begin to be framed in money terms and economic muscle is exerted by both parties. Here, the guaranteed annual wage may be traded for a nickel an hour. Compromises are worked out as deadline dates begin to exert pressure on both parties. The original real positions of the parties may be reassessed; and, as contract expiration dates become closer, the costs of the strike to both parties are estimated and reestimated with subsequent adjustments in demands or offers. The threat of strike is real at this point and the parties are down to the final stages of give-and-take bargaining. Careful tactics are called for here in presenting positions, since miscalculations could set off a chain of events ending in an unnecessary strike. Advanced preparation of data and positions give one party a sharp edge in avoiding the disadvantages resulting from hastily contrived offers made without an understanding of the climate surrounding their introduction or their possible long-run effects. In the final analysis, the face lost or gained by negotiators may be the really critical variable influencing settlement.

In the "take position," step 8, the parties are ready to settle, even though they may not have accomplished their original goals. They "take" a solution to wrap up the bargaining and obtain a contract. This often leaves both parties somewhat dissatisfied, but a compromise is accepted as a better alternative than a strike. Again, the development of plans setting parameters and outlining positions before settlement pressures dominate bargaining seems wise and prudent. "Satisficing" replaces "maximizing" in the final rush to end bargaining.

In the final step, the "alternative to settlement" is a strike, and this means that steps 5 through 8 must be repeated until the issue is settled. Once a strike occurs, the outside pressures of the market and the government become more important, and *they continue to increase* until a settlement is reached.

Unless careful preparation precedes bargaining, there is a real chance that the bargaining cushion will be obtained by the other party. The tactical aspects represented in these nine steps are the keys to successful bargaining, and the party paying the greatest attention to preparing thoroughly for each step gains a definite edge in bargaining.[14] Tactics are only part of the collective bargaining process, but their execution can directly influence the relative success or failure of an entire negotiation.

CONTRACT ADMINISTRATION

When the smoke of strategic and tactical aspects of collective bargaining is cleared away, contract administration begins. In this phase, emphasis is placed on administrative tactics, since the policies and philosophies guiding the organization should have already been built into the contract settlement. In administering the contract, labor relations officials and union leaders both have an obligation to interpret the contract in good faith, not in legalistic terms. Though this ideal may be elusive because of ambiguity of language or deliberate attempts by either or both parties to subvert the contract, the signatories should try to live up to the negotiated contract, not avoid responsibility. This attempt is equally binding on both parties, and its avoidance is the cause of enduring conflict and bitterness such as that found in the long-festering disputes between the New York City Board of Education and the teachers union (UFT).

Most of the tactical disputes in contract administration arise out of five basic sections comprising the structure of the typical labor agreement. Pressures build in each of these areas and, unless grievances and petitions are set in some sort of strategic setting, tend to be handled one at a time. Though often expeditious, this approach is hazardous, since it may allow one party to gain advantages not won during contract negotiations. One common tactic to achieve this end is the "whipsaw," in which pressure is exerted on a weak man or an ambiguous issue to gain a concession which is then cited as a precedent to justify its adoption in other areas. Once the first precedent is set, it serves to whipsaw all other areas up to its level: the net effect is to achieve gains not won through collective bargaining. Guarding against the whipsaw is one of the main reasons for establishing a set of procedural tactics for administering collective-bargaining agreements.

Of the five major contract provisions, the first deals with procedural matters and institutional factors. It typically includes the length of the contract period, the enforcement of a no-strike clause, and the nature of contract administration. The use of compulsory and/or voluntary arbitration is a subject for serious debate here, and there is also continuing discussion of varying lengths of the contract period. Perhaps the most far-reaching change in this area in recent years has been the establishment of special committees to discuss rather complex bargaining areas between normal bargaining sessions. This has allowed a much more rational discussion of complex issues. Perhaps the most

---

[14] Some means of preparing forecasts and data and relating them to objectives, goals, strategies, tactics, and plans are discussed in Chapters 3, 4, 5, and 11.

well-known committee of this type is the human relations committee in the steel industry, an approach that seems to have merit where issues are so complex that worthwhile solutions are rarely reached during the conflict-filled process of pressure bargaining.

The second major portion of the typical labor contract deals with the status and rights of unions and managements. Unions recently have become more concerned with union security mostly because of the changing nature of the labor force and constant interunion bickering. At the same time, the resistance of management to limitations on its so-called rights or prerogatives in the personnel, production, and economic areas has been much greater. These areas have generated frictions in daily contract administration. For example, even though both parties agree that work should be measured, what constitutes a "fair day's work" is always debatable. How to measure and agree upon a "fair" output is all too often decided in a climate of distrust.[15] Since this area frequently generates a great deal of emotion, it is particularly important to clarify just what limits exist and how each issue will be related to organizational objectives. Lower-level managers need such guidance before they can administer the contract with any degree of consistency or effectiveness.

Job tenure and job security are a third aspect of contract administration, with job security being perhaps the major issue of the past two decades. Pressures and disputes continue to exist in the areas of hiring, firing, transfers, promotions, layoff and recall; and technological displacements generate a range of adjustments to guarantee job security. Among the more common guarantees now used to compensate or protect workers faced by technological displacement are shorter hours for the same pay, early retirement, sabbatical leaves, supplemental unemployment benefits, expanded unemployment compensation, early collection of social security, increases in severance pay, in-company retraining, wider bases of seniority, control over plant relocations, vested pension funds, greater control over work pace, automation funds, productivity profit-sharing plans, revised incentive plans, and changed job-evaluation plans. These approaches fail to gloss over the problems of displacement, but they do provide workers with either protection against arbitrary dismissal or help to carry them through the time needed to adjust to loss of employment or to undertake training for another job. Again, guidelines and specific policies need to be shaped so that managers at all levels will be clear on how to explain contractual provisions to their subordinates.

Work schedules, work loads, and work methods are the fourth set of factors in the labor contract, and they are continually under discussion between contract periods. The methods used to adjust or change work loads and work rules have resulted in some accommodations in the agreements reached in negotiated contracts. Some adjustments made to smooth the handling of these

---

[15] Much more on work standards can be found in John G. Hutchinson, *Managing a Fair Day's Work* (Ann Arbor, Mich.: University of Michigan, Bureau of Industrial Relations, 1963) and his "Does Anyone Believe in Work Standards?", *Management of Personnel Quarterly,* Summer 1964.

knotty problems are a requirement to notify and consult the union before changes are made, the submission of proposed changes to plant or company study committees, the institution of guarantees such as broadened seniority before changes can be made, and the development of special programs such as retraining and guarantees assuring that individuals already on the job will not be replaced except by natural attrition. The principle of replacement by attrition, which seems to be gaining acceptance, was used to settle the long-lingering dispute over the removal of the railroad firemen from diesel freight trains. In addition, some of the methods outlined in Chapters 13 and 14 have been used to help carry out programs of change and displacement within the constraints of the labor contract.

Wages and hours, the fifth and final set of contractual considerations, have always been at the heart of the labor contract. The length of the work week, money wages, deferred money wages, and other fringe benefits are always discussed in great detail during negotiations and their exact interpretation continues during the contract period. Of special interest here are the development of sabbatical leaves for workers, company-financed education programs, relocation allowances, expanded supplemental unemployment benefits, and medical care, and shorter workweeks, including break times. Because of the quantitative precision associated with many of these matters, they have been implemented and controlled more exactly than most of the other areas in the contract. Differences here can usually be resolved more easily than in less quantitative sectors.

In general, the most critical clauses in labor contracts are those encroaching on management rights, particularly in the production area; those generating pressures by management to weaken union security clauses (fashioned in response to worker pressures for protection of job security), those causing or perpetuating conflict in the areas of work standards and work rules; and those exerting pressure for shorter hours and some form of worker profit sharing. Since these matters continually come up for review and negotiation, it is critically important that contract administrators consistently apply the contract in good faith, with any deviations from or interpretations of the contract recorded in writing and reported to both union officials and company managers. It is also vital for managements to develop objectives, values, strategies, and plans within which they seek to implement the labor contract in a consistent and equitable manner.

GUIDELINES FOR MANAGING UNION RELATIONS

Though no single list of guidelines can point the way to successful labor relationships under all conditions, some general principles can make major contributions to improving labor-management relations. These guidelines are listed below in program form.

1. Develop a basic philosophy or credo similar to the one already outlined in this chapter.

2. Get all the facts influencing the labor policy by analyzing key variables carefully, completely, and continually. The critical variable analysis approach outlined in Chapter 3 is ideal for this purpose.

3. Prepare strategies for bargaining based on the basic philosophy as amended by analysis of the factual variables. The analytical methods of decision making outlined in Chapters 6 and 7 should provide assistance in this evaluation phase.

4. Prepare carefully for all steps in the bargaining process by determining tactical approaches to collective bargaining in advance and by gathering information to buttress positions that may be taken in any step of the bargaining process.

5. Prepare administrative, organizational, and procedural manuals for dealing with the day-to-day administration of the labor contract and other phases of labor relations not specifically covered by the existing contract. Record and disseminate any variations from the master contract. The control and information sections in Chapters 11 and 12 contain specific means of implementing this final guideline.

In general, labor relations seem to be conducted more effectively when unions are accepted as agents representing the worker in his efforts to sell a service to management. As vendors of labor, unions are not a threat to management; rather they are a part of a supply-and-demand picture governing the procurement and use of a basic factor of production. Buying and selling are normal activities of business, and the labor union's function of selling the services of its members should be considered a normal business activity, not a continuing test of wills. If management adopts this viewpoint and develops the kinds of philosophies and approaches outlined previously, labor-management relations will be far less painful and much more harmonious.

Summary

The management of union relations involves many activities similar to those performed in dealing with other publics, but it also has some unique dimensions. Labor unions are both supported and restricted by the executive, legislative, and judicial branches of government, which also exert an effect on managerial actions as shown in Figure 16.1.

In dealing with labor unions, managements need to develop basic philosophies, strategies, and tactics along much the same lines as those governing relations with vendors, suppliers, shareholders, and nonunion employees. These basic guidelines should be anchored on a cornerstone of good faith in dealings with the union and reflect a solution-oriented approach to solving problems arising both during collective bargaining and the contract administration period between negotiations. Bargaining strategies should be based on thorough factual analysis, and the tactical steps in the bargaining process should also be buttressed by solid painstaking preparation. Critical issues such as job tenure, wages and hours, fringe benefits, and union security call for special attention because of their potentially explosive nature.

Union-management relations are almost never conducted in an aura of complete harmony, but open conflict has less chance of developing when management and union officials base their strategies and tactics on sound economic grounds and respect for both the individual and his organization.

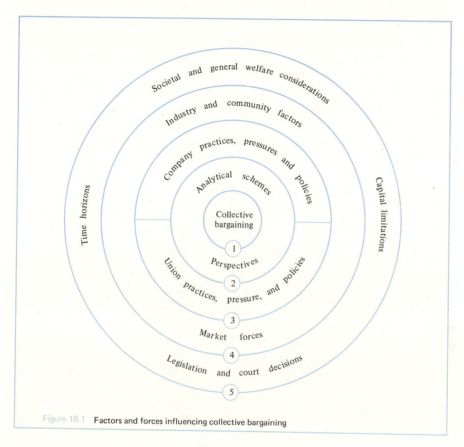

Figure 16.1   Factors and forces influencing collective bargaining

Study Questions

1. What are the major laws influencing labor-management relations? What are their key provisions?

2. Why do workers join unions? Do your personal experiences, if any, support or challenge reports by researchers? Discuss.

3. What in your mind is the real reason why workers join unions? Do you believe that contemporary union leadership helps the membership to reach its goals?

4. What are some of the benchmarks in the courts' dealings with labor relations? What influence do you believe these rulings have had on union membership?

5. What impact does unionization have on management-employee relations? Do you agree with Bakke's views? With Sayles and Strauss?

6. Evaluate the "labor relations credo" in the text. In what ways would you change it to make it more meaningful?

7. What are the major tactical steps in collective bargaining? If you can, give examples of each step from the contemporary labor scene.

8. Which of the tactical steps seem to you to be most critical? Least important? Why?

9. How might critical variable analysis as described in Chapter 3 be used to improve both the tactics and strategy of bargaining? Is it equally applicable to both unions and management?

10. What in your opinion are the most critical portions of the labor contract? How do they relate to contract administration?

11. Which of the decision-making methodologies discussed in Chapters 6 and 7 might be helpful in preparing more effective bargaining positions and viewpoints? How might they be related to the alternatives evaluated during critical variable analysis? How might they fit in with the choice of tactics used in the various phases of bargaining?

The Bing Brewing Company

Jonathan Bing, president of Bing Brewing, is considering hiring a consultant to assess employee morale and attitudes in the Lincoln, Nebraska, brewery. The consultant's proposal is to conduct and report findings of an employee survey and to make recommendations for corrective actions if necessary. The cost of this service would be $8000.

The Bing Company has two thousand employees in its brewing and distribution operations. It has only one small independent union and enjoys what Mr. Bing considers "good" labor relations. There has been some grumbling among nonunion workers recently, and the industrial relations manager knows that the Teamsters Union has been actively talking to employees. The president feels that a companywide union would not be good for Bing Brewing, but he has no plans to fight one actively if the workers choose to organize. He is, however, on the record as being willing to make a number of changes to avoid unionization.

When Mr. Bing mentioned the possibility of an attitude survey in his weekly staff conference, he received the following responses. The chief accountant stated flatly that the cost of the survey was excessive in view of expected results. The production manager felt that having a union in the plant would be a problem, but he was not sure that a survey was necessary. The marketing manager indicated that it made no difference to him whether the plant was unionized. He was also against the "wholly unjustified expense of an attitude survey." The industrial relations director held that a survey was needed to get the facts. He argued that top management never knows what workers are thinking and stated that "An outside opinion is needed to determine whether or not there are employee problems in the plant not known to the marketing, production, and accounting managers."

1. What factors should Mr. Bing consider in deciding whether to hire the consultant? What safeguards should he invoke if he plans to authorize the proposed survey?

2. Do you feel that the consultant should be engaged to conduct an attitude survey? Why or why not?

Consolidated
Electrical Supply
Company

Six months before union contract negotiations with the local electrical workers
chapter were due to start, Darrell Brown, plant manager of the South Bend,
Indiana, plant of Consolidated Electrical Supply Company (CONESCO) received
a disquieting letter from company headquarters in Chicago. The letter, which
was signed by Byron Conrad, executive vice-president in charge of manufacturing operations, stated that CONESCO was considering closing the South Bend
plant because of high operating costs. Mr. Conrad noted in the letter that
Mr. Brown could not be held accountable for the poor performance in the
plant, since he had been on the job for only three months, but costs were
"out of line with area, company, and industry productivity standards" and
labor was "too highly paid in comparison with intercompany rates and with
similar plants in the industry." These high wage rates had led CONESCO's
executive committee to a preliminary decision to close the plant within one
year unless "extenuating circumstances could be shown."

In response to this note, Mr. Brown requested he be allowed to adopt
one of the two following options: (1) prepare a comprehensive cost reduction
plan; (2) develop an initial plan for phasing out operations. Of the two options,
Mr. Brown preferred the former, since he believed that costs could be cut
to a level where a shutdown might prove unnecessary. Mr. Brown felt that
a major cost reduction program would require a series of technical and other
improvements. In the technical area, he believed it would be necessary to
replace inefficient equipment, to develop better scheduling, to improve inventory control procedures, and to tighten existing quality controls. In the nontechnical area, he recognized the need for more highly motivated supervisors
and the union's cooperation in setting more realistic output standards. On
this latter point, Mr. Brown knew that output could be improved only by
cutting existing work standards and by establishing more stringent quotas
on new operations. He called headquarters and requested that he be allowed
to prepare a cost reduction program rather than a phaseout. Mr. Conrad
agreed to consider such a plan and gave him three weeks to submit a proposal
to the executive committee.

During the next four days, Mr. Brown developed, with the production and
engineering staff, a comprehensive plan for improvement and/or replacement
of inefficient obsolete equipment. In conjunction with Benjamin Southward,
manager of industrial relations at the South Bend plant, he met with union
leaders to ask their assistance in lowering costs. These leaders, though not
enthusiastic, agreed to consider a cooperative effort in view of the urgency
of the situation. Similar presentations were made to plant management and
apparently received favorably. Following these meetings, Mr. Brown drew up

a plan which contained specific technical suggestions and general approaches to reducing supervisory and blue-collar costs.

Two weeks after submitting his tentative plan to corporate headquarters, Mr. Brown was asked to come to Chicago to talk with Keith Jonas, executive vice-president in charge of domestic operations. After a series of opening pleasantries, Mr. Jonas informed Mr. Brown that no additional funds would be committed to the South Bend operation because it was "a risky proposal." He commented, "There's no use throwing good money after bad. I've poured too much money in this particular property already. If any cost reduction program is to work, it will have to do so without additional capital investment."

Mr. Brown returned to South Bend determined to show headquarters that costs could be cut even without the required investment in new capital facilities. He felt a strong commitment to his work force and the South Bend community, and he decided to fight to keep the plant alive. His first step was to call all management personnel into the plant auditorium to inform them about his visit to Chicago. In a stormy three-hour session, he described what economies would be needed and stated flatly that some management people would have to go. Within a week after this meeting about 25 percent of the management received notices of dismissal. Anxiety was high in the plant, but those remaining felt Mr. Brown's action had been necessary. In the words of one longtime supervisor, "It's better that a few go than all of us." Said Mr. Brown, "I hate to do this, but it's the only way; otherwise we only have about four months left before we start closing the doors."

With Mr. Southward, Mr. Brown again explained the gravity of the situation to union leaders and asked for their cooperation. They listened and then asked for exact details on company finances and their role in the program. Mr. Brown agreed to discuss both items in detail the following day. True to his promise, Mr. Brown appeared the next day with the plant controller, Harold Stansky, who gave a detailed rundown of finances relating to the South Bend facility. Included in this presentation were detailed cost and profit figures; comparisons of wages, hours, productivity, working conditions, and so on in the plant with those in the South Bend area, the industry, and other CONESCO plants. Union leaders, including all of the officers, the bargaining committee, and the shop stewards, listened carefully, but were skeptical that "this plant is all that bad." The seriousness of the situation seemed to Mr. Brown to be brought home in this meeting, especially to those older union officials who might have trouble getting equally attractive jobs elsewhere if the shutdown did occur. At the close of the meeting, Mr. Brown promised to present a detailed plan of action in one week.

The meeting held to discuss a specific cost reduction program was described by one attendee as "the stormiest, most emotional meeting I've ever seen." To bring the plant "back to a competitive level of operations," Mr. Brown proposed a reduction in force of eighty of the plant's five hundred blue-collar workers, a doubling of output in over half of the existing output standards, a return to the policy of having union committeemen work on company jobs (thus giving up their status as full-time union men paid by the company), and the establishment of a policy allowing management to transfer men between jobs "if and when the company determined a man was, in the judgment of the supervisor, not productively occupied." This latter provision was particularly upsetting, since it allowed individuals to be transferred to jobs outside of their existing job descriptions. Angry oral clashes started as soon as Mr. Brown completed his talk. Charges of *union busting, speedup, dictatorship, dilution of skill,* and *fascist* were tossed out in rapid order. Indeed, these epithets were some of the more polite ones used as the meeting wore on.

After two hours of violent and noisy discussion, all the union leaders walked out. In a news release to the South Bend paper, a local union official was quoted as saying, "Management is trying to blackmail us into paying for their own inefficiency. Practices like this haven't been used since the 1930s. The only difference is that now they try to break your back with financial pressure instead of trying to crack your skull with hired goon squads."

1. Why do you think the union leadership reacted as it did?

2. If Mr. Brown persists in pursuing his present course of action, how should he proceed from here?

3. If you were Mr. Brown, what would you do now?

The Dale Corporation

Ten years ago, when job evaluation was installed in the Dale Corporation, the men in the machine shop were required to schedule their own work through the machines. This requirement was built into the descriptions of certain job classes in the machine shop. In the past five years, the scheduling function has gradually been transferred from the machine shop floor into a central production control office. In the last month, much of the production control activity has been centralized in an IBM computer.

When a headquarters team of industrial engineers came through the Dale plant in Chicago, they discovered that certain individuals in the machine shop no longer performed the scheduling function. Their recommendation was that the jobs be downgraded to reflect this lowering of skill.

When the points were removed from the job classes, the union grieved, stating that failure to uncover the change was a managerial error, and to make an adjustment now would destroy the traditional job relationships in the machine shop. The company maintained that since jobs had been upgraded in the machine shop from time to time, they should also be downgraded when necessary. The union agreed with this in principle, but said that anything that had been in effect for ten years should not be subject to change.

When the issue remained unresolved for thirty days, the union threatened to walk out. Since job evaluation disputes could not be arbitrated, a walkout seemed imminent.

1. Given the facts of this situation, with which point of view would you agree? Why?

2. What can be done in the face of such creeping change? How should it be handled?

Yale and Towne—Materials Handling Division

On August 31, 1961 the members of Lodge 1717, International Association of Machinists (IAM), struck the Philadelphia plant of Yale and Towne's materials handling division. This walkout ended in January 1962 after what the *Philadelphia Evening Bulletin* called "one of Philadelphia's most bitterly contested labor disputes in a decade." During this period of strife, the parties underwent almost every possible kind of conflict and strain upon labor-management relations.

The chronology, taken from press releases, speeches, newspaper stories, magazine articles, and other documents, traces the specific facts and forces surrounding a situation that *Business Week* characterized as one in which "an ordinary management [took] a hard line against a long established union. . . ."

TABLE 16.1 CHRONOLOGY OF THE MACHINISTS' STRIKE AT
                YALE AND TOWNE

The Prestrike Period (Prior to August 31, 1961)

1954–56	Grievances	200
	Arbitrated grievances	8
	Work stoppages (Company figures)	4
1959–61	Grievances	1360
	Arbitrated grievances	66
	Work stoppages (Company figures)	43
1955–1961	Competitive factors reported in *Forbes*	

1. The Philadelphia plant went from 15-percent return on sales before taxes to a loss position.

2. With 1960 employment up 100 people, the Philadelphia plant produced 17-percent fewer lift trucks and 100 per month fewer electric hoists than in 1955.

3. The new Y&T president, Gordon Patterson, shook up top management and placed sixteen new men in the thirty-two top posts in the company.

TABLE 16.1   CHRONOLOGY OF THE MACHINISTS' STRIKE AT
             YALE AND TOWNE (Cont.)

	4. The Philadelphia plant had a huge inventory, and the company stated it would lose less money closed than open.
	5. Consultants blamed labor troubles, poor scheduling, high costs designs, excessive manning, poor expense control, for the plant's problems.
January 1961	A communications program, previously decided upon by new management, disseminated documents stating the company's intent to change existing terms and conditions of work. This effort was given impetus by a consultant's report charging that management had lost control of its labor force. The communications program began in the face of risks of walkout and attempted to carry to the union the company's intentions either to make the Philadelphia facility competitive or to close its doors.
February 1961	Letters were sent to employees describing such factors as the company's sad profit picture, the need for changes, the highlights of the consultant's report, the possibility of future layoffs, the general state of the industry. and the dim future of the company unless increases in productivity were achieved.
April–May 1961	The company negotiating team prepared its proposals, and the union awaited the results of these deliberations.
June 1961	The company indicated an intent to adopt a radical new approach in its union dealings.
June 22, 1961	The company made a proposal to union leaders, company officers, and the board of directors. In this proposal, which was outlined orally to the union and presented in written form to company officials, the following points were stressed:
	1. Company profitability and future plans
	2. Company sales compared to industry sales
	3. Divisional profits versus company profit figures
	4. Inventory and other cost figures
	5. Directions and trends in foreign and domestic business
	6. The company's intent to take action to improve the profitability of the Philadelphia operation
June 23, 1961	The union asked for written figures, but the company refused for "competitive reasons." According to one company official's view, the union's reaction to the financial figures was "subdued but amicable."
June 25, 1961	The company attorney filed one suit for $1 million damages allegedly caused by a wildcat strike in September 1960.

TABLE 16.1 CHRONOLOGY OF THE MACHINISTS' STRIKE AT YALE AND TOWNE (Cont.)

June 27, 1961	The union filed notice of intent to terminate existing contracts and stated demands estimated by the company to equal an increase of one dollar per hour above existing labor costs. Other demands were felt by management to be further "restrictions of the right of management to manage the business."
July 3, 1961	The company outlined its proposal, which was a complete revision of the existing contract. The union's reaction to the forty-three changes was, "If we accept these changes, we honestly feel it would ruin the union at Yale and Towne."
July 6, 1961	The first negotiation was held, but no visible results were achieved.
July 10, 1961	Company letters were sent to employee homes outlining the nature of and the competitive reasons for the drastic changes proposed by the company.
July 12–August 8, 1961	Negotiations continued, but without real progress. Union officials stated they felt the company was not serious about its far-reaching demands.
August 9, 1961	The Federal Mediation and Counciliation Service entered into negotiations. The parties agreed to try to settle three hundred pending grievances in a crash program.
August 10, 1961	The company reiterated its stand in a newsletter sent to the homes of employees.
August 16, 1961	A union strike vote recorded 701 votes for a strike, six against, and two voided ballots.
August 28, 1961	The company made its final offer, which showed little change from its original offer of July 3.
August 29, 1961	The union made its last offer, which indicated that the parties were miles apart.
August 30, 1961	Meetings were held with federal mediators, but no agreement was reached. A company memo summed up its postion, "You apparently have failed to recognize the seriousness of our proposals..." The union, on the other hand, felt it had no choice but to resist changes on the basic core of the labor contract.
August 30, 1961 Midnight	The strike began.

The Strike Period (August 31, 1961–January 29, 1962)

August 31, 1961	The strike began with peaceful, orderly picketing.
September 1, 1961	Samuel Luterotty, president of Lodge 1717 said, "[the] strike will be a long one..."

TABLE 16.1   CHRONOLOGY OF THE MACHINISTS' STRIKE AT
YALE AND TOWNE (Cont.)

September 5, 1961	James Marron of Yale and Towne agreed that the strike would be a long one in a letter to employees.
September 11, 1961	*Metalworking News* reported that Yale was "living off its inventory" in meeting orders.
September 15, 1961	President Luterotty declared in a letter to union members that "We believe . . . that the new management really wanted a strike to destroy the union's strength."
September 15–30, 1961	Letters to the community and interested parties increased in number, inventory shortages began to appear, Cable King hoist operations (four hundred jobs) were transferred to Arkansas, and federal negotiators continued to push for a settlement.
October 1–31, 1961	Picketing was restricted by injunction on October 3. The union began a propaganda drive with handbills, radio shows, and an open letter to Mayor Dilworth asking him to mediate the dispute. "Volunteers" from other unions entered the picket lines. Union press releases called the company stand "Boulwarism" and asked the company to "cease its war upon its employees."
	Picketing became more vigorous. President Gordon Patterson, speaking before the New York Society of Security Analysts said, "We have had trouble convincing the IAM that the changes required to accomplish acceptable results include some improvements in work practices and contract provisions which have contributed to inefficient operations and declining productivity."
	A telegram to Secretary of Labor Goldberg from N. Zonarich of the Industrial Union Department stated, "Boulwarism is now being imposed by Yale and Towne's Vice-President Paul Hartig, who was formerly employed by General Electric."
November 1–15, 1961	Picketing became more violent, and threats of bodily harm were voiced. The *Philadelphia Evening Bulletin* and *Philadelphia Inquirer* indicated that the strike had gotten out of the hands of local authorities. Attacks were made on employees and an auto was overturned. The company protested that company property and nonunion employees were not getting proper protection. A company official was arrested after a scuffle with pickets.
November 15, 1961	Over 250 policemen appeared to stop violence under a court's direction following a newspaper report that there had been "a dismal breakdown of enforcement."
November 15–30, 1961	Vice President Hartig of Yale and Towne and Vice President DeMore of the IAM entered directly into negotiations, but little progress took place.

TABLE 16.1   CHRONOLOGY OF THE MACHINISTS' STRIKE AT
             YALE AND TOWNE (Cont.)

December 10, 1961	The latest company offer was rejected.
December 12, 1961	All union officers were re-elected.
December 16, 1961	The company issued a back-to-work offer, but had few takers.
December 27, 1961	One worker who had returned to work was assaulted at his home. President Luterotty of Lodge 1717 was charged with the attack.
December 28, 1961	The company threatened to replace workers who did not return to work by January 4, 1962. Foremen followed up on this statement. Vice-president Hartig stated, "Once you have been replaced, your jobs are lost."
January 2, 1962	Federal mediators called for efforts to settle the strike.
January 3, 1962	Director William Simkin of the Federal Counseling Service offered a proposal for settlement which the union "reluctantly" accepted. The company refused.
January 5, 1962	Negotiations, said Simkin, are in a state of "indefinite suspension."

On January 5, 1962 company officials seriously discussed the possibility of hiring replacements for union workers. Some executives felt that this action was necessary either to end the strike or to restore the plant to profitable levels of operation. Though this stand was more rigid than any the company previously had taken, it was advocated as being both feasible and economic. Another group of managers, holding that the resultant conflict could never be justified on either economic or moral grounds, opposed the concept of operating during strike conditions.

No decision was made on this matter by the close of the opening meeting. The consensus at the meeting, however, was that a decision would be made very shortly.

1. What factors and forces should the Yale and Towne management evaluate prior to deciding whether or not to operate?

2. What plans should the company prepare prior to attempting to operate during strike conditions? (Assume that the company decides to operate with replacement labor.)

3. Assuming management decided to operate during the strike, what specific plans should it follow to achieve desired objectives?

4. In your opinion, should Yale and Towne operate its plant during this strike action?

Farnell Aircraft, Inc.

James Carly, director of industrial relations at Farnell Aircraft's San Diego plant, received a telephone call from Charles Starr, director of engineering, concerning rumors about "rumblings of unionization among our engineering employees." In the course of their conversation, Carly learned that four engineering supervisors had called on Starr to discuss their belief that an independent union was gaining a foothold "in certain departments." According to Mr. Starr there were strong indications that a "grass-roots movement was afoot that might bring a union into the plant in the near future." In addition to the independent union, Starr believed that two professional unions, the United Auto Workers (UAW) and the Teamsters, were interested in organizing professional engineering employees in the plant. Starr felt that the matter was quite serious and ended the conversation with the emotional comment, "I'd quit my job if a union ever came in here. We've got to do something about this before it makes any real headway."

Carly decided to speak to the four supervisors himself to determine the nature and scope of potential union inroads. These supervisors repeated their stories and indicated that there seemed to be an increasing prounion sentiment among their engineers. Carly decided to conduct further discussions with all management personnel connected with engineering.

After completing this survey, he concluded that engineers in the San Diego area were concerned about a number of things, but they were particularly upset by eight developments. They resented the (1) high starting pay of new men. Because of the scarcity in the job market, some newly hired graduate engineers were receiving more money than senior employees. (2) New management positions had been filled by outsiders rather than from within the San Diego plant. (3) Transfers had been made between departments and between plants with very little advance notice and usually without the prior consultation of concerned individuals. This practice had caused a great stir in departments where a number of individuals had been transferred to a new facility in San Jose. (4) Cutbacks and additions had occurred in recent years without regard to seniority. The company was often accused of being arbitrary in layoffs and rehiring procedures. ("They don't care about the oldtime, long-service employees.") (5) Much engineering work was routine, and certain engineering functions, particularly drafting and design, were structured so that "it is hard for a man to make a record in these departments." This was especially true because the company had no uniform or clear-cut standards to measure engineering contributions to productivity. (6) Most engineers personally disliked the idea of joining unions, but saw no other way to meet their needs. (7) Engineers in the plant were particularly opposed to being associated with "blue-collar unions like the UAW," but "liked its muscle." (8) In general, plant engineering sentiment about unions seemed to be slightly in favor of "no union," but a solid corps of discontented engineers in the design and drafting departments appeared to be winning more converts every day. In view of these findings, Mr. Carly estimated that a forceful, continuing effort to establish a local union might bring unionization into the plant within six months. He summarized his findings in a confidential report to Division Manager A.T. Farnell, Jr., and sent copies to Mr. Starr and the other engineering supervisors.

One week later, Messrs. Farnell, Carly, and Starr met to discuss the situation. Mr. Farnell opened the meeting by stating that his own inquiries seemed to support Mr. Carly's findings. Starr reported that he had received similar feedback from other engineers under his direction. The discussion then turned to the content of the report and the problems it appeared to raise.

1. If you were Mr. Farnell, what would you do? Outline a step-by-step action program.

The Tasty Flakes Cereal Company

There are two basic groups of employees in the central purchasing department of the Tasty Flakes Cereal Company. The first, or headquarters, group, is composed of both college-trained and other specialists. This group writes material specifications, handles inventory records, develops routine sampling procedures, and analyzes inspection reports. The second group, made up of company purchasing representatives, has only college-trained personnel. The company purchasing representatives perform a series of professional services for the company and for vendors. One of their duties is value analysis, which attempts to help vendors improve their products' design and to offer lower prices on the materials and parts they sell to the Tasty Flakes Company. The second group also does some field testing of material and conducts price negotiations on contracts with vendors.

The company purchasing representatives are mostly young men fresh out of college. They do a good deal of traveling, and they are considered to be a bright ambitious group by their fellow workers. They are paid less on the average than the members of the headquarters group, and they have tightly controlled expense accounts. They continually complain about the rigidity of these controls and about the pressures of traveling. Everyone agrees that they are overworked and underpaid. It is true, however, that this group has been the testing ground for young men who have moved into positions of influence in other departments.

The headquarters group is made up principally of older employees, many of whom have long service with the company and seem to be more content than the purchasing representatives. They appear to like routine work much better than their younger colleagues, but there are very few promotions out of this group. Other employees consider the headquarters group a dead end, although they agree that it has the advantage of job security.

Earlier this year, company officials reviewed the possibility of introducing a computer installation in the company. Top management was enthusiastic about the record-keeping, payroll, and inventory control activities that could be performed by a computer. It was, however, concerned with the reactions of salaried employees to such a proposal and engaged an outside consulting firm to conduct an opinion survey to determine the nature and depth of employee reactions to computerization of certain clerical functions.

1. Based upon your understanding of human needs, how would you expect the purchasing representatives to react? The headquarters group?

2. Shortly after the announcement of the proposed purchase of the computer, a white-collar union attempted to organize the purchasing department. Union officials felt that one of the two groups was much more amenable to unionization than the other. Which group do you think is most likely to vote for a union? What reasoning underlies your answer?

Of all areas of growth in contemporary society, none surpasses that of research and development activities. Over 90 percent of the scientifically trained people who ever lived are alive today, and more students are choosing scientific and technical careers than ever before. More than half the money spent on research in the history of mankind was expended in the past ten years, and every indication points to continued increases in the foreseeable future. *Business Week* estimates that the 1970 total will soar to $20.8 billion.[1] Much of the impetus for research spending has come from the government, since over half of the research done by profit-making corporations in 1966 was concentrated in the aerospace and electrical machinery and equipment industries, the two areas in which NASA and the Defense Department sink most of their research money. On the other hand, great sums of money are spent in other industries. Even the relatively research-poor textile and apparel industry now pushes research spending.

The size and magnitude of these research expenditures point out how research and development activities are increasingly important to American industry, and possible payoffs have a similarly high potential. One major payoff occurs in terms of new product expectations. Industrial firms expect 17 percent of their 1971 sales volume will be realized from the results of research now in progress, but not yet completed. Producers of durable goods feel that 23 percent of their 1971 sales will result from work now going on in the lab. In nondurable goods industries, the estimate is 11 percent of new business will come from products now in the development stages. According to Joseph Bailey,

CHAPTER 17
Management of Research and Development

---

[1] "R & D Looms Big in Fiscal Budgets." *Business Week,* May 13, 1967, pp. 68–72.

"Though firm figures are hard to come by, the impression is strong that before another decade passes, the majority of management as well as staff positions in American big business will be occupied by men with scientific and technical training."[2] If Bailey's prediction comes true, research and development activities will spawn both new products *and* the new management force of the future. This will come about, Bailey claims, because of the "massive displacement in our working population of brawn by brains, of hands by heads."[3]

Unfortunately, management problems have developed almost as rapidly as growth in the area of research and development. According to Herbert Shepard, nine major problems are raised by the expansion of industrial research activities.[4] Shepard discusses these problems in terms of whether laboratories should be the department of today or tomorrow, whether the scientists should have a local or cosmopolitan orientation, whether the results of research should be guarded or advertised, whether budgets should be charged to company or research time, whether authority should be delegated or shared in the research function, whether research organizations should be based on project or functional groupings, whether research management should be aiming toward fulfillment or regression, whether nonprofessional workers in research activities should be caste or class, and whether professional workers should be the elite or the proletariat of the industrial organization. These points are not easy to understand or resolve in practice, but in view of the fact that research is such an important ongoing activity, they must be looked at carefully by management.

Many of the factors in Shepard's listing consider the nature and impact of research, but the others are focused on the people who conduct this research. In order to increase the yield of research efforts, management must effectively utilize the people and the resources that collectively constitute the research and development activity. How to accomplish this end is the focus of this chapter.

MANAGING RISK AND INNOVATION

Sources of research projects can vary a great deal. The bright idea, the press of competition, offshoots of innovation—these and other sources provide the projects which collectively make up research and development. Some research projects are defensive, that is, they react to something done by competitors. Other projects are offensive, since they attempt to break into new fields or to stay ahead of developments in fields in which the organization has existing interests. Research projects may originate with individuals, groups, competitive

---

[2] Charles B. Orth, Joseph N. Bailey, Francis W. Wolec, *Administering Research and Development* (Homewood, Ill.: Richard D. Irwin, Inc., 1964), p. 2.

[3] *Ibid.,* p. 5

[4] "Nine Dilemmas in Industrial Research," *Administrative Science Quarterly,* December 1965, pp. 295–309.

environments, or higher levels of management acting in research committees or formalizing problems in the operating environment. According to C.E.K. Mies, vice-president of Eastman Kodak:

> The best person to decide what research work shall be done is the man who is doing the research. The next best is the head of the department. After that, you leave the field of the best person and meet increasingly worse groups. The first of these is the research director who is wrong more than half the time, then comes the research committee which is wrong most of the time, finally, there is the committee of company VPS which is wrong all of the time.[5]

Not everyone is quite as positive as Mr. Mies about the appropriateness of individual selection of projects, but his list does pinpoint likely sources of research in the typical industrial organization.

Whatever the source of a successful invention, four steps occur during the classic innovation cycle:

1. Invention or concept
2. Rapid growth and acceptance
3. Consolidation and approach toward maturity
4. Maturity

Then the product cycle is broken and another innovative activity begins. It is not terribly important to understand the steps in the innovation cycle to realize that any project requires direction, organization, and a good, systematic development of ideas. According to Bright, the evaluation of a research project should begin with a technical and economic objective followed by an analysis of the design concept, which is then succeeded by a design and developmental prototype, which eventually becomes the product that will represent the company in the marketplace.[6] James Brian Quinn says top officials should take an active role in the project selection and management by providing meaningful objectives for research workers in terms of capital and its use, rates of growth and directions needed, sources of supply and methods of future growth.[7] They should also see that the organization is attuned to the company's long-run threats and opportunities, and they should devise a business strategy into which research is integrated. Further, he states that management should develop methods and processes to evaluate research in the light of the company's goals and should organize research operations for maximum transfer

---

[5] As quoted by R.M. Lodge, "Economic Factors in Planning of Research," in Jewkes, Sawyers, and Stillman, eds., *Sources of Invention* (New York: St. Martin's Press, Inc., 1959).

[6] James R. Bright, *Research and Development and Technological Innovation* (Homewood, Ill.: Richard D. Irwin, Inc., 1964), p. 659.

[7] "Long Range Planning of Industrial Research," *Harvard Business Review,* August 1961, p. 677.

of technology from research to operating facilities. In terms of selecting projects, Quinn says that the company must have a balance of projects taken from company goals and objectives. He suggests that research should be related either to present products or to new or foreseeable projects or to entirely new areas. He calls for a blend of offensive and defensive projects and for planning to balance the speed with which they develop. He also advocates the assignment of projects to divisions that need them most and the establishment of a system of priorities designed to achieve optimum results.

To expand upon the concept of balance more fully, the concept of risk must be considered. In order to obtain good balance between projects, risks must be assessed carefully. One classification developed by Bright lists the following risks as paramount: technical risks, marketing risks, interference risks, timing risks, obsolescence risks, and individual risks. In the technical area, scientific engineering and production problems may cause the research project to fall short of its goals. Technical risks can occur because of incomplete theory or inability to translate theory into practice or to translate working models into large-scale production. In the marketing area, competitors, consumers, sponsors, and the speed with which demand develops are important risk considerations. Interference risks are external forces in the environment such as labor, government, and technological factors beyond the control of the individual firm's research activities. Timing risks deal with the business cycle, the availability of power and materials, supplies, and the relative effectiveness of the sales force in carrying out the mission of the marketing group. Obsolescence risks are those evolving because of the pressure of competing product lines. The individual risk factor is one of the more interesting, since it involves capacities and abilities. How well people do their jobs and how well they are able to meet their goals in terms of completing stated projects are critical to any research effort. Can the people do what they claim to do? How conservative are they? These and other questions determine the dimensions of individual risk.

In practice, risk reviews tend to be negative, since the possible pitfalls in a particular research effort invariably seem to outweigh the potential returns. On the other hand, faith enters into risk evaluation and usually infuses optimism into risk evaluation, particularly when future returns seem promising.

Project management is a balancing of sources of innovation, the risks connected with developing them, and the skill with which they are administered and marketed. Good project management demands positive effort; *it does not just happen by itself.* In his book, *Research and Development Management,* Daniel J. Roman states, "What R and D is to scientific technology, management of R and D is to management technology."[8] This contention is generally borne out by the experiences of organizations engaged in extensive R&D activities. (More on the management of R&D appears later in this chapter.)

---

[8] (New York: Appleton-Century-Crofts, 1968).

MANAGEMENT OF SCIENTIFIC AND TECHNICAL PERSONNEL

One of the very critical aspects of managing any research and development organization centers on the handling of the engineers, scientists, and technicians who collectively *are* the research effort. In order to get their top research scientists to devote their best effort to project development, design, and control, it is vital for managers to know what motivates researchers positively and how they may react to various motivational stimuli. Some of the approaches in Chapters 13 and 14 designed to move people to action reflect how these concepts have been applied beyond the R&D area.

Much has been written about the "different" nature of research and development people. Psychologist Lee E. Danielson of the University of Michigan agrees that they are different and indicates that the causes of these differences are important in understanding why they do what they do. He identifies a series of personality traits and derives a set of needs that arise from these critical traits. According to Danielson, scientists and engineers are different in their approach to the job. First of all, they are more responsible, objective, and involved in their work, and they also desire supervisory patterns different from other workers.[9] They prefer supervisors who give them considerable freedom and who are themselves individualistic. In addition, engineers want greater recognition in both tangible and intangible terms. According to Danielson, the engineer's goals are broader, higher, and more definite than those of his nontechnical colleagues. And in terms of personality, Danielson finds the engineer to be generally ambitious, analytical, dynamic, competitive, creative, intense, introvertive, emotional, and with an outlook that tends to be either very narrow or very broad. He cautions that this generalized set of personality traits does not necessarily apply to all engineers and scientists; but he implies that his stereotype is reasonably accurate. Engineers' greatest needs, Danielson says, are for recognition, greater understanding of the results of their work, support from their supervision, and the desire to have their knowledge utilized effectively on meaningful work assignments.

In a study of research scientists made by Moore and Renck, one conclusion was that "the technical experts, engineers, and other professionals in industry seem to be more frustrated than satisfied."[10] The implication here is that researchers tended to strike out indiscriminantly against almost all aspects of the total work environment. According to this study, even the satisfied performers were upset by the characteristics of their supervisors; and the ineffective performers were negative, bitter, and frustrated about almost all facets of their work. The only consensus between both successful and less

---

[9] Lee E. Danielson, *Characteristics of Engineers and Scientists* (Ann Arbor, Mich.: University of Michigan, Bureau of Industrial Relations, 1960).

[10] David Moore and Richard Renck, "The Professional Employee in Industry," *Journal of Business,* January 1955, pp. 58–66.

successful subjects was that their jobs demanded much of them and that working conditions were "average." On all other matters of their job environment, including employee benefits, confidence in management, security in the job, and status and recognition, the low achievers and the high achievers were very far apart in perceptions. Productivity was also lower among the unsuccessful people than among those achieving degrees of success on the job. The conclusion here is that recognition of talent and acceptance by higher levels of management seem to be the biggest contributors to the development of professional success. According to Moore and Renck's results, management, in order to achieve maximum output and involvement, must devote a great deal of attention to nurturing and developing research personnel.[11]

Both the studies by Danielson and by Moore and Renck emphasize that participation and recognition are needed to bring out the best efforts of research and development personnel, and to this Danielson would add perception of the research job by those performing it. He claims that perceptive, well-trained, critical, skeptical, creative people have high goals and ambitions and are anxious to prove themselves. They are job-oriented, desirous of recognition, and very concerned about the way people view them on the job.[12] They have high self-expression, self-esteem, and self-determination needs, and they give high ratings to the opportunity for growth on their jobs and in their firms. It is therefore important to develop situations in which their perceived needs and received needs are in close harmony. The establishment of such a climate tends to bring forth a maximum effort.

Though most studies seem to show that engineers and scientists differ from other research personnel in their psychological makeup, a study by Taguiri seems to indicate that their value structures are not terribly different from those held by other managers.[13] Value differences do exist between managers and scientists, but they are smaller than most people think, Taguiri concluded after looking at esthetic, theoretical, political, religious, social, and economic value ratings reported by a group of scientists, managers, and attendees at a program given at the Harvard Business School for Industrial Research Institute executives. His detailed questionnaires and charts seem to indicate that "there are very small differences in the total value frameworks of these three groups of people and all three groups have relatively high theoretical, economical, and political values and relatively low aesthetic, religious, and

---

[11] At the Menninger Clinic in Topeka, Kansas, particular attention has been devoted to seminars designed to help executives spot "people problems" existing in the form of individual *hostility, personality limitations,* or personal *rigidity.* Applied in a research organization, these techniques may provide an early-warning system for identification of problem people or areas. Like most techniques used to detect psychological problems, the Menninger approach is still far from scientific, a fact managers of scientific personnel should note with care.

[12] Danielson, *op. cit.*

[13] Renato Taguiri, "Value Orientations of Engineers and Scientists," in Ralph W. Hower and Charles B. Orth, *Managers and Scientists* (Cambridge, Mass.: Harvard Business School, Division of Research, 1963).

social values."[14] This similarity of value systems does not contrast sharply with the other investigations of psychological differences and needs of managers and engineers and scientists. But it appears to show that engineers and scientists' values do differ from their psychological needs.

Are engineers and scientists really different in psychological and value traits? The consensus seems to be affirmative in the former, but unclear in the latter. In any case, special care and handling seem justified, if only because the critical services they render are in short supply. Like women, scientists and engineers are difficult to live with, but difficult to live without.

TECHNIQUES IN MANAGING RESEARCH AND DEVELOPMENT ACTIVITIES

The management of research and development is not strictly an intramural process. Research management does involve running laboratories, experiments, field tests, and motivating engineers and scientists, and it also involves such questions as whether research or innovation should be homegrown or purchased in the market. But managing research inside the house is but one phase; another is the resolution of decisions on whether to make or buy and what to buy. The considerations entering into these decisions can be enormously complex and touch on moral and social variables as well as traditional economic factors. Thus, value systems interact with judgment in the selection of methods and means of conducting R&D efforts. Some of the available methods rely primarily on a profit-centered philosophy, while others place their main emphasis on the development and utilization of people's talents and creativity. In some organizations, both approaches are embraced with emphasis shifting from time to time to best serve the demands created by specific projects or activities.

BUYING RESEARCH IN THE MARKET

One way to obtain research is to buy it on the open market. The cost of conducting research is invariably high and results typically uncertain. This means that "sure" projects can command a high price in the open market and that purchasing research sometimes may be more economical than doing it at home. The *legitimate* purchase of patent rights, licensing, franchising, or royalty arrangements are common examples of how research is bought in the open market. When a GM dealership is created, the dealer buys a share of GM's research, a situation duplicated when Coca-Cola licenses a bottler. Similarly, when IBM and Xerox offer their know-how and ideas to customers leasing or buying their computers or copiers, they too are selling the fruits of research.

Industrial espionage is a much less legitimate way to obtain results. In recent years industrial espionage has become real cloak-and-dagger stuff. Some

---
[14] *Ibid.,* p. 6.

companies, for example, do not patent highly technical processes because patenting would put them in the public domain. If competitors could read about the technology of complex operations, they could enter the market and compete on a par with the innovator or originator. The Eastman Kodak Company has for many years had a unique process for coating emulsion on films. This process, which has been kept under close lock and key, is one of the major reasons why the company has been able to maintain its position in the film market.

Industrial espionage, once little known to the general public, is now so commonplace that Hollywood got into the act by casting all-American girl Doris Day as an industrial spy in the movie *Caprice*. But industrial espionage is not considered funny in the Gulf Oil Company, where expensive exploration maps were stolen. Chemical and soap companies also have been less than joyful over the many scandals involving stolen, traded, or secretly transferred development ideas. The increase in industrial espionage bestows faint praise on the American businessmen willing to purchase stolen or fraudulently obtained properties. Nevertheless, industrial espionage is a factor that must be recognized in the management of research and development activities—even if only as a problem to be reckoned with and guarded against.

Acquisition is another way to purchase proven research results. In this day of the conglomerate merger, buying ideas is no longer novel. General Foods has done this in its overseas acquisitions. Thompson Products fused with Ramo-Wooldridge to gain entry into the electronics industry. W.R. Grace & Company made a similar move into the chemical industry. In industries such as electronics, where research and development activities are fast-moving, it has become quite common to obtain ideas and/or products through merger and acquisition.

Hiring key men away from competitors is another time-tested way to obtain either certain or close-to-certain research results. If a firm has neither the personnel nor the creativity to develop its own ideas, it may elect to raid a competitor who has the man or men able to do the desired job. Such pirating of key research people is common practice. Engineers regularly shift from company to company in defense industries, a movement given impetus by rapidly changing scientific technologies in space and other fields. Universities have pirated professors—witness Stanford's raids on Yale's scientific faculty. The brain drain from Europe to the United States has gotten tremendous publicity in recent years and probably will continue as long as personnel are willing to transfer their allegiance to environments where research is exalted.

Buying research in the market is merely a device to supplement or extend internal research and development activities; it is no substitute for a well-managed research and development effort. The main fruits of research and development do not come principally from the market, but from the organization's own laboratories.

PROJECT CONTROL

If the decision is made to conduct research and development in the house, it becomes imperative to devise ways to select projects and proposals having the greatest promise. When the most likely proposals are sorted out, methods must be chosen to carry them out successfully. "Project control" is one of the most effective means of implementing selected research and development projects.

Project control involves the selection of projects and the development of

Early phase					
Research department—Chemical division					Identification data Project 7–25 Origin Chem R&D Cost. Ref. 20–05
Item	Phase	Assignment	Estimated due date	Date completed	
1	Origin source	Chemical	–	–	Comments
2	Market potential	Sales	8/1/68	–	
3	Pricing	Sales	–	–	
4	Patents	Legal	–	–	
5	Lab rating	R & D	8/15/68	–	
6	Toxicity	R & D	9/1/68	–	
7	Pilot plant	Chem. eng.	–	–	Preliminary estimates only – final pricing not determined
8	Mfg. cost est.	Ind. eng.	–	–	
9	Packaging	Ind. eng.	–	–	
10	1st phase economic	Cost eng.	10/1/68	–	
11	Prelim. mfg. est.	Production	–	–	

Later phase (End of year)				
Research Department—Chemical division				
Item	Phase	Assignment	Estimated due date	Date completed
1	Origin source	Chemical	–	–
(2)	Market potential	Sales	8/1/68	8/1/68
(3)	Pricing	Sales	9/15/68	9/28/68
(4)	Patents	Legal	10/1/68	10/3/68
(5)	Lab rating	R & D	8/15/68	1/28/68
(6)	Toxicity	R & D	9/1/68	12/10/68
7	Pilot plant	Chem. eng.	4/1/69	–
8	Mfg. eng. est.	Ind. eng.	1/15/69	–
(9)	Packaging	Ind. eng.	11/15/68	12/20/68

(Early phase items continued, left column):
12 — 2nd phase economic
13 — Budget preparation
14 — Budget approval
15 — Development
16 — Engin. design
17 — Plant construction
18 — Marketing program
19 — Sales takeover
20 — Final progress report

completed as forecast

unexpected dealy

Figure 17.1 Sample research project progress report form annotated for greater management understanding

effective ways to measure relative and absolute progress. In practice, it assumes many forms. One fairly typical scheme manages projects through a system of reports which compare the rate of expenses incurred against actual levels of achievement. Appraisal and reappraisal of the project is made in terms of likelihood of success. Figure 17.1 illustrates the kinds of reporting used in a typical project control system. If the decision is made to continue the project, a set of technical appendices are attached to the report to indicate sales potential, how patent applications should be filed, what additional research may be indicated, and similar matters.[15] DuPont's famous research committee setup performs these functions routinely while overseeing the firm's massive research program.

Feedback from projects can be improved by the use of information retrieval which makes reports available on demand. Developments in high-speed computers with fantastically large memories have contributed a great deal to the technical feasibility of such retrieval systems; and though few firms have been able to afford them, lowered costs of computer services will permit extensive future use of retrieval banks. In firms supporting even moderately large research programs, the potential returns from information and retrieval systems probably outweigh their costs.

The real key to project control is measurement and evaluation. One of the critical points in project evaluation is the research budget, which almost all experts say should be flexible, while remaining the basic document used to evaluate research efforts. As a convention, small projects should probably be subject to cancellation or continuation on the judgment of the research director alone, while larger projects ought to be evaluated and considered by a research committee made up of research and other personnel. Some of the techniques outlined in Chapter 12 may be useful here.

Financial judgments on research projects have commonly come under the aegis of the present-value approach, used in machine replacement, and long-term capital budgeting. One of the major problems in the use of present value is that estimated payoffs and estimated discount factors are difficult to determine, particularly when time periods are long and defensive investments are being considered. In a defensive case, the return may not be a realistic indication of the importance of the project to the firm. When the corner grocery store faces competition from a new supermarket, modernization should be considered in survival terms—relative return on investment may be strictly an academic matter.

Igor Ansoff has developed one of the more comprehensive schemes for evaluating applied industrial research.[16] Ansoff talks about two factors in

---

[15] Franklin G. Moore, *Manufacturing Management,* 4th ed. (Homewood, Ill.: Richard D. Irwin, Inc., 1965).

The expected monetary value, game theory, and discounted cash flow analysis techniques described in Chapter 7 are often used to evaluate R&D proposals at various stages in their development.

[16] "Evaluation of Applied Research in a Business Firm," in Bright, *op. cit.,* p. 468.

product development evaluation: (1) the potential return on investment and (2) the associated risks, including the strategic fit of the proposed line. He also suggests the necessity of market research and advocates the use of systems and business analysis.

Ansoff's total scheme identifies the following variables in the determination of the value of a product to the sponsoring firm:

1. Average return on investment over the product's entire life cycle, including the development and production phases

2. The maximum investment that will have to be incurred by the project (drain on resources, the payout period, the time to reach maximum return on investment, the drain on resources in a time sense, the life span of the product itself, and the risks that may block return on investment)

His method sets up these relative values and attempts to develop them so that one project can be seen quickly by decision-making management. All things considered, Ansoff's approach is one of the most inclusive and utilitarian schemes now in use for evaluating research proposals.

Another thorough scheme enjoying wide usage is the government-oriented PPBS approach, the Planning-Programming-Budgeting System developed in the Pentagon. PPBS involves a detailed phase-by-phase checking of progress in an entire research project from initial feasibility studies through testing, development, engineering, and production. At each checkpoint, progress is evaluated in terms of past accomplishment and probability of continuing success. Costs and returns are given the heaviest weightings, and a cancellation can occur at any phase. In defense-related contracts, industry has had to face the fact that funds may stop at any point in a project's development, a factor influencing industry's evaluation of such contracts. PPBS has forced firms to adopt economically oriented criteria to weigh research activities. Thus, its influence has spread from government into industrial circles. Since PPBS is currently embraced by many government agencies, its use seems destined to increase, with the result that more and more research and (especially) development activities probably will have to meet more stringent economic constraints in all phases of their life cycles.

Every project control scheme, including PPBS and the Ansoff method, involves a balancing of projects and a way of evaluating results. Since research activities create cash drains in the short run, projects must be selected so that the timing of cash flows supplies returns from successful projects to help finance projects in various stages of development. Exact balance is rarely achieved in short-run and long-run flows, but control efforts do help to cut down cash flow pressures. With increasing research and development expenditures predicted for every foreseeable year in the future, the importance of careful project control is growing rapidly. Project control does not guarantee smooth execution of research programs—witness how Boeing, a sophisticated user of the most advanced project controls, ran into countless problems in almost every step of its sst program—but it does help management to move more knowingly toward correction of perceived ills in ongoing research and development programs.

MOTIVATION OF ENGINEERING AND RESEARCH PERSONNEL

Project controls collectively constitute some of the more successful economically oriented approaches to managing research and development, but they cannot function in a vacuum; they must be used in combination with the organization's chosen philosophy of leadership and motivation. There is no consensus among experts on which approaches are most effective here, and organizational philosophies reflect a wide range of ways to develop people effectively. Some managements emphasize leadership patterns and styles of leadership, while others point to the importance of organizational factors and reward systems in achieving high levels of output and morale.

Leadership and supervisory approaches to motivation now appear to be receiving greater attention than ever before. Rensis Likert argues that supervisory styles effect productive output of all managerial people but he particularly underscores their importance in the area of research and development.[17] Likert advocates loose supervisory patterns rather than tight control as the key to improved management of research efforts. Howard Baumgartel also embraces the concept of participative leadership and claims it generates better morale and higher output than directive control or authoritarian supervision.[18] Baumgartel identifies leadership climate as a critical factor in obtaining productive output of research personnel and states that shared leadership can build personal satisfaction in both creative research and developmental activities. Danielson also indicates that supervisors have and do perform an important role in obtaining better results from technical people; he says that supervisors should give a great amount of attention to their ideas and must give responsibility to them and recognize the work they do.[19] In addition, he reports that those in "research" like supportive supervisors, those in "application" seek guidance and information from supervisors, and those in "engineering" desire much more production-oriented supervisors. Danielson's findings indicate that the qualities in supervisors most cherished by research people are honesty, straightforwardness, intelligence, technical competence, approachability, and ability to supply the direction and information needed for researchers to do their jobs most efficiently. Danielson also points out that supervisors must pay close attention to their people's needs, the most important of which are current recognition and future advancement. Supervisors, he claims, are the single most important source of meeting needs and must therefore play a very active role in helping to meet employee needs.

[17] Rensis Likert, *New Patterns of Management* (New York: McGraw-Hill, Inc., 1961), *see* Chapter 1.

[18] "Leadership Style as a Variable in Research Administration," *Administrative Science Quarterly,* December 1967, pp. 344–360.

[19] Danielson, *op. cit.*

John W. Riegel also goes along with the concept of the importance of supervision in motivating engineers and scientists, but adds that systems of tangible and intangible rewards are necessary to most fully utilize their potential.[20] In particular, he emphasizes the importance of intangible rewards and spells out the relative impact of experience versus implied importance of these rewards to research application and engineering personnel. He reports that the individuals in research and development activity feel that they receive a much smaller intangible reward than they should from their firms and supervisors. Table 17.1 indicates the extent to which the experience and importance of intangible rewards was reported by 276 personnel in three technical classes when interviewed by Riegel, who was then director of the Bureau of Industrial Relations of the University of Michigan.

TABLE 17.1   DATA ON ENGINEERS AND SCIENTISTS: EXPERIENCE AND IMPORTANCE OF INTANGIBLE REWARDS

Class of Worker	Research		Engineering		Development	
Item	Impor-tance	Expe-rienced	Impor-tance	Expe-rienced	Impor-tance	Expe-rienced
1. Membership in a company which is highly regarded by people in my profession.	57	77	68	80	61	73
2. Opportunity to influence the work done on technical and scientific projects.	78	76	78	68	79	67
3. Association with other engineers and scientists of recognized ability.	81	78	70	70	71	73
4. Membership in an organization producing reputable goods or essential services.	67	78	76	84	82	85
5. A large degree of freedom to manage my own work.	86	89	90	78	87	77
6. Association with non-engineers and non-scientists of recognized ability.	36	52	54	60	48	61
7. Variety of engineering and scientific work which I do.	76	79	78	71	75	72
8. The favorable regard of top management because of my work.	79	67	81	59	79	55

[20] John W. Riegel, *Intangible Rewards for Engineers and Scientists* (Ann Arbor, Mich.: University of Michigan, Bureau of Industrial Relations, 1958).

TABLE 17.1 DATA ON ENGINEERS AND SCIENTISTS: EXPERIENCE
AND IMPORTANCE OF INTANGIBLE REWARDS (Cont.)

Class of Worker	Research		Engineering		Development	
Item	Impor-tance	Expe-rienced	Impor-tance	Expe-rienced	Impor-tance	Expe-rienced
9. The favorable regard of the community because of my work.	52	42	46	46	50	43
10. The respect of fellow engineers and scientists because of my achievements.	78	70	72	54	59	62
11. Opportunity to see my ideas put to use.	81	72	95	59	91	73
12. Opportunity to contribute to basic scientific knowledge.	79	69	54	38	43	37
13. A sense of job security due to my attainments.	71	75	77	57	68	66
14. Opportunity to work on products, processes, etc. of a highly engineered nature.	46	57	72	56	71	65
15. "Treatment as a professional" by my superior and higher management.	72	76	79	56	77	64
16. Challenge of the projects which are assigned me.	88	82	93	64	91	78

Note: All sources on this sheet are percentages of maximum possible scores. The table compares importance attached to various kinds of intangible rewards against the degree to which they were experienced by Research, Engineering, and Development workers (the application category on the chart).

SOURCE: John W. Riegel, Seminar on Intangible Rewards for Engineers and Scientists, Ann Arbor, Mich.: Sponsored by the University of Michigan, March 19-21, 1958.

Riegel's general conclusion is that intangible rewards are important for research personnel, perhaps even more than most managers believe, and these rewards are not being provided as well as they could be.

Turning to the organizational aspects of motivating research and development personnel, Louis B. Barnes reports several interesting points on how organizational arrangements seem to influence engineering inputs and productivity.[21] Barnes indicates that organizational structures may restrict an individ-

---

[21] *Organizational Systems and Engineering Groups* (Cambridge, Mass.: Harvard Business School, Division of Research, 1960).

ual to a relatively narrow subgroup and may generate competition between subgroups that blocks the organization's development and growth. He also talks about how formal organizational concepts such as the span of control can tend to retard advancement and stresses that the strict procedures, rules, and policies generated in organizational hierarchies undermine the engineering and development effort. In general, he lays great stress upon the importance of organizational constraints on the ultimate productivity of the engineering and development function. Some of the proposals discussed in Chapters 13 and 14 reflect attempts to overcome the negative aspects of such organizational blockages.

Norman Kaplan discusses organizational factors affecting productivity in terms of climate rather than structural hierarchies.[22] Reporting in *IRE Transactions on Engineering Management,* Kaplan sees the big factor in creativity stimulation as the climate generated by management's attitude toward new ideas. Pressure is important in Kaplan's view, but he isn't sure whether pressure exerts a good or bad influence on the productivity of research and development organizations. The climate that he envisions tolerates oddballs and leaves individuals freer to choose problems and to change directions. It also contains incentives designed to help develop individual creativity. His approach is much more climate-oriented than Barnes's, but Kaplan, too, discusses the organizational factors and constraints retarding or advancing research productivity. At one point in Allied Chemical's development of "Source," a new fiber of exceptional versatility, G. John Coli, then vice-president of the fibers division, faced the choice of cancelling the Source project or granting a sixty-day reprieve to his top chemist. Coli's response was favorable, and a climate of support was created that no doubt helped Allied gain its new fiber and Coli his new job as president of the division. As Coli later said, "You can read all the research reports you want, but sometimes you can look in a man's eyes and be convinced he can do it."[23]

Thomas Burns takes a structural slant in his study of research and development management when he laments the lengthening of chains of specialists and the "interpreters" lying between creation and production.[24] He believes that there should be a cutting of links between creation and production and says that fewer interfaces here would improve productivity by allowing messages and data to flow more freely. According to Burns, some scientists become isolated from company goals because of their organizational distance from top management. The goals set up by these scientists often run counter to company goals, and the firm thus derives little benefit from their presence in the organization. The linking-pin concept of Rensis Likert, described in Chapter 14, might be one way to improve communications and cooperation in such situations.

[22] "Some Organization Factors Affecting Productivity," *IRE Transactions on Engineering Management,* March 1960, pp. 24–30.

[23] "Businessmen in the News," *Fortune,* September 1968, p. 42.

[24] Thomas Burns, "Research Development and Production: Problems of Conflict and Cooperation," *IRE Transactions in Engineering Management,* March 1961, pp. 16–23.

One of the ways in which engineers and scientists have been rewarded in the past has been to move them from the laboratory into the administrative hierarchy. This reward system has been necessary because no organizational means was available to grant scientists and engineers pay raises or recognition while they were still working in engineering, development, or laboratory activities. One recent innovation designed to reward superior technical skills without pushing scientists into administration is the dual ladder, or dual hierarchy, approach. Rewards and recognition come from attaining a sort of superscientist or superengineer status, not by assuming the title of research director or taking on administrative duties. This approach has not been all milk and honey, since problems have arisen in setting it up. For example, it is difficult to establish and determine how individuals rank in the scientific ladder. Rewards are not always clear and the ladder may be used to put old-timers to pasture and to shunt ineffective performers aside, not to reward superior performance or to give extra compensation for added responsibility. Indeed, in some organizations using dual hierarchies, engineers and scientists have become uneasy because they feel they have not been given the opportunity to be managers. This desire to be recognized as managers persists even among scientists who feel supremely confident in their own technical activities and who have little real interest in performing managerial tasks.

The dual ladder is thus proving to be a somewhat ambiguous symbol. It does provide mobility, but it also tends to have a negative connotation, particularly where it has few rungs or where it allows or fosters the buildup of an inventory of out-of-date skills or esoteric specialties. In general, however, the dual hierarchy has been used more and more widely in recent years and tends to be a promising way of getting around the organizational constraints preventing the recognition of outstanding contributions by scientists or researchers.

IMPROVING CREATIVITY

Techniques and controls in organizational research activities are critical, but they can only occur after ideas are conceived and developed. How to generate and create good ideas is not easy to understand or classify. Not everyone is truly creative, and the development of individual creativity is more talked about than actual. There are, however, a number of ways to enhance creativity to the point where the individual is using his creative powers to their fullest. One does not have to be a DaVinci to take a glimmer and add what Thomas Edison called 1-percent inspiration and 99-percent perspiration to bring it to fruition. Creativity may not be creatable, but creative developments can be encouraged. The first step in enhancing creativity is to recognize what it is, and the second is to try to turn latent creativity into usable ideas.

According to Philip H. Abelson, the basic components of creativity are a slight feeling of discontent, the establishment of a stimulating group of people with the proper education and training, and a hunger to want to learn or develop something new.[25] E.I. Green says that there are several other factors involved in creativity, including knowledge, capacity for self-instruction, curiosity, observation skills, memory, intellectual integrity, skepticism, imagination, and enthusiasm and persistence.[26] Creative people recognize and relate these factors to experience to bring about some new idea. The brain creates by seeing and recognizing factors such as knowledge, skills, sentiments, and attitudes perceived in the environment and by organizing them in such a way that something new is created or something old is reviewed and restated in another form. According to Green, scientific thinking is either systematic or intuitive. Systematic thinking involves empirical, experimental, or meditative thought, from which results can develop directly in scientific fashion or through serendipity, accidental discovery. Intuitive thinking he classes as either genius or scientific hunch, two processes readily understandable to the layman.

Whether creativity comes from inherent or learned characteristics, the process of creative development must occur before the bright idea becomes operational. Professors William H. Newman and Charles E. Summer identify the four steps in the creative process as saturation, deliberation, incubation, and illumination and accommodation of ideas.[27] Their approach recommends an organized, systematized, rational approach to identifying, analyzing, classifying, and adjusting ideas to develop either new concepts or new product lines. Rudolph Flesch suggests that the creativity process can be aided by writing ideas down in plain language, discussing problems with others, making adequate reference to good sources such as libraries, keeping notes clearly and in writing, and considering reorganizing, reviewing, and rethinking concepts one has come to accept at face value.[28] If these things are done in logical, systematic fashion and patterns are set for working on creative activity, Flesch indicates that creativity will be enhanced because the individual will be better organized to perform the creative function. Further information on improving the creative process is offered by Green, who states that certain roadblocks must be overcome before the individual can be truly creative.[29] He describes things such as superficiality, false or associative thinking, wishful thinking, preoccupation with points, rejection of the new, individual reaction to discouragement, the harassment of detail, and the development of areas of limited interest that tend to yield unpromising results. He claims that if the individual recognizes these roadblocks, his ability to perform creatively will be much greater.

These insights into the creative process point to ways in which individual creativity can be enhanced. It is worth repeating that individual creativity is not always fully developed within the typical organization and that operational techniques to increase productivity can often yield great dividends. It

---

[25] Creativity in the Sciences," *Science,* June 21, 1963, p. 1271.

[26] "Creative Thinking in Scientific Work," *Electrical Engineering,* June 1954.

[27] *The Process of Management* (Englewood Cliffs, N.J.: Prentice-Hall, Inc., 1960).

[28] *The Art of Creative Thinking* (New York: Harper & Row, Publishers, 1951).

[29] Green, *op. cit.*

is ridiculous to claim that creativity can be developed in minutes or hours, but certain techniques have been utilized very effectively to generate new ideas and to introduce new ways of thinking about old situations. Some of the better known techniques are check lists, attribute listings, input-output methods, and free-association techniques such as brainstorming, buzz sessions, and the Gordon technique known as "synectics." In addition there are forced relationship devices such as focused object techniques and the catalog method. All these help to turn latent creativity into true creativity without doing much more than utilizing untapped mental capacity.

OPERATIONAL TECHNIQUES IN CREATIVITY

Few of the techniques designed to improve individual creativity have the "run it up the flagpole and see if anyone salutes" aura of Madison Avenue. Some are simply organized methods for harnessing or focusing creative efforts. *Check lists,* for example, do little more than prod the memory, but, in some circumstances, they spark a creative response. For example, check lists are often used in engineering to remind the engineer of the many ways available to arrange, simplify, group, combine, or eliminate work or motions. *Attribute listings* are not particularly exotic either, since they take key attributes and simply list (in detail) how they might be changed to bring out new ideas or developments. Manufacturers of hand appliances use attribute lists in designing products for the housewife. *Input-output techniques* state how a phenomenon is observed now and how it must be changed to bring about a desired result. The blockages that prevent movement to the new state are identified, and efforts then can be directed to ways of removing them. The obstruction is viewed in a cause-and-effect relationship, and creative research efforts are pointed toward solving the problem. The input-output technique analyzes obstacles in orderly fashion and focuses on solving them in a systematic manner. If a series of natural obstructions (blockages) prevent the use of, say, a drawbridge, a suspension bridge may be the next logical design. If this is ruled out, again by natural or cost problems, then other forms of architecture may be substituted. Similar input-output analysis can be applied in each phase of this particular design-and-construction cycle.

Free-association devices are perhaps the greatest and most publicized of all creative techniques, and brainstorming is the most familiar of the familiar. In *brainstorming,* free-wheeling ideas are discussed openly with no criticism allowed until the end of the session. In a typical session, a leader explains a particular problem to a group, which then lays out its top-of-the-head thoughts on the subject. Following the session, these thoughts are reviewed, evaluated, and rejected or pursued. Follow-up sessions may be held in which the more promising ideas are given still further brainstorming. The basic concept of brainstorming is that free-association will stimulate dormant creativity and bring forth ideas by creating the proper climate for their development.

Buzz sessions are a variation of the brainstorming technique, in which an idea is discussed in general before a group, which is then broken down into smaller groups who rediscuss it. The most promising results are then reported back to the main group by its subgroups. Again, as in brainstorming, the underlying concept is free association stimulated by discussion of suggestions and ideas which hopefully will trigger additional ideas and proposals.

In the Gordon *synetics* technique, only the leader knows the problem and he does not tell the group. He might, for example, present a topic such as bridge architecture and let the group talk about anything related to it. He alone knows that his goal is to design a better kind of ladies' foundation garment, but he keeps the group in the dark. When he has an opportunity, he may lead the group into a discussion of flexibility of materials, importance of various support concepts, and so on. Thus, he attempts to manipulate the group to a certain extent; and though creativity is unfettered, he tries to direct it toward a focused result. It was in such a session devoted to a discussion of "cutting" that the concept of the rotary power mower was developed.

Focused object techniques take two or more objects and force the individual or group to relate one to the other in either a free-form or structured framework. For example, in the so-called catalog techniques two objects or words may be taken from prepared lists and individuals or groups may be asked to relate them. This approach focuses creativity on the relationship specified and tends to direct creative efforts along desired lines. A more unstructured focused object technique selects an object, a concept, or a word and asks individuals to form free associations on it. Then this word or idea and the free association it has triggered are related to still another concept. For example, the word "money" might be selected and people's free associations and reactions to money then recorded. These reactions and associations would then be related to another word, "Jaguar," as it might be used in sales or advertising copy for the automobile. Free association such as money's relationship to power, prestige, wealth, and so on could be connected to the Jaguar automobile in the statement, "More power for less money—the prestigious Jaguar."

The techniques sketchily outlined here can add a good deal to creativity if handled well and if executed effectively. Creativity-producing techniques have particular utility in the advertising industry, in engineering applications, and in new product development. Many firms have used these techniques with excellent results; and though brainstorming and other creativity-inducing techniques are viewed by numerous managers as rather offbeat, creativity is often enhanced by their use. In a world where originality is in short supply, any technique that adds even a marginal increment to the total creative output is worth a try. Creativity is the wellspring of the ideas that develop into tomorrow's products, processes, or lifeline, and it needs to be given all available care and feeding. In Rockwell-North American, Vice-chairman Al Rockwell recognized the importance of this function by creating a "ivory tower committee" to dream up new product lines. Says Mr. Rockwell, "If we don't obsolete most of our products ourselves in five years our competition will do it for us."[30] This sentiment is perhaps not overstated in the context of today's rapidly

[30] John Mecklin, "The Rockwells Take Off For Outer Space," *Fortune*, June 1967, p. 100.

changing technological milieu. It is thus doubly important for managers of research and development activities to set the climate, the structures, and the rewards in which creativity can flourish and continue to provide the ideas which eventually germinate into results beneficial to all.

Summary

Management of research and development activities calls for guiding both projects and ideas. It also means balancing tasks, both present and future, in the light of short-run profits and long-run market and survival goals. It is important to manage research and development well, since waste can result in both monetary and human terms. It is also important in a survival sense, for without a top-notch research effort, no firm can hope to maintain its present competitive position or survive in the rapidly changing markets of the future. Better management of research and development can come about through purchase of ideas, project control, utilization of engineering and scientific personnel, and the attainment of high levels of creativity. Taken singly or in combination, these methodologies can contribute much to improving the total effectiveness of the research and development.

Study Questions

1. What are the reasons for the rapid growth in research and development expenditures? Do you expect these costs to continue to increase in both absolute and relative terms? Why or why not?

2. What are the major elements of risk on research undertakings? How can they be related to the decision-making methodologies described in Chapter 7?

3. Do you believe that engineering and scientific personnel are different from other managerial and professional people? Why do you take your particular stand? Justify it by citing examples from your experience.

4. What are the major means of improving research and development efforts? Which, if any, do you believe to be most effective? Why?

5. What are the gains available from buying research? The problems?

6. Can you relate project control to the sections in Chapter 12 on budgeting? Does project control differ in coverage and emphasis? In what specific ways?

7. What major approaches have been suggested to better motivate engineers and scientists? Which, if any, do you feel is the best approach? Why?

8. What is creativity? How can it be nurtured? Can it be created? Why or why not?

9. What are the operational techniques for obtaining higher levels of creative effort? Which seem to you to be most effective? Why?

10. Does the development of creativity tie in with the various approaches to motivating R&D personnel? How?

11. What relationships exist between government and the research and development efforts of most industrial and educational organizations? What problems does this cause in terms of economics, controls, social factors, and so on?

12. What balance should an industrial firm have between pure and applied research? What criteria should rule this choice?

Army Military Development Laboratories

The Army Military Development Laboratories has fifteen hundred employees. Over one thousand are civilians and the remainder are military personnel attached to the laboratory. Of the civilians, about half are engineers and scientists; the remainder are clerical and support personnel. Colonel Strauss, laboratory director, recently noticed that a good many of the staff arrived late to work daily. He knew the highly technical nature of the work in the laboratory did not require everyone to be present at the start of the day, but he was still concerned about the loss of time caused by tardiness. A quick check taken by security guards one Monday morning indicated that over 50 percent of the work force had arrived late. Colonel Strauss called in his civilian administrative officer, Harold Clark, and asked him to take some action to reduce the incidence of lateness.

Mr. Clark immediately notified the security force to report all latecomers to him starting on Tuesday morning. And on Wednesday afternoon he posted notices stating that each lateness would be entered into the person's file and that "chronic repetition of this offense will result in discharge."

On Wednesday, very few people arrived late, but there was a considerable amount of resentment over the way Mr. Clark had acted. Engineering personnel attached to the field test unit were particularly incensed, since they claimed that "no one ever gives us a pat on the back if we stay late to finish a test." Clark's comment was to smile and say, "Let them grumble, at least they got here on time. The troops are never really happy unless they're griping about something." The Colonel was concerned about morale, but decided to remain silent until specific grievances were voiced.

1. What do you think of Clark's solution?
2. What approach would you suggest if you disagree, even slightly, with Clark's solution?

Publish or Perish

The publish-or-perish controversy had never bothered Professor Nils Johnson, chairman of the marketing management department, until a series of events one warm March afternoon. On that afternoon he opened a letter, read a newspaper article, and received a phone call that placed him in the middle of the highly charged issue of publish or perish.

The first item affecting Professor Johnson was a letter which informed him that a prominent national marketing association had selected Dr. William Fay, assistant professor of marketing, as the "researcher of the year" for his writings in the field of consumer behavior. This honor was to be conferred at the annual meeting of the association and the letter was an invitation for Professor Johnson to attend the awards banquet. The letter noted that Dr. Fay's findings would be given prominent space in the association's journal and that the association planned to donate $20,000 to Johnson's department for further research in consumer behavior. Though the grant was to be given with "no strings attached," it was relatively clear that Professor Fay was expected to conduct some portion of the research program underwritten by the grant.

The second factor was an article in the student newspaper announcing that Tom Phillips, assistant professor of marketing, had been chosen "outstanding teacher of the year." This choice was made following a university poll conducted by the student council, and to be chosen was considered a high honor by those faculty members concerned with the quality of university teaching. Professor Johnson was pleased that Tom Phillips had received such an honor and he made a note to commend him formally on his achievement.

The phone call was the least pleasant of the three events, since it created the biggest problem Nils Johnson had yet faced as head of the marketing management department. The caller was Johnson's immediate superior, Dean Kerwin Bradley, and he wanted to inform Professor Johnson that the university committee on promotions and appointments had approved William Fay's promotion to the rank of associate professor with tenure, but had refused a similar promotion for Tom Phillips. The committee's letter to Dean Bradley noted that its decision on the Fay recommendation was based primarily on "substantial contributions to his chosen discipline as indicated in his writings and research." This citation was expanded upon in the letter, which included quotations from scholars at other universities who felt that Fay had the potential to become a leading authority in the field of consumer behavior.

The reasoning underlying Phillips's rejection was relatively involved, but Johnson believed it was based on a failure to publish. In the committee's own words, "Though the committee found him to be articulate, charming, persuasive, and knowledgeable as a teacher and conversationalist, there was little or no evidence of his ability to make any kind of enduring contribution to his chosen field of study. If his credentials had included a spark of intellectual excitement or the hint of an ability to record his innermost reflections for posterity, the final decision of this body would probably have been different."

The dean's call gave quite a jolt to Professor Johnson. Though he had backed the promotion of both Phillips and Fay, he felt that Phillips was the more deserving of the two. Johnson knew that Phillips was an infinitely superior teacher, a tireless and effective worker on curriculum problems, a cheerful and highly personable associate, and a young man with an extremely able mind who, though he had never published extensively, was currently involved in writing the results of research that might possibly be a real contribution to his field. On the other hand, Professor Johnson felt that Bill Fay had great talent for research, but was less than adequate in his other duties. Students considered Fay a poor teacher, and Johnson had often been disturbed by his cavalier attitude in observing office hours for student conferences and making adequate preparation for class meetings. Though Fay's research papers generally had been excellent, student delegations had twice visited Johnson's office to state that his performance in the classroom was not of the same high caliber. Johnson, nevertheless, decided to back Fay's bid for promotion because he believed that he could help him to overcome the alleged deficiencies in his classroom performance.

At the end of the phone call, Professor Johnson indicated that he was quite upset and asked Dean Bradley to send him a copy of the committee's letter for further study. The dean concurred saying, "Nils, I know you're concerned about the Phillips ruling, but don't do anything rash. If you decide to take any action, do it carefully and thoroughly. I know that the students will be really disturbed when they hear that Phillips hasn't been promoted, but the committee on promotions and appointments will be fighting mad if we create an undue furor over this affair. Furthermore, the administration won't be particularly happy if this thing gets to the press. Since I supported your recommendations on both of these men originally, I'll continue to back you up, but I don't want this to get out of hand. We can't afford to have the kind of publicity that Yale and Berkeley got in similar situations."

1. What course of action should Professor Johnson follow?

The Raymond Chemical Company

After receiving B.S. and M.S. degrees in industrial engineering from a well-known eastern university, Larry Jones joined the Buffalo plant of the Raymond Chemical Company. Larry, who had been the top man in his graduating class, was considered a very promising addition to the staff; and the plant manager felt Larry's knowledge of mathematical techniques would be extremely valuable in solving a number of pressing problems.

Larry was assigned to an experimental group which had earned a reputation of being able to solve the toughest technical problems. He fit in well with the group and soon was labeled a first-rate idea man in a very idea-conscious group. One of Larry's early contributions, a mathematical model of materials flows, caught the attention of Factory Manager Charlie Jenison. Jenison, who was second in command at the Buffalo plant, asked Larry to become his special staff assistant, and Larry accepted.

As Jenison's personal assistant, Larry came up with a number of interesting ideas. Though his suggestions were not always immediately workable, they were invariably thought-provoking. Jenison felt that with more practical experience Larry would soon be ready for a top-level management job. He proposed that Larry transfer to the inventory control department where he could serve under the manager, Alan Wilkinson. Though it was never mentioned by Jenison, Larry knew that Mr. Wilkinson had only four years until retirement, and he believed that he was being groomed as Wilkinson's successor. No one, however, ever explained Larry's role to Mr. Wilkinson.

In the inventory control group, things went poorly from the start. Mr. Wilkinson rode Larry at every turn and delighted in posing almost impossible problems. Wilkinson then taunted him with comments such as "Your bright ideas aren't too good under real conditions." When Larry tried to develop new approaches, Wilkinson blocked their use by saying that they weren't practical. He did allow Larry to introduce one system, but it contained some costly bugs. Wilkinson ordered it removed with the comment, "I told you it wouldn't work." After a few months, Larry felt that Wilkinson was either ignoring him or giving him only routine work.

One evening Larry had enough. He waited for Charlie Jenison after work and told him about his difficulties with Wilkinson. Jenison listened sympathetically, but said very little. When Larry asked to be reassigned, Jenison assented and suggested a transfer to the production control group. Larry agreed, and left Jenison's office feeling much less frustrated.

The following morning Larry learned that the production control group was headed by Phil Burgess, a man who had only five years left until retirement, and who, for all practical purposes, was another Wilkinson. Larry was quite upset. He wondered why Jenison, whose judgment he respected, had transferred him to Burgess's department.

1. Why do you think Jenison did what he did?

2. Assuming Larry wishes to stay with the Raymond Chemical Company, what do you suggest he do to make his new assignment less frustrating? If you were Larry would you stay with the Raymond Chemical Company? Why or why not?

3. Given a free hand, how would you have handled Larry's introduction to broader managerial responsibilities?

National Food Industries, Inc.

National Food Industries' main laboratory in San Francisco functions as the central lab facility for all NFI divisions, both domestic and international. Over four hundred technical and support people work there to improve existing product lines, develop new products, conduct pure research, and carry out development activities in food chemistry, food technology, and related chemical and biological fields. NFI President Manly Steingold has supported the research effort with "the full resources of the corporation." Time and time again he has stated, "Research is the key to continued growth and profits if NFI is to reach its goal of $2 billion sales by the mid-1970s." In support of this research, the company has committed funds to match the pronouncements of company leaders.

Lately, however, the company's top management has become concerned with both the quality and quantity of output generated by the R&D lab.[1] Dissension was allegedly rampant in the lab and an increasing turnover of key people had begun to distrub Mr. Steingold and Herman Laredo, vice-president of finance. After discussion with the executive committee and Dr. Henrick Stefanich, laboratory director, Mr. Steingold decided to call in the personnel consulting firm of Henry, Baxter, and Stolman "to look over the situation and make a preliminary report to top management."

Charles Henry, senior partner of HBS, took charge of the study and personally conducted a series of depth interviews with several members of laboratory management. After "getting the feel of the situation at San Francisco," Mr. Henry designed a full-scale, interview survey, and, with a field force of three staff consultants, set up interviews with all of the lab's 400 employees who "might be willing to talk over problems with the survey team." In all, 350 people were interviewed, a number which seemed to provide a comprehensive picture of the opinions and attitudes of laboratory personnel. Of the 50 who were not interviewed, 30 were out of town, 5 declined because of impending retirement, and 15 felt that such discussion would not be profitable or worthwhile. In the last group, 12 were clerical employees, 2 were lab technicians, and 1 was in the scientific and professional research category. Since the sample was large and the research team was composed of trained interviewers, Mr. Henry felt that the findings were a true representation of the attitudes and opinions held by the lab employees.

The principal findings compiled by Mr. Henry are reported below by occupational categories:

SUPERVISORY MANAGEMENT

1. Supervisors were concerned with their status in the eyes of management. They felt they were no longer looked upon as scientists, and this disturbed them.

2. Supervisors were not always backed up by their superiors, a failure they attributed to the "excessive profit orientation" of top management.

3. Scientific employees didn't show their supervisors enough respect and often ignored their directives.

4. Supervisory advancement was perceived to be slower in the research and development division than in the operating divisions.

---

[1] For a related case, see the Avion Aircraft case at the end Chapter 15.

5. Laboratory management was accused of overruling supervisors in favor of particular scientists (coddling them). Supervisors resented being made to "look silly."

6. Scientific personnel kept ideas to themselves too much, and an insufficient flow of ideas between supervisors and scientists tended to hinder the development of new ideas and was quite costly to the corporation.

SCIENTIFIC AND TECHNICAL PERSONNEL

1. Scientific and technical personnel claimed they did not get proper credit for work done: "The company gets all the credit for what we do."

2. Supervisors failed to back up scientists effectively because they failed to understand research activities, even though most supervisors had been research personnel themselves. Supervisors tended to shrug off promising projects too soon, instead choosing "much more rewarding projects."

3. Pay was perceived to be low by many researchers. "A scientist has to become a manager to get more money. No one really cares for research and development, only for the almighty dollar."

4. There was little incentive to inform colleagues about particular projects. No rewards were given for sharing information, and individuals who stole ideas were able to get the credit themselves.

5. Scientists too often were used on routine, unscientific work. "Yesterday, Dr. Jones was typing a letter that he couldn't get done by regular clerical help. There just isn't enough support for the research effort."

6. Laboratory administrative personnel were not scientists and failed to understand research. A typical criticism was, "He expects results quickly because he's cost conscious, but he doesn't understand what we are doing."

7. Scientists found it difficult to get support and maintenance people to do things for them. Scientists felt these personnel were lazy or so enamored with regulations that they did nothing not listed in their job descriptions.

LABORATORY TECHNICIANS

1. Laboratory technicians reported they had little or no status. They were the low men on the totem pole. "Even typists get better treatment."

2. For the most part, technicians complained that work was dull and included such things as washing test tubes and sweeping the floor.

3. Technicians perceived that they had little or no chance to advance in pay or status under the existing wage and salary regulations.

4. In times of cutbacks, lab technicians were "the first to go." Company and supervisory personnel "always sided with the scientists" in conflicts that arose between lab technicians and scientific personnel. "If they don't watch out, we'll be unionized soon," the technicians complained.

CLERICAL PEOPLE

1. Clerical personnel said their work was dull and their pay substandard.

2. Scientists were regarded as being dictatorial. "They don't care about us at all."

3. Supervisors invariably sided with the scientists and lab technicians in disputes with clerical people, reinforcing the latter's low status.

4. The one advantage noted was that "the work is real easy and not terribly demanding." Easy work was seen as only a minor compensation in view of the fact that even easy jobs were invariably routine and tedious. "When you're always typing tables and charts and stuff like that it's not much fun."

SUPPORT PERSONNEL

1. All support people (janitors, machine shop, maintenance, and so on) were unionized and let their feelings be heard through the union. One janitor stated, "We got a union here and we'll get what we want through it."

2. The machine shop attitude was, "Scientists try to push us around, but we don't have to pay any attention to them because the union has our job descriptions down cold."

3. Maintenance men were concerned with skill levels and the fact that few people appreciated their efforts. "No one really knows the kind of skill we have here. We show up those Ph.D. guys in anything practical, but nobody seems to appreciate it."

Mr. Henry reported these results orally to top management in Seattle headquarters and repeated the presentation at a joint meeting of corporate officers and laboratory management at the San Francisco facility. After an exhaustive question period in which many of the findings were discussed in depth and for the most part reaffirmed, the meeting began to turn to ways of improving the situation. As the meeting closed, Dr. Stefanich turned to Mr. Steingold and said, "It looks as though I've got a lot of work to do." Mr. Steingold agreed and suggested that Dr. Stefanich should, "get going as soon as possible."

1. What problems do you perceive in the R&D operation?

2. If you were Dr. Stefanich, what would you do?

3. What actions, if any, should Mr. Steingold initiate?

Worldwide operations are perhaps the fastest-growing phase of business and commerce. American firms are moving rapidly into both developed and underdeveloped countries. In turn, organizations based in other countries are making inroads into American markets. What returns are available? What reasons underlie these moves? Clearly, all of the traditional goals of growth and profits are at stake, as well as the human welfare and political advantages a global enterprise can bring to its country of origin.

On the profit side, returns from worldwide operations can be enormous. Reflows on investment and service accounts for U.S. firms from 1954 to 1965 were $41.2 billion in profits, dividends, royalties, rents, and fees. Professor Emile Benoit of Columbia University reckons that $72.5 billion in exports were sold by American firms and affiliates in the same period.[1] *Fortune* estimates that in 1968 direct investments by corporations outside their national boundaries was over $85 billion, a figure that the National Industrial Conference Board estimates as generating worldwide sales of $170 billion.[2] The same *Fortune* article forecasts that U.S. subsidiaries and investments will run about 25 percent of the $1 trillion of GNP expected in the free world in 1975. With foreign investment in the United States having grown to almost $10 billion in 1966, the enormity of worldwide operations is awesome. Since all projections seem to point to higher investments—Heinz, Singer, Standard Oil, and Massey-Ferguson now have over half their assets abroad and plan further expansion—and since market and profit potential overseas often exceed those in domestic markets, it seems logical that international markets will continue to develop at a fast clip.

CHAPTER 18
Management of Worldwide Operations

---

[1] "Balance of Payment Deficits: Fact, Fallacies and Fixations," *Columbia Journal of World Business,* vol. 2, no. 2, March–April 1967.

[2] Sanford Rose, "The Rewarding Strategies of Multinationalism," *Fortune,* September 1968, p. 100.

Other important by-products of such business are its political and economic impacts. From a purely economic standpoint, the spread of world business has brought about a number of important advantages. First, it has helped to spread technology in terms of both machinery and know-how. Second, employment in the host country has usually risen with a greater incidence of international trade. Third, the profits earned by the initiating company are often shared by the host country. The offshoot of these developments can be tremendous increases in good will or at the very least improvements in the ability to communicate. All companies who expand abroad exert some influence in these foreign markets, and, in some cases, industrial influences have helped to make inroads into the political arena. American technology has entered Europe with such impact that French author-journalist J.J. Servan-Schreiber predicts in *The American Challenge,* that by 1983 the third largest industrial power behind the United States and Russia will possibly be United States industry in Europe; his theme is that France and Europe must not react negatively to the American challenge, but must learn the secret of American organizational know-how or be content with second-class status forever.[3]

France's response to American industrial penetration illustrates the obvious point that not all phases of world trade have positive overtones. In some instances, the negative impact of trading activities can embarrass either the host country or the homeland of the exporting company. In extreme circumstances, more serious repercussions can result. The United Fruit Company, for example, reputedly has been instrumental in supporting or undercutting various regimes in the so-called banana republics of Central America. But since international trade often holds the key to either good or bad international relationships, nations who carefully cultivate and encourage its positive aspects are in a position to reap long-lasting benefits.

An overview of the advantages of world trade appeared in a talk by Fred Borsch, president of General Electric.[4] According to Mr. Borsch, a growing movement toward increasing world trade is almost inevitable. He calls for improved product flows and greater ease of entry into world markets, which are growing in spite of existing restrictions. It is Mr. Borsch's contention that the United States is getting more mature about world trade and is now at the threshold of the greatest opportunity for investment and flow of goods that the world has ever seen. Mr. Borsch highlights the importance of worldwide operations and hints at some of the problems and opportunities it offers to progress-minded managements and, indirectly, to the countries these managements represent.

OPPORTUNITIES AND PROBLEMS IN WORLDWIDE OPERATIONS

The development of world trade offers a number of opportunities and advantages. First, there is the potential for a greater efficiency and use of worldwide

---

[3] (New York: Atheneum Publishers, 1968).

[4] "The Maturing Phase of World Trade," reporting in a General Electric pamphlet.

resources in accordance with the basic economic principles of comparative advantage. Second, world trade helps less-developed countries to utilize their resources more fully. Finally, expansion of international trade tends to foster political harmony and the spread of understanding, thus contributing substantially to the maintenance of world peace. Add to these important points the opportunities for profit and for developing the economies of both under-populated and undercapitalized markets, and the opportunities offered by world trade are legion. But this is not to say that such trade does not have some offsetting problems.

The noted world trade expert John Fayerweather poses three major problems that continually plague worldwide operations.[5] First, he notes, problems occur in relation to the rising tide of nationalism. Possible expropriation or operating limitations here can be combated by the use of joint ventures, the sale of stock to nationals of the host country, profit sharing, and the use of resident nationals to operate and manage branch or subsidiary operations. Almost every major international organization uses one or more of these devices to promote more harmonious relations in the host country. Companies the size of Celanese, Unilever, and General Foods have used many variations of these themes to set up satisfactory management of their overseas operations. A second problem, Fayerweather states, is the identification of local executives to fill overseas management posts. These individuals are in short supply and their training in and conditioning to modern business methods may be quite sketchy. The need to train indigenous managers in modern techniques, particularly American approaches to problem solving and decision making, is a pressing and a constant challenge, and one that is not always well met. One of the greatest shortages in the management field today exists in the ranks of international management. The help wanted signs in this area are out in about every major American firm with extensive international holdings. The final problem identified by Fayerweather is the welding of international operations into an integrated unit headed and coordinated by globally oriented executives. In recent years, firms such as Joy Manufacturing, Proctor & Gamble, and Abbot Laboratories made moves to improve their management organizations, but much remains to be done before the national executive becomes the global executive.

The chairman of the giant Standard Oil Company, Michael Hader, indicates that the function and training of personnel is perhaps the most important issue faced by international marketers, and he states that Standard Oil has made progress in developing people and changing corporate concepts to meet the problems encountered in worldwide operations.[6] On the other hand, Britisher Kenneth Simmonds states that American corporations have not established a really multinational concept.[7] He asserts that power is retained in

[5] "Longrange Planning for International Operations," *California Management Review,* fall 1960.

[6] "Tomorrow's Executive, A Man for All Countries," *Columbia Journal of World Business,* winter 1966, p. 107.

[7] "Multinational? Well, Not Quite," *Columbia Journal of World Business,* fall 1966, p. 115.

corporate headquarters in the United States and that foreigners are at a disadvantage when assigned there. He points out that very few foreigners get to the top in American firms and that new ideas are discouraged in subsidiary operations or placed on trial in American markets before being used abroad; Simmonds feels that it is bad business not to have an international team at the head of an international company. In concluding, he charges that American firms, though saying they have learned this lesson, have not yet done so. General Electric's costly trip to France can serve as an example:

> Not all American firms entering international trade have reaped golden harvests. According to *Fortune* magazine, General Electric's abortive attempts to enter the French computer market have set GE back over $200 million.
>
> GE bought into France's failing Machines Bull with the expectation that it was gaining a foothold in the growing European computer market. Stockholders ratifying the GE venture shouted, "Vive les Americaines!" but from then on everything seemed to go downhill.
>
> For one thing, GE agreed as a takeover condition to retain all members of the existing work force as well as the technical staff, which the French looked upon as a national asset. Crippled by a work force far in excess of that of their competitor, IBM France, GE executives decided to increase volume to cut unit costs. This decision to produce to make work caused later woes in terms of costly inventories.
>
> GE's labor problems were then compounded by an inability to match product with market. After a costly deal with RCA (GE paid $8.5 million just to void the contract), GE launched several products which failed to dent the market. When the new designs didn't sell, GE moved to cut its work force by one fourth (2500 people). The French government, pushed by labor unions and feeling that GE had reneged on its agreement, got tough and finally allowed GE to reduce the work force, but only by 270 members. After this highly publicized negotiation, almost every move GE made generated suspicion and/or opposition.
>
> A final problem dogging GE's French venture sprang from the philosophy that a good manager can manage anything. Experts say this contention is untrue in the computer field and particularly false in French computers. GE's management team had little experience in computers, didn't speak French, and seemed to have little "feel" for the Gallic way of doing business. According to *Fortune,* GE's problems in France were clearly traceable to a failure to "master the complexities of running an integrated international business."[8]

Almost ten years ago the key problems in the international area were framed in terms of the following questions, all of which remain equally pertinent today.

---

[8] Abstracted from Gregory Wierzynski, "G.E.'s $200 Million Ticket to France," *Fortune,* July 1967, p. 92. See also Wierzynski's "G.E.'s Misadventures in France," *Fortune,* June 1967, p. 92.

1. Where is the spot in all the world where people can grow the best?

2. Where should we do research and development to capitalize on the technical capacity available in the rest of the world?

3. Where should products be made so that they will be competitive in all markets (including the United States)?[9]

Considering the United States as just another market is the real perspective of the world enterprise, and Gilbert Klee, the noted world-business authority, claims the United States still has something to learn in this area; his basic suggestions are to centralize strategic plants and to localize tactical planning by area, by country, and by regions within countries.[10]

When a much more comprehensive viewpoint is taken, the problems encountered in operating a worldwide enterprise seem almost impossible to circumvent. To name a few, there are difficulties in language, customs, misunderstandings of objectives, salary problems because of differentials between American and indigenous personnel, and conflicts of interest between local partners and parent corporations. Many of these difficulties plagued the General Electric–Machines Bull enterprise in France. As we have illustrated, this ill-starred venture had continual managerial, political, and profit troubles both prior to and after GE's takeover. Other problems occur in the form of misunderstandings about amounts and types of profit sharing, pricing decisions, legal questions relating to corporate practices and host country legislations, control of quantity and quality of output, deposition of assets, cost controls, rules concerning sales of holdings, trademarking regulations, and misinterpretations of language in written contracts.[11]

Another group of problems in world operations are the rules and regulations imposed by host governments. The problems of whom to see, where to start, how to handle red tape, exactly what to negotiate about, and, in some cases, whom to bribe or influence, are extremely important ones, but they are encountered in domestic operations, too. Dealing with the government on matters of production, finance, marketing, transportation, and distribution is not new to most businessmen, but doing so in a changing international scene adds a novel dimension. Instead of one government, some large organizations now deal with tens or even hundreds of government units. Special events or crises often complicate the nature and scope of these dealings to the point where international operations are far more complex than those domestic ones. For example, oil companies operating in the Middle East ran into many restrictions and controls following the outbreak of hostilities between Israel and the Arab states in 1967. These difficulties remained unresolved long after the fighting ended, and they still color the relationships between the affected

---

[9] Gilbert H. Klee and Alfred DiScipio, "Creating a World Enterprise," *Harvard Business Review,* November–December 1959, pp. 77–89.

[10] *Ibid.*

[11] This listing is from a detailed outline in National Industrial Conference Board, *Joint Ventures with Foreign Partners* (New York: N.I.C.B., 1966).

Arab countries and the many oil-producing firms operating within their borders. On a less grand scale, Green Giant lost large sums on a corn-canning plant in Italy when Britain was refused entry into the Common Market. Green Giant had forecast that an Italian plant would best serve the British market after anticipated tariff reductions following Britain's acceptance into the European Economic Community. When Charles deGaulle scuttled England's entry plans, Green Giant lost out on the British market, and since most Europeans see corn as animal food, the company had no market and no need for a plant in Italy. No one at Green Giant needs to be reminded of the impact of national politics and local customs on corporate profits. Cultural differences and management theories thus tend to exert divisive effects on worldwide operations, and the potential influence of these forces calls for careful study.

Cross-cultural factors include such matters as national pride; local customs, mores, and folklore; and the levels of aspiration found in various societies. Complicating the resolution of cultural variables are political pressures and economic variables such as currency and exchange restrictions and taxes such as the proposed (but not adopted) travel tax on the United States citizen abroad. Others are the lack of utilities such as electricity and water and inadequacies in transportation facilities such as those plaguing many African republics. In addition to cultural distinctions, world trading operations are affected by basic differences of opinion about philosophies of organization and control.

Organization and control problems occur in the determination of what form to use in setting up worldwide operations and in establishing the degree of tightness of control that will characterize the parent-affiliate relationships. One study comparing cross-cultural perspectives of American and Brazilian businessmen came to the conclusion that variations in perspectives are much more important sources of problems and differences than the ways in which to use so-called principles of sound management.[12] This and other studies are not surprising to students of the international scene, who have long known that problems often arise in worldwide operations because individual perspectives are colored by cultural perspectives. The sandwich-and-Coke-for-lunch engineer from Corning Glass may never really appreciate or understand the two-or-three-hour lunch with wine taken by his French associates in a St. Gobain factory in France.

Some of the more obvious cross-cultural factors and practices influencing management activities appear in relations between highly developed industrial nations and newly emerging countries. One major difference between neophyte industrial nations and their more mature counterparts is the startling contrast in comparative levels of living. In countries such as India, for example, per capita income may be as low as $50 to $60 per year, while in the United States, per capita income is in excess of $3500; and this gap will probably

---

[12] Winston Oberg, "Cross Cultural Perspectives on Management Principles," *Journal of the Academy of Management,* June 1963, pp. 129–143.

widen sharply in the next thirty years. The tremendous disparity in health, welfare, education, and outlook created by this gulf often yields bitter economic and political fruit. When populations have highly developed and sophisticated wants, as in the more economically mature countries, consumers ask for and receive a bewildering array of products. In less-developed countries, basic nutritional needs are still paramount; the concept of an adequate supply of products differs sharply from Paris to Addis Ababa. Governments in newly developing countries are vitally concerned with the kinds of industrial development they should choose to support, particularly in areas where levels of aspiration are high and the standard of living is low. In these societies, governments exert direct and close control over most phases of economic expansion and industrialization. How the conditions in host countries and the attitude of their citizens and governments can affect the foreign are clearly seen in the risky South American market:

> Every international market has its perils, but South America seems to be chancier than most. In addition to the cross-cultural, currency, and trade restrictions found almost everywhere, many South American countries have a hostile political climate, excessively high taxation, growing government interference, and/or the very real threat of expropriation.
>
> Within the recent past, the following events have caused world businessmen, particularly Americans, to view investment in South America all the more cautiously:
>
> Peru expropriated Jersey Standard's Canadian affiliate, International Petroleum Company, Ltd. (IPC), and refused to pay for the $200 million assets taken over.
>
> Columbia and Ecuador demanded a larger share of a new $100 million Texaco-Gulf Oil venture.
>
> W.R. Grace lost 30,000 acres of sugar lands as a result of an agrarian reform movement in Peru.
>
> Anaconda was forced to yield a bigger share of its copper mines in Chile to the government or face outright expropriation.
>
> In Bolivia, Gulf Oil faced governmental demands to provide at no fee 20 million cubic feet of gas daily for domestic consumption for a period of ten years.
>
> During New York Governor Nelson Rockefeller's tour of South America, anti–United States rioting occurred at almost every stop.
>
> In Brazil, United States prestige suffered when the American ambassador was kidnapped.
>
> Given these threatening circumstances, American businessmen are expressing more and more concern about investing in what seems to be a risky market. In the words of Governor Rockefeller, "private investment is very fickle.

turing is not usually performed locally. Again, problems such as transportation costs, licensing problems, and other matters may be a source of difficulty; but the branch organization allows relative ease of entry with a minimum of capital risk. Auto companies, with massive outlays needed for economies of scale have long favored the branch approach for their operations in limited markets. Since branch operations can easily be preempted by local industry or other firms willing to make heavier commitments, branch operations are subject to the same risks observed in licensing arrangements.

Joint ventures have become an increasingly popular form of overseas organization. According to the NICB, "This is the age of the joint venture."[16] The major factors affecting the success in joint operations are whether or not one partner is a local investor, the nature of the country involved, the reasons for the joint venture, the type of business to be established, the contribution of each partner in technical and dollar commitments, and the proportion of contributions of the individual partners. This list is relatively obvious to students of the international economic scene, but it still contains some very important areas to investigate and consider. Indeed, many elements differentiate the international joint venture.

The biggest factors in joint ventures are financial commitments; technical know-how; marketing and administrative abilities; good-will, or image, factors; government contracts and contacts; knowledge of or experience with politics, customs, and culture in the host country; the state of raw materials; and availability of physical plants. These aspects are certainly familiar to businessmen operating within their own national boundaries, but the development of government contacts (and thus contracts), the creation of local good will, and a general knowledge of operating methods in the host country are the novel and critical factors that must be emphasized to insure success in foreign joint ventures. Joint cooperation between local and foreign partners has been a successful format for conducting worldwide business, and almost every major firm involved in international operations (for example, Aramco Oil) has followed the joint venture route at one time or another.

The fourth approach to organizing overseas operations is the establishment of local subsidiaries. Establishment of subsidiary operations involves the highest degree of risk of expropriation, particularly if they are wholly parent-owned; but subsidiaries also hold the greatest promise of long-range profits. Many firms which invested early in subsidiary operations profited handsomely when the fruits of early entry were harvested. General Foods has followed this approach with success in some of its overseas venture. It would be false to say that all subsidiary operations have prospered, even though many have yielded favorable results. Expropriation lurks in the background to balance the lure of potentially higher profits; and local conditions which might lead to takeovers are inordinately difficult to assess accurately. Nationalism is a tide whose depth and currents are almost unmeasurable, and recent events in countries such as Ghana, Peru, Guinea, Saudi Arabia, Spain, and Indonesia

---

[16] National Industrial Conference Board, *op. cit.*

are constant reminders of the risks involved in making heavy investments in climates fraught with political conflict.

Whatever the cause, be it fear of loss or hope of gain, the subsidiary form of organization seems to be on the decline in the international arena.[17] It now seems fashionable to reject subsidiary organizations in favor of joint ventures—at least in public pronouncements. In underdeveloped countries, however, subsidiaries still enjoy wide use, primarily because local management skills are scarce and close control is needed to provide the needed direction of technical and capital inputs. Under these conditions the subsidiary's operating methods can be changed internally to adjust for developing skills or the local business climate without making changes in the organizational structure. Controls can be tightened or loosened as situations change; and if drastic problems arise, stock can be sold to nationals in amounts necessary to counteract the "foreign" onus.

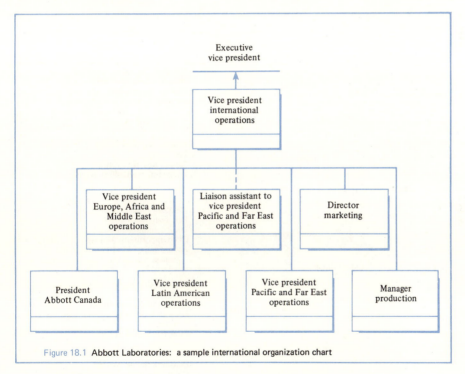

Figure 18.1 Abbott Laboratories: a sample international organization chart

Source: From National Industrial Conference Board, *The Changing Role of The International Executive* (New York: Studies in Business Policy, no. 119, 1966), p. 225.

In recent years, the tendency in international operations has been to decentralize production and marketing without relinquishing fairly tight control of finances. Figure 18.1 shows the organization chart of Abbott Laboratories,

---

[17] Perhaps one reason is that overly tight control has tended to undercut managerial freedom to manage, or, in other words, "subsidiary top management is normally a castrated top management with the entrepreneurial function removed." Simmonds, *op. cit.*

a geographically decentralized company. This middle-ground approach has provided a popular means of meeting the demands of domestic stockholders within the limitations encountered in a variety of cultures. The joint venture, the middle ground of organizational control, is popular, since it seems to provide the most flexible framework for reaching such a balance. Though generalization is difficult, decentralization through joint venture seems to be both wise and dictated by circumstances. Again, the form of organization is less critical than obtaining a working balance; and the joint venture seems quite well suited to obtaining a state of equilibrium in the control and adminis-tration of overseas activities. Figure 18.2 points out some of the major consid-erations entering into the choice of control postures.

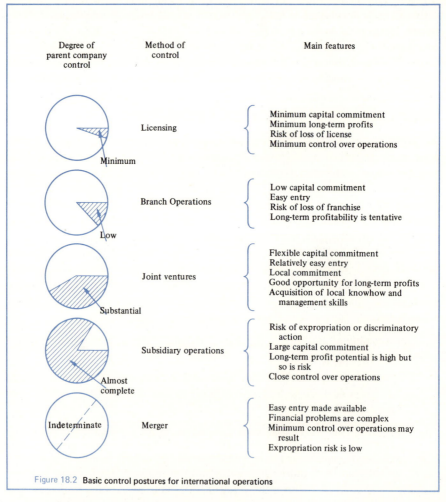

Figure 18.2 Basic control postures for international operations

One of the more interesting developments in recent years bearing on control of operations is the growth in international mergers. This trend, which began in the mid-1960s, has accelerated throughout the world. In Britain, Leyland Motors has joined with the British Motors Holdings. In Japan, the zaibatsu has come back in the form of sizable conglomerates. In the United States, Olivetti-Underwood and Joseph Seagram are examples of a long list of companies acquired by or merged with foreign enterprises. Capital is beginning to flow more freely across national borders, and this movement has generated greater worldwide activity in takeovers once considered either precarious or too complex to work out within existing financial constraints. It is now quite common for a multinational firm to use surplus growth in one country to finance expansion in another or to borrow in a country with a low-interest rate and then transfer or loan funds to another subsidiary in a country having a higher rate of interest. This kind of sophistication is relatively recent, but it has already developed to the point where international financing of international mergers is now becoming almost as routine as similar transactions conducted within national boundaries. If this trend continues, the nature of acquisitions and mergers will become important in the blending of the control philosophy designed to oversee operations of the newly acquired organization.[18]

GUIDELINES FOR WORLDWIDE OPERATIONS

As world business grows in size and importance, certain developing trends gain more attention in management circles. One is the rise of nationalism, another is the continuing emphasis placed on the development of local industries with local managements; a third is the growing use of joint ventures because of the pressures of nationalism and because of potentially severe limitations on operating practices and procedures by unfriendly or ambitious politicians. Finally, it is increasingly evident that international organizations have now started to train their people to operate differently in international markets than in domestic ones.

With these things in mind, it seems important that firms consider basic principles to guide their worldwide activities. Though no one set of guidelines is all-inclusive, the following list is a good bench mark.[19]

1. If a firm enters a local market, it should go in with the serious intent of remaining there.

2. Organizations should staff their operations with nationals as much as possible and should reinvest profits in the countries where they are earned.

---

[18] As a consequence of the trend toward international mergers, antitrust is now going international. Gillette-Braun has been sued by the U.S. Justice Department to force Gillette to sell its $50 million interest in A.G. Braun; and the Organization for Economic Cooperation and Development, composed of twenty-one major industrial nations, has agreed to ask member companies to cooperate as fully as possible in the sharing of antitrust information.

[19] This list ties in with the objectives-setting exercises in Chapters 3 and 4 and resembles the general philosophical outlines of the labor relations credo in Chapter 16.

3. Overseas markets should be treated the same as domestic markets, and people there should be given what they want, not what the company thinks they want.

4. Service and maintenance should be given important emphasis, especially in newly emerging companies, and first-hand contact should be maintained to insure that service and maintenance goals are met.

5. Overseas markets should be integrated into the company's total effort and be given the serious kind of consideration they deserve.

6. Company operations overseas should be on a permanent and full-commitment basis and not be a casual arrangement which can be terminated at any time at the convenience of the investing firm.[20]

It's small wonder that the executives able to implement the objectives implied in these guidelines are in short supply, since the ideal man would have to possess the prestige of a Winston Churchill, the business sense of Alfred Sloan, and the charm of Maurice Chevalier. Before such a man assumes the mantle of international leadership, he should be well versed in company policies, experienced in all phases of operations, able to run a major operation from a distance, willing to accept responsibility without necessarily having adequate authority, capable of getting staff help from people not under his jurisdiction, sensitive enough to direct activities performed in an environment of which he may have scant firsthand knowledge; and, finally, he should be able to accept the fact that rousing success may result in the internationalization of his company, an action that may effectively put him out of a job.[21] The few men who possess such envious personal, economic, political, language, and cultural attributes are, unfortunately, either unavailable or already employed. Even when a good man is on hand, he may be reluctant to take an assignment that would move him out of the mainstream of activities at corporate headquarters. The shortage of qualified international executives may be partially overcome by raising the status of overseas operations, but, in spite of attempts to internationalize their operations, most major companies still treat worldwide operations as overseas versions of domestic divisions. This point of view compounds the difficulties of providing the flow of executive talent needed to gain a growing and profitable share of the world's ever-widening markets.

Perhaps the most needed ingredient in the management mix as it relates to overseas operations is the ability to recognize that the factors contributing to domestic success are not necessarily paramount or even relevant in the international area. A model resembling the critical variable analysis presented in Figure 3.3 is vitally needed to assess the international scene. Following this, the approaches to goal and strategy determination described in Chapters 4 and 5 come into play. Each overseas market requires individual study, and each potential entry needs to be viewed in a generalized as well as a specific

---

[20] Adapted from Klee and DiScipio, *op. cit.*

[21] "Overseas Pilot Without a Chart," *Business Week*, September 24, 1969, p. 185.

manner. Not all firms or products are likely to succeed in all markets, and thus a decision not to enter a market can be as important as one giving a go-ahead signal. Careful setting of goals, strategies, and objectives and the construction of thorough long- and short-range plans are, if anything, more critical in international business than in domestic, where at least a modest amount of know-how is carried over even in hastily contrived marketing plans.

Summary

Worldwide operations have been growing in size and complexity over the past two decades, bringing both problems and opportunities, since such trade contains elements of risk along with its promise of profits. The necessity to cross national boundaries raises cultural, political, and economic problems not encountered in domestic operations; and solving these problems with a minimum of effort and conflict calls for the highest managerial ability.

One of the more critical problems of overseas operation is the extent of control the parent should exert over its affiliates. Another is the organizational form best suited to overseas units. Typically, a blend of loose and tight controls is used, with production and marketing controls decentralized. Licensing arrangements, branch operations, joint ventures, and subsidiaries are the primary organizational forms, listed in order of commitment. Though each has its advantages and disadvantages depending upon the weight given to the various factors in each host country, joint ventures have gained popularity because of their flexibility and because they allow a blending of local commitment and home-office control.

Recently, greater attention has been devoted to developing men capable of running worldwide operations. America, surprising as it may be to those who embrace the myth of the Ugly American, has done a superior job in preparing men for international management. European and other firms are finding it hard to keep up with American businessmen in competitive world markets, and the energetic American executive, though occasionally picking up the wrong fork, is learning to handle the complex phases of world market activities with the savoir faire of a gourmet sampling his favorite dish.

Study Questions

1. What are the advantages and disadvantages of entering extensive worldwide operations?

2. What are the potential advantages to the host country? To the homeland of the international marketer?

3. What are the major problems influencing international operations? Which of these problems do you feel is the most critical? Explain fully.

4. What are the four basic forms of control used by multinational companies? Describe the plus and minus aspects of each method.

5. Why has the joint venture been so popular? Do you feel its popularity will continue? Why or why not?

6. Do you agree that the six guidelines proposed by Klee and DiScipio are meaningful ones? Evaluate their list and discuss its strengths, weaknesses, and omissions.

7. In recruiting candidates for international management in colleges and universities, what traits should interviewers seek? Which ones are absolutely necessary? How can these traits be recognized in the recruiting and evaluation process? Which units or schools within the universities should recruiters visit? Why?

8. What kinds of programs would you suggest for developing international managers? What skills should be developed first?

9. Does a career in international management appeal to you? Why do firms have difficulty in recruiting top people to fill openings in international operations?

Consolidated Soap, Ltd.

Consolidated Soap, Ltd., is a successful marketer of soaps and detergents in Canada and the United States. Its principal sales occur in the eastern Canadian market, but large U.S. sales are recorded in the Midwest, Middle Atlantic, and New England. Consolidated's product line includes facial and beauty soaps, dish-washing powders, detergents, and industrial cleaning agents. Though Consolidated vies with giants such as Lever Brothers, Proctor & Gamble, and Colgate Palmolive, it operates profitably because of its efficient manufacturing facilities and its ability to develop product lines designed to meet the needs of specific market segments.

Company management is headed by young, progressive Harold Byrd, who recently decided to move his company into overseas markets, particularly Europe. Europe was chosen because of its growing income level, its increasing consumer sophistication, the availability of established channels of distribution, and its relatively high levels of managerial know-how. Consolidated's management knew that entry was a problem because of nationalism and restrictive legislation, but decided that a series of careful studies would allow it to choose markets most likely to react favorably to its product line.

Research conducted by Consolidated's marketing group came up with two basic points of entry into the European market: the Common Market countries and the EFTA countries. Since these areas offered certain advantages and disadvantages, a decision was made to consider both areas carefully with specific points of entry to be determined only after an additional review of opportunities available in particular countries. Management knew, however, that whatever point of access was chosen, it would have to make basic decisions concerning entry conditions and subsequent problems.

One of the basic problems posed concerned ownership and control. Involved was whether the company should attempt to use subsidiaries, joint ventures, licensed, or franchised forms of operation. After much discussion, management decided to rely on the subsidiary wherever permitted by law. Thus, the decision was made to allow the parent company to exercise close control over overseas operations, even though local management was to be retained to take advantage of local knowledge of customs and opportunities. Consolidated's management determined that the most effective method of achieving this result was to purchase established firms and use their accumulated knowledge of consumer habits to penetrate the market rapidly. Licensing and distributing were rejected because such arrangements failed to allow for adequate controls over marketing and manufacturing activities. Joint ventures were ruled out because of problems in relations with minority stockholders. Company management had no desire to be a minority partner unless legally forced to; and countries with laws limiting or prohibiting outside control were placed low on the company's preference list.

The next set of basic decisions facing Consolidated management concerned the product line. After careful deliberation, it was determined that the company should sell its product line under its own brand names in all overseas markets. This included "King Louis" beauty soaps (in king- and queen-size bars), "Sunburst" soap powders, and "Dawn" detergents. The Sunburst name was also to be used for products in the industrial cleaning line.

All consumer products were to be marketed in accordance with local customs. Area managers were allowed to retain profitable products in existing lines, but items deemed by Consolidated'a management to be unprofitable would be dropped from lines carried by subsidiaries. Consolidated'a management felt that control of product lines was vital in all marketing of high-quality consumer-oriented products; and rigid controls over quality, packaging, branding, labeling, and the quality of content of advertising media (although not local media) were to be determined by the home office. Area managers could suggest changes in product lines to meet local conditions and needs, but major product responsibility was left to the home office. According to Mr. Byrd, "Company quality and reputation must not suffer as we move into world markets."

One other area in need of clarification was the degree of autonomy allowed local managers. After extended discussion, the following guidelines were chosen. Local managers would have freedom to run their manufacturing, marketing, and financial operations within broad guidelines. They would handle all machinery, equipment, raw materials, scheduling, and operating decisions within a policy framework set by the product-engineering staff at company headquarters. They would also choose all phases of the marketing mix, except those dealing with product lines and related areas. Pricing, distribution channels, advertising and promotion, direction of the sales force, and the selection of market areas within each country would be left to the individual managers. Any marketing activities involving international shipments, however, would be controlled from headquarters.

Financial operations were placed under the close control of corporate headquarters. Quarterly profit and loss statements were to be called for and capital expenditures over $5000 would need headquarters approval. ("With operating responsibility goes profit responsibility.") The dividend policy of the subsidiaries was also to be controlled by headquarters. ("After all, the company is not in business to lose money.")

Consolidated's management considered the questions of ownership and control, product philosophy, and management philosophy to be the most crucial affecting overseas expansion. With the establishment of these guidelines, Consolidated's management planned to move rapidly into overseas markets.

1. What do you think of the planning preceding Consolidated's entry into the international market? What would you have done differently?

2. What do you think of the ownership decision? Would this be your choice? Why or why not?

3. Do you agree with all the decisions made by Consolidated's management? Would you alter their plans in any way? How?

Pantalonics, Inc.

The Pantalonics, Inc., recently developed a long-term plan to locate new manufacturing facilities in various overseas locations. As one phase of this plan, the company had finalized plans to build a plant in the Hong Kong area when Communist-inspired rioting swept the Crown colony. The decision to locate in Hong Kong had been made originally because of the low cost of labor (workers received $1.40 per day on the average in 1968), good living conditions for management, adequate banking facilities, a favorable tax setup, the relatively high productivity of labor, and the large American colony there, including General Electric, Fairchild, Motorola, Mobil Oil, and Revlon. In view of the riots, company officials decided to declare an immediate moratorium on plant construction and to reevaluate location plans at the end of six months.

At the end of this period, the Crown colony of Hong Kong appeared to be placid politically, but certain economic factors had changed. First, the United States balance of payments deficit had become more pressing and had begun to attract greater attention. Companies were now being encouraged not to invest overseas or to invest in more restrained fashion. Even though the Crown colony's government had not knuckled under pressure during the Communist riots, the threat from Communist China was now felt to be more real than ever. Coupled with the fact that the Crown colony was considered indefensible by most military experts was the high level of risk in investment there. In addition, the low-cost labor that had been available in Hong Kong was now at a competitive disadvantage to such areas as South Korea, Singapore, and Taiwan, where labor rates were 32-percent less. In addition, a tender had been received from Taiwan offering favorable tax concessions, similar to those granted by certain states in the United States to induce firms to locate within their borders.

Thus, in addition to the Red Chinese threat which was clearly visible from any Hong Kong hillside, the economic advantage of a Hong Kong location seemed diluted. Given the nature of the pressures being exerted by Pantalonics customers, the president felt he had to arrive at a location decision within one or two weeks at the latest.

1. What factors should the president weigh in deciding whether or not to locate a plant in Hong Kong?
2. Given these same conditions, what would you do?

Bea Robbins, Inc.

Bea Robbins, Inc., began its operations in Phoenix, Arizona, early in 1950. The firm started as a backroom tailor shop in which Mrs. Robert (Bea) Castle and one helper made a line of low-priced cotton dresses and suits for a major department store in the area. Later sales expanded to include a major chain store. As the firm's reputation for quality grew, it met with continuing success. Mrs. Castle soon came to the conclusion that selling to others was rather unproductive and decided to open her own store. She set up a small shop in Phoenix and when this venture proved successful, she opened several other stores in the metropolitan area. In the next few years, she established outlets in Tuscon, Arizona; Santa Fe, New Mexico; and Los Angeles and San Diego, California.

The basic policy underlying the rapid growth of Bea Robbins, Inc., was to offer reasonably fashionable goods at low prices. Bea Robbins's philosophy appeared in its motto, "High fashion at low prices." As the firm grew in size and profitability, Mrs. Castle accepted expansion as both desirable and necessary. She began to consider areas outside the United States as possible locations, and took a particular close look at the Mexican market, where income was rising along with population. After a brief study, she decided to open a shop in Nogales, Mexico, a point easy to service and control from head-quarters in Phoenix.

Since Nogales was a free port, her decision was relatively easy to implement. Local residents in both Nogales, Arizona, and Nogales, Mexico (a town much larger than its American counterpart), and the many tourists who customarily shopped at Nogales while on vacation trips to the Southwest and Mexico were to provide the customers needed to support a store. A brief search uncovered a suitable location, and a Bea Robbins shop was opened in the central shopping area in Nogales. In line with local customs, Mrs. Castle engaged a Mexican national, Mrs. Rafael Santella, as shop manager. Mrs. Santella then hired three bilingual salesgirls, all of whom lived in Nogales.

After six months, the Nogales store was the only shop in the Bea Robbins chain operating at a loss. Two major reasons were given for these losses. First, the product line was not attractive to tourists searching for something "Mexican." Second, local residents shied away from buying Bea Robbins goods because the clerks would not bargain over prices. This failure to bargain was considered to be evidence of a "high-price policy" even though prices were as low or lower than comparable goods at other stores in Nogales. Since local residents were used to haggling over price in the Nogales area, fixed prices were perceived as evidence that Bea Robbins goods were not being offered at the best possible prices. These customers frequently left the shop in a state of irritation after being told of the store's one-price policy.

Informed of this situation, Mrs. Castle commented, "fair prices are the policy that made Bea Robbins what it is, not haggling. We can't change this practice since our prices are already at rock bottom for the kinds of goods we sell." The fact remained, however, that something had to be done about the losses in the Nogales store.

1. As a consultant, what course of action would you recommend to Mrs. Castle?

International Mineral and Chemical Company

On February 10, 1968, *Business Week* reported, "five years after making a huge phosphate discovery in West Africa, Spain has lost the U.S. partner it chose to help in development. The hitch: clumsy bargaining.' In the body of the story, *Business Week* said, "After changing the ante repeatedly for three years, it [Spain] finally lost the partner it had chosen last year to develop its huge phosphate deposits in West Africa. International Minerals and Chemical Corporation (IMC), of Skokie, Illinois, pulled out of the 25–75 joint venture, leaving Madrid holding fast to the short end of a long stick, at least for the moment."

Originally, the Spanish government had invited a number of foreign firms to bid on the prospect of a partnership to remove large deposits of phosphate from the Spanish Sahara. During the bidding procedure, Spanish officials gradually tightened the requirements they would accept and eventually only one firm, International Minerals and Chemical Company, was left in the picture. A number of German, French, British, Italian, Canadian, and Japanese companies withdrew along with a series of United States companies and IMC eventually reached an apparent agreement with the Spanish government. This agreement gave IMC a 25-percent equity in the organization and control of the corporation, but allowed Spain to farm out 20 percent of the remaining ownership among several European countries.

In February 1968, the deal collapsed in what *Business Week* called a "welter of confusing cross-statements." IMC's President Nelson White attributed the withdrawal of his company to a weakening market for phosphates and the failure of the Spanish government to allow IMC to make a feasibility study to be determined by cost analysis. "What we wanted," he said, "was full control on the technical side.... With only 25 percent equity we certainly didn't expect to control the financial end." The company thus used a technical reason for breaking off its negotiations, although it seemed apparent that IMC management was exasperated by the way in which bargaining had been conducted.

According to other sources, one reason for the breakup was that other European governments, particularly France and Germany, had pressured Spain because of its willingness to allow an American firm to exercise control over the Sahara deposit. Although the real reasons for cessation of negotiations may never be known, no doubt exists that a breakdown of understanding occurred.

1. Do you feel that IMC had sufficient justification for its withdrawal?
2. What problems did IMC face that might be beyond the normal scope of problem solving and decision making techniques?

BIBLIOGRAPHY

Management of Worldwide Operations

Dale, Ernest, *Management: Theory and Practice,* New York: McGraw-Hill, Inc., 1965.

"Focus on World Business," *Fortune,* September 1968 issue.

Granick, David, *The Red Executive,* New York: Doubleday & Company, Inc., Anchor Books, 1961.

Harbison, Frederick, and Charles Myers, *Management in the Industrial World,* New York: McGraw-Hill, Inc., 1959.

Lilienthal, David, *The Multinational Corporation,* New York: Development and Resources Corporation, 1960.

Learned, Edmund, Francis Aguilar, and Robert Valtz, *European Problems in General Management,* Homewood, Ill.: Richard D. Irwin, Inc., 1963.

National Industrial Conference Board, *The Changing Role of the International Executive,* New York: Author, Studies in Business Policy, no. 119, 1966.

———, *Joint Ventures With Foreign Partners,* New York: N.I.C.B., 1966.

———, *Organization Structures of International Companies,* New York: Author, Studies in Personnel Policy, no. 198, 1965.

Robinson, Thomas, *International Management,* New York: Holt, Rinehart and Winston, Inc., 1967.

Servan-Schreiber, J.J., *The American Challenge,* New York: Atheneum Publishers, 1968.

Wadia, Maneck, ed., *The Nature and Scope of Management,* Glenview, Ill.: Scott, Foresman and Company, 1966.

Ward, Barbara, *The Rich Nations and the Poor Nations,* New York: W.W. Norton and Company, Inc., 1962.

Management of Government-Business Relations

Anderson, Martin, *The Federal Bulldozer,* New York: McGraw-Hill, Inc., 1964.

Anshen, Melvin W., and George L. Bach, eds., *Management and Corporations: 1985,* New York: McGraw-Hill, Inc., 1960.

Blough, Roger, *Free Man and the Corporation: McKinsey Lecture,* Columbia University, Graduate School of Business Administration, New York: McGraw-Hill, Inc., 1959.

Galbraith, John Kenneth, *The New Industrial State,* Boston: Houghton-Mifflin Company, 1967.

Griffin, Clare E., *Enterprise in a Free Society,* Homewood, Ill.: Richard D. Irwin, Inc., 1949.

Huxley, Aldous, *Brave New World,* New York: Bantam Books, 1932.

Jay, Anthony, *Management and Machiavelli,* New York: Holt, Rinehart and Winston, Inc., 1968.

Davis, Keith, and Robert Blomstrom, *Business and Its Environment,* New York: McGraw-Hill, Inc., 1966.

Eels, Richard, and Clarence Walton, *Conceptual Foundations of Business,* Homewood, Ill.: Richard D. Irwin, Inc., 1961.

Machiavelli, Niccolo, *The Prince,* New York: Washington Square Press, 1963.

McGuire, Joseph W., *Theories of Business Behavior,* Englewood Cliffs, N.J.: Prentice-Hall, Inc., 1964.

Mund, Vernon, *Government and Business,* New York: Harper & Row, Publishers, 1950.

Sayles, Leonard R., *Individualism and Big Business,* New York: McGraw-Hill, Inc., 1963.

Schumpeter, Joseph, *Capitalism, Socialism and Democracy,* 3rd ed., New York: Harper & Row, Publishers, 1950.

Schlender, William, William Scott, and Allan Filley, eds., *Management in Perspective,* Boston: Houghton Mifflin Company, 1965.

Sichel, Werner, *Industrial Organization and Public Policy,* Boston: Houghton Mifflin Company, 1967.

Management of Research and Development

Bright, James, *Research Development and Technological Innovation,* Homewood, Ill.: Richard D. Irwin, Inc., 1964.

Barnes, Louis B., *Organizational Systems and Engineering Groups,* Cambridge, Mass.: Harvard School of Business, Division of Research, 1960.

Burck, Gilbert, ed., *The Computer Age,* New York: Harper & Row, Publishers, 1965.

Danielson, Lee E., *Characteristics of Engineers and Scientists,* Ann Arbor, Mich.: University of Michigan, Bureau of Industrial Relations, 1960.

Dill, W., T. Hilton, and W. Reitman, *The New Managers,* Englewood Cliffs, N.J.: Prentice-Hall, Inc., 1962.

Dunlap, John, ed., *Automation and Technological Change,* Englewood Cliffs, N.J.: Prentice-Hall, Inc., 1962.

Flesch, Rudolph, *The Art of Clear Thinking,* New York: Harper & Row, Publishers, 1951.

Galbraith, John Kenneth, *The New Industrial State,* Boston: Houghton Mifflin Company, 1967.

Gardner, John W., *Self Renewal,* New York: Harper & Row, Publishers, 1964.

Jerome, William, *Executive Control-The Catalyst,* New York: John Wiley and Sons, 1961.

Kuhn, James W., *Scientific and Managerial Manpower in Nuclear Industry,* New York: Columbia University Press, 1966.

Moore, Franklin G., *Manufacturing Management,* 4th ed., Homewood, Ill.: Richard D. Irwin, Inc., 1965.

Newman, William H., and Charles E. Summer, *The Process of Management,* 2nd ed., Englewood Cliffs, N.J.: Prentice-Hall Book Company, 1960.

Orth, Charles B., Joseph Bailey, Francis Wolek, *Administering Research and Development,* Homewood, Ill.: Richard D. Irwin, Inc., 1964.

Riegel, John W., *Intangible Rewards for Engineers and Scientists,* Ann Arbor, Mich.: University of Michigan, Bureau of Industrial Relations, 1958.

Rogers, Everett, *Diffusion of Innovations,* New York: The Free Press, 1962.

Roman, Daniel J., *Research and Development Management,* New York: Appleton-Century-Crofts, 1968.

Management of Union Relations

Bakke, E. Wight, *Mutual Survival: The Goal of Union and Management,* New Haven, Conn.: Yale University, Labor and Management Center, 1946.

Barbash, Jack, *Practice of Unionism,* New York: Harper & Row, Publishers, 1956.

Bloom, G., and H. Northrup, *Economics of Labor Relations,* Homewood, Ill.: Richard D. Irwin, Inc., 1958.

Chamberlain, Neil W., *Collective Bargaining,* New York: McGraw-Hill, Inc., 1951.

———, *The Union Challenge to Management Control,* New York: Harper & Row, Publishers, 1948.

Chandler, M., *Management Rights and Union Interests,* New York: McGraw-Hill, Inc., 1964.

Dunlop, J., *Industrial Relations Systems,* New York: Holt, Rinehart and Winston, Inc., 1958.

Eels, Richard, and Clarence Walton, *Conceptual Foundations of Business,* rev. ed., Homewood, Ill.: Richard D. Irwin, Inc., 1969.

Hoxie, R.F., *Trade Unionism in the Labor Movement,* New York: Appleton-Century-Crofts, 1923.

Hutchinson, John G., *Management Under Strike Conditions,* New York: Holt, Rinehart and Winston, Inc., 1966.

———, *Managing a Fair Day's Work,* Ann Arbor, Mich.: University of Michigan, Bureau of Industrial Relations, 1963.

Markham, Charles, ed., *Jobs, Men and Machines,* New York: American Foundation on Automation and Employment, 1964.

Miernyck, William H., *Trade Unions in an Age of Affluence,* New York: Random House, Inc., 1962.

Northrup, H., *Boulwarism,* Ann Arbor, Mich.: University of Michigan, Bureau of Industrial Relations, 1964.

Perlman, M., *Labor Union Theories in America,* New York: Harper & Row, Publishers, 1958.

Reynolds, Lloyd, *Labor Relations and Labor Economics,* 4th ed., Englewood Cliffs, N.J.: Prentice-Hall, Inc., 1966.

Sayles, Leonard R., *Behavior of Industrial Work Groups,* New York: John Wiley & Sons, Inc., 1958.

————, and George Strauss, *The Local Union, Its Place in the Industrial Plant,* New York: Harper & Row, Publishers, 1953.

————, *Personnel: The Human Problems of Management,* 2nd ed., Englewood Cliffs, N.J.: Prentice-Hall, Inc., 1967.

Schel, Werner, ed., *Industrial Organization and Public Policy,* Boston: Houghton Mifflin Company, 1967.

Shils, E., *Automation and Industrial Relations,* New York: Holt, Rinehart and Winston, Inc., 1963.

Slichter, S., J. Healy, and R. Livernash, *Impact of Collective Bargaining on Management,* Washington, D.C.: Brookings Institution, 1958.

Stagner, Ross, and Hjalmar Rosen, *Psychology of Union-Management Relations,* Belmont, Calif.: Wadsworth Publishing Company, 1965.

Ullman, Lloyd, ed., *Challenges to Collective Bargaining,* Symposium held by the American Assembly, Englewood Cliffs, N.J.: Prentice-Hall, Inc., 1967.

Union Powers and Union Functions: Toward a Better Balance, New York: Committee for Economic Development, Research and Policy Committee, March 1964.

Viteles, Morris, *Motivation and Morale in Industry,* New York: W.W. Norton and Company, Inc., 1953.

INDEX